To my brother and sister-in-law, Jim and Mariann Marmel,
who always believe in me, and to the memories of my mother
Susan Marmel (1914-2003) and my father Harry Marmel
(1914-1985), who always made me feel loved and cherished.

About the Author

Elaine Marmel is President of Marmel Enterprises, LLC, an organization that specializes in technical writing and software training. Elaine has an MBA from Cornell University and worked on projects to build financial management systems for New York City and Washington, D.C. This prior experience provided the foundation for Marmel Enterprises, LLC to help small businesses implement computerized accounting systems.

Elaine left her native Chicago for the warmer climes of Arizona (by way of Cincinnati, OH; Jerusalem, Israel; Ithaca, NY; Washington, D.C.; and Tampa, FL) where she basks in the sun with her PC and her dog Josh and her cats, Cato, Watson, and Buddy, and sings barbershop harmony with the 2006 International Championship Scottsdale Chorus.

Elaine spends most of her time writing; she has authored and co-authored more than 50 books about Microsoft Project, Microsoft Excel, Microsoft Word for Windows, Microsoft Word for the Mac, QuickBooks, Peachtree, Quicken for Windows, Quicken for DOS, Windows 98, 1-2-3 for Windows, and Lotus Notes. From 1994 to 2006, she also was the contributing editor to monthly publications *Peachtree Extra* and *QuickBooks Extra*.

Credits

Project Editor
Rebecca Huehls

Acquisitions Editor
Kyle Looper

Technical Editor
Brian Kennemer

Senior Copy Editor
Barry Childs-Helton

Editorial Manager
Leah Cameron

Editorial Director
Mary C. Corder

Vice President and Executive Group Publisher
Richard Swadley

Vice President and Publisher
Andy Cummings

Senior Project Coordinator
Kristie Rees

Media Development Project Manager
Laura Moss

Media Development Assistant Project Manager
Jenny Swisher

Media Development Associate Producers
Josh Frank
Shawn Patrick
Doug Kuhn
Marilyn Hummel

Proofreading and Indexing
Sossity R. Smith
Potomac Indexing, LLC

Contents at a Glance

Contents

Contents

Contents

Contents

Contents

Contents

Part IV: Refining Your Project   339

Chapter 10: Resolving Scheduling Problems 341

Contents

Contents

Contents

Contents

Contents

Acknowledgments

No man (or woman) is an island, and this book is the product of the efforts of several people. Thank you, Kyle Looper, for your support and for making things smooth and easy and for having faith in me. Thank you, Rebecca Huehls, for keeping me on track and keeping me sane, and for keeping the manuscript readable. Thank you, Brian Kennemer, for trying to keep me technically accurate. And last, but not least, my thanks also go to the Web site team at Wiley for producing the companion Web site for this book.

Introduction

Managing projects can be as exciting as scheduling the next space shuttle or as mundane as planning routine production-line maintenance. A project can be as rewarding as striking oil or as disastrous as the maiden voyage of the *Titanic*. Projects can have budgets of $5 or $5,000,000. One thing that all projects have in common, however, is their potential for success or failure — the promise that if you do it right, you'll accomplish your goal.

Why You Need This Book

Microsoft Project is a tool for implementing project management principles and practices that can help you succeed. That's why this book provides not only the information about which buttons to press and where to type project dates but also the conceptual framework to make computerized project management work for you.

How this book is designed

This book strives to offer real-world examples of projects from many industries and disciplines. You'll see yourself and your own projects somewhere in this book. A wealth of tips and advice show you how to address, control, and overcome real-world constraints. The book is designed to work for you in two ways:

- **As a tutorial.** You can use *Project 2010 Bible* as a linear tool to learn Project — from the ground up.

- **As a reference.** You can put it on the shelf and use it as your Project reference book, to be pulled down as needed — for advice, information, and step-by-step procedures.

Either way, this book will enrich your Microsoft Project experience and make you a better project manager.

Whom this book is for

Project management software is unlike word processing or spreadsheet software; many of you may have come to project management software never having used anything quite like it before. You may also have used earlier versions of Project or other project management software.

- **If you're new to project management:** This book is for you. The early chapters explain the basic concepts of computerized project management and what it can do for you so that you have a context in which to learn Project.

- **If you're experienced with project management:** This book is also for you. It explains what's new in the latest version of Project and shows you techniques for using the software that you may not have considered before.

You will benefit most from this book if you have at least a basic understanding of the Windows environment, have mastered standard Windows software conventions, and are comfortable using a mouse. But beyond that, you need only the desire to succeed as a project manager, which this book will help you do.

The Special Features of This Book

To help you maximize your use of this book, I've included many special features in its design and conception. The following sections show you how they work.

Formatting conventions

To streamline your learning experience, I've used the following formatting conventions:

- **Text you're asked to type:** When you're asked to enter text into a Project schedule, for example, it appears in **boldface**.

- **When using the mouse:** A click indicates a left mouse-button click and right-click indicates a right mouse-button click. Double-click designates two quick, successive clicks of the left mouse button.

- **Keystroke combinations:** These look like this: Alt+Tab. Hold down the first key and, without letting it go, press the second key.

- **Menu commands:** These are shown with the command arrow — for example, Choose File ⇨ Open.

- **New terms:** When a new term or concept is introduced, it appears in *italics*.

Margin icons

Throughout the book, I've included special icons in the margins to call your attention to added information, shortcuts and advice, warnings about potentially disastrous courses of action, the new features of Project 2010, references to additional wisdom, and what you'll find on the Web site that accompanies this book. Here's how they look:

Note
The Note icon signals additional information about a point under discussion or background information that may be of interest to you. ■

Tip
A tip is a bit of advice or a hint to save you time and indicate the best way to get things done. ■

Sagacious Sidebars _____

Sidebars, such as this one, are departures into background details or interesting information. They're designed so that you may read around them if you're in a hurry to accomplish a specific task.

When you have the time for a more comprehensive approach to the subject, however, the concepts that you find in sidebars may prove invaluable — providing the context and depth necessary to achieve a fuller understanding of Project's functions.

New Feature
This icon highlights a new feature in Project 2010. ■

Cross-Reference
This helpful icon clues you in to sources of additional information on a topic under discussion. It points to another chapter or a specific heading elsewhere in the book. ■

On The Web Site
The Web site icon flags useful software and templates that you'll find on this book's companion Web site. Appendix A introduces you to all the materials on the site. ■

How This Book Is Organized

This book is organized in the same way you will use Microsoft Project: It begins with some basic concepts and progresses through the features that you need to build a typical schedule and then track its progress. The later chapters provide more advanced information for customizing Project, using it in workgroup settings, and taking Project online.

Part I: Project Management Basics

Part I of the book explains the basic project management concepts and terminology that you'll need to learn Project. In Chapter 1, you take a look at the nature of projects themselves, how Microsoft Project can help you control them, and the life cycle of a typical project. In Chapter 2, you get your first glimpse of the Project software environment.

Part II: Getting Your Project Going

Here's where you learn about the type of information that Project needs in order to do its job. In Chapter 3, you begin to build your first schedule and add tasks in an outline structure. In Chapter 4, you assign timing and construct timing relationships among those tasks. In Chapter 5, you begin assigning people and other resources to your project. This chapter is also where you learn to determine how these resources add costs to a project and how to handle issues such as overtime and shift work.

Part III: Getting Information about Projects

Before your project is ready for prime time, you need to tweak some things, just as you check spelling in a word-processed document. Chapter 6 explains how to view that information to gain perspective on your project, and Chapter 7 helps you to manipulate and customize views to make them work for you. Chapter 8 shows you how to make your project schedule look more professional by formatting the text and modifying the appearance of chart elements. In Chapter 9, you explore the power of generating reports on your projects for everyone from management to individual project team members.

Part IV: Refining Your Project

The two chapters in this part delve into the tools that Project provides to resolve conflicts in your schedule. Chapter 10 explores resolving conflicts in the timing of your schedule so that you can meet your deadlines. Chapter 11 considers the issue of resolving resource conflicts, such as overworked people and underutilized equipment.

Part V: Tracking Your Progress

Here's where you get the payoff for all your data entry and patient resolution of problems in your schedule. After you set your basic schedule and the project begins, you can track its progress and check data on your status from various perspectives. Chapter 12 gives you an overview of the tracking process. Chapter 13 shows you how to track progress on your individual tasks and view that progress in various ways. Chapter 14 shows you ways you can review the progress of your project. Chapter 15 gives advice and methods for analyzing your progress and making adjustments as needed to stay on schedule and within your budget.

Part VI: Advanced Microsoft Project

Part VI provides advice and information to make your use of Microsoft Project easier. Learn about customizing the Project environment in Chapter 16. Chapter 17 provides information on macros, which are simple programs that enable you to record and automatically play back series of steps that you use frequently, saving you time and effort. Chapter 17 also introduces how to use VBA and VBScript to customize Project so that it works the way you work. Chapter 18 deals with importing and exporting information into and out of Project. Importing information from other software can save you the time and expense of reentering existing data.

Part VII: Working in Groups

Most projects worth the effort of tracking in Project aren't done by a single person; workgroups, teams, and committees often form a day-to-day working project team. Chapter 19 shows you how to set up multiple projects to run concurrently or to consolidate smaller projects into larger schedules and includes ways to use Windows SharePoint Services to collaborate in basic ways. In

Chapters 20 through 24, you learn how to plan, implement, and manage projects using Project, Project Web Access, and Project Server, Microsoft's Web-based project-managed solution.

Part VIII: Appendices

Appendix A covers what you find on this book's companion Web site, which contains links to trial software, timesaving templates, and links to other sites of interest in the project management world — including sites for partners of Microsoft Project. Appendixes B–D provide resources and additional materials to make your work easier.

Appendix E, a glossary at the end of the book, contains many specifically project management–related terms and concepts that have evolved over time. These terms are defined when they are first used in the book, but you may want to look them up at a later date. Use this handy alphabetical listing to do so.

Part I

Project Management Basics

The Nature of Projects

Everybody does projects. Building a tree house is a project; so is putting a man on the moon. From the simplest home improvement to the most complex business or scientific venture, projects are a part of most of our lives. But exactly what is a project, and what can you do to manage all its facets?

IN THIS CHAPTER

Understanding projects

The life cycle of a project

Some projects are defined by their randomness. Missed deadlines, unpleasant surprises, and unexpected problems seem to be as unavoidable as the weekly staff meeting. Other projects have few problems. Nevertheless, the project that goes smoothly from beginning to end is rare. Good planning and communication can go a long way toward avoiding disaster. And although no amount of planning can prevent all possible problems, good project management enables you to deal with those inevitable twists and turns in the most efficient manner possible.

In this chapter, you begin exploring tools and acquiring skills that can help you become a more efficient and productive project manager. The goal of this chapter is to provide a survey of what a project is, what project management is, and how Microsoft Project 2010 fits into the picture.

Understanding Projects

When you look up the word *project* in the dictionary, you see definitions that include words and phrases such as "plan" and "concerted effort." A project in the truest sense isn't a simple, one-person endeavor to perform a task. By this definition, getting yourself dressed — difficult though that task might seem on a Monday morning — doesn't qualify as a project.

A project is a series of steps that are typically performed by more than one person. In addition, a project has the following characteristics:

- **A project has a specific and measurable goal.** You know you have finished the project when you have successfully met your project goal.
- **Projects have a specific time frame.** The success of a project is often measured by how successfully the project has been completed within the amount of time allotted to it.
- **Projects use resources.** Resources aren't just people; resources can include money, machinery, materials, and more. How well these resources are allocated and orchestrated is another key measure of a project's success or failure.
- **All projects consist of interdependent, yet individual, steps called *tasks*.** Rarely does any piece of a project exist in a vacuum. If one task runs late or over budget, it typically affects other tasks, the overall schedule, and the total cost of the project.

Projects can last for weeks, months, or even years. By their nature, projects are dynamic; they tend to grow, change, and behave in ways that you can't always predict. Consequently, you, as a project manager, have to remain alert to the progress and vagaries of your projects or you'll never reach your goals. Documentation and communication are your two key tools for staying on top of a project throughout its life.

Exploring project management

Project management is a discipline that examines the nature of projects and offers ways to control their progress. Project management attempts to organize and systematize the tasks in a project to minimize the number of surprises that you may encounter.

Project management and project managers attempt to balance project goals and objectives against the amount of time and money available to complete a project, focusing on the following key areas:

- Budgeting
- Scheduling
- Managing resources
- Tracking and reporting progress

Note

There are tasks to accomplish before a project begins, such as determining if the project is one that should be undertaken, identifying the project's stakeholders and gaining their support, and ensuring that everyone involved in the project understands its goals and objectives. While this book focuses on the use of Microsoft Project to manage a project, the Project Management Institute (PMI) offers books and education classes on all aspects of project management. ∎

To manage these aspects of projects, certain tools have evolved over the years. Some of these are conceptual, such as the critical path; others involve specific formats for displaying project organization and progress, such as a Gantt Chart. The following sections introduce some key project management concepts and tools.

Critical path and slack

The *critical path* identifies the series of tasks in a project that must be completed on time for the overall project to stay on schedule. For example, suppose you're planning a going-away party at your office and have three days to plan the party. The following table lists some of the tasks involved and indicates their time frames.

Task	Duration
Signing the good-bye card	Three days
Ordering food	One day
Reserving a room	One hour
Buying a good-bye gift	One day

The shortest task, reserving a room, takes only one hour. Assuming that plenty of rooms are available for holding the party, you can, in theory, delay reserving the room until the last hour of the third day. Delaying this task doesn't cause any delay in holding the party — as long as you accomplish this task by the end of the longest task, which is getting everyone to sign the good-bye card. Therefore the task of reserving a room isn't on the critical path. However, you can't delay the task of signing the good-bye card, which is projected to take three days to accomplish, without delaying the party. Therefore the card-signing task *is* on the critical path. (Of course, this example is very simple; typically, a whole series of tasks that can't afford delay form an entire critical path.)

The following points further define and clarify these concepts:

- **The critical path changes as the project progresses.** Remember that a *critical path* is a means of identifying tasks that have no leeway in their timing to ensure that they don't run late and affect your overall schedule. Knowing where your critical path tasks are at any point during the project is crucial to staying on track. Figures 1.1 and 1.2 show the same schedule — first with all tasks displayed and then filtered to show only the tasks that are on the critical path.

Cross-Reference

See Chapter 7 to find out how to filter for only critical tasks and to see more information about changing the view of your project. ■

- *Slack,* also called *float,* is the amount of time that you can delay a task before that task moves onto the critical path. In the preceding example, the one-hour-long task — reserving a room — has slack. This task can slip a few hours, even a couple of days, and the party will still happen on time. However, if you wait until the last half-hour of the third day to reserve a room, that task will have used up its slack and it then moves onto the critical path.

FIGURE 1.1

In this figure, all tasks appear — those with slack and those on the critical path.

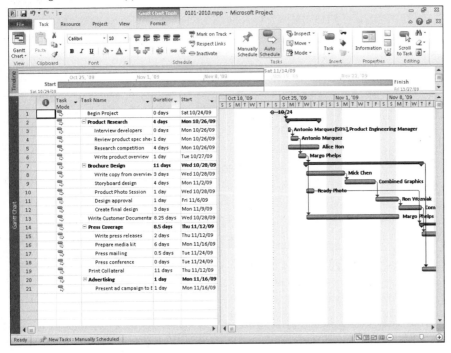

Durations and milestones

Most tasks in a project take a specific amount of time to accomplish. Tasks can take anywhere from five minutes to five months. The length of time needed to complete a task is called the task's *duration*. You should always try to break the long tasks in a project into smaller tasks of shorter duration so you can track their progress more accurately. For example, break a five-month-long task into five one-month tasks. Checking off the completion of the smaller tasks each month reduces the odds of a serious surprise five months down the road — and makes you feel as though you're getting something done.

Some tasks, called *milestones,* have no (0) duration. Milestones are merely points in time that mark the start or completion of some phase of a project. For example, if your project involves designing a new brochure, the approval of the initial design might be considered a milestone. You can assign a duration to the process of routing the design to various people for review, but assigning a length of time to the moment when you have everyone's final approval is probably impossible. Therefore this task has a duration of 0 — that is, approval of the design is a milestone that simply marks a key moment in the project.

FIGURE 1.2

When you apply the appropriate filter, only the tasks that can't afford delay appear in your schedule.

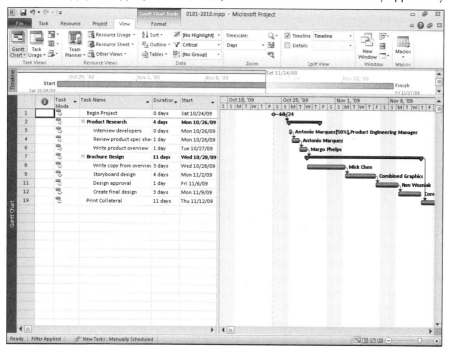

Fixed-duration tasks and resource-driven schedules

Some tasks take the same amount of time — no matter how many people or other resources you devote to them. Flying from San Francisco to New York is likely to take about five hours, regardless of how many pilots or flight attendants you add. If your project requires a test on a mixture of two solvents that must sit for six hours to react, you can't speed up the reaction by adding more solvent or by hiring more scientists to work in the laboratory. These tasks have a *fixed duration*, meaning that their timing is set by the nature of the task.

On the other hand, the number of available resources can affect the duration of some tasks. For example, if one person needs two hours to dig a ditch, adding a second person will likely cut the time in half. The task still requires two hours of effort, but two resources can perform the task simultaneously. Tasks whose durations are affected by the addition or subtraction of resources are called *resource-driven tasks*.

Note

In real-world projects, this calculation is seldom so exact. Because people have different skill levels and perform work at different speeds, two people don't always cut the time of a task exactly in half. In addition, the more people you add to a task, the more communication, cooperation, and training may be involved — each of which requires time. Microsoft Project handles additional assignments of resources strictly as a mathematical calculation, but you can still use your judgment of the resources that are involved to modify this calculation. ■

Diagrams that aid project management

Gantt Charts, network diagrams, and *work breakdown structures* (WBSs) are tools of project management that have evolved over many years. These tools are simply charts that you can use to track different aspects of your project. Figure 1.3 shows a Microsoft Project Gantt Chart, and Figure 1.4 shows a Microsoft Project network diagram. Figure 1.5 shows a typical WBS; although Microsoft Project does not include a WBS chart as one of its standard views.

FIGURE 1.3

The Gantt Chart bars represent timing of the tasks in a project.

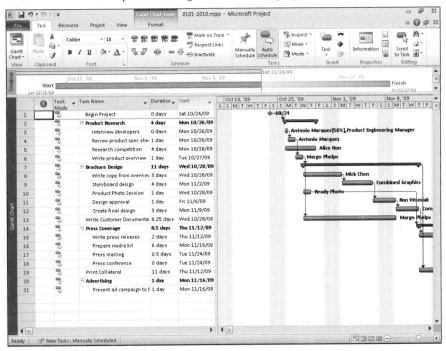

FIGURE 1.4

The network diagram resembles a flow chart for work in a project.

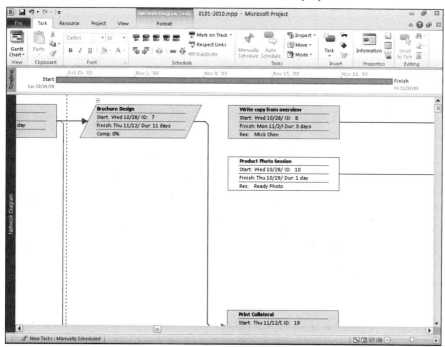

FIGURE 1.5

The work breakdown structure chart reminds you of a typical company's organization chart.

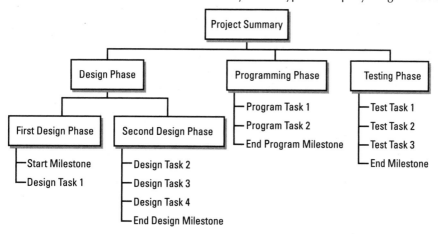

Tip

You can purchase an add-on product, WBS Chart Pro to create a WBS chart from a Microsoft Project file. On this book's Web site, you'll find a link to WBS Chart Pro. ■

Before people used computers to manage their projects, managers drew these charts by hand. Any self-respecting project war room had a 10-foot network diagram, WBS, or Gantt Chart tacked to the wall. By the end of the project, this chart was as marked up and out of date as last year's appointment calendar. Thankfully, project management software makes these charts easier to generate, update, and customize.

A Gantt Chart represents the tasks in a project with bars that reflect the duration of individual tasks. Milestones are shown as diamond shapes.

Cross-Reference

You can find out more about the elements of a Gantt Chart in Chapter 2. For this chapter's purposes, you simply need to know that a Gantt Chart enables you to visualize and track the timing of a project. ■

Network diagrams, on the other hand, don't accurately detail the timing of a project. Instead, a network diagram shows the flow of tasks in a project and the relationships of tasks to each other. Each task is contained in a box called a *node,* and lines that flow among the nodes indicate the flow of tasks.

Note

In Project 98 and prior versions of Project, network diagrams were called PERT charts. PERT stands for Program Evaluation and Review Technique. The Special Projects Office of the U.S. Navy devised this method for tracking the flow of tasks in a project when it was designing the Polaris submarine in the late 1950s. ■

The U.S. defense establishment uses the WBS as its primary tool for managing projects and describes the WBS in Military Standard (MIL-STD) 881B (25 Mar 93) as follows: "A work breakdown structure is a product-oriented family tree composed of hardware, software, services, data and facilities . . . [It] displays and defines the product(s) to be developed and/or produced and relates the elements of work to be accomplished to each other and to the end product(s)."

Note

MIL-STD 881B was superseded by MIL-HDBK 881A, 30 July 2005. The foreword of the newer document states that there were "no substantive changes in work breakdown structure definition." The full text is available on many Department of Defense sites (for example, `http://dcarc.pae.osd.mil/881handbook/881a.pdf`**). ■**

On the Web

Project doesn't contain a PERT chart view. However, on the companion Web site for this book, you can find a link to PERT Chart EXPERT, a program that converts the information in any Project file to a PERT view. ■

Dependencies

The final project management concept to master is dependencies. The overall timing of a project isn't simply the sum of the durations of all tasks, because all tasks in a project don't usually happen simultaneously. For example, in a construction project, you must pour the foundation of a building before you can build the structure. You also have to enclose the building with walls and windows before you lay carpeting. In other words, project managers anticipate and establish relationships among the tasks in a project. These relationships are called *dependencies*. Only after you have created tasks, assigned durations to them, *and* established dependencies can you see the overall timing of your project.

Cross-Reference

Chapter 4 covers the kinds of dependencies you can assign in Project. ■

Managing projects with project management software

Many people manage projects with stacks of to-do lists and colorful hand-drawn wall charts. They scribble notes on calendars in pencil, knowing — more often than not — that those dates and tasks will change over time. They hold numerous meetings to keep everyone in the project informed. People have developed these simple organizational tools because projects typically have so many bits and pieces that no one can possibly remember them all.

To manage a project effectively, you need a set of procedures. Project management software automates many of these procedures. With project management software, you can do the following:

- **Plan up front:** By preplanning the various elements of your project, you can more accurately estimate the time and resources that are required to complete the project.

- **View your progress:** By examining your progress on an ongoing basis from various perspectives, you can see whether you 're likely to meet your goal.

- **Recognize conflicts:** By identifying time and resource conflicts early, you can try out various what-if scenarios to resolve them before the project gets out of hand.

- **Make adjustments:** You can make adjustments to task timing and costs, and automatically update all other tasks in the project to reflect the impact of your changes.

- **Generate professional-looking reports:** You can create reports on the status of your project to help team members prioritize and to help management make informed decisions.

Cross-Reference

To effectively manage projects with many participants (often based in many locations), consider using Project 2010 in conjunction with its companion server product, Project Server. Using Project Server and Project 2010, you can manage projects in a Web-based environment, simplifying collaboration. For more details, see Chapters 20 through 24. You also can take advantage of Microsoft SharePoint Foundation features to collaborate on projects; see Chapter 19 for details. ■

What's required of you

Many people contemplate using project management software with about as much relish as they contemplate having surgery. They anticipate hours of data-entry time before they can get anything out of the software. To some extent, that vision is true. You have to provide a certain amount of information about your project for any software to estimate schedules and generate reports, just as you have to enter numbers for a spreadsheet to calculate a budget or a loan-payback schedule.

On the other hand, after you enter your basic project information into Microsoft Project, the ongoing maintenance of that data is far easier than generating handwritten to-do lists that become obsolete almost immediately. In addition, the accuracy and professionalism of the reports you generate with Project can make the difference between a poorly managed project and a successful one. As with a quarterly budget that you create with spreadsheet software, Project performs its calculations automatically after you enter the data. In addition, using Project enables you to spot potential problems — and test alternative solutions — quickly and easily.

So, exactly what do you have to do to manage your project with Microsoft Project? To create a schedule in Microsoft Project, you must enter the following information about your tasks:

- Individual task names
- Task durations
- Task dependencies

To track the costs of these tasks, you add certain information about resources, including the following:

- The list of human and material resources and their costs for both standard and overtime hours
- The assignment of resources to specific tasks

To track a project over its lifetime, you need to enter the following information:

- Progress on tasks
- Changes in task timing or dependencies
- Changes in resources — that is, resources that are added to or removed from the project
- Changes in resource time commitments and costs

How Microsoft Project can help

Even though you still must enter a great deal of information into your project schedule, Microsoft Project has ways to make that job easier:

- **Project templates:** If you often do similar types of projects, you can create project templates with typical project tasks already in place; you can then modify the templates for individual projects. Project comes with templates to help you get started.

On the Web

You can take advantage of some sample project templates — representing a cross-section of typical industries and project types — on this book's companion Web site. ■

- **Automate repeated tasks:** If you have tasks that recur throughout the life of your project, such as weekly meetings or regular reviews, you can create a single repeating task; Project duplicates it for you at the appropriate interval.

- **Import existing task lists:** You can create projects from tasks that you've set up in Outlook, or you can use Excel to start your project and then easily import the spreadsheet into Project. You also can use a Task List on a SharePoint site to collaboratively create a list of tasks for a project — and then import those tasks into Project. Or you can start the project itself in Project and then make the tasks available on a SharePoint site so others can modify and update the list; you can then synchronize any changes with the Project file.

Cross-Reference

See Chapter 18 for more information about starting projects in Outlook and Excel and then moving them into Project 2010. See Chapter 19 for information on using Project and SharePoint to collaborate. ■

- **Advanced reporting and analytical capabilities:** Project provides a series of text and visual reports. Project prepares the text reports and sends your project data to Visio or Excel to prepare visual reports.

- **Consolidate projects:** You can divide projects into smaller pieces that team members can use to enter and track progress. By tracking progress with this method, no individual person has to enter an overwhelming amount of data. Also, your people feel more accountable and involved in the project.

Cross-Reference

See Part VII of this book, "Working in Groups," for detailed information about working in groups in Project 2010 alone, in conjunction with SharePoint, or in conjunction with Project Server. ■

- **Compare projects:** You can compare any two projects, but the power of this feature becomes apparent when you save various versions of the same project and then compare to highlight the differences.

Cross-Reference

See Chapter 14 for details on comparing projects. ■

- **Macros:** You can take advantage of Microsoft Visual Basic to build macros that automate repetitive tasks, such as generating weekly reports.

Cross-Reference

See Chapter 17 for more information about using macros to speed your work. ■

The Life Cycle of a Project

Projects typically consist of several phases. Understanding the nature of each phase can help you relate the features of Microsoft Project to your own projects.

Identifying your goal and the project's scope

Before you can begin to plan a project, you have to identify the goal, which isn't always as obvious as it sounds. Various participants may define a project's goal differently. In fact, many projects fail because the team members are unwittingly working toward different goals. For example, is the team's goal to perform a productivity study or to actually improve productivity? Is the outcome for your project to agree on the final building design, or is it to complete the actual construction of the building? As you analyze your goal and factor in the perspectives of other team members, make sure that your project isn't just one step in a series of projects to reach a larger, longer-term goal.

To identify your goal, you can communicate in various ways, such as meetings, e-mail, and conference calls — and, if your organization uses SharePoint, you can communicate using SharePoint tools such as task lists, issues, and risks. But the people with whom you communicate are more important than the method you use to communicate. You should conduct a dialogue at various levels (from management through front-line personnel) that gets ideas on the table and answers questions. Take the time to write a goal statement and circulate it among the team members to make sure that everyone understands the common focus of the project.

Note
Be careful not to set a long-range goal that is likely to change before the project ends. Smaller projects or projects that have been divided into various phases are more manageable and more flexible. ■

Cross-Reference
See Chapter 20 for tips on avoiding pitfalls during project planning. ■

After you understand your goal, you should also gather the information that you need to define the project's scope. This endeavor may take some research on your part. The *scope* of a project is a statement of more specific parameters or constraints for its completion. The constraints of a project usually fall within the areas of time, quality, and cost, and often they relate directly to project deliverables.

The following are sample goal and scope statements:

Project A:

- **Goal:** To locate a facility for our warehouse.
- **Scope:** By October 15, to find a modern warehouse facility of approximately 5,200 square feet, with a lease cost of no more than $3,000 per month, in a location that is convenient to our main office.

Project B:

- **Goal:** To launch a new cleaning product.
- **Scope:** Includes test-marketing the product, designing packaging, and creating and launching an advertising campaign. The launch must be completed before the end of the third quarter of 2010 and can cost no more than $750,000.

Notice that the second scope statement designates major phases of the project (conducting test marketing, designing packaging, and creating an ad campaign). This statement provides a starting point for planning the tasks in the project. In fact, you may eventually decide to divide this project into smaller projects such as conducting test marketing, designing packaging, and launching an advertising campaign. Writing the scope of the project may encourage you to redefine both the goal and the scope needed to make the project more manageable.

Tip

Keep your goal and scope statements brief. If you can't explain your goal or scope in a sentence or two, your project may be overly ambitious and complex. Consider breaking up a large project into smaller projects. ■

Writing a simple goal and scope statement ensures that you've gathered key data — such as deliverables, timing, and budget — and that you and your team agree on the focus of everyone's efforts. These activities are likely to occur before you ever open a Microsoft Project file.

Planning

When you understand the goal and scope of a project, you can begin to work backward to determine the steps you need to take to reach the goal. Look for major phases first, and then break each phase into a logical sequence of steps.

Planning for resources is one aspect of planning the entire project. Resources can include equipment of limited availability, materials, individual workers, and groups of workers. Don't forget to take into account various schedule issues such as overtime, vacations, and any resources shared among projects. Time, money, and resources are closely related: You may be able to save time with more resources, but resources typically cost money. You need to understand the order of priority among time, quality, and money.

Note

There's truth to the old joke: Time, budget, or quality — pick two. Devoting resources (which usually become costs) to a project schedule can decrease the time but can also cause loss of quality control. Extending the time can improve quality but usually causes resource conflicts and added costs. Microsoft Project helps you see the trade-offs among these three important criteria throughout the life of your project. ■

Planning is the point at which you begin to enter data in Microsoft Project and see your project take shape. Figure 1.6 shows the Gantt Chart view of an initial Microsoft Project schedule.

FIGURE 1.6

The outline format of a Project schedule clearly shows the various phases of your project. Dependencies among tasks have not yet been established; every task starts at the same time, which isn't always possible.

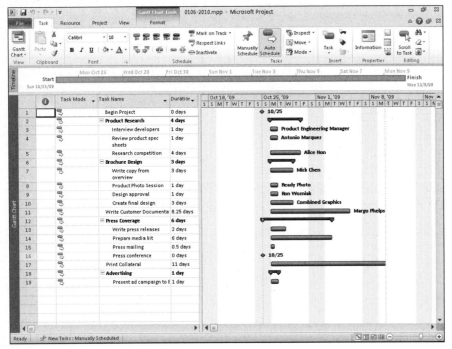

Revising

Most of the time, you send an initial project schedule to various managers or co-workers for approval or input so you can refine the schedule based on different factors. You can use the reporting features of Microsoft Project and the collaboration features of SharePoint (if your organization uses it) to generate several drafts of your plan.

Cross-Reference

Chapter 9 explains more about the reports that are available in Project; Chapter 19 describes how to use SharePoint with Project. ■

Be prepared to revise your plan after everyone has a chance to review it. You may want to create and save multiple Project files to generate what-if scenarios based on the input you receive. Seeing your plans from various perspectives is a great way to take advantage of Project's power.

Cross-Reference

Find out more about Project views that support what-if analysis in Chapter 6 and about comparing projects in Chapter 14. ∎

Finding resolutions to conflicts in timing and resource allocation is another aspect of planning and revising. Project helps you pinpoint these conflicts, which may include the following:

- A team member or resource that is booked on several projects at one time
- A task that begins before another task that must precede it
- An unusually high use of expensive equipment in one phase that is upsetting your budget

Cross-Reference

This book contains many tips and techniques for resolving conflicts. In particular, Chapters 10 and 11 focus on using Microsoft Project features to resolve scheduling and resource problems. ∎

When your project plan seems solid, you can take a picture of it, called a *baseline*, against which you can track actual progress.

Cross-Reference

Chapter 12 explains how to set (and, if necessary, clear) baselines. ∎

Tracking

You should try to solidify your tracking methods before your project begins. Ask yourself the following questions:

- Do you want to track your progress once a week or once a month?
- Do project participants track their own work or report their progress to you?
- Do you want to combine those smaller reports into a single, less-detailed report for management?

Tip

The answers to these questions can also help you determine whether you need to use Project Standard, Project Professional, or Project Server. See Chapter 2 for more information on choosing the Project product that best suits your needs. ∎

Knowing how you are going to track your project's progress, and who needs to know what and when, helps your team establish efficient tracking mechanisms from the outset, reducing frustration.

The Microsoft Project schedule shown in Figure 1.7 uses the Tracking Gantt view to show the original baseline (the bottom bar of each task) tracked against actual progress (the top bar of each task).

FIGURE 1.7

The darker portion of each upper taskbar and the percentage figure to the right of each upper taskbar indicate the percentage of each task that is complete.

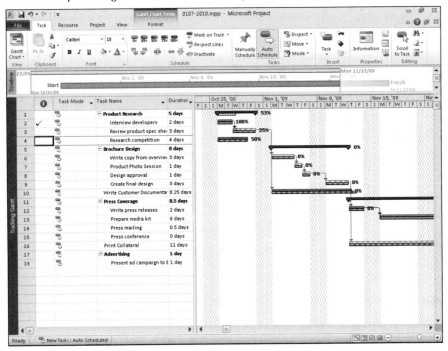

Tip

You can save interim baselines of a schedule at various points during your project. This approach helps you see where major shifts occurred and shows how you accommodated those shifts. See Chapter 12 for more information on baselines. ■

Learning from your mistakes

Learning project management software isn't the same as mastering project management, any more than learning to use a word processor is the same as learning to write. As with writing, project management as a discipline entails conceptual layers that transcend the tools and features of the software used to support it. Having the experience and wisdom to use the features effectively comes from repeated use — *and* from a seasoned professional perspective. If you don't transform right away into a proficient Microsoft Project user, just keep at it. You have to work through one or more projects before you really know the most effective way to enter information about a project. You can expect to develop efficient tracking methods over time. Don't worry — it took you time to learn all you know about managing projects. If you pay attention to what goes on during your projects when you first implement Microsoft Project schedules, you can learn from your mistakes.

Microsoft Project enables you to review your projects and to see clearly where you estimated incorrectly, made adjustments too slowly, or didn't divide phases into manageable chunks. Project keeps your original schedule's baseline, interim baselines, and your final tracked schedule in a single file. When you're planning future projects, you can use these older baselines to help gauge the duration of tasks as well as the cost of certain items and to know how many resources are enough to get the job done.

In the end, you'll be a more successful and efficient project manager. You can easily show your boss the specific actions you've taken to avoid problems and provide solutions. In addition, you'll have the tools you need to help both you and your manager understand the issues you face — and to get the support you need.

Summary

This chapter presented a survey of the discipline known as *project management* and explained the role that project management software can play to help you gain — and keep — control of your projects. It included the following topics:

- Projects involve a stated goal, a specific time frame, and multiple resources (which can include people, equipment, and materials).
- Project management seeks to control issues of time, quality, and money.
- Critical path, slack, task durations, milestones, fixed tasks, resource-driven tasks, and dependencies are elements of project management that help you build and monitor a project.
- Project management software can assist you in planning, tracking, and communicating with team members and in reporting on projects with tools such as Gantt Charts and network diagrams.
- Although using Project takes some effort on your part, this effort pays off in increased productivity and efficiency.
- Projects typically have five activities: Setting the goal and defining the scope, planning, revising, tracking, and reviewing to learn from your mistakes.

Chapter 2 takes a closer look at the Microsoft Project environment and provides information about some of the tools it provides that you can use to manage a project.

Exploring the Microsoft Project Environment

This chapter introduces Project's environment as well as the powerful tools that Project places at your disposal. You practice moving among different views, and you work with some of the tools and on-screen elements that you can use to create schedules.

Project now sports the new interface found in Word, Excel, PowerPoint, and other Office products.

IN THIS CHAPTER

Taking a first look at Project

The basics of entering information in Project

Taking a First Look at Project

Two versions of Microsoft Project 2010 are available. You can purchase Project 2010 Standard or Project 2010 Professional. These products differ only in the way that they support Project Server, which is Project's tool to manage projects on the Web.

The functionality of Project Server has again been expanded. As with Project 2007, you can't use Project Server with Project Standard. Instead, to use Project Server 2010, you must also use Project Professional 2010. In this book, I assume that you're using Project Professional.

Cross-Reference
See Part VII for more information on using Project Server. ■

What Is Project Server?

Project Server enables you to manage projects on your company's intranet or on the Internet — and only the project manager installs and uses Microsoft Project Professional. Everyone else on the project uses Project Web Access, the Web-based product that connects to the Project Server database that contains your project data. You open Project Web Access by typing the URL to the Project Server database into Internet Explorer version 8 (or later). Using Project Web Access instead of Microsoft Project, the project's resources can do the following tasks (among other things):

- View a project's Gantt Chart
- Receive, refuse, and delegate work assignments
- Update assignments with progress and completion information
- Attach supporting documentation, such as budget estimates or feasibility studies, to a project
- Receive notices about task status
- Send status reports to the project manager

Project managers can do even more than rank-and-file team members. For example, by using Project Server, project managers have access to a company-wide resource pool (called the Enterprise Resource Pool) that tracks resource allocations across projects. If a project manager finds that a specific resource is unavailable, he or she can define the requirements for the job and let Project Server tools search the Enterprise Resource Pool to find another resource with the same skills. And, those with proper security privileges can take advantage of Project Server's portfolio management features.

Note

If you're not connected to Project Server, you'll see no difference in functionality between Project 2010 Standard and Project 2010 Professional. You see commands in Project 2010 Professional that you don't see in Project 2010 Standard, but the commands aren't available for use. So if you're using Project Standard, most of this book also applies to you — just ignore any grayed-out commands you see on-screen. ■

Cross-Reference

See Part VII for more information about Project Server and Project Web Access. ■

Starting Project

When you open Microsoft Project from the Programs folder of the Windows Start menu, Project initially displays the main screen for Project 2010, as shown in Figure 2.1.

Tip

You also can open Project by double-clicking any Project file. Project files are saved with the extension .mpp. ■

The Ribbon appears across the top of the screen, and the Quick Access Toolbar appears above the Ribbon, on the program's title bar. You can customize both of these elements; see Chapter 16 for details. Clicking the File tab leads you to Backstage view, described later in this chapter.

FIGURE 2.1

Project's opening screen.

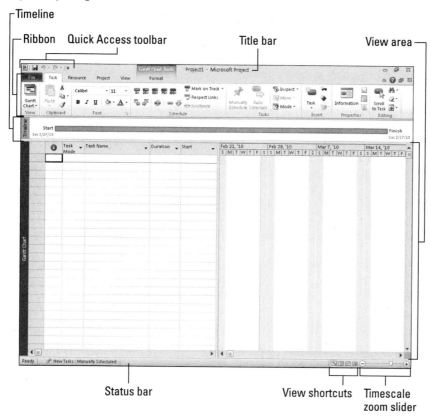

New Feature

Just below the Ribbon, the Timeline view appears by default. This new view can be used to provide a snapshot of your project's tasks and durations. You can hide the Timeline view or display a larger version of it, as needed; read more about this view in Chapter 6. ■

A *view* of your project occupies the bulk of the Project window. Views offer you different ways to review project information to help you focus on different aspects of your project. You'll find scroll bars on the right side and below most views; use the scroll bars to display different portions of your project. By default, Project displays the Gantt Chart view, which contains a table on the left side and a chart on the right; you can read more about the Gantt Chart view later in this chapter (as well as in Chapter 6, where you find samples of all the views available in Project).

At the bottom of the Project window are the Status Bar (which you can customize — see Chapter 16), the View shortcut buttons, and the timescale zoom slider. You can use the View shortcut buttons to quickly switch between the Gantt Chart view, the Task Usage view, the Team Planner view, and the Resource Sheet view. You can use the timescale zoom slider to adjust the timescale in views containing a timescale. In the Gantt Chart view, the timescale appears above the chart portion of the view on the right side of the window.

Note

Project Standard users have only three View shortcut buttons: The Gantt Chart view button, the Task Usage view button, and the Resource Sheet view button. ■

Notably missing from Project 2010 are the Project Guide, the View Bar, and the Excel-like Entry bar. The Project Guide, available in earlier versions of Project, is now available only if a developer makes it available programmatically. You can display the View Bar, which enables you to switch to the most commonly used views quickly, by right-clicking the gray bar running down the left side of the Project screen — the bar that contains the name of the currently displayed view — and choosing View Bar. Or you can use any of three controls in place of the View Bar — the View shortcuts, the Gantt Chart button on the Task tab of the Ribbon, and the Team Planner button (for Project Standard users, make that the Resource Sheet button) on the Resource tab of the Ribbon. And you can still display the Excel-like Entry bar using the Display tab of the Options dialog box; Project places the Entry bar immediately below the Ribbon. The next section offers details about using these options as a part of using the Ribbon.

Using the Ribbon

The Ribbon, shown in Figure 2.2, consists of six tabs: File, Task, Resource, Project, View, and Format; the Format tab is specific to the view currently displayed. As you click each tab, you'll find groups of buttons related to the tab's title; group names appear below the buttons on any particular tab. For example, the Task tab contains eight groups by default:

Tip

I said that the Task tab contains eight groups "by default"; you can customize the Ribbon to add or remove groups from a tab or even create your own tabs. See Chapter 16 for details. ■

FIGURE 2.2

The Ribbon consists of tabs that contain groups of buttons.

Dialog box launcher   Click to minimize Ribbon

- View
- Clipboard
- Font
- Tasks
- Schedule
- Insert
- Properties
- Editing

You click a button in a group to make Project do something; for example, you can use the chain-link button in the Tasks group to create a dependency between two tasks. If you aren't sure of a button's purpose, hover the mouse pointer over the button and Project will display a ScreenTip describing the button's function.

Tip

You can work with the Ribbon using the keyboard instead of the mouse. Press the Alt key to display letters representing a tab (or numbers representing a button on the Quick Access Toolbar, discussed in the next section). Press the letter of the tab, and Project displays additional letters — or combinations of letters — for each button on that tab. Press the letter or combination of letters, and Project performs the action associated with that button. ∎

In the lower-right corner of some groups, you see a small square button containing an arrow that points down and to the right; this button is called a *dialog box launcher* and it does exactly what its name implies — if you click a dialog box launcher button, Project displays a dialog box that contains additional options associated with the group. You can see an example of a dialog box launcher button in the Font group in Figure 2.2.

If you find the Ribbon buttons distracting, you can hide them temporarily and just display the tab names by clicking the Minimize the Ribbon button in the upper-right corner of the Ribbon. Whenever you click a tab, Project redisplays the buttons on that tab; after you click a button on the tab or simply click outside the Ribbon, Project hides the buttons again.

An arrow appears below or beside some buttons. different actions occur depending on whether you click the button or the arrow associated with it. The Gantt Chart button on the Task tab is a good example: When you click the top of the button, Project displays the Gantt Chart view. When you click the bottom of the button, however, Project displays a list of commonly used views, and you can click a view to switch to it (see Figure 2.3).

FIGURE 2.3

Buttons with arrows serve multiple purposes.

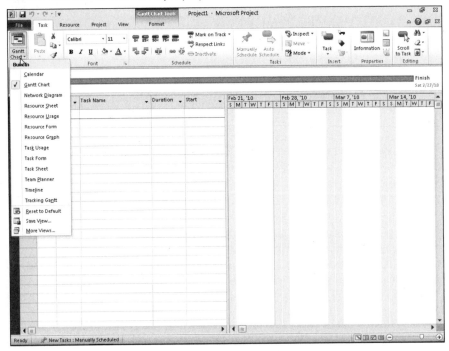

Note

The arrow can appear below the button or to the right of it; for example, the Copy button features an arrow on the right side of the button. Wherever the arrow may appear, it works the same: It causes different actions depending on where you click it. ■

Introducing the Quick Access Toolbar (QAT)

The QAT replaces all the toolbars you had in earlier versions of Project. By default, only the Save, Undo, and Redo buttons appear on the QAT, but you can quickly add more commonly used commands by clicking the Customize Quick Access Toolbar button at the right edge of the QAT (see Figure 2.4). If the command you want to add doesn't appear in the list, you can still add it to the QAT; see Chapter 16 for details.

FIGURE 2.4

You can add common commands such as New and Open to the QAT by clicking the Customize Quick Access Toolbar button.

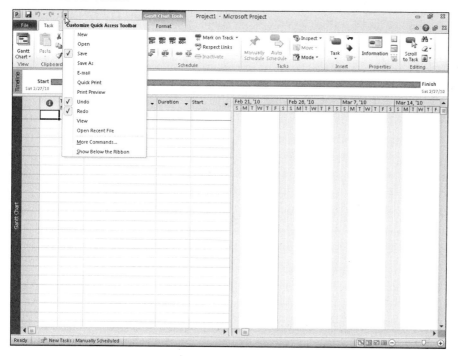

Tip

You can display the QAT below the Ribbon if you click Show Below the Ribbon.

If you aren't sure of a button's purpose, hover the mouse pointer over the button and Project will display a ScreenTip describing the button's function. ■

Working with the Mini Toolbar

The Mini Toolbar appears whenever you right-click any cell in the table portion of a view (see Figure 2.5). You can use the Mini Toolbar to perform common tasks, such as applying italics to a task name or inserting or deleting a task.

The Mini Toolbar contains commonly used commands, such as inserting or deleting a task.

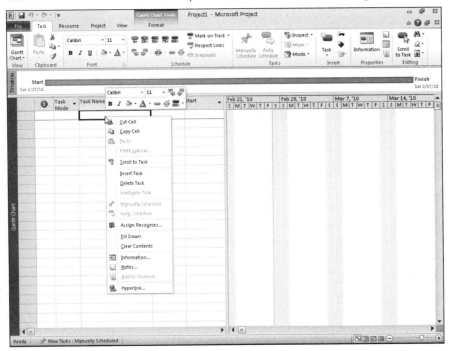

Understanding Backstage view

When you click the File tab, Backstage view appears (see Figure 2.6).

New Feature

You use Backstage view to perform many of the functions that appeared on the File menu in Project 2007 or earlier. For example, you save files, open them, close them, and print them from Backstage view. You also set options for Project and for individual Project files from Backstage view. ∎

In Backstage view, the File tab (or the Esc key on your keyboard) is your way back to your project if you decide against selecting a command in Backstage view.

Warning

In Backstage view, you might be tempted to click Exit on the lower-left side or the X in the upper-right corner of the view to get back to your project, but taking either of those actions closes the program completely. Just click the File tab to redisplay your project. ∎

FIGURE 2.6

In Project 2010, Backstage view replaces the File menu.

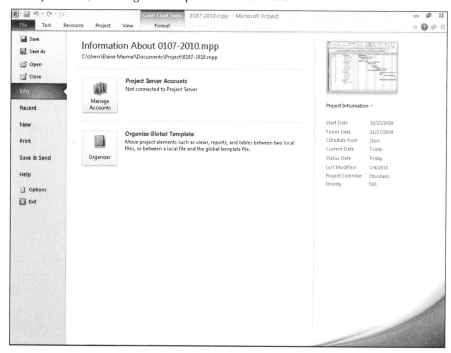

Examining the Gantt Chart view

When you open Project, the Gantt Chart view appears by default (see Figure 2.7). Project contains many other views that appear throughout this book, but you're likely to spend a great deal of your time in the Gantt Chart view. This view offers a wealth of information about your project in a single snapshot.

Cross-Reference

For details about the other views that are available in Project, see Chapter 6. ∎

The Gantt Chart view is composed of two sections: a table on the left and the Gantt Chart on the right. After you enter task information, the table displays columns of information about each task in your project, such as the task name, duration, start date, and more. The Gantt Chart presents a graphic representation that helps you see the timing and relationships among tasks.

FIGURE 2.7

When you enter information in the Gantt Chart view, the split pane displays task details in the Gantt table and bars representing tasks in the Gantt Chart.

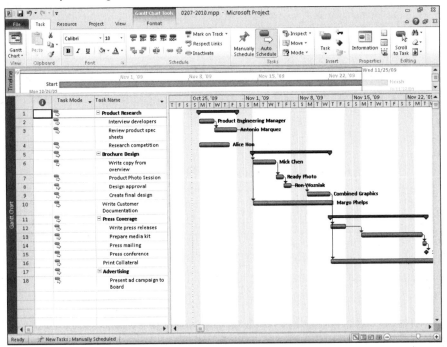

The timescale along the top of the Gantt Chart acts like a horizontal calendar. Think of it as a ruler against which you draw the tasks in your project. Instead of marking off inches, however, this ruler marks off the hours, days, weeks, and months of your project. Project enables you to display up to three timescales along the top of the Gantt Chart — a top, middle, and bottom timescale. In Figure 2.7, you see two timescales. The top timescale shows weeks; the bottom timescale shows days. Multiple timescales help you to see the multiple levels of timing simultaneously, such as the day and hour or the month, week, and day.

You can zoom in or out to view larger or smaller time increments for different perspectives of your project's schedule. You can show smaller time increments in the Gantt Chart by clicking the plus button (+) on the Zoom slider in the lower-right corner of the screen, or you can show larger increments of time by clicking the minus button (−). A daily perspective on a three-year project enables you to manage day-to-day tasks, whereas a quarterly representation of your project may be more useful when you're discussing larger issues with your management team.

Note

You have more control over the appearance of the Timescale when you use the Timescale button on the View tab or the Timescale dialog box instead of the Zoom slider bar in the lower-right corner of the screen. In Chapter 7, you can read about setting the Timescale. ■

You can modify what you see on-screen in the Gantt Chart view, and Project carries those modifications to other views. You can change views to see information about timing, budget, or resource assignments in detail, or you can just look at the big picture. You also can customize what each view shows you. For example, you can use the divider that runs vertically between the Gantt table and Gantt Chart to adjust the amount of space that each pane occupies. Dragging this divider to the right reveals more columns of project data in the Gantt table. Dragging the divider to the left displays more of the project's taskbars in the Gantt Chart.

Cross-Reference

See Chapter 7 for details on working with views, including customizing them by adding and deleting table columns or switching tables. ■

Note

Each pane of the Gantt Chart view has its own set of scroll bars at the bottom of the window. To make changes, you must use the appropriate scroll bar and select objects in the appropriate pane. ■

Most views in Project contain a table that uses a familiar spreadsheet-style interface: Information appears in columns and rows. The intersection of a column and a row is a *cell*, just as in Excel. Project assigns each task in your project an ID number, which corresponds to the task's row number running along the left of the spreadsheet. You can enter project information either in dialog boxes or directly into cells. When you select a cell, the Entry bar, which appears immediately above the column names of the table, displays the information in the cell.

Note

When you press Delete, Project deletes the contents of the selected cell. ■

If you've ever used Microsoft Excel or one of the other popular spreadsheet programs, you already know how to enter and edit information in Project. When you begin typing in a cell, the insertion point appears in the cell to the right of any text that you enter. To edit text in a cell, click once to select the cell and then press F2 or click a second time at the location in the cell where you want to begin editing. If you press F2, the insertion point appears at the right edge of the text in the cell. If you click a second time, the insertion point appears in the cell at the location where you clicked the second time.

If you display the Entry bar, then information you enter into a cell also appears in the Entry bar. The Entry bar appears directly under the Ribbon and serves the same purpose in Project as the Entry bar in Excel. You can type new text or edit existing text by clicking anywhere within the text in the Entry bar. Two buttons on the left side of the bar (an X and a check mark) enable you to cancel or accept an entry, as shown in Figure 2.8.

FIGURE 2.8

You can enter or edit text in individual cells or in the Entry bar.

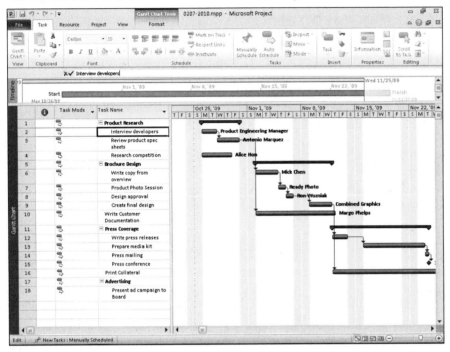

Cross-Reference

Chapter 4 covers entering and editing text in greater detail. ■

To display the Entry bar, follow these steps:

1. Click the File tab.

2. From the Backstage view that appears, click Options to display the Project Options dialog box (see Figure 2.9).

3. Click Display on the left.

4. Click the Entry bar check box on the right.

5. Click OK.

FIGURE 2.9

Use the Display options of the Project Options dialog box to enable the Entry bar in every project file.

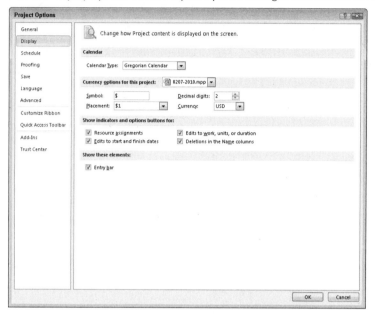

Changing views

Project offers a plethora of views in which you can display project information because a single view can't possibly show all the information that you need to see regarding timing, relationships among tasks, resource allocations, and project progress. Each view helps you focus on a different aspect of your project. Think of a project as a small business. As in any business, different people attend to various aspects of the work. The accounting department thinks mainly of the costs of doing business. The plant supervisor focuses on operations and having enough machinery and manpower to get the job done. Your human resources department thinks of people — their salaries, hours, benefits, and so on. As the owner of your project, you're likely to wear all these hats (and more) during the project. With Project, switching to another view to see your work from a different perspective is the equivalent of changing hats as you move from one responsibility to another. Each view helps you to focus on a different aspect of your project.

You can use any of four methods to switch views:

- To switch quickly between four frequently used views — Gantt Chart, Task Usage, Team Planner, and Resource Sheet — use the View shortcut buttons in the lower-right corner of the Project window (see Figure 2.10). Project Standard users see only three buttons; the Team Planner view isn't available in Project Standard.

To switch to a popular view, use View shortcut buttons in the lower-right corner or the list that appears at the bottom of the Gantt Chart button.

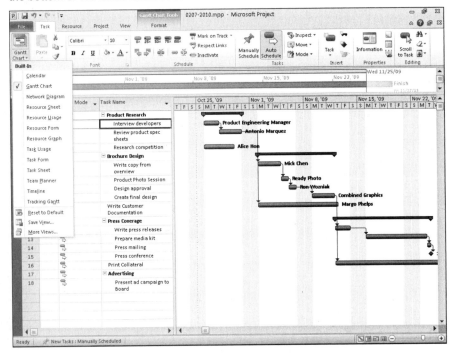

- To see additional popular views, click the Task tab and then click the bottom of the Gantt Chart button in the View group (refer to Figure 2.10). Or click the Resource tab and click the bottom of the Team Planner button (the Resource Sheet button for Project Standard users) in the View group.

- Click the View tab and use the buttons in the Task Views group and the Resource Views to switch to the most popular task and resource views (see Figure 2.11).

- Use the More Views window to select a view (see Figure 2.12). You can display the More Views window by selecting More Views from the list that appears when you click the bottom of the Gantt Chart button on the Task tab or click the bottom of any button in the Task Views group or the Resource Views group on the View tab.

FIGURE 2.11

The Task Views group and the Resource Views group (to the left of the View tab) help you switch quickly to the most popular task and resource views.

FIGURE 2.12

The More Views dialog box lists all of Project's views, as well as any you might add.

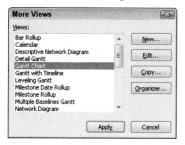

Cross-Reference

In Chapter 6, you find out more about all of Project's views and how you can use them to gain perspective on your project. In Chapter 7, you discover how to create custom views. ■

What's New in Project 2010

Most new features in Project 2010 revolve around Project Server and Project Web Access, with improvements both to the interface and under the hood. But users have anxiously awaited a few fairly powerful new features in Project Standard and Professional.

For example, Project 2010 introduces a fresh, new interface that functions like its other Office product counterparts. And Project 2010 introduces two new views: the Timeline view and the Team Planner view.

The Task Driver feature has been expanded and renamed; it's now the Task Inspector and it helps you identify, quickly and easily, the scheduling factors that drive individual tasks, providing more information than its predecessor.

In Project Professional 2010, you can make tasks inactive, keeping them in your schedule but eliminating their impact on the schedule. In both Project Standard and Project Professional, you can schedule tasks manually instead of having Project schedule them — a handy feature when you need to control task dates.

The Format tab enables you to quickly and easily format any view. For example, using the Gantt Chart Tools Format tab, you can quickly add baseline bars, select predefined bar styles from a gallery, and check boxes to display critical tasks, late tasks, and slack.

Rather than describe all the new features in Project 2010 at this point in the book, I've provided Table 2.1, which shows you where you can find more information in this book on new features.

New Feature
You can easily find the new features in the chapters in which I discuss them in detail. Simply look for the New Feature icon that appears next to the discussion of a new feature in Project. ■

Note
The features for which you find descriptions in Chapters 21–24 are not available in Project Standard. ■

TABLE 2.

New Features in Project 2010

Feature	Chapter
The Ribbon	2
QAT	2
View shortcuts	2
Zoom slider	2
Mini Toolbar	2
Backstage view	2 and 3
Schedule tasks manually	3
Schedule summary tasks manually	3 and 4
Timeline View	3 and 6
Team Planner view (available only in Project Professional)	6 and 11
Easier ways to add columns to views	7
Task Inspector	10
Make a task inactive (Project Professional only)	10
Compared versions of a project display Gantt bars	14
Copy and paste Project information into any Office program	18
Collaborate using Project Professional and SharePoint (some functionality not available in Project Standard)	20

Project Server and Project Web Access have been improved and enhanced in many ways; see Chapters 21 through 25 for details.

Summary

This chapter introduced the Project 2010 environment and the concept of views, which provide many ways to display project information. This chapter also explained how to

- Understand the Project screen
- Use the Ribbon and the Quick Access Toolbar (QAT) using both the mouse and the keyboard
- Use the Mini Toolbar
- Use Backstage view
- Understand the Gantt Chart view

Chapter 3 covers how to start a project, save Project files, and get help in Project.

Part II

Getting Your Project Going

Creating a New Project

N ow that you have some project management concepts under your belt and you've taken a stroll around Project's environment, you're ready to create your first schedule. Before you type any information into a Project schedule, however, you should first assemble the relevant information about your project. Then you can open a new Project file and begin to build your project tasks by using a simple outline structure.

In this chapter, you begin to build your first Project schedule and find out how to save your project. At the end of the chapter, you read about how to take advantage of Project's Help system.

Gathering Information

As you read in Chapter 1, several elements must be in place before you can begin to build a project schedule. In addition to determining whether the project should be undertaken, identifying the project's stakeholders, and gaining stakeholder support, you and your team must understand the overall goal and scope of the project so that you can clearly lay out the steps that lie between you and that goal. You'll find delineating the major steps of the project a good place to start. Don't worry about the order of the tasks at this point — just brainstorm all the major areas of activity. Suppose that you've been given the project of organizing an annual meeting for your company. You may take the following steps:

- Book the meeting space
- Schedule speakers
- Arrange for audiovisual equipment

- Order food

- Send out invitations

- Mail out annual reports

The last item on that list raises the question of scope: Is it within the scope of your project to create the annual report, or are you simply supposed to obtain copies of a report from the marketing department (for example) and mail them to stockholders before the meeting? In some corporations, the person who is responsible for organizing the annual meeting is also responsible for overseeing the production of the annual report. Be sure to answer questions of scope and responsibility at this stage of your planning.

For this example, assume that another department is creating the annual report. You simply need to make sure that someone mails copies of the report to all stockholders before the annual meeting.

Determining detail tasks

After you've prepared a list of major tasks — Project calls them *summary tasks* — break them into more detailed tasks. Take one of the items on the list — *Order food,* for example — and consider how you can break down this task. How detailed should you get? The following is one possible way to subdivide the *Order food* task:

- Create a budget.

- Determine a menu.

- Select a caterer.

  - Send out requests for bids.

  - Receive all estimates.

  - Review estimates and award contract.

- Give final head count to caterer.

- Confirm menu one week before the meeting.

Could you do without the detailed tasks under *Select a caterer*? Do you need more details under *Create a budget*? Those decisions are up to you; they're based on your knowledge of your project and procedures. However, keep the following points in mind:

- Create tasks that remind you of major action items, but don't overburden yourself with items of such detail that keeping track of your schedule becomes a full-time job. That's the purpose of daily to-do lists.

- Include milestones to mark off points in your project. For example, the *Review estimates and award contract* task under the summary task *Select a caterer* is a milestone — it marks a point in time by which you want to have made a major decision. If that time comes and goes and you haven't selected the caterer, will missing this deadline affect other subsequent tasks? If so, including that milestone could be vital to your success.

- Include tasks that management should know about, because you'll use the Project schedule to report progress. If your boss wants to see that you've sent out a purchase order to the caterer per your new Accounting Department procedures, you may want to include the task (even if you don't think this level of detail is all that important).

Establishing time limits

When you have a good working idea of the tasks involved in your project, you still need some idea of their timing. Should you allow two weeks for caterers to reply with bids? Not if you have only three weeks to organize the meeting. You may want to approach determining task timing by building an initial schedule in Project, assigning time to tasks, and seeing how close you can come to your deadline. If you're way off, you can go back and tweak the timing for individual tasks until your schedule works.

Caution

You may be tempted to trim time off your tasks to make them fit a deadline, but this approach tends to produce an unrealistic schedule. What should you do? Use the initial schedule to convince your boss that you need more time, money, or resources to complete this project on time. If he or she wants to trim time from a specific task to meet the deadline, you might have grounds to ask for more help. ■

At this early planning stage, get any information that you need to assign timing to tasks. For example, contact vendors or subcontractors to get their timing estimates, which you need to reflect in your schedule. If your project has a drop-dead completion date, you should be aware of it. However, you can leave it to Project to show you whether your estimates work in an overall schedule.

Lining up your resources

When you build a Project schedule, you need to know what resources are available to you, as well as their costs. You don't necessarily need to know these resources by name, but you should know, for example, that your construction project needs three engineers at a cost of $150 per hour and one piece of earthmoving equipment at a daily rental cost of $450.

Be sure to identify these resources and assign them to individual tasks early in the project-planning process. Find out anything you can about their availability: Are some of them available only half-time for your project? Will all the engineers be unavailable during the third week of August because of a professional conference? Is one resource available for most but not all of your project due to other work commitments? Research the cost and availability of resources as much as possible as you begin to build a project.

Cross-Reference

For more information about identifying resources and assigning them to individual tasks, see Chapters 5 and 25. ■

Looking at dependencies

Finally, before you enter project information into a schedule, be aware of relationships among tasks. Does the CEO have to approve the menu before you book the caterers? Are you required to wait three weeks after applying for a permit before starting construction on a building? If your project faces issues involving the order and relationships of tasks, you will save yourself some headaches down the line and build a more realistic schedule if you can identify these obstacles now.

Opening a Project File

You can start a project file in a couple of different ways. In this section, you first see the "usual" way to start a file. Then I cover how to use templates with project files.

Opening a project file — the usual way

Okay, you've done your homework. You've made some notes about your upcoming project's tasks, timing, resources, and dependencies. You're ready to start building your first schedule in Project. Choose Start ⇨ All Programs ⇨ Microsoft Office ⇨ Microsoft Project 2010. You see the main Project window, where you can begin building a task outline.

Other ways to start projects

You can base your project on one of the templates available for Project 2010. Templates contain "standard" information to help you get started quickly. Instead of entering tasks, you may need only to edit tasks. Click the File tab and, from the Backstage view, click New. From the Available Templates (see Figure 3.1), click a template in the New from Existing group or you can search at the Office Online Web site for templates by clicking the arrow button beside the Search Microsoft Office Online for templates box.

Select a template and click the Create button. If you select any template other than Blank Project, Project displays a new project that contains tasks relevant to the title of the template you selected. You can use this project as a starting point for your project and modify it as needed.

Note
You might need your Project 2010 CD to install a template. ∎

Opening projects

You can open projects by clicking the File button and, from the Backstage view, click Recent. Project displays a list of the last 17 projects you opened (see Figure 3.2); click one and Project displays it on-screen.

Tip

You can change the number of files that Project displays in the Recent list. Click the File tab and, from Backstage view, click Options. In the Project Options dialog box that appears, click the Advanced tab. In the Display section, change the number shown in the Show this Number of Recent Documents box. ■

If the project you want to open doesn't appear in the Recent Projects list, you can click Open in Backstage view. In this case, Project displays the Open dialog box shown in Figure 3.3.

Tip

If you want to open a file created in Project 2007 or earlier, you might need to set permissions. Click the File tab and, from Backstage view, click Options. In the Project Options dialog box, click the Trust Center tab and then click the Trust Center Settings button. In the Trust Center dialog box that appears, click Legacy Formats and select one of these options: (1) Prompt When Loading Files with Legacy or Non-default File Format or (2) Allow Loading Files with Legacy or Non-default File Formats. Click OK twice to save your choice. ■

FIGURE 3.1

Select a template on which to base your project.

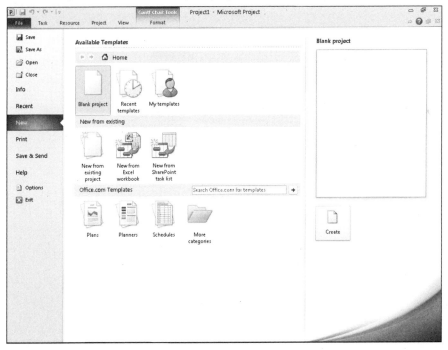

FIGURE 3.2

Click Recent in the Backstage view to see a list of the last 17 projects you opened.

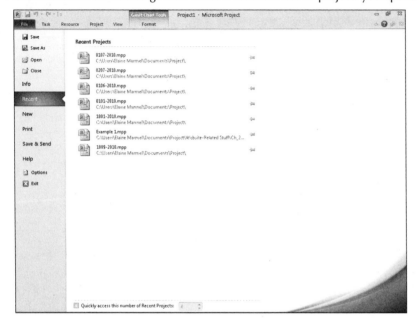

FIGURE 3.3

Use the Open dialog box to navigate to the folder where you store projects and select a project to open.

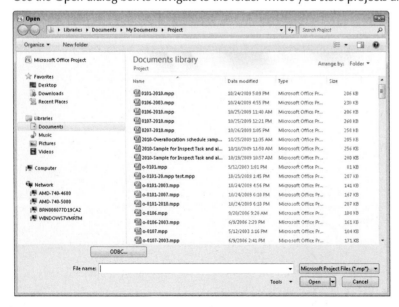

Establishing Basic Project Information

Use the Project Information dialog box (shown in Figure 3.4) to supply basic information about the new project you want to set up. If this box doesn't appear automatically, click the Project tab and, in the Properties group, click the Project Information button to display the dialog box.

FIGURE 3.4

The Project Information dialog box tracks basic information about each project.

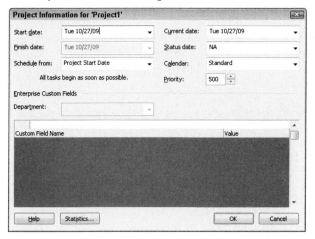

Tip

You can make the Project Information dialog box appear automatically whenever you start a new project. Click the File tab and, in Backstage view, click Options. In the Project Options dialog box that appears, click the Advanced tab. In the General section, place a check in the Prompt for Project Info for New Projects box. ■

You can enter the following eight pieces of information in the Project Information dialog box:

- **Start Date:** If you set a start date for the project, all tasks begin on that date until you assign timing or dependencies to them.

- **Finish Date:** If you know your project's deadline, you can enter it here and then work backward to schedule your project. You must change the setting in the Schedule from field to make this option available.

- **Schedule From:** You can build schedules from completion to start by setting this field to Project Finish Date. Alternatively, you can build your schedule from the start date forward by accepting the default setting, Project Start Date.

- **Current Date:** Project uses your computer's current date setting for the default entry in this field. To use a different date, change the date in this field. You can adjust this setting to generate reports that provide information on your project as of a certain date or to go back and track your project's progress from an earlier date.

- **Status Date:** Typically you set the Status Date after you set a baseline for your project and you begin tracking actual progress; that's because often the day you record the progress is not the day on which it occurred. The Status Date field sets the date used in the earned-value calculations and identifies the complete-through date in the Update Project dialog box. The Status Date also enables Project to place progress lines in your project. If you leave the Status Date set at NA, Project sets the Status Date to your computer's current date setting.

- **Calendar:** You can select the calendar on which to base your schedule. The Standard calendar is the default — it schedules work eight hours a day, five days a week.

- **Priority:** You can establish a priority for each project in addition to setting priorities for tasks. For priorities, Project uses a numerical value between 1 and 1,000. The project level priority plays a role when you use shared resources across multiple projects. Setting a project priority helps you to better control how resource leveling adjusts tasks when you share resources across projects.

Note

Leveling is a technique you can use to smooth out the use of resources so you use them most efficiently. Leveling is particularly useful when your resources are overallocated; Project can help you reallocate your resources' efforts and potentially eliminate conflicts. ■

Cross-Reference

For more information on resource leveling, see Chapter 11. ■

- **Enterprise Custom Fields:** If your organization uses Project Server, you may need to assign values to project-level custom fields or outline any codes you're using that are defined in the Project Server database. You see an asterisk (*) next to any required custom field or outline code.

Make a choice in the Schedule From field and then enter either a start or finish date — only one is available to you, depending on the choice that you've made in the Schedule From field. If you schedule from the project start date, Project defaults the constraint type for all new tasks to start As Soon As Possible (ASAP). And, as you would expect, if you schedule from the project finish date, Project defaults the constraint type for All new tasks to start As Late As Possible (ALAP). To enter one of these dates, click the down arrow next to the text box. (The arrow is not available if the Schedule From field isn't set for that choice.) Select a date from the pop-up calendar, as shown in Figure 3.5.

Caution

If you decide to schedule backward from the finish date, Project can't use tools such as resource leveling to resolve conflicts in your schedule. ■

You can change the project's start date during the planning phase, trying out alternative what-if scenarios by modifying this field. as you build your tasks going forward, if you use automatic scheduling, Project calculates the project finish date as dictated by the length of your tasks and their timing relationships. Later in this chapter, you can read more about automatic and manual scheduling.

FIGURE 3.5

Use the arrow keys at the top of this calendar to choose other months.

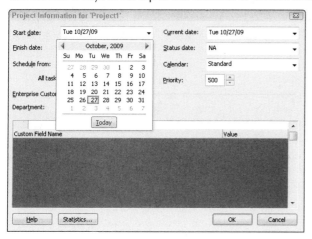

Tip

If you have already begun the project, you can set the start date to a date in the past to accurately reflect the real start date. ■

If you know the date by which something must be completed (as with the annual meeting project in the earlier example, or a Christmas party that must happen on December 25), you can schedule tasks by moving backward from the finish date. When you do this and use automatic scheduling, Project builds the tasks going back in time. You may be surprised when Project generates a schedule telling you that you should have started three weeks earlier to finish on time. In that case, you can either add resources to get the work done faster or reduce the scope of the project.

Cross-Reference

In Chapters 10 and 11, you can read about techniques that can help you resolve scheduling and resource problems. ■

When beginning a new schedule, you typically accept the default settings for Current date and Status date. After your project is under way, changing these default settings affects project tracking — as well as the material that is generated in project reports.

For now, you can keep all the default settings (that is, scheduling from the start of the project, having the current date be today, and starting the project today, as well as basing your schedule on the standard calendar). Click OK to close the Project Information dialog box.

Looking at Project Calendars

The Project Information dialog box enables you to set the basic parameters of the project's timing. Those parameters — and the information you're about to enter for specific tasks — are based on the Standard calendar, also called the *base calendar* because it serves as the basis for the calendar-scheduling calculations Project makes.

You can create a Standard calendar for each group of resources in your project. For example, if the plant employees work a nine-hour day from 6:00 a.m. to 3:00 p.m., and the office employees work an eight-hour day from 8:00 a.m. to 5:00 p.m., you can create two calendars. When you assign one day of an office employee's time, Project understands it to be an eight-hour day. In the Project Information dialog box, you designate whether you want your project to use a standard, 24-hour, or night-shift calendar for most of your work assignments.

Note

If you're using Project Standard, the preceding information is absolutely true. If you're using Project Professional, it's almost all true. When using Project Professional, you can create your own calendars (for both projects and tasks) if you're working offline and storing the project locally (that is, not in the Project Server database). If you store the project in the Project Server database, you can create calendars only if the administrator has given you the rights to do so. ∎

Project also supports resource calendars and task calendars you can use when a resource's calendar or a task's calendar don't follow the Standard calendar for the project. Resource and task calendars work well for resources or tasks in your project with work hours that differ from the rest of the resources or tasks.

Cross-Reference

You find out more about task calendars in Chapter 4 and more about resource calendars in Chapter 5. ∎

Setting calendar options

Project makes default assumptions about certain items that form the basis of the default project calendar. For example, Project assumes that the default week contains five working days and 40 working hours. Project uses this calendar for resources unless you assign a different calendar to them. You can see the assumptions that Project uses when you click Schedule in the Project Options dialog box.

Note

These options do not affect scheduling. The options you see in this dialog box show you the defaults that Project uses to convert durations into corresponding time amounts. For example, if you enter 1mo for a task's duration, Project assumes you're allotting the equivalent of 20 days for that task. ∎

To view the default calendar options, click the File tab and, from Backstage view, click Project Options. Click Schedule in the Project Options dialog box (see Figure 3.6).

Caution

Any changes you make to these options apply to the current schedule only. To save your current changes and make them apply to all new project schedules, open the Calendar Options for this Project list and select All New Projects. ■

You can select any day of the week as your start day. For example, if you run a restaurant that closes on Sundays and Mondays, you might want to designate a work week of Tuesday through Saturday. In that case, you would set the Week Starts On field to Tuesday.

If your company uses a fiscal year other than the calendar year (January through December), you can set the Fiscal Year Starts In option. This setting is especially useful when you generate reports that show costs per quarter or year.

The other five Calendar options enable you to designate specific start and end times for each day, the number of hours in a day and in a week, and the number of days in a month. For example, you can set the work day to start at 9:00 a.m. and end at 6:00 p.m., assign 9 hours to your work day (no lunch for you!), and end up with a 45-hour week.

FIGURE 3.6

By reviewing the Calendar settings in the Project Options dialog box, you ensure that you and Project are speaking the same language when you enter task-duration information.

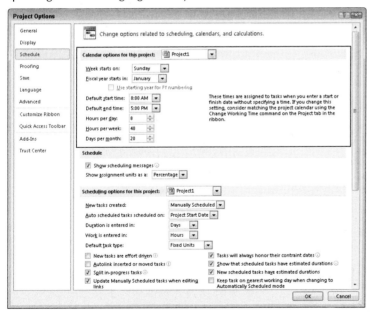

Setting schedule options

You also can modify the way in which Project enters task information. In the Project Options dialog box (if it isn't open, click the File tab and, in the Backstage view, click Options), click Schedule and then use the options shown in Figure 3.7 to change the default settings for entering tasks. You determine

- Whether Project shows scheduling messages that give you guidance about scheduling conflicts you might accidentally impose (select or deselect the Show Scheduling Messages check box).

- Whether Project displays assignment units as percentages or decimals. (In Figure 3.7, I've selected percentage.)

- Whether Project enters tasks without dates, uses the project Start Date, or uses the current date.

- The default unit of time for entering task durations (the default is days) and work time (hours).

When setting the last two options, suppose you're working on a five-year project in which most tasks run for months, not days. You might want to change the default setting for the Duration Is Entered In field. If you prefer to have any new tasks begin no earlier than the current date, you can adjust the setting for New tasks. As you gain experience with entering information, you'll find ways to customize Project to match your work style.

FIGURE 3.7

The Schedule tab is where you modify the default settings for entering tasks.

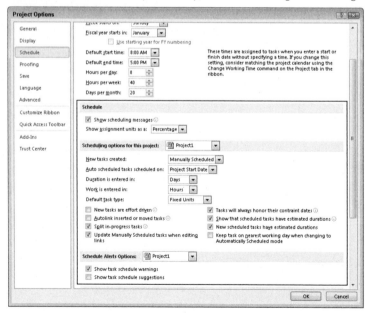

You also can use the check boxes to set Project behavior concerning tasks; Chapter 4 explains many of the concepts associated with the task behavior referenced in these options:

- **New Tasks Are Effort Driven:** If you check this box, Project schedules new tasks so that the work on the task remains constant as you add or remove assignments. See Chapter 4 for more information on effort-driven tasks, but, in general, assigning additional resources to an effort-driven task shortens the task duration.

- **Autolink Inserted or Moved Tasks:** If you check this box, Project automatically reestablishes a dependency between contiguous tasks that you move or insert.

- **Split In-Progress Tasks:** If you check this box, you allow Project to reschedule remaining duration and work when a task slips or when you report progress on a task ahead of its schedule. In this case, Project creates a *split task* — a task whose schedule is interrupted. Checking this box helps ensure that the progress you record appears when it actually takes place; if you remove the check from this box, the progress information you enter appears on the originally scheduled dates.

- **Tasks Can Be Manually Scheduled:** If you check this box, you have the option to schedule a task manually which gives you control over its dates or let Project schedule it automatically for you, according to the dependencies and constraints you've specified.

New Feature

The Task Mode field, which enables you to choose between automatic and manual scheduling for a task, is new to Project 2010. You can read more about it later in this chapter. ■

- **Update Manually Scheduled Tasks When Editing Links:** If you check this box, Project will make appropriate changes to manually scheduled tasks if you edit links that affect them.

- **Tasks Will Always Honor Their Constraint Dates:** If you check this box, Project schedules tasks according to their constraint dates and doesn't move them. See Chapter 4 for more information on constraints.

- **Show That Scheduled Tasks Have Estimated Durations**: If you check this box, Project displays a question mark (?) after the duration unit of any task for which you set a tentative duration rather than one that you want to establish firmly. The question mark provides a visual clue that the duration is only an estimate.

- **New Scheduled Tasks Have Estimated Durations:** If you check this box and enter a scheduled task, Project displays a question mark, indicating an estimated duration.

- **Tasks Can Be Made Inactive:** In Project Professional, if you check this box, you can opt to make a task inactive as necessary. Inactive tasks remain in the schedule but do not affect it.

New Feature

Creating inactive tasks is a new feature in Project Professional 2010. You can read more about them in Chapter 10. ■

- **Keep Task on Nearest Working Day When Changing to Automatically Scheduled Mode:** If you check this box and then change a manually scheduled task to an automatically scheduled task, Project schedules the task on the working day closest to the manually established date.
- **Show Task Schedule Warnings:** If you check this box, Project uses a red squiggly underline to identify tasks that might need to happen later than you expect.
- **Show Task Schedule Suggestions:** If you check this box, Project uses a green squiggly underline to identify tasks that might be able to happen sooner than you expect.

New Feature

Task schedule warnings and suggestions are new to Project 2010. ■

When you are satisfied with the settings on the Schedule tab, click OK to close the Project Options dialog box.

Creating a new calendar

The Standard calendar might not work for your project under all circumstances. For example, suppose you run a print shop and each project you complete requires you to use the printing press, but the press requires cleaning and maintenance each week for two hours on Thursday afternoon. To make sure that each printing project takes into consideration the scheduled maintenance requirement of the printing press, you can create a Press calendar that covers the need to shut down the press for cleaning and maintenance. Then you can assign the Press calendar to the Press Time task that you create for each project.

Note

As previously mentioned, if you're using Project Standard, everything you're about to read works automatically. However, if you're using Project Professional, you can create your own calendars (for both projects and tasks) if you're working offline and storing the project locally (not in the Project Server database). If you store the project in the Project Server database, you can create calendars only if the administrator has given you the rights to do so. Also, note that having the privilege to create calendars still doesn't permit you to change the Standard calendar. ■

To create a new, project-wide calendar, click the Project tab and, in the Properties group, click Change Working Time to display the Change Working Time dialog box shown in Figure 3.8. The Legend panel on the left side of the dialog box identifies Working, Nonworking, and Edited Working Hours, as well as exception days and nondefault work weeks. If other calendars exist, you see them listed in the For Calendar list box at the top of the dialog box.

Tip

Although you can make changes to the Standard calendar, I suggest that you make a copy of the Standard calendar rather than modify it. That way, you can always use the original Standard calendar if you need it. ■

FIGURE 3.8

By default, Project displays the settings for Standard (Project Calendar) in the Change Working Time dialog box.

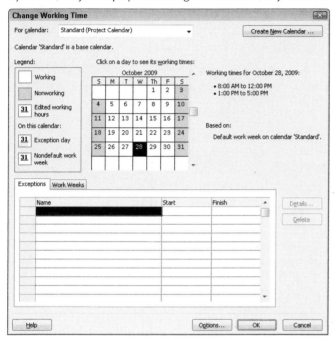

You can create a custom calendar by clicking the Create New Calendar button. Project then displays the Create New Base Calendar dialog box (see Figure 3.9) and suggests the name "Copy of Standard."

FIGURE 3.9

From the Create New Base Calendar dialog box, you can create a copy of an existing calendar or you can create a new Standard calendar.

To model your calendar on an existing calendar, select the existing calendar from the Make a Copy Of drop-down box. Provide a name for the new calendar in the Name box (as I did in Figure 3.9) and click OK to create the new calendar.

Adjusting the calendar

You can define the work week or create exceptions to the Standard calendar or any other calendar using the tabs at the bottom of the Change Working Time dialog box. To accommodate the maintenance time needed for the printing press, you would modify the work week for the printing press by following these steps:

1. Click the Work Weeks tab.

2. Click the [Default] work week already defined for the calendar by Project (see Figure 3.10).

3. Click Details. Project displays the Details dialog box (see Figure 3.11).

4. Select the day you want to change from the Select Day(s) list on the left side of the dialog box.

5. On the right side of the box, select the appropriate option; for this example, I chose Set Day(s) to These Specific Working Times.

6. In the grid section, define the working time for the selected day.

7. Click OK. Project redisplays the Change Working Time dialog box.

FIGURE 3.10

To modify the default work week, select [Default] on the Work Weeks tab.

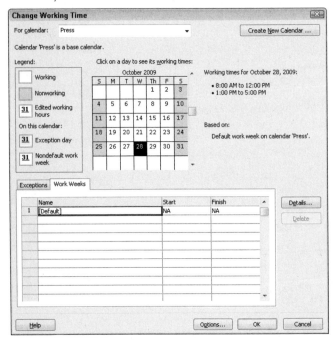

FIGURE 3.11

Use this dialog box to redefine a work week.

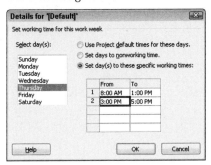

When you change the work week, the change you make is not considered an exception; instead, it's considered the new normal work week. You won't see any changes to the calendar showing up in the Change Working Time dialog box. You can, however, identify the working time for any day by clicking that day on the calendar; the working time appears to the right.

Suppose, however, that your child has swimming lessons every Wednesday afternoon during the month of July and you, as the owner of the business, have decided to close the shop and take your child to swimming lessons because business is slow in the summer anyway. To set up a working time exception like this one, follow these steps:

1. Click the Exceptions tab in the Change Working Time dialog box.

2. In the Name column, type a name that helps you remember the purpose of the exception.

3. In the Start column, select the date on which the exception starts.

4. In the Finish column, select the date on which the exception ends. Project sets every day between the starting and ending dates as an exception on the calendar, and the Details button and the Delete button become available (see Figure 3.12).

5. Click the Details button. Project displays the Details For dialog box shown in Figure 3.13.

6. In the top section of the dialog box, click the Working Times option button and then set the working times; in this example, I set the working time from 8:00 a.m. to 1:00 p.m.

7. To repeat this working time pattern every Wednesday, click Weekly in the Recurrence pattern section and check the Wednesday check box.

8. In the Range of Recurrence section, set the starting and ending dates for the working time exception using the dates you supplied in Steps 3 and 4. You can change these dates if you want.

9. Click OK. When Project redisplays the Change Working Time dialog box, every Wednesday between the beginning and ending dates you specified appears as an exception on the calendar (see Figure 3.14).

FIGURE 3.12

To set up a working time exception, type a name for the exception and set dates.

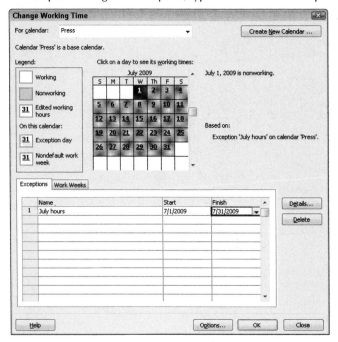

FIGURE 3.13

Use this dialog box to define the working time exception.

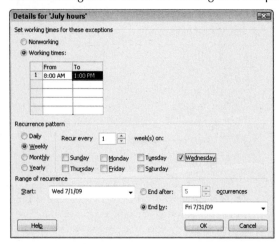

FIGURE 3.14

Project marks exceptions to the typical schedule with an underscore.

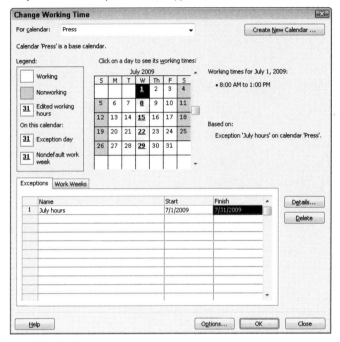

Working with Tasks

Tasks are the heart and soul of every project. You'll spend much of your time in Project adding and modifying tasks. In this section, you get started creating a project by entering major tasks into a project schedule. Then you refine the major tasks by adding detail tasks that help you accomplish the major tasks — and, in the process, you build an outline of your project.

In this section, you also explore adding tasks to the timeline and how the use of manually scheduled tasks compares with using automatically scheduled tasks.

Note

Project 2010 contains a new task mode that allows you to manually schedule tasks; in the past, the only task mode available was to allow Project to automatically calculate Start Date, Finish Date, Work and Duration values for a task based on dependencies, constraints, calendars, and other factors. Because the power of project management software lies mostly in its ability to calculate your project's schedule and cost, I make the assumption throughout this book that you use Project 2010 predominantly in the Auto Schedule task mode; that's where Project's behavior is much like that of its predecessors. Later in this chapter, I show you an example of using the Manually Schedule task mode. ■

Entering tasks

To begin building a project, enter the major steps to reach your goal in roughly the same order that you expect them to occur. (Don't worry if you're not quite accurate about the sequence of events; Project makes it easy to reorganize tasks in your schedule at any time.) For the sample project (organizing a corporate annual meeting), follow these steps to create your first task — booking the meeting space:

1. Click the Task Name column in the first row of the Gantt table.

2. Type **Book Meeting Space**. The text appears in the cell.

3. Press Enter to accept the text.

Information begins to appear in your schedule. Project lists the task name in the Task Name column and makes a corresponding entry in the Duration column. The question mark in the Duration column represents an estimated duration. According to the Start column, the task begins today, and a task bar in the chart portion of the Gantt Chart view reflects the one-day duration of the task graphically. And, as you work, Project highlights any change you make that affects the schedule; because I added a task, the Duration and Start Date appear highlighted in Figure 3.15.

FIGURE 3.15

Project highlights the duration and dates of any changes you make that affect the project schedule.

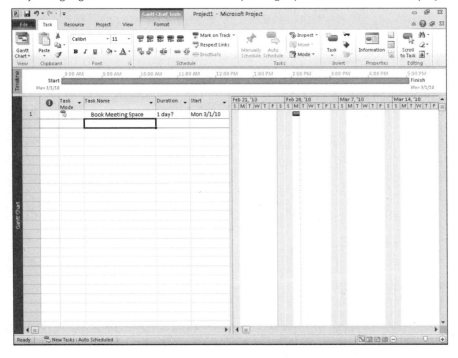

Cross-Reference

Chapter 4 contains more information about estimated durations. ■

New Feature

The Task Mode column displays an image that identifies whether a task is being scheduled automatically or manually. Figure 3.15 shows an automatically scheduled task. ■

You can use the scroll bar located at the bottom of the Gantt table to move to the right and view the Finish Date entry. Because this is a one-day task, it will be completed by the end of the day.

Tip

You also can drag the bar that divides the Gantt table from the Gantt Chart to expand the visible area of the Gantt table. ■

In the second row in the Task Name column and enter **Schedule Speakers** as the next task. Then enter the following tasks on the next four rows: **Arrange for Audio/Visual Equipment**, **Order Food**, **Send Invitations**, and **Mail Annual Reports**. Your schedule should now look like that shown in Figure 3.16.

FIGURE 3.16

Note that each task is the same length by default, and each begins on the project's start date.

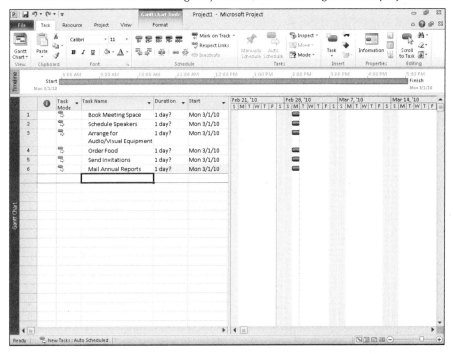

Note

If you make a mistake, you can click the Undo button on the Quick Access Toolbar in the upper-left corner of the screen. Each time you click the Undo button, Project 2010 displays an earlier version of your project. You can click the Undo button multiple times to undo multiple prior actions. ■

Adding detail tasks

After you enter the major tasks in your project, you can begin to flesh out the details by adding subordinate tasks, also referred to as *subtasks* or *detail tasks* to each major task. When you add detail tasks, the upper-level task becomes a *summary task*. Summary tasks and detail tasks provide an easy-to-apply outline structure for your schedule, and summary tasks often represent phases of projects.

Project's outline approach also enables you to display and print your project information with various levels of detail. For example, with only summary tasks showing, you see a higher-level overview of the project that you may want to present to management. On the other hand, you can reveal the details of only one or two phases of a project so you can discuss those tasks with the people who will be performing them. The outline structure gives you a lot of flexibility in working with your schedule.

When you insert a new task, it appears above the currently selected task. Begin by adding detail tasks under the Book meeting space task. Follow these steps to insert a new detail task:

1. Click the Schedule Speakers task.

2. Click the Task tab and, in the Insert group, click the top portion of the Task button. Row 2 displays the beginning of a new task, with a prompt for a task name appearing in the Task Name column. All the other tasks move down one row (see Figure 3.17).

Note

If you click a blank row in the project and then click the top of the Task button, Project adds the new row below the last completed row. ■

3. Type **Request purchase order** and press Enter to accept the new task.

4. To indent the detail task, select it, click the Task tab and, in the Schedule group, click the Indent button (see Figure 3.18). The task above the selected task — Book Meeting Space in this example — becomes a *summary task* and appears in boldface type. The selected task appears indented below the summary task.

Notice that the summary task (Book Meeting Space) now displays a black bar on the chart portion of the Gantt Chart view, with a down arrow shape marking its beginning and end. When you work with automatically scheduled tasks and a task becomes a summary task (that is, when it contains detail tasks), the timing of the summary task reflects the total amount of time required to complete all of its detail tasks.

FIGURE 3.17

When you insert a task, Project prompts you to type a name for the new task.

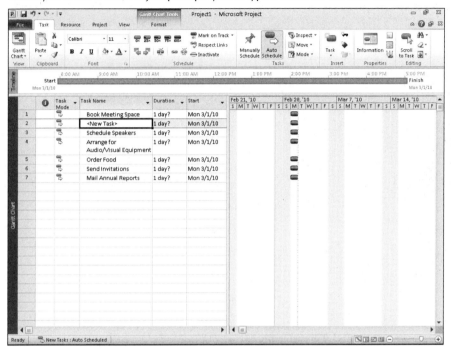

Note

If a task has a duration assigned to it and you make it into a summary task, the timing of the detail tasks overrides the assigned duration. If you change the timing of a detail task, the summary task duration changes to reflect the change. ∎

New Feature

Along the way, you might discover that you need a new major heading instead of a new detail task. No problem — and accomplished more easily than in earlier versions of Project. Select the task you want to appear below the new summary task. Then click the Task tab and, in the Insert group, click the Insert Summary Task button. Project inserts the summary task above the selected task, indents the selected task, and prompts you for a name for the summary task. ∎

FIGURE 3.18

The summary task now appears in boldface type.

Indent button

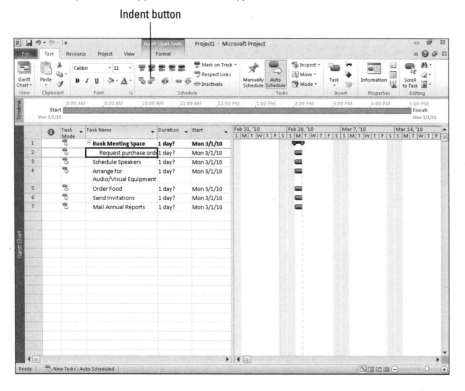

You can add other detail tasks by following these steps:

1. Click the Schedule Speakers task.

2. Press the Insert key on your keyboard (which is a shortcut for clicking the Task button on the Ribbon).

   A new blank row appears.

3. Type **Select Room** and press Enter to accept the new task.

   The new task uses the same level of indentation as the task above it.

4. Press Insert. A new blank row appears.

5. Type **Confirm Space** and press Enter to accept the new task.

   The new task uses the same level of indentation as the task above it.

6. Press Insert.

7. Type **Order Flowers** and press Enter to accept the new task.

Each of these new tasks indents to the subordinate level. However, the third new task — Order Flowers — is not a detail task of the Book Meeting Space summary task. To move the task higher in the outline hierarchy, simply click in the Task Name column of that task (or any column of the task) to select it and, on the Task tab in the Tasks group, click the Outdent button (which does the opposite of indenting as it promotes the task to a higher level).

Note

Project won't use any Change Highlighting, a feature that highlights all tasks affected by changes you make to any single task, when you outdent a task if outdenting doesn't affect any task dates or durations. ■

Your schedule now looks like the schedule shown in Figure 3.19. Adding details is as simple as inserting new tasks wherever you want them and then moving the tasks in or out in the outline structure.

You can come back later and add more information to your tasks; explore the kinds of information you can add in Chapter 4.

FIGURE 3.19

The outline structure enables you to see summary tasks and subtasks as manageable chunks of work.

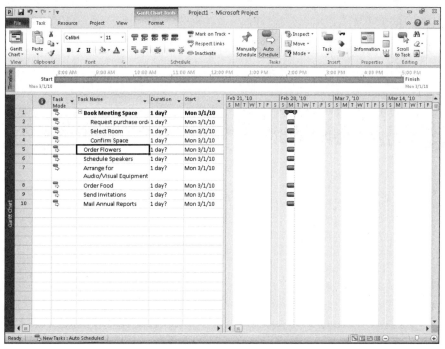

New Feature

If you're using Project Professional and you find you don't need a particular task in your project at some point, you can make it inactive instead of deleting it. (See Chapter 10 for details on using inactive tasks.) ■

Adding tasks to the timeline

You can use the Timeline that appears above the view area to present an overview picture of a project. Project doesn't display all tasks on the Timeline by default; instead, Project lets you identify the tasks to include.

Tip

If the Timeline doesn't appear between the bottom of the Ribbon and the top of the View area, click the View tab and, in the Split View group, place a check in the Timeline box. ■

You can easily add a task to the Timeline using any of the following techniques:

- Click the task to select it; then, on the Task tab, in the Properties group, click the Add Task to Timeline button.
- Right-click the task and choose Add to Timeline.
- Double-click the task to display the Task Information dialog box; then, on the General tab, place a check in the Display on Timeline check box.

In Figure 3.20, I've added the summary tasks to the Timeline. Using the scroll bars below the right portion of the Gantt Chart view, I can see different time periods of my project, and the information on the Timeline changes to match whatever dates I view.

Tip

If you decide later that you don't want a particular task to appear on the Timeline, right-click that on the Timeline and choose Remove from Timeline. ■

In addition to displaying the Timeline in Project, you can copy it in a couple of different ways and then paste it into other Office programs. At the top of the Timeline, just below the Ribbon, you'll see a light blue bar; right-click that bar, point at Copy Timeline and click For E-mail, For Presentation, or Full Size (see Figure 3.21). Each copy produces a slightly different size of the Timeline that you can paste into a file in another Office program (such as a Word document, a PowerPoint slide, or an Outlook e-mail message).

Cross-Reference

You also can display the Timeline as a view without any other view; see Chapter 6 for details. ■

FIGURE 3.20

The Timeline can present an overview snapshot of your project.

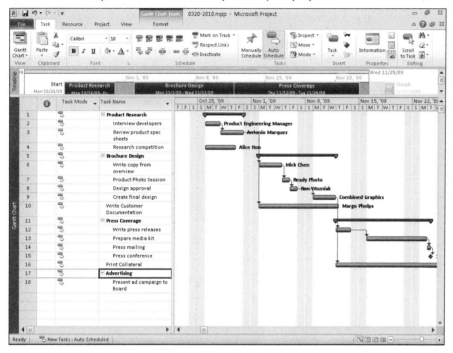

Manual or automatic scheduling?

In Project 2010 contains a new task mode that allows you to manually schedule tasks. Previous versions of Project offered only one task mode: You had to let Project to calculate Start Date, Finish Date, Work, and Duration values automatically for each task based on their dependencies, constraints, calendars, and other factors. The power of project management software lies in its ability to calculate your project's schedule and cost; manual scheduling is a useful, but subsidiary, feature. That's why, throughout this book, I assume you're using Project 2010 primarily in Auto Schedule task mode, where Project behaves much like its predecessors.

You might find manually scheduled tasks useful when you first start a project. When you add manually scheduled tasks to a project, you don't need to supply a duration, a start date, or a finish date; you can simply create a list. You can use manually scheduled tasks to work on your project's outline structure, creating summary tasks and indenting and outdenting as needed. You also might find manually scheduled tasks useful when setting up tasks in a project with a very long timeline; you can use automatically scheduled tasks for the early part of the project and use manually scheduled tasks for the later portion of the project, when timeframes are not as clear.

FIGURE 3.21

You can copy the Timeline to other Office programs.

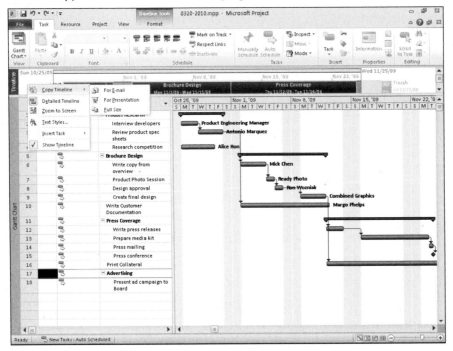

Note

For you Project Server users, be aware that manually scheduled tasks cannot be updated by team members in the same ways that automatically scheduled tasks can be updated. For example, team members cannot update status by supplying number of hours worked per day or week. Also important is that manually scheduled tasks cannot be updated in PWA in the same ways as automatically scheduled tasks. A resource you assign to a manually scheduled task cannot update status in a timescaled way (number of hours per day or week); only total Actual work or % complete updates are available. ■

Project enables you to do much more with manually scheduled tasks; for example, you can set dependencies between manually scheduled tasks and you can, if you want, supply duration or date information. However, it's important to remember that manual scheduling gives you complete control over your tasks; Project has no control over manually scheduled tasks.

Caution

You can easily change a manually scheduled task to an automatically scheduled task — and vice versa. However, depending on how your options are set, switching back and forth can introduce constraints you didn't intend. If you use manually scheduled tasks to set up dependencies, you might unintentionally introduce scheduling conflicts. Exercise care when using manually scheduled tasks; they might produce a schedule that won't work — and Project won't adjust manually scheduled tasks to make your schedule functional. ■

Cross-Reference

You can read more about dependencies and constraints in Chapter 4. ■

Creating manually scheduled tasks

Suppose you want to start a new project and you're at the point where you want to list all the tasks without worrying about their durations, start dates or end dates. You can set the default scheduling mode for the current project by using the Task Mode button on the Status bar.

At the left edge of the Status Bar, the Task Mode button identifies how Project treats new tasks in the current project for scheduling purposes. Click the button (see Figure 3.22) to select the scheduling mode you'd like to use by default in the current project. The out-of-the-box default is Manually Scheduled.

FIGURE 3.22

Select a scheduling mode for all new tasks in a project.

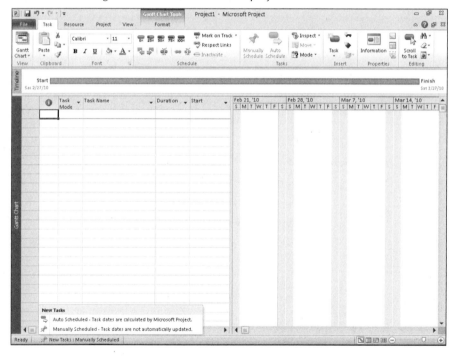

Note

The choice you make affects only new tasks; it doesn't affect any tasks already in the project. ∎

Next, enter manually scheduled tasks the same way that you enter automatically scheduled tasks:

- Click in the Task Name column on the row where you want to enter a task, type a name for the task, and press Enter. Or,

- Click the row on which you want to enter a task, click the Task tab, and then click the top of the Task button in the Insert group.

Compare Figure 3.23 with Figure 3.24. The two projects contain the same tasks, but I set up Figure 3.23 using manually scheduled tasks and Figure 3.24 using automatically scheduled tasks.

FIGURE 3.23

A project that uses manually scheduled tasks.

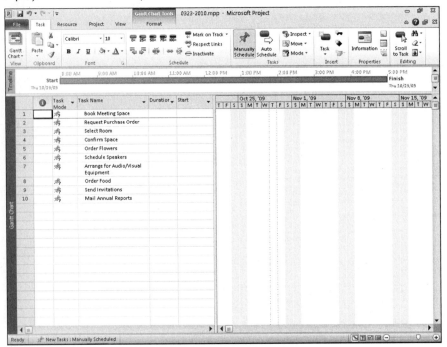

FIGURE 3.24

A project that uses automatically scheduled tasks.

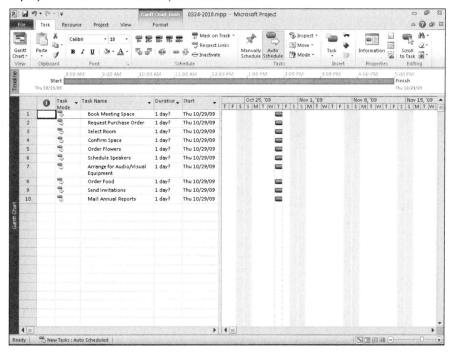

Note that the image in the Task Mode column in Figure 3.23 is different from the image shown in Figure 3.24.

In addition, in Figure 3.23, no bars appear in the chart portion of the Gantt Chart view; the bars represent duration and start and finish dates — but because I didn't supply that information, Project has no information to use to create any bars for the chart. In Figure 3.24, Project assigned an estimated duration of 1 day to each task and supplied bars in the chart portion of the view.

In Figure 3.25, I indented the tasks on Rows 2, 3, and 4 in the project that uses manually scheduled tasks. Project converts the Book Meeting Space summary task to an automatically scheduled task, assigns an estimated duration of 1 day to the task, and displays a summary task bar beside the summary task that reflects the estimated duration. Note, however, that Project doesn't make any changes to the other manually scheduled tasks.

FIGURE 3.25

Changing the outline structure of a project that uses manually scheduled tasks converts the summary task to an automatically scheduled task.

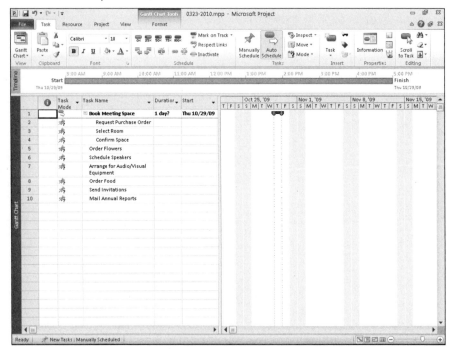

Switching a task's scheduling mode

If you want to use a mixture of manually scheduled and automatically scheduled tasks in your project, select the Task Mode (using the Status Bar button) for the majority of tasks in your project. Then you can change the scheduling mode for an individual task in one of two ways:

- You can click in the Task Mode column and select the appropriate mode for that task (see Figure 3.26).
- You can select the task by clicking in the Task Name column and then using the Manually Schedule and Auto Schedule buttons in the Tasks group on the Task tab to set the task mode for the selected task.

Caution

In the Project Options dialog box, placing a check next to Keep Task On Nearest Working Day when Changing to Automatically Scheduled Mode can cause Project to create constraints if you change a manually scheduled task to an automatically scheduled task. ∎

FIGURE 3.26

Change the scheduling mode of a task using either the Task Mode column or the buttons in the Schedule group on the Ribbon.

These buttons are available when you don't open the list in the Task Mode column.

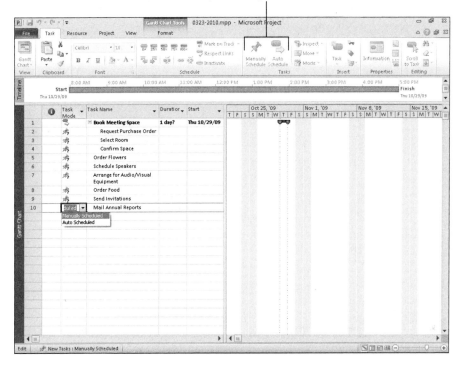

Setting the default scheduling mode

If you expect to use one scheduling mode more than the other for all new projects, you can set that mode as the default scheduling mode in the Project Options dialog box. Follow these steps:

1. Click the File tab.

2. In the Backstage view, click Options to display the Project Options dialog box.

3. Click Schedule on the left.

4. Open the list box beside Scheduling Options in This Project and select All New Projects.

5. To set the default scheduling mode, open the New Tasks Created list box (see Figure 3.27) and select Manually Scheduled or Auto Scheduled.

6. Click OK.

7. Repeat these steps for the current project (that is, in Step 4, select the current project instead of selecting All New Projects).

FIGURE 3.27

The New Tasks Created list box controls whether Project uses manual or automatic scheduling by default.

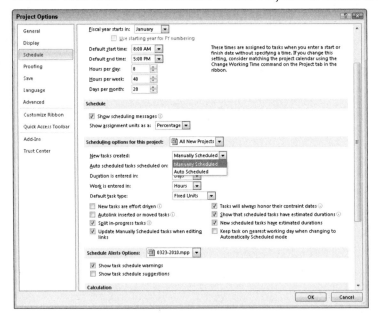

Saving Project Files

Of course, you should always save your work frequently. Information centralized in a Project file is often mission-critical, which makes frequent saving even more important. When saving Project files, you have the option of setting up protection for them. You can also save your files as *templates* — files on which you can base other schedules.

Saving files

To save a Project file for the first time, click the Save tool on the QAT or click the File tab and, in the Backstage view, click Save. In the Save As dialog box that appears, specify the name of the file, where to save the file, and what format you want to use (see Figure 3.28).

In the File Name box, type a name for the file. Use the options in the left pane to navigate to the folder in which to save the file.

Note

Project 2003, Project, 2002, and Project 2000 all use the same file format, but Project 2007 uses a different format from its predecessors, and Project 2010 uses yet another different file format. If you need to share your files with users of earlier versions of Project, you can save your file using the file format for Project 2000 – 2003. Any features or formatting exclusive to Project 2010 will be lost. Also note that Project 2007 and 2010 cannot save to the Project 98 file format. ■

FIGURE 3.28

Use the Save As dialog box to tell Project where to save a file and what format to use.

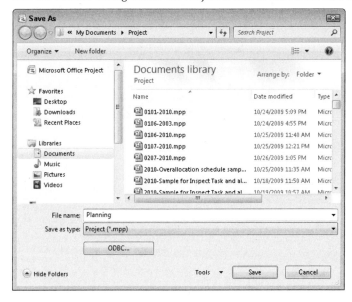

By default, Project saves files in Project 2010 format with the extension .mpp. To save a file in a different format, such as a Project 2007 file (also .mpp) or a Project 2000 – 2003 file (also .mpp), you can select that format in the Save as Type drop-down list. After you enter a name for your file and designate its location and type, click the Save button to save the file.

Note

After you save a project for the first time, you can simply click the Save button to save the file; Project doesn't display this dialog box. If you want to change a setting or save the file with a new name, click the File tab and — in Backstage view — click Save As to display this dialog box again. ■

Saving files as templates

Here's another place where manually scheduled tasks might come in handy: You can use them to set up a template of a project that you perform often. In a template, you set up the tasks for the project and create the project outline. The template then forms a great starting place for others who use it to manage a project. A template file saves all the settings that you may have made for a particular project, such as formatting, commonly performed tasks, and calendar choices. Keeping template files on hand can save your coworkers (and you) from having to reinvent the wheel each time that you want to build a similar project.

To save a project file as a template, use the Save As dialog box (shown in the preceding section); in the Save as type list, select Template (*.mpt). Project prompts you to remove baselines, actual values, resource rates, fixed costs, and any information indicating whether tasks have been published to Project Server. As needed, check these boxes — and then click Save.

To create a new schedule based on a template, click the File tab and, from the Back Stage view, click New. Click My Templates to view a list of templates you've created, select one, and click OK. Project opens a new file that contains all the information you saved in your template. When you save your new project, be sure to supply a new name and select Project from the Save As Type list.

Protecting files

Some projects are as "top secret" as an FBI file. In such a case, some people within the organization — and certainly people from outside the organization — should not have access to project details. If your projects fit this mold, you need a way to keep your Project files secure from prying eyes. You can set a measure of security for Project 2010 files; click the File tab and choose Save As from the Backstage view to display the Save As dialog box. Click the Tools button and choose General Options to display the Save Options dialog box, as shown in Figure 3.29.

Caution
Don't use your phone extension, birthday, spouse's name, or similar quick choice as a password — such passwords are much too easy to break! ■

Assign a password in the Protection password box to safeguard the file from being opened by anyone who doesn't know the password. If you assign a Write Reservation password, on the other hand, anyone can open the file without a password, but as a *read-only* file (that is, anyone can look, but only those who know the Write Reservation password can make changes to the file). Finally, if you check the Read-Only recommended option, Project displays a message recommending that anyone opening the file not make changes to it. However, this choice doesn't prevent someone from making changes.

Tip

What kind of passwords should you use? Consider two factors: You must be able to remember the password, and you must make it something that the average person can't guess. (No password is perfect; if someone really wants to break into your files, he or she will.) Try using passwords such as an address or phone number that you had as a child — information that you remember but others are not likely to know. The longer the password, the harder it is to break. ■

FIGURE 3.29

The Save Options dialog box.

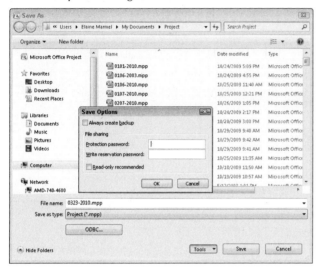

Caution

Both the Protection password and Write reservation password are case-sensitive. If you assign JoeS as a password, you can't open the file if you enter joes. ■

Closing Project

When you're finished working in Project, you can save your files as described previously and then use one of the following methods to close the program:

- Click the Close button in the upper-right corner of the Project window.
- Click the File tab and, in the Backstage view, click Exit.

If you haven't saved any open files, Project prompts you to do so.

Working with a Project Outline

After you build a project outline, reorganizing the order of individual tasks is easy. You also can manipulate the outline to show either more or less detail about your project. Outlining features work the same way in many software products. For example, Microsoft Word, PowerPoint, and Project all have the same outlining tools and features. In Project, you can move, copy, hide, and display tasks.

Adjusting tasks in an outline

To illustrate adjusting tasks in the outline, I use the project shown in Figure 3.30.

To move tasks in an outline, you can cut and paste (as in the following Steps 1 through 4) or you can drag and drop (as in the following Steps 5 through 7). You also can change the relative position of tasks in the hierarchy of the outline by promoting or demoting them (outdenting or indenting). In Step 8, you see an example of demoting a task.

To move tasks, you must first select them. Use any of the following techniques to select tasks:

Tip
You can select a task by clicking its Gantt bar. ■

FIGURE 3.30

I refer to this project as I make adjustments to the outline.

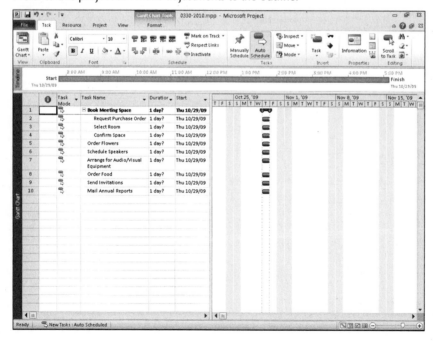

- To select a single task, click its ID number. As you hover the mouse pointer over an ID number, the pointer changes to a right-pointing arrow.

- To select several contiguous tasks, select the first task. Then hold down Shift and click the last task that you want to select.

- To select several noncontiguous tasks, hold down Ctrl as you click the ID numbers of the tasks that you want to select.

Moving summary tasks and detail tasks can be a little tricky. Although you can move tasks wherever you like, it's important to remember that when you move a summary task, its detail tasks move with it. Furthermore, if you move a task at the highest level of the outline to a new location just below a summary task that has detail tasks, Project demotes the task that you move. Similarly, if you move a detail task so it appears below a task at the highest level of the outline, Project promotes the detail task that you move. To get a feel for this behavior, try the following steps:

Note

To move a summary task only — without moving any of its detail tasks — you must first promote all its detail tasks to the same level as the summary task. ∎

1. Click the ID number in the leftmost column for the task you want to move (in my example, it's Task 5, the Order Flowers task). Project highlights (selects) the entire row.

2. Click the Task tab and, in the Clipboard group, click the Cut tool. The task disappears from the project.

3. Click the Gantt bar for the task that should appear below the task you're moving. In my example, I click Task 8, the Send Invitations task. Project selects the row.

4. On the Task tab in the Clipboard group, click the top of the Paste button. The task you selected in Step 1 (Order Flowers) appears selected in its new location above the Send Invitations task (see Figure 3.31).

5. Click the ID number of the next task to move; for this example, I clicked Task 2, the Request Purchase Order task.

6. Move the mouse pointer over the ID number of the selected task; the pointer changes to a four-way arrow.

7. Press and hold down the left mouse button while you drag the task to its new position; in this example, I dragged the Request Purchase Order task below the Order Food task. A horizontal gray line appears on-screen, indicating the new proposed position as you drag (see Figure 3.32). When you release the mouse button, Project moves the task and promotes the Request Purchase Order task in accordance with its new position in the outline.

8. To demote the Request Purchase Order task, click either the ID number or the task name to select the task, and then click the Task tab and, in the Tasks group, click the Indent button.

Tip

You can promote or demote tasks by dragging. Dragging a task to the left promotes the task in the project outline. Similarly, dragging a task to the right demotes the task. When you promote or demote tasks, you see the same gray line (only it's vertical) that you see when you move tasks up or down in the outline. ∎

FIGURE 3.31

The project after cutting a task and pasting it in a new location.

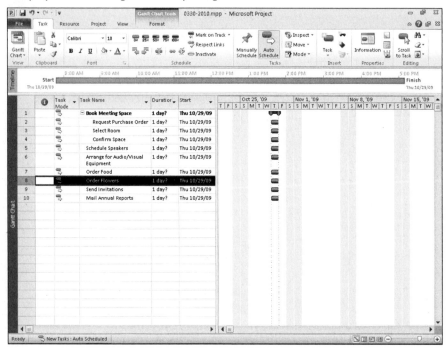

Note

You also can promote or demote by dragging. Move the mouse pointer over the first few letters of the subtask's name until the pointer becomes a double arrow. Then drag the task to the left or right. ∎

Your schedule now has two tasks with detail tasks beneath them (see Figure 3.33).

Copying tasks

Copying tasks also is simple to do and can come in handy while building a project outline. For example, suppose you were entering tasks in a project to test various versions of a compound to see which works best as a fixative. You may repeat the same series of tasks (Obtain Compound Sample, Test in Various Environments, Write Up Test Results, Analyze Results, and so on) several times. Instead of typing those tasks 10 or 20 times, you can save time by copying them.

Warning

While you run no risks copying tasks to create new ones, you should avoid cutting and pasting tasks, particularly if you use Project Server, because cutting and pasting changes the unique ID's Project assigns to each task. ∎

FIGURE 3.32

Project indicates the proposed position of the task with a horizontal gray line.

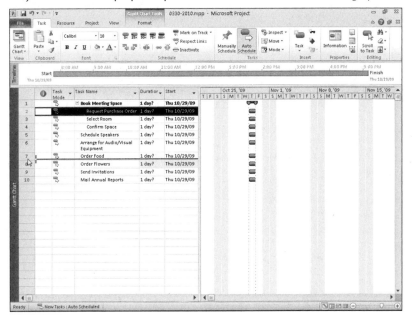

FIGURE 3.33

Both Book Meeting Space and Order Food tasks have detail tasks beneath them.

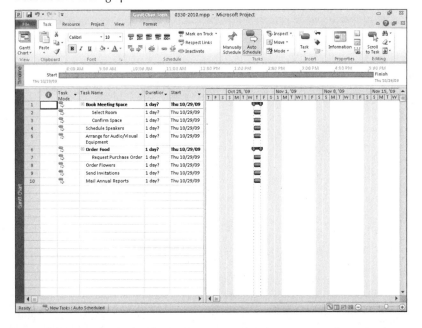

To copy tasks, you must first select them, using any of the techniques described in the previous section. To copy tasks, use the generic steps:

1. Select the tasks you want to copy.

2. Click the Task tab and, in the Clipboard group, click the Copy button to copy the selected tasks.

3. Click the task in the schedule that you want to appear below the tasks you're copying.

4. Click the Task tab and, in the Clipboard group, click the top of the Paste button. Project pastes the tasks you selected in Step 1 above the selected task.

Tip

To copy a summary task and its detail tasks, you need only select the summary task and copy it. Project automatically copies the summary's detail tasks for you. ■

If you have several repetitive phases of a project, such as the development and production of several models of a single product, you can use the fill handle to copy the tasks. Figure 3.34 shows three tasks: Design, Development, and Production. To copy a group of tasks such as Development and Production, follow these steps:

FIGURE 3.34

Take advantage of the fill handle for contiguous copy tasks.

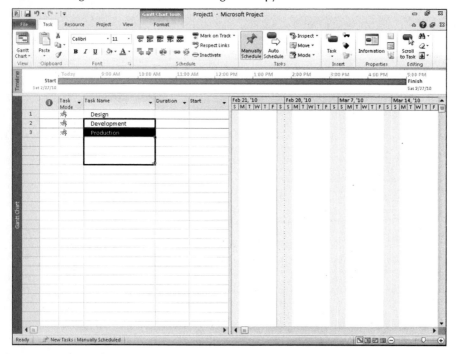

1. Select their task names.

2. Place the mouse pointer over the fill handle in the lower-right corner of the selection.

   The mouse pointer changes to a plus sign (+).

3. Drag the fill handle down until you've selected the group of rows that you want to contain the repetitive tasks.

   When you release the mouse pointer, Project copies the tasks into the selected range, as shown in Figure 3.35.

FIGURE 3.35

Project fills the range with the selected tasks.

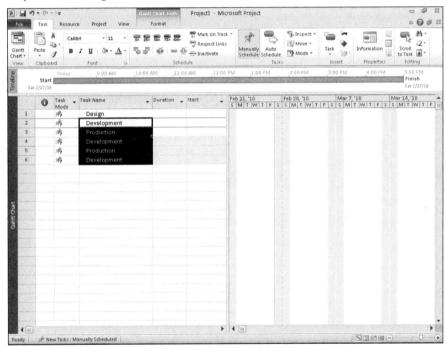

Caution

The fill handle copies tasks into a contiguous range. However, if the range already contains information, using the fill handle to copy overwrites the existing information. To avoid this problem, insert blank rows in the project before using the fill handle. Select the task that you want to appear beneath the tasks you intend to copy. To insert more than one blank row, select the number of rows you want to insert. Then press the Insert key or click the Task tab and, in the Insert group, click the top of the Task button. ■

Displaying and hiding tasks

The outline structure enables you to view your project at different levels of detail by expanding or collapsing the summary tasks. You can use the Show Outline button on the View tab in the Data group to quickly hide or display detail tasks (also called *subtasks*) based on their level in the outline (see Figure 3.36). You also can quickly display all the detail tasks in your schedule.

FIGURE 3.36

Use the Show button on the View tab to easily determine the level of detail that you want to view in a project.

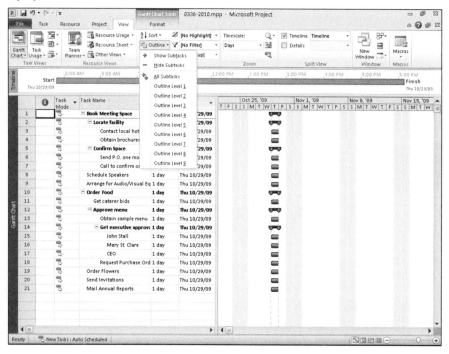

Figure 3.37 shows a minus sign (–) appearing to the left of each summary task. This symbol indicates that all subtasks are in view. If you click the minus sign, any subtasks disappear from view and a plus sign replaces the minus sign next to the summary task name. The plus sign indicates that the task is associated with some hidden detail tasks. Click the plus sign to reveal the "hidden" subtasks.

How many levels of detail can an outline have? Just about as many as you need. For example, the schedule that is shown in Figure 3.37 has several levels of detail regarding the annual meeting project. Any task that has subtasks also has the plus and minus sign mechanism for displaying or hiding the subtasks.

Caution

Using too many levels of outline indentation (usually more than three or four) makes it difficult to see your entire schedule on-screen. In fact, a very detailed project outline may indicate that you need to rethink the scope of the project and break it into smaller, more manageable projects. ■

You can use the hide and show features of the outline to focus on just the amount of detail you want. You can take the schedule shown in Figure 3.37, for example, and show just the highest level of detail for a report to management to summarize project activity (see Figure 3.38).

FIGURE 3.37

You can expand or collapse any task that has a subtask.

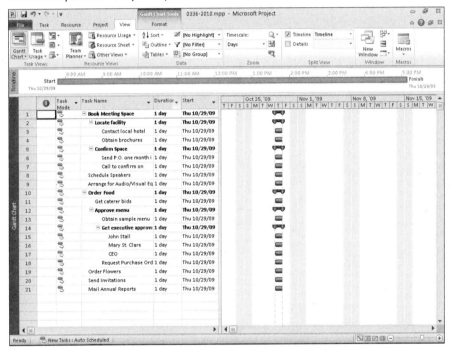

FIGURE 3.38

The detail tasks are now hidden. The plus signs and the summary-style bars in the chart portion of the Gantt Chart view, however, indicate that more is here than meets the eye.

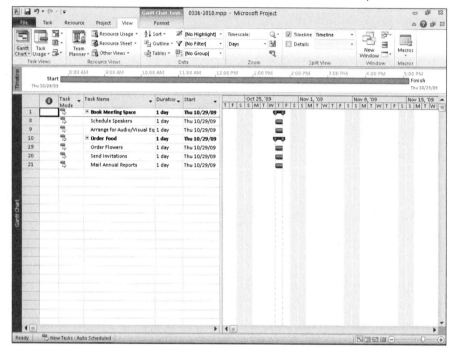

Getting Help

As you begin to build tasks in a schedule, you're likely to have questions about using Project 2010 that the Help system can answer. Project's Help is similar to the Help feature in Microsoft Office 2010 products.

Using the Help system

You click the Microsoft Project Help button located above the Ribbon at the right edge of the screen — beside the Minimize Ribbon button — to display the Help window (see Figure 3.39).

From the Help window, you can click a subject on which you want help, and Project displays a list of topics associated with the subject you selected (see Figure 3.40).

Tip

If you don't see a topic that interests you, click the Home button (the one that looks like a house) to return to the Help window shown in Figure 3.39. ■

FIGURE 3.39

You can use the Project Help window to search both online and offline sources for help.

When you click a topic, Project displays the Help text associated with that topic (see Figure 3.41).

If you prefer, you can type a keyword in the Search box at the top of the Help window and click the Search button next to the box; Project searches for Help topics that include your keyword (see Figure 3.42).

The Table of Contents is a good way to view the structure of the Project Help file and see the topics under each subject. Click the Show Table of Contents button on the Help window toolbar to display the Help System's Table of Contents. Click any book in the Table of Contents to see the topics associated with that subject. To hide the Table of Contents, click the Hide Table of Contents button on the Help window toolbar.

Tip

Use the buttons across the top of the Help window to move back and forward between Help topics — or click the Home icon to return to the opening Help window. ■

FIGURE 3.40

Project displays a list of topics after you select a subject.

FIGURE 3.41

A typical Help topic.

FIGURE 3.42

Use the Help system's search engine to find Help topics on a subject.

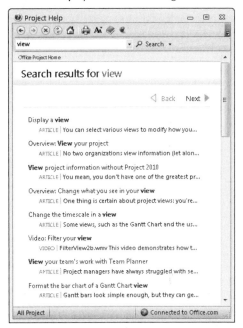

Finding online help

On the Internet, you can find a world of support, information, and even freeware, shareware, or products for sale that work along with Project.

Using your browser, you can start your search at the Project Home Page:

```
http://Office.microsoft.com/en-us/project
```

At this site, you can find things such as update information, files to download, and software companies that provide add-on products or specialize in the use of Microsoft Project. You also can find links on this page to the Microsoft Project discussion groups, experts, and solution providers.

Summary

In this chapter, you started to build your first project by creating summary tasks and detail tasks, also called subtasks. You learned about the following aspects of Project:

- Gathering the data that you need to begin creating your schedule
- Entering Project information and setting up some calendar defaults
- Creating summary and detail tasks
- Using manual or automatic scheduling
- Saving files and closing Project
- Working with the outlining hierarchy to move, copy, and display detail tasks
- Using the Help system to search for information and obtain online help

In Chapter 4, you begin to add details about task types, add timing, and establish relationships among your tasks.

Building Tasks

Hesiod, that classic Greek project manager, once said, "Observe due measure, for right timing is in all things the most important factor." You could do worse than to use this truism from around 700 B.C. as your personal project management mantra today. When it comes to projects, timing is, indeed, everything.

In Chapter 3 you created several tasks and used the outlining feature of Project to organize them. If you used automatic scheduling, every task in your schedule has the default length (one estimated day), and they all occur on the same day. If you used manual scheduling, no task has any length. In essence, you have listed the steps to get to your goal, but with no related timing information, and your schedule is more like a to-do list than a project schedule.

You have to add durations to your tasks. In other words, you must establish how long (or how many hours of effort) each task will take. However, timing consists of more than determining how many hours, days, or weeks it takes to complete each task. Timing for your project becomes clear only when you've set a duration for each task and when you've established the relationships, called *dependencies,* among the tasks. Only then can you accurately predict the amount of time that you will need to complete the project.

Note
Unless I state otherwise, I use automatic scheduling for the task mode throughout this chapter. ∎

Establishing Timing for Tasks

In real life, you make estimates about task durations every day. Your boss asks how long it will take to write that report, and you tell her it will take about a week. Your coworker calls and asks when you will be finished repairing the computer network, and you tell him it will take another day. You know your own business, and you're probably pretty good at determining how long to allow for everyday tasks based on many factors.

Exactly how do you figure out the timing for a task in a project? The method is virtually identical to the seemingly automatic process you go through when someone asks you how long it will take to complete a task, such as placing an order for materials. Consider the following example:

1. You estimate that you'll spend about 40 minutes doing the research and performing the calculations to determine how many square feet of lumber you'll need for the job.

2. You consider how long the actual task (placing a phone order for materials) will take. This duration could be a matter of only minutes, but if you factor in playing a few rounds of phone tag, you may want to allow half a day.

3. You also think about what's involved in getting a purchase order. With your system, cutting a purchase order can take up to four days. Some of that time requires your presence, but most of it consists of waiting.

So how long is your task? You could say that you need exactly four days, four hours, and 40 minutes, but just to be safe, you should probably allow about five days. In addition, Project uses some specific methods that you need to understand to estimate task durations accurately.

In Project, you can create three different types of tasks: Fixed Unit, Fixed Work, and Fixed Duration. Project's behavior when you change the amount of resource effort you assign to the task varies, depending on the task's type.

Fixed Unit tasks

By default, using automatic scheduling, Project creates *Fixed Unit tasks* that are not affected by effort supplied by resources. That is, any changes you make do not affect the amount of any resource assigned to a task.

This task type ensures that resource allocations remain constant on the task. So, if you assign two resources — one at 100% and one at 50% — to a task and you remove the resource you assigned at only 50%, Project will not change the other resource's allocation to compensate.

Caution

This behavior is new in Project 2010; in prior versions, all new tasks were Fixed Unit, effort-driven tasks. You can change Project 2010's behavior to emulate earlier versions if you prefer to work that way; see "Changing Task Type Default Behavior" later in this chapter. ■

To Pad or Not to Pad?

Although most people agree that delays are inevitable and that you should allow for them, people who schedule projects accommodate these delays in various ways.

Some schedulers build in extra time at the task level, adding a day or two to each task's duration — just in case. Unfortunately, padding each task may leave you with an impossibly long schedule, and it may suggest to your boss that you're not very efficient. Why should it take two days to run a three-hour test? It doesn't — but because you know that setting up the test parameters properly the first time is an error-prone process, you allow a couple of work days to complete the testing. Just make sure that your boss understands that you're building a worst-case scenario; when you bring the project in early, he or she will be glad to share the praise.

One school of thought on estimating task duration suggests that you take your estimate, double it, and then add 10%. If you are new to estimating, you might want to try this approach — as long as your project fits within the timeframe allotted for it — until you have an opportunity to track the progress of a few projects and learn just how accurately you estimate.

Some project managers add one long task, maybe two weeks or so in duration, at the end of the schedule, and they name it something like Critical Issues Resolution Period. This task acts as a placeholder that covers you if individual tasks run late. This approach can help you see how the overall time left for delays is being used up as the project proceeds. For example, if the final two-week task is running a week late because of earlier delays, you know that you've eaten up half of the slack that the task represents.

Or, you can build a schedule with best-case timing. Then you can document any problems and delays that occur, and request additional time as needed. In the case of a project that you must complete quickly, you may need to work this way. However, best-case timing sets you up for potential missed deadlines. Estimating a schedule with worst case timing sounds safe, because you're unlikely to run out of time. But, if the estimate you provide is too long, the project might never happen because upper management will find better ways to spend the money.

Which approach should you use? Possibly a combination. For example, try building a best-case schedule. If the completion date is one week earlier than your deadline, by all means add a little time to the tasks that are most likely to encounter problems, such as those that are performed by outside vendors.

Fixed Work tasks

When you create a *Fixed Work task*, you set the duration of the task, and Project assigns a percentage of effort that is sufficient to complete the task in the time that is allotted for each resource that you assign to the task. For example, if you assigned three people to work on a one-day task, Project would say that each person should spend 33 percent of his or her time on the task to complete it in one day. Similarly, a task may take 48 hours to complete (its Fixed Work value). With one resource assigned working eight hours a day, the task will require six days to complete. With two resources assigned working eight hours a day, the task will require three days to complete. In either case, the amount of work that's required remains constant. The task's duration changes based on the number of resources that are assigned to the task. Fixed Work tasks are always effort driven; in just a moment, you read more about effort-driven tasks.

Fixed Duration tasks

You also can use the *Fixed Duration task* type in Project. The number of resources does not affect the timing of this type of task. To allow a week for a committee to review the company's new ad campaign — no matter how many people are on the committee — give the task a fixed duration. You can't shorten the task's duration by adding resources to it. In fact, adding people to the review process may lengthen the task, because their effort has no impact on getting the work done more quickly, and coordinating their efforts can add time.

Effort-driven tasks

Almost every task is affected by the effort supplied by resources. Here's a simple example: Suppose you have to plant a tree. One person needs two hours to plant a tree. If you add another person (another resource), then it's reasonable to assume that together they need only one hour to complete the task. That is, two resources, each putting in an hour of effort, complete the two hours of work in only one hour. With resource-driven scheduling, when you add resources, the task duration becomes shorter; if you take away resources, the task takes longer to complete. And, on the flip side, the resource assignments to a task don't change when the work increases or decreases.

Caution

The reduction of time required on a resource-driven task is strictly a mathematical calculation in Project. for example, ten people get work done in one-tenth the time of one person. However, whenever two or more people work on a task, the time savings are seldom so straightforward. You must also factor in the time for those people to communicate, miscommunicate, hold meetings, and so on. ■

Every Fixed Work task you create in Project is effort-driven by default, and you cannot change that task type to not be effort-driven. For Fixed Duration and Fixed Unit tasks, you can tell Project to modify the percentage of total work that is allocated to each resource, based on the number of assigned resources, if the number of resources changes. In effect, you create an *effort-driven task*. The work that's required to complete the task remains the same, but Project redistributes the work equally among all assigned resources. Table 4.1 summarizes Project's behavior for each task type in relation to effort-driven scheduling.

TABLE 4.1

Effort-Driven Scheduling and Task Types

Task Type	When Effort-Driven	When Not Effort-Driven
Fixed Work	If you add resources, Project shortens the task's duration.	Not applicable, because all Fixed Work tasks are effort-driven.
Fixed Unit	If you add resources, Project shortens the task's duration.	Adding resources doesn't affect the task's units or duration, but Project increases the task's total work.
Fixed Duration	Because the task's duration is fixed, adding resources doesn't affect the task's duration, but Project reduces the allocation of each resource.	The task's duration and all resource allocations remain the same when you add resources, but Project increases total work.

Note

In this book, I change Project's default settings so that the durations that you assign to tasks are resource-driven and a five-day task requires five days of resource effort to complete. See the next section to find out how to change Project's default settings. In Chapter 5, you find out more about how resource assignments modify task timing. ∎

Changing Task Type Default Behavior

In earlier editions of Project, the default task type was Fixed Unit, effort-driven. In Project 2010, the default task type is *not* effort-driven. If you prefer the behavior of earlier versions of Project, you can change the default settings. Here's how:

1. Click the File button.

2. From the Back Stage view, click Options.

3. In the Project Options dialog box (see Figure 4.1), click Schedule on the left.

4. In the Scheduling Options For This Project list box, select All New Projects.

FIGURE 4.1

Changing Project options to make all new tasks effort-driven.

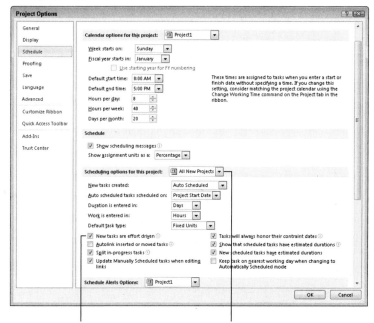

Check this box   Select All New Projects

Tip

If you enter predominantly Fixed Work tasks or Fixed Duration tasks, click the Default Task Type list-box arrow and select the appropriate task type. ■

> **5.** Click New Tasks Are Effort-Driven.
>
> **6.** Click OK.

Repeat these steps for the current project; that is, in Step 4, select the current project instead of All New Projects.

For the remainder of this book, I set up Project to insert new tasks that are, by default, Fixed Unit, effort-driven tasks.

Assigning Task Timing

You now understand the basics of estimating task timing, and you understand how task timing relates to effort that is expended on the task by resources. The actual process of assigning durations is simple. To assign a duration to a task, you can use one of the following three methods:

- Enter a duration in the Duration column of the Gantt table.
- Use the Task Information dialog box to enter and view information about all aspects of a task, including its timing, constraints, dependencies, resources, and priority in the overall project.
- Use your mouse to drag a task bar to the required length.

Note

You also can enter the work value after assigning the resources to the task. Project then calculates the duration and provides smart tag help, giving you the option to change the method of calculation. ■

Using the Gantt table

To enter a task's duration in the Entry table portion of the Gantt Chart view, simply click the Duration column and enter the duration. Using automatic scheduling, you might have noticed that Project uses estimated durations — a question mark (?) — by default when you type a task name but no duration. Even though Project initially assigns estimated durations to tasks, when you type a duration, Project assumes that you want a planned rather than an estimated duration — unless you enter a question mark (?).

Tip

You can change Project's default behavior (and use planned rather than estimated durations) on the Schedule tab of the Options dialog box. See the next section for more information. ■

You can enter a duration in a few different ways. For example, Project recognizes all the following entries as three weeks: 3 w, 3 wks, 3 weeks.

Tip

To assign the same duration to several contiguous tasks, enter the duration once and then use the fill handle in the Duration column to copy the duration to the other tasks. ■

When you type a duration, Project uses the Change Highlighting feature to show you the other tasks in your project that are affected by the scheduling change you made (see Figure 4.2). In this example, the task I changed — Acquire Materials — and the summary task, Phase One Testing, were both affected by the duration I entered. In particular, the finish dates of both tasks were changed by the duration I provided.

FIGURE 4.2

When you change a task's duration, Project highlights other tasks affected by the change.

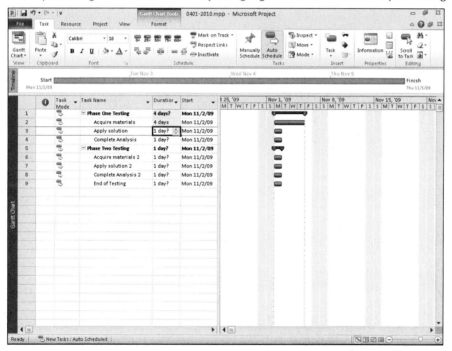

Tip

If the information you enter has results you weren't expecting, you can click the Undo button on the QAT to reverse the effects. In Project 2010, each time you click the Undo button, Project reverses the effects of each change you made, in the order you made them. If you click Undo enough times, Project can return your file to the state in which it appeared when you last saved the file. ■

Using the Task Information dialog box

Follow these steps to assign durations from the Task Information dialog box:

1. Display the Gantt Chart view by clicking the Gantt Chart view shortcut at the right edge of the Status Bar.

2. Double-click a task name to open the Task Information dialog box (see Figure 4.3).

FIGURE 4.3

If you double-click a task name you already entered, it appears in the Name field in this dialog box. If you double-click a blank task-name cell, you can fill in the name here.

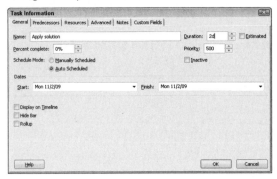

Tip

You can also display this dialog box if you click the Task Information button in the Properties group of the Task tab or right-click either the task name or the task's Gantt bar and select Task Information. ■

3. Click the arrows in the Duration field to increase or decrease the duration from the default setting of one day. Each click changes the duration by one day.

Note

If you change the duration in the Task Information dialog box, Project assumes you want a planned duration and also removes the check from the Estimated box. ■

To enter a duration in increments other than a day, you can click the Duration field, highlight the current entry, and type a new duration using any of the following abbreviations: *m* for minutes, *h* for hours, *w* for weeks, and *mo* for months.

Note

Project uses the Schedule tab of the Project Options dialog box to determine the number of days in a month. ∎

4. Click OK to establish the task duration. The task's Gantt Chart bar reflects the new task length (see Figure 4.4).

FIGURE 4.4

Task bars become more meaningful after you assign durations.

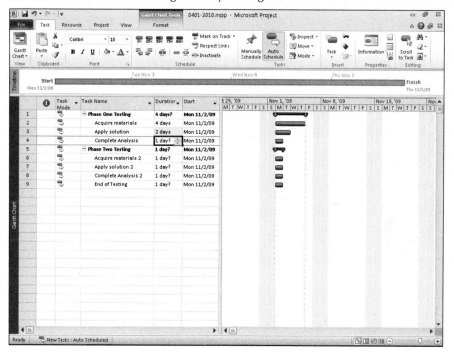

Start and finish versus duration

You can use the Start and Finish fields in the Task Information dialog box to set a start date and finish date for the task rather than enter a duration. However, If you use the Start and Finish dates, Project uses only working days in that date range. If you enter a duration, Project calculates the beginning and end of the task, taking into consideration weekends and holidays. These two methods can have different results and most often, you'll find that using durations produces better results that using Start and Finish dates.

For example, suppose you have a five-day task that starts on December 22, 2009 and you've set up the project's calendar to make December 25 a nonworking day. The following table shows how that week and the following week look on a calendar: December 25, 2009, falls on a Friday.

Sun	Mon	Tues	Wed	Thurs	Fri	Sat
20	21	22	23	24	25	26
27	28	29	30	31		

If you entered 12/22/09 as the start date and 12/28/09 as the finish date, Project would calculate that as an estimated four-day task, with work on December 22, 23, 24 and 28. However, if you enter four days in the Duration field, the calculated start and finish dates would be 12/22/09 and 12/29/09, respectively — taking into account both the Christmas holiday and a weekend. In this example, the work days are December 22, 23, 24, 28, and 29.

If a task has immutable timing, such as a Christmas celebration on Christmas day, use the Start and Finish fields. Except for days you establish as non-working days, Project will force the task to start on the Start Date you establish and expect it to finish on the Finish Date you set, which could upset the timing of both earlier and later tasks. If you know how many work days a task will require, but not the days on which the work will occur, use the Duration field to set timing, and let Project calculate the actual work dates based on the calendar.

Using your mouse and the task bar

Finally, follow these steps to adjust a task's duration using your mouse and the task bar:

1. Place your mouse pointer on the right edge of a task bar until the pointer becomes a vertical line with an arrow extending to the right of it.

2. Click and drag the bar to the right. As you do, Project displays the proposed new task duration and finish date, as shown in Figure 4.5.

3. Release the mouse button when the duration you want appears in the information box.

Note

When you use the mouse to set a task duration, Project does not make the duration a planned duration; instead, the duration remains an estimated one. To change the duration from estimated to planned, you must make the change using one of the two preceding methods described — the Gantt table or the Task Information dialog box. ■

FIGURE 4.5

If you're a visually oriented person, dragging task bars to change durations might be the best method for you.

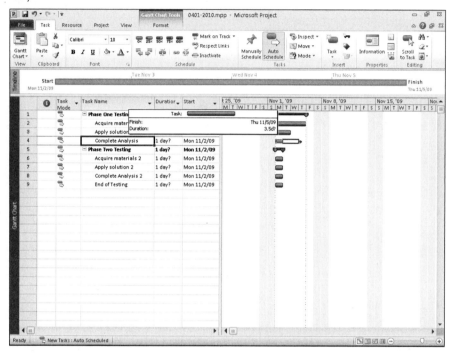

Setting scheduling options

You aren't limited to entering resource-driven tasks or estimated durations on the Gantt table. You can change the default task type and other default scheduling settings for your project. Click the File tab and, in the Back Stage view that appears, click Options. On the left side of the Project Options dialog box, click Schedule to change the default settings for entering tasks (see Figure 4.6).

In the section Scheduling Options in This Project section of the Project Options dialog box, you determine default information such as the default unit of time for new task durations (the default is days), the work time (hours), and whether Project schedules new tasks to start on the project start date or on the current date. If, for example, you don't want to use estimated durations for new tasks, remove the check mark from the New Scheduled Tasks have Estimated Durations check box. Or, if you're working on a five-year project in which most tasks take months — not days — change the default setting for the Duration Is Entered In field. If you prefer that new tasks begin no earlier than the current date, you can open the New Tasks Created list box and select Scheduled On Current Date.

FIGURE 4.6

Use the Scheduling Options section in the Project Options dialog box to change Project's default behavior when scheduling tasks.

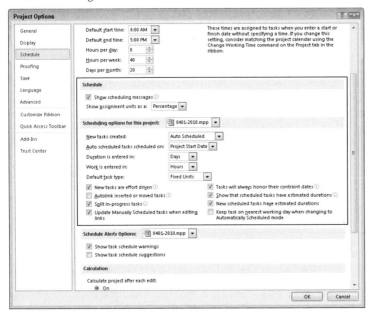

As you gain experience in entering information, you'll find ways to customize Project to match your work style. When you are satisfied with the settings in the Schedule tab, click OK to close the Project Options dialog box.

Assigning a calendar to a task

You can assign a calendar to a task by using the same steps that you used to create the Press calendar, described in detail in Chapter 3. Click the Project tab and, in the Properties group, click Change Working Time to display the Change Working Time dialog box. Click the Create New Calendar button to create the calendar, and then provide a name for the new calendar. Then create the calendar exceptions that apply to the task and click OK to save the calendar.

Cross-Reference
For more detailed steps on creating a new calendar and calendar exceptions, see Chapter 3. ■

To assign a calendar to a task, double-click the task name to open the Task Information dialog box for that task. Click the Advanced tab and open the Calendar list box to assign a special calendar for the task (see Figure 4.7).

FIGURE 4.7

Assign a calendar to a task from the Advanced tab of the Task Information dialog box.

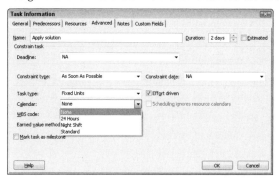

Creating milestones

Managers often use milestones to mark key moments in a project, such as the completion of a phase or the approval of a product or activity. In Project, milestones are tasks that usually have zero duration. The symbol for a milestone on the Gantt Chart is a diamond shape. For example, the diamond in the Gantt Chart shown in Figure 4.8 indicates that the End of Testing task is a milestone.

FIGURE 4.8

A milestone typically marks a noteworthy point in your project; a milestone is usually a task of no duration.

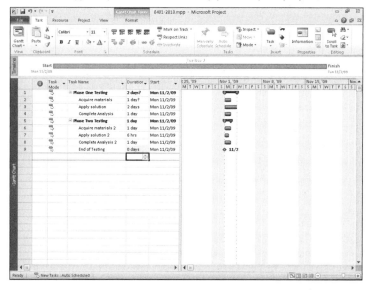

A task doesn't have to have a zero duration to be a milestone; you can mark any task as a milestone. On the Advanced tab of the Task Information dialog box, place a check mark in the Mark Task As Milestone check box. In this case, the task duration doesn't change to zero. However, the element that represents the task in the Gantt Chart changes from a bar, reflecting the task's duration, to a milestone diamond symbol, representing the task as a moment in time.

Note

For milestones with durations longer than zero, the diamond appears at the beginning of the duration. ■

Timing for summary tasks

How do you assign durations for summary tasks? You don't have to assign a duration to a summary task and, if you want your summary task to represent the total timing of its subtasks, then don't enter a duration for a summary task. For example, if three subtasks occur one right after the other and each is three days long, the summary task above them takes nine working days from beginning to end if you don't assign a duration to it (see Figure 4.9). If you do change the duration of any of those tasks, Project will update the summary task accordingly.

FIGURE 4.9

Using a summary task to represent the total timing of its subtasks.

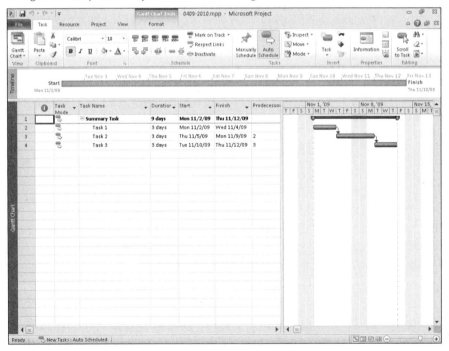

Note, however, that you can assign a duration to a summary task — and you might want to make such an assignment in certain cases. Suppose, for example, that you're starting a project and you can easily identify that it has five phases. You also know that Phase 1 can last six weeks, and you know some of the tasks in that phase, but they only account for three weeks of the phase. In this case, enter your phases and, under each phase, enter the tasks you know.

Tip

You can use manually scheduled or automatically scheduled tasks and you don't need to enter durations for the tasks. ■

Indent the known tasks under each phase, establishing the phase task as a summary task (see Figure 4.10). In the duration column for the summary task, enter the phase's duration; Project automatically makes the summary task a manually scheduled task, as you can see in the Task Mode column, and Project accounts for the duration of the phase by the length of the summary task bar in the chart portion of the Gantt Chart view.

Because the summary task is a manually scheduled task, Project respects any dates or durations you assign and won't change them, even if you make changes to a detail task under the summary task. But Project tracks your manually entered information along with information it calculates; if you hover your mouse on the summary task bar, Project displays the planned dates for the summary task as well as the calculated dates for the detail tasks (see Figure 4.11). And whether you use manually scheduled tasks, automatically scheduled tasks, or a mix of both, Project still displays both sets of dates.

FIGURE 4.10

You can assign a duration to a summary task.

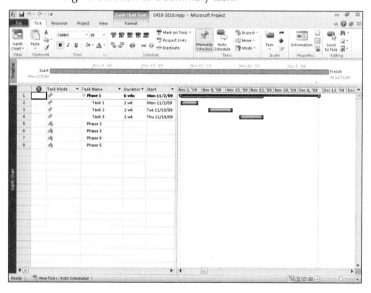

FIGURE 4.11

Project tracks the information you assign to a summary task along with its calculations for the associated detail tasks.

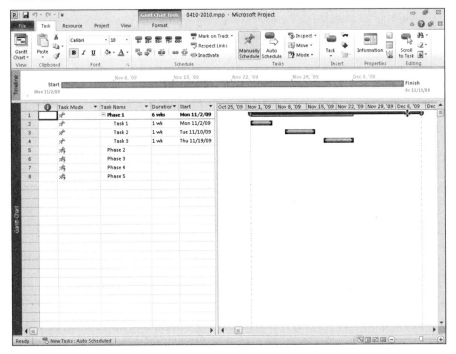

Note

If you edit the duration of an automatically scheduled summary task, Project converts it to a manually scheduled task. ∎

Using this approach, you can create a schedule that you plan from the top down and, if you use manually scheduled tasks, you can control all the dates in the schedule. You can create tasks that begin before the start of a phase and tasks that end after the end of the phase. But remember: You don't need to use a manually scheduled task to assign a duration to a summary task. If you assign a duration to an automatically scheduled task, Project converts the task to a manually scheduled task.

Note

You can have Project display a summary task for your entire project. The project summary task displays the total time for a project, and, using a project summary task and a Cost Resource, you can establish a budget for your entire project. To learn more about Cost Resources, see Chapter 5. To learn more about project budgets, see Chapter 12. ∎

Using Recurring Tasks

Projects often have tasks that occur on a regular basis. Weekly staff meetings, quarterly reports, or monthly budget reviews are examples of these recurring tasks. Rather than create, for example, 20 or so weekly staff-meeting tasks over the life of a five-month project, you can use Project's Recurring Task feature. This feature enables you to create the meeting task once and assign a frequency and timing to it. Follow these steps to create a recurring task:

1. Because Project inserts tasks above the selected task, select the task that you want to appear below the recurring task.

2. Click the Task tab and, in the Insert group, click the bottom of the Task button; from the menu that appears, choose Recurring Task button to open the Recurring Task Information dialog box, as shown in Figure 4.12.

3. Type a name for the recurring task.

4. Set the task duration in the Duration field. For example, does the meeting run for two hours, or does a report take a day to write?

5. Set the occurrence of the task by selecting one of the Recurrence Pattern option buttons: Daily, Weekly, Monthly, or Yearly. Depending on the recurrence you select, the timing settings to the right of the control buttons change. Figure 4.12 shows the Weekly settings.

6. Select the appropriate settings for the recurrence frequency. For a Weekly setting, place a check mark next to the day(s) of the week on which you want the task to occur. For example, the task shown in Figure 4.12 occurs every Tuesday. For the Monthly or Yearly setting, select the day of the month on which you want the task to occur.

Note

For a daily task, you have only one choice: whether you want it to occur every day or only on scheduled workdays. For example, to schedule a computer backup for every day of the week — regardless of whether anyone is at work — you can have the task occur every day. (Ask your IT department how to automate the process so it occurs even when nobody is at work.) ∎

7. Set the *Range of recurrence* — the period during which the task should recur — by entering Start and End After or End By dates. If you need to repeat a test weekly for only one month of your ten-month project, you can set Start and End After or End By dates that designate a month of time.

Tip

If you set the End After number of occurrences, Project calculates the date range required to complete that many occurrences of the recurring task and automatically displays the ending date in the End By box. This method can be useful if one of these events falls on a holiday; if that happens, Project displays a box that allows you to skip the occurrence or to schedule it on the next working day. For a weekly staff meeting, you can skip that meeting or schedule it on a different day. On the other hand, if you must repeat a test 16 times during the project cycle, you can schedule the test to occur on the next working day to compensate for the holiday. Therefore be sure you set the number of occurrences rather than the time range. ∎

8. Click OK to create the task. Project creates the appropriate number of tasks and displays them as subtasks under a summary task with the name that you supplied in Step 2. In Figure 4.13, I expanded the view of the summary task so you can see each recurring task; note the recurring task symbol in the Indicators column of Row 6.

FIGURE 4.12

If a task occurs at regular intervals during the life of a project, you can save time by creating it as a recurring task.

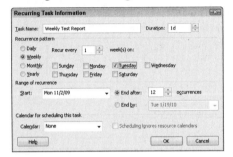

FIGURE 4.13

Task bars appear for each occurrence of the recurring task in the Gantt Chart.

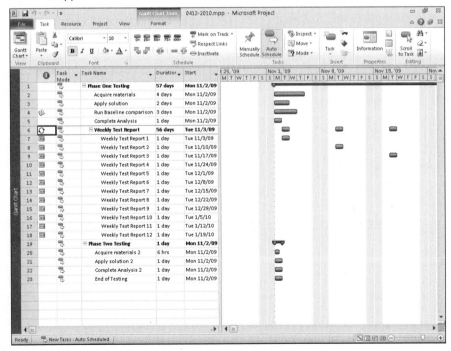

Mysterious Icons in the Indicator Column

The symbol next to each Weekly Test Report task in the schedule shown in Figure 4.13 represents a task with a timing constraint applied. Project applies this constraint automatically as you enter settings for the recurring task.

If you move your mouse pointer over one of these symbols, as I did in the following figure, you can see an explanation of that constraint. For example, each Weekly Test Report task has a Start No Earlier Than constraint, based on the timing you set in the Recurring Task Information dialog box. The first recurring task can start no earlier than the From date entered there, and each task occurs weekly thereafter. You find out more about setting timing constraints in the next section.

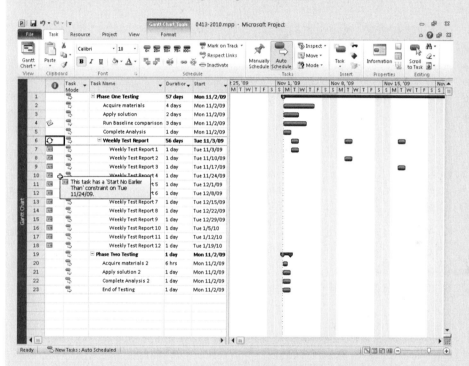

Constraints affect the timing of a task relative to the start or end of your project, or relative to some other specified date. Setting a deadline date in Project provides you with a visual reminder if you don't complete a task by the deadline date that you establish.

Establishing Constraints and Deadline Dates

Constraints affect the timing of a task relative to the start or end of your project or to a specific date. Setting a deadline date in Project provides you with a visual reminder if you don't complete a task by the deadline date that you establish.

Understanding constraints

By default, Project sets all automatically scheduled tasks to start with an As Soon As Possible constraint. Barring any dependency relationships with other tasks (see the "Establishing Dependencies Among Tasks" section later in this chapter), the task would start on the first day of the project. You can set other constraints as follows:

- **As Late As Possible:** This constraint forces a task to start on a date such that its end occurs no later than the end of the project.

- **Finish No Earlier Than/Finish No Later Than:** This constraint sets the completion of a task to fall no sooner than or later than a specific date.

- **Must Finish On/Must Start On:** This constraint forces a task to finish or start on a specific date.

- **Start No Earlier Than/Start No Later Than:** This constraint sets the start of a task to fall no sooner or later than a specific date.

Only the Must Finish On/Must Start On settings constrain a task to start or end on a particular date. All the other settings constrain the task to occur within a specified time frame.

Using deadline dates

You also can establish a deadline date for a task. The deadline date differs from a constraint in that Project doesn't use the deadline date when calculating a project's schedule. Instead, the deadline date behaves as a visual cue to notify you that a deadline date exists (the down-arrow symbol that you see next to the *Acquire materials 2* task bar in Figure 4.14). If you place your mouse over the deadline indicator, Project displays the deadline information. If the task finishes after the deadline date, you also see a symbol in the Indicators column. Keep in mind that you won't see an indicator if you complete the task prior to the deadline date.

Although deadline dates don't affect the calculation of a project schedule, they do affect a Late Finish date and the calculation of total slack for the project. Also, be aware that you can assign both a deadline date and a constraint to a task. In a project that you schedule from a beginning date, a deadline date has the same effect as a Finish No Later Than constraint in the calculation of slack. If you assign deadline dates to tasks in projects that you schedule from an ending date, those tasks will finish on their deadline dates unless a constraint or a dependency pushes them to an earlier date.

FIGURE 4.14

When you set a deadline date for a task, Project displays an indicator to alert you that you've set the deadline.

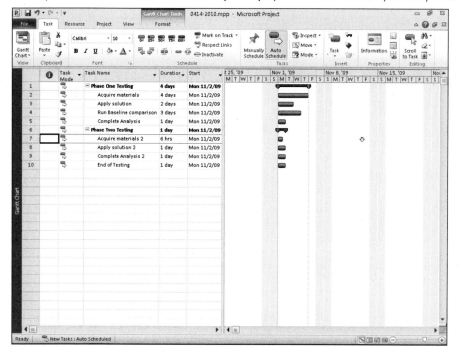

Setting constraints and deadline dates

You set constraints on tasks in your project by using the Advanced tab of the Task Information dialog box (see Figure 4.15). Select a constraint type from the Constraint type drop-down list. For all settings in the type list other than As Late As Possible and As Soon As Possible, designate a date by clicking the arrow next to the Constraint Date field and choosing a date from the drop-down calendar that appears. Set a deadline date by clicking the arrow next to the Deadline field and choosing a date from the drop-down calendar that appears.

Under what circumstances would constraints be useful? Consider the following situations:

- A project involves preparing a new facility for occupancy, and you want the final inspection of that facility to happen as late as possible.

- The approval of a yearly budget must finish no later than the last day of the fiscal year, ready to begin the new year with the budget in place.

- Billing of a major account must start no sooner than the first day of the next quarter so the income doesn't accrue on your books this quarter.

- Presentation of all severance packages for laid-off employees must finish on the day that a major takeover of the company is announced.

FIGURE 4.15

Click the arrow next to the Constraint Type field to see the various constraints.

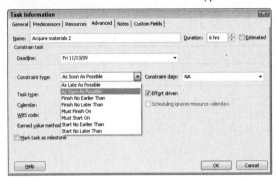

Deadline dates would be useful in the following situations:

- You need to prepare the annual budget by a deadline date to ensure approval in time to begin the new year with the budget in place.

- You need to prepare severance packages for laid-off employees so you can present the packages on the day that a major takeover of the company is announced.

You see how constraints and dependencies interact in establishing the timing of tasks in the section "Establishing Dependencies Among Tasks," later in this chapter.

Entering Task Notes

You can attach notes to individual tasks to remind you of certain parameters or details for the task. For example, if a task involves several subcontractors, you may want to list their contact information here so it's close at hand when you're working on the project schedule. Or you can use the Notes field to document company regulations that are relevant to that type of procedure. When you add a note to a task, you can display the note on-screen and include the note in a printed report.

Cross-Reference
You can also attach notes to individual resources and to their assignments, as you find out in Chapter 5. ■

To enter a note for a task while viewing the Gantt Chart, follow these steps:

1. Double-click a task to open the Task Information dialog box.
2. Click the Notes tab, as shown in Figure 4.16.
3. Type your note in the area provided. You can use the tools provided just above the description box to format your note text.

FIGURE 4.16

The Notes tab provides simple word processing, such as tools for formatting your notes.

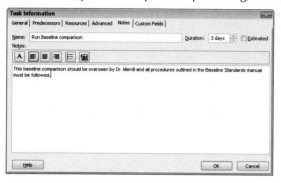

4. Click OK to attach the note to your task.

   A Note icon now appears in the Indicators column of the Gantt table (see Figure 4.17). Move the mouse pointer over this icon to display the note.

FIGURE 4.17

Project automatically adds an icon for the note to the Indicators column.

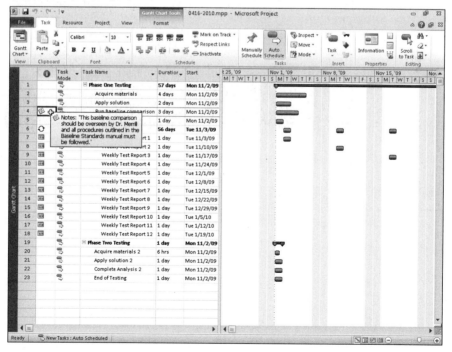

You can print notes along with your schedule. To print the Gantt Chart view and task notes, follow these steps:

1. Click the File tab and, in the Back Stage view, click Print.

2. Click the Settings button.

   Project displays settings you can select when printing a project (see Figure 4.18).

FIGURE 4.18

Notes appear on a separate page after printing your Gantt Chart when you check the Print Notes option.

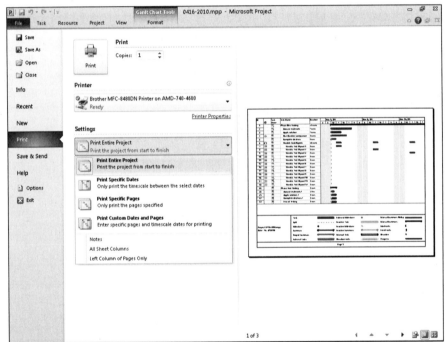

3. Click Notes to have Project print notes for tasks.

4. Select any other settings you want.

5. Click the Print button.

   Project prints notes on a separate page after printing the Gantt Chart view.

Establishing Dependencies Among Tasks

Whereas constraints tie tasks to the project start or end or to particular dates, dependencies tie tasks to the timing of other tasks in the project. Dependencies are central to visualizing the true length of a project.

Dependencies exist because all tasks in a project rarely can happen simultaneously; usually some tasks must start or finish before others can begin. Tasks happen at different times for many reasons; resources might be unable to work on more than one task at a time, a piece of necessary equipment might be unavailable, or the nature of the tasks themselves might drive the timing of the tasks — for example, you can't start construction until you receive a construction permit.

You can't know the total time needed to complete a project until you establish durations and dependencies. For example, a project that comprises five 10-day-long tasks — with no dependencies among the tasks — takes 10 days to complete. If the tasks must happen one after the other, the project requires 50 days. And if some tasks can happen simultaneously while others must happen one after the other, you won't know the total time needed to complete the project until you establish the durations and dependencies for all tasks in the project.

Understanding dependencies

A task that must occur before another task is a *predecessor task*. The task that occurs later in the relationship is a *successor task*. Each task can have multiple predecessors and successors. Tasks with dependency relationships are *linked*. Gantt Charts show these links as lines running between task bars; an arrow at one end points to the successor task. Some dependency relationships are as simple as one task ending before another can begin — but some relationships are much more complex. For example, if you're moving into a new office and the first task is assembling cubicles, you don't have to wait until all the cubicles are assembled before you begin moving in furniture. You might work in tandem, using the first morning to set up cubicles on the first floor. Then you can begin to move chairs and bookcases into the first-floor cubicles while the setup task continues on the second floor.

Understanding the interactions between constraints and dependencies

Both constraints and dependencies drive the timing of a task. Consider for a moment how constraints and dependencies might interact when you apply one of each to a task. Suppose you have a task — the opening of a new facility — that has a constraint set so it must start on November 6. You then set up a dependency that indicates that the task should begin after another specified task — fire inspection — that is scheduled for completion on November 10. When you try to set up such a dependency, Project displays a Planning Wizard dialog box that indicates a scheduling conflict (see Figure 4.19). Project displays this dialog box when a conflict exists among dependencies or between constraints and dependencies.

FIGURE 4.19

Multiple dependencies or a combination of dependencies and constraints can cause conflicts in timing.

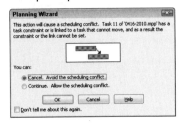

If a conflict exists between a constraint and a dependency, the constraint drives the timing of the task; the task does not move from the constraint-imposed date. You can modify this functionality in the Project Options dialog box. Click the File tab and, from the Back Stage view, click Options. Then, click Schedule and, in the Scheduling Options In This Project section, remove the check mark from the Tasks Will Always Honor Their Constraint Dates check box. When you change this option, dependencies — rather than constraints — will determine timing.

Cross-Reference

See Chapter 10 for more information about resolving timing conflicts. ■

You can create dependencies in one of the following three ways:

- You can select two tasks and click the Link Tasks button in the Schedule group of the Task tab on the Ribbon. The first task you select becomes the predecessor in the relationship.

- You can open the successor task's Task Information dialog box and enter predecessor-task information on the Predecessors tab.

- You can click the Gantt bar of a predecessor and drag it to the Gantt bar of a successor task.

Tip

To link a whole range of tasks so they're consecutive (one finishes, the next begins, and so on down through the list of tasks), select the range of tasks (drag from the ID number of the first task to the ID of the last task). Then use the Link Tasks button to create a string of such relationships. ■

Allowing for delays and overlap

Although many dependency relationships are relatively clear-cut — Task A can begin only when Task B is complete, or Task C can start only after Task B has started — some are more finely delineated. These relationships involve delay and overlap, and these relationships are supported in Project by adding lag time or lead time to the dependency relationship.

To understand these two concepts, consider the following examples. Suppose your project tests a series of metals. In the first task, you apply a chemical solution to the metal, and in the second task, you analyze the results. But time can be a factor here, so you want the analysis to begin only when several days have passed after the application of the chemical solution. You build in a delay between the finish of the first task (the predecessor) and the start of the second (the successor). Figure 4.20 shows a relationship with some lag — delay — between the two tasks. The line between the two tasks indicates the dependency, and the space between the bars indicates the delay in time between the finish of one task and the start of the next.

You create lag or lead time using the Predecessors tab of the Task Information dialog box. You create lag time by entering a positive duration in the Lag field, and you create lead time by entering a negative duration in the Lag field.

Note

Some people prefer to build a task to represent lag rather than to modify a dependency relationship. For example, instead of placing a dependency between application of the solution and analysis, you can create a three-day-long task called Solution Reaction Period. Then create a simple dependency relationship between Solution Reaction Period and the analysis so that the analysis task won't begin until Solution Reaction Period is complete. Adding the lag tasks can generate a very long schedule with multiple tasks and relationships to track. But in a simpler schedule, this approach enables you to see relationships as bars on the Gantt Chart. You can try both methods and see which works best for you. ■

FIGURE 4.20

Here, after you apply the chemical solution, you must wait four days before analyzing the results.

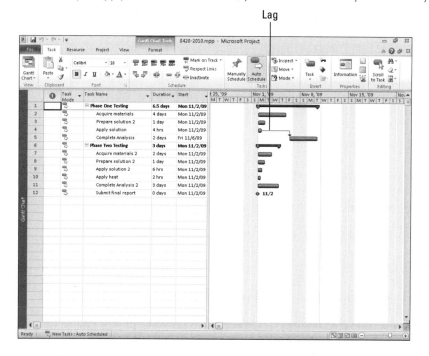

Another test in your project involves applying both a solution and heat. You first want to apply the solution for three days, but one day before you finish applying solution, you want to begin to apply heat as well. Notice the overlap between the tasks: the predecessor task — applying the solution — begins on November 12 and runs through November 14. The successor task — Applying Heat — begins one day before the end of the predecessor task, on November 14. The project shown in Figure 4.21 has some overlap between tasks, created by adding one day of lead time to the successor task.

Dependency types

Four basic dependency relationships define the relationship between the start and finish of tasks: start-to-finish, finish-to-start, start-to-start, and finish-to-finish. You can set these dependency relationships on the Predecessors tab of the Task Information dialog box, as shown in Figure 4.22.

FIGURE 4.21

Some overlap — lead time — occurs between the application of the chemical solution and the application of heat in this testing project.

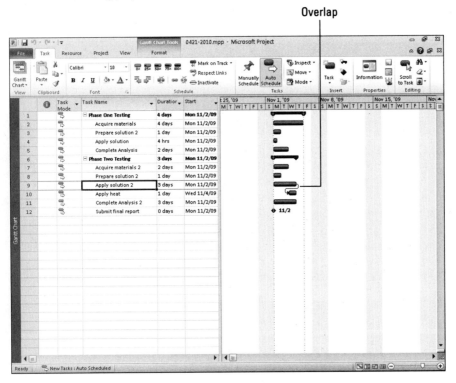

FIGURE 4.22

Four types of dependencies enable you to deal with every variable of how tasks can relate to each other's timing.

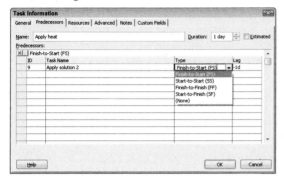

Tip

Use the Lag column on the Predecessors tab of the Task Information dialog box to create lag or lead time between tasks, entering a positive number for lag time or a negative number for lead time. ■

The first timing mentioned in each relationship name relates to the predecessor task and the second to the successor. Therefore, a start-to-finish dependency relates the start of the predecessor to the finish of the successor, and a finish-to-start relationship relates the finish of the predecessor to the start of the successor. Project refers to these relationships by their initials, such as *SS* for a start-to-start relationship.

Tip

As you view the figures in the following sections, take note of the direction that the arrow points between tasks. The direction of the arrow provides important visual clues about the type of dependency. ■

Finish-to-Start (FS)

A finish-to-start relationship is the most common type of dependency and is, in fact, the only relationship that you can create by using your mouse or the Link Tasks tool or command. In the finish-to-start relationship, the successor task can't start until the predecessor task finishes. Examples of this relationship are as follows:

- You must write a report before you can edit it.

- You must have a computer before you can install your software.

In Figure 4.23, you see examples of the FS relationship in which the successor task can start as soon as its predecessor is finished. The following tasks have a finish-to-start relationship:

- Task 2 and Task 3
- Task 3 and Task 4
- Task 4 and Task 5

Note

The relationship between Tasks 4 and 5 also contains some lag time, as discussed the section "Allowing for delays and overlap," earlier in this chapter. ■

Start-to-Finish (SF)

With the start-to-finish relationship, the successor task cannot finish until the predecessor task starts. The following are some examples:

- You can finish scheduling production crews only when you start receiving materials.
- Employees can start using a new procedure only when they have finished training for it. If the use of the new procedure is delayed, you also want to delay the training so that it occurs as late as possible before the implementation.

FIGURE 4.23

In the FS relationship, successor tasks can't start until predecessor tasks finish.

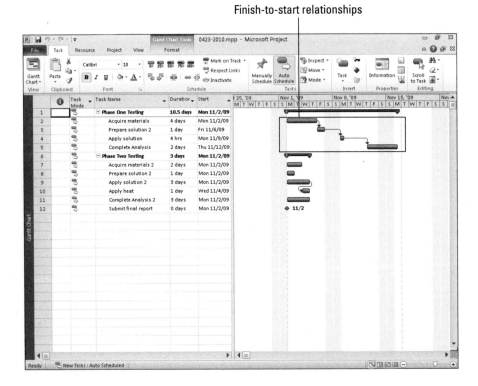

Note

Can you set up this start-to-finish example as a finish-to-start relationship? Not really. The idea is to allow no delay between training and implementation. If you set the new procedure to start only when the training finishes, the new procedure can start any time after the training ends, depending on how other relationships may delay it. If the training task has to finish just before the other task starts, delays of the later task (implementation) also delay the earlier task. This fine distinction will become clearer as you see more real-world projects in action. ■

Figure 4.24 shows a start-to-finish relationship between acquiring materials for Phase Two Testing and completing the analysis of Phase One Testing. Assuming that the test results of Phase One determine the materials that you'll need for Phase Two, you can't begin acquiring materials for Phase Two Testing until you have completed the analysis of Phase One Testing. Notice the direction of the arrow that connects the two tasks; it provides a visual clue of the type of dependency that exists between the tasks. In fact, the direction of the arrow in *all* dependencies provides you with valuable information.

FIGURE 4.24

The successor task can't finish until the predecessor task starts.

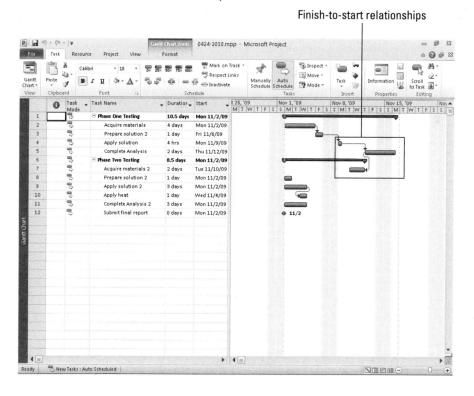

Start-to-Start (SS)

In a start-to-start relationship, the successor can't start until the predecessor starts. Consider the following examples:

- When you start getting results in an election, you can begin to compile them.
- When the drivers start their engines, the flagger can start the race.

In Figure 4.25, Tasks 10 and 11 have a start-to-start relationship. Although you'll need three days to complete the analysis, you can start the analysis as soon as you begin applying heat.

Finish-to-Finish (FF)

In the finish-to-finish dependency, the successor task can't finish until the predecessor task finishes. Consider the following examples:

- You finish installing computers at the same time that you finish moving employees into the building so that the employees can begin using the computers right away.
- Two divisions must finish retooling their production lines on the same day so that the CEO can inspect the lines at the same time.

FIGURE 4.25

The successor task can't finish until the predecessor task starts.

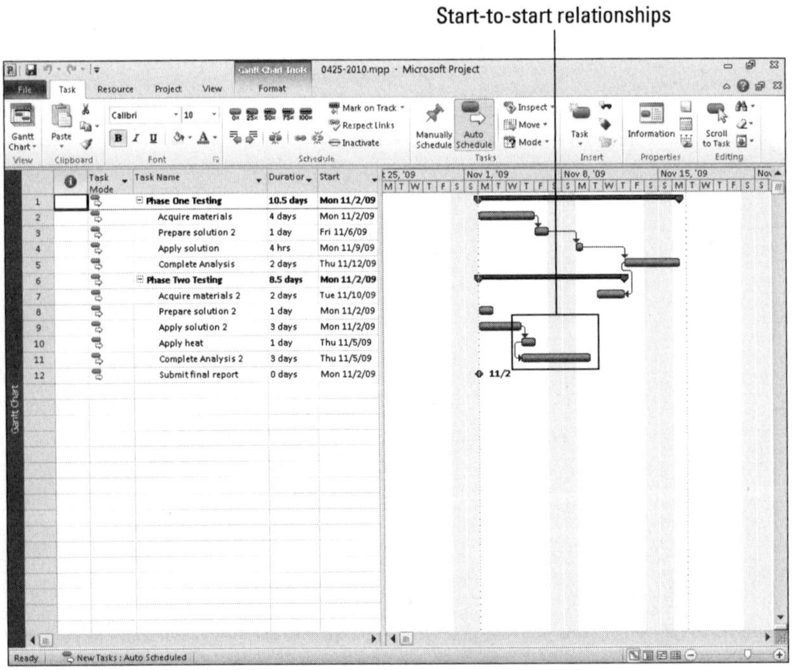

Start-to-start relationships

Suppose that, in Phase Two of the testing shown in Figure 4.26, you can begin preparing the chemical solution (Prepare solution 2) while you're still acquiring materials (Acquire materials 2). Note, however, that you can't finish preparing the chemical solution *until* you finish acquiring the materials. Therefore, set up a finish-to-finish dependency between these two tasks to make sure that you don't finish preparing the solution if you experience a delay in acquiring materials.

Establishing dependencies

As previously mentioned, you can set dependencies in several different ways. If you use the tasks in the Gantt table or the bars on the Gantt Chart to set dependencies, you must establish finish-to-start relationships. To establish more complex relationships, including lag and lead, use the Task Information dialog box.

FIGURE 4.26

The successor task can't finish before the predecessor task finishes.

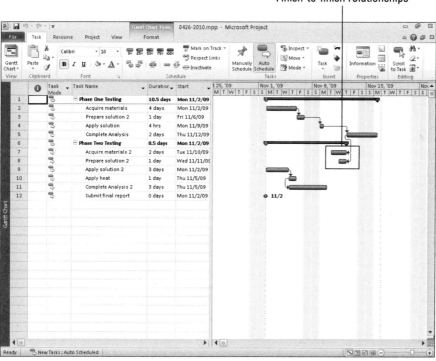

Project enables you to use summary tasks when setting dependencies with some limitations. You can set dependencies between two summary tasks or between a summary task and a detail task in another task group, regardless of the task mode (automatic or manual scheduling) of the tasks involved in the relationship. When you're setting dependencies between summary tasks, you can use either a finish-to-start or a start-to-start dependency; you cannot use any other type of dependency. You also cannot set dependencies between a summary task and any of its own subtasks. When you set a dependency between a summary task and a detail task in *another* task group, however, you can set any type of dependency you choose.

Setting finish-to-start dependencies

With the Gantt Chart displayed, you can use your mouse to drag between Gantt bars or click the Link Tasks button to set finish-to-start dependencies. Use the following steps to set a simple finish-to-start relationship by dragging between Gantt bars:

1. Place your mouse pointer over the predecessor task until the pointer turns into four arrows pointing outward.

2. Drag the mouse pointer to the second task. An information box describes the finish-to-start link that you are about to create, and the mouse pointer changes to a chain link (see Figure 4.27).

3. Release your mouse button when you're satisfied with the relationship, and Project establishes the link.

FIGURE 4.27

The relationship isn't established until you release the mouse button. If you have second thoughts, just drag the pointer back to the predecessor task before releasing your mouse button.

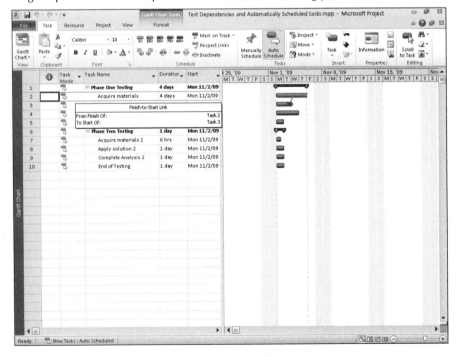

To use the Link Tasks button, simply follow these steps:

1. Select the tasks you want to link.

   To select adjacent tasks, drag through their ID numbers in the Gantt Chart table.

   To select nonadjacent tasks, hold down Ctrl as you click the ID numbers of the tasks that you want to link.

2. Click the Task tab and, in the Schedule group, click the Link Tasks button.

   Project establishes the link.

Setting other types of dependencies

You can use either the Task Information dialog box or the Task Dependency dialog box to set any type of dependency. Use the Task Dependency dialog box shown in Figure 4.28 to establish dependency types or lag or lead times between tasks. To open the Task Dependency dialog box, double-click the line that connects the tasks you want to change. Remember, you set lag time using a positive number in the Lag box, and set Lead time by supplying a negative number in the Lag box.

FIGURE 4.28

Use this dialog box to establish task dependencies or lag time.

You also can use the Task Information dialog box to establish dependencies and lag or lead times. If you choose to use the Task Information dialog box, open the dialog box for the successor task and build the relationship on the Predecessors tab.

Follow these steps to create a task dependency:

1. Double-click the task that you want to make a successor. When the Task Information dialog box appears, select the Predecessors tab.

2. Click the Task Name column; an arrow appears at its far end.

3. Click the arrow to the right of the column to display the drop-down list of task names, as shown in Figure 4.29.

4. Click the task that you want to identify as the predecessor to this task.

5. Click the Type field; a list box arrow appears.

6. Click the arrow to display a list of dependency types and select the type of dependency that you want to establish, such as start-to-start or start-to-finish.

FIGURE 4.29

Every task you create for your project appears on this list.

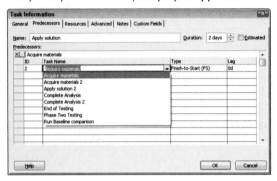

To establish a dependency with no lag or lead, click OK at this point to create the relationship. To establish a delay, click the Lag column and supply an amount of time for the delay. To establish an overlap, simply enter a negative number in the Lag column. For example, if you want the successor to finish one week before the predecessor finishes, use a finish-to-finish relationship and enter **1 week** in the Lag column. To establish lead time, supply a positive number in the Lag column.

Tip

Here's a quick way to create Finish to Finish, Start to Finish, or Start to Start relationships. Create the default Finish to Start relationship for the tasks. Then double-click the link line to open the Task Dependency dialog box and change the relationship. ■

Viewing Dependencies

After you've established several dependencies in a project, you can study them in several ways. You can, of course, open each task's Task Information dialog box and look at the relationships listed on the Predecessor tab. You can also view the lines drawn between tasks to see dependencies. You can scroll to the right in the Gantt table, or you can reduce the size of the Gantt Chart to see more of the Gantt table and display the Predecessors column, as shown in Figure 4.30. This column lists any relationships, using the two-letter abbreviations for the dependency type and positive and negative numbers to show lag and overlap.

Or, you can use the Task Inspector pane, shown in Figure 4.31, to explore the relationships among your tasks. To display the Task Inspector pane, click the Task tab and, in the Tasks group, click the Inspect button. Project displays information for the currently selected task, and you can click any task in the project schedule to see its information.

FIGURE 4.30

Display the Predecessors column to show all the relationships for a task.

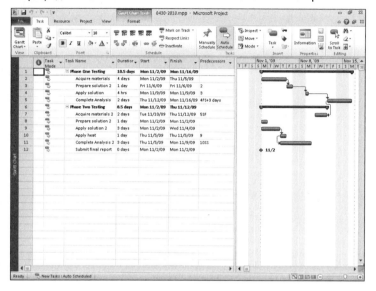

FIGURE 4.31

You can use the Task Inspector pane to explore task relationships.

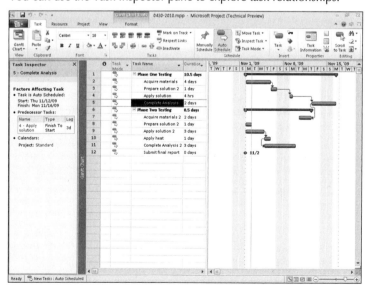

Cross-Reference

You can read more about the Task Inspector in Chapter 10. ■

The information that appears in the Task Inspector pane changes, depending on whether the task is scheduled manually or automatically and depending on whether you've set a baseline for your project and recorded actual information.

New Feature

The Task Inspector pane replaces the Task Driver pane introduced in Project 2007. ■

Cross-Reference

For more information on setting a baseline and recording actual information, see Chapters 12 and 13. ■

Deleting Dependencies

You can delete dependencies in several ways:

- Open the Task Information dialog box for the successor task, select the Predecessors tab, click the task name for the link that you want to break, and press Delete.

- Display the Predecessors column in the Gantt table, click the Predecessors cell for the successor task, and either press Delete to delete all relationships or edit the predecessor information in the cell.

- Select the tasks that are involved in the dependency you want to delete, click the Task tab, and then (in the Schedule group) click the Unlink Tasks button.

- Double-click the dependency line, and click the Delete button in the Task Dependency dialog box.

Note

If you delete a dependency for an automatically scheduled task, the task bars shift accordingly to reflect any new timing. If you delete a dependency for a manually scheduled task, Project makes no changes to the task's timing — honoring the duration, start date, and finish date you supplied or created when you first established the dependency. ■

Summary

In this chapter, you read more about the timing of tasks, including how to set task durations and dependencies. You now should know how to do the following things:

- Differentiate between resource-driven and fixed scheduling
- Establish task durations
- Assign calendars to tasks
- Create recurring tasks
- Establish constraints and deadline dates
- Add and view task notes
- Set, view, and delete dependencies

In Chapter 5, you begin to assign resources to tasks and to find out more about the relationship between resource assignment and task timing.

Creating Resources and Assigning Costs

T he "management" portion of the term *project management* suggests that you are overseeing and, supposedly, controlling what goes on during the project's lifetime. In the last chapter, you found out how to build the tasks that comprise the project. Now you need to identify the resources for each task. Some tasks require people only; other tasks may also require equipment.

As you create resources, you see that you can associate various rates with a resource. As you assign the resource to a task in your project, Microsoft Project automatically begins to calculate the cost of your project.

Understanding Resources

Resources are the people, supplies, and equipment that enable you to complete the tasks in your project. In Project, you can define four types of resources:

- Work resources
- Material resources
- Generic resources
- Cost resources

Work resources are people or equipment that consume time when working on a task. When you set up work resources, you define the amount of time that the resources have to spend on a project (100 percent is full-time).

Similarly, when you assign a work resource to a task, you indicate the amount of time that you want the work resource to spend on the task (100 percent is full-time).

Material resources are items that are consumed while working on a project. Material resources use, well, materials such as gasoline or wood — as opposed to time. When you assign a material resource to a task, you specify the amount of the material resource that you intend to use in units that are appropriate for the material resource. You can also indicate whether the amount of material used is based on time. For example, the number of gallons of water that are used when watering a lawn depends on the amount of time that you run the water and the number of gallons per hour that flow from the faucet. Or, you can indicate that the amount of material is fixed. For example, you need five 2 x 4's to construct a bench — regardless of how long you take to build the bench.

Generic resources are resources (as defined by you) that aren't specific people, equipment, or materials, but rather descriptions of the skills that you need for a task when you don't know what specific resources are available. Although this generic resource feature was designed to work in conjunction with the Resource Substitution Wizard and Enterprise Resources (available in Project Server), you may find generic resources handy even if you don't use Project Server. For example, you can use generic resources when you don't care who does the work — you simply want to track the work that is completed on a project.

Cross-Reference

If you're using Project Server, you can also take advantage of three related features. You can define Enterprise Resources — resources that are available company-wide for projects. You can use the Build Team page to help you select resources for your project from the Enterprise Resource pool, and you can use the Resource Substitution Wizard to replace generic resources with actual resources. Read more about all these features in Chapter 22. ∎

Using a *cost resource*, you can add a fixed cost to a task without making the cost depend on work performed. If one or more tasks in your project require that you rent a storage unit during part of the project, you can set up the storage unit as a cost resource that you can assign to tasks during the appropriate periods to account for the cost of the storage unit as part of the task. Or, suppose that a resource needs to fly from Salt Lake City to Chicago to complete a task; you can set up the airline tickets as a cost resource and add them to the task.

Resources cost money and therefore affect the cost of the project. To manage a project effectively, you should define resources and assign those resources to tasks in the project. Thus, you need to know how Project uses those resource assignments to change the duration and length of your project.

Tip

If you're not using Project Server and expect to use the same resources for several projects, consider setting up those resources in a special project that contains no tasks. Then you can use Project's resource-pooling feature and the "resource project" to share the same resources across multiple projects. This approach enables you to set up resources once and then use them repeatedly on many different projects. For more information about resource pooling, see Chapter 19. If you use Project Server, see Chapter 22 for more information about setting up Enterprise Resources. ∎

How resources function in Project

By defining and then assigning resources in Project, you accomplish the following goals:

- You can keep track of the tasks that are being performed by resources — because Project identifies the resources that are assigned to each task.

- You can identify potential resource shortages that may force you to miss scheduled deadlines and possibly extend the duration of your project.

- You can identify underutilized resources. If you reassign these resources, you may be able to shorten the project's schedule.

- You can determine the cost of each task and your project as a whole.

When the tasks that you create are effort-driven, the resources that you assign to a task affect the duration of the task. For example, if you assign two people to do a job, typically the job gets done in less time than if you assigned only one person to the job. But, you ask, what about the cost? Does the use of additional resources increase the project's cost? Perhaps yes — perhaps no. You may find that completing the project in less time (by using more resources) saves you money because you can accept more projects. Or you may be eligible for a bonus if you complete the project earlier than expected, and the bonus may cover or exceed the cost of the additional resources that you used.

How Project uses resource information to affect the schedule

For effort-driven tasks, Project uses the resource information that you provide to calculate the duration of the task and, consequently, the duration of the project. However, if you set up a task with a fixed duration, Project ignores the resources that you assign to the task when calculating the duration of the project. Similarly, if you don't assign resources, Project calculates the schedule using only the task duration and task dependency information that you provide.

Cross-Reference
See Chapter 4 for information on task durations and task dependencies. ∎

Assigning a resource to a task can affect the duration of the project because work on the task can't begin until the resource is available. Project uses a resource calendar to define the working days and times for a resource, but the resource's availability also depends on other tasks to which you've assigned the resource.

If the work assigned to a resource exceeds the time that is available, Microsoft Project assigns the resource to the task and indicates that the resource is overallocated. This technique enables you to see the problem and decide how to fix it.

How Project gathers cost information

When you assign rates to resources and then assign resources to tasks, Project can calculate the cost of tasks as well as the project. In addition to resource-associated costs, Project also handles fixed costs, which you read more about near the end of this chapter.

Cross-Reference

You can assign rates to resources when you define them, as you see in "Creating a Resource List," later in this chapter. ■

Assigning costs enables you to monitor and control the money you're spending on a project. Project shows you where and how you're spending your money so you can control when a project's costs accrue — which, in turn, helps you predict the cash flow needed to pay bills. The cost-related information that Project provides helps you verify the following items:

- The cost of resources and materials for any task
- The cost of any phase of your project, as well as the cost of the entire project

Tip

Cost information that you gather on one project might help you calculate bids for future projects. ■

Creating a Resource List

Note

If you intend to upload your project into the Project Server database, you may want to assign resources from the Enterprise Resource pool, a company-wide group of resources. See Chapter 22 for details on assigning resources from the Enterprise Resource pool. ■

Project gives you the option of creating resources one at a time, as you think of them, or entering all (or most) resources by using the Entry table of the Resource Sheet. To display the Resource Sheet, shown in Figure 5.1, click the Resource Sheet view shortcut button at the right edge of the Status Bar. By default, Project displays the Entry table of the Resource Sheet.

Tip

There are lots of ways to get to the Resource Sheet. For example, you can click either the Task or the Resource tab on the Ribbon and, in the View group, click the bottom of the Gantt Chart button or the Team Planner button (Project Standard users, where there is no Team Planner, click the Resource Sheet button) and select the Resource Sheet view. As an alternative, of course, you can click the View tab and, in the Resource Views group, click the Resource Sheet button. ■

FIGURE 5.1

The Resource Sheet displays a list of the resources available to your project.

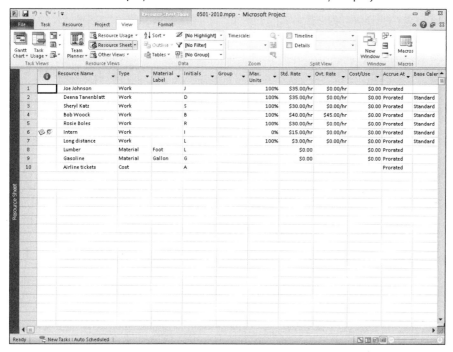

	ⓘ	Resource Name	Type	Material Label	Initials	Group	Max. Units	Std. Rate	Ovt. Rate	Cost/Use	Accrue At	Base Caler
1		Joe Johnson	Work		J		100%	$35.00/hr	$0.00/hr	$0.00	Prorated	
2		Deena Tanenblatt	Work		D		100%	$35.00/hr	$0.00/hr	$0.00	Prorated	Standard
3		Sheryl Katz	Work		S		100%	$30.00/hr	$0.00/hr	$0.00	Prorated	Standard
4		Bob Woock	Work		B		100%	$40.00/hr	$45.00/hr	$0.00	Prorated	Standard
5		Rosie Boles	Work		R		100%	$30.00/hr	$0.00/hr	$0.00	Prorated	Standard
6	📝	Intern	Work		I		0%	$15.00/hr	$0.00/hr	$0.00	Prorated	Standard
7		Long distance	Work		L		100%	$3.00/hr	$0.00/hr	$0.00	Prorated	Standard
8		Lumber	Material	Foot	L			$0.00		$0.00	Prorated	
9		Gasoline	Material	Gallon	G			$0.00		$0.00	Prorated	
10		Airline tickets	Cost		A						Prorated	

Note

You can switch tables by clicking the View tab and, in the Data group, clicking the Tables button. Each table contains columns pertinent to its name. For example, the Cost table shows columns that pertain to a resource's cost. ∎

If you use the Resource Sheet to define most of the resources for your project, the process of assigning resources goes much faster because you don't have to stop to create the resource first. Also, using the Resource Sheet is a safe way to define resources; the visual presentation helps you avoid accidentally creating the same resource twice. For example, if you've defined both Vicki and Vickie, Project sees two resources, even though you may have simply misspelled the name the second time.

You can enter the basics for the resource by filling in the Resource Sheet; simply press Tab to move from field to field (cell to cell). The Resource Sheet shown in Figure 5.1 does not show all the fields described in this section. Scroll to the right to see the rest of the Entry table of the Resource Sheet.

Tip

You can customize the Resource Sheet to show many additional fields that you may want to set up for each resource. For example, if you need to manually enter e-mail addresses for each resource, you can easily add the E-mail Address column to the Resource Sheet. ■

Cross-Reference

See Chapter 7 to find out how to insert a column in a table. ■

A *field* is a cell in a table into which you type appropriate information. All table and form views contain fields. Each field on the Resource Sheet serves a specific purpose, as follows:

- **Indicators:** Although you can't type in the `Indicators` field, icons appear there from time to time. Some of the icons appear as Project's response to an action you've taken. For example, you might see an indicator for an overallocated resource. In other cases, the indicator appears because you entered a note about the resource. See the "Adding notes to a resource" section, later in this chapter, for more information.

Tip

If you rest your mouse over an indicator, Project displays the information that is associated with the icon. ■

- **Resource Name:** Type the name of the resource. For a person, you can type the person's name or you can type a job description, such as Product Analyst 1 or Product Analyst 2.
- **Type:** Use this column to specify whether you're defining a human, material, or cost resource.

Tip

Project refers to human resources as Work resources. ■

- **Material Label:** For material resources, specify the unit of measure. You can set up any label you want. For example, you can use *minutes* for long-distance phone time, *feet* for lumber, or *miles* for vehicle usage.
- **Initials:** Type initials for the resource, or accept the default that Project provides, which is the first letter of the resource name. This designation appears on any view to which you add the Initials field. Typically, a resource's name appears, but you can customize the view to display initials if you prefer.
- **Group:** Assign resources to groups if they share some common characteristic, such as job function. Then you can use this field as a filtering or sorting mechanism and display information about the group (in this example, a particular job function) as opposed to a specific resource. Just type a name to create a group.

Tip

Be sure to spell the group name the same way every time you use it if you want to filter or sort resource information by group later on. ■

- **Max. Units:** Project expresses the amount of a Work resource you have available for assignment as a percentage of time spent at work. For example, 100 percent equals one unit, or the equivalent of all the working time one resource can provide (which can be part-time or full-time); normally over 100 percent is the point at which a resource is considered overallocated. By the same token, 50 percent equals one-half of a unit, or one-half of a full-time resource's available working time; 200 percent equals the available work time of two full-time resources.

- **Std. Rate:** The *standard rate* is the rate typically charged for a resource's work. Project calculates its default standard rate in hours, but you can specify other time increments. (For Work resources, you can use minutes, days, weeks, months, or years. For material resources, think of the charge as per unit based on the Material Label.) To specify a time increment other than hours, type a forward slash and then the first letter of the word representing the time increment (for example, to charge a resource's use in days, type **/d** after the rate you specify).

- **Ovt. Rate:** The overtime rate is the rate charged for any overtime work that a Work resource provides. Again, Project calculates the default rate in hours, but you can change the default unit just as you can for the standard rate.

- **Cost/Use:** In the Cost/Use column (read as "cost per use"), you supply a rate for costs charged for each use of a particular resource. Resource costs may be based on the Standard rate (which is calculated by multiplying the number of hours times the cost per hour), on the Cost/Use rate (a fixed fee for use of the resource), or on a combination of the two. Project uses a combination of the Cost/Use field and the Std. Rate field when it calculates the cost of a task. If you rented a piece of equipment that costs you $25/hour plus a setup charge of $100, you would assign a Std. Rate of $25/hour and a Cost/Use of $100.

- **Accrue At:** This field specifies how and when Project charges resource costs to a task at the standard rate or the overtime rate. The default option is Prorated, but you also can select Start or End, with the following results:

  - If you select Start and assign that resource to a task, Project calculates the cost for a task as soon as the task begins.

  - If you select End and assign that resource to a task, Project calculates the cost for the task when the task is completed.

  - If you select Prorated and assign that resource to a task, Project accrues the cost of the task as the assigned resource completes scheduled work.

  If you set the cost-per-use rate for a particular resource and assign that resource to a task, Project will use the Accrue At field to determine whether the cost is applied at the beginning or end of the task. If you set the Accrue At field to Start or Prorated, Project charges the cost at the beginning of the task. If you set the Accrue At field to End, Project charges the cost at the end of the task.

- **Base Calendar:** Here you identify the calendar that Project should use when scheduling the resource. The calendar identifies working and nonworking time. Project assumes that each resource uses the Standard calendar, but as you read later in this chapter, you can create calendars for resource groups (perhaps to handle shift work) or you can modify an individual resource's calendar to reflect vacation or other unavailable time (such as jury duty).

- **Code:** You can use this field as a catch-all field to assign any information that you want to associate with a resource, using an abbreviation of some sort. For example, suppose that your company uses cost-center codes. You may want to supply the appropriate cost-center code for the resource in the Code field. You can sort and filter information by the abbreviations that you supply in the Code field.

Note
After you create a resource, Project displays the resource's ID number on the left edge of the Resource Sheet, to the left of the Indicator column. ∎

Modifying Resource Information

You just learned a quick way to set up a resource — by entering it on the Resource Sheet. In addition, you can use the Resource Information dialog box to fine-tune any resource's definition. To display the Resource Information dialog box, double-click any resource on the Resource Sheet or click the Resource tab and, in the Properties group, click Resource Information.

Using the Resource Sheet, you already provided most of the information on the General tab, so this section discusses the fields in the dialog box that didn't appear by default on the Entry table of the Resource Sheet.

Assigning a communication method

In the Resource Information dialog box, use the Email field (see Figure 5.2) to supply the e-mail address of a particular resource.

FIGURE 5.2

Use the General tab of the Resource Information dialog box to add information about a resource, such as an e-mail address or availability.

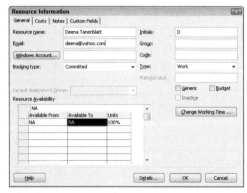

Note

If you're using Outlook and you've stored the resource's e-mail address in your address book, you can click the Details button in the Resource Information dialog box. When you do, Project tries to access Outlook — you must provide permission — and opens the appropriate Outlook Contact record. You can then copy the e-mail address from the Contact record and, in Project's Email field in the Resource Information dialog box, press Ctrl+V to paste the e-mail address. ■

Specifying resource availability

Suppose that you set up a resource to represent a specific job, such as Intern, as shown in Figure 5.3. And suppose that you have more than one person who can serve as this resource, but not at all times. Using the Resource Availability table (refer to Figure 5.3), you can specify the time periods for which the resource will be available. Figure 5.3 shows that three interns are available from June 1 through July 31 and only one intern is available from August 1 through August 31.

FIGURE 5.3

Use the Resource Availability table to identify when a resource is available.

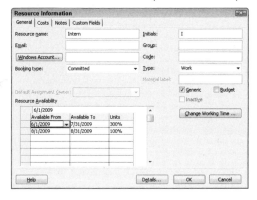

Note

You can contour the availability of resources you have identified for your project; see Chapter 11 for more information. ■

Specifying a booking type

You can specify a booking type for a resource assignment. Booking types are most useful in an enterprise environment that has implemented Project Server, where you are utilizing the Enterprise Resource Pool.

The Booking Type field offers you two choices: Committed and Proposed (see Figure 5.4). When you *commit* a resource, you are officially assigning the resource to the project. When you *propose to use* a resource, you are indicating that the resource is not yet officially assigned to the project — which leaves the resource's calendar untouched by the proposed assignment to your project.

Note

Project does not consider proposed bookings when calculating resource allocation. Thus another project manager could commit the same resource to a different project for the same time frame, and Microsoft Project would not identify the resource as being overallocated. ■

FIGURE 5.4

Specify whether to commit a resource or simply propose its use.

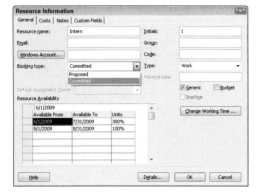

Tip

The Booking type you choose for a resource applies to all tasks in your project to which you assign the resource. ■

Creating a Generic resource and assigning custom fields

The Intern resource discussed in the previous section is essentially a generic resource — it's a job description, not a person (at least not yet). To mark a resource as generic, place a check mark in the Generic box on the General tab of the Resource Information dialog box (refer to Figure 5.4). Your company may have set up custom fields in Project that apply to your generic resource. To assign the appropriate custom fields, click the Custom Fields tab and assign any appropriate values to your generic resource, as shown in Figure 5.5.

FIGURE 5.5

You can assign custom fields to Generic resources to describe the skills that are required.

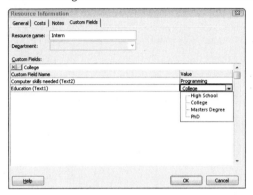

Cross-Reference

See Chapter 16 for more information about creating custom fields. ■

When you click OK to close the dialog box, you see an icon in the Indicator column like the one shown in Figure 5.6. This icon signifies that the resource is Generic.

Creating a budget resource

You also can set up a *budget resource* — another useful stand-in for a real resource, this one made of estimated costs. Project provides budget resources so you can specify how work or costs will be allocated during the project. Suppose, for example, that you want to create a budget for the cost of a storage unit required during the life of your project. You would create a resource for the storage unit, setting its type as Cost, and then check the Budget check box on the General tab of the Resource Information dialog box to make it a budget resource (see Figure 5.7).

Project doesn't allow you to enter any cost information for a budget resource on the Resource Sheet. To assign a value to the budget resource, you first assign it to the project summary task — but Project won't let you assign a value as you assign the budget resource. Instead, you supply a value by adding the Budget Cost field to the table in the Task Usage view or the Resource Usage view.

FIGURE 5.6

Identify Generic resources by the icon that's shown in the Indicator column.

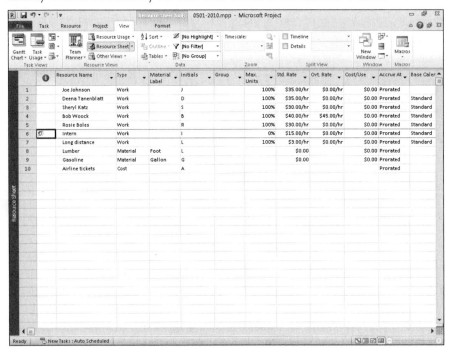

FIGURE 5.7

If you set up a Cost resource as a budget resource, you can use it to budget for your project.

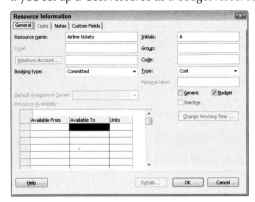

Tip

Project doesn't display the project summary task by default. To display it, start in a task-oriented view such as the Gantt Chart view. Click the Format tab for the view — in my example, click the Gantt Chart Tools Format tab — and, in the Show/Hide group, select the Project Summary Task check box. Note that the Task Mode for the project summary task is Auto Schedule, and you cannot change that value. ■

Cross-Reference

See Chapter 7 for details on inserting columns to add a field to a view. ■

You also can set up a work budget resource that you can use to budget for the number of hours of work you intend to perform for the entire project. You then assign the Work budget resource to the project summary task. To record the number of hours of work you want to budget for the entire project, add the `Budget Work` field to the Task Usage view or the Resource Usage view and enter your budget value. As you track the work for your project's tasks, you can compare the work performed with the budgeted work.

Adding notes to a resource

Click the Notes tab of the Resource Information dialog box. The Notes text box, shown in Figure 5.8, is a free-form text box in which you can type any information that you want to store about the resource. For example, you may want to store a reminder about a resource's upcoming vacation or an explanation about resource availability.

After you type text in this box and click OK, a Note indicator icon appears in the Indicator column on the Resource Sheet, as shown in Figure 5.9.

FIGURE 5.8

Use this text box to store information about a resource.

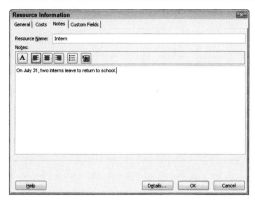

FIGURE 5.9

No need to reopen the Resource Information dialog box to read a note. Instead, place your mouse pointer over the icon in the Indicator column to display the contents of the note.

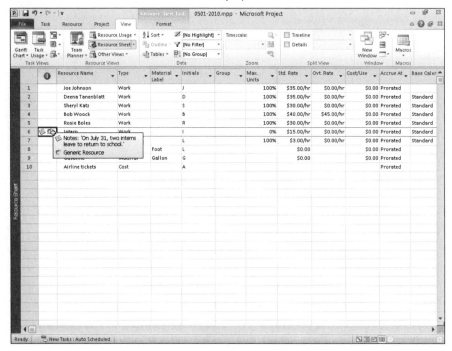

Note

If more than one indicator appears in the Indicator column, Project displays information about all indicators when you point to the Indicator column. ■

Calendars and resources

Project uses a base calendar called the Standard calendar to calculate the timing of the project. When you first create a resource for your project, Project uses the Standard base calendar as the default (an eight-hour day and a 40-hour week) if you haven't selected a different calendar in the Project Information dialog box. You can modify working times and create calendar exceptions for resources to accommodate a different work week or planned vacation time.

Note

The entire project has a Standard calendar, and each resource also has his or her individual Standard calendar. Tasks can also have calendars; see Chapter 4 for information on task calendars. ■

Modifying a resource's working hours

Suppose that a specific resource won't be available all day on a given day, or even on several specified days. For example, suppose that all the interns work from 1:00 p.m. to 6:00 p.m. on weekdays. You can change the working hours of a resource by using the Resource Information dialog box. To change the work week for Interns, follow these steps:

1. Double-click the resource on the Resource Sheet to open the Resource Information dialog box.

2. On the General tab, click the Change Working Time button.

   Project displays the resource's calendar with today's date selected. Current working times appear to the right of the calendar.

3. Click the Work Weeks tab (see Figure 5.10).

4. Click the [Default] work week already defined for the calendar by Project.

FIGURE 5.10

To modify the default work week, select [Default] on the Work Weeks tab.

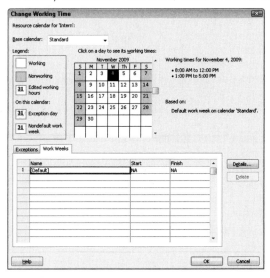

5. Click the Details button. Project displays the Details dialog box (see Figure 5.11).

6. Select the day(s) you want to change on the left side of the dialog box.

FIGURE 5.11

Use this dialog box to redefine a work week.

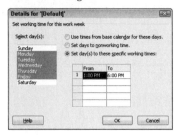

Tip

To select multiple days, use Windows selection techniques. To select contiguous days, click the first day. Then, press and hold the Shift key while clicking the last day. To select noncontiguous days, press and hold Ctrl as you click each day you want to select. ■

7. Select the Set Day(s) to These Specific Working Times option.

8. In the Working Times section, define the working time for the selected day.

9. Click OK. Project redisplays the Change Working Time dialog box.

When you change the work week, the change you make is not considered an exception; instead, it's considered the normal work week. So you won't notice any changes to the calendar in the Change Working Time dialog box. However, you can identify the working time for any day by clicking that day on the calendar; the working time appears to the right.

Cross-Reference

To avoid overallocating a resource that works part of a day, level the resource on a day-by-day basis. Read more about leveling and handling overallocations in Chapter 11. ■

Blocking off vacation time

In the real world, human resources take time off from work. To avoid overallocating a person by assigning work during a vacation period, you should mark vacation days as an exception on the team member's calendar. Follow these steps:

Again, by comparing the date to the Legend panel, you can tell the reason for the exception.

1. Double-click the resource on the Resource Sheet to open the Resource Information dialog box.

2. On the General tab, click the Change Working Time button. Project displays the resource's calendar with today's date selected.

3. Click in the Name column on the Exceptions tab and type a name that helps you remember the purpose of the exception (see Figure 5.12).

FIGURE 5.12

To set up a working time exception, type a name for the exception and set dates.

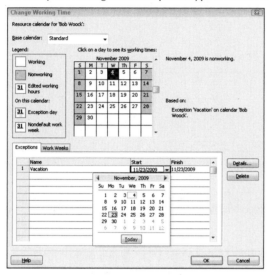

4. Click in the Start column and select the date on which the exception starts.

5. Click in the Finish column and select the date on which the exception ends.

   Click anywhere outside the Finish column, and Project sets every day between the starting and ending dates as an exception on the calendar. In addition, the Details button and the Delete button become available (see Figure 5.13).

Note

By default, Project sets any exception you create as nonworking time, but if you need to describe the exception more fully, click the Details button. In the Details dialog box, you can define the details of a working time or a nonworking time exception. For example, you can change a resource's working time for a particular day by using the Details dialog box. Also, if appropriate, you can set up the exception as a recurring exception. ■

6. Click OK twice to save the exception.

FIGURE 5.13

Project uses underscores to mark exceptions to the resource's regular calendar.

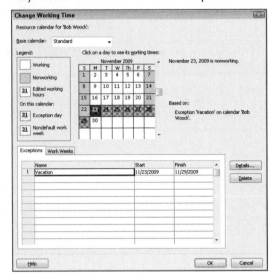

Assigning Resources to Tasks

You've spent a lot of time in this chapter defining resources and fine-tuning your resource definitions. Now you can finally assign resources to tasks. As noted earlier in this chapter, defining your project's resources helps you to manage your project more effectively, both in scheduling and in cost.

Assigning resources to tasks

You can easily assign resources to tasks from the Gantt Chart view. Click the Gantt Chart view shortcut at the right edge of the Status Bar or click the top of the Gantt Chart button in the View group on the Task tab of the Ribbon to switch to the Gantt Chart view. Then follow these steps to assign resources to tasks:

1. Select the task to which you want to assign a resource.

    You can click the task bar on the Gantt Chart, or you can click any column in the Gantt table.

2. Click the Resource tab and, in the Assignments group, click the Assign Resources button to open the Assign Resources window (see Figure 5.14).

FIGURE 5.14

Use the Assign Resources window to assign a resource to the task identified at the top of the box.

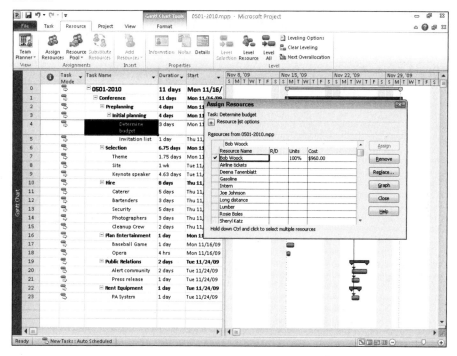

3. Select the resource you want to assign from the Resource Name list of the Assign Resources dialog box.

Tip

Did you forget to define a resource you're trying to assign? You don't need to return to the Resource Sheet. Just enter the name of the resource in the Resource Name column of the Assign Resources dialog box. ■

4. (Optional) If you're using Project Server and you intend to use the Resource Substitution Wizard, in the R/D field enter an **R** for Request to indicate that any resource with the required skills can work on the task. Or, enter a **D** for Demand to indicate that the selected resource is specifically required to work on the task.

Cross-Reference

For more information about resource substitution, see Chapter 22. ■

5. Do one of the following to assign the amount of a resource:

   - To assign any amount other than 100 percent of a resource, type the quantity as a percentage in the Units column. (Project applies units in percentages, so 100 percent equals one unit of the resource.)

   - To assign one unit (100 percent) of a resource, leave the Units column blank, because Project assigns 100 percent by default.

Note

You don't need to type the percent sign (%); Project assumes percentages. For example, if you enter 50, Project converts your entry to 50%. Keep in mind that you can't assign less than 1% of a resource's time. ■

6. Click Assign.

   Project places a check mark in the leftmost column of the Assign Resources window to indicate that the resource is assigned to the selected task, and Project calculates the resource's cost using the cost you supplied when you defined the resource.

7. Repeat Steps 3, 4, and 5 to assign additional resources to the selected task, or to select another task in the project; then repeat Steps 3, 4, and 5.

8. When you finish assigning resources, click Close.

Assigning a budget resource

To assign a budget resource to your project, you must first display the project summary task. Start in any task view; for this discussion, I'll start in the Gantt Chart view. Click the Format tab of the view; in my example, I click the Gantt Chart Tools Format tab. Then, in the Show/Hide group, select the Project Summary Task check box (see Figure 5.15). The first task in your project bears the filename of the project.

After you make sure the project summary task is displayed, follow these steps to assign a budget resource:

1. Click the project summary task and then click the Resource tab on the Ribbon.

2. In the Assignments group, click the Assign Resources button to open the Assign Resources window (see Figure 5.16).

3. Click the budget resource and click Assign. Project places a check in the leftmost column beside the resource to indicate that the resource is assigned to the selected task. You cannot assign any value to the budget resource at this point, so click Close.

FIGURE 5.15

To assign a budget resource, you must display the project summary task.

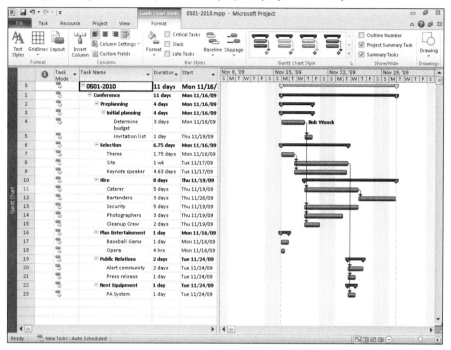

Note

While the project summary task is selected, the Assign button will not be available for any resource other than a budget resource. ∎

4. To assign a value to a budget resource, switch to the Task Usage or the Resource Usage view (use the view shortcut buttons at the right edge of the Status Bar or click the View tab on the Ribbon and select a view); in Figure 5.17, I'm using the Task Usage view.

5. To add the budget resource value on a specific day, add the Budget Cost or Budget Work fields to the Details section of the view and enter the budget value. To add the budget resource value to the project, regardless of the timeframe, add the Budget Cost and Budget Work fields to the table portion of the view and enter the budget value for the budget cost or budget work resource.

FIGURE 5.16

You use the Assign Resources window to assign a budget resource to the project summary task.

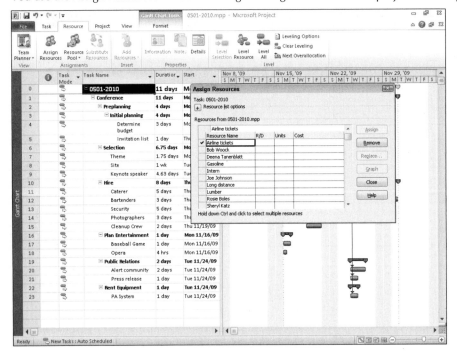

Cross-Reference

See Chapter 7 for details on adding fields like Budget Cost or Budget Work to a view. ■

Getting help while selecting resources to assign

You may have noticed a plus sign (+) next to Resource List options at the top of the Assign Resources window. If you click the plus sign, the box expands to provide you with ways to make selecting resources easier (see Figure 5.18).

If you check the Filter By check box, Project presents a long list of ways you can limit the resource list. For example, you can search for only material resources — or you can search for resources in a particular group. (Remember that you can assign resources to groups if the resources share a common characteristic.) If you don't find the filter that you want to use, you can create your own filter by clicking the More Filters button — and, in the More Filters dialog box that appears, clicking New.

FIGURE 5.17

You can use the Task Usage view or the Resource Usage view to assign budget-resource values to the project summary task.

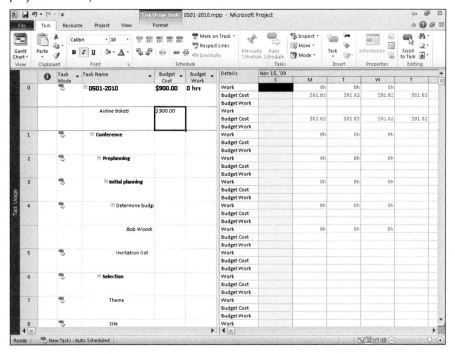

FIGURE 5.18

You can narrow your search for resources by filtering, and you can make additional resources available.

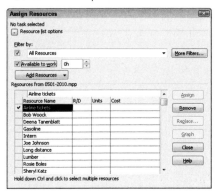

How Project Calculates Available to Work Time

Project calculates the value for Available To Work time by using the resource's calendar, availability contour, and the duration of the task. Based on the resource's calendar, Project calculates the number of working hours for the selected task. Because the resource's availability may be reduced by the availability contour and by other assignments, Project multiplies available working hours by the availability contour value and then subtracts existing assignment work hours to determine Available To Work hours.

To see how this works, assume that you have a task to accomplish within a ten-day window and the calendar provides for an eight-hour work day. If Day 3 is a holiday and Days 6 and 7 are the weekend, you have only seven days to complete the task. If you assigned one resource to this task full-time, that resource would be allocated for 56 hours. But if the resource's availability contour were set to 50 percent, then resource's availability would be reduced to 28 hours. And if the resource were already assigned to another task for 25 percent of the time on Days 1 and 2 (4 hours), then the resource's Available To Work hours would be down to 24 hours.

Cross-Reference

See Chapter 7 for information about creating custom filters. ∎

If you check the Available to Work box, you can specify the number of hours you need the resource to work. Project calculates the remaining available hours of each resource for the duration of the task and then compares the results of the calculation with the number of hours that you specified. Resources having available hours equal to or greater than the number you supplied appear in the list, along with the resources that are already assigned to the selected task.

Tip

If you need a resource for 12 days, enter 12d in the Available to work box, and Project converts the value to 96 hours. ∎

You can click the Add Resources button to display a list of sources from which you can select a resource. These sources include the Active Directory, your address book (if you use a MAPI-compliant e-mail program such as Microsoft Outlook or Windows Mail), or Microsoft Project Server— the items that are available in the list depend on your working environment.

Note

When you click Add Resources, one of the options that appears is the Active Directory, a Windows network feature. In a Windows network, the administrator can set up an Active Directory that contains a list of people and the contact information for these people. ∎

The Assign Resources window also contains a Graphs button that you can use to get a graphic representation of a resource's availability. Be aware that these graphs don't relate particularly to a task for which you're considering assignment; instead, they focus on the resource.

Note

Although technically you can select multiple resources to graph, this action may not be very useful when you're trying to select resources to assign to a task. ■

The Work variation of the Resource Graph appears in a split view when you click the Graph button in the Assign Resources window (see Figure 5.19). This graph shows the amount of work (regardless of the task) assigned to the selected resource on a day-by-day basis.

If you right-click the graph, you can select a different view for the selected resource. For example, you can select Work Availability and you'll see basically the inverse of the Work variation of the Resource Graph: Each bar represents *available* time instead of *allocated* time.

You can use the scroll bar on the left side at the bottom of the view to scroll through resources; you don't need to use the Assign Resources window to select a resource.

FIGURE 5.19

This graph shows the amount of work assigned to the resource you selected in the Assign Resources window for the time period displayed.

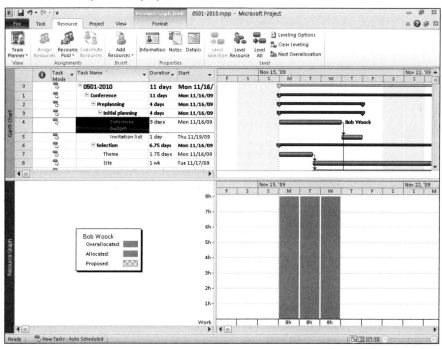

Some tips about resource assignments

Use the following tips when working in the Assign Resources window to assign resources to tasks:

- **You can assign several different resources to the same task by simply selecting each resource.** You can select a single resource and immediately click Assign, or you can use standard Windows selection techniques to select several resources and then click Assign only once.

- **You can assign a resource to a task on a part-time basis by assigning less than 100 in the Units column.** The number you type here represents the percentage of working time that you want the resource to spend on the task.

- **You can assign more than one resource by assigning more than 100 in the Units column.**

- **You can consume material resources in two ways: fixed and variable.**

  When you use *fixed consumption,* you indicate that — no matter how long the task lasts — you'll use the same quantity of the material. For example, to build a swimming pool, you need two tons of concrete — no matter how long it takes you to pour the concrete.

  When you use *variable consumption,* you indicate that the length of time needed for the task does affect the amount of the material you expect to use. For example, when you mow the lawn with a gas mower, the amount of gas you consume depends on how long you run the mower.

You designate fixed or variable consumption in the Units column of the Assign Resources dialog box. To differentiate between fixed and variable consumption, supply the time rate at which you consume a variable resource, such as "per hour" or "per day." In Figure 5.20, gasoline is a material resource that is being consumed at a variable rate of $2.75/gallon for 6 hours. Project recognizes the variable consumption because I entered the "per hour" designation as I assigned the units of the resource and Project calculates the cost of using the resource at $33.00 ($2.75/gallon per hour for six hours). If I had simply typed "2 gal," I would have indicated a fixed consumption rate and Project would have calculated a cost of $5.50 (two gallons at $2.75/gallon) for the material resource, with no concern for the length of time I use it.

After you assign a resource to a task, the resource name appears next to the task bar on the Gantt Chart by default. Depending on the task type that you set, you may be able to use resource assignments to modify not only individual task lengths, but also the entire project schedule. For example, if you assign additional resources to an effort-driven, fixed-unit task, Project shortens the duration of the task. As explained in Chapter 4, the amount of work to be done doesn't change, but the extra concurrent effort shortens the time necessary to get the work done. Or, if you assign a resource to work part-time on an effort-driven task, you may find you can complete several tasks at the same time.

Tip
If you overallocate a resource by assigning more of the resource than you have available, Project displays the resource in red on the Resource Sheet view. Chapter 10 explains how to handle these problems. ∎

FIGURE 5.20

Indicate variable consumption by supplying the time rate when you specify the amount that you'll use.

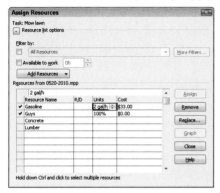

Removing or replacing a resource assignment

To remove a resource assignment, follow these steps:

1. Using the Gantt Chart view, select the task from which you want to remove the resource assignment.

2. Click the Resource tab and, in the Assignments group, click the Assign Resources button to display the Assign Resources dialog box.

3. Highlight the resource you want to remove from the task.

   You should see a check mark next to the resource in the leftmost column of the dialog box.

4. Click Remove, as shown in Figure 5.21.

FIGURE 5.21

Remove resources from tasks by selecting them in the Assign Resources window and clicking Remove.

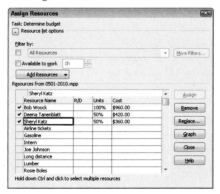

You can be sure that at some point in your project, you will want to change resource assignments. Follow these steps to switch from one resource to another on a particular task:

1. Select the task for which you want to switch resources.

2. Open the Assign Resources dialog box. (Step 2 in the preceding steps list explains how.)

3. Highlight the resource that you want to remove from the task; a check mark appears next to the assigned resource.

4. Click Replace. Project displays the Replace Resource dialog box, which enables you to easily select replacement resources, as shown in Figure 5.22.

FIGURE 5.22

The Replace Resource dialog box looks very similar to the Assign Resources dialog box.

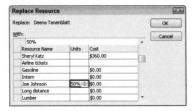

5. Highlight each resource that you want to assign, and supply units.

6. Click OK.

Handling Unusual Cost Situations

If you're trying to figure out how long it will take to complete a project, resources go hand in hand with tasks. If you assign costs to your resources, those costs also affect the cost of your project. Assigning a cost to a resource, however, is not the only way to assign a cost to a project. For example, projects can have fixed costs associated with them. This section starts with a quick look at overall project costs — and then focuses on handling unusual cost situations.

Looking at the project's cost

You've seen how to assign costs to resources. You've also seen how to assign resources to tasks — and, by the transitive property of equality (remember that one from high school algebra?), assigning a resource to which you have assigned a cost causes your project to have a cost. Are you wondering what that cost is? Click the Project tab and, in the Properties group, click Project Information to open the Project Information dialog box. Then click the Statistics button to open the Project Statistics dialog box (see Figure 5.23).

FIGURE 5.23

Check the cost of your project in the Project Statistics dialog box.

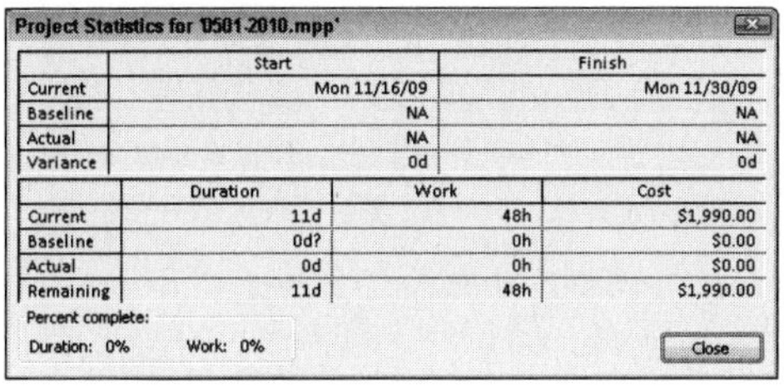

Project Statistics for '0501-2010.mpp'				
	Start		Finish	
Current		Mon 11/16/09		Mon 11/30/09
Baseline		NA		NA
Actual		NA		NA
Variance		0d		0d

	Duration	Work	Cost
Current	11d	48h	$1,990.00
Baseline	0d?	0h	$0.00
Actual	0d	0h	$0.00
Remaining	11d	48h	$1,990.00

Percent complete:
Duration: 0%   Work: 0%   [Close]

Cross-Reference

Part V covers tracking, recording work done, and analyzing and reporting on progress. Chapter 15 explains additional ways to view project costs. The following sections consider ways to assign unusual costs to a project. ■

Assigning fixed costs

This chapter has, to this point, focused on resources, and on how to assign costs to a resource. But the costs of some tasks need to be calculated differently. In Project, you can assign a fixed cost to a task or you can assign a fixed resource cost to a task.

Assigning a fixed cost to a task

Some tasks are fixed-cost tasks. That is, you know that the cost of a particular task stays the same regardless of the duration of the task or the work performed by any resources on the task. For example, your catering service, as part of each job, washes linens. You own the washing machine, and you've done the calculation on the amount of water plus electricity used (plus wear and tear) each time you run the machine for a wash cycle. Or, you're renting a site for a meeting for a flat fee. In cases like these, you assign the cost directly to the task. If you assign a cost to a task, Project adds the fixed cost of the task to the cost of any resource work that you assign to the task when calculating costs for the project.

Note

Remember that assigning a fixed cost to a task does not necessarily make the total cost of the task equal to the fixed cost that you assigned. You can, for example, assign more than one fixed cost as well as variable costs to a task. ■

To assign a fixed cost to a task, use the Gantt Chart view and apply the Cost table. Follow these steps:

1. Click the Gantt Chart view shortcut at the right edge of the Status Bar to switch to the Gantt Chart view.

2. Click the View tab and, in the Data group, click the Tables button; from the list that appears, select Cost to switch to the Cost table view of the Gantt Chart (see Figure 5.24).

FIGURE 5.24

Use the Cost table view of the Gantt Chart to assign costs to tasks.

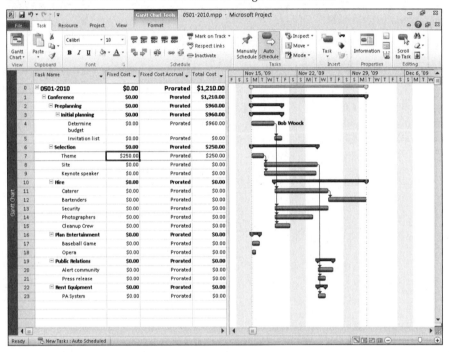

3. Select the task to which you want to assign a fixed cost.

4. In the Fixed Cost column, type the cost for that task and press Enter.

You can control how Project accrues the fixed cost for a task from the Fixed Cost Accrual column. Your choices are Start, Prorated, and End. These choices have the same meaning as the accrual choices for resources discussed in the "Creating a Resource List" section earlier in this chapter.

Tip

To control how Project accrues all fixed costs, use the Project Options dialog box. Click the File tab button and, in Backstage view, click Options. Click Schedule on the left side of the Project Options dialog box. Then, use the Default Fixed Cost Accrual list box to select an accrual method. ■

Assigning a fixed resource cost to a task

Suppose you hire a consultant to perform a task for a fixed amount of money. You can assign the consultant to the task as a *fixed-cost resource*. First, set up the resource in the Resource Sheet view. If the resource has some sort of "per unit" cost (an hourly or daily rate), assign that rate in the Std. Rate field. Otherwise, assign a standard rate of $0, as I did in Figure 5.25. Supply the fixed-cost amount in the Cost/Use field.

Tip

To keep this example clear, I assigned a Std. Rate of $0 to show you how Project calculates the cost of using the resource as the value you assign in the Cost/Use field, regardless of the amount of time the resource spends working on the task. If your resource has a standard rate, be sure to assign it in the Std. Rate field to make Project add the Cost/Use value to the amount of time the resource spends working on the task. ■

FIGURE 5.25

Setting up a fixed-cost resource.

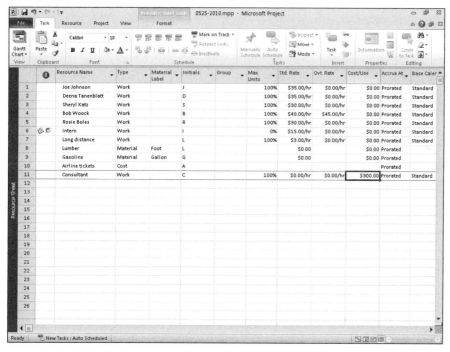

Next, you can add the resource to the task using the Assign Resources window; click the task to select it. Then click the Resource tab and, in the Assignments group, click the Assign Resources button. In the Assign Resources window, be sure to assign a percentage of units to the resource, even if the resource has a $0 standard rate. After you click Assign, Project automatically adds the fixed cost in the Cost column (see Figure 5.26).

Caution

If you don't assign units, Project converts the task to a milestone, causing the task to lose its duration. ■

To view the costs of your tasks — and to see how Project treated the cost of the task to which you assigned a cost/use (cost-per-use) resource, change the table of the Gantt Chart view from the Entry table to the Cost table by clicking the View tab and, in the Data group, clicking the Tables button; from the list that appears, select Cost.

FIGURE 5.26

When you assign a resource with a cost/use to a task, Project displays that cost in the Assign Resources window.

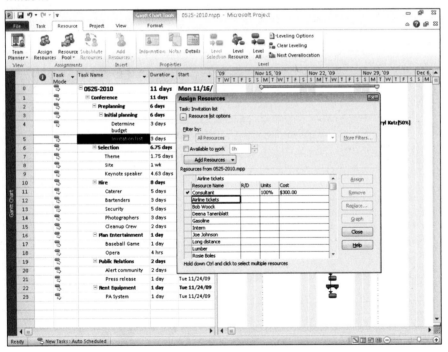

In the Total Cost column, Project assigns the resource's cost using the rate/hour you supplied in the Std. Rate field on the Resource Sheet *plus* the cost you assigned in the Cost/Use field, as shown in Figure 5.27. The task's total cost does not depend entirely on the time that a resource spends working on the task.

Accounting for resource rate changes

In some situations, you must charge different rates on different tasks for the same resource. Or you may expect a resource's rate to change during the life of your project. Project uses cost-rate tables to accurately reflect resource costs as they change. On cost-rate tables, you can identify up to 125 rates for a single resource, and you can identify the effective date of each rate. Cost-rate tables help you to account for pay increases or decreases to human resources during the life of your project, and enable you to charge the same resource at different rates, depending on the task.

FIGURE 5.27

Project assigns the cost per use to the task when you assign a resource defined with a cost-per-use value.

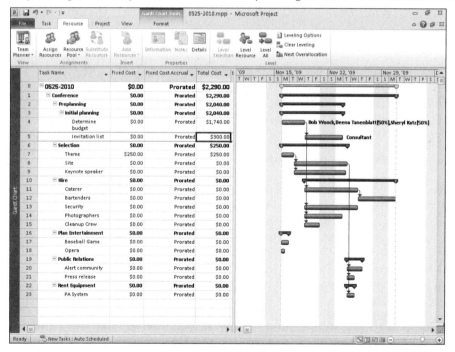

To assign multiple rates to a resource, use the Costs tab of the Resource Information dialog box. On the Resource Sheet view, double-click the resource for which you want to assign multiple rates. Click the Costs tab in the Resource Information dialog box (see Figure 5.28).

Use cost-rate tables to assign different rates to a resource.

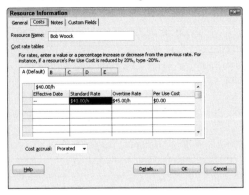

The Costs tab displays five cost-rate tables (tabs A through E) that you can use to assign different rates to a resource for use on different dates throughout a project's life. On each cost-rate table, you can enter up to 25 rates for the selected resource and indicate an effective date for each rate. Project uses the effective dates that you supply to apply the correct rate to a resource at different times during the project.

Tip

If you're specifying a new rate as an increase or decrease of an existing rate, you can specify the new rate in a percentage (such as +10% or –10%); Project calculates the value of the rate for you. You must enter the percent sign. ■

If you charge different amounts for resources depending on the type of work they perform, you may want to use each cost-rate table tab to represent sets of rates for different kinds of work.

To assign the correct resource cost-rate table to a task, follow these steps:

1. Assign the resource to the task by using the Assign Resources window as discussed in "Assigning resources to tasks" section, earlier in this chapter.

2. Click the Task Usage view shortcut at the right edge of the Status Bar to switch to the Task Usage view (see Figure 5.29).

FIGURE 5.29

The Task Usage view shows you the amount of time that a resource is assigned to a particular task.

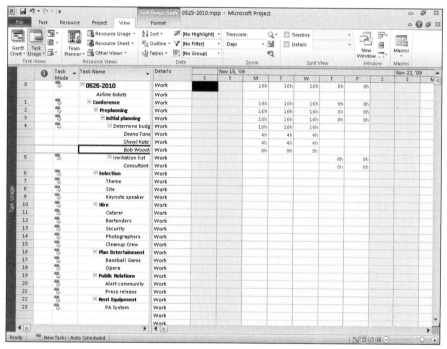

3. In the Task Name column, double-click the resource for which you want to select a cost-rate table.

The Assignment Information dialog box appears.

4. Click the General tab, shown in Figure 5.30, to select a cost-rate table.

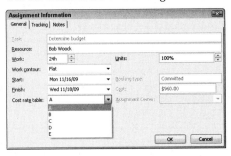

FIGURE 5.30

Use the General tab of the Assignment Information dialog box to select a cost-rate table.

5. Select the correct cost-rate table from the Cost Rate Table drop-down list.

6. Click OK.

Tip

If you use cost-rate tables a great deal, you may want to add the Cost Rate Table column to the table portion of the Task Usage view. Doing so makes it easy to select a cost-rate table without opening the Assignment Information dialog box. See Chapter 7 for details on inserting a column. ■

Summary

This chapter detailed more about using resources in Project, including how to create and assign resources to your project. The following topics were covered:

- Creating a resource list
- Modifying resource information, including using calendars for resources
- Assigning resources to tasks and removing resource assignments
- Handling fixed costs, both for individual tasks and for resources
- Assigning either a fixed or variable cost to a material resource
- Setting up different rates for resources to account for pay increases or decreases or for charging resources at different rates on different tasks

Chapter 6 presents the basics of using the standard views in Project.

Part III

Getting Information about Projects

Understanding the Basics of Views

A project is like a small business: Different people attend to various aspects of the work. The Accounting department thinks mainly of the costs of doing business. The plant supervisor focuses on deadlines and having enough machinery to get the job done. Your Human Resources department thinks of people — their salaries, hours, benefits, and so on.

As the owner of your project, you're likely to wear all these hats (and more) during the project. Changing views in Project is the practical way of changing hats. You switch to another view to see and work with your project from a different perspective. Each view helps you to focus on a different aspect of your project.

Views in Project enable you to enter, organize, and examine information in various ways. Project provides a variety of views, and this chapter provides you with a basic understanding of the default views. The next chapter covers techniques you can use to customize views and make them work for you.

What Is a View?

A *view* is a way to examine and update your project. Different views enable you to focus on different aspects of the project. Project uses three types of views and typically uses them in combination, as follows:

- **Chart or graph views:** These views present information by using pictures. You've already seen the Gantt Chart view, which is a chart view.

- **Sheet views:** These views present information in rows and columns, similar to the way a spreadsheet program presents information. The Task Sheet view and the Resource Sheet view are both sheet views: Each row on the sheet contains all the information about an individual task or resource in your project. Each column represents a field that identifies the information you're storing about the task or resource.

- **Forms:** These views present information in a way that resembles a paper form. You saw the Task Form view in Chapter 5. A form displays information about a single item (or task) in your project.

Tip
Shortcut menus are available in many views. Right-click the view to see a shortcut menu. ■

You can modify the default views by switching what appears on-screen. You can also create custom views. The next two sections describe these common ways of manipulating views:

- Switching the table of any view that includes a table

- Adding or changing the details that appear in any view that contains a Details section

Cross-Reference
You can also create a combination view, in which you see one format in one pane of the window and another format in another pane. Read more about creating custom views and combination views in Chapter 7. ■

Changing a table

If a view contains a table, you can use the Select All button to switch quickly to another table. The Select All button appears in the upper-left corner of the table portion of the view. Right-click the Select All button to open the menu that appears in Figure 6.1.

If you prefer, you can click the View tab and, in the Data group, click the Tables button to see the list of available tables.

Note
Project displays different choices on the menu; the choices you see depend on the view that's displayed when you open the menu. ■

Choose More Tables to open the More Tables dialog box, which displays all the tables available in Project (see Figure 6.2). By default, Project shows the tables available in task views; click the Resource option button at the top of the box to see the tables available in resource views.

FIGURE 6.1

Switch tables by choosing from the menu that appears when you right-click the Select All button.

Select All button

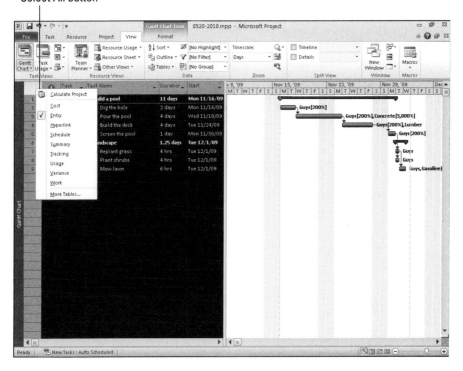

FIGURE 6.2

The More Tables dialog box shows the tables to which you can switch in task views; click the Resource option to view the corresponding tables in resource views.

Changing a Details section

You also can add fields to the Details section of the Task Usage and Resource Usage views. In either view, right-click an existing field to view a list of commonly used fields and click one to add it to the view (see Figure 6.3). To view other available fields, choose Detail Styles from the list; Project then displays a dialog box showing the many fields that you can add to the Details section of a usage view; see Chapter 7 for details.

Note

Project adds rows to the Details section when you select fields from this menu. To remove a row, repeat the process; that is, right-click an existing field and select the item that you want to remove. ∎

FIGURE 6.3

Change the information that appears in the Details section of the view by selecting from this list.

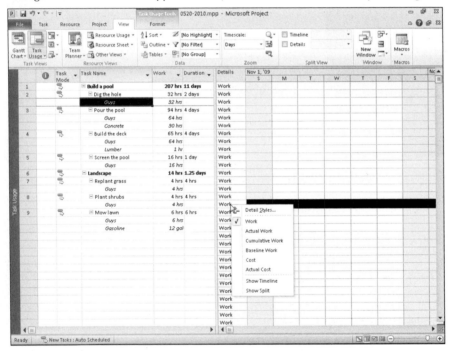

Examining Indicators

Indicators are icons that appear in the Indicator column on table views; the Indicator column appears to the right of the ID column. Indicators represent additional information about the row in which they appear. For example, a Notes indicator appears in the indicator field on the resource sheet if you assign a note to a particular resource.

Cross-Reference

For more information about assigning notes to resources, refer to Chapter 5. ■

Different icons represent different types of indicators:

- **Constraint indicators:** These indicators identify the type of constraint that is assigned to a task. For example, a task can have a flexible constraint, such as Finish No Later Than, if the task is scheduled from the finish date. Or, a task can have an inflexible constraint, such as Must Start On, for tasks that are scheduled from the start date. Constraint indicators also show that the task hasn't been completed within the time frame of the constraint.

- **Task type indicators:** These indicators may identify special conditions about a task, such as whether the task is a manually scheduled task, an automatically scheduled task, a recurring task or whether the task has been completed.

- **Deliverable indicator:** This indicator identifies tasks that have a deliverable associated with them.

- **Dependency indicators:** This indicator appears beside tasks that are dependent on tasks in other projects.

Cross-Reference

You can find out more about tasks with cross-project dependencies in Chapter 20. ■

- **Contour indicators:** These indicators identify the type of contouring used to distribute the work assigned to the task.

Cross-Reference

Read more about contouring in Chapter 11. ■

- **Miscellaneous indicators:** These indicators identify items, such as a note or a hyperlink, that you created; a calendar that's been assigned to a task; or a resource that needs leveling.

Tip

To identify the purpose of an indicator, hover the mouse pointer over it. Project tells you what the indicator means or displays additional information to remind you of important details. ■

Admiring the Views

Here is a list of the default views available in Project:

- Bar Rollup
- Calendar
- Descriptive Network Diagram
- Detail Gantt
- Gantt Chart
- Gantt with Timeline
- Leveling Gantt
- Milestone Date Rollup
- Milestone Rollup
- Multiple Baselines Gantt
- Network Diagram
- Relationship Diagram
- Resource Allocation
- Resource Form

- Resource Graph
- Resource Name Form
- Resource Sheet
- Resource Usage
- Task Details Form
- Task Entry
- Task Form
- Task Name Form
- Task Sheet
- Task Usage
- Team Planner (Project Professional only)
- Timeline
- Tracking Gantt

Deciding which of Project's 27 built-in views (or any of your custom views) suits a particular purpose can be tricky. As you become more familiar with the features of Project and the way that you apply project management concepts and terms to Project, you'll get more comfortable selecting views by name. You can find the most commonly used views in several locations:

- Click the bottom of the Gantt Chart button on the Task tab.
- Click the bottom of the Team Planner button (Resource View button for Project Standard users) on the Resource tab.
- Click the arrow beside the buttons that appear in the Task Views and Resource Views groups on the View tab, and then right-click the view name that appears in a gray bar running down the left side of the Project window. (I like this method best, because it involves the fewest mouse clicks.)

You can find all available views listed in the More Views dialog box (see Figure 6.4). You can open the More Views dialog box if you take any of the actions listed in the preceding bullet points and then click More Views from the list that appears.

Note

Project 2010 contains no PERT views. At the Project Bible Web site, you'll find information about PERT Chart Expert, a product that uses Project data and creates PERT charts. Visit http://www.wiley.com/ and search for Project 2010 Bible. ■

The following sections describe how these views enable you to look at different aspects of your project. Notice the wealth of detail about your project that is available to you.

FIGURE 6.4

The More Views dialog box lists all views available in Project.

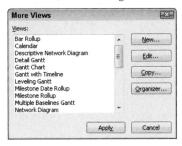

Calendar

Calendar view in Project 2010, (shown in Figure 6.5) closely resembles the Calendar view in Outlook 2010. You can easily display a weekly or monthly calendar by clicking the buttons at the top of the calendar. You also can set custom dates to view.

FIGURE 6.5

The Calendar view features a familiar, easy-to-read format.

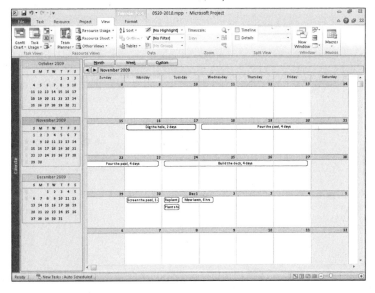

The familiar format of the Calendar view makes it easy to use; a black box surrounds the currently selected day. Using a monthly calendar format, the Calendar view indicates the length of a task with a bar running across portions of days, or even weeks. In the Calendar view, nonworking days appear shaded. Although a taskbar may extend over nonworking days, such as Saturday and Sunday in this example, the work of the task doesn't progress over those days. Don't forget that every project has a calendar (not to be confused with the Calendar view) that tells Project how to handle events, such as 24-hour shifts, weekends, and holidays off, over the life of your project.

The Calendar view is useful for entering a simple project and for reviewing what needs to be done on a given day. You can move from month to month by using the arrow buttons beside the month name, underneath the Month, Week, and Custom button above the calendar.

Cross-Reference

See Chapter 8 for information on some of the kinds of formatting you can use on the Calendar. ∎

Detail Gantt

The Detail Gantt view shows a list of tasks and related information, as well as a chart that displays *slippage* as a thin bar between tasks (as shown in Figure 6.6). Choose this view from the More Views dialog box (right-click the gray bar running down the left side of the Project window and choose More Views).

FIGURE 6.6

The Detail Gantt view.

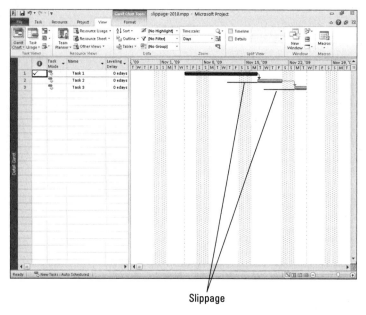

Slippage

The thin bar that appears at the left edge of the second and third tasks represents slippage. The number of days appears in both cases. Slippage results whenever progress at a given date is less than expected at that date. For example, slippage happens if you save a baseline on a project initially and then record actual dates or durations for tasks, and the resulting actual finish dates or durations for the task are later than the baseline finish dates or durations. In the figure, the actual start date of the second task was later than the baseline start date; because the third task depends on the second task, both the second and the third tasks are affected. Slippage can also occur if, for example, the date for a scheduled task has passed and you have not recorded any progress to the task. In this case, you don't even need a baseline to know that your project is behind schedule. Instead, the current date or the status date can give you that information.

This view is most useful for evaluating slippage. The default table in the Detail Gantt view is the Delay table. Use the techniques described in the section "Changing a table," earlier in this chapter, to change the table.

Gantt Chart

Chapter 2 covers the Gantt Chart view, shown in Figure 6.7, in detail. This view makes it easy for you to create a project, link tasks to create sequential dependencies, see how your project is progressing over time, and view tasks graphically while still having access to details.

FIGURE 6.7

The Gantt Chart view.

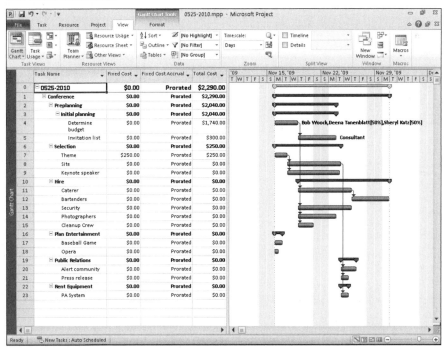

New Feature

In Project 2010, you can format the Gantt Chart to display slippage or a baseline. See Chapter 14 for details. ∎

Gantt with Timeline

The Gantt with Timeline view lets you simultaneously display a high-level and a detailed picture of your project. The timeline, which appears just below the Ribbon, is completely customizable; that is, you determine which tasks appear on the timeline. In Figure 6.8, I added major phase summary tasks to the timeline.

Cross-Reference

You can read about adding tasks to the timeline in Chapter 3. ∎

FIGURE 6.8

The Gantt with Timeline view simultaneously presents a high-level view and a detailed view of a project.

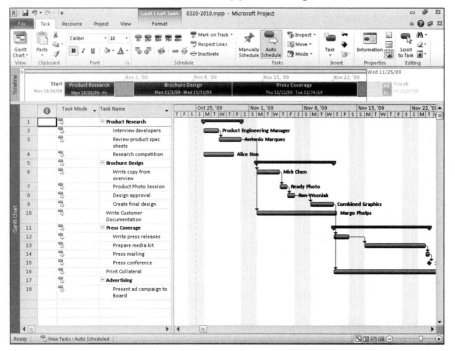

Leveling Gantt

The Leveling Gantt view, shown in Figure 6.9, focuses on task delays. This view provides a graphic representation of delayed tasks while still providing task detail information. The chart portion of the view shows the effects before and after leveling. The default table that appears in the Leveling Gantt view is the Delay table, but you can change the table by using the techniques described in an earlier section of this chapter ("Changing a table"). You can use the Delay table to add or remove delay time and see the effects of your changes.

Note

Leveling (also called resource leveling) is the process of resolving resource conflicts or overallocations by delaying or splitting certain tasks. You can read more about resource leveling in Chapter 11. ■

The top bar represents the task prior to leveling; the bottom bar represents the task after leveling. The bar to the left of the *Keynote speaker* task represents delay, and the bar to the right of the *Invitation list* task and the *Site* task represents slack.

FIGURE 6.9

The Leveling Gantt view.

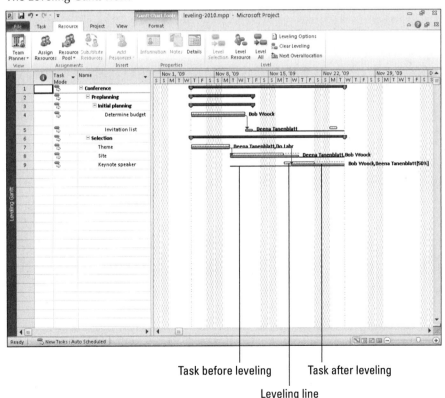

Task before leveling   Task after leveling

Leveling line

Tracking Gantt

The Tracking Gantt view is also based on the Gantt Chart view. The Tracking Gantt view provides a great visual way to evaluate the progress of individual tasks — and of the project as a whole. By using the Tracking Gantt view, you can see how your project has shifted from your original estimates — and then decide how to adjust your plans to accommodate delays. Theoretically, if a project ever goes faster than you've anticipated, you can also see how much extra time you've bought yourself as a result of your efficiency. (Realistically, however, projects so seldom go faster than projected that I won't show that option here!)

Figure 6.10 shows a standard Gantt view of a project that has had some activity. The standard Gantt view shows the progress on tasks as a black bar within the Gantt task bar. A check mark appears in the Indicators column beside each completed task.

FIGURE 6.10

The standard Gantt view shows you the reality of your project timing at the moment, based on actual work done.

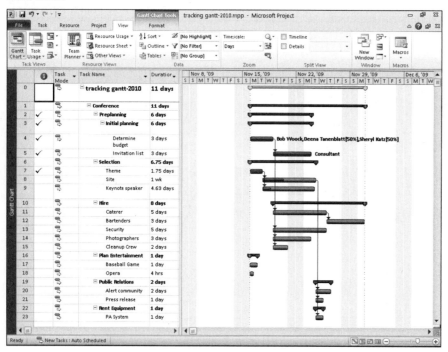

Figure 6.11, on the other hand, shows the same schedule using the Tracking Gantt view with the Tracking table (the default table is the Entry table). The Tracking table enables you to update your project by supplying actual information. On the chart portion of the view, you see two bars for every task. The bottom bar reflects baseline settings. The top bar reflects current scheduled start and finish dates if a task has not yet been started. If a task *has* started — that is, if you have supplied some amount of work that has been completed — the top bar represents actual information. Project fills in the top bar and makes it solid to represent completed work. Tasks in progress display a small vertical line dividing the top bar; the placement of the vertical line helps represent the progress of the task (look closely at Tasks 8 and 9; the line is difficult to see, but it's there).

In the Tracking Gantt view, you can see that the Determine budget, Invitation list, and Theme tasks have been completed; the *Site* task is 50 percent complete; and the *Keynote speaker* task is 25 percent complete. No other tasks have been started, so the top bars on all other tasks represent scheduled start and finish dates, based on progress made so far in the project.

FIGURE 6.11

The Tracking Gantt view shows the discrepancy between your estimates and the real-world activity in your project.

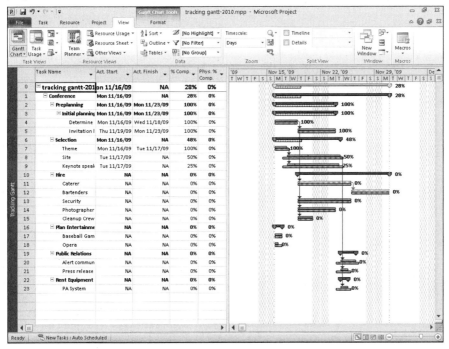

Multiple Baselines Gantt

The Multiple Baselines Gantt view is also based on the Gantt Chart view. The Multiple Baselines Gantt view enables you to see the first three baselines you save for your project; each baseline is represented by a different color. In Figure 6.12, you see two baselines; two lines represent each task in the chart portion of the view.

The default table for the Multiple Baselines Gantt view is the Entry table, but you can change the table to any table you want, using the techniques described in the section "Changing a table," earlier in this chapter.

Cross-Reference

You can read more about baselines in Chapter 12. ■

FIGURE 6.12

The Multiple Baselines Gantt view helps you compare the first three baselines you save.

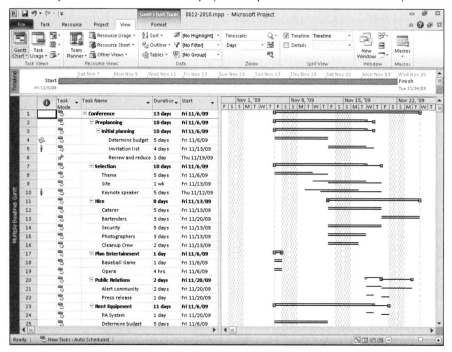

Network Diagram

Project's Network Diagram view will remind you of a PERT Chart.

Tip

Project no longer produces any PERT charts, but you can use an add-on product — PERT Chart Expert. Try a sample using the demo that's available at `http://www.criticaltools.com/download.htm`. ∎

The Network Diagram view, shown in Figure 6.13, has less to do with timing than with the general flow of work and the relationships between tasks in your project. This view makes it easy for you to evaluate the flow of your project and to check task dependencies.

Each node in the Network Diagram view represents a task in your project. A node contains the task name, duration, task ID number in the sequence of the project outline, start date, finish date, and, if assigned, the resource(s); in Figure 6.14, I used the Zoom Slider at the right edge of the Status Bar to enlarge each node so that you can see its details. The color and shading of each node represent different types of tasks; for example, critical tasks are red, noncritical tasks are blue, and manually scheduled tasks are filled with a hatch pattern. You can determine (and change) the meaning of node shapes in the Box Styles dialog box, which you'll see in a moment. The lines that flow between the nodes represent dependencies. A task that must come after another task is completed, called a *successor task*, appears to the right or sometimes below its predecessor.

FIGURE 6.13

The Network Diagram view.

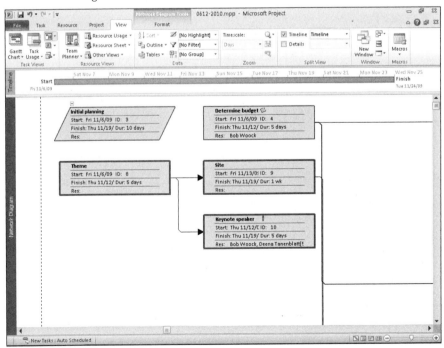

FIGURE 6.14

You can see task details when you examine the nodes of the Network Diagram.

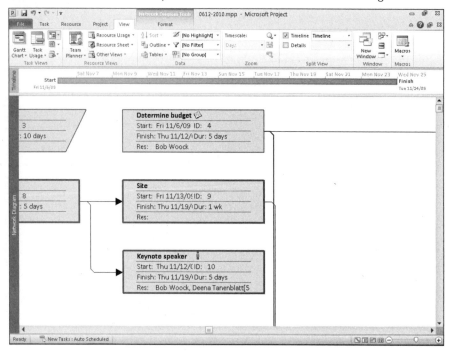

You can filter the Network Diagram to display only a certain kind of information; for example, you can hide all non-critical tasks and display only critical tasks.

You also can group tasks in the Network Diagram view; this is similar to the way that you can group tasks in the Gantt view. Colored bands separate the nodes. For example, in Figure 6.15, you see tasks grouped by duration; the group names appear along the left side of the view in the yellow bars that separate the groups. You also can create your own groups.

Tip
Manually scheduled tasks to which you've assigned no duration appear in a separate group: the Duration: No Value group. ∎

Cross-Reference
You can read more about filtering and grouping in Chapter 7. ∎

FIGURE 6.15

You can group tasks in a variety of ways in the Network Diagram view.

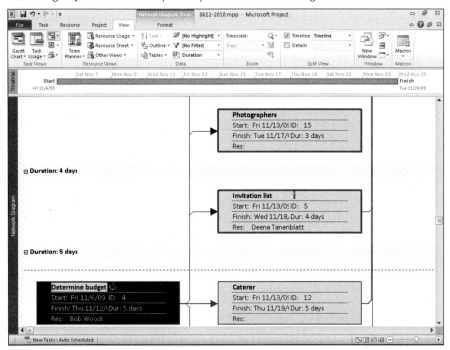

You can also display indicators and custom fields in Network Diagram nodes. You add the node information to an existing node template, or you create a new template. Follow these steps to display indicators or custom fields in nodes:

1. In the Network Diagram view, click the Network Diagram Tools Format tab and, in the Format group, click Box Styles. The Box Styles dialog box appears.

2. Click the More Templates button to display the Data Templates dialog box (see Figure 6.16).

3. In the Data Templates dialog box, you can edit an existing template, make a copy of an existing template and edit the copy, or create a new template. To edit or create a copy of an existing template, select it in the Templates in Network Diagram list — and then click either Copy or Edit. To create a new template, click New. For this example, I copied the Standard template. In all cases, Project displays the Data Template Definition dialog box, shown in Figure 6.17.

Note

You can't edit the Standard template, but you can copy it and edit the copy. ■

4. Click in the cell where you want either indicators or a custom field to appear, making sure that you click in an empty cell. Project adds a list box indicator to the cell, thus enabling you to open the list and select the information that you want to appear in that cell of the node. In Figure 6.17, I'm adding the Indicators field beside the Name field.

5. Click OK to redisplay the Data Templates dialog box.

6. Click Close to redisplay the Box Styles dialog box (see Figure 6.18).

7. In the Style Settings For list, select the types of tasks to which you want to apply the template.

Tip

You can use Windows selection techniques to select several tasks simultaneously. Click the first task that you want to select. Then, to select contiguous tasks, press Shift and click the last task. To select noncontiguous tasks, press and hold Ctrl while you click each task. ■

FIGURE 6.16

Add information to a cell of the Network Diagram node.

FIGURE 6.17

Use this dialog box to add indicators or a custom field to a Network Diagram node.

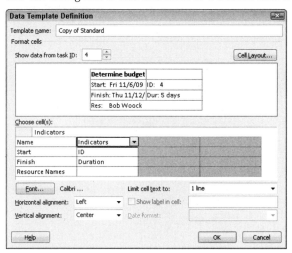

FIGURE 6.18

In this dialog box, select the template you want to apply to selected types of tasks.

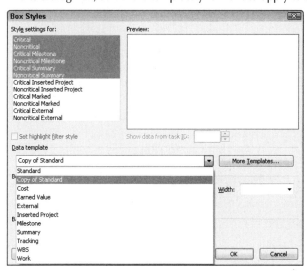

8. From the Data Template list, select the template that you edited or created.

9. Click OK.

You see the new field on appropriate nodes. In Figure 6.19, a Note indicator appears in the *Determine budget* task and a Resource Overallocation icon appears in the *Keynote speaker* task. As in the Gantt Chart view, you can hover the mouse pointer over an indicator to see information about it.

FIGURE 6.19

A Network Diagram that displays indicators in the nodes.

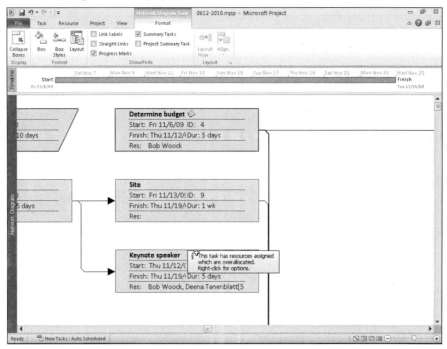

Descriptive Network Diagram

The Descriptive Network Diagram, shown in Figure 6.20, is a cousin of the Network Diagram — and so it focuses on the general flow of work and the relationships among tasks in your project.

As with the Network Diagram, each node in the Descriptive Network Diagram view represents a task in your project. If you compare Figures 6.13 and 6.20, you see more detail in the nodes of the Descriptive Network Diagram than you see in the Network Diagram. The Descriptive Network Diagram also indicates whether the task is critical and how complete the task is.

FIGURE 6.20

The Descriptive Network Diagram view.

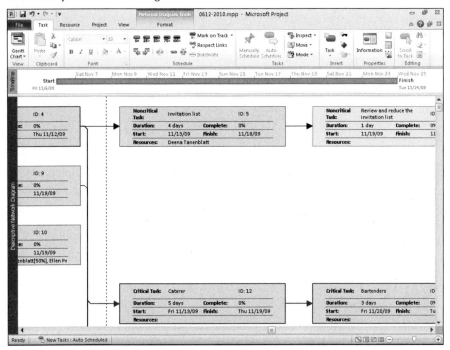

Relationship Diagram

This special version of the Network Diagram view, the Relationship Diagram (see Figure 6.21), displays the current task in the center of the pane, with the task's predecessors to the left and its successors to the right. When you're working on a large project, this graphic view helps you to focus on one task and the tasks that are linked to it.

Resource Allocation

The Resource Allocation view is a combination view. In Figure 6.22, the Resource Usage view appears in the top pane and the Leveling Gantt Chart view appears in the bottom pane. Note that the names of each view appear in the bar that runs down the left side of the screen.

FIGURE 6.21

The Relationship Network Diagram view helps you focus on a single task and the tasks linked to it.

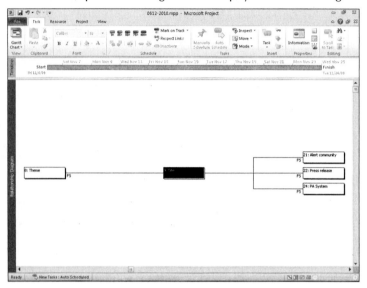

FIGURE 6.22

The Resource Allocation view displays resource allocation relative to the project timing.

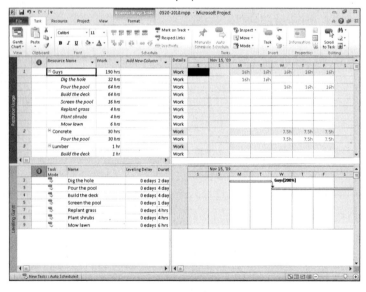

Cross-Reference

See the section "Leveling Gantt," earlier in this chapter, for a discussion of the Leveling Gantt Chart view. Refer to the section "Resource Usage," later in this chapter, for information about the Resource Usage view. ■

The default table that appears on the Resource Usage view (the upper pane of the combination view) is the Usage table. The default table that appears on the Gantt Chart view (the lower pane of the combination view) is the Delay table. As you select tasks in the top pane, the bottom pane changes to display information about the selected task. You can use the techniques described in the section "Changing a table," earlier in this chapter, to change either table.

Resource Form

The Resource Form view displays detailed information about one resource at a time, as shown in Figure 6.23.

Use the Next and Previous buttons in the upper-right corner of the view to display different resources. If you haven't sorted or filtered resources, Project shows them to you in ID-number order.

FIGURE 6.23

The Resource Form view.

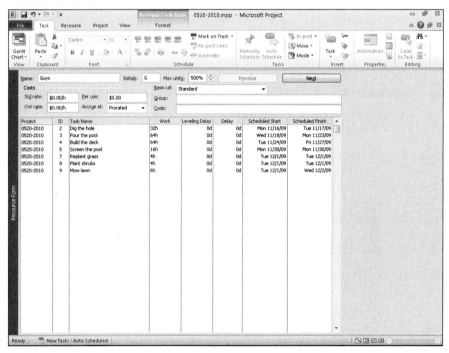

Resource Graph

The Resource Graph view shows how a particular resource is being used on a project. You can use the Resource Graph view to spot and correct resources that are inappropriately allocated. Note that the Resource Graph view shows information for one resource at a time. To view a different resource, click the scroll arrows that appear below the left pane in this window. This view works well as part of a combination view.

The Resource Graph view highlights resource conflicts: people, equipment, or other resources that are being overworked or underutilized. Looking at the Resource Graph view as both a single and combination view can show you how assignments on individual tasks are affecting a resource's utilization on a project. Figure 6.24 shows the main Resource Graph view. Figure 6.25 shows a combination view, with the Resource Form providing details of the tasks being performed shown at the bottom of the Project window. You can create this view by clicking the View tab and, in the Split View group, placing a check in the Details box; then, use the list box beside Details to select the view Project should display in the bottom portion of the window.

FIGURE 6.24

The percentage of a resource's available work time is tracked and displayed as overallocated or underallocated.

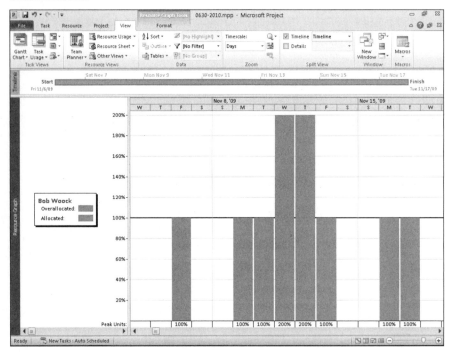

FIGURE 6.25

Displaying task information beneath a Resource Graph shows you the work assignments that are keeping the resource busy.

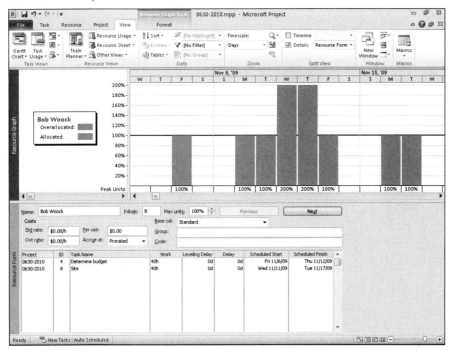

Project displays a resource's total work hours on any particular day as a bar. A bar that falls short of the 100 percent mark indicates that a resource isn't working full-time and may be underutilized. A bar that extends beyond 100 percent indicates that someone is working too many hours in a day. The percentage of the workday that the resource is working appears at the bottom of the usage bars.

Note

Underutilization may indicate that a resource is busy with other projects the rest of that day, and overutilization may signal occasional and acceptable overtime. See Chapter 8 for more information about interpreting these bars. See Chapter 10 for more details about resolving conflicts in resource time. ■

Resource Name Form

The Resource Name Form view is a simplified version of the Resource Form view (compare Figure 6.26 with Figure 6.29). None of the cost information appears in this view, nor do you see the resources' maximum units, base calendar, group, or code.

The Resource Name Form view.

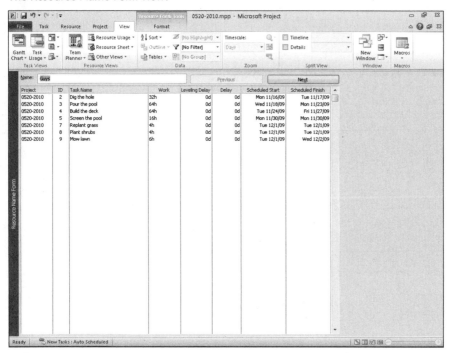

You can use this view to set up basic information about resources for a project — this can give you a good idea about a resource's workload. Use the Previous and Next buttons to view different resources.

Resource Sheet

The Resource Sheet view, shown in Figure 6.27, gives you a wealth of information about the resources assigned to your project, including standard and overtime rates, availability for overtime work, and fixed costs.

Tip

By assigning group designations to resources, such as Marketing, Facilities, or Temporary Help, you can use filters to study resource information for just one or two groups at a time. ■

This columnar interface is a great way to prepare to assign resources if, for example, you want to assign lower-cost people to most tasks and higher-cost people to certain mission-critical tasks. This view clearly shows to which group a resource belongs. If overallocations exist, you see a warning flag in the Indicator column in the far left of this view. Switch back to the Resource Graph to get resource-by-resource details on these problems.

FIGURE 6.27

You can view both standard and overtime rates in the Resource Sheet view.

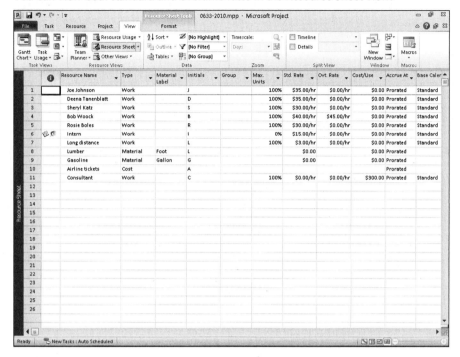

			Resource Name	Type	Material Label	Initials	Group	Max. Units	Std. Rate	Ovt. Rate	Cost/Use	Accrue At	Base Caler
1			Joe Johnson	Work		J		100%	$35.00/hr	$0.00/hr	$0.00	Prorated	Standard
2			Deena Tanenblatt	Work		D		100%	$35.00/hr	$0.00/hr	$0.00	Prorated	Standard
3			Sheryl Katz	Work		S		100%	$30.00/hr	$0.00/hr	$0.00	Prorated	Standard
4			Bob Woock	Work		B		100%	$40.00/hr	$45.00/hr	$0.00	Prorated	Standard
5			Rosie Boles	Work		R		100%	$30.00/hr	$0.00/hr	$0.00	Prorated	Standard
6			Intern	Work		I		0%	$15.00/hr	$0.00/hr	$0.00	Prorated	Standard
7			Long distance	Work		L		100%	$3.00/hr	$0.00/hr	$0.00	Prorated	Standard
8			Lumber	Material	Foot	L			$0.00		$0.00	Prorated	
9			Gasoline	Material	Gallon	G			$0.00		$0.00	Prorated	
10			Airline tickets	Cost		A						Prorated	
11			Consultant	Work		C		100%	$0.00/hr	$0.00/hr	$300.00	Prorated	Standard

Tip

The default table that appears on the Resource Sheet view is the Entry table, but you can change this table by using the techniques described in the section "Changing a table," earlier in this chapter. ■

Resource Usage

The Resource Usage view, shown in Figure 6.28, displays each resource and the tasks that are assigned to it. You can use the Resource Usage view to enter and edit resource information, and you can assign or reassign tasks to resources in this view by dragging the tasks among resources.

The Resource Usage view is also useful when you want to do the following:

- Check resource overallocations
- Examine the number of hours or the percentage of capacity at which each resource is scheduled to work
- View a resource's progress or costs
- Determine how much time a particular resource has for additional work assignments

FIGURE 6.28

The Resource Usage view organizes task assignments by resource so you can easily figure out who's doing what and when it's being done.

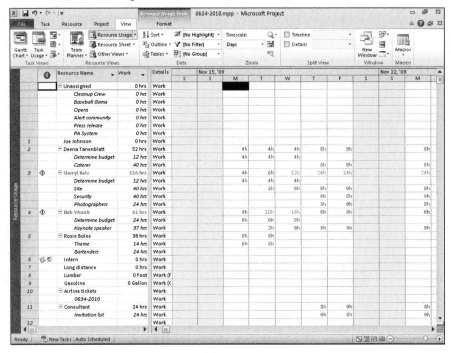

The default table on the left side of this view is the Usage table. You can use the Table Selection button, described in the section "Changing a table," earlier in this chapter, to switch to a different table. Similarly, you can right-click in the Details section and choose an item to add or remove to the Details section (Work is the default selection).

Rollup views

You can display symbols on a summary task bar that represent subtask dates, effectively "rolling up" the subtasks onto a summary task bar when you collapse the outline of the Gantt view. Rollup behavior is most useful when task start dates aren't close together, because it enables you to see your project's phases as long horizontal lines. When task dates are close together, task names over-write each other, making it difficult or impossible to read them.

Note
Rollup behavior operates at the project level. Project 2010 no longer supports rollup using individual selected tasks, nor does it provide the Rollup_Formatting macro available in earlier versions of the product. ∎

Enabling rollup behavior

While viewing the Gantt Chart view of your project, click the Gantt Chart Tools Format tab and, in the Format group, click the Layout button. Project displays the Layout dialog box (see Figure 6.29).

Select the Always Roll Up Gantt Bars check box — unless you don't want to see the rollup bars when you expand the project outline to view all tasks. In that case, also select the Hide Rollup Bars When Summary Expanded check box.

Using the summary task bar

When you enable rollup behavior and collapse the outline, Project displays a summary task bar that contains symbols that represent subtasks. Compare Figures 6.30, 6.31, and 6.32, which show various effects of collapsing the outline and rollup behavior. In particular, compare Figures 6-31 and 6-32.

Tip
To expand and collapse the outline, use the Show Outline button in the Data group on the View tab. ∎

FIGURE 6.29

Use this dialog box to enable rollup behavior for all tasks in your project.

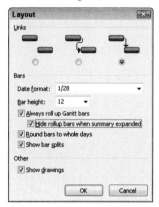

FIGURE 6.30

In this figure, the outline is completely expanded.

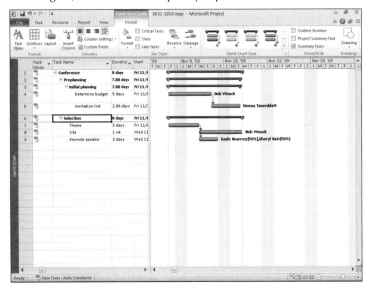

FIGURE 6.31

In this figure, I collapsed the outline for the Selection task, but I didn't enable rollup behavior.

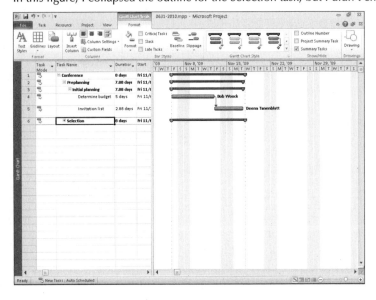

FIGURE 6.32

In this figure, I collapsed the outline for the Selection task and enabled rollup behavior.

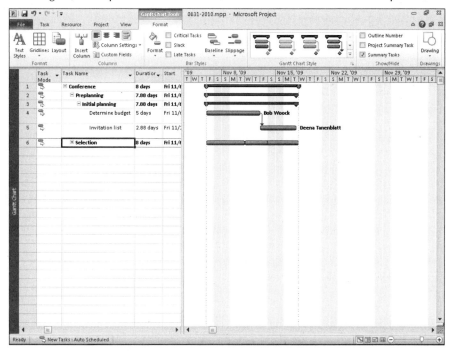

You also can use one of three different "rollup" views, in addition to the Gantt Chart view, to display different symbols on the summary rollup bar. In Figure 6.33, you see the Bar Rollup view; the detail tasks below a collapsed summary task are rolled up onto that summary task; Project represents the summary task as a bar. Each task's name appears along the bar.

Caution

If your start dates are close together, Project overwrites the task names, thus making them difficult or impossible to read. ∎

In Figure 6.34, I switched to the Milestone Rollup view. In this view, no bar — summary or task — appears; instead, each task's name appears as a milestone along an imaginary horizontal bar. The task's start date determines its relative position on this imaginary bar.

Finally, you can use the Milestone Date Rollup view, shown in Figure 6.35. This view is essentially the same as the Milestone Rollup view, except Project displays each task's name and its start date along the imaginary horizontal bar.

FIGURE 6.33

The Bar Rollup view.

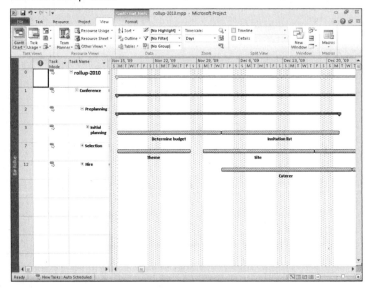

FIGURE 6.34

The Milestone Rollup view.

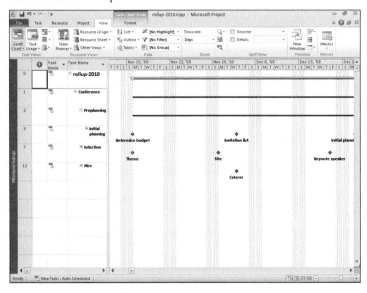

FIGURE 6.35

The Milestone Date Rollup view.

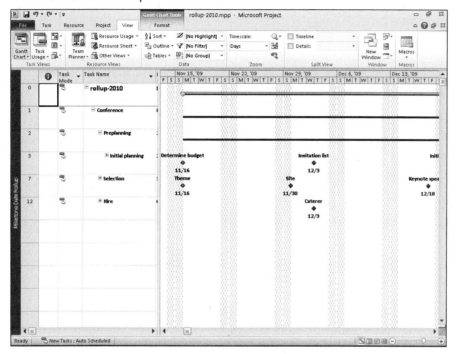

Tip

To redisplay all detail tasks, click the View tab and, in the Data group, click the Show Outline button; from the list that appears, click All Subtasks. ∎

Task Details Form

The Task Details Form view closely resembles the Task Form view and the Task Name Form view. The Task Details Form view, shown in Figure 6.36, enables you to view and edit tracking information about one task at a time.

Use the Previous and Next buttons in the upper-right corner of this view to switch from task to task. If you haven't sorted or filtered tasks, Project displays them in order of ID number. The Task Details Form view is a good choice for part of a combination view.

FIGURE 6.36

The Task Details Form view.

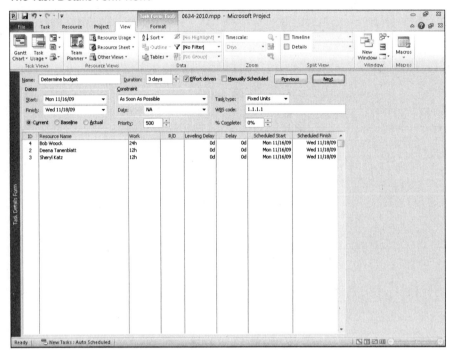

Task Entry

The Task Entry view is a combination view. In Figure 6.37, the Gantt Chart view appears in the top pane, and the Task Form view appears in the bottom pane. To see information about a task in the Task Form view, select the task in the Gantt Chart view. You can see this view easily if you select the Gantt view and then click the View tab and, in the Split View group, place a check in the Details box.

Only the Gantt Chart view in the top pane uses a table. The default table is the Entry table, but you can use the techniques that are described in the section "Changing a table," earlier in this chapter, to change the table.

Task Form

The Task Form view appears on the bottom portion of the Task Entry view, shown previously in Figure 6.37. The Task Form view closely resembles the Task Details Form view, shown previously in Figure 6.36.

FIGURE 6.37

The Task Entry view.

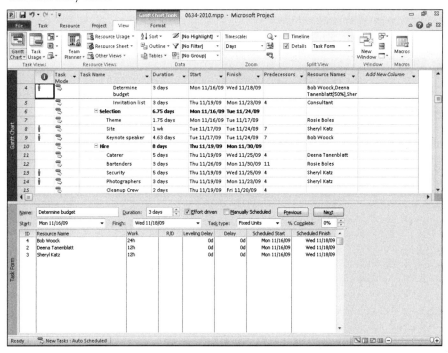

The Task Form view provides more resource information (such as costs) than the Task Details Form view; the Task Details Form view provides more task information (such as predecessors) than the Task Form view. Use the Previous and Next buttons to switch between tasks. The Task Form view also closely resembles the Task Name Form view.

Task Name Form

The Task Name Form view is a cousin to the Task Details Form view and the Task Form view. This simplified version displays the basic characteristics of tasks, one task at a time (see Figure 6.38).

Use the Previous and Next buttons to switch between tasks. Again, if you compare Figures 6-36, the bottom portion of 6-37, and 6-38, you can see how closely these views resemble each other. The Task Name Form view works well as part of a combination view.

FIGURE 6.38

The Task Name Form view.

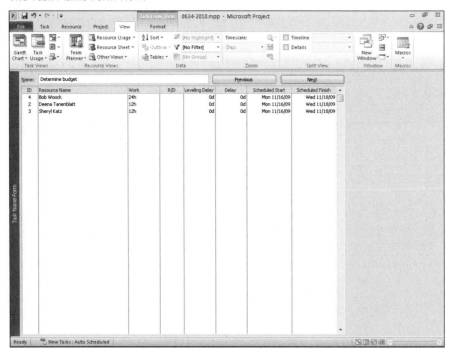

Task Sheet

The Task Sheet view is the counterpart of the Resource Sheet view in that the Task Sheet view displays task information in a spreadsheet-like format. In this view, you can create tasks, link tasks (establishing dependencies), and even assign resources (see Figure 6.39).

This view closely resembles the left side of the Gantt Chart view and makes it easy to view tasks in chronological order. The default table that appears on the Task Sheet view is the Entry table, but you can use the techniques described in the section "Changing a table," earlier in this chapter, to change the table.

Task Usage

This powerful view, shown in Figure 6.40, enables you to focus on how resources affect the task by showing resource assignments for each task. Use this view to organize resources by task, evaluate work effort and cost by task, and compare scheduled and actual work and costs.

FIGURE 6.39

The Task Sheet view helps you to see tasks in chronological order.

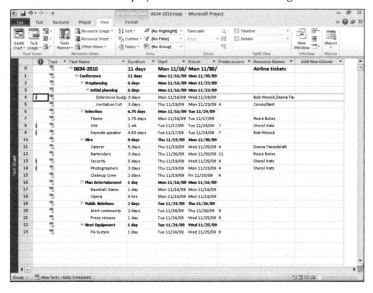

FIGURE 6.40

The Task Usage view shows resources grouped under the tasks to which they are assigned.

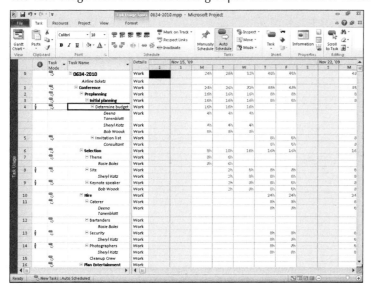

The default table for the left side of the Task Usage view is the Usage table, but you can display other tables by using the Table Selection button, as described in the section "Changing a table," earlier in this chapter. Also, by default, Project shows Work in the Details section on the right. Again, you can select any item from the menu that appears when you right-click in the Details section or from the Details Styles dialog box (click the Format tab and, in the Details section, click Add Details).

Note

How can you do 16 hours of work in one eight-hour day, as indicated for the Determine Budget task in the sample project shown in Figure 6.40? Remember that this view shows total resource hours for the task: As the figure shows, two people worked four hours and one other person worked eight hours. ■

Team Planner

The Team Planner view, shown in Figure 6.41, is available only in Project Professional and can be particularly helpful when you're working on resource allocations.

New Feature

The Team Planner is new to Project Professional 2010. ■

FIGURE 6.41

The Team Planner view.

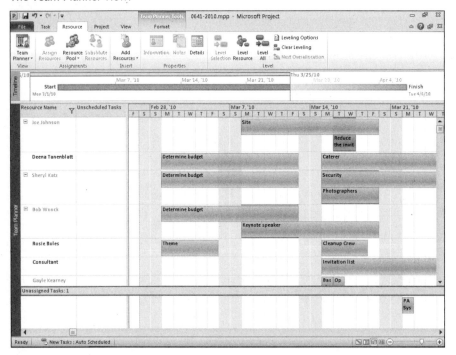

In this view, each resource appears on a row in the first column. The second column displays any unscheduled tasks — tasks to which you've assigned no start or finish dates. On the right side of the view, tasks with scheduled start and finish dates appear on the row associated with the resource(s) assigned to them; if a given task has more than one resource assigned, it appears on more than one row. At the bottom of the view, you find tasks to which no resources have been assigned.

I know we're in black and white here, but on-screen, you might see tasks in blue and turquoise; blue tasks are automatically scheduled tasks, while turquoise tasks are manually scheduled tasks. Overallocations are represented by red; overallocated resource names appear in red in the left column, and, on the right, time periods where overallocations exist display red backgrounds.

If you hover the mouse pointer over any task, you see basic information about that task; to change the details of either a task or a resource, double-click it and Project displays the Task Information dialog box or the Resource Information dialog box, as appropriate. You can insert tasks and resources into your project; in the Insert group of the Task tab and the Resource tab, use the Insert Task and Add Resources buttons.

You can change a task's dates by dragging the task horizontally. If you want to reassign a task, you can drag it vertically or you can right-click it and, from the menu that appears, point at Reassign To and choose a resource. When you drag a task, it "snaps" into its new location, and you won't see any gaps in the timescale.

You can record progress from the Team Planner view; click the task (Project surrounds it with an orange outline) and use the buttons in the Schedule group on the Task tab or right-click the task and those same buttons appear as part of the context menu (see Figure 6.42). When you record progress, Project changes the color of the completed portion of the task from light blue to dark blue.

Cross-Reference

You can read more about recording progress in Chapter 13. ■

You can use the Format tab of this view to modify Team Planner view in various ways, including these:

- Change the colors assigned to automatically scheduled tasks, manually scheduled tasks, late tasks, external tasks, and progress.

- Hide unassigned tasks.

- Hide unscheduled tasks.

- Roll up tasks so you can visualize related tasks as a single item and get a high-level overview of work. Project displays the summary task name and the task bar extends over the total time needed to complete the detail tasks under the summary task.

Cross-Reference

Read more about using Team Planner view in Part IV and Part V. ■

FIGURE 6.42

Recording progress on the Team Planner view.

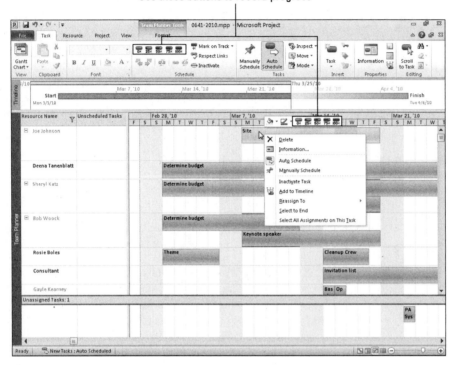

Timeline

The Timeline view can help you communicate, in a graphic way, the high-level project schedule.

New Feature

The Timeline view is new to Project 2010. ∎

You can display the timeline at any time above any view in Project, as shown in Figure 6.43. Click the View tab and, in the Split View group, place a check in the Timeline box.

If you prefer, you can display the timeline alone, as shown in Figure 6.44. Right-click the gray bar running down the left side of the Project window and, from the menu that appears, click Timeline.

FIGURE 6.43

The Timeline appears above the Gantt Chart view.

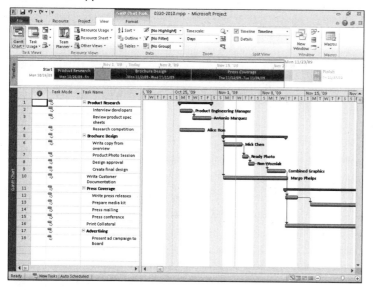

FIGURE 6.44

A full screen view of the Timeline.

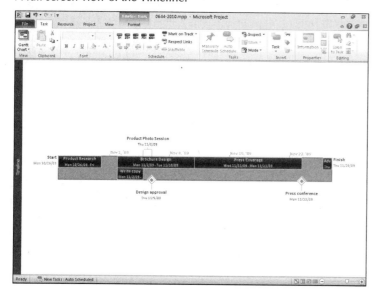

Only tasks that you add to the Timeline appear on it. Typically, you add summary tasks so you can present a high-level view of the project, but you can add detail tasks. If you do so, they appear below the associated summary task.

Chapter 3 describes several ways of adding tasks to the timeline when it appears above another view. When you select the Timeline as a full-screen view, the Format tab contains Timeline tools you can use to modify the appearance of the timeline. For example, you can change the format of the dates Project displays in each task box, or you can opt to hide dates altogether.

Using buttons on the Format tab, you can:

- Add existing tasks and milestones to the timeline.
- Create new tasks or milestones that Project adds automatically to the timeline.
- Add or display a callout task that appears above the timeline, like the *Product Photo Session* callout task shown in Figure 6.44.
- Change the color of each task that appears on the timeline.
- Copy the timeline and paste it into files open in other Office programs, such as Word documents, PowerPoint slides, or Outlook e-mail messages.

Cross-Reference

See Chapter 3 for details on adding tasks to the Timeline and copying the Timeline into other Office programs. See Chapter 8 for more information on formatting the appearance of the Timeline. ■

Summary

This chapter covered the standard views that are available in Project. You saw a sample of each view and found out how to print in Project.

Chapter 7 takes you beyond the basics in views. You find out how to customize and filter views and show other available information in views.

Using Views to Gain Perspective

In Chapter 6, you saw samples of the built-in views that come with Project. And although you may never need any view other than those, you're not limited to just those views. The potential variations for viewing information about your project are almost mind-boggling; you can use the built-in views, you can create variations of the built-in views, and you can create your own views. In this chapter, you explore ways to make views work for you.

Customizing Views

You can customize the views in Project so they show you the information that you need. You can fiddle with the tables in views that contain tables or tinker with the views themselves.

Changing tables

In views containing tables, you can make changes as simple as modifying the height of the rows or switching to a different table. Or you can modify the appearance of the default table by moving columns around — hiding or adding columns — and save your changes in a new table.

Changing row height and column width

By default, Project automatically adjusts the height of rows in your project to accommodate the text you type in the Task Name column. If a task name is longer than the current width of the Task Name column, Project widens the task's row and wraps the text. In Figure 7.1, the names of Tasks 5 and 7 are wrapped in the Task Name column.

FIGURE 7.1

By default, Project widens rows to accommodate long task names.

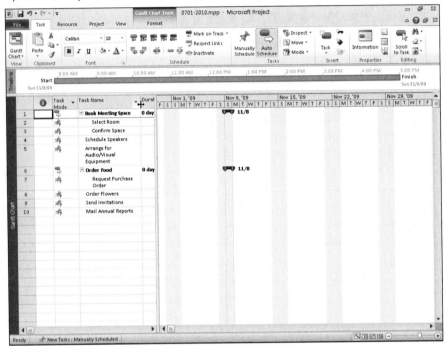

If you find that Project is widening more rows than you like, you can make the Task Name column wider. Just move the mouse pointer into the column heading area and over the bar on the right side of the task name column. When the mouse pointer changes to a pair of arrows pointing left and right (refer to Figure 7.1), drag the bar to the right. When you release the mouse button, Project widens the Task Name column.

Note

You can double-click the bar to make the column wide enough to accommodate the longest entry in the column, but your Task Name column might get so wide that you might have trouble working effectively with the rest of the information in the table. ■

Tip

If you see pound signs (#) in a column such as the Start Date column, the column isn't wide enough to display the information stored in the field and you should widen the column. ■

If you make the column wide enough, the text in the Task Name column re-wraps itself and you see what appears to be a blank row within a particular task name. After I widen the Task Name column, both Tasks 5 and 7 appear to have extra space below their names (see Figure 7.2).

FIGURE 7.2

If you widen the Task Name column enough, some rows can appear wider than they need to be.

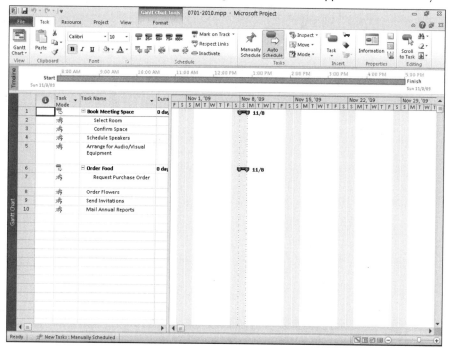

To eliminate the extra white space, you can make the rows narrower. You use the same technique to change the height of a row as you use to change the width of a column. Move the mouse pointer into the Task ID number column at the bottom of the row you want to change. The mouse pointer changes to a pair of arrows pointing up and down. Drag up to make the row narrower or down to make the row wider. When you release the mouse button, Project changes the height of the selected row and, if appropriate, changes the wrapping of the text in the row.

Tip

To change the height of more than one row, select each row that you want to change. Use Windows selection techniques to select the rows. For example, to select two noncontiguous rows, click the ID of the first row and then press and hold down Ctrl while you click the ID of the second row. ∎

Note

Project changes row heights only in full row increments. In other words, you can make a row twice its original size but not one and a half times its original size. ∎

You might have been wondering if you have any control over Project's default behavior that wraps text in the Task Name column; you do: Click anywhere in the column, click the Format tab and, in the Columns group, click the Column Settings button (see Figure 7.3). Click the Wrap Text command to eliminate automatic text wrapping. Project doesn't wrap text automatically in any column other than the Task Name column, but you can enable text wrapping for any column by using this technique.

New Feature

Your ability to control text wrapping in fields is new in Project 2010. ∎

FIGURE 7.3

To control whether Project wraps text in a column, right-click over the column heading and use the Wrap Text command.

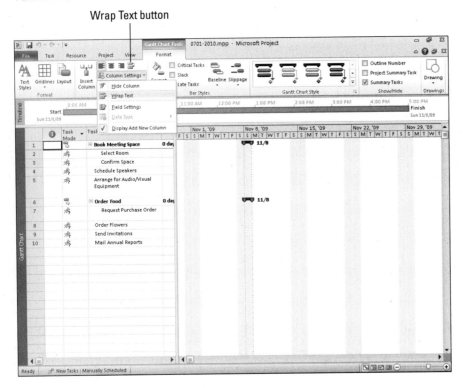

You also can control text wrapping for an individual task name: Click that task name and, on the Format tab in the Columns group, click the Wrap Text button (refer to Figure 7.3).

Hiding and inserting columns

You can remove a column from a table temporarily by hiding it — and the key word here is "temporarily," because Project doesn't remove the actual data residing in the column from the file; instead, Project simply hides that data from view.

Click anywhere in the column you want to hide. Then click the Format tab and, in the Columns group, click the Column Settings button. From the menu that appears, choose Hide Column (see Figure 7.4).

New Feature

The method of hiding and displaying columns described in this section is new to Project 2010. ∎

FIGURE 7.4

You can safely hide the information in any column.

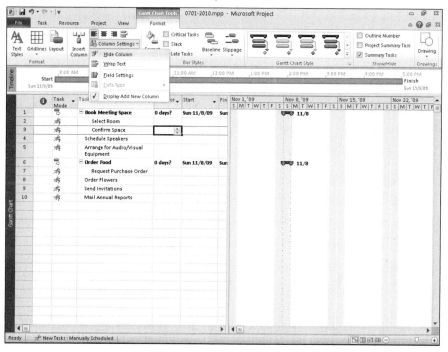

To redisplay the column's information, follow these steps:

1. Click anywhere in the column that you want to appear to the right of the column that you intend to insert; for this example, I clicked in the Start column, because I intend to redisplay the Duration column to the left of the Start column.

2. Click the Format tab.

3. In the Columns group, click the Insert Column button. Project inserts a column in your project and displays a list of column names you can insert (see Figure 7.5).

4. Type the first few letters of the name of the column you want to display or click its name in the list. Project displays the column and any data that it contains.

Tip
Typing the first few letters helps you find the field faster because you narrow the list. ∎

FIGURE 7.5

Inserting a column in between existing columns.

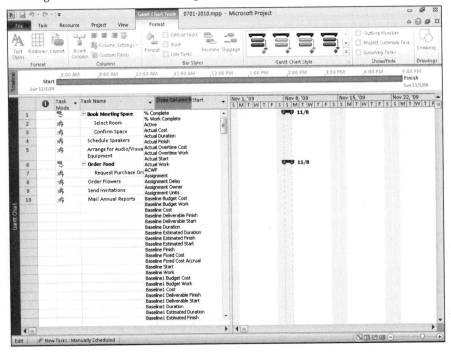

Note
Are you longing to see the Column Definition dialog box available in earlier versions of Project? Click anywhere in the column that concerns you. Then click the Format tab and, in Columns group, click the Column Settings button. From the list that appears, click Field Settings. ∎

You also can simply add a new column to the right edge of the table; at the right edge of the table, Project displays, by default, a spare column you can use to quickly add new information to the table. Just click the down arrow beside the column heading "Add New Column" (see Figure 7.6), and Project displays the list of available columns you can add to the table (refer to Figure 7.5). Select the column you want to add by typing the first few letters of the column you want to display or click its name in the list.

FIGURE 7.6

You can use the Add New Column feature to add a new column to the right edge of the table.

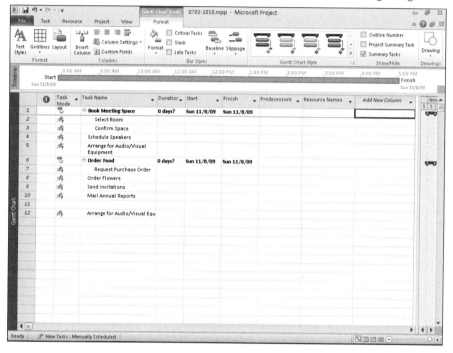

Tip

To see the right edge of the table, use the scroll bar below the table or, if you're working in the Gantt Chart view, drag the vertical bar that separates the table from the chart to the right. ∎

Adding fields to a usage view

By default, the Work field appears in the Details section of both usage views; you can easily add the Actual Work, Cumulative Work, Baseline Work, Cost, and Actual Cost fields by right-clicking anywhere in the Details section and then choosing the appropriate field from the shortcut menu that appears.

But, you can add many other fields to the Details section of a usage view using the Detail Styles dialog box shown in Figure 7.7. Suppose, for example, that you want to take advantage of the budget resource and enter values for a budget work resource or a budget cost resource:

1. Start in either usage view — the Task Usage view or the Resource Usage view — and click the Format tab.

2. In the Details group, click Add Details, and Project displays the Detail Styles dialog box.

FIGURE 7.7

The Detail Styles dialog box supplies additional choices that you can display in the Details section of a view.

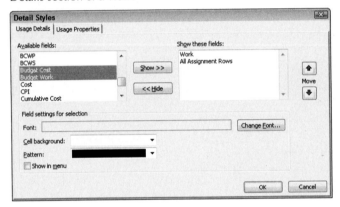

3. Click a field — such as the Budget Cost field — in the Available fields list (you can use Windows selection techniques to select more than one field simultaneously, as I've done in Figure 7.7).

4. Click the Show button, and the field then appears in the Show These Fields list.

5. When you click OK, Project displays a row for the field in the Details portion of the view.

Tip

To select two noncontiguous fields, click the first field and then press and hold Ctrl while you click the second field. To select contiguous fields, click the first field and then press and hold Shift while you click the last field. ■

You can hide fields in the Details portion of a usage view; right-click anywhere in the Details section, and from the context menu that appears, click the field you want to hide (see Figure 7.8). Project removes the field from the Details portion of the view.

FIGURE 7.8

You can hide fields in a Details section of a usage view by selecting the field from the shortcut menu that appears when you right-click in the Details section.

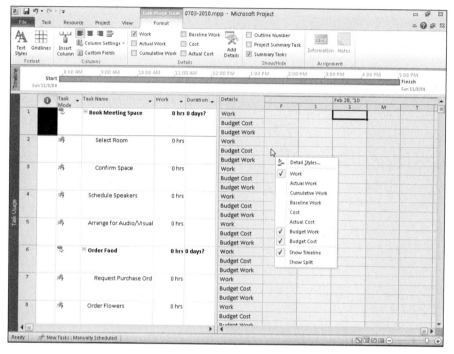

Note

The Work, Actual Work, Cumulative Work, Baseline Work, Cost, and Actual Cost fields remain available from the context menu even after you hide them. But if you add a field to the Details portion of a usage view using the Detail Styles dialog box and then subsequently hide that field, it will not appear on the context menu. To use it again, you must use the Detail Styles dialog box to display it again. ■

Switching tables

Tables don't appear in every view. For example, neither the Network Diagram view nor the Resource Graph view has a table that displays columns of information. However, views that do have tables, such as the Task Usage view or the Gantt view, also have a Select All button (see Figure 7.9). Right-click the Select All button to select all the information in the table and list the standard tables that you can display as well as the More Tables option.

Tip

Clicking (instead of right-clicking) the Select All button selects all information in the table portion of the view. ■

FIGURE 7.9

Switch to a different table by selecting it from this shortcut menu.

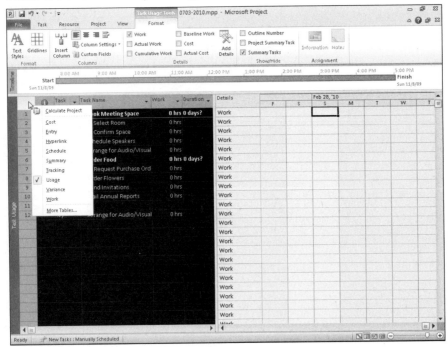

If you're a Ribbon person, you can switch tables in a view that contains a table if you click the View tab and, in the Data group, click the Tables button. Select a table from the list that appears or click the More Tables option.

Creating new tables or editing existing tables

As with views, discussed in Chapter 6, Project has dozens of built-in tables, offering a wide variety of information to help you focus on issues of scheduling, resources, tracking, and so on. The More Tables window enables you to switch to tables that don't appear on the shortcut list of tables. You also can use the More Tables window to modify the fields of information displayed in the columns of tables, and even to create new tables. Creating new tables in Project is remarkably similar to editing existing tables; you use the same dialog box for both operations.

Tip

How do you decide whether to create a new table or modify an existing one? If you can find a predefined table that has several of the fields you want to include, start with a copy of that table. Then delete, rearrange, modify, or add fields as needed. If you can't find an appropriate model, you may need to create a new table. I suggest using a copy of the table because someone else who is using your schedule will expect to find the default fields in Project's original tables instead of the fields that you establish. ■

Suppose that the view would be more meaningful if the columns appeared in a different order than the order in which Project shows them. For example, many tables list baseline information first and then list actual information, resulting in this sequence of columns: Baseline Start, Baseline Finish, Actual Start, Actual Finish. You might find this information easier to compare if you create a table that presents the information in the following order: Baseline Start, Actual Start, Baseline Finish, Actual Finish — and so on.

Or perhaps you want to add the table to the list of tables on the shortcut menu that appears when you right-click the Select All button. You might even want to add or delete some fields of information (columns) from the table. You can either edit an existing table or make a copy of it and edit the copy.

Caution

The More Tables window does not have a Table reset button; consequently, any changes you make are permanent. I advise you to always make a copy of a table that you want to modify, and edit the copy rather than the original table. That way the original tables remain intact. ■

Follow these steps to create a new table or edit an existing table:

1. Click the View tab and, in the Data group, click Tables; from the menu that appears, click More Tables. Project displays the More Tables window shown in Figure 7.10.

FIGURE 7.10

Select a table to use, edit, or copy from this dialog box.

2. Click the New button to create a new table, or select a table that you want to edit. You can use the Task or Resource option buttons at the top of the dialog box to display the type of table you want. Then click either the Edit button to edit the original table or the Copy button to edit a copy of the table. The Table Definition dialog box appears (see Figure 7.11).

Note

If you create a copy, you may want to rename it in the Name box instead of using the default "Copy of" name that Project supplies. ■

FIGURE 7.11

Use the Table Definition dialog box to make changes to the appearance of a table. When you create a new table, no information appears in the bottom portion of the dialog box.

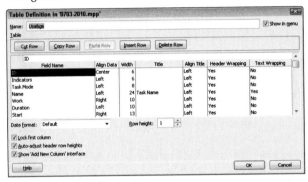

3. Enter a name for the table in the Name text box. To show this table in the shortcut menu that appears when you right-click the Select All button, you can select the Show in Menu check box.

4. To add a field to the table, click a blank space in the area under the Field Name column; an arrow appears on the right side of the field. Click the arrow to display the drop-down list of available fields and select a field name.

Tip

Use the Insert Row and Delete Row buttons to add rows in between existing rows or to remove existing rows. To insert a row, click the row below the row you want to add and click Insert Row. ■

5. In the same row, click in the Align Data column. Project displays the default settings for alignment of data and title as well as the width of the column. Click the arrow on the right side of the field; then select Left, Center, or Right alignment for the data in the column.

6. Click the Width column and, if necessary, modify the width of the column to accommodate the type of information you think will typically go there.

Tip

If you aren't sure about the ideal column width, just accept the default. You can easily adjust column widths when the table is on-screen by dragging the edge of the column heading to the right or left. ■

7. Click the Title field and enter a title for the column if you don't want to use the default field name. Otherwise skip this step.

8. Click the Align Title column and select a different alignment for the column title if you like.

9. The Header Wrapping field — a Yes or No choice — controls whether long titles wrap within the column heading. If you set the Header Wrapping field to No, Project hides that portion of a column title that doesn't fit within the allotted space for the column.

10. Click in the Text Wrapping field and select Yes to allow Project to wrap text in the field if the text exceeds the width assigned in the Width column in Step 6. Select No to disable text wrapping.

New Feature

Controlling text wrapping in fields is a new feature in Project 2010. ∎

11. Repeat Steps 4 through 10 to add more fields to your table. To reorganize your table, use the Cut Row, Copy Row, and Paste Row buttons.

12. For any columns that include dates, such as Start or Finish information, you can modify the date format by using the Date Format drop-down list. You can also modify the height of all the rows with the Row Height setting.

13. If you want the first column of your table to remain on-screen while you scroll across your page, select the Lock First Column check box. Typically the Task ID column is the one locked in place in a table.

14. Click OK when you finish. Then click Apply in the More Tables dialog box to display the new table on your screen.

New Feature

By default, changes you make to tables appear in all Project files — new ones or ones you created previously. This behavior is new in Project 2010; in prior versions, you had to use the Organizer function to make new or edited tables available to other projects. ∎

Working with views

As you discovered in Chapter 6, views display a variety of information: tables with several fields of data, task bars, network diagram nodes, and so on. Microsoft has provided a plethora of views, meeting just about every information need. Nevertheless, you may want to create a variation on one of those views to look at information from a different perspective. For example, you might want to change the timescale of a view to look at more or less of your project. Or you might want to create a second Network Diagram view in which you set the nodes to display a different set of information than the standard Network Diagram view. Then, instead of having to modify the nodes in the original Network Diagram view each time to see different information that you call on frequently, you can simply display the new view to use the alternative Network Diagram view. You can base an alternative view on any of the existing views and then change the information that Project displays by default to include only the information that you need.

Adjusting the timescale

Many views contain timescales, including the Gantt Chart view or any of its cousins (such as the Tracking Gantt), in the Team Planner view, and in the usage views, just to name a few. In views containing a timescale, you might find it useful to change the timescale. In effect, when you change the timescale, you display either more or less of your project's timeframe on-screen. You change the timescale in any view containing a timescale using the same technique, so I'll work with the Gantt Chart view in this section.

One quick and easy way to see more or less of your project is to use the Zoom slider in the lower-right corner of the Project window. You can zoom in or out in controlled increments by clicking the plus (+) or minus (-) signs at either end of the Zoom slider, or you can simply drag the Zoom slider in either direction. Figure 7.12 shows a timescale that displays each day of each week. In Figure 7.13, I clicked the minus sign on the Zoom slider twice to zoom out and view more of my project.

FIGURE 7.12

A timescale that shows each day of the week.

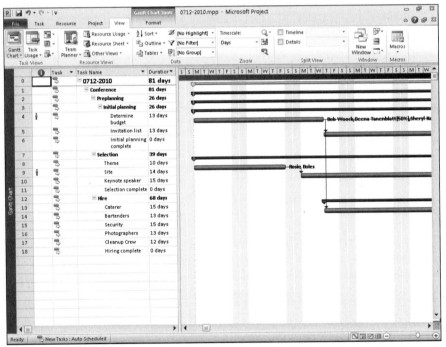

FIGURE 7.13

The same project after using the Zoom slider to zoom out.

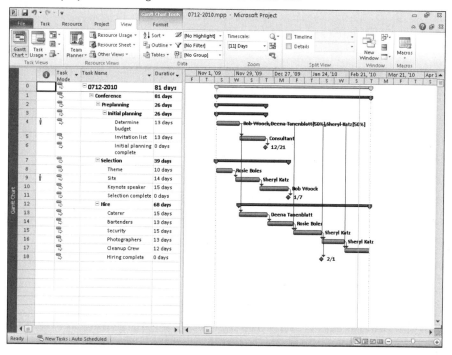

If you prefer to have more control of the timescale, use the Timescale dialog box shown in Figure 7.14. From this dialog box, you can set the timescale to view up to three levels, and you can modify the increments of time displayed in the timescale itself. Double-click the timescale to display the dialog box.

You can change the units for the top tier, the middle tier, and the bottom tier to help you concentrate on a particular period in your project or to view larger increments with less detail. The Count field controls how many instances of the unit Project marks off on your Gantt Chart.

Figure 7.15, for example, shows a top-tier timescale in months, a middle-tier timescale in weeks, and a bottom-tier timescale in days. The count for each tier is 1: one month with each of its four or five weeks, and each week's seven days.

FIGURE 7.14

In the Timescale dialog box, adjust the units to display and set the heading labels and alignment.

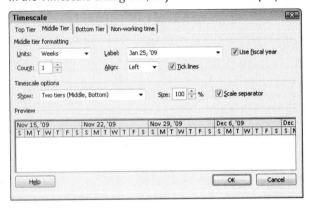

FIGURE 7.15

When you specify 1 week in the Count field of the Timescale dialog box, Project marks off every week on the portion of the timescale that displays weeks.

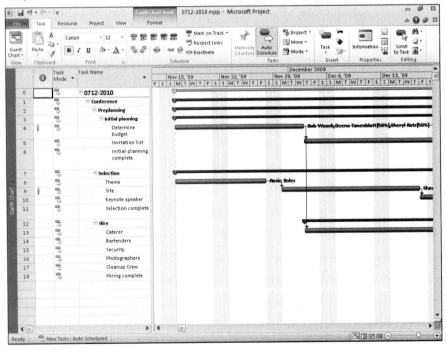

If you change the count for the middle tier — weeks — to 2, the weekly timescale displays two-week increments (see Figure 7.16).

FIGURE 7.16

Changing the number of weeks to 2 in the Count field causes Project to mark off weeks in two-week chunks.

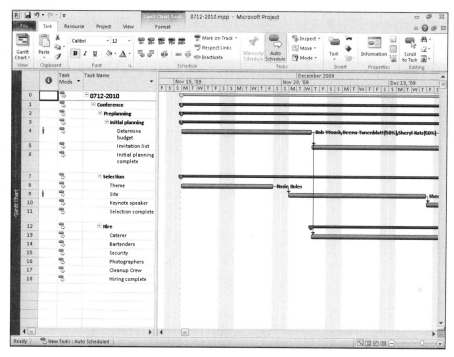

To show more of the project on-screen, consider displaying only two tiers on the timescale and set them to Months and Weeks respectively.

Tip

To shrink the timescale even more (that is, to see more of your project on-screen), use the Size setting in the Timescale dialog box. This setting enables you to view the timescale at a percentage of its full size. ∎

You can set the use of the fiscal year for any tier of the timescale. To make this feature work, you should set up a fiscal year calendar by following these steps:

1. Click the File tab and, in the Backstage view that appears, click Options.

2. In the Project Options dialog box, click the Schedule tab.

3. In the Calendar Options For This Project section, change the starting month from January to your fiscal year's starting month.

Adding views

When you create a new view, you can make it available in the More Views dialog box only or you can include it on the shortcut menu of views that appears when you click right-click the gray bar running down the left side of the Project window and containing the current view's name. That same menu also appears when you click the bottom of the Gantt Chart button or the Team Planner button (the Resource Sheet button for Project Standard users).

Caution

You can edit an existing view instead of creating a new view. But, as with the More Tables dialog box, the More Views dialog box does not have a View reset button; consequently, any changes you make are permanent. As I previously suggested, make a copy of a view you want to modify instead of editing the original view. That way, the original views remain intact. ■

To add a new view to your copy of Project, follow these steps:

1. Right-click the View bar if you've displayed it or right-click the gray bar running down the left side of Project and click More Views.

2. Click the New button in the More Views dialog box. The Define New View dialog box appears (see Figure 7.17).

Tip

If you can, base your new view on a copy of an existing view by selecting that view and clicking Copy — you'll have less to do to create the view. ■

FIGURE 7.17

A simple choice awaits you in the Define New View dialog box: a single or combination view.

3. Select the Single view option and click OK. The View Definition dialog box opens (see Figure 7.18).

Note

If you select the Combination view option, the View Definition dialog box requests slightly different information. ■

FIGURE 7.18

Use this dialog box to name and describe your new view.

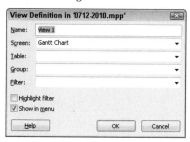

4. In the Name box, enter a name for the new view that describes the information you'll show in the view.

5. Using the Screen drop-down list, select a view on which to base the new view.

6. If the screen you chose in Step 5 gives you the option of selecting a table to include with it, select that table from the Table drop-down list. Otherwise skip this step.

7. Open the Filter list box to choose a filter to apply to the view. By default, Project applies the All Tasks filter; therefore all tasks appear in the view. To apply a selective filter so Project highlights only filtered tasks, select the Highlight Filter check box at the bottom of the View Definition dialog box.

Note

You can set filters to hide tasks from the display if they don't meet the filtering criteria, or you can set filters simply to highlight tasks that meet the criteria. ■

8. Select the Show in Menu check box to make the new view available as a selection in lists where you can select a view. If you don't check this box, you must display the view by selecting it from the More Views dialog box.

9. Click OK and then click Apply in the More Views dialog box to save the new view and display it on-screen.

Creating a combination view

You can display a single view or you can display a combination of two views simultaneously. Combination views display the entire project as well as information about the selected task. Figure 7.19 shows a combination view of the Network Diagram at the top of the screen and the Task Form view at the bottom of the screen. The Task Form view shows details of the task selected in the Network Diagram view.

FIGURE 7.19

A combination view displays information for selected tasks.

Split bar

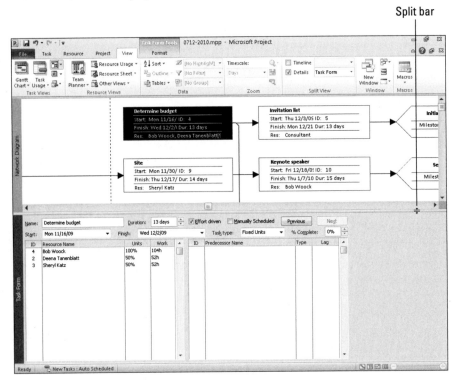

You can use the Split Bar to both display and hide a combination view. In Figure 7.19, I moved the mouse pointer onto the Split Bar at the bottom of the vertical scroll bar. To hide or display a combination view, move your pointer to the split bar until the pointer becomes two horizontal lines with arrows; then double-click or drag. While viewing a combination view, you can double-click the split bar to display only the view that appears in the top portion of the screen.

You can always identify the portion of the split view that has Project's focus by paying attention to the gray bar that appears on the left side of the Project window. The active view's bar is darker in color than the inactive view's bar; in Figure 7.19, the Network Diagram has Project's focus. If you switch views while displaying a combination view, the new view also appears as a part of the combination view, replacing the portion of the combination view that was active when you switched views.

Suppose you want to create a combination view that you can display at any time. Follow these steps to create a new combination view that includes the two views you want to see together:

1. Right-click the gray bar that runs down the left side of the Project window and choose More Views to display the More Views dialog box.

2. Click New to display the Define New View dialog box.

3. Choose the Combination view option to display the dialog box shown in Figure 7.20.

FIGURE 7.20

In the combination view version of the View Definition dialog box, select the two views to place on-screen.

4. Name the view and designate which view should appear at the top of the screen and which view should appear at the bottom using the Primary View and the Details Pane lists respectively.

5. To be able to display the view by choosing it from a list of views, select the Show in Menu check box.

6. Click OK when you finish.

Ordering Tasks in a View

You can think of project management as the attempt to comprehend a large job by breaking the job into progressively smaller pieces — until the job is a collection of tasks. You want to organize the tasks so you can estimate schedules, resource requirements, and costs. You can sort tasks and assign WBS codes or outline numbers to help you organize the project.

Sorting tasks

Sometimes sorting information in a different way helps you to get a better handle on a problem or even to see things that you might not have seen otherwise. In Project, you can sort a project from most views in almost any way you want.

For example, in the Gantt Chart view, Project sorts tasks by ID number automatically. But you might find it easier to view your project information if you sort by Finish Date.

Click the AutoFilter arrow that appears beside the heading of the column by which you want to sort; in this example, I clicked the AutoFilter arrow beside the Finish column. Project displays a list that you can use to both sort and filter (see Figure 7.21). If you select Sort Latest to Earliest, Project reorders the Gantt Chart view so tasks are ordered by Finish Date from latest to earliest date (refer to Figure 7.21); note that the Task IDs are no longer in ascending numerical order.

FIGURE 7.21

Using commands from the Sort submenu, you can sort a project by Task Finish Date.

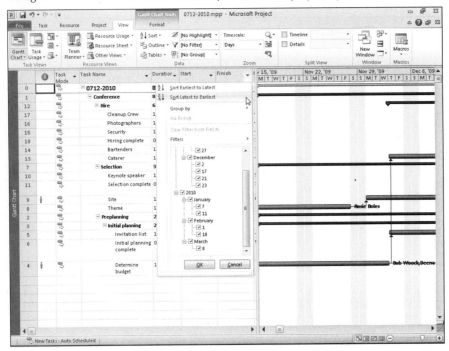

If you want more control over sorting options, choose the Sort By command at the bottom of the Sort menu; the Sort dialog box appears (see Figure 7.22). From this dialog box, you can sort down to three levels. That is, if Project finds a "tie" at the first level, it uses the second sort that you specify to break the tie. And if Project finds a tie at the second level, it uses the third sort that you specify to break the tie. Using the check boxes at the bottom of the dialog box, you can make your sort choices permanent by reassigning Task IDs, and you can choose to retain the outline structure of the project.

FIGURE 7.22

Use the Sort dialog box to set up a more complex sort structure.

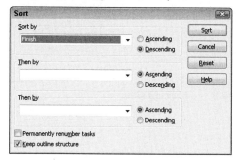

Creating WBS codes

The U.S. defense establishment initially developed the *work breakdown structure* (WBS), and you find it described in Section 1.6 of MIL-HDBK-881A (30 July 2005) as follows:

- A product-oriented family tree is composed of hardware, software, services, data, and facilities. The family tree structure results from systems engineering efforts during the acquisition of a defense material item.

- A WBS chart displays and defines the product, or products, to be developed and/or produced. It relates the elements of work to be accomplished to each other and to the end product. In other words, the WBS is an organized method of dividing a product into sub-products at lower levels of detail.

- WBS can be expressed down to any level of interest. Generally, the top three levels are sufficient unless the items identified are high cost or high risk. In that case, be sure to take the WBS to a lower level of definition.

More simply put, a WBS chart shows a numbered list of the tasks you must complete to finish a project.

In Project 2010, you can't produce a WBS graphic representation of your project that is similar to the one shown in Figure 7.23. You can, however, assign WBS codes to each task. WBS codes can be letters and numbers (or combinations of letters and numbers) that help you identify the relationship among tasks and organize the project.

FIGURE 7.23

The WBS chart is reminiscent of a company organization chart.

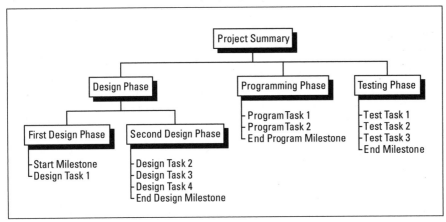

Tip

WBS Chart for Project, an add-on product for Project, creates a WBS chart from a Microsoft Project file. To check out a sample of the program, point your browser to `http://www.criticaltools.com/download.htm` **and click the link to download the demo version of WBS Chart Pro.** ∎

You can use any numbering system you want for your WBS code structure. Suppose you assigned codes to your project that are similar to those shown in Figure 7.24. Here the task numbered 1.1.2.3 identifies the first box in Level 2, the second box in Level 3, and the third box on Level 4 of the outline structure of the project. Although Project doesn't produce the graphic representation, it assigns the numbers based on the task's level within the project outline.

To assign WBS numbers to a project, follow these steps:

1. Click the Project tab and, in the Properties group, click the WBS button.

2. From the menu that appears, click Define Code. Project displays the WBS Code Definition dialog box. The Code preview box shows you the format of the WBS code that you're designing as you design it — and therefore remains blank until you make selections in this dialog box.

3. Use the Project Code Prefix box to apply a prefix to all WBS codes that you assign. For example, you may want to use the initials of the project name.

4. In the Sequence column at the bottom of the box, select the type of character you want to use for each level of the WBS code. In Figure 7.25, I've selected Numbers (ordered) for both Levels 1 and 2, but you can also include Uppercase Letters or Lowercase Letters. If you choose Characters (unordered), Project inserts an asterisk at that position of the WBS code.

FIGURE 7.24

WBS numbering shows you the hierarchical relationship of tasks in the project.

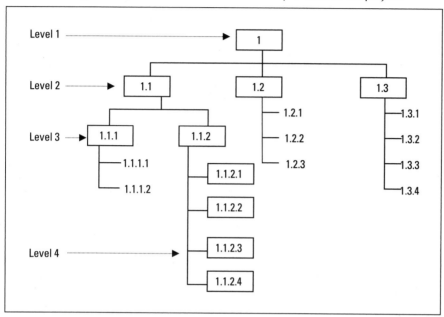

FIGURE 7.25

Use the WBS Code Definition dialog box to define the type of WBS code you want to use.

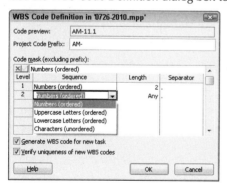

Note

If you choose Characters (unordered) in the Sequence column, you can enter any characters that you want into that part of the WBS code. For example, suppose you use a mask of Numbers (ordered) Length 1, Numbers (ordered) Length 1, Characters (unordered) Length 3. For any third-level task, you can enter any three characters you want for the third part of the WBS code. In this example, when you enter a third-level task, you initially see a WBS of 1.1.***. However, you can change it to something like 1.1.a#3. ■

5. Open the list box in the Length column and choose the length for the level of the WBS code. In Figure 7.25, I set Level 1 to two digits, but I allowed any number of digits for Level 2. You can choose Any, select from the predefined list of numbers 1–10, or enter any other number.

Note

For the technically curious, I tested the number 100, and Project accepted it, but using a 100-digit number in a WBS code isn't particularly practical. ■

6. In the Separator column, use the list box to select period (.), dash (–), plus (+), or slash (/), or enter any character that is not a number or a letter (such as =).

7. Repeat the previous steps for each level you want to define.

8. Click OK when you finish.

Tip

You should probably select both check boxes at the bottom of the WBS Code Definition dialog box; doing so ensures that all tasks are assigned WBS codes and that the codes are unique. ■

The WBS codes don't appear by default in the Gantt Chart view; to view the WBS codes, you must add the WBS column. To add the WBS column to the left of the Task Name column, right-click the Task Name column. Project selects the column and displays a shortcut menu. Choose Insert Column from the shortcut menu; Project inserts a column and displays a list of fields from which to choose. Type WBS and press Enter. The WBS column appears in the table portion of the Gantt Chart view (see Figure 7.26).

Note

If you had added the WBS column before defining WBS codes, you would have seen outline numbering that corresponded to the task's position in the project outline. ■

Tip

By default, Project assigns incremental WBS codes to each new task you add to the project or any tasks you copy within the project. ■

FIGURE 7.26

When you display the WBS column, Project displays the WBS codes for each task in your project.

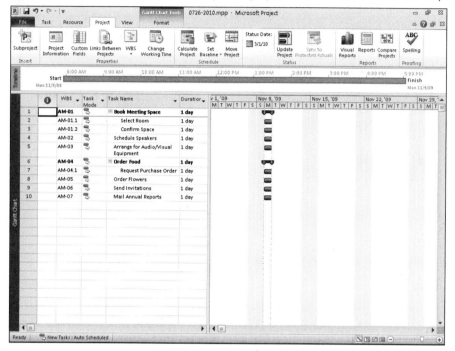

Renumbering WBS codes

WBS codes *don't* automatically renumber themselves in all cases when you change the structure of the project outline. WBS Codes *do* automatically renumber themselves if you change the level of a task within the outline structure of the project. That is, if you promote or demote the task, or if you move it so it appears at a new level in the outline, or you move a subtask to a new parent task, Project assigns the task a new WBS code. However, if you drag a Level 1 task to a new Level 1 location or if you drag a subtask to a new location beneath its original parent task, both tasks retain their original WBS code number. You can test the premise by dragging Request Purchase Order so it appears before Order Food. Each task retains its original WBS code, and Project assigns a new WBS Code — AM-08 — to Request Purchase Order (see Figure 7.27). In Figure 7.26, Request Purchase Order had a WBS Code of AM-04.1.

FIGURE 7.27

Because I moved tasks around, the WBS codes are no longer sequential.

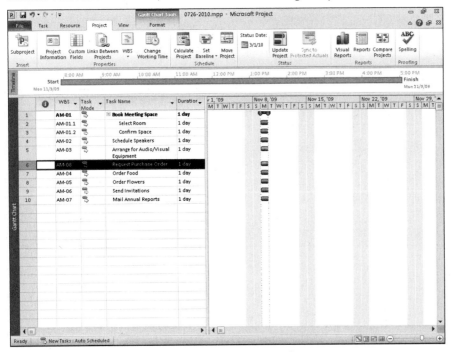

Note

If you're working on a government contract for which you and the government have agreed to a numbering scheme and you don't want WBS codes to change, even if you move tasks around, use Outline codes, which are static. You can assign both an Outline code and a WBS code to a task. (You read about Outline codes later in this chapter.) ■

At times, you'll want to renumber the WBS codes, even though Project didn't renumber them automatically — and you can. In fact, you can renumber the entire project or only selected portions of the project. If you choose to renumber selected portions, you must select the tasks before starting the renumbering process.

Caution

You can't undo renumbering WBS codes, so save your project before you start this operation. That way, if you don't like the results, you can close the project without saving it and reopen it in the state it was in before you renumbered it. ■

To renumber selected tasks in the project shown in Figure 7.27, follow these steps:

1. Select the tasks you want to renumber; in this example, I selected Rows 5-10.

2. Click the Project tab and, in the Properties group, click WBS. From the menu that appears, click Renumber. Project displays the dialog box shown in Figure 7.28.

FIGURE 7.28

Use this dialog box to renumber the project.

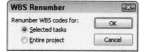

3. Click OK. If you opt to renumber the entire project, Project prompts you before renumbering.

4. Click Yes. Project reassigns all WBS numbers.

Defining outline numbers

In the preceding section, I offered a scenario in which you're working on a government contract, and you and the government have agreed to a numbering scheme. In a case such as this, you *don't* want WBS codes to change — even if you move tasks around. So don't rely on WBS codes in Project; instead, use outline codes, which are static.

Note
You can assign both an outline code and a WBS code to a task. ■

Outline codes work similarly to the way that WBS codes work. However, outline codes are customizable, and they are not tied to the outline structure of your project. For example, you may want to assign a department code to a task so you can view the project organized by department. Or, you may want to assign a company cost code to a task so you can view tasks by cost code.

You can enter outline code information in an ad-hoc manner, with no particular rhyme or reason, but most people create a list of valid outline codes for users to enter so the outline codes assigned are meaningful and consistent.

Outline codes work as you would expect: You define codes at the highest level — we'll call that Level 1 — and then additional codes at various subordinate levels — Level 2, Level 3, and so on. Level 2 codes would appear subordinate to Level 1, Level 3 subordinate to Level 2, and so on.

Tip
Try not to get carried away defining subordinate levels of outline codes; stacking codes deeply makes them harder to use. ■

To define outline codes, follow these steps:

1. Click the Project tab and, in the Properties group, click Custom Fields. Project displays the Custom Fields dialog box.

2. Open the Type drop-down list and choose Outline Code (see Figure 7.29).

FIGURE 7.29

Select an outline code to customize.

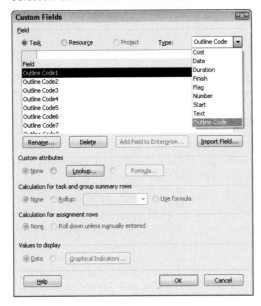

Cross-Reference

Read more about customizing fields in Chapter 16. ∎

3. Choose an Outline Code to customize.

4. To provide a meaningful name for the code, click the Rename button and enter the new name. Then click OK to redisplay the Custom Fields dialog box.

5. Click the Lookup button; Project displays the Edit Lookup Table dialog box (see Figure 7.30).

6. To define a mask for the lookup table, click the plus sign (+) beside Code Mask. The plus sign (+) changes to a minus sign (−), and displays the top potion of the Edit Lookup Table dialog box. Click the Edit Mask button to display the Code Mask Definition dialog box (see Figure 7.31).

FIGURE 7.30

Use this dialog box to define the allowable lookup codes.

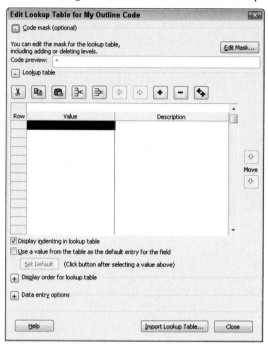

FIGURE 7.31

The Code Mask Definition dialog box looks and operates like the WBS Code Definition dialog box.

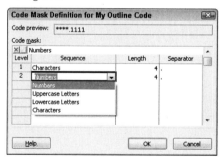

7. In the Sequence column, select the type of character you want to use for each level of the outline code.

8. In the Length column, use the list to choose the length for the level of the outline code.

9. In the Separator column, use the list box to select period (.), dash (–), plus (+), or slash (/), or enter any character that is not a number or a letter (such as =).

10. Repeat the previous steps for each level of the mask that you want to define.

11. Click OK to redisplay the Edit Lookup Table dialog box.

12. On Row 1 of the Value column, enter a permissible outline code for the first level of your outline — call it Level 1 — and press Enter.

13. On the second line, type an outline code for the second level that is permissible under Level 1 and press Enter; after Project displays the code, move the pointer back into Row 2 and click the Indent button (the right arrow) at the top of the dialog box to indent the code.

14. On the third line, enter another acceptable Level 2 outline code.

    If you need a Level 3 outline code under a Level 2 outline code, simply enter the code on a blank line below the Level 2 outline code, press Enter, move the pointer back to the line on which you just typed the code, and click the Indent button again.

    To supply another Level 1 code, enter the code, place the pointer on the code's row, and click the Outdent button (the left arrow) as many times as necessary, depending on the last code you entered.

    If you forget to include a code, highlight the code that you want to appear *below* the code you'll add, and then click the Insert Row button at the top of the dialog box. If a code becomes invalid at some later date, reopen this dialog box, highlight the code, and click the Delete Row button.

    You can click the plus sign (+) beside Display Order for Lookup Table to control the order in which lookup table codes appear. Similarly, you can click the plus sign (+) beside Data Entry Options to allow users to add codes to the lookup table or to force entry of only Level 1 codes. In both cases, when you click the plus sign (+), it changes to a minus sign (–) and displays your options.

15. Click Close to redisplay the Custom Fields dialog box.

16. Click OK to save your outline code settings.

Next, you need to insert a column in a table to display outline codes. To do so, follow the same process you used to display the column for the WBS code. Right-click the column you want to appear to the right of the Outline Code column, and then choose Insert Column. After Project inserts a column, type a few letters of your outline code's name until Project highlights it in the list so you can select it.

If you followed the preceding steps to create a lookup table of permissible outline codes, you can now enter codes by clicking in the outline code column; Project displays a list-box arrow. When you open the list, the entries from the lookup table appear (see Figure 7.32).

FIGURE 7.32

You can enter outline codes using the entries listed in the lookup table.

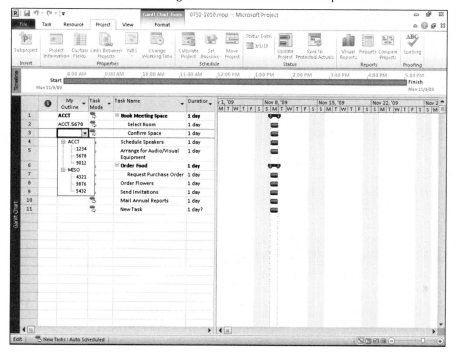

Filtering Views to Gain Perspective

Filters help you to focus on specific aspects of your project. For example, suppose you want to view only the tasks assigned to certain resources or you want to display only the tasks that are on the critical path of your project. You can apply filters to views to limit the information that you see and to help you focus on a particular issue.

Project filters come in two varieties: task filters, which enable you to view specific aspects of tasks, and resource filters, which enable you to view specific aspects of resources. In Table 7.1, you find a description of the default task filters, and in Table 7.2, you find a description of the default resource filters. Many of the filters perform similar functions.

TABLE 7.1

Default Task Filters

Filter	Purpose
All Tasks	Displays all the tasks in your project.
Active Tasks	Displays all active tasks and hides inactive tasks.
Completed Tasks	Displays all finished tasks.
Cost Greater Than	Displays the tasks that exceed the cost you specify.
Cost Overbudget	Calculated filter that displays all tasks with a cost that exceeds the baseline cost.
Created After	Displays all tasks that you created in your project on or after the specified date.
Critical	Displays all tasks on the critical path.
Date Range	Interactive filter that prompts you for two dates and then displays all tasks that start after the earlier date and finish before the later date.
In Progress Tasks	Displays all tasks that have started but haven't finished.
Incomplete Tasks	Displays all tasks that haven't finished.
Late Tasks	Displays only those tasks that are not on schedule.
Late/Overbudget Tasks Assigned To	Prompts you to specify a resource. Then Project displays tasks that meet either of two conditions: (a) tasks assigned to that resource that exceed the budget you allocated for them, or (b) tasks that haven't finished yet and will finish after the baseline finish date. (Note that completed tasks do not appear when you apply this filter, even if they are completed after the baseline finish date.)
Linked Fields	Displays tasks to which you have linked text from other programs.
Manually Scheduled Tasks	Displays only tasks created using the Manually Scheduled mode.
Milestones	Displays only milestones.
Resource Group	Displays the tasks assigned to resources that belong to the group you specify.
Should Start By	Prompts you for a date and then displays all tasks not yet begun that should have started by that date.
Should Start/Finish By	Prompts you for two dates: a start date and a finish date. Then Project uses the filter to display those tasks that haven't started by the start date and those tasks that haven't finished by the finish date.
Slipped/Late Progress	Displays two types of tasks: (a) those that have slipped behind their baseline scheduled finish date and (b) those that are not progressing on schedule.
Slipping Tasks	Displays all tasks that are behind schedule.
Summary Tasks	Displays all tasks that have subtasks grouped below them.
Task Range	Shows all tasks that have ID numbers within the range that you provide.
Tasks with a Task Calendar Assigned	Shows only those tasks to which you've assigned a task calendar.
Tasks with Attachments	Displays tasks that have objects attached or a note in the Notes box.

Filter	Purpose
Tasks with Deadlines	Displays all tasks to which you have assigned deadline dates.
Tasks with Estimated Durations	Displays all tasks that have the `Estimated Duration` field checked or tasks for which the default duration estimate has not been changed.
Tasks with Fixed Dates	Displays all tasks that have a start or finish date you entered into the `Start` or `Finish` date field directly instead of allowing Project to calculate the `Start` and `Finish` dates.
Tasks Without Dates	Displays only those tasks that have no dates assigned.
Tasks/Assignments with Overtime	Displays the tasks or assignments that have overtime.
Top Level Tasks	Displays the highest-level summary tasks.
Unstarted Tasks	Displays tasks that haven't started.
Using Resource in Date Range	Displays tasks assigned to a specified resource that start after the first date you specify and finish before the second date you specify.
Using Resource	Displays all tasks that use a resource you specify.
Work Overbudget	Displays all tasks with scheduled work greater than baseline work.

TABLE 7.2

Default Resource Filters

Filter	Purpose
All Resources	Displays all the resources, in your project.
Budget Resources	Displays resources set up as budget resources
Cost Greater Than	Displays the resources that exceed the cost that you specify.
Cost Overbudget	A calculated filter that displays all resources with a cost that exceeds the baseline cost.
Created After	Displays resources created after a date you specify.
Date Range	An interactive filter that prompts you for two dates and then displays all tasks and resources with assignments that start after the earlier date and finish before the later date.
Group	Prompts you for a group and then displays all resources that belong to that group.
In Progress Assignments	Displays all tasks that have started but haven't finished.
Linked Fields	Displays resources to which you have linked text from other programs.
Non-budget Resources	Displays resources *not* set up as budget resources.

(continued)

TABLE 7.2 *(continued)*

Filter	Purpose
Overallocated Resources	Displays all resources that are scheduled to do more work than they have the capacity to do.
Resource Range	An interactive filter that prompts you for a range of ID numbers and then displays all resources within that range.
Resources – Cost	Displays only those resources with a type of Cost.
Resources – Material	Displays only those resources with a type of Material.
Resources - Work	Displays only those resources with a type of Work.
Resources with Attachments	Displays resources that have objects attached or a note in the Notes box.
Resources/Assignments with Overtime	Displays the resources or assignments that have overtime with Overtime.
Should Start By	Prompts you for a date and then displays all tasks and resources with assignments not yet begun that should have started by that date.
Should Start/Finish By	Prompts you for two dates: a start date and a finish date. Then, Project uses the filter to display those tasks or assignments that haven't started by the start date and those tasks or assignments that haven't finished by the finish date.
Slipped/Late Progress	Displays two types of resources: those that have slipped behind their baseline scheduled finish date and those that are not progressing on schedule.
Slipping Assignments	Displays all resources with uncompleted tasks that are behind schedule because the tasks have been delayed from the original baseline plan.
Unstarted Assignments	Displays confirmed assignments that have not yet started.
Work Complete	Displays resources that have completed all their assigned tasks.
Work Incomplete	Displays all resources with baseline work greater than scheduled work.
Work Overbudget	Displays all resources with scheduled work greater than baseline work.

Applying a filter to a view

By applying a filter to a view, you specify criteria that Project uses to determine which tasks or resources appear in that view. Project then selects information to display and either highlights the selected information or hides the rest of the information. To apply a filter and hide all other information, follow these steps:

1. Display the view that you want to filter.

2. Click the View tab and, in the Data group, click the drop-down arrow beside the Filter button.

3. Choose the filter that you want from the menu. If the filter doesn't appear in the list, or to apply a highlighting filter, continue with Step 4.

Note

Because Project enables you to apply task filters to task views only and resource filters to resource views only, the menu shows either task or resource filters, depending on the view that you display before starting these steps. ■

4. Click More Filters. Project displays the More Filters dialog box (see Figure 7.33).

FIGURE 7.33

Use the More Filters dialog box to apply a filter that doesn't appear on the Filtered For list or to apply a highlighting filter.

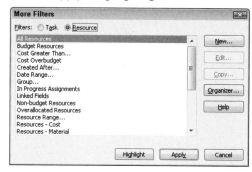

5. Click the Task option button to select and apply a task filter; select the Resource option button to apply a resource filter.

Caution

Remember that Project doesn't let you apply a task filter to a resource view or a resource filter to a task view. ■

6. Select a filter name from the list.

7. Click Apply to apply the filter or click Highlight to apply a highlighting filter. If the filter you want to apply is interactive, type the requested values.

Tip

To turn off a filter, use the Ribbon. Click the View tab and, in the Data group, open the Filter list and select [No Filter]. ■

Creating custom filters

If none of Project's default filters meet your needs, you can create a new filter or modify an existing filter by customizing a particular filter's criteria from the More Filters dialog box. To edit an existing filter, follow these steps:

1. Display the view you want to filter.

2. Click the View tab and, in the Data group, click the drop-down arrow beside the Filter button.

3. Click More Filters. Project displays the More Filters dialog box.

4. Select the option button of the type of filter you want to use: Task or Resource.

5. Highlight the filter you want to modify, and click the Copy button. Project displays a Filter Definition dialog box, similar to the one shown in Figure 7.34.

FIGURE 7.34

The Filter Definition dialog box enables you to edit an existing filter.

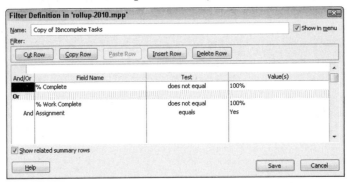

Caution

The More Filters dialog box does not have a "filter reset button"; consequently, any changes that you make are permanent. For this reason, I advise you to click the Copy button to make a copy of a filter that you want to modify, instead of clicking the Edit button to edit the original filter. That way the original filters remain intact. ■

6. Click in the Field Name column; Project displays a list box arrow to the right of the field.

7. Select a field from the list.

8. Repeat Steps 6 and 7 for the Test column and supply a comparison operator.

9. Repeat Steps 6 and 7 in the Value(s) column and supply a filtering value.

10. Repeat Steps 6 through 9 for each criterion you want to create; also supply an And/Or operator if you supply additional criteria. Remember, And means the filter displays information only if the task or resource meets *all* criteria, whereas Or means the filter displays information if a task or resource meets *any* of the criteria.

11. Click Save to redisplay the More Filters dialog box.

12. Click Apply to apply the filter.

Note

To create a new filter from scratch, click New Filter in the Filter drop-down list in the Data group on the View tab of the Ribbon. The Filter Definition dialog box appears, displaying the name Filter 1 in the Name box and no information appears at the bottom of the box. For the new filter, you need to supply a name and some filtering criteria. To have your new filter appear in the Filtered For list, select the Show in Menu check box. ■

Each line that you create in the Filter Definition dialog box is called a *statement*. To evaluate certain statements together but separate from other statements in your filter, group the statements into a set of criteria. To group statements, leave a blank line between sets of criteria and select either operator in the And/Or field for the blank row.

If your filter contains three or more statements within one criteria group, Project evaluates all And statements before evaluating Or statements. Across groups, Project evaluates And conditions in the order in which they appear.

Using AutoFilters

AutoFilters are similar to regular Project filters, but you can access them directly on the sheet of any sheet view instead of using a menu or a window. By default, the AutoFilters option is on when you create a project, but you can turn it off by clicking AutoFilter at the bottom of the Filter list (click the View tab and then click the drop-down list beside the Filter button).

To use an AutoFilter, click the drop-down list beside a column heading name. Project displays filters that are appropriate to the column (see Figure 7.35).

FIGURE 7.35

Select an AutoFilter.

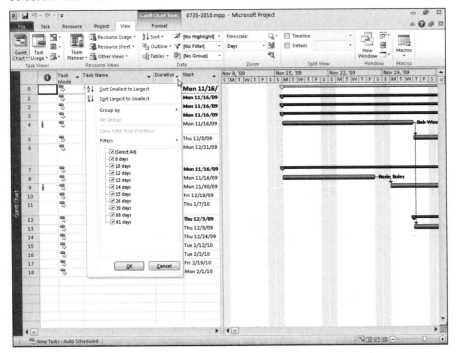

Using grouping

Grouping is another technique you can use to view information about your project. You may be able to solve a problem if you group tasks by some common denominator. In Figure 7.36, for example, I've grouped tasks by duration to help identify shorter versus longer tasks.

To quickly group information for any column appearing in the view, click the AutoFilter arrow beside the column name, point at Group By, and make a selection.

FIGURE 7.36

Group tasks in a view to help you identify information about your project.

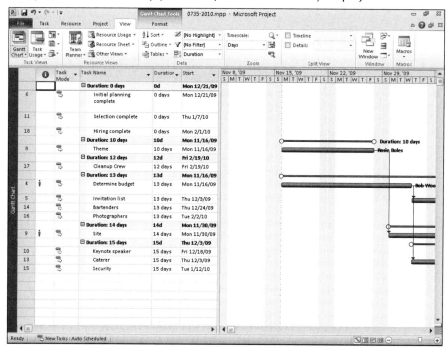

In addition, you can use one of the predefined groups Project contains. To use one of these groups to arrange tasks in a view, follow these steps:

1. Display the view you want to use to group tasks.

2. Click the View tab and, in the Data group, click the drop-down arrow beside the Group By button (see Figure 7.37).

3. Choose the group you want.

Note

Project only lets you group tasks in task views and resources in resource views. Thus the Group By menu shows either task groupings or resource groupings, depending on the view you displayed in Step 1. ■

FIGURE 7.37

Select a way to group information in the view.

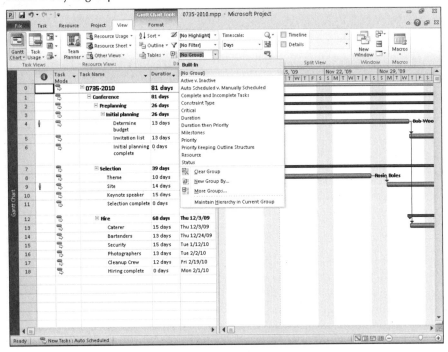

If you think of a way you'd like to group information, and your way doesn't appear in the Group By list, you can create a new grouping. Although you can start from scratch by choosing New Group By from the Group By list, it's often easier to base your new group on an existing group. Follow these steps:

1. Display the view that you want to use to group tasks.

2. Click the View tab and, in the Data group, click the drop-down arrow beside the Group By button.

3. Click More Groups, and Project displays the More Groups dialog box (see Figure 7.38).

4. Select the Task option button to apply a task grouping; select the Resource option button to apply a resource grouping.

Tip

Project doesn't let you apply a task group to a resource view or a resource group to a task view. ■

5. Select a group name from the list.

FIGURE 7.38

Use the More Groups dialog box to apply a group not on the Group By list or to create a new group by copying and editing an existing group.

6. Click Copy to make a copy of a group so you can edit it. Project displays the Group Definition dialog box (see Figure 7.39).

Caution

As with its cousins, the More Groups dialog box has no "group reset" button; consequently, any changes you make are permanent. I advise you to click the Copy button to make a copy of a group that you want to modify, and edit that copy instead of the original group. That way the original groups remain intact. ■

FIGURE 7.39

Use this dialog box to create a custom group based on an existing group.

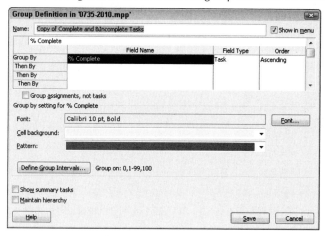

7. Assign a name to the group that you're creating, and select the Show in Menu box if you want the group to be available from the Group By menu.

8. Open the Field Name list box, and select a field on which you want Project to group.

9. In the Order column, choose Ascending or Descending.

10. (Optional) Select a font for the grouping title information.

11. (Optional) Change the cell background and the pattern that Project displays for the field.

12. (Optional) Click the Define Group Intervals button to display the Define Group Interval dialog box, as shown in Figure 7.40. In this dialog box, you can control the grouping intervals that Project uses. Click OK when you finish to redisplay the Group Definition dialog box.

FIGURE 7.40

Use this dialog box to specify the intervals at which you want Project to group the fields.

13. Select the Show Summary Tasks check box to include summary tasks in the grouping.

14. Click Save to save your choices and redisplay the More Groups dialog box.

15. Click Apply to apply the group that you just defined.

Working from a usage view, you also can group on assignment fields. Complete the steps just given here — but be sure to select the Group Assignments, Not Resources check box *before* you click Save. Then, in the Field Type column, select whether to group by assignment or by resource. In Figure 7.41, I started working from the Task Usage view, but I copied a resource grouping. If you select a task grouping, the name of the check box changes to refer to tasks instead of resources, and, in the Field Type list, you choose whether to group by assignment or by task.

Tip

To turn off grouping, click the View tab and, in the Data group, open the Group By list and select [No Group]. ■

FIGURE 7.41

Use this dialog box to group by assignment fields.

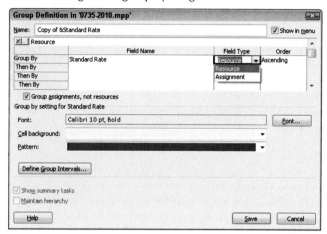

Summary

This chapter covered techniques that you can use to get more information from Project's views. You learned the following:

- How to work with tables
- How to customize views
- How to order tasks in a view
- How to assign WBS codes and outline codes to tasks
- How to filter information while working
- How to group information while working

You can use the skills you've picked up here to make Project work in the way that's most comfortable for you.

Chapter 8 explains how to change the appearance of your project by formatting elements and inserting visual elements.

Modifying the Appearance of Your Project

A fter you enter the information for your project, you may want to take the time to format the individual elements of the schedule. After all, you may be working with this project for months or even years. Why not get it to look just right?

Project has dozens of ways to format the appearance of elements, from text to task bars, link lines, and network diagram nodes. Some of these changes are practical; others simply provide shapes or styles that may be more pleasing to you. You can use color and insert drawings or pictures into your schedule to make a visual point. You can also copy pictures of your Project file into other Office documents — for example, to include in a report. So get ready: This chapter is where you can get visually creative!

IN THIS CHAPTER

Changing Project's looks

Using the Gantt Chart Wizard

Formatting elements one by one

Inserting drawings and objects

Changing Project's Looks

Beyond the obvious motivation of making the lines and colors in your schedule more appealing, you may have a practical reason for modifying a schedule's appearance. You may, for example, want to do any of the following to make information about your project more accessible:

- Display information, such as the start and end dates or resources assigned to the task, in text form alongside task bars. This technique is especially useful for longer schedules in which a task bar may appear on the printed page far to the right of the task information in the Gantt table.

- Use a bolder color for tasks that are on the critical path (tasks that, if delayed, will delay the final completion of the project). This method helps you keep an eye on tasks that are vital to meeting your deadline.

- Modify the display of baseline timing estimates versus actual progress on tasks so that you can more clearly see any divergence.

Consistency Counts

Displaying an abundance of elements on a schedule can be a mixed blessing. For example, highlighting critical tasks, displaying resource names, and showing baseline, actual lines, and progress lines as well as slack time will probably result in a chart that is visually confusing. Although it may feel good to format to satisfy your penchant for a particular color, remember that you're formatting elements to make project information easier to read.

You'll help everyone in your organization read and understand Project schedules if you make the formatting consistent across your organization. If your coworkers and management see the same formatting in various schedules, they will quickly learn to read the symbols and be less likely to misread a schedule. Set standards for formatting projects in your workgroup and your division (even across your company) and stick to them.

Cross-Reference

You can store multiple baselines. You may want to format your project schedule to distinguish various baselines more easily. See Chapter 12 for more information on multiple baselines. ■

- Display or hide dependency lines between tasks. In a project with many complex dependency relationships, multiple lines can obscure task-bar elements or network diagram nodes.

In short, beyond mere cosmetics, paying attention to the format of your schedule elements can help you focus on your project. Keep in mind that these changes pertain only to the currently open schedule; any changes you make to the format of these elements appear both on-screen and on any corresponding printed versions of the project.

Tip

You can change formats whenever you like and then change them back again without changing the data in your project. For example, you may decide not to display dependency lines to print a report of resource assignments for your boss because printing the lines can obscure the list of resources next to each task bar. You can always redisplay the dependency lines later. ■

Using the Gantt Chart Wizard

You can make changes to specific elements in several Project views. However, the Gantt Chart view has its own wizard to help you format the various pieces. Running through the Gantt Chart Wizard highlights some of the options.

By default, the Gantt Chart Wizard does not appear on either the Ribbon or the Quick Access Toolbar (QAT). But you can add the wizard's button to either location; for this exercise, we add it to the QAT.

Note

A wizard is an interactive series of dialog boxes that require you to answer questions or make selections. Project uses your input to create or modify some aspect of your project (in this case, the formatting that is applied to your Gantt Chart). The Microsoft Office family of products uses wizards to automate many functions. ■

To add a button to the QAT to run the Gantt Chart Wizard, follow these steps:

1. Click the File tab and, from the Back Stage view that appears, click Options to display the Project Options dialog box.

2. On the left side of the Project Options dialog box, click Quick Access Toolbar.

3. Above the left column, open the Choose Commands From list and select Commands Not in the Ribbon (see Figure 8.1).

FIGURE 8.1

Find the Gantt Chart Wizard in the list on the left and click Add to display the entry in the list on the right.

Click here to Select Commands Not in Ribbon

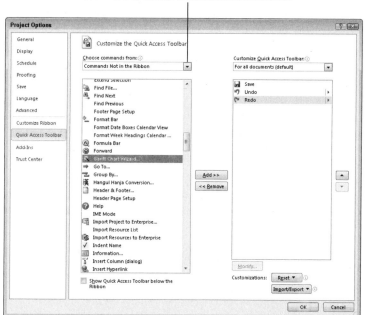

4. In the list that Project displays, scroll to and select Gantt Chart Wizard.

Tip

Project lists the commands in alphabetical order. ■

5. Click the Add button.

   Project displays the Gantt Chart Wizard button at the bottom of the list on the right.

6. Click OK.

   A new button representing the Gantt Chart Wizard appears at the right edge of the QAT.

You can use the Gantt Chart Wizard from any Gantt Chart view. Because Gantt Chart Wizard changes apply only to the project file that's open when you run the wizard, start by displaying the project you want to format. Then follow these steps to run the Gantt Chart Wizard:

Note
If you don't like the changes you made to the project using the Gantt Chart Wizard, you can Undo the changes that the Gantt Chart Wizard applies to your project if you click Undo before you save your project. ∎

1. Click the Gantt Chart Wizard button on the QAT.

   A dialog box appears, welcoming you to the Gantt Chart Wizard.

Note
The four buttons at the bottom of this dialog box appear at the bottom of every wizard dialog box. Click Cancel to leave the wizard without saving any settings, click Back to move back one step, and click Finish to complete the wizard with results based on the information you've provided to that point. ∎

2. Click Next to move to the next step. In the second wizard dialog box (see Figure 8.2), indicate the category of information you want to display. You can select only one item here; the choice you make determines which dialog boxes Project displays as you walk through the rest of the Gantt Chart wizard. Try clicking each of the following choices to see a preview of its style on the left of the dialog box:

   - **Standard:** Shows blue task bars, black summary task bars, and a black line superimposed over the task bars to indicate progress on tasks.

   - **Critical path:** The Standard layout, with critical-path tasks in red.

   - **Baseline:** Displays baseline task bars and progress task bars separately rather than superimposed (as they are in the Standard setup, shown in Figure 8.2).

FIGURE 8.2

The preview provides an idea of how each option formats your Gantt Chart.

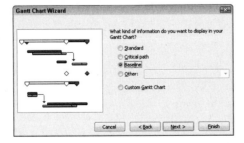

- **Other:** Displays a drop-down list that contains several alternative, predefined chart styles for the categories of Standard, Critical Path, Baseline, and Status.

- **Custom Gantt Chart:** Displays several additional screens to enable you to create a highly customized Gantt Chart.

Tip

Highlighting critical tasks in a project helps you to pay special attention to them when reviewing or tracking progress. If you don't want to format the Gantt Chart to treat critical tasks differently, try using a filter to temporarily display only critical tasks (as I discuss in Chapter 7). ∎

3. For this example, click the option button for Other and use the List box to select styles to preview. When you find one you like, click the Next button.

4. In the third wizard dialog box that appears, (see Figure 8.3), you can choose a type of task information to display with your Gantt bars: Resources and dates (the end date only), Resources, Dates, None (of the choices), or Custom Task Information. When you choose Dates, as I did in Figure 8.3, Project displays the start date and end date on either end of each Gantt bar. If you choose this setting, you don't need to show the corresponding columns for start date and end date in the Gantt table, so this option can help you modify the size of your schedule printout.

FIGURE 8.3

Placing text alongside task bars can be useful with larger schedules.

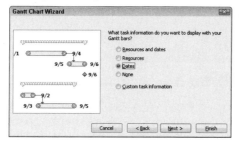

5. Click Next: Using the wizard's dialog box shown in Figure 8.4, you can decide whether you want to show link lines between dependent tasks.

6. Click Next to preview the formatting options you have selected (see Figure 8.5).

   You can use the Back button to go back and make changes.

7. Click the Format It button to apply your choices.

   Project displays a final dialog box to tell you that your formatting is complete.

8. Click the Exit Wizard button to close the dialog box and see your changes.

   If you decide you don't like the changes, click the Undo button.

FIGURE 8.4

Decide whether to display link lines to indicate dependent tasks.

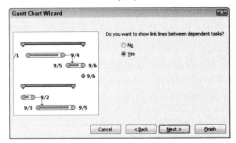

FIGURE 8.5

If you don't like what you see, move back to the dialog box in which you made the original setting, change the setting, and then move forward to this dialog box again.

When Enough Is Too Much

If you select the Custom Gantt Chart option in the Gantt Chart Wizard (refer to Figure 8.2), the wizard asks if you want to display different bars for critical and non-critical tasks; if you answer yes, the Gantt Chart Wizard asks you to select options for critical task bars and then for non-critical task bars. The Gantt Chart Wizard then prompts you to select options for summary task bars and milestones. You then have the option of displaying additional Gantt bars representing baselines, total slack, or both. At this point, the wizard displays the dialog box shown in Figure 8.3 — where, if you select Custom Task Information, you can specify information to appear to the left, to the right, and inside each task bar. The information ranges from task name, duration, and priority to percentage of work complete and types of constraints — and you could end up with a lot of information in and around your various task bars, making your Gantt Chart unreadable. However, consider this scenario: Put the task name inside both summary and normal task bars, put the start date to the left and the finish date to the right of normal task bars, and put the cost of summary tasks to the right of their bars. (The final element is a total of the cost of all tasks beneath the summary tasks.)

You can also modify the information that is available to someone viewing your schedule if you change the columns that appear in the Gantt table pane of the Gantt Chart view.

Formatting Elements One by One

The Gantt Chart Wizard enables you to make changes to several common elements, such as summary task bars or dependency lines. But Project also enables you to format each of these elements separately — and with even more options.

Working with text

You may want to change text to be more readable; for example, some people prefer a larger font to make views easy to read. Perhaps you want to use boldface for row and column titles or a distinctive font for summary tasks. Or perhaps you want to change the background color behind text to call attention to certain tasks.

Note

You format text the same way for any view. You can't format fonts in the Calendar view, but you can format categories of text. ■

Suppose, for example, that you want to apply boldface to the task name of a milestone called Grand Opening, but you don't want to affect any other milestone task names.

Formatting selected text

To format selected text, follow these steps:

1. Display any view that contains a table of columns (for example, the Gantt Chart, Task Usage, or Resource Sheet views).

2. Click the cell containing the text you want to format. To format more than one adjacent cell, click the first cell. Then drag your mouse to highlight cells above, below, to the left, or to the right.

3. Click the Task tab and use the buttons in the Font group to make changes to the cell.

   If you're a dialog-box kind of person, click the dialog box launcher to open the Font dialog box shown in Figure 8.6. From the three lists across the top of this dialog box, you can select a new font, select a font style such as Italic or Bold (Regular is normal text that has neither italic nor bold applied), or change the font size. Select the Underline check box to apply underlining to text, or select a color from the Color and Background Color drop-down palettes. A preview of your selections appears in the Sample area.

Note

You can apply a background pattern to a cell, but exercise care, because a background pattern can make text harder to read. ■

4. Click OK to save your changes.

Note

You cannot apply background patterns from the Ribbon; instead, use the Font dialog box. ■

FIGURE 8.6

From the Font dialog box, you can control the style, size, and color of fonts, as well the background appearance of cells.

Applying formatting to categories of text

You can use text styles to change the format of text for one cell in a table or to apply a unique format to an entire category of information, such as all task names for milestones. Text styles are identical to the formatting options for text that were described in the preceding section, but you can apply text styles to specific categories of text.

Follow these steps to use text styles to modify text:

1. Click the Gantt Chart Tools Format tab and, in the Format group, click Text Styles to open the Text Styles dialog box (see Figure 8.7).

FIGURE 8.7

The default in the Item to Change list box is All (that is, all the text in your project schedule).

2. Click the down arrow next to the Item to Change field to display the options. (This field is the only element that distinguishes the Text Styles dialog box from the Font dialog box you saw earlier.)

3. Click a category of text to select it. You can format text for categories such as row and column titles, summary tasks, tasks on the critical path, and milestones.

4. Select the settings you want for the text — including the font, font size, style, color, and script (see the preceding set of steps in the section, "Formatting selected text").

5. Click OK to apply the formatting.

Using the Item to Change list box, you can format categories of text to add emphasis to certain key items, such as critical tasks and milestones, or to make your schedule more readable by enlarging text or choosing easy-to-read fonts. Figure 8.8 shows a schedule with separate text styles applied to critical and noncritical tasks. Critical tasks have red backgrounds and italic text; noncritical tasks have pale blue backgrounds.

Caution

Good advice bears repeating: Don't go overboard with multiple fonts or colors on a single view. You can make a project harder to read by using too many different formats. Avoid using more than one or two fonts or colors, and vary the text by using bold or italic between items. Also, try to set up company-wide standards for formatting so that all your project schedules have a consistent, professional look. ■

FIGURE 8.8

Here task names in italics with a red background indicate critical tasks; noncritical tasks have a pale blue background.

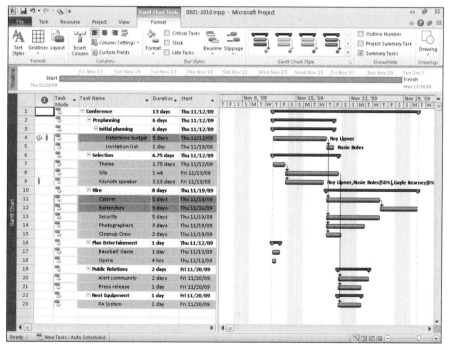

Changing task bars

In addition to changing text styles in your schedule, you can modify the look of the task bars. You can make changes to the shape, pattern, and color of bars, as well as to the style of the shape that appears on either end of the task bar.

Formatting task bars

Formatting task bars is similar to formatting text. You can format either an individual task bar or a category of task bars, such as milestones or critical tasks.

- **To format just one task bar:** Click a particular task and then click the Gantt Chart Tools Format tab. Then, in the Bar Styles group, click the Format button and select Bar to open the Format Bar dialog box.

- **To format categories of task bars:** Click the Format tab. Then, in the Bar Styles group, click the Format button and select Bar Styles to open the Bar Styles dialog box.

Tip

The settings you can modify are the same either way. You can open the Format Bar dialog box by right-clicking the bar you want to modify and choosing Format Bar from the shortcut menu that appears. You can open the Bar Styles dialog box by right-clicking a blank spot in the chart portion of the Gantt Chart and choosing Bar Styles from the shortcut menu that appears. ■

Figure 8.9 shows the Format Bar dialog box; Figure 8.10 shows the Bar Styles dialog box. The bottom half of the Bar Styles dialog box has two tabbed sheets called Text and Bars. Counterparts to these tabbed sheets appear at the top of the Format Bar dialog box and are called Bar Shape and Bar Text. The Bar Styles dialog box has a table from which you can designate the category of task bar that you want to modify and the changes that you want to make.

You can modify the appearance of an individual task bar to draw attention to it.

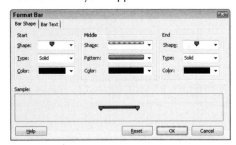

FIGURE 8.10

Use the Bars tab of the Bar Styles dialog box to change the appearance of an entire category of tasks.

Tabs for bar formatting

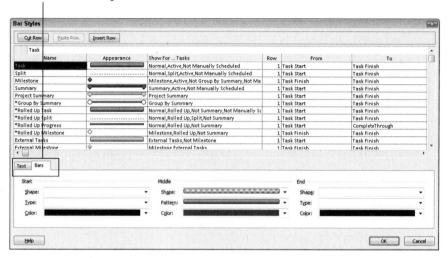

You can use the Bars tab at the bottom of the Bar Styles dialog box or the Bar Shape tab in the Format Bar dialog box to set the shape, type or pattern, and color for the bar and its end shapes. Use the Text tab in the Bar Styles dialog box or the Bar Text tab in the Format Bar dialog box to add text to the chart portion of the Gantt Chart view. In the steps that follow, I use the Bar Styles dialog box to make changes for a category of tasks, and I point out differences if you are using the Format Bar dialog box to change a selected task.

1. If you're working in the Format Bar dialog box, skip to Step 2. In the table at the top of the Bar Styles dialog box, click in the Name column of the category of task you want to change.

Tip

Immediately following these steps is an explanation of the type of information that appears in each column of the table. ∎

2. Click the Text tab (the Bar Text tab in the Format Bar dialog box) to select the information you want to display to the left, to the right, above, below, or inside the selected category of task bar (see Figure 8.11).

FIGURE 8.11

Be careful not to place too much information around task bars or you'll create a cluttered, illegible Gantt Chart.

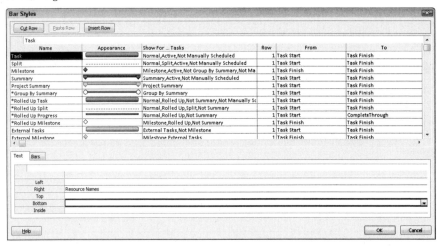

3. On the Text tab (the Bar Text tab in the Format Bar dialog box), click in the box beside the location where you want to display additional text.

   Project displays a drop-down arrow in the box.

4. Click the drop-down arrow and select the text you want to display on the chart portion of the Gantt Chart view for the selected category.

5. Click OK to save your changes.

The columns in the Bar Styles table at the top of the dialog box are as follows:

- **Name:** This column specifies the task bar category. To create a new task-bar category name, click the Insert Row button at the top of the dialog box and enter a name. This name appears in a legend for your chart when you print it.

- **Appearance:** This column provides a sample of the current formatting settings for the bar.

Note

When you click in any of the next four columns, Project displays a list box arrow at the right edge of the column. Open the list box to identify valid choices for these columns. ∎

- **Show For . . . Tasks:** This column defines the types of tasks that the specified formatting affects. You can specify the type of task to affect by selecting the category from a drop-down list or by entering a category name directly in the cell or in the entry bar. To specify more than one category, add a comma (,) after the first type and then select or type a second category. For example, to specify Normal tasks that are critical and in progress as a new category of task-bar style, choose or type in one of the following: Normal, Critical, In Progress.

Note

You can type directly in a Bar Styles table cell; you don't need to type in the Entry bar. ∎

- **Row:** The Row column specifies how many rows of bars (as many as four) that you want to display for each task. If you have only one row and you are showing a bar for both the baseline timing and progress, the bars overlap each other. If you want two separate bars, you need two rows. You also can add extra rows to accommodate text above or below task bars.

Tip

If a task fits in several categories, what happens? Project tries to display multiple formatting settings. (For example, if one category is solid blue and the other is a pattern, you get a blue pattern.) If Project can't display the formats together, the formatting for the item that is higher in this listing takes precedence. To modify the formatting precedence, use the Cut Row and Paste Row features to rearrange the rows in the Bar Styles dialog box. ∎

- **From and To:** These columns define the time period shown by the bar. The Progress bar, for example, shows the actual date that the task started and how much of the task was completed through today. Select the time frames from drop-down lists in each of these fields.

Figure 8.12 shows a schedule with expanded rows: The baseline duration appears beneath normal task bars; resource names appear to the right of task bars. To display the expanded rows and the baseline duration beneath normal tasks, I used the settings shown in Figure 8.13. In the top of the dialog box, I changed the Row setting for Task from 1 to 2; in the bottom of the dialog box, on the Text tab, I displayed Baseline Duration on the bottom of the tasks and Resource Names to the right of tasks.

Adding rows to each task can make your schedule easier to read.

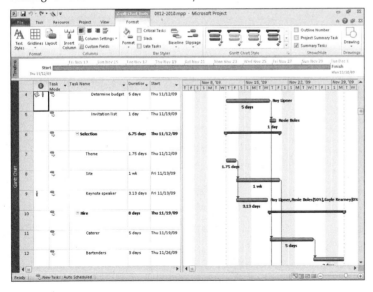

FIGURE 8.13

In the table, I changed the number of rows for Normal tasks. At the bottom of the dialog box, I added Baseline Duration to the bottom row of Normal tasks.

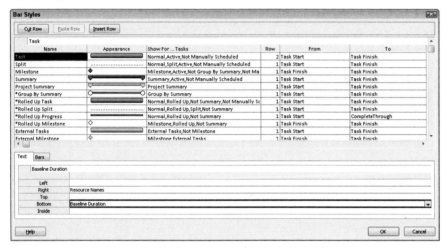

The settings in the Bar Styles dialog box enable you to modify, in great detail, the appearance of your schedule and how Project displays or prints it. If you print a legend along with your schedule, the legend reflects these changes. However, remember that modifying task bar colors isn't of much use in black-and-white printouts of schedules, and creating too many kinds of formatting with too many variables can make your schedule difficult to read. The advice given previously about standardizing these settings across your organization also holds for changes you make to formatting your task bars.

Changing the color of task bars

You can modify bar colors in both the Timeline view and the Team Planner view. You can, if you want, assign a different background color to each task that appears on the Timeline. In the Team Planner view, you can assign different colors to different categories of tasks. In Figure 8.14, I chose to use the Timeline view to simplify the screen.

Note
Project retains the changes you make if you display the Timeline above another view. ■

To assign a color to a task on the Timeline, click the task. Then click the Timeline Tools Format tab and use the buttons in the Font group to modify the appearance of the selected task. You can, for example, change the font, font size, and font color of the selected task, using the same techniques described earlier in this chapter in the section, "Formatting selected text."

Click the arrow beside the Background color button and click a color on the color palette that Project displays. Repeat the process for each task on the Timeline.

FIGURE 8.14

Assign different colors to tasks on the Timeline.

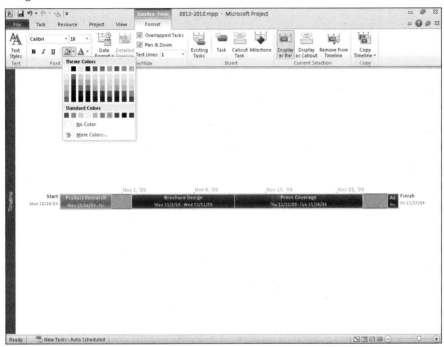

In the Team Planner view, you can assign colors to the bars that distinguish between the following types of tasks:

- Automatically scheduled tasks
- Manually scheduled tasks,
- Tasks on which work has been performed
- Tasks in other projects linked to your project
- Tasks that are late

Project assigns colors to each type of task by default, but you can change the colors. Click the Team Planner view shortcut button at the right edge of the Status Bar to switch to the view. Then click the Team Planner Tools Format tab and click the buttons in the Styles group to change both the inside and outside colors of a category of task (see Figure 8.15).

Any color changes you make to the Team Planner view apply only to that view in the current project.

FIGURE 8.15

Change the border and fill color of tasks in the Team Planner view.

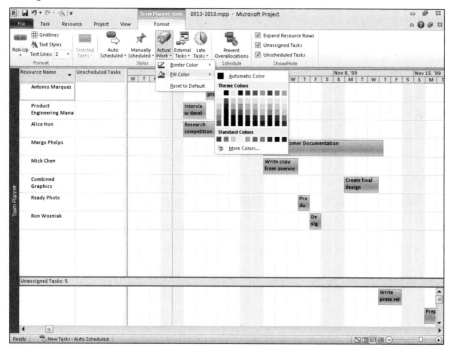

Changing the layout of the Gantt Chart

The layout of a Gantt Chart refers to the appearance of link lines, date formats used for information displayed near task bars, the height of task bars, and how Project displays certain characteristics of task bars.

Note

In views other than the Gantt Chart view, layout affects different elements. For example, in the Calendar view, layout affects the order in which Project lists multiple tasks on one calendar day and how it splits date bars. And, layout in the Network Diagram Chart view affects link lines and how Project handles page breaks. ■

To modify the layout of the Gantt Chart view, switch to the Gantt Chart view by clicking the Gantt Chart view shortcut at the right edge of the Status bar. Then click the Gantt Chart Tools Format tab and, in the Format group, click the Layout. Project displays the Layout dialog box shown in Figure 8.16.

FIGURE 8.16

Because layout affects different elements in different views, the Layout dialog box for the Gantt Chart view is different from the Layout dialog box for the Network Diagram and Calendar views.

You can set these options for the Gantt Chart layout:

- **Links:** Click one of these option buttons to display either no link lines or to use one of the available styles. Remember, link lines graphically show dependency relationships among tasks.

- **Date format:** Use this drop-down list to select a date or time format. Two interesting date formats include a week number (W4/4 and W4/4/09 12:33 PM) of the year and the day of the week. Therefore, W47/2/09 is November 23, 2009 (the second day of the 47th full week of 2009).

Note

Your nation or industry may use conventions for numbering weeks that differ from what Project produces. ∎

- **Bar Height:** Select a height in points for the task bars in your Gantt Chart.

The check boxes in the Layout dialog box have the following effects:

- **Always Roll Up Gantt bars:** This setting gives you the freedom to display your Gantt schedule by rolling up tasks onto summary bars.

- **Hide Rollup Bars when Summary Expanded:** This check box works with the preceding check box to hide rollup behavior if your schedule is completely expanded.

Cross-Reference

See Chapter 6 for more on Project's rollup capabilities. ∎

- **Round Bars to Whole Days:** This option works well on longer schedules but not as well on schedules with tasks that tend to run in hourly or half-day increments.

- **Show Bar Splits:** This option provides graphic representation of split tasks on the Gantt Chart.

Note

Split tasks are tasks that start, stop for a time, and then start again. For example, if you expect to begin hiring employees for the project, but you know that your company imposes a two-week hiring freeze during the last two weeks of the year for accounting purposes, you can create a split task (see Chapter 10). The setting for splits in the Layout dialog box simply enables you to choose to show the split task as separate task bars or as one continuous task bar. ■

- **Show Drawings:** If you select this check box, Project displays any drawings you've inserted into your chart.

Make any choices in the Layout dialog box and click OK to implement them.

Changing gridlines

Gridlines are those lines in the Gantt Chart and the Gantt table that mark off periods of time, rows and columns, pages in your schedule, and regular intervals in the chart. In Figure 8.17, gridlines mark off regular intervals across the chart; this format can help you read across the page on a long schedule. Also, the vertical line that marks the current date appears as a dashed line, rather than as the typical small-dotted line that you've seen in other figures in this chapter.

FIGURE 8.17

Displaying additional gridlines can make a schedule easier to read.

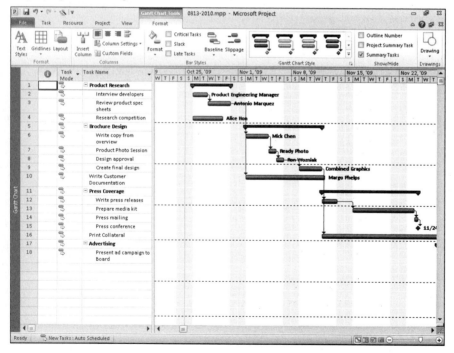

To modify gridlines, follow these steps:

1. Click the Gantt Chart Tools Format tab and, in the Format group, click the Gridlines button.

2. From the drop-down list that appears, click Gridlines. The dialog box shown in Figure 8.18 appears.

3. In the Line to Change list, the options Gantt Rows, Sheet Rows, and Sheet Columns enable you to set gridlines at regular intervals. For example, the project in Figure 8.17 has the Gantt Rows set to show at an interval of every four rows. You can change the line type and color only (not the interval) for the other choices in the Line to Change list. To modify these settings, highlight the kind of line that you want to change and then select the desired settings from the Type and Color drop-down lists.

FIGURE 8.18

You can choose gridlines from five different styles.

Tip

If you make substantial changes in the Gridlines dialog box, consider saving the file as a template for everyone else in your organization to use for their projects. This template not only saves you and your coworkers the effort of repeating the changes, but also helps to enforce consistency throughout your organization. ■

Changing network diagrams

You can change a network diagram in various ways, including these:

- Format the nodes, control their size and shape, and set the number of fields per node.
- Control the layout and adjust the thickness and color of the line that defines text boxes.
- Modify the style of text placed in boxes in the diagram.

In short, you have lots of control over the appearance of a network diagram.

Formatting nodes in a network diagram

You can modify the boxes that form the various nodes displayed in the Network Diagram view, in much the same way you format task bars in the Gantt Chart:

- You can format the color and line style of the box itself for each type of task.

- You can control the number of fields per node, the shape of the node, the horizontal and vertical alignment of text within the node, and the font used in each cell of the node.

Use these settings to draw the reader's attention to categories of nodes that you want to emphasize.

Note

As with task text and task bars in the Gantt Chart view, you can undo changes you make here. But be aware that Project has its own color and line scheme for various types of tasks, and you run the risk of formatting one category to look just like another category by mistake. Because interpreting the information in a project chart is so vital to its success, be careful about changing formatting defaults. ■

Modifying node box styles

You can change the formatting of network diagram boxes individually, or you can change the formatting of a particular category of boxes. To change an individual box, select the box in the network diagram, click the Network Diagram Tools Format tab, and choose Box from the Format group to display the dialog box shown in Figure 8.19.

FIGURE 8.19

To modify the appearance of a single box in the network diagram, use this dialog box.

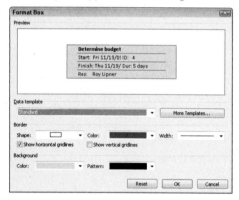

Use the Shape list to select one of ten shapes for the box. Similarly, use the Color list to identify the color for the lines of the box, and use the Width list to specify the width of the box's border. You also can use the lists in the Background section of the dialog box to set a background color and pattern for the node. Project combines all your changes; watch the Preview to determine their effects. When you finish, click OK to save the changes.

To format a category of box, such as all Critical Milestones, use the Box Styles dialog box, shown in Figure 8.20. You can display this dialog box by clicking the Network Diagram Tools Format tab and choosing Box Styles from the Format group. In the Style Settings For list at the left side of the dialog box, Project highlights the style of the Network Diagram node you selected before you opened the Box Styles dialog box, but you can make changes to any type of box by selecting it in the Style Settings For list.

FIGURE 8.20

Use this dialog box to select a category of box to format.

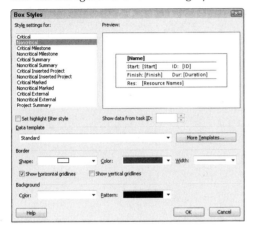

The current settings for the type of box selected in the Style Settings For list appear in the Preview window. The rest of the options in this dialog box are the same as the options shown in the Format Box dialog box, except for the Set Highlight Filter Style check box. You can filter information on the network diagram as described in Chapter 7. Selecting the Set Highlight Filter Style check box enables you to set the color that Project uses when you filter tasks on the network diagram.

Tip

Make Name one of the pieces of information that you display. Otherwise the flow of tasks in the network diagram chart is nearly incomprehensible. ■

Formatting fields that appear on nodes

Network diagram nodes display the following information by default: Task Name, Duration, ID, Start and Finish Dates, Percent Complete, and Resource Name, if assigned. However, you can display up to 16 fields of information. For example, to focus on costs in today's staff meeting, change the network diagram node information to Task Name, Baseline Cost, Actual Cost, Actual Overtime Cost, and Cost Variance. If your manager wants a network diagram chart report so he or she can see whether the project schedule is on track, change this information to Task Name, Critical, Free Slack, Early Finish, and Late Finish.

Caution

Just because you can do something doesn't mean you should do it. Although you can specify up to 16 pieces of information, beware of information overload. Providing too much information in a node makes the network diagram difficult to read and evaluate, and your reader may miss your point. ■

To modify a node, you can change the information shown in a node, the font used to display the information, and the horizontal and vertical alignment of the information. Follow these steps to modify a node:

1. Open either the Format Box or Box Styles dialog box.

2. Click the More Templates button. Project displays the Data Templates dialog box (see Figure 8.21).

FIGURE 8.21

Select a template to modify or copy, or create a new template.

Note

A template contains previously established node format settings. ■

3. Highlight the template that you want to change and click the Edit button.

Alternatively, you can create a new template by clicking the New button, or you can copy an existing template and make changes to the copy by clicking the Copy button. For this exercise, I copy the Standard template by clicking the Copy button. Regardless of whether you click the New, Edit or Copy button, Project displays the Data Template Definition dialog box (Figure 8.22).

Note

As you can see in Figure 8.21, you cannot edit the Standard template — the Edit button is not available. To base your changes on the Standard template, you must copy it, as I did in Step 3. ■

FIGURE 8.22

Use this dialog box to change the information you show in network diagram nodes.

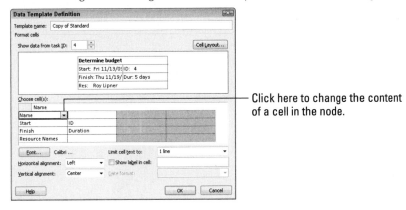

Click here to change the content of a cell in the node.

Note

The picture at the top of the dialog box provides a preview of the current structure of the cell. In this figure, the node contains eight cells — two on each row and four in each column. Project merges blank cells (one each in the top and bottom rows) with nonblank cells. ■

4. To change the contents of a cell of the node, click the corresponding cell in the middle of the dialog box.

    A list box arrow appears to the right of the cell. Open the list box to select a new field for the selected cell.

5. To change the font for a particular cell, select that cell and click the Font button.

    A dialog box appears, from which you can select a new font, the font size, and font attributes, such as boldface or italics.

6. Use the Horizontal Alignment and Vertical Alignment list boxes to change the alignment of text within its cell.

7. Use the Limit Cell Text To list box to specify the number of lines for each cell; a cell can have as many as three lines.

8. Select the Show Label in Cell check box to include an identifier in the cell for the type of information.

    For example, if you select the cell containing Name and then select the Show Label in Cell check box, the title of the task contains Name: followed by the title of the task.

Tip

You also can change the label text that appears in the box after you click the Show Label in Cell text box. ■

9. To increase or decrease the number of cells in the node, click the Cell Layout button to display the dialog box shown in Figure 8.23; in this dialog box, specify the number of cells for all nodes.

    After you click OK, Project redisplays the Data Template Definition dialog box, with the appropriate number of cells available for formatting.

FIGURE 8.23

Use this dialog box to change the number of cells in a node.

10. Click OK to close the Data Template Definition dialog box, click Close to close the Data Templates window, and click OK to close the Box Styles dialog box.

Changing the layout of the network diagram

A significant number of layout controls are available for the network diagram. As Figure 8.24 demonstrates, you can control the layout mode, the box arrangement, the link style and color, and several overall options for the network diagram from the Layout dialog box. To display the Layout dialog box, click the Network Diagram Tools Format tab and, in the Format group, click Layout.

FIGURE 8.24

You can control layout mode, box arrangement, and link style for the network diagram.

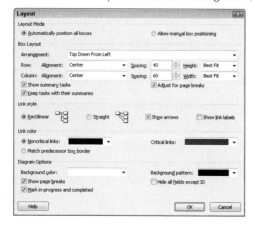

By default, Project automatically positions all boxes on the diagram, but you can position the boxes manually if you choose Allow Manual Box Positioning at the top of the Layout box.

Using the Arrangement list box, you can change the order in which Project displays the boxes. Choose from Top Down From Left, Top Down By Day, Top Down By Week, Top Down By Month, Top Down – Critical First, Centered From Left, and Centered From Top. The varying arrangements change the number of pages required to print your network diagram.

You also can change the row and column alignment and spacing as well as row height and column width. Using check boxes in the Box Layout section, you can hide or display summary tasks, keep tasks with their summaries, and adjust for page breaks.

From the Link Style section, you can control the style of the link lines, and you can choose to show arrows and link labels — which, by default, show the type of link dependency existing between two tasks (Finish-to-Start, Finish-to-Finish, and so on). And you can select different colors for both critical and noncritical links.

Cross-Reference

For more information on types of links, see Chapter 4. ■

Tip

To choose a background color or pattern for individual nodes, use the Format Box or Box Styles dialog box; you saw the Box Styles dialog box in Figure 8.20. ■

You use the options in the Diagram Options section of the Layout dialog box to format the network diagram as a whole (not the individual nodes):

- You can choose a background color and pattern.
- You can mark in-progress tasks with half an X and completed tasks with an entire X.
- If you hide all information on the nodes except the ID, Project reduces the size of the nodes on your network diagram — which reduces the number of pages that print.
- You can also choose to show page breaks, which appear as dotted lines on-screen in the Network Diagram view.

In Figure 8.25, I've included link labels and hidden all task information except the ID. A page break appears at the right side of the diagram (shown as a vertical dotted line in the figure).

Remember, creating too many kinds of formatting with too many variables can make your schedule difficult to read. The advice given previously in this chapter about standardizing these settings across your organization also holds for changes that you make to network diagram layouts.

FIGURE 8.25

By adjusting the layout of the network diagram, you can dramatically change its appearance.

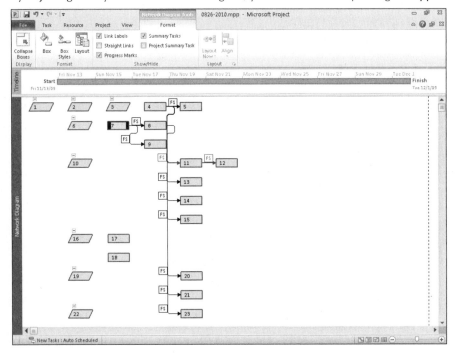

Formatting the Calendar view

Project's Calendar view looks and acts like the Calendar view in Outlook, giving you weekly and monthly views of your project. If you want, you can create your own view to help you focus on the tasks for a specific time frame.

As I mention earlier in the chapter, you format text in the Calendar view just as you would format text in any other view. Although you can't format the text of individual items in the Calendar view, you can format categories of text using the Text Styles dialog box (see "Applying formatting to categories of text," earlier in this chapter). To open the Text Styles dialog box, click the Calendar Tools Format tab and, in the Format group, click Text Styles.

You also can change the gridlines that Project uses to separate days using the techniques I describe earlier in this chapter in the section, "Changing gridlines." To display the Gridlines dialog box, click the Calendar Tools Format tab and, in the Format group, click Gridlines.

Note
You cannot apply background color to the bars on the Calendar, but you can apply color to the bar outline and to the text. ■

Formatting the Calendar entries

By default, when you display the Calendar view, entries appear in boxes that Project calls bars. You can change the style of these bars. For example, you can make all critical tasks appear on the Calendar in red. Click the Calendar Tools Format tab and, in the Format group, click Bar Styles to display the dialog box shown in Figure 8.26. Select a type of task from the list at the left. As you make changes in the Bar Shape area and the Text area, watch the Sample window at the bottom of the box to see the effects of your changes.

FIGURE 8.26

Use this dialog box to change the appearance of the Calendar view. Assign different font colors to different task types, or use a line instead of a bar to represent the task's duration.

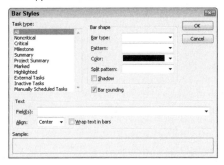

In the Bar shape area, use the Bar type box to control how Project displays tasks. Select Line, Bar, or None; choosing None hides the selected task type from the Calendar view. If you choose Bar from the Bar type box, you can open the Pattern list box and select a pattern, which appears inside the bar for the task type. You can also choose a pattern for Project to display between split tasks from the Split pattern box. Select the Shadow box to display a shadow behind a bar. (This option is available only if you choose Bar from the Bar type box.)

Select the *Bar rounding* check box to tell Project to draw the bar for tasks that take less than one day so that the task's duration is implied. For example, use bar rounding to tell Project to draw a bar that extends three-quarters of the width of the day to represent a task that takes 0.75 days. If you don't use bar rounding, Project doesn't imply the duration of the task by the length of the bar.

In the Text area (refer to Figure 8.26), you can include Project fields for each task type; to include more than one field, separate fields from each other with commas. You can use the Align list box to center, left-align, or right-align text.

If you chose Bar as the Bar Type, you can select the Wrap Text in Bars check box to have Project wrap text so that it fits within the box. For example, if you show the task name and duration in the bar, and the task name is fairly long but the task lasts only one day, Project wraps the text so that the task occupies more than one row when it appears on the calendar — and you'll be able to read all displayed information about every task. If you don't select the Wrap Text in Bars check box,

Project displays only as much information as it can fit in a bar sized to match the task's duration. In the example just described, you may not see the entire task name, and you certainly won't see the task duration, because the bar spans only one day.

Changing the Calendar layout

You can view your project a month at a time or a week at a time, or you can create a custom view. Click the Month button or the Week button to view your project in those increments. You can then use the arrows just below the buttons to move forward or backward by the selected increment.

In Figure 8.27, I created a custom view that shows two weeks. To create a custom view, click the Custom button; the Zoom dialog box appears (see Figure 8.28).

FIGURE 8.27

You can create custom Calendar views to help you focus on a specific time period.

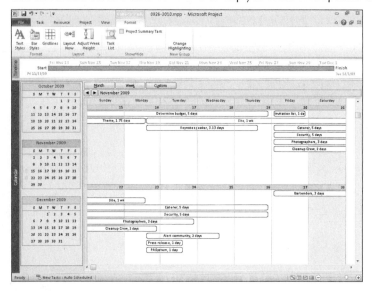

FIGURE 8.28

Use this dialog box to specify a time frame to display in the Calendar view.

You can use the Layout dialog box, shown in Figure 8.29, to change the layout of tasks in the Calendar view. By default, Project displays tasks in the Calendar view using the currently sorted order of tasks. To display the Layout dialog box, click the Calendar Tools Format tab and then click the dialog-box-launcher button in the lower-right corner of the Layout group.

Use the Layout dialog box to change the way that Project presents tasks in the Calendar view.

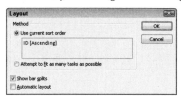

Cross-Reference

You can read about sorting tasks in Chapter 7. ■

Remove the check from the Show Bar Splits check box to hide the designation for split tasks from the Calendar view. Select the Automatic Layout check box to have Project automatically adjust the Calendar view to accommodate tasks that you add or delete.

If you don't want tasks to appear in the Calendar view using the currently sorted order, select the Attempt to Fit as Many Tasks as Possible option button. Project sorts tasks by Total Slack and then by Duration (longest task first) to try to fit the maximum number of tasks into the rows for a week without overlapping bars.

When multiple tasks fall on the same day, a small arrow pointing down appears in the upper-left corner of the day; you can click the down arrow to see a list of tasks scheduled for that day. In Figure 8.30, for example, multiple tasks appear on Friday, November 20 through Wednesday, November 25; I opened the list on November 24.

FIGURE 8.30

When multiple tasks appear on the same day, Project displays a small black arrow in the upper-left corner of the day.

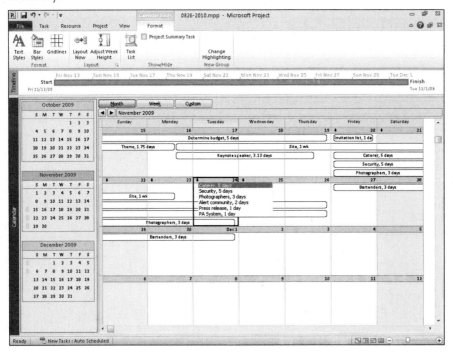

Inserting Visuals

We're living in the age of multimedia. Visual elements have a way of getting a message across that simple text often can't match; not surprisingly, statistics show that 75 percent of the world learns visually. In Project, you can insert graphic images (for example, photos, illustrations, or diagrams) in the following places:

- In a Gantt Chart, in the task bar area
- In notes (task, resource, or assignment)
- In headers, footers, and chart legends
- In resource or task forms

You also can copy your Project schedule into other Office products.

Copying pictures

Suppose you've written a report in Microsoft Word and you would *really* like to include your Gantt Chart in the report. You can print it on a separate page, but you can also insert it as a picture in the appropriate place in your Word document. Or suppose you want to post a picture of your Project schedule on the Web. You can easily create a picture for either of these purposes by using the Copy Picture dialog box.

Cross-Reference

The Copy Picture to Office Wizard is no longer available in Project 2010. However, you can accomplish much of what you might need to do by using techniques described in Chapter 18. ∎

Using the Copy Picture command, you copy your Project schedule to the Windows Clipboard and then paste it into any application as a graphic image. This technique copies only a picture without Project fields. Follow these steps:

1. Switch to the Gantt Chart view and click the Task tab. In the Clipboard group, click the down arrow beside the Copy button and select Copy Picture (see Figure 8.31).

FIGURE 8.31

Select Copy Picture to create a graphic image you can paste into any application.

Click here to Select Copy Picture

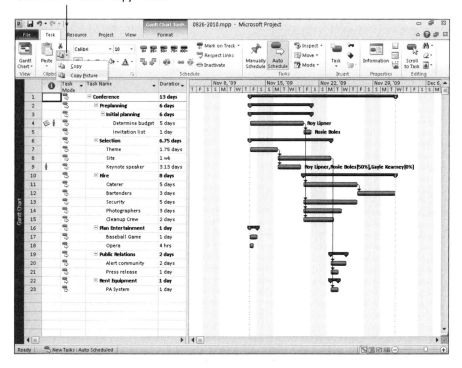

2. When Project displays the Copy Picture dialog box shown in Figure 8.32, click the For Screen button in the Render Image section and then click OK. If the image you're copying will fit well into another document, Project simply copies the picture to the Windows Clipboard. But if the picture you're copying is especially large, Project warns you — and displays a dialog box that gives you the opportunity to change the size of the picture before saving or pasting it. To create a graphic image file that you can use on a Web page or in a document, select the *To GIF image file* option in the Copy Picture dialog box.

FIGURE 8.32

Choose the For Screen option to copy a Project schedule to the Windows Clipboard.

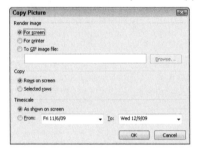

3. After you've copied the picture, simply switch to the other document in which you want to place the picture and click the Paste button in that document.

   Figure 8.33 shows a Gantt Chart in Microsoft Word.

When you use the Paste button, you place a graphic image in your document. The image is not linked to Project in any way, which imposes limits on what you can do from in the program into which you pasted the chart:

- You can't edit the chart to make scheduling changes.
- You can't double-click the image to open the chart in Project.

Note

Even if you choose the Paste Special command, the image you copied from Project is exactly that — an image. It is not a Project file that you can link to from another application. ∎

When you render the image for a printer, Project copies the image to the Windows Clipboard but formats the image using your printer driver. If you have a black-and-white printer, the image appears in shades of gray rather than in the colors you see on-screen. If you have a color printer, the image appears in color, much the same as it looks on-screen. You can view the image by pasting it into another application.

FIGURE 8.33

After you use the Copy Picture command to render an image for the screen, you can paste the image into any document.

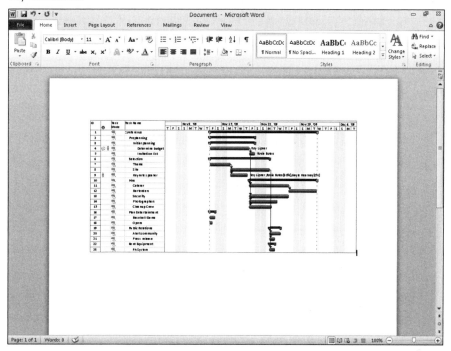

Using visuals in schedules

Because project management is often a serious, information-oriented business, you don't want to overdo the visuals. Remember: Both the Gantt Chart and the network diagram are visuals. Pictures of bunnies and curly doodads aren't likely to sit well with the head of your engineering division. However, used judiciously, images can reinforce the information about your project and lend a professional look to your reports.

Consider using graphics in the following ways:

- Add a company logo to the header of your schedule so that it appears at the top of every page.

- Add a photograph of each of your project's key resources in his or her resource note. The photo helps you get to know all the team members in a large-scale project so that you can address them by name when you see them.

- If a particular task involves a schematic or diagram of a product or other data related to the task, place a copy of or link to the diagram or other data in the task notes for reference.

Caution

Placing graphics in a schedule makes your file larger and possibly increases calculation time; for this reason, use graphics sparingly and only as needed. ■

Note

Graphic objects come in a variety of file formats, depending on the type of graphic and the program in which it was created. You can use scanned images, photo files, illustrations such as clip art, a chart that you've created in Excel, a Word table, or even a video clip. Check the Internet for sources of graphics files, or use the images that are available to the Microsoft Office family of products. ■

To insert an object into a header, footer, or legend, click the File tab and, in the Back Stage view, click Print. Click the Page Setup button to display the Page Setup dialog box shown in Figure 8.34. Click the appropriate tab and use the Insert Picture button to open a dialog box that enables you to select a picture file to insert.

FIGURE 8.34

You can click this button to open the Insert Picture dialog box and add a picture to a header.

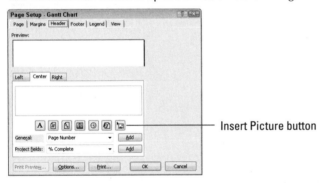

Insert Picture button

On the Notes tab in the Task Information dialog box and the Resource Information dialog box, you can add a link to another file and display that link as either a graphic image or an icon; once inserted, you can double-click the link to open the file. Suppose that you have an Excel worksheet that provides information that you need for a budgeting task. You can insert a link to the worksheet on the Notes tab of the Task Information dialog box for the budgeting task. Follow these steps to insert a graphic object link to worksheet data:

1. Double-click the task with which you want to associate the worksheet.

2. Click the Notes tab.

3. Click the Insert Object button — the rightmost button on the toolbar that appears above the area where you can type a note. The Insert Object dialog box appears (see Figure 8.35).

FIGURE 8.35

Select the file you want to associate with a task.

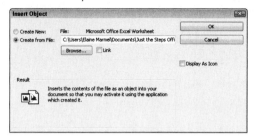

4. Select the Create from File option.

5. Click the Browse button to select the worksheet.

6. Click the OK button.

The worksheet information appears as a graphic on the Notes tab, as shown in Figure 8.36.

FIGURE 8.36

The information in the file appears as a graphic object on the Notes tab of the Task Information dialog box.

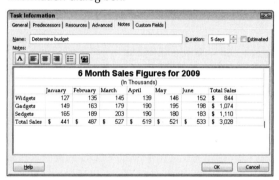

You can double-click the graphic image to open the workbook containing the information.

Instead, suppose you want to see a chart of the information on the Notes tab. Logically, you create the chart in the worksheet and then use the steps just given. But if you try this approach, you'll find that you get the entire worksheet — both numbers and chart. To place *just* the chart on the Notes tab, follow these steps:

1. Select the chart in Excel and click the Copy button to copy the chart to the Clipboard.

2. Switch to Project.

3. Double-click the appropriate task to open the Task Information dialog box.

4. Click the Notes tab.

5. Right-click in the area where the note would appear, and from the submenu that appears, click Paste.

   The chart alone appears on the Notes tab (see Figure 8.37).

FIGURE 8.37

You can copy any image that you placed on the Windows Clipboard into Project.

Tip

You can place any image directly on the Gantt Chart. Don't open the Task Information dialog box. Instead, copy the image to the Clipboard; then, after you switch to Project, click the Paste button. ∎

Summary

In this chapter, you discovered many ways to do the following:

- Format text for individual selections or globally by category of task.
- Format task bars and the information that is displayed near them.
- Format network diagram boxes and change the information that you display in the Network Diagram view.
- Control the appearance of the Calendar view.
- Insert visuals in task notes or project headers and footers.

Chapter 9 explains how to report on a project's progress.

Reporting on Progress

A s shown in Chapters 6 and 7, Project contains various views that help you evaluate the progress of your project, identify areas with problems, and even resolve problems. Although you can print views, sometimes you want to present information in a format that isn't available in any view. This chapter explores printing views and examines the use of reports for presenting your Project information.

In addition to printing views, you can use your project's data to create two kinds of reports:

- Traditional text reports, typically in row-and-column format. These types of reports have long been available in Project.

- Visual reports, which present pictures of your project's data in the form of charts and diagrams. Visual reports export your project data to either Excel or Visio.

Setting Up to Print a View or Report

You can print the various views in Project, or you can print reports. Regardless of what you're printing, you use the same process to set up to print.

Tip

To print a Project view, select the view that you want to print. To select a report to print, see the subsequent sections of this chapter. ■

Click the File tab and, in Backstage view, click Print; your screen will look similar to the one shown in Figure 9.1.

FIGURE 9.1

You set up print information in the Backstage view.

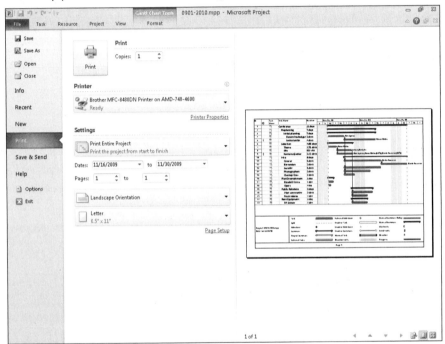

The information is interactive; you click buttons to make selections. For example, click the Printer button to select a printer. In the Settings section, you can click the button at the top of the section to select whether to print your entire project or only selected dates or pages; you also can opt to print Notes, All Sheet Columns, and Left Column of Pages Only.

Below that button, you can select a date range and a page range to print.

Use the other two buttons in the Settings section to specify your paper orientation and size.

When you click the Page Setup button, Project displays the Page Setup dialog box (see Figure 9.2). From the Page tab, you can set orientation and scaling. Using scaling, you may be able to fit the printed text onto one page.

FIGURE 9.2

The Page tab of the Page Setup dialog box.

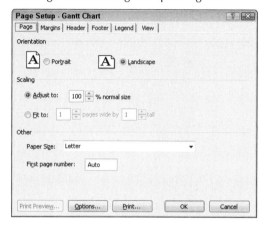

Note

You can set the first page number of the printed product. For example, suppose your project is 10 pages long but you intend to print only pages 5 and 6. Typically you'd want to number those pages as 1 and 2 — and you can do exactly that by entering 1 in the First page number box. ■

From the Margins tab, shown in Figure 9.3, you can change the margins for your printed text and determine whether a border should appear.

FIGURE 9.3

The Margins tab of the Page Setup dialog box.

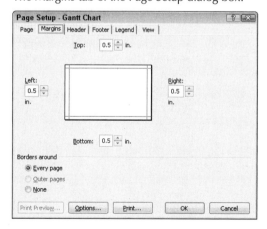

From the Header tab, shown in Figure 9.4, you can define and align header information to appear at the top of every page you print. Use either the buttons at the bottom of the box or the list box to add information you want Project to update automatically, such as page numbers.

The Header tab of the Page Setup dialog box.

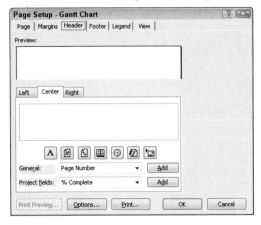

Tip

You can include Project level fields in the header, footer, or legend of your printed product. From the appropriate tab of the Page Setup dialog box, use the Project fields list box to select the field you want to include. ∎

The Footer tab works just as the Header tab does. You can align and include the same kind of updating information in the footer on each page of your printed text.

The Page Setup dialog box changes just slightly, depending on the view you were using when you opened the dialog box. For example, the Legend tab (see Figure 9.5) is available only when you're printing a Calendar, Gantt Chart, or Network Diagram view. The Legend tab works just the same as the Header and Footer tabs; you can align and include the same kind of updating information.

The View tab, shown in Figure 9.6, enables you to control what Project prints, such as all or only some columns.

FIGURE 9.5

The Legend tab of the Page Setup dialog box.

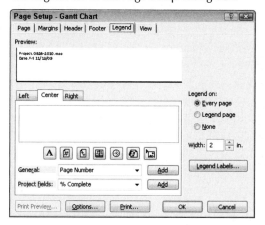

FIGURE 9.6

The View tab of the Page Setup dialog box.

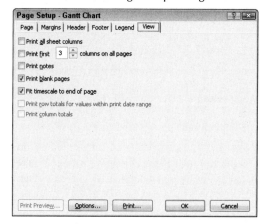

Two check boxes — Print Column Totals and Print Row Totals for Values Within Print Date Range — appear on the View tab in views where they apply: the Task Usage view and the Resource Usage view (the boxes are unavailable in all other views). When you select the Print Column Totals check box, Project calculates totals in memory and adds a row to the printed page showing totals for timephased data as well as for sheet data. You can take advantage of the Print Row Totals for Values Within Print Date Range check box when you're printing a Usage view. Selecting this box tells Project to add a column to the printed page that shows totals for the timephased data with the date range you specify in the Print dialog box. The totals print on the same page as the last rows or columns of data, before any Notes pages.

Tip

In many cases, you can add a column to a table that gives you the same information you can get in the row totals. The column prints where you place it, whereas the row totals print on a separate page. ∎

When you're ready to print the report, specify the number of copies to print in Backstage view (refer to Figure 9.1) and then click the Print button. If you change your mind and don't want to print the report, click the File tab to return to Project.

Creating Text Reports

All text reports in Project have certain common characteristics. For example, you can print any report or you can review the report on-screen.

Note

Project organizes text reports into categories of reports that are related to the same subject; for example, all cost reports fall into the Costs category. ∎

Follow these steps to display the reports that are available in a particular category:

1. Click the Project tab and, in the Reports group, click Reports to open the Reports dialog box (see Figure 9.7).

FIGURE 9.7

Select a report category from the Reports dialog box.

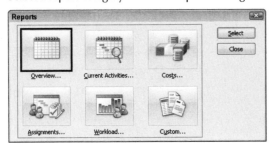

2. Click the category of report you want.
3. Click Select. Project displays the reports available in that category.
4. Select a report.
5. Click Select. Project displays the report on-screen in Backstage view (see Figure 9.8).

Use the buttons in the lower-right corner of the screen to move around the report. From left to right, the three buttons at the right edge of the screen offer these capabilities:

- Zoom to view the report in the size it will print.
- View the report one page at a time.
- View multiple pages of the report at the same time.

Tip

If you click directly on a report page, Project displays the same view that you see if you click the second button at the bottom-right corner of the screen. If you click a second time, Project zooms in to display the report in the size it will print. ■

If your report contains multiple pages, you can use the small arrows in the lower-right corner to navigate through the report. To print the report, use the information in the preceding section, "Setting Up to Print a View or Report" to help you.

FIGURE 9.8

A preview of a report in Backstage view.

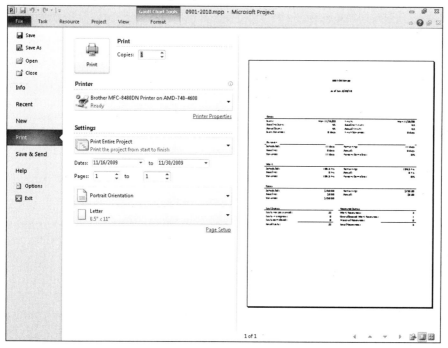

Looking at the big picture

When you select Overview in the Reports dialog box, Project displays the top-level, summary-type reports (see Figure 9.9).

Note

You can use the Edit button to change the information that appears on the report. You can also use the Edit button to customize the report, which I describe near the end of the discussion of text reports. ∎

FIGURE 9.9

The reports available in the Overview category.

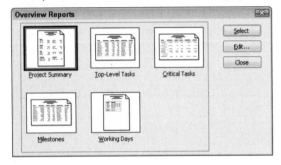

Project Summary

The Project Summary report (see Figure 9.10) shows top-level information about your project. This report presents summarized information about dates, duration, work, costs, task status, and resource status.

Top Level Tasks

The Top Level Tasks report (see Figure 9.11), shows — as of today's date — the summary tasks at the highest level in your project. You can see scheduled start and finish dates, the percentage complete for each task, the cost, and the work required to complete the task.

FIGURE 9.10

The Project Summary report.

reports-2010

as of Fri 2/26/10

Dates

Start:	Mon 2/22/10	Finish:	Tue 3/9/10
Baseline Start:	NA	Baseline Finish:	NA
Actual Start:	Mon 2/22/10	Actual Finish:	NA
Start Variance:	0 days	Finish Variance:	0 days

Duration

Scheduled:	12 days	Remaining:	10.29 days
Baseline:	0 days?	Actual:	1.71 days
Variance:	12 days	Percent Complete:	14%

Work

Scheduled:	362.5 hrs	Remaining:	289.13 hrs
Baseline:	0 hrs	Actual:	73.38 hrs
Variance:	362.5 hrs	Percent Complete:	20%

Costs

Scheduled:	$250.00	Remaining:	$200.00
Baseline:	$0.00	Actual:	$50.00
Variance:	$250.00		

Task Status

Tasks not yet started:	22
Tasks in progress:	6
Tasks completed:	2
Total Tasks:	30

Resource Status

Work Resources:	7
Overallocated Work Resources:	1
Material Resources:	0
Total Resources:	8

FIGURE 9.11

The Top Level Tasks report.

Top Level Tasks as of Sat 11/14/09
reports-2010

ID	Task Mode	Task Name	Duration	Start	Finish	% Comp.	Cost	Work
1	Auto Scheduled	Conference	11 days	Mon 2/22/10	Mon 3/8/10	0%	$0.00	0 hrs
2	Auto Scheduled	Preplanning	11 days	Mon 2/22/10	Mon 3/8/10	41%	$0.00	72 hrs
9	Auto Scheduled	Selection	8 days	Mon 2/22/10	Wed 3/3/10	34%	$250.00	117.5 hrs
14	Auto Scheduled	Hire	9 days	Thu 2/25/10	Tue 3/9/10	0%	$0.00	130 hrs
21	Auto Scheduled	Plan Entertainment	2.5 days	Thu 2/25/10	Mon 3/1/10	0%	$0.00	11 hrs
25	Auto Scheduled	Public Relations	3 days	Wed 3/3/10	Fri 3/5/10	0%	$0.00	24 hrs
29	Auto Scheduled	Rent Equipment	1 day	Wed 3/3/10	Wed 3/3/10	0%	$0.00	8 hrs

Critical Tasks

The Critical Tasks report (see Figure 9.12) shows the status of the tasks on the critical path of your project — those tasks that make the project late if you don't complete them on time. This report displays each task's planned duration, start and finish dates, the resources assigned to the task, and the predecessors and successors of the task.

FIGURE 9.12

The Critical Tasks report.

Critical Tasks as of Sat 11/14/09
reports-2010

ID	Indicators	Task Mode	Task Name	Duration	Start	Finish	Predecessors	Resource Names
14		Auto Scheduled	Hire	9 days	Thu 2/25/10	Tue 3/9/10		
15		Auto Scheduled	Caterer	5 days	Thu 2/25/10	Wed 3/3/10	4	Donna Ballioux

Day	Hours	Standard Rate	Lag
16	Bartenders	FS	0 days

ID	Indicators	Task Mode	Task Name	Duration	Start	Finish	Predecessors	Resource Names
16		Auto Scheduled	Bartenders	3 days	Thu 3/4/10	Mon 3/8/10	15	Carla West

Day	Hours		Standard Rate	Lag
20	Complete hiring phase		FS	0 days

ID	Indicators	Task Mode	Task Name	Duration	Start	Finish	Predecessors	Resource Names
20		Auto Scheduled	Complete hiring phase	1 day	Tue 3/9/10	Tue 3/9/10	16	

Milestones

The Milestones report (see Figure 9.13) shows information about each milestone in your project. If you marked summary tasks to appear as milestones in the Task Information dialog box, summary tasks also appear on this report as milestones. For each milestone or summary task, Project displays the planned duration, start and finish dates, predecessors, and the resources assigned to the milestone.

FIGURE 9.13

The Milestones report.

Milestones as of Sat 11/14/09
reports-2010

ID	Indicators	Task Mode	Task Name	Duration	Start	Finish	Predecessors	Resource Names
2		Auto Scheduled	Preplanning	11 days	Mon 2/22/10	Mon 3/8/10		
3		Auto Scheduled	Initial planning	11 days	Mon 2/22/10	Mon 3/8/10		
9		Auto Scheduled	Selection	8 days	Mon 2/22/10	Wed 3/3/10		
5		Auto Scheduled	Settle on a budget	1 day	Thu 2/25/10	Thu 2/25/10	4	
14		Auto Scheduled	Hire	9 days	Thu 2/25/10	Tue 3/9/10		
21		Auto Scheduled	Plan Entertainment	2.5 days	Thu 2/25/10	Mon 3/1/10		
24		Auto Scheduled	Complete entertainment phase	1 day	Fri 2/26/10	Mon 3/1/10	23	
13		Auto Scheduled	Complete selection phase	1 day	Wed 3/3/10	Wed 3/3/10	11	
25		Auto Scheduled	Public Relations	3 days	Wed 3/3/10	Fri 3/5/10		
28		Auto Scheduled	Complete public relations phase	1 day	Fri 3/5/10	Fri 3/5/10	26,27	
8		Auto Scheduled	Complete initial planning	1 day	Mon 3/8/10	Mon 3/8/10	7	
20		Auto Scheduled	Complete hiring phase	1 day	Tue 3/9/10	Tue 3/9/10	16	

Working Days

As Figure 9.14 demonstrates, the Working Days report shows the base calendar information for your project. You can see the name of the base calendar for the project and the working hours established for each day of the week, along with any exceptions you defined.

FIGURE 9.14

The Working Days report.

Base Calendar as of Sat 11/14/09
reports-2010

BASE CALENDAR:	Standard
Day	Hours
Sunday	Nonworking
Monday	8:00 AM - 12:00 PM, 1:00 PM - 5:00 PM
Tuesday	8:00 AM - 12:00 PM, 1:00 PM - 5:00 PM
Wednesday	8:00 AM - 12:00 PM, 1:00 PM - 5:00 PM
Thursday	8:00 AM - 12:00 PM, 1:00 PM - 5:00 PM
Friday	8:00 AM - 12:00 PM, 1:00 PM - 5:00 PM
Saturday	Nonworking
Exceptions:	None

Generating reports on costs

When you select Costs in the Reports dialog box, Project displays thumbnail sketches of the reports that describe the costs associated with your project (see Figure 9.15).

FIGURE 9.15

The reports available in the Cost category.

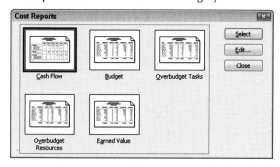

Note

You can use the Edit button to change the information that appears on the report. You can also use the Edit button to customize the report, which I discuss near the end of the discussion of text reports. ■

Cash Flow

The Cash Flow report (see Figure 9.16) is a tabular report that shows, by task, the costs for weekly time increments.

FIGURE 9.16

The Cash Flow report.

Cash Flow as of Sat 11/14/09
reports-2010

	2/21/10	2/28/10	3/7/10	3/14/10	Total
Conference					
Preplanning					
Initial planning					
Determine budget					
Settle on a budget					
Invitation list					
Send out invitations					
Complete initial planning					
Selection					
Theme					
Site	$250.00				$250.00
Keynote speaker	$500.00				$500.00
Complete selection phase					
Hire					
Caterer					
Bartenders					
Security					
Photographers					
Cleanup Crew					
Complete hiring phase					
Plan Entertainment					
Baseball Game					
Opera					
Complete entertainment phase					
Public Relations					
Alert community					
Press release					
Complete public relations phase					
Rent Equipment					
PA System	2/21/10	2/28/10	3/7/10	3/14/10	Total
Total	$750.00				$750.00

If you click Cash Flow in the Cost Reports dialog box (previously shown in Figure 9.16) and then select Edit before you choose Select ➪ Project, the Crosstab Report dialog box opens (see Figure 9.17). On the Definition tab, you can change the time increments.

FIGURE 9.17

Use the Crosstab Report dialog box to change the default settings for the report.

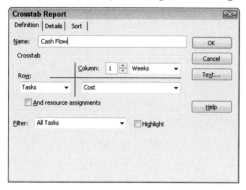

See the section "Customizing reports," later in this chapter, for more information about the Crosstab Report dialog box.

Earned Value

The Earned Value report (see Figure 9.18) shows you the status of each task's costs when you compare planned to actual costs. Some column headings in this report may seem cryptic; see Table 9.1 for translations.

FIGURE 9.18

The Earned Value report.

Earned Value as of Sat 11/14/09
reports-2010

ID	Task Name	Planned Value PV (BCWS)	Earned Value EV (BCWP)	AC (ACWP)	SV	CV	EAC	BAC	VAC
1	Conference	$12,087.50	$0.00	$0.00	($12,087.50)	$0.00	$0.00	$12,087.50	$12,087.50
4	Determine budget	$1,200.00	$1,200.00	$0.00	$0.00	$1,200.00	$0.00	$1,200.00	$1,200.00
5	Settle on a budget	$0.00	$0.00	$0.00	$0.00	$0.00	$0.00	$0.00	$0.00
6	Invitation list	$640.00	$320.00	$0.00	($320.00)	$320.00	$0.00	$640.00	$640.00
7	Send out invitations	$1,120.00	$0.00	$0.00	($1,120.00)	$0.00	$0.00	$1,120.00	$1,120.00
8	Complete initial planning	$0.00	$0.00	$0.00	$0.00	$0.00	$0.00	$0.00	$0.00
10	Theme	$640.00	$640.00	$0.00	$0.00	$640.00	$0.00	$640.00	$640.00
11	Site	$2,250.00	$450.00	$50.00	($1,800.00)	$400.00	$250.00	$2,250.00	$2,000.00
12	Keynote speaker	$752.50	$188.13	$0.00	($564.38)	$188.13	$0.00	$752.50	$752.50
13	Complete selection phase	$0.00	$0.00	$0.00	$0.00	$0.00	$0.00	$0.00	$0.00
15	Caterer	$1,000.00	$0.00	$0.00	($1,000.00)	$0.00	$0.00	$1,000.00	$1,000.00
16	Bartenders	$720.00	$0.00	$0.00	($720.00)	$0.00	$0.00	$720.00	$720.00
17	Security	$2,000.00	$0.00	$0.00	($2,000.00)	$0.00	$0.00	$2,000.00	$2,000.00
18	Photographers	$260.00	$0.00	$0.00	($260.00)	$0.00	$0.00	$260.00	$260.00
19	Cleanup Crew	$310.00	$0.00	$0.00	($310.00)	$0.00	$0.00	$310.00	$310.00
20	Complete hiring phase	$0.00	$0.00	$0.00	$0.00	$0.00	$0.00	$0.00	$0.00
22	Baseball Game	$240.00	$0.00	$0.00	($240.00)	$0.00	$0.00	$240.00	$240.00
23	Opera	$75.00	$0.00	$0.00	($75.00)	$0.00	$0.00	$75.00	$75.00
24	Complete entertainment phase	$0.00	$0.00	$0.00	$0.00	$0.00	$0.00	$0.00	$0.00
26	Alert community	$320.00	$0.00	$0.00	($320.00)	$0.00	$0.00	$320.00	$320.00
27	Press release	$240.00	$0.00	$0.00	($240.00)	$0.00	$0.00	$240.00	$240.00
28	Complete public relations phase	$0.00	$0.00	$0.00	$0.00	$0.00	$0.00	$0.00	$0.00
30	PA System	$320.00	$0.00	$0.00	($320.00)	$0.00 ,	$0.00	$320.00	$320.00
		$24,175.00	$2,798.13	$50.00	($21,376.88)	$2,748.13	$250.00	$24,175.00	$23,925.00

Note

Even printed in landscape format, the columns of this report don't fit on one page. The EAC, BAC and the VAC columns appear on Page 2 of the report. ■

Cross-Reference

For more information about how Project handles earned value, see Chapter 15. ■

TABLE 9.1

Headings in the Earned Value Report

Heading	Translation
BCWS	Budgeted Cost of Work Scheduled
BCWP	Budgeted Cost of Work Performed
ACWP	Actual Cost of Work Performed
SV	Schedule Variance
CV	Cost Variance
BAC	Budgeted at Completion
EAC	Estimate at Completion
VAC	Variance at Completion

Project calculates BCWS, BCWP, ACWP, SV, and CV through the project status date. SV represents the cost difference between current progress and the baseline plan, and Project calculates this value as BCWP minus BCWS. CV represents the cost difference between actual costs and planned costs at the current level of completion, and Project calculates this value as BCWP minus ACWP. EAC shows the planned costs based on costs already incurred plus additional planned costs. VAC represents the variance between the baseline cost and the combination of actual plus planned costs for a task.

Budget

The Budget report (see Figure 9.19) lists all tasks and shows the budgeted costs as well as the variance between budgeted and actual costs.

Note

This report doesn't have much meaning unless you've saved a baseline of your project; the values in the variance column change from $0.00 as you complete tasks. ■

FIGURE 9.19

The Budget report.

Budget Report as of Sat 11/14/09
reports-2010

ID	Task Name	Fixed Cost	Fixed Cost Accrual	Total Cost	Baseline	Variance	Actual	Remaining
11	Site	$250.00	Prorated	$250.00	$2,250.00	($2,000.00)	$50.00	$200.00
1	Conference	$0.00	Prorated	$0.00	$12,087.50	($12,087.50)	$0.00	$0.00
4	Determine budget	$0.00	Prorated	$0.00	$1,200.00	($1,200.00)	$0.00	$0.00
5	Settle on a budget	$0.00	Prorated	$0.00	$0.00	$0.00	$0.00	$0.00
6	Invitation list	$0.00	Prorated	$0.00	$640.00	($640.00)	$0.00	$0.00
7	Send out invitations	$0.00	Prorated	$0.00	$1,120.00	($1,120.00)	$0.00	$0.00
8	Complete initial planning	$0.00	Prorated	$0.00	$0.00	$0.00	$0.00	$0.00
10	Theme	$0.00	Prorated	$0.00	$640.00	($640.00)	$0.00	$0.00
12	Keynote speaker	$0.00	Prorated	$0.00	$752.50	($752.50)	$0.00	$0.00
13	Complete selection phase	$0.00	Prorated	$0.00	$0.00	$0.00	$0.00	$0.00
15	Caterer	$0.00	Prorated	$0.00	$1,000.00	($1,000.00)	$0.00	$0.00
16	Bartenders	$0.00	Prorated	$0.00	$720.00	($720.00)	$0.00	$0.00
17	Security	$0.00	Prorated	$0.00	$2,000.00	($2,000.00)	$0.00	$0.00
18	Photographers	$0.00	Prorated	$0.00	$260.00	($260.00)	$0.00	$0.00
19	Cleanup Crew	$0.00	Prorated	$0.00	$310.00	($310.00)	$0.00	$0.00
20	Complete hiring phase	$0.00	Prorated	$0.00	$0.00	$0.00	$0.00	$0.00
22	Baseball Game	$0.00	Prorated	$0.00	$240.00	($240.00)	$0.00	$0.00
23	Opera	$0.00	Prorated	$0.00	$75.00	($75.00)	$0.00	$0.00
24	Complete entertainment phase	$0.00	Prorated	$0.00	$0.00	$0.00	$0.00	$0.00
26	Alert community	$0.00	Prorated	$0.00	$320.00	($320.00)	$0.00	$0.00
27	Press release	$0.00	Prorated	$0.00	$240.00	($240.00)	$0.00	$0.00
28	Complete public relations phase	$0.00	Prorated	$0.00	$0.00	$0.00	$0.00	$0.00
30	PA System	$0.00	Prorated	$0.00	$320.00	($320.00)	$0.00	$0.00
		$250.00		$250.00	$24,175.00	($23,925.00)	$50.00	$200.00

Overbudget reports

Project contains two Overbudget reports: one for tasks and one for resources. Neither report prints if you haven't yet indicated that some tasks are at least partially completed and you haven't assigned costs to resources. Instead, you see a message that indicates Project has no data to print.

The Overbudget Tasks report (see Figure 9.20) shows cost, baseline, variance, actual, and remaining information about tasks that exceed their budgeted amounts.

FIGURE 9.20

The Overbudget Tasks report.

Overbudget Tasks as of Sat 11/14/09
reports2-2010

ID	Task Name	Fixed Cost	Fixed Cost Accrual	Total Cost	Baseline	Variance	Actual	Remaining
10	Keynote speaker	$0.00	Prorated	$5,750.00	$500.00	$5,250.00	$5,750.00	$0.00
9	Site	$250.00	Prorated	$3,850.00	$250.00	$3,600.00	$3,850.00	$0.00
		$250.00		$9,600.00	$750.00	$8,850.00	$9,600.00	$0.00

The Overbudget Resources report (see Figure 9.21) displays resources whose costs will exceed baseline estimates, based on the current progress of the project.

The Overbudget Resources report.

Overbudget Resources as of Sat 11/14/09
reports2-2010

ID	Resource Name	Cost	Baseline Cost	Variance	Actual Cost	Remaining
5	Gayle Kearney	$3,920.00	$500.00	$3,420.00	$500.00	$3,420.00
		$3,920.00	$500.00	$3,420.00	$500.00	$3,420.00

Producing reports related to time

By using the Current Activities reporting category, you can produce reports on the timing of your project. Click Current Activities in the Reports dialog box. Choose Select to open the Current Activity Reports dialog box (see Figure 9.22) and view the reports available in this category.

The reports available in the Current Activities category.

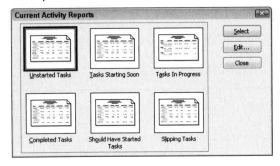

Unstarted Tasks

The Unstarted Tasks report (see Figure 9.23) lists the tasks that have not yet started, sorted by the scheduled start date. For each task, Project displays the duration, start and finish dates, predecessor, and resource information (if you assigned resources).

FIGURE 9.23

The Unstarted Tasks report.

Unstarted Tasks as of Sat 11/14/09
reports-2010

ID	Indicators	Task Mode	Task Name	Duration	Start	Finish	Predecessors	Resource Names
1		Auto Scheduled	Conference	11 days	Mon 2/22/10	Mon 3/8/10		
5		Auto Scheduled	Settle on a budget	1 day	Thu 2/25/10	Thu 2/25/10	4	
15		Auto Scheduled	Caterer	5 days	Thu 2/25/10	Wed 3/3/10	4	Donna Ballioux
		Day Hours Standard Rate Lag Start Rem. Cost						
17		Auto Scheduled	Security	5 days	Thu 2/25/10	Wed 3/3/10	4	Roy Lipner
		Day Hours Standard Rate Lag Start Rem. Cost						
18		Auto Scheduled	Photographers	1 day	Thu 2/25/10	Thu 2/25/10	4	Joe Johnson[50%],Intern
		Day Hours Standard Rate Lag Start Rem. Cost						
19		Auto Scheduled	Cleanup Crew	2 days	Thu 2/25/10	Fri 2/26/10	4	Intern,Joe Johnson[50%]
		Day Hours Standard Rate Lag Start Rem. Cost						
22		Auto Scheduled	Baseball Game	1 day	Thu 2/25/10	Thu 2/25/10	4	Carla West
		Day Hours Standard Rate Lag Start Rem. Cost						
23		Auto Scheduled	Opera	4 hrs	Fri 2/26/10	Fri 2/26/10	4,22	Joe Johnson[75%]
		Day Hours Standard Rate Lag Start Rem. Cost						
24		Auto Scheduled	Complete entertainment phase	1 day	Fri 2/26/10	Mon 3/1/10	23	
7		Auto Scheduled	Send out invitations	4 days	Tue 3/2/10	Fri 3/5/10	6	Gayle Kearney
		Day Hours Standard Rate Lag Start Rem. Cost						
13		Auto Scheduled	Complete selection phase	1 day	Wed 3/3/10	Wed 3/3/10	11	
26		Auto Scheduled	Alert community	2 days	Wed 3/3/10	Thu 3/4/10	11	Intern
		Day Hours Standard Rate Lag Start Rem. Cost						
27		Auto Scheduled	Press release	1 day	Wed 3/3/10	Wed 3/3/10	11	Do Lahr
		Day Hours Standard Rate Lag Start Rem. Cost						
30		Auto Scheduled	PA System	1 day	Wed 3/3/10	Wed 3/3/10	11	Rosie Boles
		Day Hours Standard Rate Lag Start Rem. Cost						
16		Auto Scheduled	Bartenders	3 days	Thu 3/4/10	Mon 3/8/10	15	Carla West
		Day Hours Standard Rate Lag Start Rem. Cost						
28		Auto Scheduled	Complete public relations phase	1 day	Fri 3/5/10	Fri 3/5/10	26,27	
8		Auto Scheduled	Complete initial planning	1 day	Mon 3/8/10	Mon 3/8/10	7	
20		Auto Scheduled	Complete hiring phase	1 day	Tue 3/9/10	Tue 3/9/10	16	

Tasks Starting Soon

When you print the Tasks Starting Soon report (see Figure 9.24), Project displays the Date Range dialog boxes. The information you provide in these two dialog boxes tells Project the date range to use when selecting tasks for this report. In the first dialog box, specify the earlier date; in the second dialog box, specify the later date, using the mm/dd/yy format. On the report, Project includes tasks that start or finish between the two dates you specify.

The information that appears on the report is similar to the information you find on the Unstarted Tasks report: the duration, start and finish dates, predecessors, and resource information (if you assigned resources). Completed tasks also appear on this report; the check mark that appears in the Indicators column on the report identifies completed tasks.

FIGURE 9.24

The Tasks Starting Soon report.

Tasks Starting Soon as of Sat 11/14/09
reports-2010

ID	Indicators	Task Mode	Task Name	Duration	Start	Finish	Predecessors	Resource Names
1		Auto Scheduled	Conference	11 days	Mon 2/22/10	Mon 3/8/10		
4	✓	Auto Scheduled	Determine budget	3 days	Mon 2/22/10	Wed 2/24/10		Roy Lipner
		Day Hours Standard Rate Lag Start Rem. Cost						
10	✓	Auto Scheduled	Theme	2 days	Mon 2/22/10	Tue 2/23/10		Rosie Boles
		Day Hours Standard Rate Lag Start Rem. Cost						
11		Auto Scheduled	Site	5 days	Wed 2/24/10	Tue 3/2/10	10	Intern,Do Lahr
		Day Hours Standard Rate Lag Start Rem. Cost						
12		Auto Scheduled	Keynote speaker	2.69 days	Wed 2/24/10	Fri 2/26/10	10	Gayle Kearney
		Day Hours Standard Rate Lag Start Rem. Cost						
5		Auto Scheduled	Settle on a budget	1 day	Thu 2/25/10	Thu 2/25/10	4	
15		Auto Scheduled	Caterer	5 days	Thu 2/25/10	Wed 3/3/10	4	Donna Ballioux
		Day Hours Standard Rate Lag Start Rem. Cost						
17		Auto Scheduled	Security	5 days	Thu 2/25/10	Wed 3/3/10	4	Roy Lipner
		Day Hours Standard Rate Lag Start Rem. Cost						
18		Auto Scheduled	Photographers	1 day	Thu 2/25/10	Thu 2/25/10	4	Joe Johnson[50%],Intern
		Day Hours Standard Rate Lag Start Rem. Cost						
19		Auto Scheduled	Cleanup Crew	2 days	Thu 2/25/10	Fri 2/26/10	4	Intern,Joe Johnson[50%]
		Day Hours Standard Rate Lag Start Rem. Cost						
22		Auto Scheduled	Baseball Game	1 day	Thu 2/25/10	Thu 2/25/10	4	Carla West
		Day Hours Standard Rate Lag Start Rem. Cost						

Tasks in Progress

As Figure 9.25 shows, the Tasks in Progress report lists tasks that have started but not yet finished. You see the tasks' duration, start and planned finish dates, predecessors, and resource information (if you assigned resources).

FIGURE 9.25

The Tasks in Progress report.

Tasks In Progress as of Sat 11/14/09
reports-2010

ID	Indicators	Task Mode	Task Name	Duration	Start	Finish	Predecessors	Resource Names
February 2010								
11		Auto Scheduled	Site	5 days	Wed 2/24/10	Tue 3/2/10	10	Intern,Do Lahr
		Day Hours Standard Rate Lag Start Rem. Cost						
12		Auto Scheduled	Keynote speaker	2.69 days	Wed 2/24/10	Fri 2/26/10	10	Gayle Kearney
		Day Hours Standard Rate Lag Start Rem. Cost						
6		Auto Scheduled	Invitation list	2 days	Fri 2/26/10	Mon 3/1/10	5	Rosie Boles
		Day Hours Standard Rate Lag Start Rem. Cost						
March 2010								
11		Auto Scheduled	Site	5 days	Wed 2/24/10	Tue 3/2/10	10	Intern,Do Lahr
		Day Hours Standard Rate Lag Start Rem. Cost						
6		Auto Scheduled	Invitation list	2 days	Fri 2/26/10	Mon 3/1/10	5	Rosie Boles
		Day Hours Standard Rate Lag Start Rem. Cost						

Completed Tasks

The Completed Tasks report (see Figure 9.26) lists tasks that have completed. You can see the actual duration, the actual start and finish dates, the percent complete (always 100 percent — if a task is only partially complete, it won't appear on this report), the cost, and the work hours.

FIGURE 9.26

The Completed Tasks report.

Completed Tasks as of Sat 11/14/09
reports-2010

ID	Task Mode	Task Name	Duration	Start	Finish	% Comp.	Cost	Work
February 2010								
4	Auto Scheduled	Determine budget	3 days	Mon 2/22/10	Wed 2/24/10	100%	$0.00	24 hrs
10	Auto Scheduled	Theme	2 days	Mon 2/22/10	Tue 2/23/10	100%	$0.00	16 hrs

Should Have Started Tasks

When you print the Should Have Started Tasks report (see Figure 9.27), you must supply a date by which tasks should have started. Project uses this date to determine which tasks appear on the report.

FIGURE 9.27

The Should Have Started Tasks report.

Should Have Started Tasks as of Sat 11/14/09
reports-2010

ID	Task Mode	Task Name	Start	Finish	Baseline Start	Baseline Finish	Start Var.	Finish Var.
1	Auto Scheduled	Conference	Mon 2/22/10	Mon 3/8/10	Mon 6/26/06	Mon 7/10/06	955 days	955 days
2	Auto Scheduled	Preplanning	Mon 2/22/10	Mon 3/8/10	Mon 6/26/06	Thu 7/6/06	955 days	957 days
3	Auto Scheduled	Initial planning	Mon 2/22/10	Mon 3/8/10	Mon 6/26/06	Thu 7/6/06	955 days	957 days
5	Auto Scheduled	Settle on a budget	Thu 2/25/10	Thu 2/25/10	NA	NA	0 days	0 days

Day	Hours	Standard Rate	Lag
6	Invitation list	FS	0 days

ID	Task Mode	Task Name	Start	Finish	Baseline Start	Baseline Finish	Start Var.	Finish Var.
14	Auto Scheduled	Hire	Thu 2/25/10	Tue 3/9/10	Thu 6/29/06	Mon 7/10/06	955 days	956 days
15	Auto Scheduled	Caterer	Thu 2/25/10	Wed 3/3/10	Thu 6/29/06	Wed 7/5/06	955 days	955 days

Day	Hours	Standard Rate	Lag
16	Bartenders	FS	0 days

ID	Task Mode	Task Name	Start	Finish	Baseline Start	Baseline Finish	Start Var.	Finish Var.
17	Auto Scheduled	Security	Thu 2/25/10	Wed 3/3/10	Thu 6/29/06	Wed 7/5/06	955 days	955 days
18	Auto Scheduled	Photographers	Thu 2/25/10	Thu 2/25/10	Thu 6/29/06	Thu 6/29/06	955 days	955 days
19	Auto Scheduled	Cleanup Crew	Thu 2/25/10	Fri 2/26/10	Thu 6/29/06	Fri 6/30/06	955 days	955 days
21	Auto Scheduled	Plan Entertainment	Thu 2/25/10	Mon 3/1/10	Thu 6/29/06	Fri 6/30/06	955 days	956 days
22	Auto Scheduled	Baseball Game	Thu 2/25/10	Thu 2/25/10	Thu 6/29/06	Thu 6/29/06	955 days	955 days

Day	Hours	Standard Rate	Lag
23	Opera	FS	0 days

ID	Task Mode	Task Name	Start	Finish	Baseline Start	Baseline Finish	Start Var.	Finish Var.
23	Auto Scheduled	Opera	Fri 2/26/10	Fri 2/26/10	Fri 6/30/06	Fri 6/30/06	955 days	955 days

Day	Hours	Standard Rate	Lag
24	Complete entertainment phase	FS	0 days

ID	Task Mode	Task Name	Start	Finish	Baseline Start	Baseline Finish	Start Var.	Finish Var.
24	Auto Scheduled	Complete entertainment phase	Fri 2/26/10	Mon 3/1/10	NA	NA	0 days	0 days

For each task on the report, Project displays planned start and finish dates, baseline start and finish dates, and variances for start and finish dates. Successor task information appears when a task on the report has a successor defined.

Slipping Tasks

The Slipping Tasks report (see Figure 9.28) lists the tasks that have been rescheduled from their baseline start dates.

FIGURE 9.28

The Slipping Tasks report.

Slipping Tasks as of Sat 11/14/09
reports-2010

ID	Task Mode	Task Name	Start	Finish	Baseline Start	Baseline Finish	Start Var.	Finish Var.
1	Auto Scheduled	Conference	Mon 2/22/10	Mon 3/8/10	Mon 6/26/06	Mon 7/10/06	955 days	955 days
2	Auto Scheduled	Preplanning	Mon 2/22/10	Mon 3/8/10	Mon 6/26/06	Thu 7/6/06	955 days	957 days
3	Auto Scheduled	Initial planning	Mon 2/22/10	Mon 3/8/10	Mon 6/26/06	Thu 7/6/06	955 days	957 days
9	Auto Scheduled	Selection	Mon 2/22/10	Wed 3/3/10	Mon 6/26/06	Tue 7/4/06	955 days	956 days
11	Auto Scheduled	Site	Wed 2/24/10	Tue 3/2/10	Wed 6/28/06	Tue 7/4/06	955 days	955 days

	Day	Hours		Standard Rate	Lag			
	13	Complete selection phase	FS		0 days			
	26	Alert community	FS		0 days			
	27	Press release	FS		0 days			
	30	PA System	FS		0 days			

ID	Task Mode	Task Name	Start	Finish	Baseline Start	Baseline Finish	Start Var.	Finish Var.
12	Auto Scheduled	Keynote speaker	Wed 2/24/10	Fri 2/26/10	Wed 6/28/06	Fri 6/30/06	955 days	955 days
14	Auto Scheduled	Hire	Thu 2/25/10	Tue 3/9/10	Thu 6/29/06	Mon 7/10/06	955 days	956 days
15	Auto Scheduled	Caterer	Thu 2/25/10	Wed 3/3/10	Thu 6/29/06	Wed 7/5/06	955 days	955 days

	Day	Hours		Standard Rate	Lag			
	16	Bartenders	FS		0 days			

ID	Task Mode	Task Name	Start	Finish	Baseline Start	Baseline Finish	Start Var.	Finish Var.
17	Auto Scheduled	Security	Thu 2/25/10	Wed 3/3/10	Thu 6/29/06	Wed 7/5/06	955 days	955 days
18	Auto Scheduled	Photographers	Thu 2/25/10	Thu 2/25/10	Thu 6/29/06	Thu 6/29/06	955 days	955 days
19	Auto Scheduled	Cleanup Crew	Thu 2/25/10	Fri 2/26/10	Thu 6/29/06	Fri 6/30/06	955 days	955 days
21	Auto Scheduled	Plan Entertainment	Thu 2/25/10	Mon 3/1/10	Thu 6/29/06	Fri 6/30/06	955 days	956 days
22	Auto Scheduled	Baseball Game	Thu 2/25/10	Thu 2/25/10	Thu 6/29/06	Thu 6/29/06	955 days	955 days

	Day	Hours		Standard Rate	Lag			
	23	Opera	FS		0 days			

ID	Task Mode	Task Name	Start	Finish	Baseline Start	Baseline Finish	Start Var.	Finish Var.
6	Auto Scheduled	Invitation list	Fri 2/26/10	Mon 3/1/10	Thu 6/29/06	Fri 6/30/06	956 days	956 days

	Day	Hours		Standard Rate	Lag			
	7	Send out invitations	FS		0 days			

ID	Task Mode	Task Name	Start	Finish	Baseline Start	Baseline Finish	Start Var.	Finish Var.
23	Auto Scheduled	Opera	Fri 2/26/10	Fri 2/26/10	Fri 6/30/06	Fri 6/30/06	955 days	955 days

	Day	Hours		Standard Rate	Lag			
	24	Complete entertainment phase	FS		0 days			

ID	Task Mode	Task Name	Start	Finish	Baseline Start	Baseline Finish	Start Var.	Finish Var.
7	Auto Scheduled	Send out invitations	Tue 3/2/10	Fri 3/5/10	Mon 7/3/06	Thu 7/6/06	956 days	956 days

	Day	Hours		Standard Rate	Lag			
	8	Complete initial planning	FS		0 days			

ID	Task Mode	Task Name	Start	Finish	Baseline Start	Baseline Finish	Start Var.	Finish Var.
25	Auto Scheduled	Public Relations	Wed 3/3/10	Fri 3/5/10	Wed 7/5/06	Thu 7/6/06	955 days	956 days
26	Auto Scheduled	Alert community	Wed 3/3/10	Thu 3/4/10	Wed 7/5/06	Thu 7/6/06	955 days	955 days

	Day	Hours		Standard Rate	Lag			
	28	Complete public relations phase	FS		0 days			

ID	Task Mode	Task Name	Start	Finish	Baseline Start	Baseline Finish	Start Var.	Finish Var.
27	Auto Scheduled	Press release	Wed 3/3/10	Wed 3/3/10	Wed 7/5/06	Wed 7/5/06	955 days	955 days

	Day	Hours		Standard Rate	Lag			
	28	Complete public relations phase	FS		0 days			

ID	Task Mode	Task Name	Start	Finish	Baseline Start	Baseline Finish	Start Var.	Finish Var.
29	Auto Scheduled	Rent Equipment	Wed 3/3/10	Wed 3/3/10	Wed 7/5/06	Wed 7/5/06	955 days	955 days
30	Auto Scheduled	PA System	Wed 3/3/10	Wed 3/3/10	Wed 7/5/06	Wed 7/5/06	955 days	955 days
16	Auto Scheduled	Bartenders	Thu 3/4/10	Mon 3/8/10	Thu 7/6/06	Mon 7/10/06	955 days	955 days

	Day	Hours		Standard Rate	Lag			
	20	Complete hiring phase	FS		0 days			

This report displays the same information as the information you saw on the Should Have Started Tasks report, but the presentation of the information changes the focus of your attention.

Preparing reports on work assignments

Using the Assignments reporting category of the Reports dialog box, you can produce reports on the resource assignments in your project. Click the Assignments category. Choose Select to open the Assignment Reports dialog box (see Figure 9.29) and view the reports available in this category.

FIGURE 9.29

The reports available in the Assignments category.

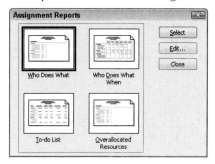

Who Does What

The Who Does What report (see Figure 9.30) lists resources and the tasks to which they are assigned, the amount of work planned for each task, and the planned start and finish dates.

FIGURE 9.30

The Who Does What report.

Who Does What as of Sat 11/14/09
Reports

ID	ⓘ	Resource Name				Work	

1		Roy Lipner				64 hrs	
	ID	Task Name	Units	Work	Delay	Start	Finish
	4	Determine budget	100%	24 hrs	0 days	Mon 02/22/10	Wed 02/24/10
	17	Security	100%	40 hrs	0 days	Thu 02/25/10	Wed 03/03/10
2		Rosie Boles				40 hrs	
	ID	Task Name	Units	Work	Delay	Start	Finish
	6	Invitation list	100%	16 hrs	0 days	Fri 02/26/10	Mon 03/01/10
	10	Theme	100%	16 hrs	0 days	Mon 02/22/10	Tue 02/23/10
	30	PA System	100%	8 hrs	0 days	Wed 03/03/10	Wed 03/03/10
3		Gayle Kearney				53.5 hrs	
	ID	Task Name	Units	Work	Delay	Start	Finish
	7	Send out invitations	100%	32 hrs	0 days	Tue 03/02/10	Fri 03/05/10
	12	Keynote speaker	100%	21.5 hrs	0 days	Wed 02/24/10	Fri 02/26/10
4		Intern				72 hrs	
	ID	Task Name	Units	Work	Delay	Start	Finish
	11	Site	100%	40 hrs	0 days	Wed 02/24/10	Tue 03/02/10
	18	Photographers	100%	8 hrs	0 days	Thu 02/25/10	Thu 02/25/10
	19	Cleanup Crew	100%	8 hrs	0 days	Thu 02/25/10	Thu 02/25/10
	26	Alert community	100%	16 hrs	0 days	Wed 03/03/10	Thu 03/04/10
5		Do Lahr				48 hrs	
	ID	Task Name	Units	Work	Delay	Start	Finish
	11	Site	100%	40 hrs	0 days	Wed 02/24/10	Tue 03/02/10
	27	Press release	100%	8 hrs	0 days	Wed 03/03/10	Wed 03/03/10
6		Joe Johnson				13 hrs	
	ID	Task Name	Units	Work	Delay	Start	Finish
	18	Photographers	50%	4 hrs	0 days	Thu 02/25/10	Thu 02/25/10
	19	Cleanup Crew	50%	6 hrs	0 days	Thu 02/25/10	Fri 02/26/10
	23	Opera	75%	3 hrs	0 days	Fri 02/26/10	Fri 02/26/10
7		Carla West				32 hrs	
	ID	Task Name	Units	Work	Delay	Start	Finish
	16	Bartenders	100%	24 hrs	0 days	Thu 03/04/10	Mon 03/08/10
	22	Baseball Game	100%	8 hrs	0 days	Thu 02/25/10	Thu 02/25/10
8		Donna Ballioux				40 hrs	
	ID	Task Name	Units	Work	Delay	Start	Finish
	15	Caterer	100%	40 hrs	0 days	Thu 02/25/10	Wed 03/03/10

Who Does What When

The Who Does What When report (see Figure 9.31) also lists resources and the tasks to which they are assigned. This report, however, focuses your attention on the daily work scheduled for each resource on each task.

FIGURE 9.31

The Who Does What When report.

Who Does What When as of Sat 11/14/09
Reports

	02/22	02/23	02/24	02/25	02/26	02/27	02/28	03/01	03/02	03/03	03/04	03/05	03/06	03/07	03/08	03/09	03/10
Roy Lipner	8 hrs	8 hrs	8 hrs	8 hrs	8 hrs			8 hrs	8 hrs	8 hrs							
Determine budget	8 hrs	8 hrs	8 hrs														
Security				8 hrs	8 hrs			8 hrs	8 hrs	8 hrs							
Rosie Boles	8 hrs	8 hrs			8 hrs			8 hrs		8 hrs							
Invitation list					8 hrs			8 hrs									
Theme	8 hrs	8 hrs															
PA System										8 hrs							
Gayle Kearney			8 hrs	8 hrs	#######				8 hrs	8 hrs	8 hrs	8 hrs					
Send out invitations									8 hrs	8 hrs	8 hrs	8 hrs					
Keynote speaker			8 hrs	8 hrs	#######												
Intern			8 hrs	24 hrs	8 hrs			8 hrs	8 hrs	8 hrs	8 hrs						
Site			8 hrs	8 hrs	8 hrs			8 hrs	8 hrs								
Photographers				8 hrs													
Cleanup Crew				8 hrs													
Alert community										8 hrs	8 hrs						
Do Lahr			8 hrs	8 hrs	8 hrs			8 hrs	8 hrs	8 hrs							
Site			8 hrs	8 hrs	8 hrs			8 hrs	8 hrs								
Press release										8 hrs							
Joe Johnson				8 hrs	5 hrs												
Photographers				4 hrs													
Cleanup Crew				4 hrs	2 hrs												
Opera					3 hrs												
Carla West				8 hrs							8 hrs	8 hrs			8 hrs		
Bartenders											8 hrs	8 hrs			8 hrs		
Baseball Game				8 hrs													
Donna Ballioux				8 hrs	8 hrs			8 hrs	8 hrs	8 hrs							
Caterer				8 hrs	8 hrs			8 hrs	8 hrs	8 hrs							

Tip

You can use the Edit button in the Assignment Reports dialog box to change the timescale on the report from daily to some other increment, such as weekly. Also, you may want to change the date format on the Details tab to a wider format if you see pound signs (###) in your report. See the section "Customizing reports," later in this chapter, for more information. ■

To Do List

The To Do List report (see Figure 9.32) lists, on a weekly basis, the tasks assigned to a resource you select. When you are ready to print this report, Project first displays the Using Resource dialog box, which contains the Show Tasks Using list box. When you open the list box, you see a list of your resources. Select a resource, and click OK. The To Do List report shows the task ID number, duration, start and finish dates, predecessors, and a list of all the resources assigned to each task.

FIGURE 9.32

The To Do List report.

To Do List as of Sat 11/14/09
Reports

ID	ⓘ	Task Name	Duration	Start	Finish	Predecessors	Resource Names
Week of February 21							
10	■	Theme	2 days	Mon 02/22/10	Tue 02/23/10		Rosie Boles
11		Site	3.67 days	Wed 02/24/10	Mon 03/01/10	10	Intern,Do Lahr,Rosie Boles
6		Invitation list	2 days	Fri 02/26/10	Mon 03/01/10	5	Rosie Boles
Week of February 28							
11		Site	3.67 days	Wed 02/24/10	Mon 03/01/10	10	Intern,Do Lahr,Rosie Boles
6		Invitation list	2 days	Fri 02/26/10	Mon 03/01/10	5	Rosie Boles
30		PA System	1 day	Mon 03/01/10	Tue 03/02/10	11	Rosie Boles

Overallocated Resources

The Overallocated Resources report (see Figure 9.33) shows the overallocated resources, the tasks to which they are assigned, and the total hours of work assigned to them. You can also see the details of each task, such as the allocation, the amount of work, any delay, and the start and finish dates.

FIGURE 9.33

The Overallocated Resources report.

Overallocated Resources as of Sat 11/14/09
Reports

ID	❶	Resource Name				Work		
3	◇	Gayle Kearney				77.5 hrs		
	ID	Task Name	Units	Work	Delay	Start	Finish	
	7	Send out invitations	100%	32 hrs	0 days	Tue 03/02/10	Fri 03/05/10	
	12	Keynote speaker	100%	21.5 hrs	0 days	Wed 02/24/10	Fri 02/26/10	
	16	Bartenders	100%	24 hrs	0 days	Mon 03/01/10	Thu 03/04/10	
2	◇	Rosie Boles				61.33 hrs		
	ID	Task Name	Units	Work	Delay	Start	Finish	
	6	Invitation list	100%	16 hrs	0 days	Fri 02/26/10	Mon 03/01/10	
	10	Theme	100%	16 hrs	0 days	Mon 02/22/10	Tue 02/23/10	
	30	PA System	100%	8 hrs	0 days	Mon 03/01/10	Tue 03/02/10	
	11	Site	100%	21.33 hrs	1 day	Thu 02/25/10	Mon 03/01/10	
1	◇	Roy Lipner				84 hrs		
	ID	Task Name	Units	Work	Delay	Start	Finish	
	4	Determine budget	100%	24 hrs	0 days	Mon 02/22/10	Wed 02/24/10	
	17	Security	100%	40 hrs	0 days	Thu 02/25/10	Wed 03/03/10	
	15	Caterer	100%	20 hrs	0 days	Thu 02/25/10	Mon 03/01/10	

222.83 hrs

Reporting on workloads

You can use the Workload category to produce reports on task and resource usage in your project. Click Workload in the Reports dialog box and choose Select to open the Workload Reports dialog box (see Figure 9.34).

FIGURE 9.34

The Workload Reports dialog box.

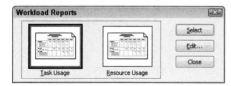

Task Usage

The Task Usage report (see Figure 9.35) lists tasks and the resources assigned to each task. It also displays the amount of work that's assigned to each resource in weekly time increments.

FIGURE 9.35

The Task Usage report.

Task Usage as of Mon 11/16/09
reports2-2010.mpp

	2/21/10	2/28/10	3/7/10	3/14/10	3/21/10	Total
Conference						
Preplanning						
Initial planning						
Determine budget	32 hrs	32 hrs				64 hrs
Roy Lipner	32	32				64
Invitation list		8 hrs	16 hrs			24 hrs
Rosie Boles		8	16			24
Send out invitations						
Selection						
Theme	24 hrs					24 hrs
Rosie Boles	24					24
Site	32 hrs	14 hrs				46 hrs
Intern	16	4				20
Do Lahr	16	10				26
Keynote speaker	13.5 hrs	13 hrs				26.5 hrs
Roy Lipner	6	13				19
Rosie Boles	7.5					7.5
Gayle Kearney						
Hire						
Caterer		8 hrs	32 hrs			40 hrs
Gayle Kearney		8	32			40
Bartenders			8 hrs	16 hrs		24 hrs
Gayle Kearney			8	16		24
Security		16 hrs	24 hrs			40 hrs
Roy Lipner		8	12			20
Joe Johnson		8	12			20
Photographers		12 hrs				12 hrs
Rosie Boles		4				4
Intern		8				8
Cleanup Crew		12 hrs	4 hrs			16 hrs
Intern		8				8
Joe Johnson		4	4			8
Plan Entertainment						
Baseball Game	8 hrs					8 hrs
Gayle Kearney	8					8
Opera	4 hrs					4 hrs
Gayle Kearney	4					4
Public Relations						
Alert community		16 hrs				16 hrs
Do Lahr		16				16
Press release		8 hrs				8 hrs
Do Lahr		8				8
Rent Equipment						
PA System						
Events						
Baseball Game						
Opera						
Total	113.5 ...	139 hrs	84 hrs	16 hrs		352.5 hrs

Tip

You can change the time increment by clicking Edit in the Workload Reports dialog box. See the section "Customizing reports," later in this chapter, for more information about editing reports. ∎

Resource Usage

The Resource Usage report (see Figure 9.36) lists resources and the tasks to which they are assigned. As does the Task Usage report, this report shows the amount of work assigned to each resource for each task in weekly time increments, but this report focuses your attention on the resource.

FIGURE 9.36

The Resource Usage report.

Resource Usage as of Mon 11/16/09
reports2-2010.mpp

	2/21/10	2/28/10	3/7/10	3/14/10	3/21/10	Total
Roy Lipner	38 hrs	53 hrs	12 hrs			103 hrs
Determine budget	32 hrs	32 hrs				64 hrs
Keynote speaker	6 hrs	13 hrs				19 hrs
Security		8 hrs	12 hrs			20 hrs
Rosie Boles	31.5 hrs	12 hrs	16 hrs			59.5 hrs
Invitation list		8 hrs	16 hrs			24 hrs
Theme	24 hrs					24 hrs
Keynote speaker	7.5 hrs					7.5 hrs
Photographers		4 hrs				4 hrs
Intern	16 hrs	20 hrs				36 hrs
Site	16 hrs	4 hrs				20 hrs
Photographers		8 hrs				8 hrs
Cleanup Crew		8 hrs				8 hrs
Do Lahr	16 hrs	34 hrs				50 hrs
Site	16 hrs	10 hrs				26 hrs
Alert community		16 hrs				16 hrs
Press release		8 hrs				8 hrs
Gayle Kearney	12 hrs	8 hrs	40 hrs	16 hrs		76 hrs
Keynote speaker						
Caterer		8 hrs	32 hrs			40 hrs
Bartenders			8 hrs	16 hrs		24 hrs
Baseball Game	8 hrs					8 hrs
Opera	4 hrs					4 hrs
Joe Johnson		12 hrs	16 hrs			28 hrs
Security		8 hrs	12 hrs			20 hrs
Cleanup Crew		4 hrs	4 hrs			8 hrs
Total	113.5 ...	139 hrs	84 hrs	16 hrs		352.5 hrs

Note

Two variations of the Resource Usage report exist: the Resource Usage (material) and Resource Usage (work) reports. Both reports look identical to the Resource Usage report but, as you would expect, one shows only material resources whereas the other shows only work resources. Both reports are custom reports; to print them, follow the instructions in the next section. ■

Customizing reports

Project contains some custom reports. In addition to printing these custom reports, you can customize any of the other reports described in this chapter. Click the Custom category in the Reports dialog box and choose Select to open the Custom Reports dialog box (see Figure 9.37).

FIGURE 9.37

The Custom Reports dialog box.

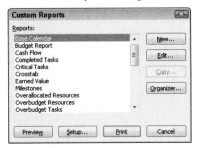

The reports listed in the Custom Reports dialog box include three custom reports as well as all the standard reports described earlier in this chapter. You can print any of the standard reports either from this dialog box or as described earlier in this chapter. Remember, though, that you must use this dialog box to print the three custom reports.

Note

You can create your own reports by clicking the New button in the Custom Reports dialog box. When you define a new custom report, Project offers you four formats. Three formats are based on the reports discussed in this section: the Task report format, the Resource report format, and the Crosstab report format. The fourth format, the Monthly Calendar format, functions just like the Working Days report discussed earlier in this chapter. ■

Task report

The Task report (see Figure 9.38) shows task information, such as the ID number, task name, indicator icons, task duration, planned start and finish dates, predecessors, and (if resources have been assigned) resource names.

FIGURE 9.38

The Task report.

Task as of Mon 11/16/09
reports2-2010.mpp

ID	Indicators	Task Mode	Task Name	Duration	Start	Finish	Predecessors	Resource Names
4		Auto Scheduled	Determine budget	9 days	Mon 2/22/10	Thu 3/4/10		Roy Lipner
5		Auto Scheduled	Invitation list	3 days	Fri 3/5/10	Tue 3/9/10	4	Rosie Boles
6		Auto Scheduled	Send out invitations	4 days	Mon 2/22/10	Thu 2/25/10		
8		Auto Scheduled	Theme	3 days	Mon 2/22/10	Wed 2/24/10		Rosie Boles
9		Auto Scheduled	Site	0.65 wks	Thu 2/25/10	Tue 3/2/10	8	Intern,Do Lahr
10		Auto Scheduled	Keynote speaker	4.13 days	Wed 2/24/10	Thu 3/4/10	8	Roy Lipner,Rosie Boles[50
12		Auto Scheduled	Caterer	5 days	Fri 3/5/10	Thu 3/11/10	4	Gayle Kearney
13		Auto Scheduled	Bartenders	3 days	Fri 3/12/10	Tue 3/16/10	12	Gayle Kearney
14		Auto Scheduled	Security	2.5 days	Fri 3/5/10	Tue 3/9/10	4	Roy Lipner,Joe Johnson
15		Auto Scheduled	Photographers	1 day	Fri 3/5/10	Fri 3/5/10	4	Rosie Boles[50%],Intern
16		Auto Scheduled	Cleanup Crew	2 days	Fri 3/5/10	Mon 3/8/10	4	Intern,Joe Johnson[50%]
18		Auto Scheduled	Baseball Game	1 day	Mon 2/22/10	Mon 2/22/10		Gayle Kearney
19		Auto Scheduled	Opera	4 hrs	Mon 2/22/10	Mon 2/22/10		Gayle Kearney
21		Auto Scheduled	Alert community	2 days	Wed 3/3/10	Thu 3/4/10	9	Do Lahr
22		Auto Scheduled	Press release	1 day	Wed 3/3/10	Wed 3/3/10	9	Do Lahr
24		Auto Scheduled	PA System	1 day	Wed 3/3/10	Wed 3/3/10	9	
26		Auto Scheduled	Baseball Game	0 days	Fri 3/5/10	Fri 3/5/10		
27		Auto Scheduled	Opera	0 days	Mon 3/8/10	Mon 3/8/10		

Resource report

As you can see from the report sample shown in Figure 9.39, the Resource report shows resource information. On Page 1, you find the resource ID number; indicator icons; the resource name, type, initials, material label, group, and maximum units. On the second page of the report, Project displays rate information; accrual information; base calendar information; and code information.

FIGURE 9.39

The Resource report.

Resource as of Mon 11/16/09
reports2-2010.mpp

ID	Indicators	Resource Name	Type	Material Label	Initials	Group	Max. Units	Std. Rate	Ovt. Rate	Cost/Use	Accrue At	Base Calendar	Code
1		Roy Lipner	Work		R		100%	$50.00/hr	$0.00/hr	$0.00	Prorated	Standard	
2		Rosie Boles	Work		R		100%	$50.00/hr	$0.00/hr	$0.00	Prorated	Standard	
3		Intern	Work		I		100%	$20.00/hr	$0.00/hr	$0.00	Prorated	Standard	
4		Do Lahr	Work		D		100%	$40.00/hr	$0.00/hr	$0.00	Prorated	Standard	
5		Gayle Kearney	Work		G		100%	$45.00/hr	$0.00/hr	$0.00	Prorated	Standard	
6		Joe Johnson	Work		J		100%	$40.00/hr	$0.00/hr	$0.00	Prorated	Standard	

You'll find two variations of the Resource report: the Resource (material) and Resource (work) reports. Both reports look identical to the Resource report but, as you would expect, one shows only material resources whereas the other shows only work resources.

Crosstab report

The Crosstab report (see Figure 9.40) is a tabular report that shows task and resource information in rows and time increments in columns.

Tip

Much of the information on the Crosstab report also appears on the Task Usage report and the Resource Usage report. These reports give you more formatting options, such as the time period the report covers and the table that's used in the report. ∎

FIGURE 9.40

The Crosstab report.

Crosstab as of Mon 11/16/09
reports2-2010.mpp

	2/21	2/28	3/7	3/14	3/21
Conference					
Preplanning					
Initial planning					
Determine budget	$1,600.00	$1,600.00			
Roy Lipner	$1,600.00	$1,600.00			
Invitation list		$400.00	$800.00		
Rosie Boles		$400.00	$800.00		
Send out invitations					
Selection					
Theme	$1,200.00				
Rosie Boles	$1,200.00				
Site	$1,085.00	$605.00			
Intern	$320.00	$80.00			
Do Lahr	$640.00	$400.00			
Keynote speaker	$1,175.00	$650.00			
Roy Lipner	$300.00	$650.00			
Rosie Boles	$375.00				
Gayle Kearney	$500.00				
Hire					
Caterer		$360.00	$1,440.00		
Gayle Kearney		$360.00	$1,440.00		
Bartenders			$360.00	$720.00	
Gayle Kearney			$360.00	$720.00	
Security		$720.00	$1,080.00		
Roy Lipner		$400.00	$600.00		
Joe Johnson		$320.00	$480.00		
Photographers		$360.00			
Rosie Boles		$200.00			
Intern		$160.00			
Cleanup Crew		$320.00	$160.00		
Intern		$160.00			
Joe Johnson		$160.00	$160.00		
Plan Entertainment					
Baseball Game	$360.00				
Gayle Kearney	$360.00				
Opera	$180.00				
Gayle Kearney	$180.00				
Public Relations					
Alert community		$640.00			
Do Lahr		$640.00			
Press release		$320.00			
Do Lahr		$320.00			
Rent Equipment					
PA System					
Events					
Baseball Game					
Opera					

Customizing an existing report

You can customize almost every report you've seen in this chapter. For a few reports, such as the Working Days report, the only item you can change is the font information that Project uses to print the report. For other reports, however, you can change the table or the task or resource filter to change the content of the report. Click the Edit button when preparing to print the report to make any of these changes; Project then opens the dialog box that corresponds to the report you selected. For example, if you select the Working Days report in the Overview Reports dialog box and then click Edit, Project opens the Report Text dialog box (see Figure 9.41).

Similarly, if you select the Tasks Starting Soon report from the Current Activities dialog box and then click Edit, Project opens the Definition tab of the Task Report dialog box (see Figure 9.42).

FIGURE 9.41

Use the Report Text dialog box to change the font of the report items.

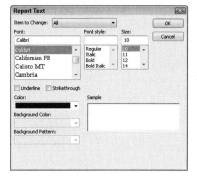

FIGURE 9.42

Use the Definition tab to change the report's table or filter.

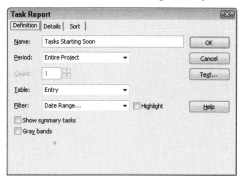

From the Details tab (see Figure 9.43), select the information you want to include on the report. You may want to display predecessors for tasks or place a gridline between details.

Use the Details tab to specify the information you want to include on the report.

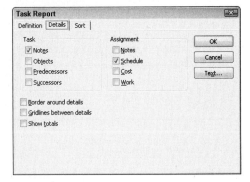

Note

The options on the Details tab change from report to report. ■

From the Sort tab, shown in Figure 9.44, select the sort orders for the report.

Select a sort order for the report.

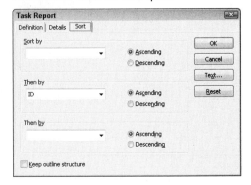

The Report Type Determines the Dialog Box

Remember that the type of report you select initially determines the dialog box you see when you click Edit in the report's category dialog box (for example, the Overview Reports dialog box or the Cost Reports dialog box). In addition to the dialog boxes you've seen in this chapter, you may also see the Resource Report dialog box or the Crosstab Report dialog box, each of which contains slightly different options (primarily on the Definitions tab) from those in the Task Report dialog box.

For example, when you edit the Who Does What report before printing it, Project opens a Resource Report dialog box. On the Definitions tab of this dialog box, you can select filters related to resources, whereas the filters in the Task Report dialog box pertain to tasks. Or, if you edit the Cash Flow report before printing it, Project opens a Crosstab Report dialog box from which you can select the information you want to appear on each row; the default information is Tasks and Cost.

Taking Advantage of Visual Reporting

The visual reports you create in Project use Project data to build PivotTables in Excel and PivotDiagrams in Visio. After you produce a report, you can manipulate it in Excel or Visio, using techniques available in those programs you would normally use to manipulate any Excel PivotTable or Visio PivotDiagram. You'll always see two tabs at the bottom of the Excel and Visio windows; one contains the visual report and the other contains the PivotTable or PivotDiagram data on which the report is based.

Note

To create visual reports in Project 2010, you need Excel 2010 and Visio 2010. ■

You produce visual reports from the Visual Reports – Create Report window (see Figure 9.45). You can open this window by clicking the Project tab and, in the Reports group, clicking Visual Reports.

FIGURE 9.45

Use this window to create visual reports.

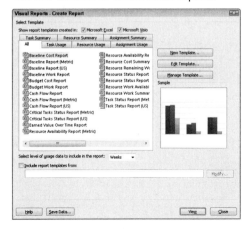

You'll find the reports broken into six categories:

- Task Usage
- Resource Usage
- Assignment Usage
- Task Summary
- Resource Summary
- Assignment Summary

The reports that appear in the Visual Reports – Create Report window are the templates that come with Project, but you also can create your own reports if you don't find a report that suits your needs.

In this section, I describe each of the report templates that come with Project. Then, at the end of this section, I walk you through creating your own visual report.

Task Usage reports

Only one report appears in the Task Usage category of reports: the Cash Flow Report. The Cash Flow report, an Excel PivotTable, uses timephased data to produce a bar graph similar to the one shown in Figure 9.46. The PivotTable data appears on the Task Usage tab of the workbook.

FIGURE 9.46

The Excel-based Cash Flow Report.

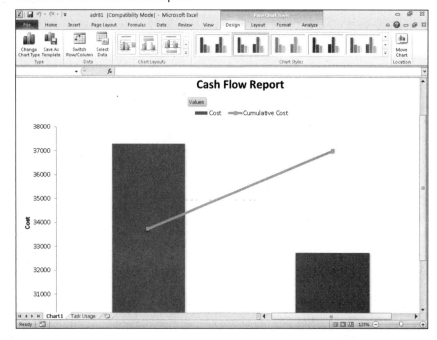

Resource Usage reports

The Resource Usage visual report category contains five reports. For two of the reports, the Cash Flow Report and the Resource Availability Report, you'll find both Metric and US versions.

Cash Flow Report

You'll find a Metric and a US version of the Cash Flow Report, a Visio PivotDiagram. Using your project data, this report produces a diagram (see Figure 9.47) that shows planned and actual costs for your project over time and breaks down the information by resource type, showing work, material, and cost information.

FIGURE 9.47

The Visio-based Cash Flow Report.

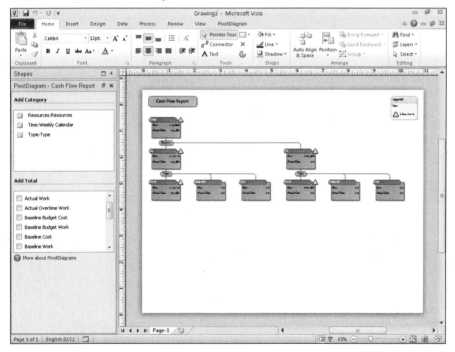

Resource Availability Report

You'll find a Metric and a US version of the Resource Availability Report, a Visio PivotDiagram. Using your project data, this report produces a diagram (see Figure 9.48) that shows total capacity, work, and remaining availability for work resources.

Resource Cost Summary Report

The Resource Cost Summary Report, an Excel PivotTable, produces a pie chart (see Figure 9.49) that divides resource costs among resource types.

FIGURE 9.48

The Resource Availability Report.

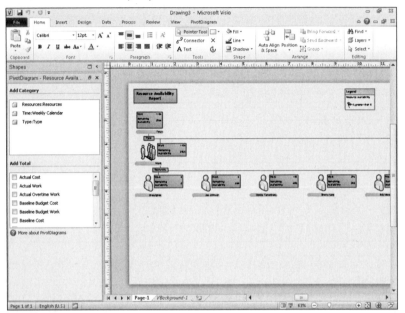

FIGURE 9.49

The Resource Cost Summary Report.

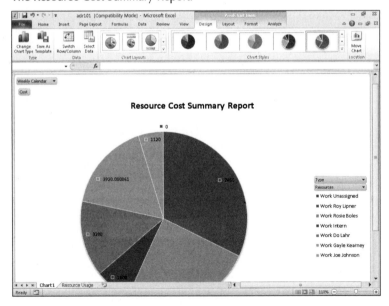

Resource Work Availability Report

The Resource Work Availability Report is an Excel PivotTable that produces a column chart (see Figure 9.50) showing work availability, work, and remaining availability over time. By default, the chart doesn't show each individual resource, but using the PivotChart tools, you can display the information for individual resources.

FIGURE 9.50

The Resource Work Availability Report.

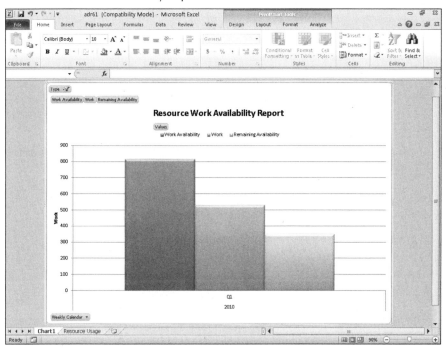

Resource Work Summary Report

The Resource Work Summary Report is an Excel PivotTable that produces a column chart (see Figure 9.51) showing work availability, work, remaining availability, and actual work for each work resource assigned to your project.

Assignment Usage reports

The Assignment Usage visual report category contains six reports. For one of the reports, the Baseline Report, you'll find both Metric and US versions.

FIGURE 9.51

The Resource Work Summary Report.

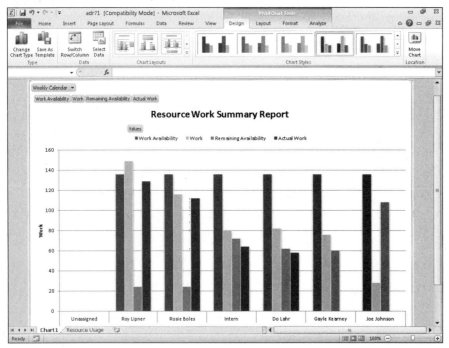

Baseline Cost Report

The Baseline Cost Report is an Excel PivotTable that produces a column chart (see Figure 9.52) that compares baseline cost, planned cost, and actual cost.

Baseline Report

You'll find a Metric and a US version of the Baseline Report, a Visio PivotDiagram. Using your project data, this report produces a diagram (see Figure 9.53) that shows baseline and actual work and costs for your project over time. The report flags instances in which planned work exceeds baseline work and planned cost exceeds baseline cost.

FIGURE 9.52

The Baseline Cost Report.

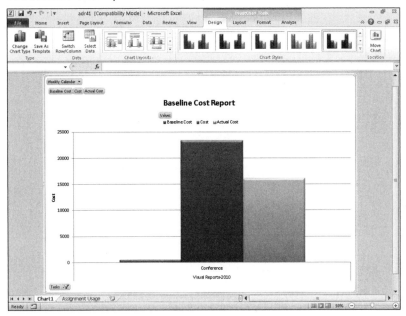

FIGURE 9.53

The Baseline Report.

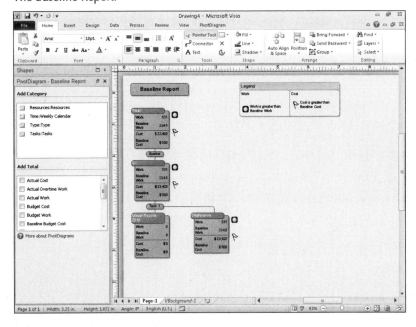

Baseline Work Report

As is its cousin the Baseline Cost Report, the Baseline Work Report is an Excel PivotTable that produces a column chart (see Figure 9.54) comparing baseline work, planned work, and actual work.

Budget Cost Report

The Budget Cost Report is an Excel PivotTable that produces a column chart (see Figure 9.55) comparing budget cost, baseline cost, planned cost, and actual cost.

Budget Work Report

Similar to its cousin the Budget Cost Report, the Budget Work Report is an Excel PivotTable that produces a column chart comparing budget work, baseline work, planned work, and actual work.

Earned Value Over Time Report

The Earned Value Over Time Report, an Excel PivotTable, uses timephased data to produce a chart that plots actual cost of work performed (ACWP), Planned Value – PV (BCWS), and Earned Value – EV (BCWP) over time, similar to the one shown in Figure 9.56.

FIGURE 9.54

The Baseline Work Report.

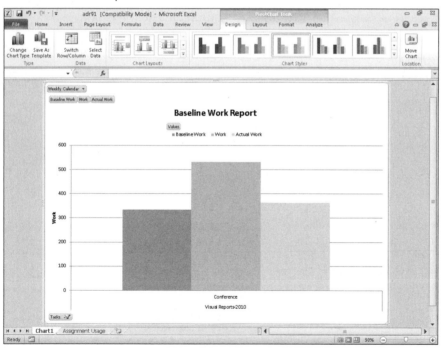

FIGURE 9.55

The Budget Cost Report.

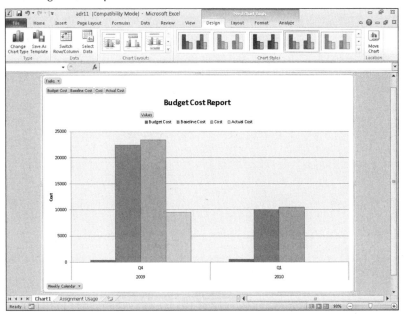

FIGURE 9.56

The Earned Value Over Time Report.

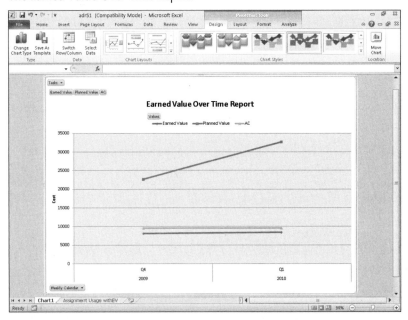

Summary reports

Finally, you'll find two task summary visual reports, one resource summary visual report, and two assignment summary visual reports. US and Metric versions exist for the task summary reports and for the assignment summary report.

Critical Tasks Status Report

This task summary report comes in a Metric version and a US version. A Visio PivotDiagram, the Critical Tasks Status Report (see Figure 9.57) shows the work and remaining work for both critical and noncritical tasks, along with the percent of work complete.

FIGURE 9.57

The Critical Tasks Status Report.

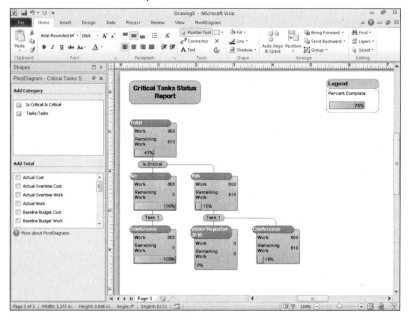

Task Status Report

This task summary report also comes in a Metric version and a US version. A Visio PivotDiagram, the Task Status Report (see Figure 9.58) shows work and percent of work complete for tasks at the highest level in your project outline. Using PivotDiagram tools, you can show more detail.

Resource Remaining Work Report

A resource summary report, the Resource Remaining Work Report is an Excel PivotTable that produces a column chart (see Figure 9.59) showing work, remaining work, and total work for each work resource on your project.

FIGURE 9.58

The Task Status Report.

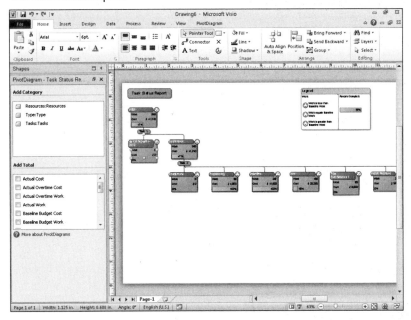

FIGURE 9.59

The Resource Remaining Work Report.

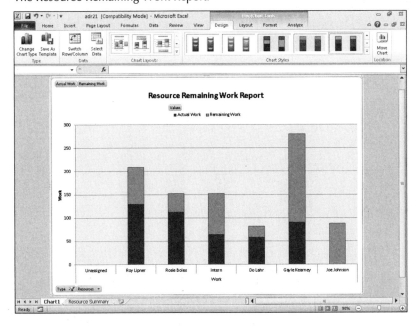

Resource Status Report

This assignment summary report also comes in a Metric version and a US version. A Visio PivotDiagram, the Resource Status Report (see Figure 9.60) shows work and cost values for each of your project's resources.

The Resource Status Report.

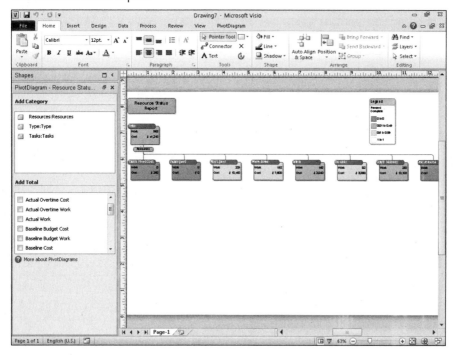

Customizing visual report templates

Because of the variety of available report templates, the odds are good that you won't need to create your own template. But you can create a new template or edit an existing template to suit your needs.

When you create a new template, Project bases it on an existing template. To create a new custom visual report template, follow these steps:

1. Click the Project tab and, in the Reports group, click Visual Reports to display the Visual Reports – Create Report dialog box.

2. Click the New Template button. Project displays the Visual Reports – New Template dialog box (see Figure 9.61).

FIGURE 9.61

Use this dialog box to describe the new template you want to create.

3. Choose Excel or Visio as the application that will display the report. If you select Visio, choose between Visio (Metric) or Visio (US Units).

4. Open the Choose the Data on Which You Want to Report list box and select an existing visual report to act as the foundation for your new report.

Tip
To include timephased data on your report, select Task Usage, Resource Usage, or Assignment Usage. ∎

5. Click the Field Picker button. Project displays the Visual Reports – Field Picker dialog box (see Figure 9.62). The fields that appear in this dialog box change depending on the report template you selected in Step 4. But the dialog box functions the same, regardless of the choice you make in Step 4. The columns on the right show the fields currently included in the report template, and the columns on the left show the fields available to add to the template.

6. To include a new field, click it in one of the columns on the right and click the Add button. To remove an existing field from the report, click it in one of the columns on the left and click Remove. When you finish selecting fields, click OK twice. Project begins to go through the process of building the report that you described. Either an Excel window or a Visio window appears to enable you to establish the PivotTable or PivotDiagram. Figure 9.63 shows an empty Excel PivotTable with fields on the right I can drag and drop into the appropriate places on the PivotTable.

7. When you finish setting up the template, click the File tab and, in Backstage view, click Save As. In the Save As dialog box, navigate to the default location for Excel or Visio templates. Provide a name for the template and click Save.

FIGURE 9.62

Use this dialog box to select the fields you want to include in your Visual Report template.

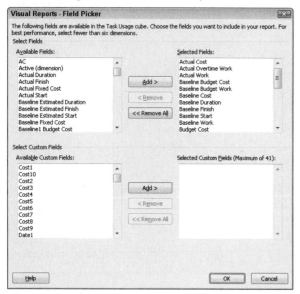

FIGURE 9.63

A blank PivotTable or PivotDiagram appears so you can format your report.

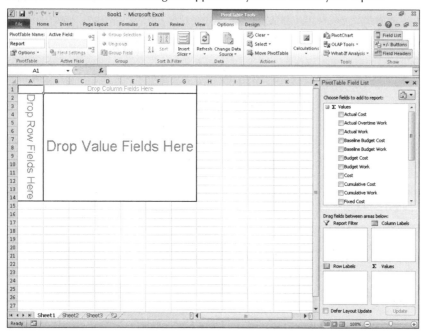

You also can export data as an OLAP cube or as a reporting database; see Chapter 18 for details.

Summary

In this chapter, you found out how to produce text reports and visual report in Project, and you examined samples of the text and visual reports available in Project. In addition, you should now know how to customize any standard text report or visual report in Project. The next chapter shows you how to analyze your project's progress.

Chapter 10 explains how to fine-tune timing to resolve scheduling conflicts.

Part IV

Refining Your Project

Resolving Scheduling Problems

S cheduling conflicts are the bane of the project manager's existence. By
and large, scheduling conflicts typically fall into one of two categories:

- Your project is taking longer than you had planned.

- Your resources are overassigned.

This chapter considers the first problem and focuses on identifying and then
resolving scheduling problems; Chapter 11 focuses on the second problem.

IN THIS CHAPTER

Identifying scheduling problems

Resolving scheduling conflicts

Using the critical path to shorten a project

Identifying Scheduling Problems

Scheduling conflicts announce themselves in a number of ways. Changing
views and filtering information by using the techniques described in
Chapters 6 and 7 may identify some glaring problem inherent in your original logic. For example, if you filter your project to view only incomplete
tasks or slipping tasks, you may spot some problems. Or, you might
unknowingly create a problem by using a *task constraint,* as explained later in
this chapter.

In addition to views and reports, Project contains two features you can use to
help you identify scheduling problems:

- Warnings and Suggestions
- The Task Inspector

Working with Warnings and Suggestions

Manually scheduled tasks offer you complete control over a task's dates. For example, if a task is delayed, Project won't move out manually scheduled successor tasks automatically, because doing so would introduce the possibility of unintentionally creating scheduling conflicts. You, as the project manager, get the opportunity to re-evaluate the dependency and determine whether you need to move the successor task. The Warnings and Suggestions feature in Project help you find and resolve these potential conflicts.

New Feature

Warnings and Suggestions are new to Project 2010. ■

For manually scheduled tasks, Project makes a background calculation of the task's probable start and finish date using information such as dependencies and project, task, and resource calendars. Project then compares these background calculation dates to those you enter for the manually scheduled task.

When Project identifies a possible conflict, a red, squiggly line appears under the task's Start and/ or Finish dates (see Figure 10.1) in any table view that displays the Start and Finish dates.

FIGURE 10.1

The red squiggly line under the Start or Finish dates of the top-level task in this figure implies a scheduling problem.

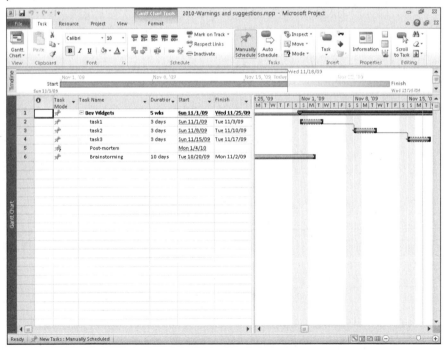

To help you resolve a potential scheduling problem, right-click any date under which a red squiggly line appears to display a context menu and see options you can select to help you resolve the schedule issue (see Figure 10.2). You can take various actions, including these:

- Change the task from manually scheduled task to an automatically scheduled task.

- If a predecessor task is slipping, you can opt to have Project respect the links you've established.

- Use the Task Inspector, discussed in the next section, to help you resolve the issue.

- Simply opt to ignore the problem; while that might feel good momentarily, remember that the problem isn't going to go away by itself.

In Figure 10.1, a green squiggly line appears under the Finish dates of the tasks that appear on Rows 3 and 4 (although that's hard to see in the grayscale figures in this book). The green squiggly line helps you identify tasks that you might be able to change to optimize your schedule. Project doesn't display optimization suggestions by default (as it does warnings). Instead, you must choose to display optimization suggestions if you want to see them — and you can choose to show them only for the current project or for all projects. Follow these steps:

FIGURE 10.2

The context menu contains options you can use to help you resolve the scheduling problem.

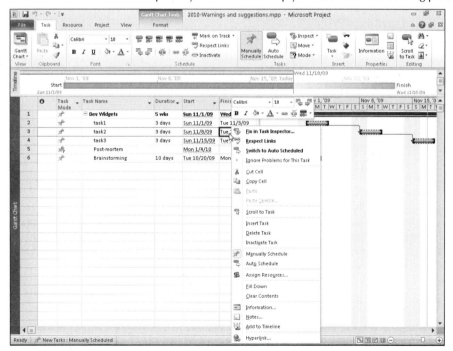

1. Click the File tab and, in the Backstage view that appears, click Options.

2. In the Project Options dialog box (see Figure 10.3), click Schedule on the left.

You can opt to hide or display warnings and suggestions.

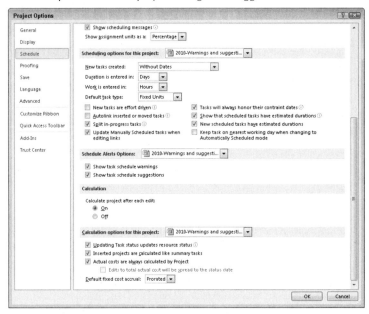

3. In the Schedule Alerts Options section, use the list box arrow to set options for the current project or for all projects.

4. Place a check in the Show Task Schedule Suggestions box.

5. Click OK to save your settings.

Tip

You can hide or display warnings and suggestions from the Inspect button in the Tasks group on the Task tab. Click the down arrow beside the button; Project displays a menu. Clicking the choices on this menu toggles on or off warnings, suggestions, and ignored problems. To review suggestions, once again, right-click a task date under which a squiggly line appears and choose one of the options that appears on the context menu. ∎

Using the Task Inspector

The Task Inspector is the successor to the Task Driver, which appeared in Project 2007 and provided information about factors affecting the selected task. The Task Inspector goes beyond the Task Driver, because it offers not only information about the task but suggestions on changes you can make.

You can inspect any task, not just those that show a red or green squiggly line under Start or Finish dates:

- On tasks Project highlights for your review (using red and green squiggly lines), right-click the task and choose Fix In Task Inspector.

- For tasks Project has not highlighted for your review, click the Task tab and, in the Tasks group, click the Inspect button.

In both cases, Project displays the Task Inspector pane (see Figure 10.4).

FIGURE 10.4

The Task Inspector offers both information about the selected task and changes you can make.

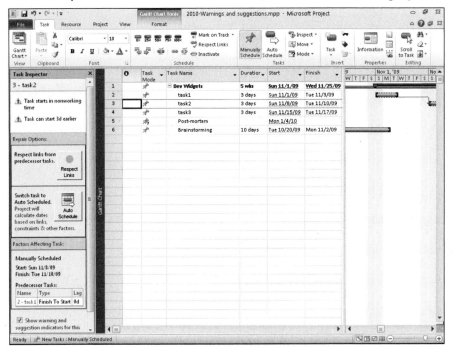

Resolving Scheduling Conflicts

Project provides several techniques you can use to resolve scheduling conflicts. This section covers the following strategies:

- Adding resources
- Using overtime
- Adding time

- Making a task inactive
- Adjusting slack
- Changing constraints
- Adjusting dependencies
- Splitting a task

Adding resources to tasks

Adding resources to a task can decrease the time that's necessary to complete it. On the Advanced tab of the Task Information dialog box (see Figure 10.5), set the task type to Fixed Units. In this instance, adding resources to the task reduces the duration of the task. Also, remember that a check mark appears by default in the Effort Driven check box of the Task Information dialog box. When you use the Effort Driven option, Project reallocates the work among the assigned resources.

To open the Task Information dialog box, simply double-click the task.

FIGURE 10.5

The Advanced tab of the Task Information dialog box controls the task type and shows whether the task is effort-driven.

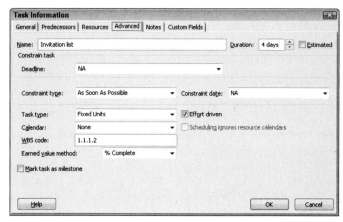

Using overtime

In the best of all worlds, you have unlimited resources and can add resources to resolve scheduling problems. After performing a reality check, though, you'll discover that you don't have unlimited resources, and adding resources may not be an option. But you may be able to use overtime to shorten a task's duration, which is the next strategy you can use to resolve scheduling problems.

Cross-Reference

For information on resolving resource conflicts, see Chapter 11. ■

Overtime in Project is defined as the amount of work that is scheduled beyond an assigned resource's regular working hours. Overtime hours are charged at the resource's overtime rate. Overtime work does not represent additional work on a task; instead, it represents the amount of time that's spent on a task outside regular hours. For example, if you assign 30 hours of work and 12 hours of overtime, the total work is still 30 hours. Of the 30 hours, 18 hours are worked during the regular work schedule (and charged to the project at the regular rate), and 12 hours are worked during off hours (and charged to the project at an overtime rate). Therefore, you can use overtime to shorten the time that a resource takes to complete a task.

To enter overtime, follow these steps:

1. Display the Gantt Chart view by right-clicking the gray bar at the left edge of the Project screen and choosing Gantt Chart.

2. Click the task to which you want to add overtime.

3. Click the Task tab, and, in the Properties group, click the Display Task Details button to display the Task Details Form in the bottom pane of the Project window. Information about the task you selected in Step 2 appears in the Task Details Form.

4. Click the Task Details Form to make it the active pane.

5. Click the Task Form Tools Format tab.

6. In the Details group, click the Work button to display work fields, including the Ovt. Work field.

7. Fill in the overtime amount for the appropriate resource (see Figure 10.6).

8. Click OK. Project adjusts the schedule.

Tip
After you finish entering overtime, you can hide the Task Details Form clicking the Display Task Details button again. ■

Adding time to tasks

You can also solve scheduling conflicts by increasing the duration of a task. Again, in the best of all worlds, you have this luxury; in reality, you might not. But if you can increase the duration of a task, you may find that once-scarce resources are now available to complete the task — given the task's new timing.

As you know, you can change the duration from several different views, such as the Task Usage view or the Gantt Chart view. You can also use the Task Information dialog box to complete this task (see Figure 10.7). To open the Task Information dialog box, double-click the task; then, use the Duration box to change the duration.

FIGURE 10.6

Adding overtime to a resource on a task.

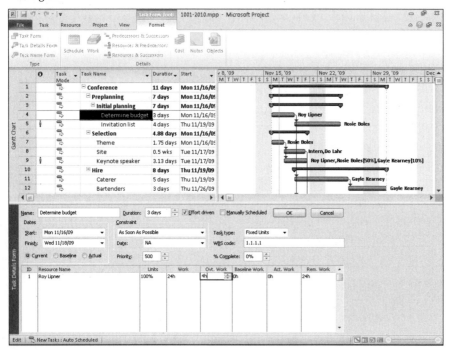

FIGURE 10.7

Change the duration from the Task Information dialog box.

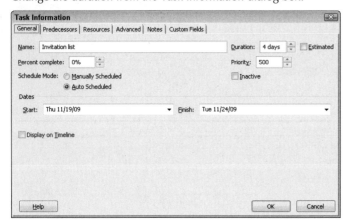

Making a task inactive

You might be able to shorten your schedule — and thereby eliminate a scheduling conflict — if you can make one or more of your project's tasks inactive.

New Feature

Making a task inactive is new to Project 2010. ■

Making a task inactive is the equivalent of putting the task on hold. When you make a task inactive, you remove the *effect* of the task from your project schedule, but you don't actually remove the task. You retain all of the information about the task, but the task has no impact on the project schedule.

Suppose, for example, that management decides to put one portion of your project on the back burner and focus on completing the rest of the project. Effectively, management is changing the scope of the project — indicating that the portion of your project they are willing to delay isn't really essential right now, but they will want to address it at a later date.

In a case like this, you could delete the tasks or perhaps cut and paste them into a new, separate project, or, you can make inactive the tasks affected by the change in direction. When you make them inactive, they remain in the schedule, but nothing about them affects the schedule or resource availability.

Suppose that your schedule is 70 days long, as the first task in the schedule shown in Figure 10.8 indicates. Further suppose that management has approved putting the group of tasks on lines 17, 18, and 19 on hold.

The effect of making tasks inactive is easy to see in the Gantt Chart view. To make a task or group of tasks inactive, select them — you can drag over their names — and then click the Task tab. In the Schedule group, click the Inactivate button.

You can see the results in Figure 10.9. In the table portion of the view, Project changes the text to a light gray and draws lines through the task information — the task names, durations, dates, and so on. In the chart portion of the view, the task bars are no longer blue and the summary bar is no longer black; instead, they are white and gray respectively. And if you look closely, the task bars appear to have lines drawn through them, as if they were crossed out. Finally, the duration of the project has dropped to 56 days, as the Duration field of the first task in the project indicates.

By making the tasks inactive, you've shortened the schedule by 14 days, but you haven't lost any of the information about the tasks you made inactive. That extra 14 days just might resolve some scheduling problems for you.

FIGURE 10.8

Before making any tasks inactive, your schedule is 70 days long, as the Duration of the first task indicates.

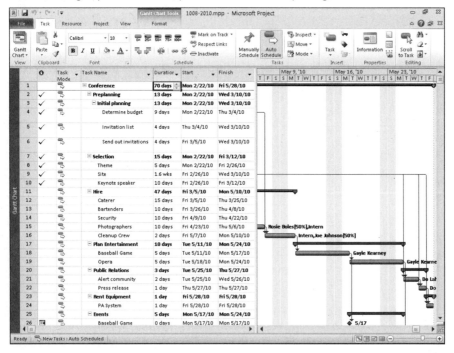

Adjusting slack

Slack time is the amount of time that a task can slip before it affects another task's dates or the finish date of the project. *Free slack* is the amount of time that a task can be delayed without delaying another task. Most projects contain *noncritical tasks with slack* — tasks that can start late without affecting the schedule. If you have slack in your schedule, you may be able to move tasks around to balance phases of the schedule that have no slack with phases that have too much slack. Therefore you can use tasks with slack to compensate for tasks that take longer than planned or to help resolve overassignment of resources.

Note

Slack values can also help you identify inconsistencies in the schedule. For example, you see a negative slack value when one task has a finish-to-start dependency with a second task, but the second task has a Must Start On constraint that is earlier than the end of the first task. ■

Almost by definition, you create slack time if you use the Must Start On constraint when you create your task. You set constraints on the Advanced tab of the Task Information dialog box (see Figure 10.10). To display the Task Information dialog box, double-click the task in your schedule. When the dialog box appears, select the Advanced tab.

FIGURE 10.9

The schedule after making three tasks inactive.

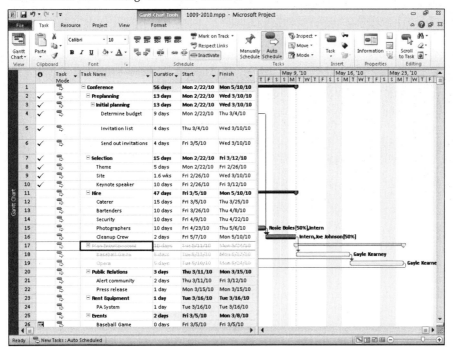

FIGURE 10.10

Constraints can often create slack time.

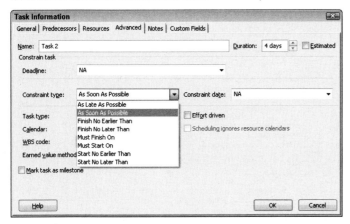

To avoid creating slack time, use the As Soon As Possible constraint whenever possible. To identify tasks with slack time, follow these steps:

1. Display the Gantt Chart view.

2. Click the Gantt Chart Tools Format tab.

3. In the Bar Styles group, place a check in the Slack box. Project displays thin lines extending out of the right side of the bar of each task that has slack time (see Figure 10.11).

To see a numerical representation of slack, use the Schedule table. Right-click the Select All button and select Schedule from the list of tables. Drag the divider bar to the right to view more of the table and see the Free Slack and Total Slack fields (see Figure 10.12).

Changing task constraints

Task constraints are the usual culprits when projects fall behind schedule. By default, Project uses the Planning Wizard to warn you when you are about to take an action that is likely to throw your project off schedule. For example, if you impose a Must Start On task constraint on a task that has no slack time and does have other tasks linked to it, Project displays the Planning Wizard dialog box (see Figure 10.13).

FIGURE 10.11

Slack is represented by a thin line extending from task bars in the Gantt Chart.

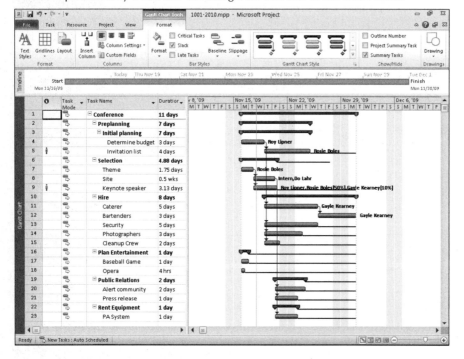

FIGURE 10.12

You can see slack time represented in numbers by using the Schedule table.

Select All button

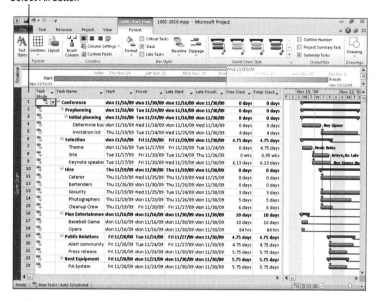

Similarly, if you impose an illogical start date on a task when you're recording dates, Project displays a Planning Wizard dialog box. For example, you see a Planning Wizard dialog box if you accidentally enter a start date for Task 2 that is earlier than Task 1, and Task 2 is linked to and succeeds Task 1.

FIGURE 10.13

The Planning Wizard appears by default when you apply a constraint that is likely to lengthen your project schedule.

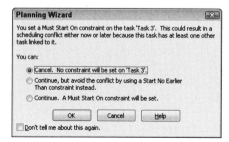

Notice that you can turn off the Planning Wizard warnings by placing a check in the Don't Tell Me About This Again check box at the bottom of the Planning Wizard dialog box. (Some people just don't like to have wizards popping up all the time.)

If you turn off the Planning Wizard, Project still warns you if you take actions that cause scheduling problems. Instead of the Planning Wizard, Project displays a more traditional message that describes actions you can take to avoid these kinds of conflicts — suggestions that all refer to the predecessor task. But, in contrast to the Planning Wizard, this message box does not give you the option of canceling your action.

So, although you may find the Planning Wizard annoying at some levels, it can actually save you effort at other levels. Sorry you turned it off? To turn it on again, click the File tab and, in the Backstage view that appears, click Options. Click Advanced on the left side of the Project Options dialog box and make sure checks appear in the Planning Wizard section (see Figure 10.14).

FIGURE 10.14

You can control whether the Planning Wizard appears from the Project Options dialog box.

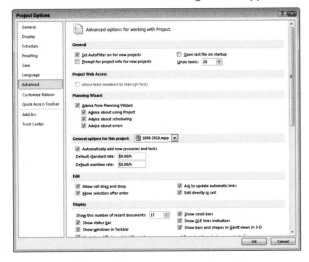

Adjusting dependencies

By changing task dependencies, you can tighten the schedule and eliminate scheduling conflicts. If you inadvertently link tasks that don't need to be linked, you may create a situation in which you don't have the resources necessary to complete the tasks — and as a result, the project schedule falls behind. If you discover unnecessary links, you can remove them. When you remove the dependencies, you may find holes in the project schedule where work can be performed. After you remove unnecessary dependencies, you may be able to move tasks around and fill those holes.

You can use the Task Inspector pane (see Figure 10.15) to identify the predecessor task that drives the timing of an individual task. Click the Task tab and, in the Tasks group, click Inspect to display the pane. Select a task and, in the Task Inspector pane, Project displays the predecessor task that drives the timing of the selected task.

You can view dependencies graphically if you use the Relationship Diagram view in combination with the Gantt view (see Figure 10.16). The Relationship Diagram view shows you the selected task and its immediate predecessor and successor. Use the following steps to set up the combined view:

1. Click the Task tab.

2. Click the Gantt Chart button to display the Gantt Chart view.

3. In the Properties group, click the Display Task Details button.

   Project splits the view and displays the Task Details Form in the bottom of the window.

4. Click the bottom pane.

5. Right-click the gray bar running down the left side of the bottom pane and choose More Views.

6. Select Relationship Diagram from the More Views window and click Apply.

7. In the upper pane, click each task in your project to review its dependencies graphically in the lower pane.

FIGURE 10.15

Use the Task Inspector pane to identify the predecessor task responsible for the timing of a selected task.

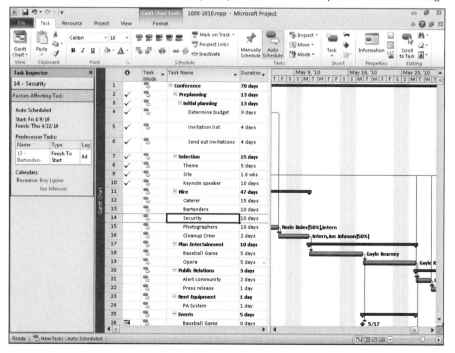

FIGURE 10.16

Use the Relationship Diagram view to review task dependencies.

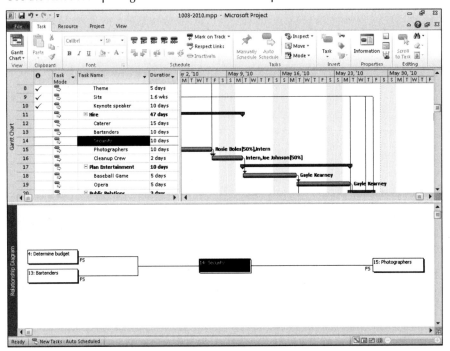

As you review the tasks, ask yourself the following questions:

- Do I really need to complete Task A before Task B begins?
- Can I perform the tasks concurrently?
- Can I do one of the tasks later without harming the project?

Splitting a task

Splitting a task can sometimes be the best way to resolve a scheduling conflict. You may not be able to complete the task on consecutive days, but you can start the task, stop work on it for a period of time, and then come back to the task. Project enables you to split a task any time you determine that you need to make this type of adjustment. Remember that splitting a task creates a gap, which you see in the task's Gantt bar. Follow these steps to split a task:

1. Switch to the Gantt Chart view.

2. Click the Task tab and, in the Schedule group, click the Split Task button.

    The mouse pointer changes shape, and a screen tip tells you how to split a task (see Figure 10.17).

3. Move the mouse pointer along the bar of the task that you want to split.

   As the mouse pointer moves, dates representing the split date appear in the screen tip.

4. Click when the screen tip shows the date on which you want to split the task.

   Project inserts a one-day split.

Tip

If you want the split to last longer than one day, drag to the right instead of clicking. ∎

FIGURE 10.17

Use the Split Task button to divide a task.

After you split a task, it will look similar to Task 5 in Figure 10.18: Dotted lines appear between the two portions of the split. If you decide that you want to remove a split, drag the inside portions of the split together so that they touch.

Note

If you change your mind about splitting a task before you click, press Esc. ∎

FIGURE 10.18

Task 5 on this Gantt Chart is a split task.

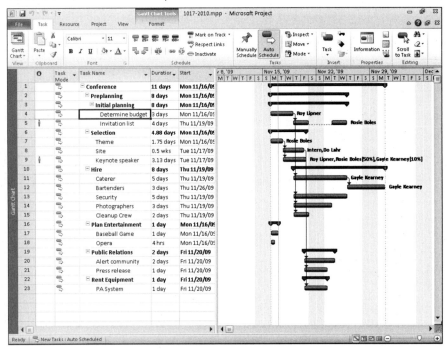

Using the Critical Path to Shorten a Project

Earlier in this chapter, you examined ways to resolve the scheduling conflicts that may develop. But what about simply shortening the time frame that you originally allotted for the entire project, thus becoming a hero? How would you accomplish that goal? You would evaluate — and try to shorten — the critical path.

The *critical path* shows the tasks in your project that must be completed on schedule in order for the entire project to finish on schedule — and these tasks are called *critical tasks*. Most tasks in a project have some slack, and you can delay them some without affecting the project finish date. If you delay critical tasks, however, you affect the project finish date. As you use the techniques described earlier in this chapter to modify tasks to resolve scheduling problems, be aware that any changes you make to critical tasks affect your project finish date.

Note

Noncritical tasks can become critical if they slip too much. You can control how much slack that Project allows for a task before defining the task as a critical task. Click the File tab and, from the Backstage view, click Options. In the Project Options dialog box, click the Advanced tab. In the Calculation Options For This Project section, enter the number of slack days in the Tasks Are Critical If Slack Is Less Than or Equal To box. To make the setting apply to all new projects, open the Calculation Options For This Project list and select All New Projects. ∎

Identifying the critical path

You can see the critical path in a variety of ways. In this section, you explore various ways to identify the critical path.

You can use the Gantt Chart Wizard to format your project to highlight the critical path. You'll find a complete discussion of the Gantt Chart Wizard in Chapter 8.

Using formatting to identify the critical path

Project 2010 provides you with a quick and easy way to display critical tasks in your project in red. Follow these steps:

1. Display the Gantt Chart view and then click the Gantt Chart Tools Format tab.
2. In the Bar Styles section, place a check in the Critical Tasks check box.

    Project changes the color of all critical tasks to red.

Because this book isn't in color, you might find it a bit difficult to distinguish the difference between critical and noncritical tasks in Figure 10.19; the tasks on Rows 4, 11, and 12 are critical — delaying any of them will result in delaying the end date of the project.

Note

The formatting you apply carries to some of the other Gantt Chart views — but not to any other views. If you use the Gantt Chart Wizard described in Chapter 8 to format critical tasks, the formatting carries to all other views. ∎

You can apply your own formatting to identify critical tasks. When you apply formatting to critical and noncritical tasks, this formatting appears in all views in which you can see task bars. The formatting identifies critical tasks with a Yes in the bar of the tasks and noncritical tasks with a No.

To apply formatting, follow these steps:

1. Display the Gantt Chart view.
2. Click the Gantt Chart Tools Format tab.
3. In the Bar Styles group, click the Format button and select Bar Styles.

    Project displays the Bar Styles dialog box.

FIGURE 10.19

Checking the Critical Tasks box on the Gantt Chart Tools Format tab quickly and easily displays critical tasks in red.

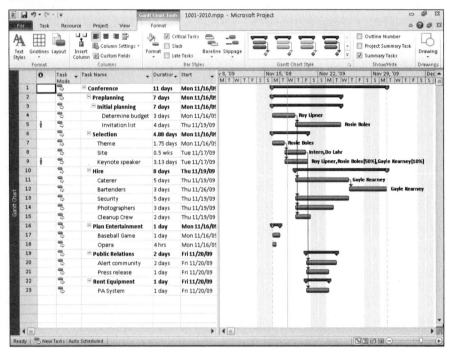

4. Select Task from the list at the top of the Bar Styles dialog box to apply formatting to noncritical tasks.

5. Click the Text tab at the bottom of the dialog box.

6. Select a position for the formatting: Left, Right, Top, Bottom, or Inside.

   When you click a position, a list-box arrow appears.

7. Click the list-box arrow and scroll to select Critical (see Figure 10.20).

8. Click OK.

FIGURE 10.20

Use the Text tab of the Bar Styles dialog box to apply formatting that distinguishes critical from noncritical tasks.

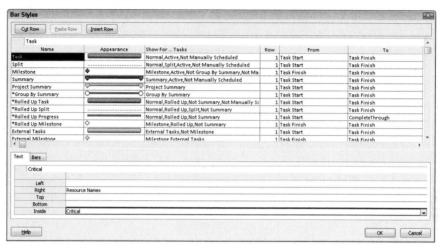

After you apply the formatting, the Gantt Chart shows critical and noncritical tasks (see Figure 10.21). Because I placed critical information inside task bars, No appears inside noncritical tasks, and Yes appears inside critical tasks.

Note

If you apply your own formatting and also check the Critical Tasks box on the Gantt Chart Tools Format tab, Project displays No for noncritical tasks but does not display Yes for critical tasks. ■

Using filters to identify the critical path

If your project contains many tasks, you might find filtering a more effective method to focus on critical tasks. As Chapter 7 explains, you can apply the Critical filter to any task view to display only critical tasks (see Figure 10.22). Display the view that you want to filter and then click the View tab. In the Data group, open the Filter list box and choose Critical.

FIGURE 10.21

The formatting in this Gantt Chart identifies critical and noncritical tasks.

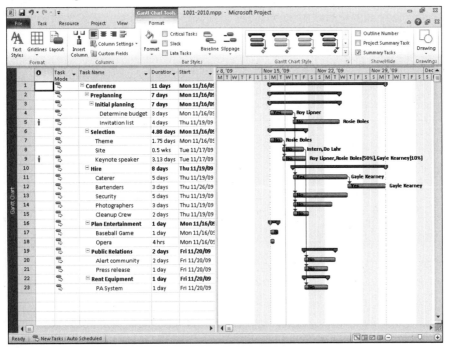

Tip

Filtering is an effective tool to display only certain aspects of the project, but sometimes you need to view all the tasks in your project and still identify the critical ones. If you use formatting, you can always distinguish between critical and noncritical tasks. ■

Shortening the critical path

Shortening the time allotted on the critical path shortens your project's duration. The converse is also true: Lengthening the time allotted on the critical path lengthens the project. In all probability, you, as the project manager, are also responsible (at least to some extent) for the cost of a project. Typically, the longer a project goes on, the more it costs. Therefore, shortening the critical path is often the project manager's goal.

FIGURE 10.22

You can filter to display only critical tasks.

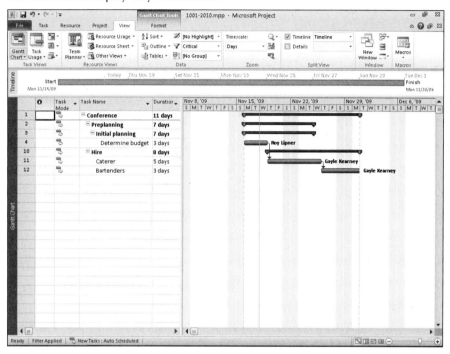

Shortening a project's duration can result in an earlier finish. But it also can mean starting later. Obviously, the second alternative is riskier, particularly if you're not confident in your estimates. If you are new to project management, you probably should not plan to start later; instead, use project management tools to help you evaluate the accuracy of your estimating skills. Over time (and multiple projects), you'll know how accurate your estimates are — and then you can take the risk of starting a project later than initially planned.

To reduce the time allotted on the critical path, you can do one or both of the following:

- Reduce the duration of critical tasks
- Overlap critical tasks to reduce the overall project duration

To reduce the duration of critical tasks, you can do any of the following:

- Reassess estimates and use a more optimistic task time.
- Add resources to a critical task.

  Remember, however, that the task must not be a fixed-duration task; adding resources to a fixed-duration task does not reduce the time needed to complete the task.

- Add overtime to a critical task.

To overlap critical tasks, you can do one or both of the following:

- Adjust dependencies and task date constraints.
- Redefine a finish-to-start relationship to either a start-to-start or a finish-to-finish relationship.

After you know the techniques that you can apply to adjust the critical path, you need to ask the important question: What's the best way to identify tasks that you want to change and then make the changes? The answer: Select a view and filter it to show only critical tasks.

I prefer the combination view of the Gantt Chart and the Task Details Form view, because the top pane graphically presents the project and, in the bottom pane, you can display most of the fields that you may want to change for any given task (see Figure 10.23).

FIGURE 10.23

The combination of the Gantt Chart view, filtered for critical tasks, and the Task Details Form view is probably the easiest view to use when you are trying to adjust the critical path.

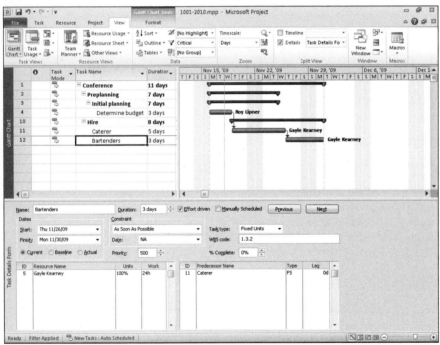

To display this view, follow these steps:

1. Display the Gantt Chart view.

2. Filter the view for critical tasks by clicking the View tab and, in the Data group, selecting Critical from the Filter list.

3. Create the combination view by clicking the Task tab and, in the Properties group, clicking the Display Task Details button.

If you don't see the Predecessor information in the Task Details Form, right-click anywhere in the Task Details Form window and choose Resources & Predecessors from the context menu that appears. You also can use this context menu to change the fields that appear on the Task Details Form (see Figure 10.24).

You're now ready to click each critical task in the top portion of the view to evaluate it and make changes to it in the bottom portion of the view.

FIGURE 10.24

Using the context menu in the Task Details Form, you can change the fields displayed in the Task Details Form.

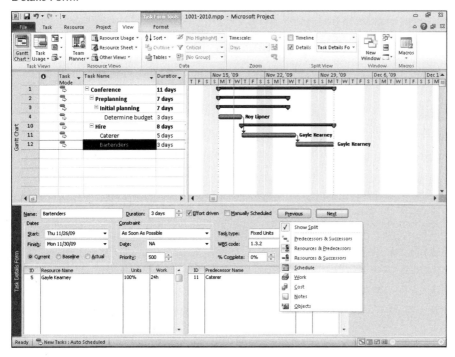

Using multiple critical paths

Project enables you to view more than one critical path in a project. This feature comes in handy when you have lots of tasks that are driving other tasks and you want to find out which ones are truly critical to finishing the network of tasks on time.

By default, when you view only one critical path, you're viewing the tasks that must be completed to finish the project on time. These tasks have no total slack. (*Total slack* is the amount of time that you can delay a task without delaying the completion of the project.)

Suppose, however, that your project contains many subtasks — and, within the subtasks, you have dependencies. You may start wondering, within a given network of tasks, which ones are really critical. In this case, view your project with multiple critical paths, where Project displays a separate critical path for each network of tasks.

Consider the project that appears in Figure 10.25. In this figure, you see the following four networks of tasks:

- Network 1: Task IDs 2, 3, and 4
- Network 2: Task IDs 6 and 7
- Network 3: Task IDs 9 through 13
- Network 4: Task IDs 15 through 18

Using the Bar Styles dialog box, I made the critical path for the project appear with a cross-hatched pattern (on-screen, it's also red); the critical path revolves around the tasks in the first two networks.

When you display multiple critical paths, you see a critical path for each network of tasks (see Figure 10.26). For each unique task, Project sets its late-finish date equal to its early finish date. When a task has no links, it is critical because its late-finish date is equal to its early-finish date. If a network of tasks contains slack, such as Network 3, some tasks are not critical but others are critical. When you view multiple critical paths, you can determine which tasks within a network of tasks must be completed on time to avoid delaying the network.

By default, Project displays only one critical path, but you can change this default. Follow these steps:

1. Click the File tab and, in the Backstage view that appears, click Options to display the Project Options dialog box.
2. Click Advanced on the left and, on the right, scroll to the bottom.
3. In the Calculation Options for the Project section, select the Calculate Multiple Critical Paths check box and click OK (see Figure 10.27).

FIGURE 10.25

This project contains four networks of tasks.

FIGURE 10.26

When you view multiple critical paths, you see the critical tasks within each network of tasks in your project.

FIGURE 10.27

Display multiple critical paths within a project from the Calculation tab of the Options dialog box.

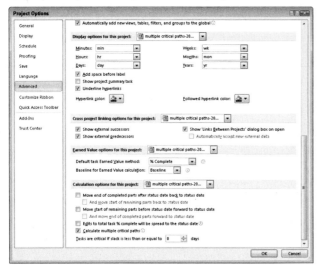

Over time, the critical path of your project may change as tasks on the critical path are completed either ahead of schedule or behind schedule. If your schedule contains slack — the amount of time you can delay tasks before affecting other tasks or the project end date — you may be able to adjust your schedule to get it back on track. Use the Detail Gantt view with the Schedule table to help evaluate the slack in your schedule. On the Gantt Chart, slack appears as thin bars on the right side of task bars. In the Schedule table, you'll find fields for Free Slack and Total Slack.

Summary

This chapter described the following techniques that you can use to identify and resolve scheduling conflicts and shorten the length of your project:

- Working with Project's warnings and suggestions to identify scheduling conflicts
- Adding resources to tasks
- Using overtime
- Finding and adjusting slack
- Changing task constraints and dependencies
- Adjusting the length of the critical path

In Chapter 11, you find out how to resolve conflicts that occur with resources.

Resolving Resource Problems

R esource allocation is the process of assigning resources to tasks in a project. Because the potential for resource overallocation always accompanies resource assignment, this chapter explores the causes of resource overallocation and suggests methods to resolve the conflicts.

Understanding How Resource Conflicts Occur

As you assign resources to tasks, Project checks the resource's calendar to make sure that the resource is working. However, Project doesn't assess whether the resource is already obligated when you assign the resource to a new task; Project enables you to make the assignment. If, indeed, the resource is already obligated, the additional assignment will probably lead to overallocating the resource. Overallocation occurs when you assign more work to a resource than the resource can accomplish in the time that you've allotted for the work to be completed.

For example, if you assign Gayle to work full-time on two tasks that start on the same day, you're actually assigning Gayle to 16 hours of work in an 8-hour day — not possible unless Gayle is a really dedicated employee who has no life outside work. On the other hand, if you have a group of three mechanics and you assign two mechanics to work on two tasks that start on the same day, you still have one spare mechanic and no overallocation.

Figure 11.1 shows a series of tasks under the Plan Entertainment and Public Relations tasks that begin on the same day. By assigning the same resource to them, an overallocation is inevitable. And overallocations can cause delays in the project schedule if the assigned resources can't complete the tasks in the time allotted.

FIGURE 11.1

Assigning the same resource to tasks that run simultaneously causes an overallocation.

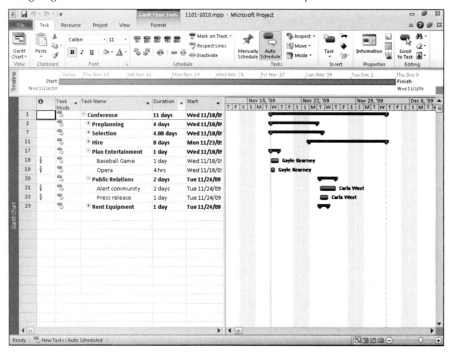

To calculate the scheduled start date for a task, Project checks factors such as the task's dependencies and constraints. Project then checks the resource's calendar to identify the next regular workday and assigns that date as the start date for the task. If you haven't assigned resources to the task, Project uses the project's calendar to calculate the next regular workday. Note, however, that when Project calculates the task's start date, it does not consider other commitments that the resource may have.

Spotting Resource Conflicts

Before you can resolve resource conflicts, of course, you have to spot them. You can use views or filters to help you identify resource-overallocation problems.

Using views to spot resource conflicts

You can spot resource conflicts in almost any view. In the Gantt Chart view (see Figure 11.2) or the Task Usage view, a red indicator that looks like a person appears in the Indicators column.

FIGURE 11.2

The red person in the Indicators column flags a task containing overallocated resources.

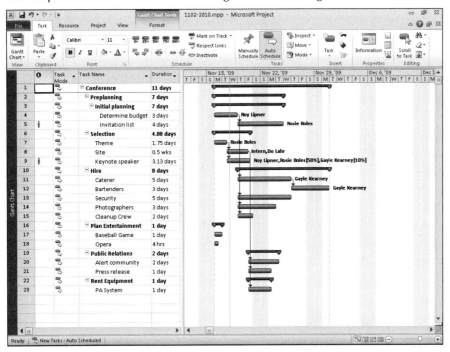

In resource views such as the Resource Usage view shown in Figure 11.3 or the Resource Sheet, a Caution sign appears in the indicator column beside an overallocated resource; in addition, the resource's name and hours appear in bold red type.

You also can see a graphic representation of a resource's allocation by switching to the Resource Graph view. To display the view that appears in Figure 11.4, right-click the gray bar running down the left side of the Project window and choose Resource Graph. Scroll through the resources assigned to tasks in your project by clicking the left and right scroll arrows that appear at the bottom of the left pane where the resource's name appears.

If you're using Project Professional, you can also review the Team Planner view to spot resource conflicts. In the Team Planner view shown in Figure 11.5, an overallocated resource's name appears in red, and a red bar highlights overallocated tasks and timeframes.

New Feature

The Team Planner is new to Project Professional 2010. ∎

FIGURE 11.3

The Resource Usage view displays overallocated resources in red; a Caution sign appears in the Indicator column.

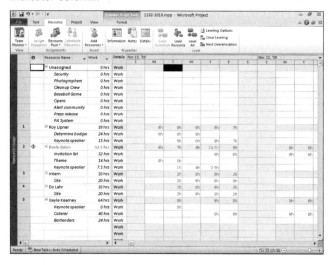

FIGURE 11.4

The Resource Graph view provides a picture of a resource's allocation.

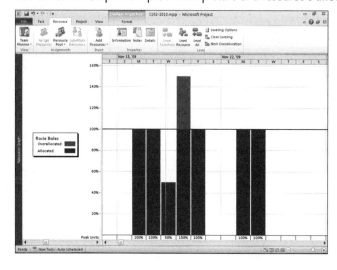

FIGURE 11.5

You can spot overallocated resources in the Team Planner view.

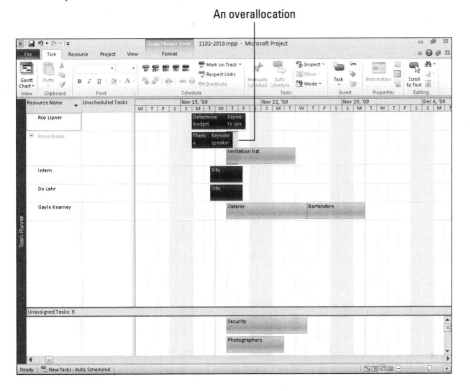

The Resource Allocation view, shown in Figure 11.6, is useful for working with overallocations; the Resource Usage view appears in the top pane, and the Leveling Gantt Chart in the lower pane shows the tasks assigned to the resource that you select in the Resource Usage pane. Tasks that start at the same time overlap in the Leveling Gantt Chart pane. This view helps you pinpoint the tasks that are causing the resource's overallocation. The top portion of the view in Figure 11.5 shows that Rosie Boles is overallocated on Thursday, November 19. If you examine that day more closely, you'll notice that Rosie is scheduled to work 10.5 hours that day. In the bottom portion of the view, the two tasks to which she's assigned 100 percent of the time are Invitation List and Keynote Speaker — and the Gantt view makes it easy to see the overlap of the two tasks on that Thursday.

Tip

In any view that displays an Indicator column, you can see a message about the overallocation if you use your mouse to point at the indicator. For information on addressing overallocations, see "Delaying tasks by leveling resource workloads," later in this chapter. ■

FIGURE 11.6

The Resource Allocation view uses the Gantt Chart format to show the tasks assigned to the resource selected in the top pane.

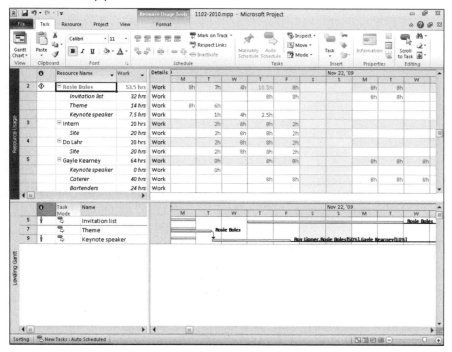

Using filters to spot resource conflicts

Filtering is another simple technique you can use to identify resource conflicts. If you filter the Resource Usage view to display only overallocated resources (see Figure 11.7), the problems become even more apparent. To filter the view in this way, follow these steps:

1. Click the View tab and, in the Resource Views group, click the Resource Usage button.

2. Click the list box arrow beside the Filter button in the Data and choose Overallocated Resources.

3. Add the Overallocation field to the view to identify the extent of the resource's overallocation: Right-click anywhere in the Details portion of the view and choose Overallocation.

   As Figure 11.8 shows, Project adds a row to the timescale portion of the view to show you the number of hours that you need to eliminate to correct the overallocation.

FIGURE 11.7

You can filter the Resource Usage view to show overallocated resources only.

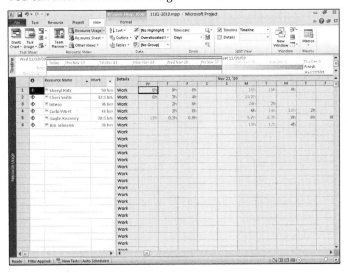

FIGURE 11.8

Add the Overallocation field to the Resource Usage view to find out how many hours you need to eliminate.

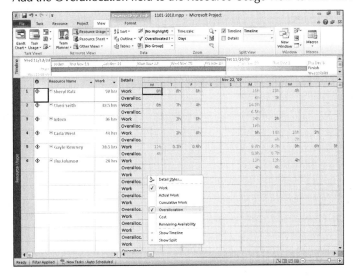

Resolving Conflicts

After you find the overallocations, you need to resolve the conflicts. Project managers use several methods to resolve conflicts.

Changing resource allocations

If you play around with resource allocations, you may be able to resolve a resource conflict. Adding a resource is one obvious way to resolve an overallocation. For example, suppose that Task 3 is an effort-driven task that has a resource conflict with Task 4. The two tasks don't run concurrently, but Task 3 is continuing when Task 4 is supposed to start. Suppose also that you need the same resource, Rosie Boles, to work on both tasks. Adding a resource (Do Lahr) to Task 3 reduces the amount of time that it takes to finish Task 3, which can eliminate Rosie's conflict between Tasks 3 and 4.

Getting Help While Trying to Resolve Conflicts

Often the hardest part of resolving conflicts is figuring out what your options are. Throughout the rest of this section, I describe many ways you can resolve resource conflicts, but Project might be able to head you in the right direction.

In any task view, right-click the Overallocation icon in the Indicators column. As you can see in the figures, Project displays a context menu that makes suggestions you might find useful in your situation. The options on the context menu differ, depending on what's causing the overallocation, as you can see by comparing the following two figures.

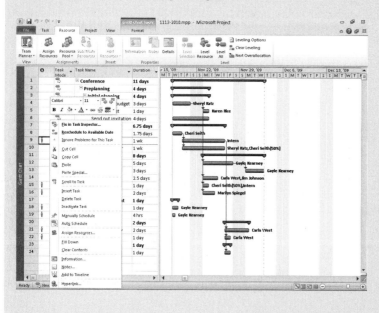

One suggestion you'll always see, however, is the one to fix the problem in the Task Inspector. When you select that option, Project displays more details about the overallocation that might help you decide how to approach solving it, as shown in the next figure.

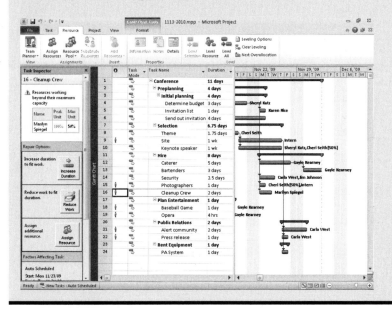

Cross-Reference

You can add a resource by using the techniques described in Chapter 5, or you can add a resource to a task by using the Resource Usage view (described in the section "Adding a task assignment to a resource," later in this chapter). ■

Switching resources

You also can resolve resource conflicts by switching resources. You can use this technique when one resource is overallocated but you have another resource available that's capable of doing the job. You switch resources by replacing resources on the task in question.

Project Standard users should start in the Resource Usage view, where you can focus on resource conflicts (refer to Figure 11.3; Figures 11.6 and 11.7, all based on the Resource Usage view). To switch resources, I suggest you create a combination view that shows the Gantt Chart in the top of the view and the Resource Usage view in the bottom of the view (see Figure 11.9).

FIGURE 11.9

Using a combination of the Gantt view and the Resource Usage view helps focus on correcting resource overallocations.

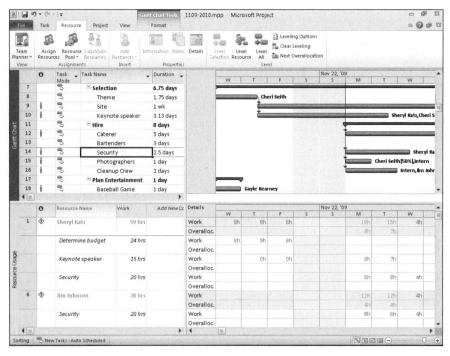

Cross-Reference

See Chapter 6 to learn how to create a combination view. ■

Then follow these steps:

1. In the upper pane, find and click the task for which you want to switch resources.

   In the bottom of the window, Project displays all the tasks assignments for each resource assigned to the selected task.

2. Click the Resource tab and, in the Assignments group, click the Assign Resources button to open the Assign Resources window.

3. Highlight the resource you want to switch.

4. Click the Replace button.

   The Replace Resource dialog box appears (see Figure 11.10).

5. Select the resource you want to use on the task.

FIGURE 11.10

Use the Replace Resource dialog box to substitute one resource for another.

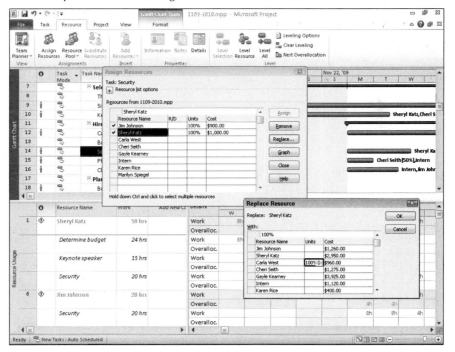

6. Fill in the Units column.

7. Click OK in the Replace Resource dialog box.

Note

Depending on your option settings, you may see a message from the Planning Wizard. Read the message and click OK to continue. ∎

8. Click Close in the Assign Resources window.

Project changes the assignment without affecting historical actuals, and no resources are affected other than the ones involved in the switch.

Project Professional users can use the method just described, or, they can do their work graphically in the Team Planner view. As you can see from Figure 11.11, Sheryl Katz is overallocated on November 23 because she has two simultaneous task assignments: Keynote Speaker and Security. However, Carla West has no assignments that day.

FIGURE 11.11

The Team Planner view displays task assignments graphically by resource.

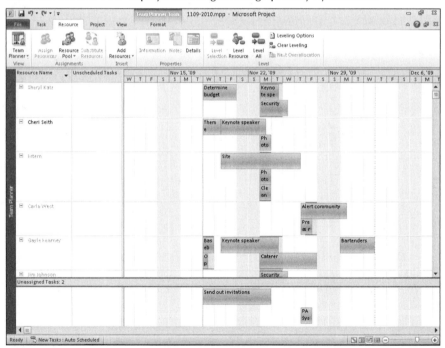

You can drag a task to a different resource to effectively replace one resource with another. In this case, I reassign the Security task to Carla by simply dragging it straight down and dropping it beside her name (see Figure 11.12). Be aware that you can drag a task left or right in this view — and that horizontal dragging changes the task's dates.

FIGURE 11.12

After dragging the Security task from Sheryl to Carla, Sheryl no longer displays an overallocation.

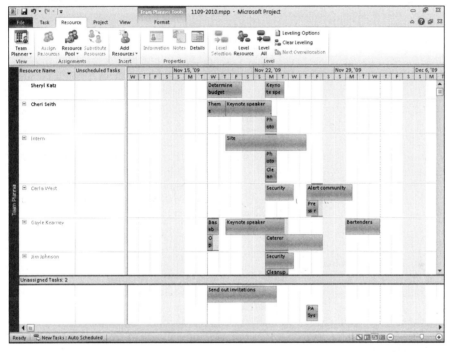

Tip

If you hover the mouse pointer over a task in the Team Planner view, Project displays details of the task. ■

Cross-Reference

If you're using Project Server, you can take advantage of the Resource Substitution Wizard to substitute generic resources automatically. See Chapter 22 for more details. ■

Adding a task assignment to a resource

You add a task assignment to a resource by using essentially the same process as I describe in the preceding section, "Switching resources" — except you don't replace one resource with another. Here are the general steps:

1. Set up the combination view where the Gantt Chart appears in the top pane and the Resource Usage view appears in the bottom pane.

2. In the upper pane, find and click the task to which you want to add a resource.

   In the bottom of the window, Project displays all the tasks assignments for each resource assigned to the selected task.

3. Open the Assign Resources window, highlight the resource you want to add, fill in the Units column, and click Close.

   Project adds the resource to the task.

Adding or deleting a resource assignment

You can add or delete a resource assignment using a number of techniques. For example, you can use the Assign Resources window, or you can work in the Gantt Chart view and then split the view to display the Task Details Form view in the bottom pane (see Figure 11.13).

FIGURE 11.13

You can work in the combination of the Gantt Chart view and the Task Details Form view to add or delete resource assignments.

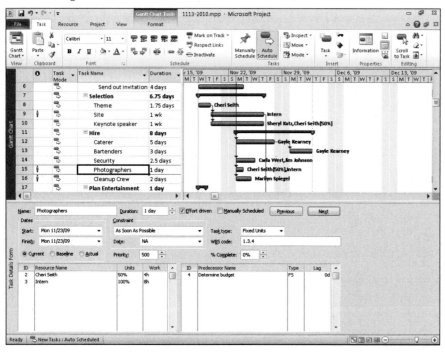

Select a task in the Gantt Chart view and then do any of the following:

- To add a resource assignment, select the resource from the list box that appears when you click the Resource Name column of the Task Details Form view.

- To delete a resource assignment, select the resource's ID number in the Task Entry view and press Delete.

- To switch resources, use the Replace Resource dialog box (see "Switching resources," earlier in this chapter, for more details).

Tip
Working in the Gantt Chart view is effective, but the Resource Usage view helps you to focus on resource conflicts. ■

Caution
You shouldn't delete a resource assignment that contains actual work. If you do, you will see misleading information about the task. Suppose, for example, that you assign one resource to a task, the resource completes the task, and then you delete the resource assignment. Project shows the task as completed, but you won't complete any work or actual work at the task level. ■

Scheduling overtime

You also can resolve a resource conflict by scheduling overtime for the resource. *Overtime* in Project is the amount of work that is scheduled beyond an assigned resource's regular working hours, and overtime hours are charged at the resource's overtime rate. Overtime work does not represent additional work on a task; instead, it represents the amount of time spent on a task during nonregular hours. Scheduling overtime may enable a particular resource to finish the task faster and therefore eliminate the conflict. As you read in the last chapter, you assign overtime from the Gantt Chart view. Use the following steps to schedule overtime:

1. Display the Gantt Chart view.
2. Click the Task tab and, in the Properties group, click the Show Task Details button to split the view, displaying the Gantt Chart in the top pane and the Task Details Form in the bottom pane.
3. Click the Task Details Form to make it the active pane.
4. Click the Task Form Tools Format tab and, in the Details group, click Work. Project displays the Ovt. Work column in the Task Details Form pane (see Figure 11.14). In this column, 0h means that you have not yet assigned overtime.

FIGURE 11.14

Use the Task Details Form, and display the Overtime column to add overtime.

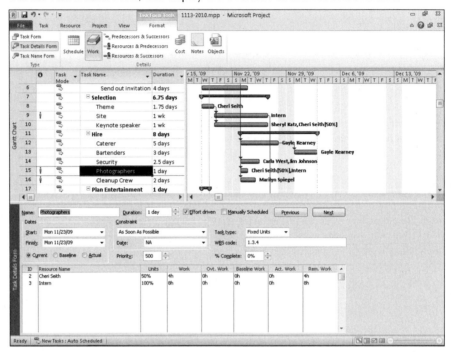

5. In the top pane, select the task to which you want to assign overtime.

6. In the bottom pane, fill in the overtime amount for the appropriate resource.

Tip

When you finish entering overtime, you can hide the Task Details Form by repeating Step 2 in the preceding steps list. ■

Redefining a resource's calendar

You may have the option of redefining a resource's calendar so that hours typically considered nonworking (and therefore charged at an overtime rate if worked) become working hours. If a resource has a conflict and the number of hours in conflict on a given day is low enough, you can eliminate the conflict by increasing the working hours for the resource for that day.

Note

You can make this kind of change to any resource — Project won't stop you. But you need to consider the effects on the cost of your project. If your company pays a resource at an overtime rate for working during nonworking hours, you don't want to change nonworking hours to working hours in Project. If you do, you will understate the cost of your project. ■

To change a resource's working calendar, follow these steps:

1. Display the Resource Usage view.

2. Identify the resource that has a conflict and note the number of hours that the conflict involves.

3. Double-click the resource that has a conflict.

   The Resource Information dialog box for that resource.

4. Click Change Working Time to view that resource's calendar (see Figure 11.15).

FIGURE 11.15

Open the Change Working Time dialog box from the Resource Information dialog box to change the standard working hours for a specific resource.

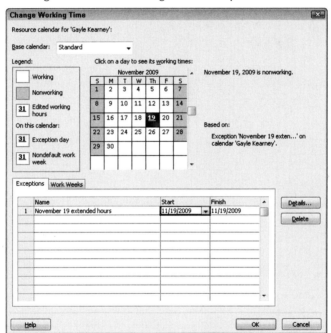

5. Click the Exceptions tab.

6. Click the first date on which the resource is overallocated.

7. In the Name column, type a name for the exception you're about to create and click outside the Name column.

   Project displays the date you clicked in Step 6 in both the Start and Finish columns.

8. Click the Details button.

9. Click the Working times option button and use the From and To boxes to set up non-standard working hours for the resource.

10. If you want to change the resource's standard working hours for more than one day, select an option in the Recurrence Pattern section and then set a date range in the Range of Recurrence section. In Figure 11.16, I set the workday to last 10.5 hours for two days: November 19 and November 20.

FIGURE 11.16

Set nonstandard working hours during a specified time period for a particular resource.

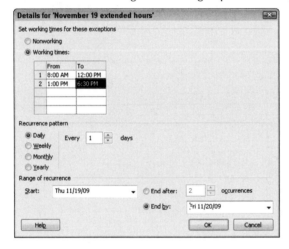

11. Click OK to redisplay the Change Working Time dialog box; the working hours for the specified dates will appear if you click those dates on the calendar.

12. Click OK to save the exception to standard working hours for the resource.

13. Click OK to close the Resource Information dialog box.

Assigning part-time work

Suppose that a resource is assigned to several concurrent tasks and is also overallocated. Suppose also that, for varying reasons, you don't want to add other resources, switch to a different resource, or add overtime. You can assign the resource to work part-time on each of the tasks to solve the conflict, although the tasks may take longer to complete by using this method. Or, you may want to use this method in conjunction with additional resources to make sure that you can complete the task on time.

To assign a resource to work part-time, you can change the number of units of the resource that you apply to the task. by default, Project sets task types to Fixed Units. therefore, if you change the amount of time that a resource works on a task, Project changes the duration of the task accordingly.

Note

To retain the duration and assign a resource to work part-time on a task, change the task type to Fixed Duration. by making this change, however, you are indicating that the task can be completed by the resource in the allotted amount of time — effectively, you are shortening the amount of time that it takes to complete the task because you're applying less effort during the same time frame. ∎

To change a task's type to Fixed Duration and then assign a resource to work on the task part-time without changing the task's duration, follow these steps:

1. Display the Task Usage view by clicking the View shortcut at the lower-right edge of the Status Bar.
2. Double-click the task you want to change.

   Project displays the Task Information dialog box.
3. Click the Advanced tab (see Figure 11.17).

FIGURE 11.17

Use the Advanced tab of the Task Information dialog box to change the task type.

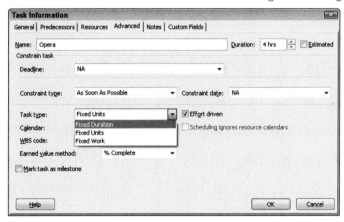

4. Open the Task type list box and select Fixed Duration.
5. Click OK.
6. Under the task you just changed, double-click the resource to whom you want to assign part-time work.

   Project displays the Assignment Information dialog box (see Figure 11.18).

FIGURE 11.18

Use the Assignment Information dialog box to change a resource's workload to part-time.

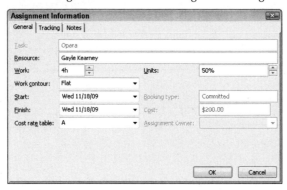

7. Change the default value in the Units box (100%) to reflect the percentage of time that you want the resource to spend on the task.

   In this example, the value should be less than 100%.

8. Click OK.

Controlling when resources start working on a task

If you've assigned more than one resource to a task, consider staggering the times that the resources begin working on the task to resolve resource conflicts. When you delay a resource's start on a task, Project recalculates the start date and time for that resource's work on the task. To stagger start times for resources, work in the Task Usage view and follow these steps:

Note
This technique can extend the duration of the task, which may not be a viable option for you. ■

1. Display the Task Usage view by clicking the View shortcut at the lower-right edge of the Status Bar.

2. In the Task Name column, double-click the resource whose work time you want to delay. Project displays the General tab of the Assignment Information dialog box (as shown previously in Figure 11.18).

3. Change the dates in the Start or Finish boxes.

4. Click OK.

Tip
You also can alter the assignment start and finish dates directly in the Task Usage table. ■

Delaying tasks by leveling resource workloads

If you have scheduled several tasks to run concurrently and you now find resource conflicts in your project, you can delay some of these tasks to *level* — that is, spread out — the demands you're making on your resources. Leveling is the process of resolving resource conflicts by delaying or splitting tasks to accommodate the schedules of assigned resources. You can ask Project to select the tasks to delay or split by using its leveling feature, or you can control the process manually by examining the project to identify tasks that you are willing to delay or split.

Letting Project level resource loads

When Project does the leveling for you, it redistributes a resource's assignments and reschedules them according to each resource's working capacity, assignment units, and calendar. Project also considers the task's duration, constraints, and priority.

What is a task's *priority*? Well, leveling typically results in Project's delaying some tasks, and you can use the task's priority to control the order in which Project levels tasks to try to avoid delaying certain tasks. By default, Project assigns all tasks a priority of 500. When you assign different priorities to tasks, Project considers the priorities of each task when you level and attempts to avoid delaying tasks in order of their priority, from highest to lowest — the higher the number, the higher the priority. Effectively, Project delays tasks with lower priorities before delaying tasks with higher priorities; if everything else is equal, Project will delay a task with a priority of 5 before it will delay a task with a priority of 15. So, before you start to use the automatic-leveling feature, consider how you want to prioritize tasks.

Tip

The priority of 1000 is treated in a special way; Project will not consider delaying any task to which you assign a priority of 1000. ■

To set a priority, follow these steps:

1. Click the Gantt Chart View shortcut at the lower-right edge of the Status Bar.
2. Double-click the task for which you want to set a priority.

   Project displays the Task Information dialog box.
3. Use the General tab to set a priority (see Figure 11.19).

Tip

You might prefer to set priorities from the table portion of the Gantt Chart view or the Task Usage view, where you can easily see the priorities of neighboring tasks. ■

FIGURE 11.19

Setting a priority for a task.

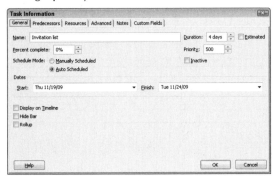

Tip

After you prioritize tasks — but before you level — you can sort tasks by priority to view the tasks that Project is most likely to level. ∎

If you don't want to review leveling options, you can skip the steps that follow and simply click the Resource tab and, in the Level group, click Level All. However, if you want to review and control the way Project levels, follow these steps:

1. Click the Resource tab and, in the Level group, click Leveling Options to open the Resource Leveling dialog box (see Figure 11.20).

FIGURE 11.20

From the Resource Leveling dialog box, you can set resource-leveling options.

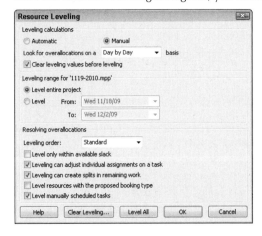

2. Select Automatic or Manual leveling.

   If you selection the Automatic option button, Project automatically levels resources, if necessary, whenever you make a change to your schedule. Select the Manual option if you prefer to perform leveling only when you click the Level Now button in this dialog box.

3. Use the Look for Overallocations on a . . . Basis list box to select a basis.

   The *basis* is a time frame, such as Day by Day or Week by Week. (The Indicator box in the Resource Usage view may contain a note that suggests the appropriate basis.)

4. Select the Clear Leveling Values before Leveling check box to make Project reset all leveling delay values to 0 before leveling.

   If you don't check this box, Project does not reset leveling values but builds upon the values. During leveling, the scheduling for previously leveled tasks will probably not change.

5. In the Leveling Range For area, select either to level the entire project or to level only for specified dates.

6. In the Leveling Order list box, select the order that you want Project to consider when leveling your project:

   - If you choose ID Only, Project delays or splits the task with the highest ID number.

   - If you choose Standard, Project looks at predecessor dependencies, slack, dates, and priorities when selecting the best task to split or delay.

   - If you choose Priority, Standard, Project looks first at task priority and then at all the items that are listed for the Standard leveling order.

7. Select any of the following options:

   - Level Only Within Available Slack: This avoids changing the end date of your project.

   - Leveling Can Adjust Individual Assignments on a Task: In this case, leveling adjusts one resource's work schedule on a task independent of other resources that are working on the same task.

   - Leveling Can Create Splits in Remaining Work: This allows leveling to split tasks to resolve resource conflicts.

   - Level Resources with the Proposed Booking Type: Check this box to have Project include tasks containing proposed resources during the leveling process.

   - Level manually scheduled tasks: Check this box to include manually scheduled tasks when you level resource assignments.

8. Click Level All to apply leveling.

You can review the effects of leveling from the Leveling Gantt Chart view (see Figure 11.21). Right-click the gray bar that runs down the left side of the Project window and choose More Views. In the More Views window, select Leveling Gantt and then click Apply. Project shows light-green bars above blue bars in the Gantt Chart; the light-green bars represent the duration of tasks before leveling and the blue bars represent the tasks after leveling. Depending on the nature of your project, Project may build more slack into your tasks. If Project can't resolve an overallocation by leveling, you'll see a message to that effect during the leveling process and the overallocation indicator will remain for that task.

FIGURE 11.21

The Leveling Gantt Chart view shows how leveling affects your project.

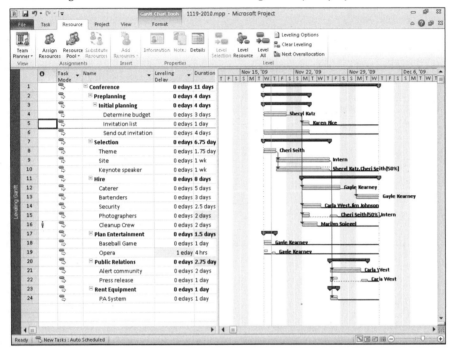

To remove the effects of leveling, reopen the Resource Leveling dialog box (on the Resource tab in the Level group, click Leveling Options) and click the Clear Leveling button. A subsequent dialog box enables you to clear leveling for the entire project or for selected tasks only.

Note

If you're scheduling from a finish date, you still can level to resolve resource conflicts. Project calculates the delay by subtracting it from a task's or assignment's finish date, causing the finish date to occur earlier. ■

Making adjustments to leveling

You can adjust leveling when automatic leveling doesn't provide acceptable results or when you have just a few resource conflicts to resolve. To make leveling adjustments to resources in Project, follow these steps in the Resource Allocation view:

1. Right-click the gray bar that runs down the left side of the Project window and choose More Views.

   In the More Views window, select Resource Allocation and then click Apply.

2. In the top pane, select a resource.

3. In the bottom pane, highlight the task that you want to delay.

4. Enter an amount in the Leveling Delay field. Project delays the task accordingly and reduces the resource's conflict.

Figures 11.22 and 11.23 show "before" and "after" pictures for manual leveling. I used a simple situation to demonstrate the effects of manual leveling: I set up a project with only two tasks that run simultaneously and one resource, and I assigned the same resource full-time to both tasks. Notice that manually leveling the second task delays the second task so that it starts when the first task finishes.

Contouring resources

Contour is the term that Project uses to refer to the shape of a resource's work assignment over time. Contours come in several flavors; the most common are Flat, Back Loaded, Front Loaded, and Bell. The default contour is Flat, which means that a resource works on a task for the maximum number of hours that he or she is assigned to the task for the duration of the assignment. You can use different contours to control how much a resource is scheduled to work on a task at a given time — and possibly resolve a conflict.

FIGURE 11.22

The Resource Allocation view before manual leveling.

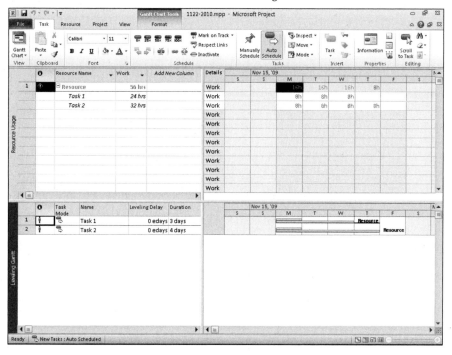

FIGURE 11.23

The Resource Allocation view after manually leveling the second task.

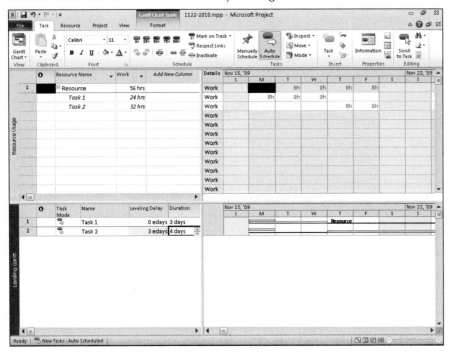

Tip

Add the Peak Units field to the Resource Usage view to display the maximum effort — as distributed over time — that a resource is expected to work. This field is particularly useful when you have selected a contour other than the default (Flat). ■

The Flat contour assigns a resource to work the maximum number of hours per time period throughout the duration of the task. By changing the contour, you can more accurately reflect the actual work pattern for the resource while working on a task.

To better understand contours, think of dividing each task into 10 equal timeslots. By using the various contours, Project assigns percentages of work to be done in each timeslot. Contours help you to assign work to a task, based on when the task requires the effort. For example, if a task requires less effort initially, consider using a Back Loaded contour. If a task requires most effort in the middle of the task, consider using a Bell, Turtle, or even an Early Peak contour.

Caution

If you start changing contours from the default Flat contour, you may inadvertently create a resource conflict. Therefore, viewing any contours you set can help you resolve resource conflicts. ■

Setting a contour pattern

To set a contour pattern, follow these steps:

1. Click the Task Usage view shortcut at the lower-right edge of the Status Bar. In the sheet portion of the view, Project displays each task in your project, along with the resources that are assigned to it listed below the task, showing the number of hours per day that a resource is assigned to a task.

2. In the Task Name column, double-click the resource whose contour you want to change. Then click the General tab of the Assignment Information dialog box (see Figure 11.24).

FIGURE 11.24

Use the General tab of the Assignment Information dialog box to select a contour.

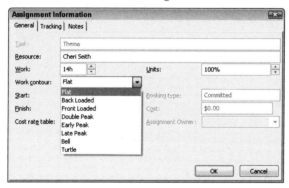

3. Open the Work contour list box and select a contour.
4. Click OK.

Tip

To change the start and end dates for the resource's work on the task, use the Start and Finish list boxes. ■

When you select a contour other than Flat, an indicator showing the type of contour appears next to the affected resource in the Indicator column. If you hover the mouse pointer over the indicator, Project identifies the contour that was applied to the resource (see Figure 11.25).

FIGURE 11.25

Project displays an icon in the Indicator column next to a resource for which you've specified a contour other than Flat.

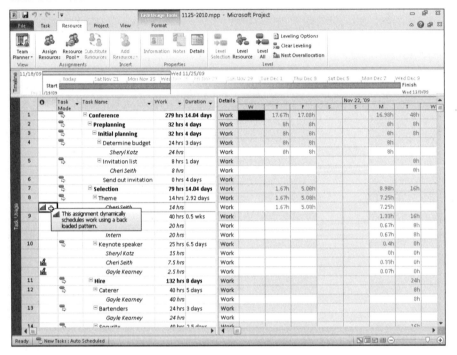

Tip

The same icon appears in the Indicator column in the Resource Usage view. ∎

Keep the following points in mind when working with contours:

- Suppose you apply a contour other than the default Flat contour to a task, and later you add new Total Work values to the task. Project automatically reapplies the contour pattern to the task and the resources first by distributing the new task work values across the affected time span and then by assigning new work values to the resources that are working on the task.

- If you set a contour and then change the start date of the task — or the start date of a resource's work on that task — Project automatically shifts the contour and reapplies it to include the new date, thus preserving the pattern of the original contour.

- If you increase the duration of a task, Project stretches the contour to include the new duration.

- Suppose you apply a contour other than the default contour to a task. If you manually edit a work value on the portion of a view that displays the contour, Project no longer applies the contour pattern automatically. Note however, that you can reapply the contour to redistribute the new values.

- If you enter actual work and then change the task's Total Work or Total Remaining Work, Project automatically redistributes the changes to the remaining work values and not to the actual work.

Contouring a resource's availability

You can contour a resource's availability using the General tab of the Resource Information dialog box (see Figure 11.26). In the Resource Availability list box, set Available From and Available To dates for the selected resource. You'd use this feature if a particular resource is available to work on your project only part-time during a specified time frame. Or suppose you have five computer programmers, but only three are available in August and one retires in September. Use the Resource Availability section to specify the availability of your resources, which will influence your project's schedule.

FIGURE 11.26

Set dates that represent the resource's availability so that you can assign the resource to a task by using only the dates that the resource is available.

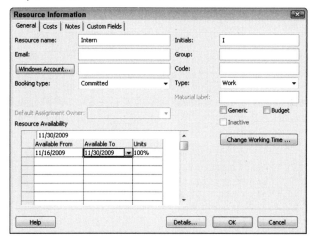

Pooling resources

Finally, you can try to solve resource conflicts by using a resource pool. A *resource pool* is a set of resources that are available to any project. You can use resources exclusively on one project, or you can share the resources among several projects.

Typically, resource pooling is useful only if you work with the same resources on multiple projects and you don't use Project Server. Different project managers can share the same resources. Because resource pooling is so closely tied to the topic of managing multiple projects, I postpone further discussion until Chapter 19; in that context, I believe that you'll better understand the application of resource pooling to resolving resource conflicts.

If you're using Project Server, you don't need to use resource pooling. Instead, you'll be more interested in using Enterprise resources and the Resource Substitution Wizard to resolve resource conflicts. See Chapter 22 for more information.

Summary

This chapter explained how to identify and resolve resource conflicts that can delay a project. The techniques involved include the following:

- Changing resource allocations
- Scheduling overtime
- Redefining a resource calendar
- Assigning part-time work
- Controlling resource start times
- Leveling resource workloads
- Contouring resources

In the next chapter, you discover the art of tracking your progress by comparing your project to its baseline.

Part V

Tracking Your Progress

Understanding Tracking

This chapter marks something of a turning point in this book and in your use of Project. Up to this point, you've been in the planning phase: building a project schedule, entering tasks, adding resources, and shifting things around so resource assignments don't conflict and tasks have the proper relationships to each other. You've even tweaked details such as text formatting and the appearance of taskbars. You now have a workable, good-looking project in hand — and now you are ready to start the project.

Tracking is the process of comparing what actually happens during your project to your estimates of what would happen. To track, you need to take a picture of your project schedule at the moment your planning is complete; this moment is called a *baseline*. But you also have to understand what steps are involved in tracking and how to set up efficient procedures to handle these steps.

Note
You can store up to 11 baselines for any project. ■

Because you control manually scheduled tasks completely and Project controls automatically scheduled tasks, the bulk of the information in this chapter focuses on describing Project's behavior with automatically scheduled tasks.

Understanding the Principles of Tracking

A good plan is only half the battle. How you execute that plan is the key. Think of yourself as the quarterback in a football game. If you run straight down the field toward the goalpost, never swerving to avoid an oncoming opponent, you won't get very far. Project tracking is similar: If you don't swerve and make adjustments for the changes in costs and timing that are virtually inevitable in any human endeavor, you're not playing the game correctly.

Project management software greatly enhances your ability to quickly see problems and revise the plan to minimize any damage. Project enables you to compare what you thought would happen to what actually happens over the course of the project.

Estimates versus actuals

The plan you've been building is an estimate of what can occur. It's your best guess (an educated one, I hope) about how long tasks may take, how one task affects another, how many resources you need to complete the work, and what costs you expect your project to incur. Good project managers keep good records of their estimates and actuals to become better project managers. By comparing these two sets of data, you can see where your estimates were off and then use this information to make your next plan more realistic. You can also use data on actual costs and timing to make the changes in your strategy that are necessary to keep you on track, within budget, and meet your current project's goals.

Tracking in Project consists of entering information about actuals, such as the actual start date, the actual finish date, and the actual duration of a task. You enter actual time that is worked by resources and actual costs that are incurred. When you enter information about actuals, Project shows you a revised schedule with projections of how the rest of the schedule is likely to play out, based on your actual activity.

Project managers usually track activity on a regular basis, such as once a week or every two weeks. This tracking includes information about tasks in progress as well as about tasks that have been completed.

This tracking activity also enables you to generate reports that show management where your efforts stand at any given point in time. By showing managers the hard data on your project's status — rather than your best guess — you can make persuasive bids for more time, more resources, or a shift in strategy if things aren't going as you expected. Figure 12.1 shows a Tracking Gantt view using the Tracking table.

Cross-Reference
Chapter 13 explains the specific steps for updating a project to reflect actual progress. ■

FIGURE 12.1

Use the Tracking Gantt view to display the progress of your project.

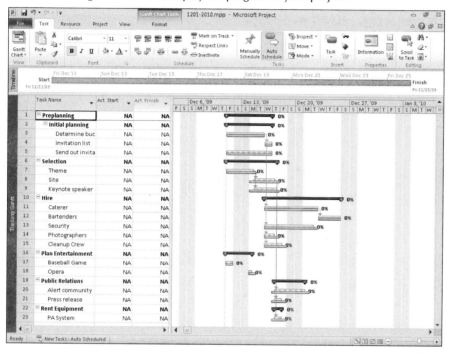

Making adjustments as you go

Tracking isn't something that you leave to the end of the project, or even to the end of individual tasks. Tracking tasks in progress on a regular basis helps you to detect any deviation from your estimates. The earlier you spot a delay, the more time you have to make up for it. In the following discussion, I focus primarily on Project's behavior when you use automatic scheduling; if your schedule includes manually scheduled tasks, Project makes no adjustments.

If you use automatic scheduling and Project determines that you're running late on a task, it automatically moves dependent tasks into the future. For example, suppose you estimated that a task would take three days, but you've already put four days of effort into it and it's still not complete. Project not only tells you that you're running late but also moves automatically scheduled future tasks that depend on this task farther out in the schedule. Project also shows any resource conflicts that result when resources have to put in more work than you estimated in resource views, such as the Resource Sheet and Resource Graph view. Project clearly shows how one delay ripples through your schedule.

How Much Have You Accomplished?

As I describe in Chapter 13, you record activity on a task by entering an estimate of the percentage of the task that's complete, actual resource time spent on the task, or actual costs incurred (such as fees or equipment rentals paid), or by entering the hours of work done per time period. Estimating "the completeness" of a task is not an exact science, and different people use different methods.

With something concrete, such as a building under construction, you can look at the actual building and estimate fairly accurately how far along the project has progressed. Most projects aren't so straightforward. How do you estimate how far along you are in more creative tasks, such as coming up with an advertising concept? You can sit in meetings for five weeks and still not find the right concept. Is your project 50 percent complete? Completion is hard to gauge from other, similar projects on which you've worked — perhaps on the last project, you came up with the perfect concept in your very first meeting.

Don't fall into the trap of using money or time spent as a gauge. It's (unfortunately) easy to spend $10,000 on a task estimated to cost $8,000 and still be only 25 percent of the way to completion. You probably have to use the same gut instincts that put you in charge of this project to estimate the progress of individual tasks. Hint: If your project has individual deliverables that you can track, document them and use them consistently when you make your estimate.

Tip
Project adjusts your project's cost as you track to reflect the effect of higher-than-expected costs. ∎

Project also shows the effect of unanticipated costs on the total budget if the costs you track on early tasks are higher than anticipated. Project displays your projected total costs based on a combination of actual costs and the remaining estimates. Project shows you exactly how much of your budget you have used and how much you have remaining, so you can revise your resource allocations to stay within your overall budget.

Using Baselines

You complete the planning phase of your project by setting a baseline. You have seen this term in previous chapters, but take a moment to grasp its significance in the tracking process.

What is a baseline?

A *baseline* is a snapshot of your project that you take when you complete the planning phase, or sometimes at the end of some other critical phase. The baseline is a set of data saved in the same file where you track actual progress data. Project enables you to save up to 11 baselines and an equal number of interim plans during your project. You can show a wide variety of information about your baseline(s), or you can choose not to display baseline information.

Some projects, particularly shorter ones that run only a few weeks or even a couple of months, may have one baseline set at the outset and may proceed close enough to your estimates that they can run their course against that single baseline. Other projects, especially longer ones, may require you to set several baselines along the way, particularly if the original estimate is so out of line with what has transpired in the project that the original is no longer useful. You can modify the entire baseline if changes are drastic and occur early in the project, or you can modify the baseline estimates only going forward from a particular point in the project.

For example, if your project is put on hold shortly after you complete the schedule and you actually start work three months later than you had planned, you would be wise to set a new baseline schedule before restarting. If, however, you're six months into your project and it is put on hold for three months, you may want to modify the timing of future tasks and reset the baseline only for tasks going forward to help you retain the ability to accurately assess how well you estimated for the tasks on which work was performed before the project was placed on hold.

Costs can change a baseline, too. For example, what if you save a baseline that is set to fit within a $50,000 budget and, before you start work, cost-cutting measures hit your company and your budget is cut to $35,000? You would be wise to make the changes to your resources and costs, and then reset your baseline. Setting interim baselines keeps your projects from varying wildly from your estimates when mitigating circumstances come into play.

Setting a baseline

In most cases, you need to save the project file — without setting the baseline — several times during the planning phase.

When you're ready, you can use the Set Baseline dialog box to save up to 11 baselines and 10 interim plans for your project. Each baseline is a picture of your project at the time that you save it, and each baseline you set includes information about tasks, resources, and assignments. For tasks, Project saves duration, start and finish dates, work, timephased work, cost, and timephased cost. For resources, Project saves work, timephased work, cost, timephased cost, budget work, timephased budget work, budget cost, and timephased budget cost information with the baseline. For assignments, Project saves start and finish dates, work, timephased work, costs, and time-phased costs.

When you save interim plans, Project saves less information than when you save a baseline. For each interim plan, Project saves a set of task start and finish dates that you can compare with another interim plan or with a baseline plan, which helps you to keep an eye on progress or slippage. Saving baselines and interim plans can help you compare current information (found in the start and finish fields) with baseline information (found in the baseline fields). The distinction between baselines and interim plans in Project is the amount and type of information that Project saves.

To control the settings when you set a baseline, follow these steps:

1. Set up the baseline project that you want to save.
2. Click the Project tab.

3. In the Schedule group, click Set Baseline.

4. From the drop-down menu that appears, click Set Baseline to display the Set Baseline dialog box shown in Figure 12.2.

FIGURE 12.2

Use this dialog box to save a baseline or interim plan.

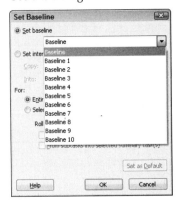

5. Open the Set Baseline list box and select the baseline that you want to set.

6. Click OK.

When you set baselines for selected tasks, you can choose to roll up baselines to all summary tasks and from subtasks into their parent summary task(s) — thus helping to maintain accurate baseline information (see Figure 12.3). The relationship between the tasks in the project and the task(s) that you select prior to opening the dialog box determines the effect of these check boxes.

FIGURE 12.3

You can control Project's behavior when rolling up baseline information for selected tasks.

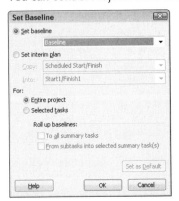

For example, suppose you have a project set up like the one shown in Figure 12.4. Furthermore, suppose you select Task 6, a child of Task 1 and the parent of Tasks 7 and 8, before you open the Set Baseline dialog box. If you select only the From Subtasks into Selected Summary Task(s) check box, Project rolls up the information from Tasks 7 and 8 to Task 6. If you select only the To All Summary Tasks check box, Project rolls up baseline information from Task 6 without regard to the baseline information that is stored for Tasks 7 and 8. If you select both check boxes, Project rolls up baseline information from Tasks 7 and 8 to Task 6 and then rolls up that information to Task 1.

Suppose you want to update the baseline to reflect approved changes to the project, such as added tasks, or changes to existing tasks that affect the cost or schedule of the tasks. Highlight the added or changed tasks and the parent summary task and then set the baseline. In the Set Baseline box (refer to Figure 12.3), choose the Selected Tasks option and check both boxes in the Roll Up Baselines section. Project will update the baseline for the changed tasks and then change all the summary levels to reflect the change.

FIGURE 12.4

Ancestry determines baseline information rollup behavior. In this sample project, Tasks 3 and 6 are children of Task 1, and Task 6 is the parent of Tasks 7 and 8.

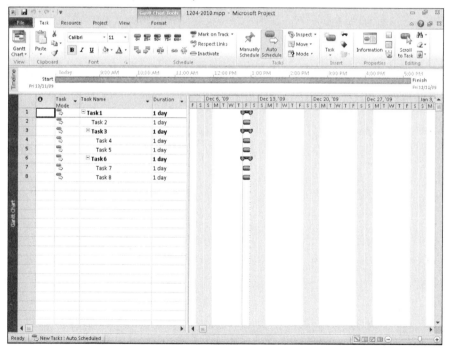

Changing the Baseline

Most of the time, you *don't* want to make changes to a baseline. It's a moment that's frozen in time, a record against which you can compare your progress. If you change a baseline on a regular basis, you are defeating its purpose.

That said, sometimes — for strategic reasons — you need to modify a baseline project, reset the baseline or set a second or third baseline to document major shifts in the project. However, if you are overriding the original baseline, you must do so in a thoughtful and efficient way. This section discusses some of the times when changes to a baseline are necessary and explains how you can make those changes.

Adding a task to a baseline

It's fairly common to set your baseline plan and then realize that you left out a task, or then decide to break one task into two tasks. Perhaps your company institutes a new requirement or process, and you have to modify a task to deal with the change. You don't want to reset your whole project baseline, but you want to save that one task along with the original baseline. You can make this change after you set the original baseline.

To add a task to your baseline so that you can track its progress, follow these steps:

1. Do one of the following:
    - To add a new task to the schedule and then incorporate it into the baseline, first add the task in the Task Name column on your Gantt Chart and then select it.
    - To save modifications to an existing task, first make the changes and then select the task.
2. Click the Project tab.
3. In the Schedule group, click Set Baseline, and, from the drop-down menu that appears, click Set Baseline.

    The Set Baseline dialog box appears.
4. Select the baseline that you want to modify from the Save baseline list.
5. Choose the Selected Tasks option button, as shown in Figure 12.5.
6. Choose the appropriate Roll Up Baselines settings (see the preceding section for details on these options).
7. Click OK to save the baseline, which now includes the new task.

Note

You can add tasks to the baseline by entering them in the Gantt table, using columns such as Baseline Duration and Baseline Start or Finish. However, adding baseline data this way does not enable all baseline calculations. For example, adding a task at the end of the project with this method doesn't affect a change in the baseline finish date. ∎

FIGURE 12.5

Make modifications to tasks and save them in an already established baseline.

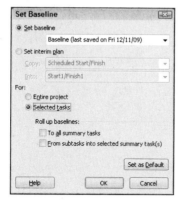

Using interim plans

You can use the baseline in different ways. You can refer to it as your original estimate and compare it with actual results at the end of the project to see how well you guessed, and to learn to make better guesses on future projects. But the baseline also has an important practical use during the project: It alerts you to shifts so that you can make changes to accommodate them. The second use may prompt you to save interim plans.

The initial baseline(s) may quickly take on more historical than practical interest. You should not change the initial baseline(s) because that record of your original planning process is important to retain for your education. However, if timing shifts dramatically away from the baseline plan, all the little warning signs that Project gives you about being off schedule become useless. A project that starts six months later than expected will show every task as late and every task as critical. To continue generating useful project information, you need to revise the schedule to better reflect reality. Only by setting interim plans can you see how well you're meeting your revised goals.

Note

Remember that interim plans contain a set of task start and finish dates that you can compare with another interim plan or with a baseline plan, which helps you keep an eye on progress or slippage. A baseline includes much more information — duration, start and finish dates, work, and cost information about tasks, resources, and assignments. Setting baselines and interim plans helps you to compare current information, found in the start and finish fields, with baseline information, found in the baseline fields. ∎

You can set interim plans for all the tasks in the project. However, you should usually set an interim plan only for tasks going forward. For example, if a labor strike pushes out a manufacturing project by two months, you should keep the baseline intact for all the tasks that were completed at the time the strike started and save an interim plan for all the tasks that must still be performed when the strike ends.

Tip

You also can use interim plans to copy baseline information from one baseline to another. ∎

You can set an interim plan by following these steps:

1. Select various tasks to include in the interim plan.

2. In the Schedule group, click Set Baseline, and, from the drop-down menu that appears, click Set Baseline.

   The Set Baseline dialog box appears.

3. Select the Set interim plan option button. Project makes the Copy and Into fields available.

4. Open the Copy list.

   In Figure 12.6, I've opened the Into list, which contains basically the same choices as you'll find in the Copy list.

FIGURE 12.6

The choices in the Copy and Into lists enable you to save several sets of start and finish dates in interim plans.

5. Select Scheduled Start/Finish from the Copy drop-down list to copy the current start and finish dates.

6. Open the drop-down list for the Into field and select an item, such as Start1/Finish1, to copy the dates into new fields, thus creating an interim plan.

7. Select the Entire project option button to create an interim plan for the whole project, or choose the Selected tasks option button to create an interim plan that retains the original interim plan or baseline information for any tasks that you didn't select, yet saves new baseline information for the tasks that you have selected.

8. Click OK to save the interim plan.

Remember that you can use the various numbered Start/Finish items to set up to 10 interim plans plus the original, for a total of 11 interim plans over the life of your project.

Clearing a baseline or interim plan

Inevitably, you set a baseline or an interim baseline and then find a reason to clear it. Suppose, for example, that you thought you finished the planning stage of the project. The project hasn't yet started, and you attend a meeting in which you inform everyone that you're "good to go" for next Monday. Naturally, your announcement triggers discussion and, by the time the discussion ends, the scope of the project has expanded (or contracted) considerably. You now need to work again on the planning phase of your schedule — and you really don't want to adjust the baseline. Instead, you want to get rid of it. After you make all your changes, you can set the correct baseline.

To clear a baseline, click the Project tab and, in the Schedule group, click the Set Baseline button. From the drop-down menu that appears, choose Clear Baseline. Project displays the Clear Baseline dialog box (see Figure 12.7). In this dialog box, you can choose to clear a baseline plan or an interim plan for the entire project or for selected tasks.

FIGURE 12.7

Set the baseline too soon? Clear it from this dialog box so that you can make adjustments and set the baseline correctly.

Understanding Tracking Strategies

As you use Microsoft Project on real projects, your tracking skills will improve. However, if you follow certain basic principles of tracking from the start, you can save yourself a lot of aggravation in your first few projects.

Tackling the work of tracking

First, update your project schedule frequently and at regular intervals. Many people see tracking as a monumental task: All the details of each task's progress and duration, as well as all the resources and costs associated with each task must be entered one by one. You have to gather that data through resource timecards, reports from other project participants, and vendor invoices. You must type in all the information that you gather. I won't kid you: Tracking can be hard work. However, the more often you track, the less the tracking data will pile up and the less likely it is to overwhelm you.

Help yourself with the tracking task by assigning pieces of the updating to various people in your project. If a particular resource is in charge of one phase of the project, have him or her track the activity on just that phase. You can use various methods of compiling those smaller schedules into a master schedule.

Cross-Reference

Part V of this book provides ideas for compiling several schedules and managing schedules with workgroups. ■

If you have a resource available, such as an administrative assistant who can handle the tracking details, all the better. Make sure you provide this assistant with appropriate training (and a copy of this book) so he or she understands the tracking process well enough to be accurate and productive. However, this resource probably does not need to be a Project expert to take on some of the work.

Tip

To help you remember to track, you can enter tracking as a recurring task, occurring once every week or two, within your project file. And don't forget to include required meetings (such as progress meetings and performance reviews) in your schedule. ■

Keeping track of tracking

Using task notes to record progress and changes can be another good strategy for effective tracking. If an important change occurs that doesn't merit changing your baseline, use the task notes to record it. When you reach the end of the project, these notes help you to document and justify everything from missed deadlines to cost overruns.

Tip

Try to set some standards for tracking in your organization. For example, how do you determine when a task is complete? How do you measure costs, and what is the source of information on resource time spent on a task? Project becomes a much more effective management tool if each project manager uses identical methods of gauging progress and expenditures, just as your company's accounting department uses standards in tracking costs. ■

Setting multiple baselines is useful, but how do you decide when to save each iteration? You may want to consider setting a different baseline for each major milestone in your project. Even long projects usually have only four or five significant milestones, and they are likely to occur after you have accomplished a sizeable chunk of work.

Summary

This chapter explored some of the fundamental concepts of tracking activity on a project. You became familiar with the following:

- How to set, modify, and clear baselines
- Tracking strategies you can use to record tracking information

Chapter 13 covers the mechanics of tracking, recording the actuals, and streamlining the entry of this data.

Recording Actuals

A ctuals represent what has, in fact, occurred during your project. In Microsoft Project, you can record actual information about the cost of a task and about the time spent completing the task. By recording actual information, you accomplish the following things:

- For automatically scheduled tasks, you let Project automatically reschedule the remainder of your project.

- You provide management with a way to measure how well your project is going.

- You provide yourself with valuable information on your estimating skills — information that you can apply to the remainder of the current project and to your next project.

You also can record progress for manually scheduled tasks, and you find information in this chapter on the process. Because you control the behavior of manually scheduled tasks and Project controls the behavior of automatically scheduled tasks, Project behaves just a little differently when you record progress for manually scheduled tasks.

Organizing the Updating Process

Before you launch into the mechanics of updating a project, you should take a moment to examine the updating process. Updating a project can become complicated, particularly for large projects with many resources assigned to them. You need to establish efficient manual procedures for collecting information in a timely fashion, and then you need to determine the best ways to enter that information into Project.

Individuals working on tasks should answer the following questions regularly:

- Is the task on schedule?
- How much is done?
- Is a revised estimate available on the duration of the task?
- Is a revised estimate available on the work that is required to complete the task?

Tip

If your organization has forms and processes in place to capture actuals and status information, use those forms and processes as much as possible. Although the organization's forms and processes may not currently capture project information, sometimes it is easier to ask for a little more information using current forms than it is to create new forms and processes. ■

You may want to create a form for participants to use for their regular reports. Their reports should provide the information that you need to update your project plan in Project. You may be able to use one of the reports in Project (or customize one of Project's reports) to provide the necessary information.

Cross-Reference

If you use Project Server, you can take advantage of electronic tracking and reporting capabilities. See Chapter 22 for more information. ■

You also should decide how often you need to receive the collection forms. If you request the reports too frequently, your staff may spend more time reporting than working. On the other hand, if you don't receive the reports often enough, you won't be able to identify a trouble spot early enough to resolve it before it becomes a major crisis. As the manager, you must decide on the correct frequency for collecting actual information for your project.

Tip

You can use the timephased fields in Project to track actual work and costs on a daily or weekly basis. Read more about timephased cost tracking in the section "Using timephased fields efficiently," later in this chapter. ■

When you receive the reports, you should evaluate them to identify unfinished tasks for which you need to adjust the planned duration, work, and costs. You'll find that these adjustments are easiest to make if you make them before you record a task's actual dates or percentage of completion.

Also, remember that recording actual information enables you to compare estimates to actuals; this comparison often proves to be quite valuable. To make this comparison, make sure that you set a baseline for your project.

Cross-Reference

See Chapter 12 for more information on setting baselines. ■

Understanding Calculation Options

You need to understand the calculation options that you can set in Project; they affect the "bottom line" of both the project's cost and schedule. You can review and change calculation options in the Options dialog box. Click the File tab and, from the Backstage view that appears, click Options to display the Options dialog box. Calculation options appear in two places. Click Schedule on the left and then scroll to the bottom to view the first set of calculation options (see Figure 13.1).

Note

Because you completely control the behavior of manually scheduled tasks, the calculation options described in this section are the ones that Project uses when dealing with automatically scheduled tasks. ■

- **Calculation options:** You can control whether Project calculates changes that you make to the project as you make those changes. If you choose Off and you make a change to, say, a task duration, the task bar will expand or contract to reflect your change. But, Project will not re-schedule subsequent dates for dependent tasks in your Project until you click the Calculate Project button in the Schedule group on the Project tab. Automatic calculation is the default, but if your project is very large, calculating can take quite a while; under these circumstances, you may want to switch to manual calculation to save time. When your project is set to manual calculation, you see Calculate: Off in the status bar as a reminder to calculate the project when you finish making changes.

FIGURE 13.1

You can set some of the options that Project will use to calculate your project's schedule and cost.

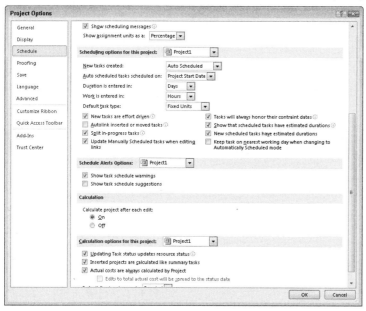

- **Updating Task Status Updates Resource Status check box:** Selected by default, this box tells Project to update resource status to correspond with any updated task status. (This option works in reverse, too. If you update a resource's status, Project also updates task status accordingly.) Suppose, for example, that you update the percentage of completion for a task. When you select this box, Project also updates the % Complete field for the resource and the assignment.

- **Inserted Projects Are Calculated Like Summary Tasks check box:** When this box is selected (as it is by default), Project treats inserted projects like summary tasks when calculating the project schedule, instead of treating them like a separate project.

Cross-Reference
See Chapter 19 for more information about inserting projects. ■

- **Actual Costs Are Always Calculated by Project check box.** When you select this check box, Project calculates actual costs. You can't enter actual costs until a task is 100% complete; Project will overwrite any costs that you enter prior to 100% completion as it recalculates costs. You also can't import actual cost values.

- **Default Fixed Cost Accrual list box:** Use this list box to choose a method for Project to accrue fixed costs for new tasks. You can have Project accrue fixed costs at the start of a task or at the end of a task, or you can prorate the costs throughout the duration of the task.

Click Advanced on the left and then scroll to the bottom to find additional calculation options that you can set (see Figure 13.2).By default, when tasks begin late or early, Project doesn't change the task start dates or adjust the remaining portions of tasks. The following four check boxes enable you to change this default behavior so that Project updates the tasks in relation to the Status Date — the "as of" date you use when recording information:

- Move End of Completed Parts after Status Date Back to Status Date

- And Move Start of Remaining Parts Back to Status Date

- Move Start of Remaining Parts before Status Date Forward to Status Date

- And Move End of Completed Parts Forward to Status Date

Tip
You can find the project's status date in the Project Information dialog box (on the Project tab, click Project Information in the Properties group). If the status date isn't set, Project uses the current date. ■

The check boxes work in pairs — that is, the first two check boxes work together and the second two check boxes work together. To better understand Project's behavior and the first pair of check boxes, suppose that the Status Date is December 9 and you have a task with a Start Date of December 14 and a duration of four days. Furthermore, suppose that the task actually starts on December 7. If you select the first check box, Project moves the task start date to 12/7, sets the percent complete to 50%, and schedules the start of the remaining work for 12/16 — thus creating a split task. If you also select the second check box, Project makes the changes that I just described *and* moves the start of the remaining work to 12/9.

FIGURE 13.2

Additional calculation options appear when you click Advanced on the left and then scroll down.

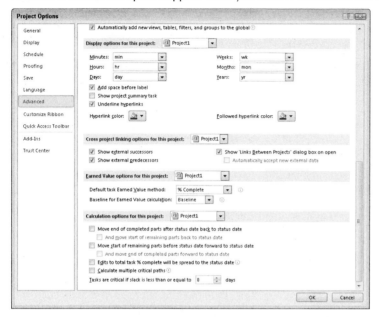

Now consider the second pair of check boxes. Again, suppose the Status Date is December 9 and you have a task with a Start Date of December 1 and a duration of four days. Further, suppose the task actually starts on December 7. If you select the third check box, Project leaves the task start date at 12/1, sets the percent complete to 50%, and schedules the start of the remaining work for 12/9 — again creating a split task. If you also select the fourth check box, Project makes the changes that I just described but also moves the task's actual start date to 12/7.

Note

These options don't apply when you record actual information on Summary tasks. These options apply only when you make total actual value edits, including task total actual work, task actual duration, total percent complete, and percent work complete. The settings of these check boxes don't apply if you use timesheet information from Project Server to update your project. ■

Other calculation options include the following:

- **Edits to Total Task % Complete Will Be Spread to the Status Date check box:** By default, this box is not selected, which makes Project distribute changes to the task percentage of completion to the end of the actual duration of the task. If you select this check box, Project instead distributes the changes evenly across the schedule to the project status date.

- **Calculate Multiple Critical Paths check box:** When you select this check box, Project calculates and displays separate critical paths in the project — and sets the late finish date for tasks without successors or constraints to their early finish date. By changing the finish dates of these tasks, Project makes these tasks critical. When you deselect this box, Project sets the late finish date for these tasks to the project finish date, which leaves these tasks off the critical path.

- **Tasks Are Critical If Slack Is Less Than or Equal to *x* Days list box:** By default, Project sets this value to 0; only tasks with no slack appear on the critical path. You can force tasks in your project onto the critical path by increasing this value.

Throughout the rest of this chapter, I use the default settings in Project to demonstrate the effects of updating a project.

Setting the Project Status Date

The first step in the updating process should be to establish the date on which the updates are effective, and you accomplish this by setting the project status date. If you don't set the project status date, Project uses the current date as the effective date for all updates you enter.

Follow these steps to set the project status date:

1. Click the Project tab.

2. In the Properties group, click the Project Information button to display the Project Information dialog box (see Figure 13.3).

FIGURE 13.3

Use the Project Information dialog box to set the project status date before recording actual.

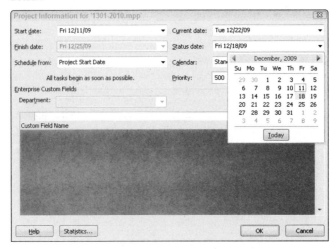

3. Click the list box arrow beside the Status Date field to display a calendar.

4. Click the date you want Project to use to record actual information.

Note
You can record progress as of December 18 on December 22 by setting the Status Date to December 18. ■

5. Click OK to save your changes.

Updating Tasks to Reflect Actual Information

Using a variety of techniques, you can record actual information for a project by filling in the following fields for each task that tracks the progress of your project:

- Actual start date
- Actual finish date
- Actual duration
- Remaining duration
- Percentage complete

Note
The fields mentioned previously are one possible set of fields that you can use to record actual information; there are other alternatives. For example, some people focus on updating only Actual Work and Remaining Work; in this case, Project updates the fields listed previously. ■

You can record progress for both manually scheduled tasks and automatically scheduled tasks. For the most part, Project's behavior for both types of tasks is the same; to read about the ways in which Project behaves differently for manually scheduled tasks, see the section, "Recording progress for manually scheduled tasks."

In some cases, when you enter information into one of these fields, Project calculates the values for the other fields. For example, if you enter a percentage complete for a task, Project calculates and supplies an actual start date, an actual duration, a remaining duration, and an actual work value.

Setting actual start and finish dates

The Gantt Chart view displays projected start and finish dates for tasks. In this section, you find out how to enter and view actual start and finish dates (and compare current, baseline, and actual dates) in the Task Details Form view, as shown in Figure 13.4.

FIGURE 13.4

Use the Task Details form to enter actual information.

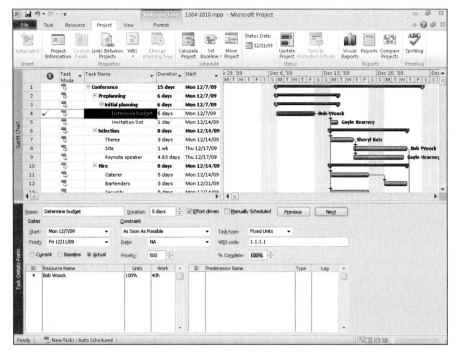

Starting from the Gantt Chart view, follow these steps to set up your screen:

1. Click the Task tab.

2. In the Properties group, click the Display Task Details button. Project splits the screen, displaying the Gantt Chart view in the top pane and the Task Details Form in the bottom pane. The Task Details Form shows information for the currently selected task in the Gantt Chart view.

3. In the top pane, select the task for which you want to record actuals.

4. In the Dates section of the bottom pane, select the Actual option button to identify the type of dates that you want to enter.

   The three option buttons (Current, Baseline, and Actual) refer only to the dates that you can view and set. In other words, you don't see baseline assignments at the bottom of the view if you click Baseline.

5. Record either a Start or a Finish date. If the task has been started but not yet completed, you can supply a % Complete value; you can read more about supplying a % Complete value in the section, "Setting the Percent Complete Value" later in this chapter.

6. Click OK.

Project initially sets the Actual Start Date and Actual Finish Date fields to NA to indicate that you have not yet entered a date. When you update your project to provide actual start and finish dates, Project changes the projected start and finish dates to the actual dates that you enter. When you enter an actual start date, Project changes only one other field — the projected start date. However, when you enter an actual finish date, Project changes several other fields: the Percent Complete field, the Actual Duration field, the Remaining Duration field, the Actual Work field, and the Actual Cost field. If you didn't set an actual start date, Project also changes that field.

To remove the split view, drag the horizontal split divider down to the bottom of the screen, or you can click the Task tab, and, in the Properties group, click the Display Task Details button again.

Recording actual durations

The *actual duration* of a task is the amount of time that was needed to complete the task. To record an actual duration, you can use the Update Tasks dialog box. Select the task for which you want to record progress. Then, click the Task tab and, in the Schedule group, click the arrow beside the Mark on Track button. From the drop-down list that appears, click Update Tasks to display the Update Tasks dialog box (see Figure 13.5).

FIGURE 13.5

Use the Update Tasks dialog box to set the actual duration for a task by filling in the Actual Dur field.

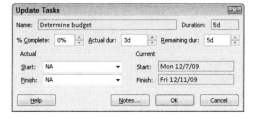

When you set an actual duration that is less than or equal to the planned duration, Project assumes that the task is progressing on schedule. When you click OK after setting an actual duration, Project sets the actual start date to the planned start date — unless you previously set the actual start date. In that case, Project leaves the actual start date alone. In either case, Project also calculates the percentage complete and the remaining duration for the task.

Note

To see the updated Remaining Duration and % Complete fields, reopen the Update Tasks dialog box. ∎

If you set an actual duration that is greater than the planned duration, Project assumes that the task is finished but that it took longer than expected to complete. Project adjusts the planned duration to match the actual duration and changes the Percent Complete field to 100% and the Remaining Duration field to 0%.

You can set an option in the Project Options dialog box to have Project update the status of resources when you update a task's status. Click the File tab and, from the Backstage view, click Options. In the Project Options dialog box that appears, click Schedule on the left. Scroll down to find the Updating Task Status Updates Resource Status check box. If you set this option and then supply an actual duration, Project also updates the work and cost figures for the resources.

Cross-Reference
You find out more about this option in the section "Overriding resource cost valuations," later in this chapter. ■

Note
Don't change the actual duration of a task if you use effort-driven scheduling. Instead, change the number of resource units that are assigned or the amount of the resource assignment. Remember that the duration of effort-driven tasks is affected by resource assignments. ■

Setting the Percent Complete value

Before I dive into a discussion of the Remaining Duration field, take a look at the Tracking table, which contains, in table form, all the fields into which you can enter actual information. In the two preceding sections, you saw that you can use the Task Details Form view and the Update Tasks dialog box to record and view actual information. The Task Details Form view provides a limited way to update tasks using the Start and Finish Date fields and the % Complete field. Although the Update Tasks dialog box provides a complete way to enter actual information (including entering Remaining Duration), I find that it's easiest to enter all actual information into Project by using the Tracking Table view (see Figure 13.6).

If you previously displayed the Task Details Form, you can remove the split view by dragging the horizontal split divider down to the bottom of the screen, or you can click the Task tab, and, in the Properties group, click the Display Task Details button.

To display the Tracking Table view, right-click the Select All button and choose Tracking from the menu that appears. Project displays the Tracking Table view in the left portion of the Gantt Chart view.

Tip
To see all the columns that are available on the Tracking Table view, narrow the chart portion of the window by dragging the vertical split divider. ■

On the Web site
On the Web site, look for the `Status Date Field and Current Date Field Example.mpp` **file.** ■

FIGURE 13.6

The Tracking Table view helps you view and enter actual values for tasks.

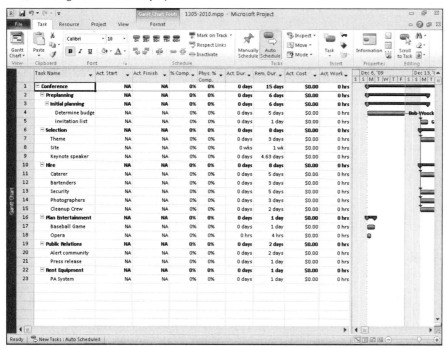

You can establish the progress of work performed on a task by assigning a Percent Complete value to the task. Any value less than 100 indicates that the task is not complete. You can set Percent Complete value from the Task Details Form view, from the Update Tasks dialog box, or from the Tracking table. Or, you can select the task from any task view and use the percentage buttons in the Schedule section of the Task tab (see Figure 13.7).

FIGURE 13.7

Use these buttons to set a task's actual progress at 0%, 25%, 50%, 75%, or 100% complete or to indicate that a task is on track.

Customize the Tracking Table

Project calculates some of the fields that store actuals when you enter information in other fields that store actuals. For this reason, I recommend that you create your own version of the Tracking table that displays the fields into which you will enter information in contiguous columns. Placing the fields side-by-side on a customized Tracking table will make your data entry much easier — and provide an easy way for someone other than you to enter the data. (See Chapter 6 for details on customizing a table.) You might want to consider including the project's status date and the current date on your Tracking table to help you easily find any tasks not completed prior to the status date, identifying work that needs to be rescheduled. To include this information, you need to create custom fields. This book's Web site contains a file called `Status Date Field and Current Date Field Example.mpp`. In this file, you'll find a sample Tracking table that also contains the Status Date and Current Date fields and the formulas you need to create these fields. To view and use the formulas, follow these steps:

1. On each field's column heading, right-click and choose Custom Fields. Project displays the Custom Fields dialog box with the highlighted field selected.

2. Click the Formula button to view the formula for that field.

3. In your own project file, create custom fields using these formulas.

Cross-Reference

For information on creating custom fields, see Chapter 16. ■

If you enter a Percent Complete value, Project assigns an Actual Start Date (unless you had entered one previously). Project also calculates the Actual Duration and Remaining Duration values. If you set your options to update resource information when you update tasks, Project also calculates the Actual Cost and Actual Work values. If you enter 100 in the Percent Complete column, Project assigns the planned finish date to the Actual Finish Date column. If this value is not correct, don't enter a Percent Complete value; instead, enter an Actual Finish Date.

If a task is running on track, click the Mark on Track button. For example, suppose that you have a five day task that starts on Monday and is expected to finish on Friday. Further suppose that on Wednesday, you record progress and the task is still anticipated to finish on Friday. If you click the Mark on Track button, Project fills in the Actual Start Date, supplies a % complete of 60%, and fills in an Actual Duration of 3 days, a Remaining Duration of 2 days, and an Actual Work value of 24 hours. If you pro-rate costs for the task, Project also assigns 60% of the task cost to the Actual Cost field.

Setting work completed

Sometimes, you must schedule tasks based on the availability of certain resources. In these cases, tracking progress on a task is easiest if you update the work completed. Updating this value also updates the work each resource is performing.

In the same way that Project calculates duration information when you fill in a duration field, Project updates the work remaining by subtracting the work performed from the total work scheduled.

Use the Tracking Table view to enter information into the Act. Work (Actual Work) column, but start in the Task Usage view so you can enter actual work performed by specific resources. Click the Task Usage view shortcut; then, to apply the Tracking table, right-click the Select All button, and choose Tracking from the shortcut menu that appears. You can drag the divider bar almost completely to the right edge of the screen to reveal the Act. Work column. In Figure 13.8, I also display the Actual Work field in the Details portion of the Task Usage view, and I moved the Actual Work column to the left to reveal the part of the Details section of the Task Usage view affected when I enter 20 hours as the Actual Work value. The Project Status Date is set for Friday and the task on Row 4 began on Monday of that week. Project fills in Actual Work hours in the Details portion of the view for Monday, Tuesday, and Wednesday.

Note

If you are scheduling tasks according to the availability of resources in general instead of the availability of specific resources, you can still use this view to record actual work. However, you need to enter the value on the same row as the task, rather than on the individual rows for the resources. Project divides the actual and remaining work among the resources. ■

FIGURE 13.8

The Tracking Table view with resources displayed.

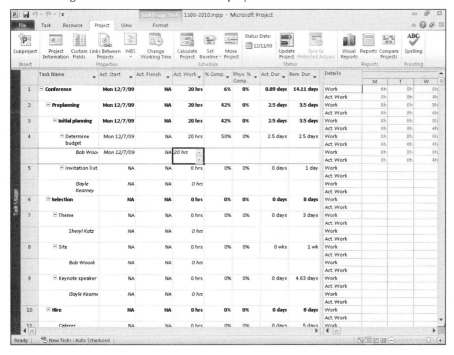

Setting remaining durations

The Rem. Dur. (Remaining Duration) field shows how much more time you need to complete a task. If you change only the value in the Remaining Duration field so that it is higher or lower than the existing figure, Project assumes that you are changing the planned duration of the task instead of tracking actual progress for the task. In this case, Project adjusts the schedule based on the new planned duration.

But if you enter a value into the Rem. Dur. (Remaining Duration) column after entering an Act. Dur. value, Project assumes that the work for the task will be completed based on the remaining duration value. Therefore Project sets the % Comp. (Percent Complete) value based on a combination of the remaining duration value that you supplied and the original planned duration.

In Figure 13.9, the planned duration for Task 4 was originally five days. I recorded an actual duration value of 3 days, and Project updated the % Comp. field to reflect that the task was 60% complete. I then recorded a remaining duration of 1 day, and Project adjusted the % Comp. field from 60% complete to 75% complete; recording the remaining duration value adjusted the project schedule for all automatically scheduled tasks.

Similarly, if you enter information into the % Comp. field and the Rem. Dur. field, Project adjusts the Act. Dur. field using a combination of the remaining duration value and the original planned duration.

FIGURE 13.9

When you set the remaining duration value after setting an actual duration, Project updates the task's percent-complete field.

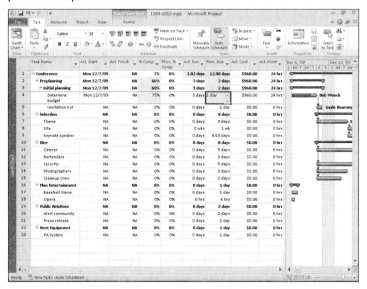

If you have entered actual duration information or percent complete information, entering 0 in the Rem. Dur. (Remaining Duration) column is the same as entering 100% in the Percent Complete column; that is, Project assigns the planned finish date to the Actual Finish Date column. If this value is not correct, change the Actual Finish Date.

Recording progress for manually scheduled tasks

You can record progress for manually scheduled tasks. Because you control the behavior of manually scheduled tasks and Project controls the behavior of automatically scheduled tasks, Project behaves just a little differently when you record progress for manually scheduled tasks.

The most significant difference is a completely logical one: when you record progress on a manually scheduled task that does not match any planned dates you might have entered, Project does not reschedule any manually scheduled successor tasks.

You enter progress on a manually scheduled task using any of the methods described earlier in this chapter except that you cannot record progress using timephased views. You can enter Actual Start and Actual Finish dates, % Complete information, actual and remaining duration information, or actual and remaining work information. In Figure 13.10, I created a summary task and three manually scheduled tasks. In this example, I assigned planned durations, start and finish dates, and resources to the tasks, and set up dependencies among the three tasks. I also set a baseline.

FIGURE 13.10

Manually scheduled tasks with planned durations in a project.

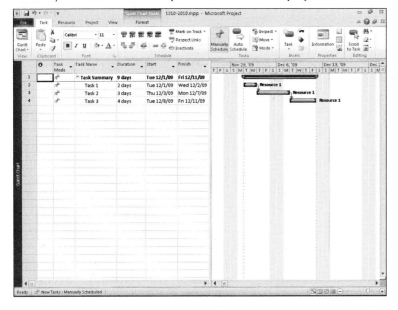

Figure 13.11 displays the Tracking table for the same project as I begin to record progress using a Status Date of December 4. For Task 1, I set an Actual Start date and an Actual Finish date, and the task took longer than planned. In cases like this one, a few things happen:

- As with automatically scheduled tasks, Project fills in related fields, such as the % Complete field, the Actual Duration and Remaining Duration fields, and the Actual Cost and Actual Work fields.

- Unlike automatically scheduled tasks, Project does not adjust dates for dependent successor tasks.

- Project updates the summary task to reflect the actual information.

For Task 2, I simply marked the task 25% complete, and Project treats the manually scheduled task the same way it treats automatically scheduled tasks, filling in the Actual Start date using the planned start date. Project also calculates the Actual Duration, Remaining Duration, Actual Cost and Actual Work fields using planned values and updates the summary task with the additional progress information. If I had supplied an Actual Start date and click the Mark on Track button, Project would have set the task to 67% complete — the three day task began on December 3, and on December 4, it's on track to complete on December 5, making it 2/3 complete.

FIGURE 13.11

Recording progress for manually scheduled tasks with planned durations.

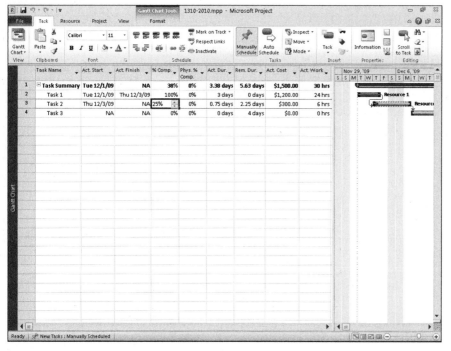

Note

If you do not supply an Actual Start date, clicking the Mark on Track button has no effect. ■

Project handles manually scheduled tasks for which you do not supply planned start and finish dates and durations a bit differently when you record progress. In Figure 13.12, I set up a project that starts on December 1 with a Status Date of December 11 and contains a summary task and two manually scheduled tasks. I supplied a planned start date for the Task 2, but no planned duration or finish information. For Task 1, I supplied only a Task Name. I didn't set any dependencies because, for this example, I didn't want Project to establish a planned duration of one day for the tasks — the preceding example showed you how Project handles manually scheduled tasks with planned durations.

FIGURE 13.12

Manually scheduled tasks with no durations and limited start date information.

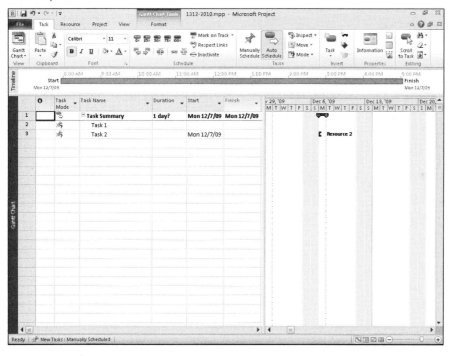

Remember the following facts about manually scheduled tasks:

- When you don't supply either a planned duration or both a planned start and a planned finish date, Project does not display a bar for the task on the chart portion of the Gantt Chart. Any resources you assigned won't appear on-screen because the Gantt bar doesn't appear.

- Summary tasks are always automatically scheduled tasks.

- Project assigns an estimated duration of 1 day to the summary task of manually scheduled tasks with no duration information.

- Project sets the planned start date of the summary task to the planned start date of a manually scheduled subtask.

- If you don't set any planned start dates for manually scheduled tasks, Project assigns the project start date to their summary tasks.

In Figure 13.13, I switched to the Tracking table for the project and I entered marked Task 1 as 50% complete and Task 2 as 100% complete. Remember, the method you use to record actual information doesn't matter; Project still updates related fields. What does matter in this case is the way Project treats manually scheduled tasks that have limited date information and no duration information.

For both tasks, Project used the summary task's planned start date — which Project set to be the same as the planned start date of Task 2 — as the Actual Start date. When you don't supply any duration information (or both a planned start and a planned finish date) for a manually scheduled task, Project assumes that a task's duration is one day. So, Project calculates the information for the related fields (Actual and Remaining Duration, Actual Work, Actual Cost and all other "actual" fields) based on the one day duration. You can see this clearly in the case of Task 2, which I marked Complete; in this case, Project also supplied an Actual Finish date that is the same as the task's Actual Start date.

FIGURE 13.13

Recording actual data for manually scheduled tasks that contain no duration and limited date information.

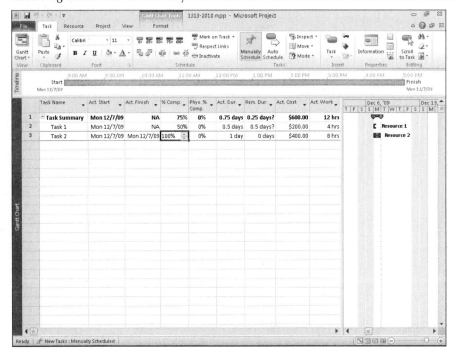

Actuals and Costs

Except for fixed-cost tasks, Project uses the cost of the resources that are assigned to a task over the duration of the task to calculate a task's cost. Costs are accrued, and total project costs are the sum of all resource and fixed costs. Therefore, if you previously set up and assigned resources to your tasks, Project has been calculating and accruing the costs for you; all you need to do is review and analyze the costs.

Alternatively, you may have chosen not to assign resources to your tasks, or you may have changed your default options so that Project wouldn't calculate costs. How can you do that? Click the File tab and, from the Backstage view that appears, click Options to display the Project Options dialog box. Click Schedule on the left and scroll to the bottom (see Figure 13.14). If the Updating Task Status Updates Resource Status check box is not selected, Project has not been calculating your project's costs. Remember, however, that this check box is selected by default, as you see in the figure.

If you did not assign resources or you changed the defaults, Project can't calculate the cost of your project unless you provide additional information after the task is completed. You can review and update your project's costs from one of two cost tables: the Cost table for tasks or the Cost table for resources. You can also override the costs that Project assigns.

FIGURE 13.14

From the Project Options dialog box, you can tell whether Project has been calculating your project's costs.

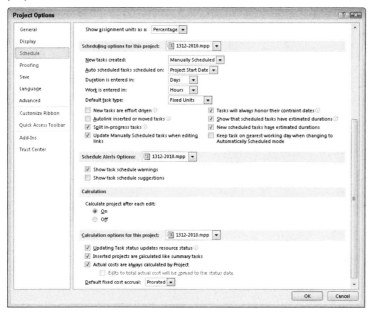

Using the Cost table for tasks

The Cost table for tasks, shown as part of the Gantt Chart view in Figure 13.15, displays cost information based on each task in your project; to display this table in the Gantt Chart view, right-click the Select All button and choose Cost. This table shows you the baseline cost (the planned cost), the actual cost, the variance between planned and actual costs, and the remaining cost of the task.

If you assign a fixed cost to a task in this table (as I did to the Site task in Row 8), Project adds that fixed cost to the calculated cost for the task. To display this table, click the Gantt Chart view shortcut. Then right-click the Select All button to display the shortcut menu of tables and choose Cost. You might also need to slide the vertical pane divider to the right to see all the fields on the Cost table for tasks.

The Cost table for tasks is most useful if you saved a baseline view of your project, because it enables you to compare baseline costs with actual costs.

FIGURE 13.15

The Cost table for tasks.

Select All button

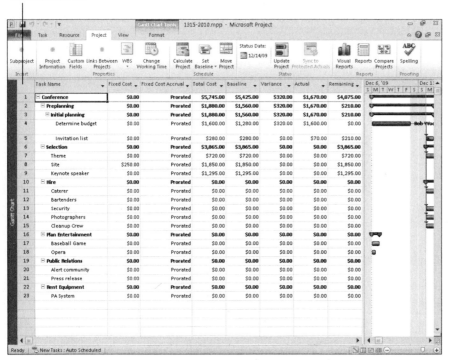

Using the Cost table for resources

The Cost table for resources is similar to the Cost table for tasks, except it displays a breakdown of costs by resource rather than by task, as shown in Figure 13.16.

To display this table, start in a resource view such as the Resource Sheet view; you can click the Resource Sheet view shortcut to display the Resource Sheet. Then right-click the Select All button and choose Cost from the shortcut menu that appears.

As is the Cost table for tasks, the Cost table for resources is most useful if you saved a baseline view of your project, because it enables you to compare baseline costs with actual costs.

Overriding resource cost valuations

Project's default settings automatically update costs as you record progress on a task. Project uses the accrual method that you selected for each resource when you created the resource.

The Cost table for resources.

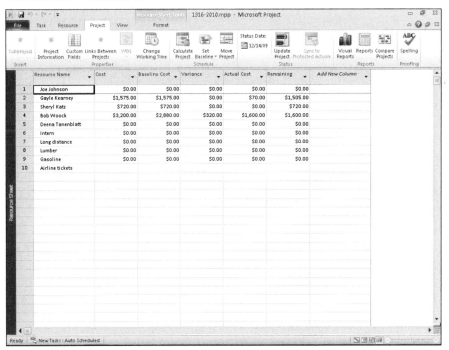

Cross-Reference

For more information about setting a resource's accrual method, see Chapter 5. ■

Alternatively, you can enter the actual costs for a resource assignment, or you can track actual costs separately from the actual work done on a task. To do so, after the task is completed, you must enter costs manually to override Project's calculated costs. Before you can override the costs that Project calculated, however, you must turn off one of the default options. Follow these steps to adjust Project's default settings so you can override calculated costs:

1. Click the File tab and, from the Backstage view, choose Options to display the Project Options dialog box.

2. Click Schedule on the left.

3. Scroll to the bottom and remove the check from the Actual Costs Are Always Calculated by Project check box (see Figure 13.17).

FIGURE 13.17

Revise the default settings to override Project's calculated costs.

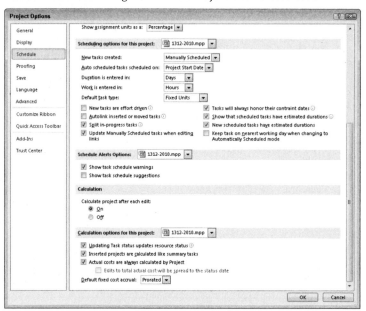

Note

The Edits to Total Actual Cost Will Be Spread to the Status Date check box becomes available. Check this box if you want Project to distribute the edits that you intend to make through the Status Date. If you don't check the box, Project distributes the edits to the end of the actual duration of the task. ■

4. Click OK.

5. Click the Task Usage view shortcut.

6. Right-click the Select All button to display the table shortcut menu and choose Tracking. Project displays the Tracking table in the Task Usage view (see Figure 13.18).

FIGURE 13.18

The Tracking Table view with the Act. Cost (Actual Cost) column visible.

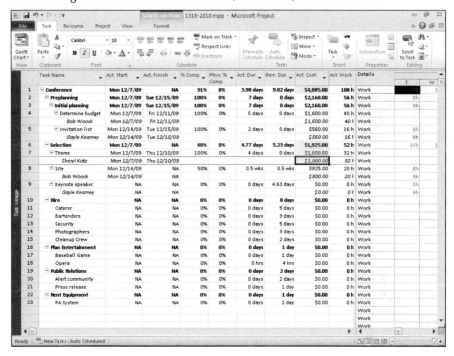

7. Drag the divider bar to the right so that you can see all the columns.

8. Select the task or resource to which you want to assign a cost.

9. Enter the cost in the Act. Cost (Actual Cost) column.

Tip

If you change your mind and want Project to calculate costs as it originally did, repeat Steps 1 and 2 and select the Actual Costs Are Always Calculated by Project check box to restore the default calculation method. Project warns you that it will overwrite any manually entered costs when you click OK. ∎

Techniques and Tips for Updating

Project users can find ways to accelerate the updating process. For example, you can do the following:

- Use Project's timephased fields to easily and efficiently update your project
- Update the progress of several tasks simultaneously
- Reschedule incomplete work so that it starts on the current date

Note

You can speed the data-entry process if you create a custom Tracking table that groups the fields into which you enter actual information. You might want to consider including the project's status date and the current date on your tracking table to help you easily find any tasks not completed prior to the status date, identifying work that needs to be rescheduled. To include this information, you need to create custom fields. ■

Cross-Reference

See Chapter 6 for details on creating customized tables. For information on creating custom fields, see Chapter 16. ■

On the Web site

On the Project 2010 Bible Web site, you'll find the Status Date Field and Current Date Field Example.mpp file, which contains the formulas you need to create these fields. On each field's column heading, right-click and choose Custom Fields to open the Custom Fields dialog box; then, click the Formula button to view the formula for that field. ■

Using timephased fields efficiently

Project's timephased fields enable you to update the progress of your project on a regular basis, such as daily or weekly. To use timephased fields efficiently to record progress information for resources, start by displaying the Resource Usage view by clicking the View tab and, in the Resource Views group, clicking the Resource Usage button. Then change the table: In the Data group, click the Tables button and select Work from the drop-down list that appears.

You'll to want to use most of the right side of the view, but on the left side of the view, you really need only the Actual Work column, which is called "Actual" in the Work table and is hidden by the right side of the view. The easiest way to set up the table so that you can use the Actual Work column is to move that column so that it appears between the Resource Name column and the % Comp. (Percent Complete) column. To move the column, follow these steps:

1. Drag the vertical divider to the right so that you can see the Actual column.
2. Click the title of the Actual column to select the entire column.
3. Move the mouse pointer over the column title so that it changes to a pointer with arrows pointing in four directions attached.
4. Drag the column to the left; as you drag, Project displays a vertical bar that marks the current location of the column (see Figure 13.19).

FIGURE 13.19

Moving the Actual Work column in the Work table.

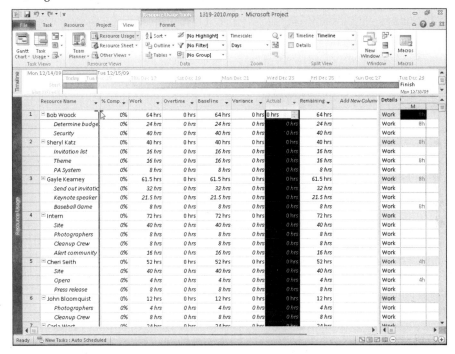

5. Drop the column when the vertical bar appears on the right edge of the Resource Name column. The vertical bar that marks the current location of the column disappears and the column appears to the right of the Resource Name column (see Figure 13.20).

6. Drag the vertical split bar to the left so that, in the Work table, the only visible columns are the Resource Name, Actual, and % Comp. columns (refer to Figure 13.20).

Tip

This move affects only the current project. To use this version of the Work table in all new projects, create a new Work table. Chapter 7 explains how to create new tables. ■

Next, you should decide the timeframe for which you want to provide actual values. To provide daily values, you don't need to make any changes to the timescale on the right side of the window. But if you want to provide weekly values (or use some other frequency), you need to change the timescale. This example doesn't require any timescale changes, but if you wanted to change the timescale to weekly (for example), click the View tab and, in the Zoom group, open the Timescale drop-down list and select Weeks (see Figure 13.21).

FIGURE 13.20

The Resource Usage view using a modified Work table.

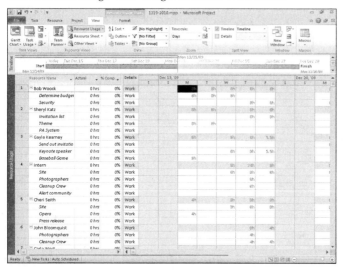

FIGURE 13.21

If necessary, change the timescale.

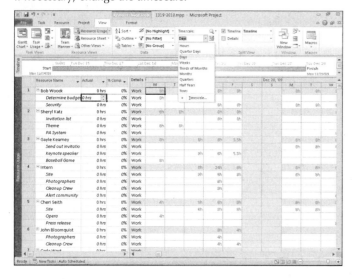

Last, you can see the results as you update the schedule if you add a timephased field for Actual Work. Click the Resource Usage Tools Format tab and, in the Details group, select Actual Work. Project adds a row for every task on the right side of the view (see Figure 13.22).

To enter hours worked for a particular day, click the letter of the column representing that day to select the entire day (refer to Figure 13.22). Then click in the Actual column in the table — the column you moved so that it appears to the right of the Resource Name column — beside a task listed under a particular resource and enter the hours worked on that task by that resource on the selected day. As long as the day for which you are entering actual work remains selected, you can type and press Enter. Project simply records the hours on the selected day for the task and resource and moves down one row so that you can type actual work on the next task for the same resource. If you have no hours to record for the next task, just press Enter again.

This entire process also works if you are updating costs on a daily basis, with the following minor changes:

- Begin in the Task Usage view instead of the Resource Usage view.
- Use the Tracking table instead of the Work table.

FIGURE 13.22

Add actual work information for a specific day.

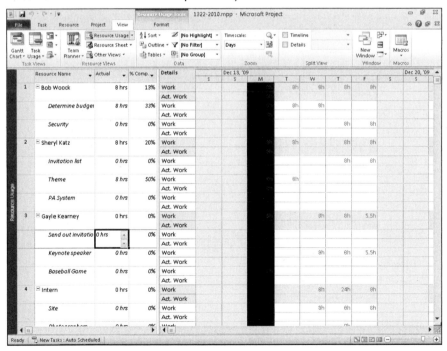

Remember, though, that you can't add costs to override Project's automatically calculated costs unless you open the Project Options dialog box by clicking the File tab and, from the Backstage view that appears, clicking Options; then you click Schedule on the left and remove the check from the Actual Costs Are Always Calculated by Project check box.

Accelerating the updating process

If you have several tasks that are on schedule or were completed on schedule, you can update these tasks simultaneously by following these steps:

Note
Project updates both automatically scheduled and manually scheduled tasks. ■

1. Set the project status date by clicking the Project tab. In the Status group, click the Status Date button. In the Status date dialog box that appears, click the list box arrow, select the appropriate status date, and click OK.

2. Click the Gantt Chart view shortcut.

Tip
If you want to update the entire project, don't select any tasks. ■

3. In the Task Name column, select the tasks that you want to update. For example, Figure 13.23 shows three tasks selected for updating.

Note
You can select tasks by using the same techniques that you use in Windows Explorer. To select two or more contiguous tasks, click the first task, hold down Shift, and click the last task. To select two or more noncontiguous tasks, hold down Ctrl as you click each task that you want to select. ■

4. Click the Project tab and, in the Status group, click Update Project to display the Update Project dialog box (see Figure 13.24). The status date appears in the list box next to the Update Work As Complete Through option button.

5. Select one of the following:

   - **Set 0% – 100% Complete:** This option tells Project to calculate the Percent Complete for each task.

   - **Set 0% or 100% Complete Only:** Select this option to have Project mark completed tasks with 100% and leave incomplete tasks at 0%.

6. Specify whether to update the entire project or selected tasks by selecting the appropriate option.

7. Click OK.

FIGURE 13.23

Selecting tasks to update.

FIGURE 13.24

Use the Update Project dialog box to update your project.

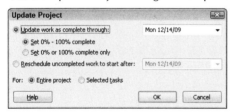

Letting Project reschedule uncompleted work

If you updated your project and you had partially completed tasks, you can guarantee that no remaining work is scheduled for dates that have already passed. You can make sure that all remaining work is scheduled for future dates by rescheduling the work to start on the current date.

Note

In Project 2000 and earlier, if you rescheduled work by using the technique that I describe in this section, Project would remove task constraints that you had applied. For example, suppose you rescheduled the work for a task that had a Must Finish On constraint, and rescheduling moved the finish date beyond the constraint date. Project 2000 and earlier did not honor the constraint date; instead, these versions changed the constraint to As Soon As Possible. To preserve a task's constraints, you had to reschedule the remaining work manually.

Starting in Project 2002, Project changed so that it does not remove constraints and reschedule tasks without progress. However, be aware that this behavior may leave your project in an infeasible situation. Project displays a message if this situation occurs, and you can make changes manually as needed. ■

Follow these steps to tell Project to reschedule remaining work for future dates:

1. Select the Gantt Chart view.

2. Go to the Task Name column and select the tasks you want to update. See the previous section for techniques that you can use to select tasks.

3. Click the Project tab and, in the Status group, click Update Project to display the Update Project dialog box (see Figure 13.25).

FIGURE 13.25

Use this dialog box to reschedule incomplete work to start today.

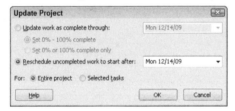

4. Select the Reschedule Uncompleted Work To Start After option button and choose the date from which you want to reschedule all unfinished work. By default, Project suggests the status date.

Note

Project 2000 introduced the ability to set a date from which you wanted to reschedule uncompleted work. However, if you rescheduled work twice, Project 2000 ignored all dates except the first rescheduling date you supplied. Starting in Project 2002, Project reschedules selected tasks for your project each time you change the date. ■

5. Specify whether to update the entire project or selected tasks by selecting the appropriate option button.

6. Click OK.

When you reschedule a partially completed task using the technique just described, Project automatically splits the task into a completed portion and a remaining portion. Therefore the Gantt Chart may display a split task that has a gap between its two parts because the completed portion may have finished sometime before the remaining portion is scheduled to start.

Summary

In this chapter, you found out how to record actual information about tasks and resources. For example, you should now be able to do the following:

- Set actual start and finish dates
- Set actual and remaining durations
- Set the percent complete for a task
- Set the work completed for a task
- Use cost tables for tasks and resources

In addition, this chapter contains a section that helps you record actual information efficiently. Chapter 14 shows you how to review progress on your project.

Ways to Review Progress

O nce you start recording actuals, you'll want to review the progress of your project — and Project can help you. You can use a variety of techniques to review progress, including

- Views
- Tables
- Progress lines
- Comparing versions of a project

Cross-Reference

As you review progress, the facts of project management life dictate that you will find problems in your schedule that you need to resolve. Life happens, and reality brings changes to even the most carefully planned schedule. Review Chapters 10 and 11 for techniques you can use to resolve problems you encounter. ∎

Viewing Tasks That Are Slipping

The baseline is the staple of determining if your project is on schedule. You use baseline information to compare your plans to what is actually happening. For any baseline you set for your project, you can quickly and easily identify tasks that are slipping from their planned start dates at any time on any Gantt view. In this example, I use the basic Gantt Chart view.

To display slippage information on the Gantt Chart view, follow these steps:

1. Click the Gantt Chart view shortcut in the lower-right corner of the Project window.
2. Click the Gantt Chart Tools Format tab.

3. In the Bar Styles group, click the Slippage button.

4. From the list of available baselines, select the baseline containing the information you want to see.

   On the left side of the bars of tasks that are slipping, Project adds lines in the chart portion of the view. In the project shown in Figure 14.1, only the Baseball Game and Opera tasks on Rows 17 and 18 are not slipping.

The slippage lines help you identify how much any given task is slipping from its planned start dates along with its calculated finish dates.

To hide slippage information, repeat the preceding steps.

FIGURE 14.1

You can view tasks that are slipping from their planned start dates on any Gantt view at any time.

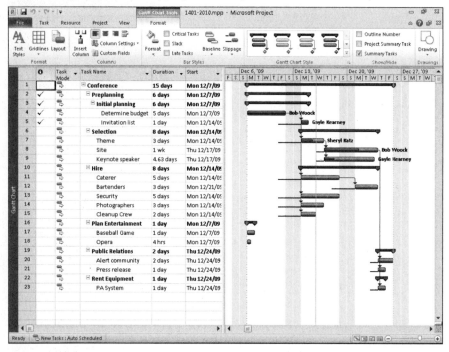

Viewing with Baseline Information

Viewing slipping tasks, described in the preceding section, helps you focus on tasks that might not start as planned, but doesn't show you information related to when you planned each task to finish.

But, using baseline information, you identify not only those tasks that might not finish when you planned, but you also can see the planned finish information you provided for each task. You can view baseline information quickly and exceedingly easily at any time on any Gantt view. In this example, I use the basic Gantt Chart view.

New Feature

The option to view baseline information on any Gantt view without manually editing bar styles is new to Project 2010. ■

To display baseline information on the Gantt Chart view, follow these steps:

1. Click the Gantt Chart view shortcut in the lower-right corner of the Project window.

2. Click the Gantt Chart Tools Format tab.

3. In the Bar Styles group, click the Baseline button.

4. From the list of available baselines, select the baseline containing the information you want to see.

   Project adds gray baseline bars in the bottom portion of the bars that appear in the chart portion of the view. In Figure 14.2, several tasks look like they aren't going to start on time, and you also can compare their planned finish dates to the finish dates Project has calculated based on progress.

To hide the baseline information, repeat the preceding steps.

FIGURE 14.2

You can view baseline information on any Gantt view at any time using the Baseline button on the Gantt Chart Tools Format tab.

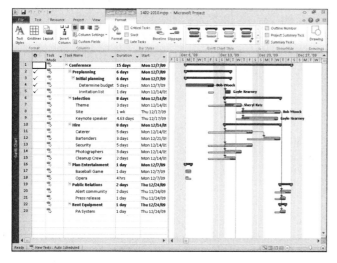

Taking Advantage of the Tracking Gantt View

Baselines help you to see how your estimates differ from actual activity in the project. Project enables you to see this variance both graphically, with baseline and actual taskbars, and through data displayed in tables in various views, helping you understand the status of your project.

Cross-Reference

In Chapter 12, you find out how to set a baseline, and in Chapter 13, you find out how to enter tracking data. ∎

Interpreting the Tracking Gantt view

The Tracking Gantt view (see Figure 14.3) is most useful in viewing progress against your baseline estimates. To display the Tracking Gantt view, right-click the gray bar that runs down the left side of the Project screen and, from the shortcut menu that appears, click Tracking Gantt.

If a task is finished, a check mark appears in the Indicator column on the left side of the view next to the task.

FIGURE 14.3

The Tracking Gantt view helps you understand the progress of your project.

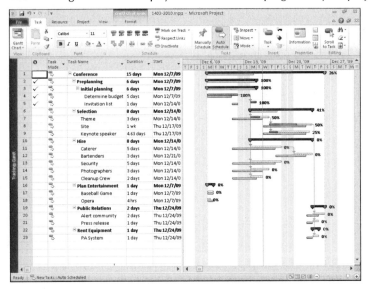

The chart portion of the Tracking Gantt provides a wealth of information:

- The bottom bar on the chart portion of the view (light gray on your screen) represents the baseline dates for each task. The top bar spans either the scheduled start and finish dates or (if a task has been completed) the actual start and finish dates for each task.

- The top bar of tasks not on the critical path and not yet started appears light blue; if the task has been started or completed, the completed portion of the top bar appears medium blue.

- The top bar of tasks on the critical path and not yet started appears light red; if the task has been started or completed, the completed portion of the top bar appears medium red.

- For partially completed tasks, the distinction between the completed and uncompleted portion is easy to see.

- The percent complete appears on the right side of each task.

The Tracking table

The default table for the Tracking Gantt view is the Entry table, but you can add or remove fields (columns), or you can display other tables of information. In Figure 14.4, I chose to display the Tracking table, and I added columns to include Baseline Duration and Baseline Cost information. I also opted to hide the Physical % Complete field that appears in the default Tracking table since I'm not using it in this example.

FIGURE 14.4

The Tracking Gantt displaying the Tracking table can provide a wealth of information.

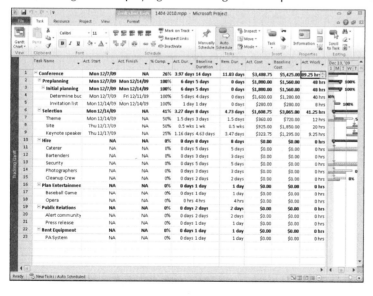

Cross-Reference

Review Chapter 7 for more information about changing and modifying tables. ∎

Using the Baseline Duration, Baseline Cost, Actual Duration, and Actual Cost fields, you can compare estimated versus actual timing and costs.

The default Tracking table also contains the following information:

- **% Complete:** This field shows the progress of various tasks in the schedule. If you refer to just the chart portion of Figure 14.1, you can see that two tasks — the ones on Rows 4 and 5 — are complete, along with their summary tasks, which appear on Rows 2 and 3. In addition, three more tasks, appearing on Rows 7, 8, and 9, are partially complete, and their summary task on Row 6 reflects the progress of that phase of the project.

- **Physical % Complete:** You can use this field to calculate BCWP (budgeted cost of work performed). Project calculates the % Complete field for you based on Total Duration or Actual Duration values you enter, but Project allows you to enter a value for the Physical % Complete field. Use this field to calculate BCWP when the % Complete value would not accurately represent the real work performed on a task. You can read more about this field in Chapter 15.

- **Remaining Duration:** This field reflects the amount of time needed to complete an unfinished task. You can enter a value into this field or you can allow Project to calculate it for you by entering a value into either the Actual Duration field or the % Complete field. If you enter a value for Remaining Duration, Project calculates a new % Complete value and a new Duration value; Project changes the Duration value to equal the sum of Actual Duration and Remaining Duration, leaving Actual Duration untouched.

- **Actual Work:** In the Actual Work field, you'll see the amount of work that has been performed by resources. There are Actual Work fields for tasks, resources, and assignments, as well as timephased Actual Work fields for tasks, resources, and assignments.

Using Tables to View Progress

Project contains a number of tables you can use to help you evaluate progress, both of tasks and of resources. In this section, you review these tables:

- The Task Variance table
- The Task Cost table
- The Task Work table
- The Resource Work table

The Task Variance table

The Variance table highlights the variance in task timing between the baselines and actuals. To display this table, shown in Figure 14.5, click View tab and, in the Data group, click the Tables button. Choose Variance from the list of tables that appears.

FIGURE 14.5

If you're behind schedule, you can easily see the truth in the Variance table.

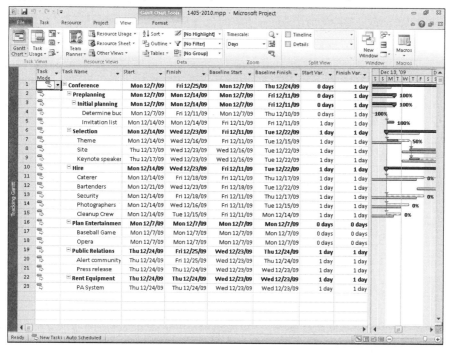

You can easily compare the Baseline Start and Baseline Finish and the actual Start and Finish columns that show actual data for tasks on which you have tracked progress as well as baseline data for tasks with no progress. This table also contains fields to show you the Start Variance (how many days late or early the task started) and the Finish Variance (how many days late or early the task ended). If you're behind schedule, you'll see negative values in the Start Variance and Finish Variance columns.

The Task Cost table

The Task Cost table is most useful for pointing out variations in money spent on the project. Figure 14.6 shows a Task Cost table for a project in progress, with some costs incurred and others yet to be expended. Project takes the following factors into account when calculating cost variances:

- Actual resource time worked

- The estimate of days of resource time still to be expended to complete the task

- Actual costs (such as fees and permits) that have been tracked on the task

Compared to a baseline estimate of $1,600.00, the Determine Budget task on Row 4 is under budget by $320.00, a delightful surprise. On the other hand, the Site task is over budget by $1,280.00, so, the overall project is currently over budget by $960.00.

FIGURE 14.6

The Task Cost table shows where you've spent too much and where you have a lot more money to spend.

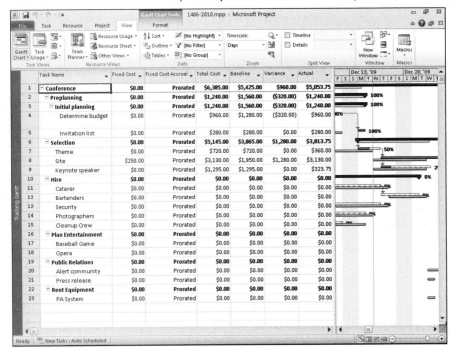

The Task Work table

The Work table for tasks, shown in Figure 14.7, shows the total time that is required from all resources to complete the task and includes baseline information so you can compare your progress to your original estimate. Work differs from task duration because:

- Work measures how many hours of effort are needed to complete a task.
- Task duration measures the amount of time (number of days) that is allotted to the task.

If the total work for an effort-driven task is 16 hours but the task duration is only one day, you either need to add another resource (meaning that two people can complete the task in one day) or extend the task's duration.

The Work table of the Tracking Gantt view focuses on the number of work hours put in by resources that are working on tasks. For example, the Baseline work for the Site task on Row 8 was 40 hours. However, the task took 72 hours to complete. Therefore the Variance field (the difference between the baseline hours of work and the actual hours spent) shows a loss of 32 hours, displayed as a positive number. On the other hand, the Baseline estimate for the Determine Budget task was 40 hours, and the task was completed in 24 hours. The Variance column shows a saving of 16 hours; the negative value indicates that fewer hours were used than were estimated in the baseline.

FIGURE 14.7

To determine whether a task is taking much more effort than you estimated, check the Task Work table.

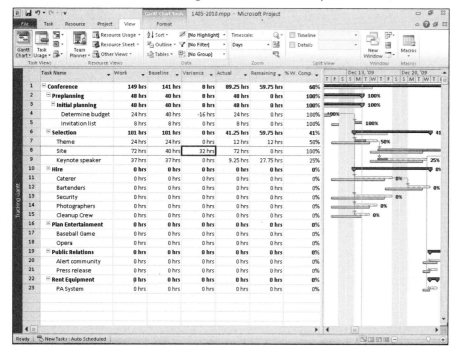

The Resource Work table

The Work table for resources displays work information for resources. Again, work represents the total time that is required from all resources to complete the task. The Work table for resources also includes baseline information so you can compare your progress to your original estimate.

You can apply the Work table for resources to the Resource Sheet view or the Resource Usage view. In Figure 14.8, I displayed the Resource Sheet using the view shortcut in the lower-right corner of the Project window, and then I applied the Work table by clicking the View tab. In the Data group, I clicked the Tables button and selected Work from the list that appeared.

FIGURE 14.8

The Work table for resources.

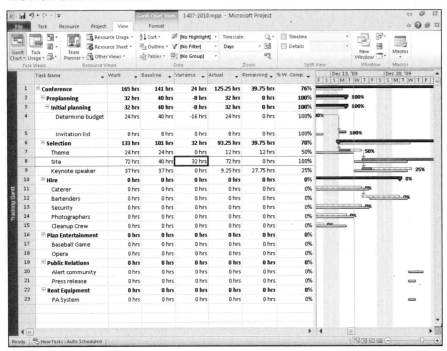

Viewing Progress Lines

Project contains another tool you can use to show the progress you're making on your project if you have saved a baseline of your project. If you add progress lines to the Gantt Chart of your project, as I did in Figure 14.9, Project draws a line that connects in-progress tasks. The progress line creates a graph of your project with peaks pointing to the right for work that is ahead of schedule and peaks pointing to the left for work that is behind schedule. The distance between the peaks and the line indicates the degree to which the task is ahead of or behind schedule.

A Gantt Chart with a progress line added.

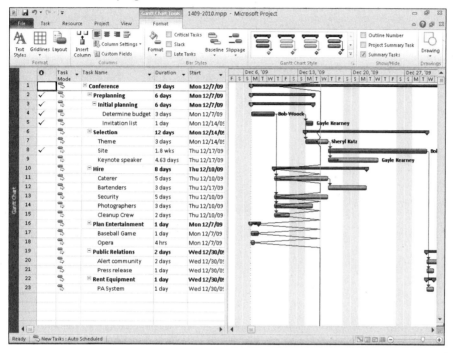

To add a progress line, follow these steps:

1. Click the Gantt Chart view shortcut in the lower-right corner of the Project screen.

2. Click the Gantt Chart Tools Format tab and, in the Format group, click the Gridlines button. From the drop-down list that appears, select Progress Lines to open the Progress Lines dialog box and display the Dates and Intervals tab.

3. Select the Display check box in the Selected Progress Lines section on the right to activate the Progress Line Dates list.

4. Click once in the Progress Line Dates list. Project displays a list box arrow.

5. Click the list-box arrow, and a small calendar appears (see Figure 14.10).

6. Select a date for the progress line; typically, you use the status date.

7. Select either Actual Plan or Baseline Plan in the Display Progress Lines In Relation To section.

8. Click OK.

    Project adds the progress line to your Gantt Chart, which looks like the progress line shown previously in Figure 14.9.

FIGURE 14.10

The Dates and Intervals tab of the Progress Lines dialog box.

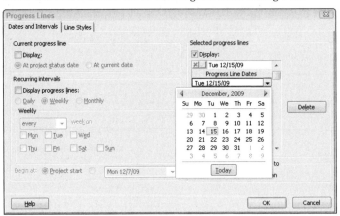

As you can imagine, a progress line on a project with a large number of tasks can begin to look messy. But if you decide that you like progress lines, you can display them at varying intervals, as shown previously in Figure 14.10. You also can add specific dates to the Progress Line Dates list on the right side of the Progress Lines dialog box to display multiple progress lines on the Gantt Chart. If you decide to display more than one progress line, you may want to use the Line Styles tab of the Progress Lines dialog box to format the lines so you can tell them apart (for example, you can change their colors or use different styles of lines).

To stop displaying progress lines, reopen the Progress Lines dialog box and deselect any check boxes on the Dates and Intervals tab.

Comparing Versions of Projects

You can compare versions of the same project to review their differences. Suppose your original plan has become sufficiently different from real life that you've decided to make changes and save a new baseline. After making the changes and saving the baseline, if you save the file using a new file name, Project can provide you with a detailed report showing you the differences between the original file and the newly created file.

Tip

This tool doesn't depend on whether you have saved a baseline, and you can use this tool with projects during the planning phase as well. For example, you can save different versions of the same project so you can compare the differences in plans and find the one most likely to work for you. ■

When you compare projects, Project creates a separate file that contains the comparison information. You can select a task table and a resource table to use in the comparison; the information that Project provides is limited specifically to those two tables. For each field in the two tables you select, Project includes, in the report, columns for each Project file version as well as a "difference" column that identifies the variations between the two files.

You initiate a comparison from one of the two files you want to compare, and Project assumes that you start in the latest version of the project. Although you can start in either project file, you might find it less confusing to open the latest version of the project and start the comparison process from that project, because Project uses terms like "previous" in the comparison report it produces.

You must open at least one of the projects you want to include in the comparison. You don't need to open both files, but I suggest that you do, because doing so saves you a step while setting up the comparison.

Suppose you want to compare two versions of the same project, and that they look like the projects shown in Figure 14.11 and 14.12.

FIGURE 14.11

I'll use this project as the older version in my comparison.

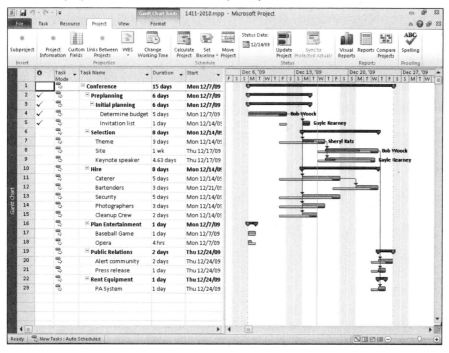

FIGURE 14.12

The project I'll use as the newer version in my comparison.

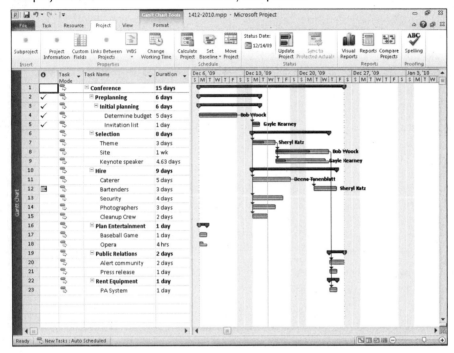

To compare two files, follow these steps:

1. Open the two projects you want to compare.

2. Display the project you consider to be the later version of the two projects you want to compare.

   In this example, I start in the project shown in Figure 14.12.

3. Click the Project tab.

4. In the Reports group, click the Compare Projects button.

   Project displays the Compare Project Versions dialog box (see Figure 14.13).

5. Click the list-box arrow at the top of the dialog box and select the other file you want to use in your comparison.

Note

If you didn't open both files before you started, click the Browse button at the top of the dialog box and navigate to and select the other file you want to use in your comparison. ∎

FIGURE 14.13

Use this dialog box to establish the parameters of your comparison.

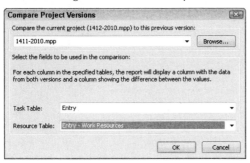

6. Open the Task Table list box and select a table to compare for the tasks in both projects. If you don't want to compare task information, select None.

7. Open the Resource Table list box and select a table to compare for the resources in both projects. If you don't want to compare resource information, select None.

Note

You must select at least one table to compare in the two projects, but you do not need to compare both a Task table and a Resource table. ■

8. Click OK. Project creates a separate file that contains the results of comparing the selected files (see Figure 14.14).

The Comparison file displays its own tab on the Ribbon — the Compare Projects tab. Below the Ribbon, in the Comparison Report portion of the screen, the legend for the Comparison Report appears. Beside the Legend, you see the report results, which include three columns for each column in the table you compared: a Current column, a Previous column, and a Difference column.

Below the Comparison Report, you see each of the files you compared. The information in the report's Current column refers to the data in the file on the bottom-left side of the screen, and the information in the report's Previous column refers to the data in the file on the bottom-right side of the screen.

You can scroll through the Comparison Report portion of the window to spot differences; when you do, you can click the Go to Item button in the Compare group on the Ribbon, and Project displays the same item in each of the project files at the bottom of the screen (see Figure 14.15).

FIGURE 14.14

A typical comparison file.

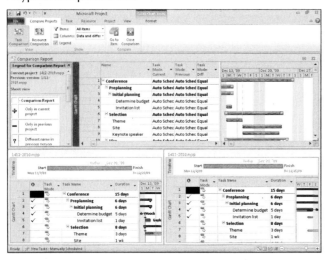

FIGURE 14.15

Find a difference and then click the Go to Item button on the Ribbon.

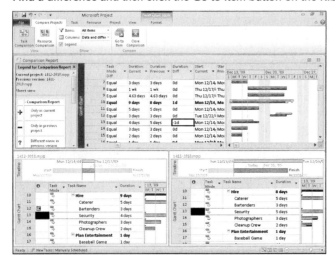

You can reduce the number of columns Comparison Report displays to make finding differences easier. Right-click the Select All button in the Comparison Report table and select Comparison Report: Task Differences Columns (see Figure 14.16).

Note

You can switch tables, but Project only compared information for the two tables you selected in Steps 6 and 7. ■

You also can limit the information displayed in the Comparison Report using the Items drop-down list in the Show group; from this drop-down list, you can view all differences, all changed items, all unchanged items, all items the two projects have in common, all items unique to the current version of the project, and all items unique to the previous version of the project.

If you opted to view data for both tasks and resources, you can use the buttons in the View group of the Compare Projects tab to switch between the two comparisons Project made.

To close the window that displays the Comparison Report and the two files you compared, click the Close Comparison button on the Ribbon. Project displays the comparison report in a window of its own; the two files you compared are also still open.

FIGURE 14.16

Control the columns displayed in the Comparison Report.

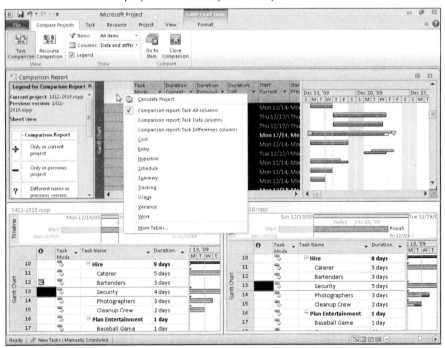

To save the Comparison Report information, click the File tab and, from the Backstage view, click Save As. Project suggests the name Comparison Report.mpp; you can accept the suggestion or provide a name of your own. You might want to include the names of the two files you compared in the file name so that you can identify the comparison information later when you reopen the file.

Note
When you work with the data from the Comparison Report file outside of the comparison process, you don't have the same options. For example, Project doesn't display the Compare Projects tab and you cannot selectively hide information. ■

Summary

In this chapter, you found out how to review progress on a project. For example, you should now be able to do the following:

- Display baseline and slippage information on any Gantt view
- Work with the Tracking Gantt to review progress
- Use various tables to review progress
- Compare two versions of a project

Chapter 15 shows you how to analyze your project's financial progress.

Analyzing Financial Progress

When you analyze the progress of your project, you must measure not only the progress of the schedule but also the progress based on the costs you incur. You do the latter by measuring the earned value of your project.

Understanding Earned Value

Earned value is the measurement that project managers use to evaluate the progress of a project based on the cost of work performed up to the project status date. When Project calculates earned value, by default it compares your original cost estimates to the actual work performed to show whether your project is on budget. You can think of earned value as a measurement that indicates how much of the budget should have been spent, when comparing the cost of the work performed thus far to the baseline cost for the task, resource, or assignment.

Note

You can calculate earned value by manually recording the Physical % Complete instead of letting Project calculate % Complete, which is Actual Duration divided by Total Duration. ∎

To work with and use earned value information effectively for both automatically and manually scheduled tasks, you must first do the following:

- Assign resources and their costs to tasks in your project
- Save a baseline for your project
- Complete some work on your project

Understanding earned value fields

The fields that appear as headings in the Earned Value report you saw in Chapter 9 also appear on various earned value tables. *Earned value fields* are currency fields that measure various aspects of earned value. The following table translates the acronyms that Project uses to represent the earned value fields.

Acronyms	Earned Value Fields
PV (also called BCWS)	Planned Value (BCWS stands for Budgeted Cost of Work Scheduled)
EV (also called BCWP)	Earned Value (BCWP stands for Budgeted Cost of Work Performed)
AC (also called ACWP)	Actual Cost (ACWP stands for Actual Cost of Work Performed)
SV	Schedule Variance
CV	Cost Variance
BAC	Budgeted at Completion
EAC	Estimate at Completion
VAC	Variance at Completion

Three of the preceding fields are really at the heart of earned value analysis:

- PV (or BCWS) measures the budgeted cost of individual tasks based on the resources and fixed costs that are assigned to the tasks when you schedule them.

- EV (or BCWP) indicates how much of a task's budget should have been spent, given the actual duration of the task. For example, suppose you have a task budgeted at $100, work has been performed for one day, and you find 40 percent of the work completed after one day. You would expect that 40 percent of the cost of the task, or $40, would also be incurred. Therefore the EV for the task is $40.

- AC (or ACWP) measures the actual cost that is incurred to complete a task. During the completion process, AC represents the actual costs for work performed through the project's status date.

PV, EV, AC, SV, and CV are all calculated through today or through the project status date. SV represents the cost difference between current progress and the baseline plan, and Project calculates this value as EV minus PV. CV represents the cost difference between actual costs and planned costs at the current level of completion, and Project calculates this value as EV minus AC. EAC shows the planned costs based on costs that are already incurred plus additional planned costs. VAC represents the variance between the baseline cost and the combination of actual costs plus planned costs for a task.

Note

Project calculates EV at the task level differently from the way it calculates EV at the assignment level. Because Project rolls the task-level EV values into summary tasks and the project summary task, I suggest that you use the task-level EV values. ■

Project uses PV, EV, AC, SV, and CV as task fields, resource fields, and assignment fields; Project also uses timephased versions of each field. BAC, EAC, and VAC, however, are task fields only.

In addition to the earned value fields I've already described, Project supports some additional earned value fields, some of which appear by default on earned value tables. Using the techniques described in Chapter 7, you can also add any of these fields to any table:

- **Physical % Complete:** This field represents your estimate of the progress of a task, regardless of actual work or time, and is not a timephased field. Project uses Physical % Complete to calculate EV on subtasks and rolls up EV to associated summary tasks. See the next section for details on having Project use Physical % Complete as the method for calculating earned value.

Note
You may be wondering about the difference between the % Complete field and the Physical % Complete field. Project calculates % Complete by dividing actual task duration by total duration. Physical % Complete is your estimate of where a task stands and has no connection to duration. ■

- **CPI:** CPI stands for *Cost Performance Index,* and Project calculates CPI by dividing EV by AC. This field appears by default in the Earned Value Cost Indicators table and is a time-phased field.

- **SPI:** SPI stands for *Schedule Performance Index,* and Project calculates SPI by dividing EV by PV. This field appears by default in the Earned Value Schedule Indicators table and is a timephased field.

- **CV%:** CV% stands for *Cost Variance %,* and Project calculates this field by dividing CV by EV and multiplying the result by 100. This field appears by default in the Earned Value Cost Indicators table and is a timephased field.

- **SV%:** SV% stands for *Schedule Variance %,* and Project calculates this field by dividing SV by PV and multiplying the result by 100. This field appears by default in the Earned Value Schedule Indicators table and is a timephased field.

- **EAC:** EAC stands for *Estimate at Completion,* and Project calculates this field by using the following formula: AC + (BAC − EV) / CPI. This field appears by default in the Earned Value for Tasks and the Earned Value Cost Indicators tables and is not a timephased field.

- **TCPI:** TCPI stands for *To Complete Performance Index,* and Project calculates this field by using the following formula: (BAC − EV) / (EAC − AC). This field appears by default in the Earned Value Cost Indicators table and is not a timephased field.

Using the Physical % Complete method to calculate earned value

Project can use the % Complete method or the Physical % Complete method to calculate earned value. Unless you specify otherwise, Project uses the % Complete method.

You can set Physical % Complete as the default earned value calculation method for your project by following these steps:

1. Click the File tab and, from the Backstage view that appears, click Options to display the Project Options dialog box

2. Click Advanced on the left.

3. In the Earned Value Options for this Project section, open the Default Task Earned Value Method list and select Physical % Complete (see Figure 15.1).

Choose the method you want Project to use for calculating earned value.

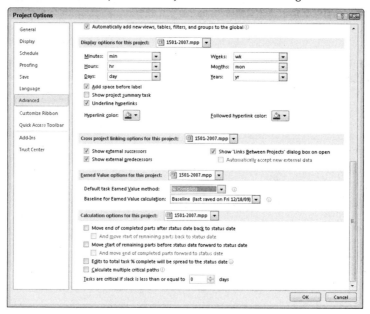

4. From the Baseline for Earned Value calculations list box, choose a baseline (Project stores 11 baselines for earned value).

Note

Clearing a baseline after entering Physical % Complete values does not clear those values. ■

5. Click OK to save the settings.

The preceding steps set the default for all new tasks that you enter in your project. If your project already contains tasks (or if you want to use the Physical % Complete method for some but not all tasks), set the earned value calculation method on a task-by-task basis. Follow these steps to do so:

1. Select the task(s) for which you want to set the earned value calculation method to Physical % Complete.

2. Click the Task tab.

3. In the Properties group, click the Information button.

   The Multiple Task Information dialog box appears.

4. Click the Advanced tab.

5. From the Earned Value Method list box, choose Physical % Complete (see Figure 15.2).

Assign the Physical % Complete method as appropriate to tasks in the Task Information dialog box.

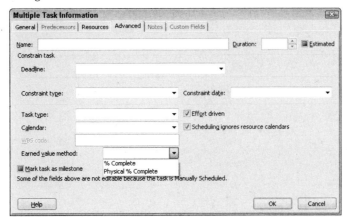

To record Physical % Complete, use the default Tracking table, shown in Figure 15.3, or add the field as a column on a table view and then enter appropriate amounts for tasks. If you add the Physical % Complete field to an Earned Value table, you'll see other Earned Value fields update accordingly when you update the Physical % Complete field.

Tip

To insert a column, right-click the heading of the column to the right of the column you are inserting, and then choose Insert Column. ■

Setting the date for earned-value calculations

By default, Project uses today's date to calculate earned-value information. However, you can set a project status date for Project to use instead of today's date when it calculates earned value. Click the Project tab and, in the Status section, click the Status Date button to open the Status Date dialog box; then select the date you want Project to use when it calculates earned value and click OK (see Figure 15.4).

FIGURE 15.3

Record Physical % Complete values on the Tracking table or on any table to which you have added the field.

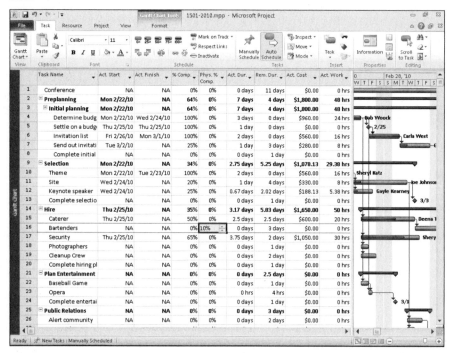

FIGURE 15.4

Use this dialog box to set a date for Project to use when calculating earned value.

Using Earned Value tables

Project contains four Earned Value tables you can use to compare your expected costs with your actual costs: Earned Value for Tasks, Earned Value Cost Indicators, Earned Value Schedule Indicators, and Earned Value for Resources. These four tables help you evaluate the relationship between work and costs. You can use the Earned Value tables to forecast whether a task will finish within the budget; such a forecast is based on a comparison of actual costs incurred for the task to date with the baseline cost of the task.

Using the Earned Value table for tasks

When you use the Earned Value table for tasks, you can compare the relationship between work and costs for tasks. This table helps you evaluate your budget to estimate future budget needs and prepare an accounting statement of your project. You can use the information in the table to determine whether sufficient work is getting done for the money you're paying, whether tasks need more money or less money, or perhaps should be cut. That is, the information in the Earned Value for tasks table helps you assess whether the money you're spending on a task is enough money, too much money, too little money, or perhaps wasted money.

To display the Earned Value table for tasks, follow these steps:

1. Start in a task view that includes a table, such as the Gantt Chart view or the Task Usage view.

2. Click the View tab and, in the Data group, click the Tables button.

3. From the list that appears, choose More Tables.

4. In the More Tables dialog box that appears, select Earned Value.

5. Click Apply. Project applies the Earned Value table for tasks to the view (see Figure 15.5).

FIGURE 15.5

The Earned Value table for tasks.

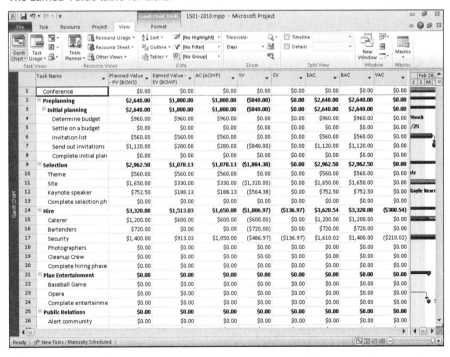

All the fields on this sheet are calculated. However, you can type values in the BAC field to change information in the table.

Using the Earned Value table for resources

When you use the Earned Value table for resources, you can compare the relationship between work and costs for resources. This table also helps you to evaluate your budget to estimate future budget needs and prepare an accounting statement of your project. You can use the information in the table to determine whether the work is getting done for the money that you're paying or whether you need more or less of a particular resource.

To display the Earned Value table for resources (see Figure 15.6), follow the same steps you used in the preceding section to display the Earned Value table for tasks, but start in a resource view that contains a table, such as the Resource Sheet view.

All the fields in this sheet are calculated. However, you can enter values in the BAC field to change information in the table.

FIGURE 15.6

The Earned Value table for resources.

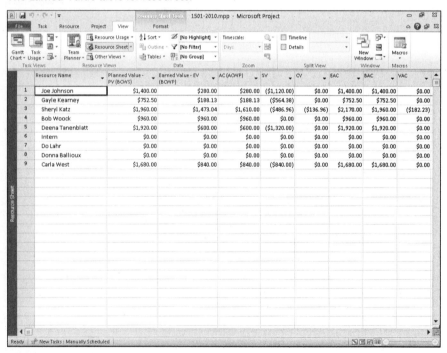

Using the Earned Value Cost Indicators and Earned Value Schedule Indicators tables

The Earned Value Cost Indicators and Earned Value Schedule Indicators tables are similar to their cousin, the Earned Value for Tasks table. The Earned Value Cost Indicators table enables you to compare the various cost factors related to tasks in your project (see Figure 15.7). The Earned Value Schedule Indicators table for tasks enables you to focus on the effects of scheduling variances on the cost of your project (see Figure 15.8).

To display the Earned Value Cost Indicators table, start in a task view that contains a table. Then, right-click the Select All button and choose More Tables from the shortcut menu that appears. In the More Tables dialog box, select Earned Value Cost Indicators and click Apply.

To display the Earned Value Schedule Indicators table, start in a task view that contains a table. Then right-click the Select All button and choose More Tables from the shortcut menu that appears. In the More Tables dialog box, select Earned Value Schedule Indicators and click Apply.

FIGURE 15.7

The Earned Value Cost Indicators table closely resembles the Earned Value for Tasks table but focuses on different earned-value fields.

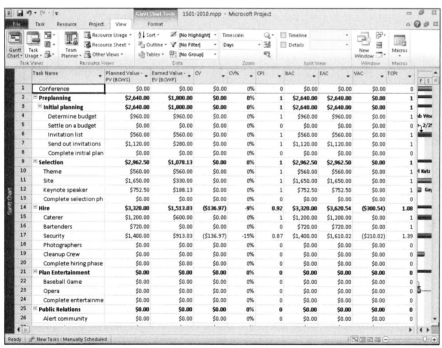

The Earned Value Schedule Indicators table closely resembles the Earned Value for Tasks table but focuses on different earned-value fields.

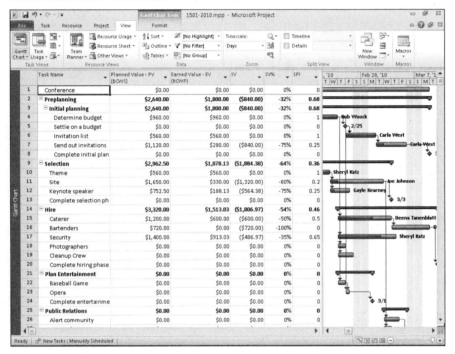

Evaluating Cost Information

If you own Microsoft Excel, you can use it to assist you in evaluating cost information. By exporting information to Excel, you can chart earned value or create PivotTables.

Charting earned value

The saying goes, "A picture is worth a thousand words." And when you look at earned-value information, you may find it easier to understand the information if you use a picture rather than studying Project's earned-value tables. You can export the earned-value information to Microsoft Excel (you must be using Excel version 5.0 or later) and then use Excel's charting tools to create charts of earned-value information.

Cross-Reference

To find out more about Project's capabilities to export and import data, see Chapter 18. ∎

When you export earned values from Project to Excel, you create an Excel workbook that contains a task ID, a name, and the various earned values for each task (see Figure 15.9).

FIGURE 15.9

An Excel workbook that was created by exporting earned-value information from Project to Excel.

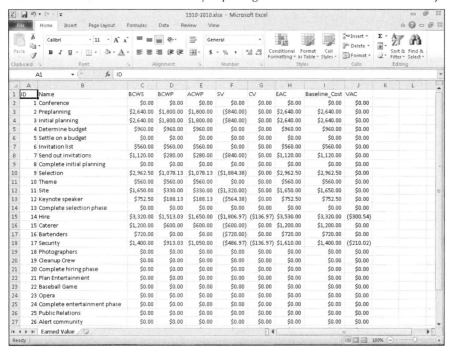

ID	Name	BCWS	BCWP	ACWP	SV	CV	EAC	Baseline_Cost	VAC
1	Conference	$0.00	$0.00	$0.00	$0.00	$0.00	$0.00	$0.00	$0.00
2	Preplanning	$2,640.00	$1,800.00	$1,800.00	($840.00)	$0.00	$2,640.00	$2,640.00	$0.00
3	Initial planning	$2,640.00	$1,800.00	$1,800.00	($840.00)	$0.00	$2,640.00	$2,640.00	$0.00
4	Determine budget	$960.00	$960.00	$960.00	$0.00	$0.00	$960.00	$960.00	$0.00
5	Settle on a budget	$0.00	$0.00	$0.00	$0.00	$0.00	$0.00	$0.00	$0.00
6	Invitation list	$560.00	$560.00	$560.00	$0.00	$0.00	$560.00	$560.00	$0.00
7	Send out invitations	$1,120.00	$280.00	$280.00	($840.00)	$0.00	$1,120.00	$1,120.00	$0.00
8	Complete initial planning	$0.00	$0.00	$0.00	$0.00	$0.00	$0.00	$0.00	$0.00
9	Selection	$2,962.50	$1,078.13	$1,078.13	($1,884.38)	$0.00	$2,962.50	$2,962.50	$0.00
10	Theme	$560.00	$560.00	$560.00	$0.00	$0.00	$560.00	$560.00	$0.00
11	Site	$1,650.00	$330.00	$330.00	($1,320.00)	$0.00	$1,650.00	$1,650.00	$0.00
12	Keynote speaker	$752.50	$188.13	$188.13	($564.38)	$0.00	$752.50	$752.50	$0.00
13	Complete selection phase	$0.00	$0.00	$0.00	$0.00	$0.00	$0.00	$0.00	$0.00
14	Hire	$3,320.00	$1,513.03	$1,650.00	($1,806.97)	($136.97)	$3,530.00	$3,320.00	($300.54)
15	Caterer	$1,200.00	$600.00	$600.00	($600.00)	$0.00	$1,200.00	$1,200.00	$0.00
16	Bartenders	$720.00	$0.00	$0.00	($720.00)	$0.00	$720.00	$720.00	$0.00
17	Security	$1,400.00	$913.03	$1,050.00	($486.97)	($136.97)	$1,610.00	$1,400.00	($210.02)
18	Photographers	$0.00	$0.00	$0.00	$0.00	$0.00	$0.00	$0.00	$0.00
19	Cleanup Crew	$0.00	$0.00	$0.00	$0.00	$0.00	$0.00	$0.00	$0.00
20	Complete hiring phase	$0.00	$0.00	$0.00	$0.00	$0.00	$0.00	$0.00	$0.00
21	Plan Entertainment	$0.00	$0.00	$0.00	$0.00	$0.00	$0.00	$0.00	$0.00
22	Baseball Game	$0.00	$0.00	$0.00	$0.00	$0.00	$0.00	$0.00	$0.00
23	Opera	$0.00	$0.00	$0.00	$0.00	$0.00	$0.00	$0.00	$0.00
24	Complete entertainment phase	$0.00	$0.00	$0.00	$0.00	$0.00	$0.00	$0.00	$0.00
25	Public Relations	$0.00	$0.00	$0.00	$0.00	$0.00	$0.00	$0.00	$0.00
26	Alert community	$0.00	$0.00	$0.00	$0.00	$0.00	$0.00	$0.00	$0.00

To create an Excel workbook like the one shown in Figure 15.9, follow these steps:

1. In the Project file containing the information that you want to use in Excel, click the File tab and, from the Backstage view that appears, choose Save As to open the Save As dialog box.

2. Type a name for the Excel workbook in the File Name list box.

   Don't worry about the file extension; Project supplies it.

3. Open the Save As Type list box and select Microsoft Excel Workbook. The Save As dialog box should resemble the one shown in Figure 15.10.

4. Click Save, and Project starts the Export Mapping Wizard.

5. Click Next.

6. Choose Selected Data in the next box of the wizard and then click Next.

7. Choose Use existing map in the next box of the wizard and then click Next.

FIGURE 15.10

The Save As dialog box as it appears after you choose to save an Excel workbook file.

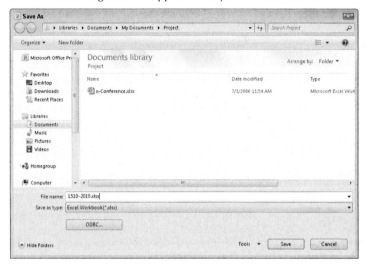

8. Choose Earned Value Information from the list of available maps in the Export Wizard dialog box (see Figure 15.11).

9. Click Finish.

FIGURE 15.11

Choose Earned value information as the map from the Export Wizard dialog box.

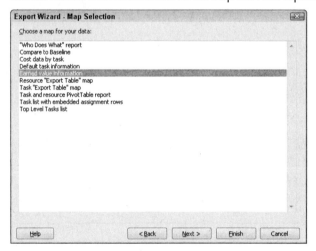

Note

You can continue clicking Next in the wizard, but to chart earned value in Excel, you usually don't need to make any changes in the remaining dialog boxes that the wizard presents. ∎

Open Microsoft Excel and then open the workbook you just created by clicking the File tab and, from the Backstage view that appears, clicking Open. In the Open dialog box that appears, navigate to open the workbook you just created. You can use Excel's charting tools to create as many charts from this data as you want. For example, the chart in Figure 15.12 compares the budgeted cost of work performed with the actual cost of work performed for three tasks.

To create a chart like the one shown in Figure 15.12, follow these steps:

1. Select the cells you want to chart.

   For the example chart, I selected the cells C11.E13.

2. Click Insert and then click Column to open the Column gallery (see Figure 15.13).

FIGURE 15.12

An Excel chart comparing two earned values for selected tasks.

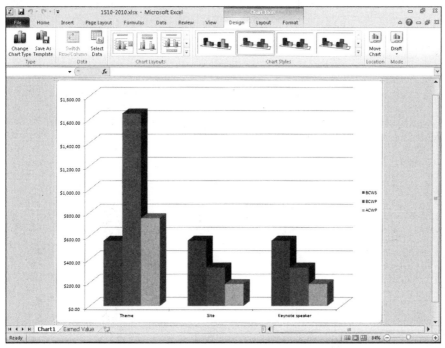

FIGURE 15.13

Select a column chart style for the selected data.

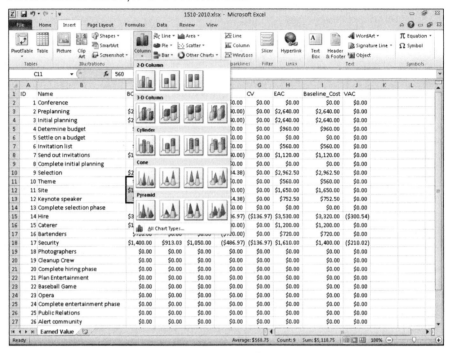

3. Select a column style. Excel inserts the chart in your spreadsheet; the chart is selected. Chart Tools appear on the Ribbon.

4. Click Select Data on the Ribbon to display the Select Data Source dialog box (see Figure 15.14).

5. Click an entry in the Legend Entries list; in the example, I clicked Series1.

6. In the Legend Entries area, click Edit. Excel displays the Edit Series dialog box (see Figure 15.15).

7. Click the Series Name Collapse Dialog button at the right edge of the Series Name box. Excel collapses the dialog box so you can select a cell in the spreadsheet.

FIGURE 15.14

Use this dialog box to assign meaning labels to the data in the chart.

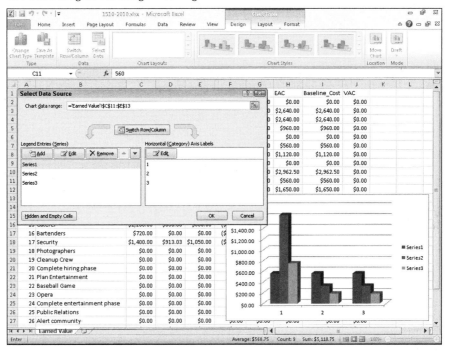

FIGURE 15.15

Use this dialog box to select a legend label.

Collapse Dialog button

8. Click the column heading for the value represented by the leftmost bar; in the example, I clicked C1, which contains the label for PV (BCWS). Excel changes the information in the collapsed Edit Series dialog box to match your selection (see Figure 15.16).

FIGURE 15.16

The collapsed Edit Series dialog box containing a legend label selection.

9. Click the Collapse Dialog button to redisplay Edit Series dialog box; then click OK to redisplay the Select Data Source dialog box.

Excel shows the name change in the Legend Entries list in the dialog box and on your chart (see Figure 15.17).

FIGURE 15.17

The legend for the first set of values now displays a name instead of the generic title "Series1" that Excel assigns.

The name change appears here

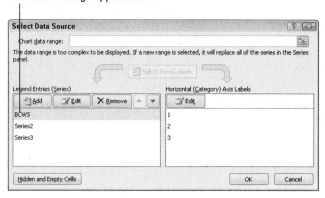

10. Repeat Steps 5 to 9 for each series in the Legend Entries list.

11. For the entries in the Horizontal Axis Labels list, repeat Steps 5 to 9 to select row headings to use as X-axis labels, *with one exception:* Select all row labels simultaneously.

In the example, when I repeated Step 8, I selected cells B11.B13 to replace the numbers 1, 2, and 3 that Excel assigned to the X axis of the chart. You complete Step 11 only *once;* this step assigns labels to all three entries in the Horizontal Axis Labels list simultaneously. When you complete this step, the Select Data Source dialog box will resemble the one shown in Figure 15.18.

12. Click OK.

FIGURE 15.18

The Select Data Source dialog box after you have assigned labels to the horizontal axis and the legend.

In the chart shown previously in Figure 15.12, I placed the chart in its own sheet by making sure that the chart was selected and clicking Move Chart in the Location group at the right edge of the Design tab on the Ribbon. In the Move Chart dialog box that appeared, I clicked the New sheet option.

Using PivotTables for analysis

Excel PivotTables can be interesting and useful when you want to analyze Project earned-value data. The PivotTable is an interactive table that summarizes large amounts of data in a cross-tabular format. When you use Project to create a PivotTable in Excel, you get two PivotTables in the same workbook: a Task PivotTable and a Resource PivotTable. The Task PivotTable shows the project's resources, the tasks to which the resources are assigned, and costs for each resource per task. The Resource PivotTable summarizes resources by showing work assigned to each resource and the total cost of each resource. In addition to the PivotTable worksheets, the same Excel workbook also includes two worksheets — Tasks and Resources — that Excel uses to create these two PivotTables.

To export Project information to create PivotTables in Excel, follow these steps:

1. Start in any view of your project.
2. Click the File tab and, in the Backstage view that appears, click Save As to open the Save As dialog box.
3. In the File Name box, type a name for the Excel workbook that you want to create.

   Don't worry about the file extension — Project supplies it.
4. Select Microsoft Excel from the Save As Type list box.
5. Click Save to start the Export Mapping Wizard.
6. Click Next.

7. Choose Use Existing Map and click Next.

8. Select Task and Resource PivotTable Report as the map that Project should use and then click Finish (see Figure 15.19). The hourglass icon for the mouse pointer appears, indicating that you should wait while action takes place. You'll also hear action on your hard drive.

FIGURE 15.19

The Map Selection portion of the Export Wizard dialog box.

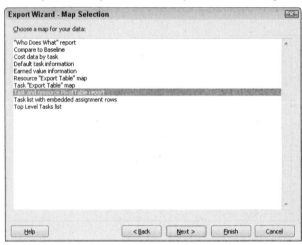

Note
You can continue clicking Next in the wizard, but to chart earned value in Excel, you usually don't need to make any changes in the remaining dialog boxes that the wizard presents. ∎

To view the PivotTables and their source data, start Excel and open the file that you just created. The workbook contains four sheets that should resemble the sheets shown in Figures 15.20, 15.21, 15.22, and 15.23.

Tip
You may need to widen columns in Excel to see all the data. Double-click the right border of the column letter to do so. ∎

FIGURE 15.20

The Resource PivotTable.

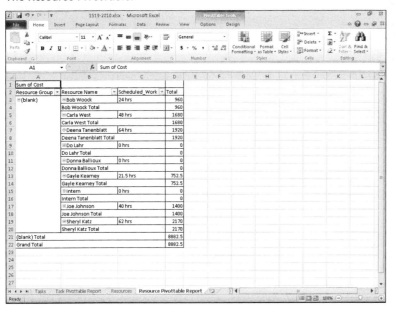

FIGURE 15.21

The Resources sheet that Excel used to create the Resource PivotTable.

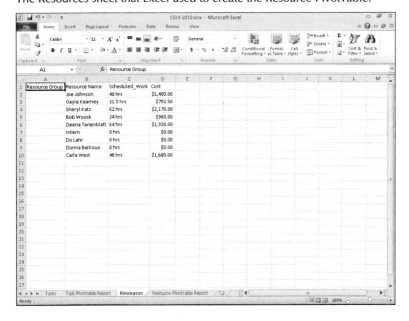

FIGURE 15.22

The Task PivotTable.

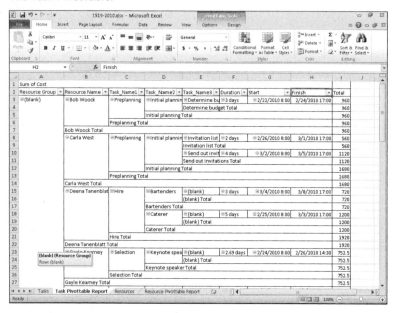

FIGURE 15.23

The Tasks sheet that Excel used to create the Task PivotTable.

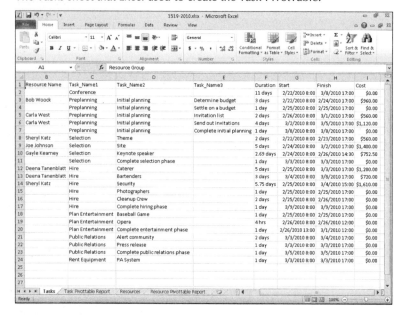

Making Adjustments During the Project

Now that you've seen the various ways you can collect and analyze financial data about your project, you need to use that information to make improvements to your project. You can use many of the same techniques that you used to change your project because of scheduling problems or resource conflicts.

Cross-Reference

Find out how to deal with scheduling problems by using the techniques that are discussed in Chapter 10. You'll find help resolving resource conflicts in Chapter 11. ■

Changing the schedule

After evaluating earned value information, you may want to change the schedule. For example, you may want to do the following:

- Add resources to tasks
- Use overtime
- Increase task duration
- Adjust slack
- Change task constraints
- Adjust dependencies
- Split tasks
- Adjust the critical path

You may also need to make changes to the baseline project you saved.

Cross-Reference

For more information on adjusting the baseline, see Chapter 12. ■

Modifying resource assignments

Your evaluation of earned value information may prompt you to make changes to resource assignments on your project. For example, you may need to do the following:

- Change resource allocations
- Schedule overtime
- Redefine a resource's calendar
- Assign part-time work
- Control when resources start working on a task

- Level workloads
- Contour resources
- Pool resources

Tip
When you're working on an unusually large project, you may find it easier to break your project into smaller, more manageable portions called subprojects. In Project, you can create subprojects and then consolidate them into the larger project to see the bigger picture (see Chapter 19). ■

Summary

This chapter explained how to analyze the costs in your project. After reading this chapter, you should know the following:

- How to use Project's Earned Value tables
- How to chart earned-value information and use Project information to create PivotTables in Microsoft Excel
- How to make adjustments to your project

Part VI

Advanced Microsoft Project

Customizing Microsoft Project

You can customize the Project working environment in several ways. For example, you can change the way various elements appear on-screen and how you use Project's tools and commands. Suppose you use a particular command for sharing resources all the time; you can perform that action quickly if you add it to the Quick Access Toolbar (QAT) or the Ribbon. Or maybe you never use the Task Note tool and prefer to get it off the Ribbon. Or perhaps you'd like to create your own tab on the Ribbon that contains all the buttons you use most often — that way you don't need to switch tabs on the Ribbon to do the work you do most often. In addition, you can use custom fields to store and manipulate custom data in a project file.

Microsoft Project enables you to customize most of its elements. This chapter shows you how to make changes to the behavior of the Project interface, create and modify Ribbon tabs and groups, add buttons to and remove buttons from the QAT, and create and use custom fields to make Project work the way that's best for you.

Modifying Project's Behavior and Interface

Project contains dozens of ways you can customize its interface — way too many for me to cover here. In this section, I'll cover just a few of the options I think you might find useful in making Project support the way you work.

Customizing the status bar

You can use Project's status bar to change the appearance and behavior of various Project elements. For example, by default, Project displays no indicator that you are recording a macro. If you want to see that indicator, you can add it to the status bar. Then you'll see one version of the indicator when you are recording a macro and another when you aren't. To add the indicator to the status bar, right-click the status bar to display the Customize Status Bar menu (see Figure 16.1). Click Macro Recording, and Project adds the Macro Recording indicator to the status bar (see Figure 16.2). Click outside the Customize Status Bar menu to close it. If you right-click the status bar again, a check appears beside Macro Recording to point out that the indicator is visible on the status bar.

Setting levels of Undo

Project allows you to undo actions you take while working in a Project file, and you can set the number of times you can click Undo to any number between 1 and 99.

By default, Project lets you undo your last 20 actions, but you can change that number. Click the File tab and, in the Backstage view that appears, click Options. Click Advanced on the left and use the Undo Levels box in the General section to control the number of actions you can undo (see Figure 16.3).

FIGURE 16.1

Control elements that appear on the Status Bar.

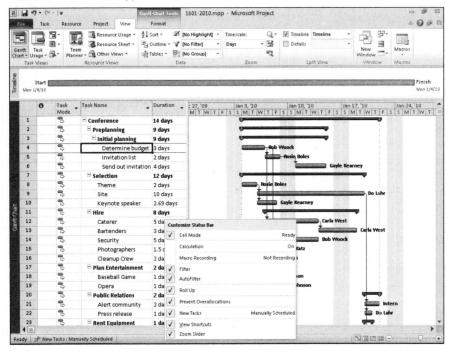

FIGURE 16.2

The Macro Recording indicator appears between the Cell Mode indicator and the New Tasks indicator.

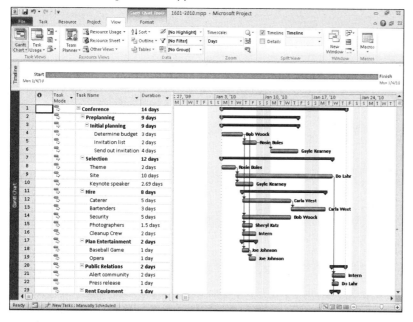

FIGURE 16.3

Use this field to control the number of times the Undo button will work.

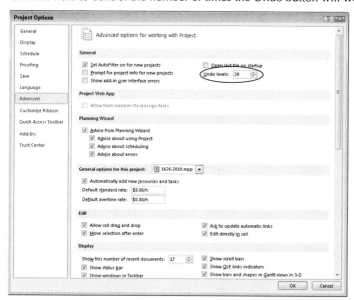

Windows taskbar icons

By default, Project displays an icon in the Windows taskbar for each open project. Windows itself controls whether the icons for each project appear individually on the taskbar or stacked on one icon on the taskbar.

If you don't want to see icons for all open projects, you can limit the number of icons appearing on the Windows taskbar to only one — the one for the project you are currently using. Open the Project Options dialog box (click the File tab and, from the Backstage view that appears, click Options) and click the Advanced tab. Scroll down and, in the Display section, deselect the Show Windows in Taskbar option (see Figure 16.4).

FIGURE 16.4

To display only one icon on the Windows taskbar for the project you are currently viewing, deselect the Windows in Taskbar check box.

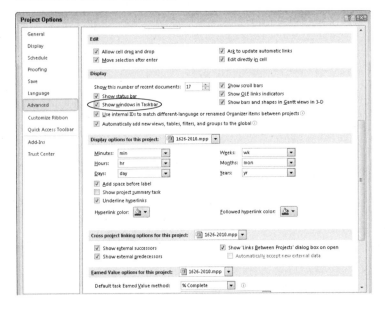

Note

Regardless of the behavior you choose in the Options dialog box, all open Project files appear when you click the Switch Windows button on the View tab in the Window group. You can switch among Project files by using the Switch Windows button in Project or the Windows taskbar. ■

Saving Project files

Using the Save tab of the Options dialog box (see Figure 16.5), you can set the following defaults:

Project has several features associated with saving files.

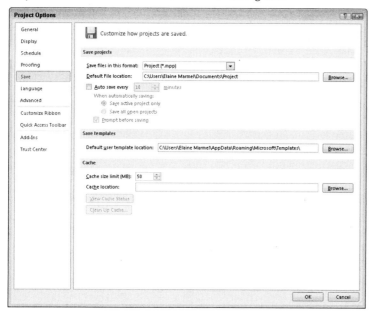

- By opening the Save Files In This Format list box, you can specify the default file format for each new Project file you save. For example, you might want to save all Project 2010 files in Project 2000 – 2003 format if you regularly share files with someone who uses one of those versions of Project.

Caution

If you save files created in Project 2010 in the format of Project 2000 – 2003, you may lose information. For example, background cell formatting doesn't exist in any version of Project prior to Project 2007. If you apply background formatting to cells in a file and then save the file in Project 2000 – 2003 format, you'll lose the formatting. ■

- You can set a default file location to save all files and user templates. By setting these locations, you don't need to navigate to the correct folder each time you want to save a new file or template.
- Use the Auto Save feature to save project files on a regular basis. The Auto Save feature is particularly valuable to people who tend to work extensively, forget to save regularly, and

become victims of power failures or server crashes. If you use Auto Save, you can open your file as of the last automatic save.

Using the Organizer

Project uses the Organizer to help you share views, tables, forms, reports, and more among projects. To display the Organizer box, click the File tab and then click Info (see Figure 16.6). Click the Organizer button to display the Organizer window shown in Figure 16.7).

Tip
You'll also find an Organizer button in the More Views window. ■

Use the various tabs in the Organizer dialog box to copy elements from the Global template (`Global.mpt`) to the current project. You also can copy elements from the current project to the Global template or simply between projects. First, open the Project file that contains the element you want to copy and the Project file into which you want to copy the information. Then, in the Organizer box, use the list boxes at the bottom of each tab to select the file containing the information and the file that should receive the information.

FIGURE 16.6

You can display the Organizer by clicking the Organizer button in the Backstage view.

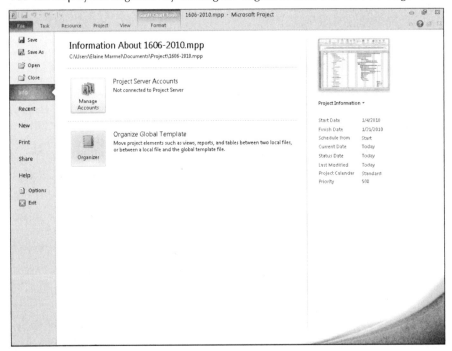

FIGURE 16.7

All views in the Global template (Global.mpt) file are available to every file that is based on the Global.mpt file.

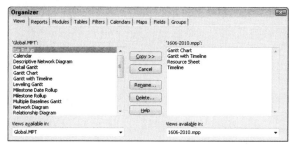

Note

When you copy an element to the Global template, that element becomes available to all files created with your copy of Project. ■

Customizing the Quick Access Toolbar

You can customize the Quick Access Toolbar (QAT) by changing its location and its content. By default, the QAT's default location is on the program title bar. If you prefer, you can position the QAT below the Ribbon.

You also can add buttons to the QAT and remove buttons from the QAT.

Changing the placement of the QAT

The QAT's default location is on the program title bar, just above the File tab, but you can reposition it so it appears below the Ribbon. Some people find that positioning the QAT below the Ribbon brings the buttons closer to the working area.

Click the Customize Quick Access Toolbar button — the down arrow-like button that appears at the right edge of the QAT. From the menu of choices that appears, select Show Below the Ribbon. In Figure 16.8, I moved the QAT so it appears below the Ribbon. Notice that the Show Below the Ribbon command changes to the Show Above the Ribbon command — and you can use that command to move the QAT back above the Ribbon.

FIGURE 16.8

You can reposition the QAT so it appears below the Ribbon.

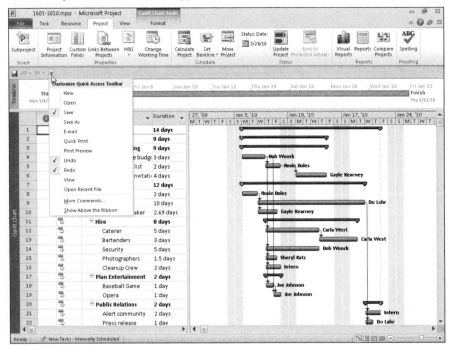

Adding buttons to and removing buttons from the QAT

You can add buttons to the Quick Access Toolbar, remove buttons from the QAT, and reorganize the order in which buttons appear on the QAT.

The Customize Quick Access Toolbar menu contains some commonly used buttons you might want to add to the QAT; click the down arrow-like button at the right edge of the QAT to display the menu and select any command on it to add a button for that command to the QAT. Commands with checks beside them already appear on the QAT (refer to Figure 16.8).

You can add buttons to the QAT for commands you don't see on the Customize Quick Access Toolbar menu. Using the following steps, you also can control the order in which the buttons appear.

1. Click the down arrow-like button at the right edge of the QAT to display the Customize Quick Access Toolbar menu.

2. Click More Commands to display the Project Options dialog box, showing the Quick Access Toolbar customization options (see Figure 16.9).

FIGURE 16.9

Use the Quick Access Toolbar tab of the Project Options dialog box to customize the QAT.

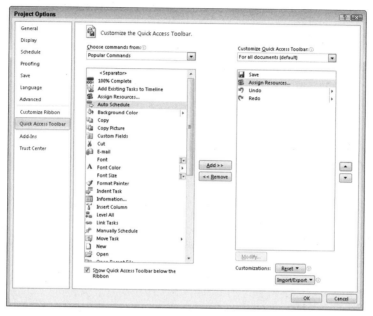

3. Click a command in the list on the left to the QAT. If the command you want to add does not appear in the list, click the list box arrow above the list (which, by default, displays Popular Commands) and select All Commands.

4. Click the Add button. Project displays the button in the list on the right, which contains commands already on the QAT.

5. Repeat Steps 3 and 4 for each command you want to add to the QAT.

Tip
Using the list box above the list on the right, you can customize the QAT for all documents or just the current document. ■

6. To reorder the buttons on the QAT, click a command in the right-hand column.

7. Click the Move Up or the Move Down buttons, which appear to the right of the list on the right.

8. Click OK to save your changes.

Tip

You can quickly add any button that appears on the Ribbon to the QAT if you right-click the button and choose Add to Quick Access Toolbar. You'll still need to use the Project Options dialog box to control the button's position on the QAT. ∎

If you decide you don't like any of the changes that you made to the QAT, you can reset it from the Project Options dialog box. Repeat Steps 1 to 2 to reopen the dialog box and, in the lower-right corner of the dialog box, click Reset. From the menu that appears, click Reset only Quick Access Toolbar.

You can remove a button from the Quick Access Toolbar by right-clicking it and then clicking Remove from Quick Access Toolbar.

Customizing the Ribbon

You can customize the Ribbon in several ways. For example, you can hide all the buttons on the Ribbon and display only tabs; when you need a button, you click a tab and Project redisplays all the buttons.

You also can reorganize the information on the Ribbon by adding predefined groups from one tab to another, by creating custom groups, and by creating your own Ribbon tabs.

Hiding and displaying buttons

If screen real estate is important to you and you want to be able to see more of your project while you work, you can hide the buttons on the Ribbon and display only the Ribbon tabs. When you need the buttons on the Ribbon, you can easily redisplay them by simply clicking any tab. Hiding the buttons on the Ribbon can make your screen appear less crowded.

To hide Ribbon buttons and display only Ribbon tabs, click the Minimize Ribbon button in the upper-right corner of the Project window or press Ctrl+F1. In Figure 16.10, I've hidden the Ribbon buttons.

When you display Ribbon buttons, the Minimize the Ribbon button arrow points up; when the Ribbon buttons are hidden as in the figure, the button arrow points down.

Adding pre-defined groups to a Ribbon tab

Many people find they use only a few groups of buttons on any given tab. You can work more efficiently if you customize the Ribbon to place the groups of buttons that you use most often on a single tab.

For example, suppose that most of the buttons you need appear on the Task tab, but you often use the Task Views group on the View tab to switch task views. You can add the Task Views group to the Task tab.

Note

You cannot add or delete a button to one of the default groups on the Ribbon. But you can create your own group that contains only those buttons you want to use — and then hide the default group Project displays. See "Creating your own Ribbon group" later in this chapter. ∎

FIGURE 16.10

Click the Minimize the Ribbon button or press Ctrl+F1 to display only Ribbon tabs.

Click here to minimize Ribbon

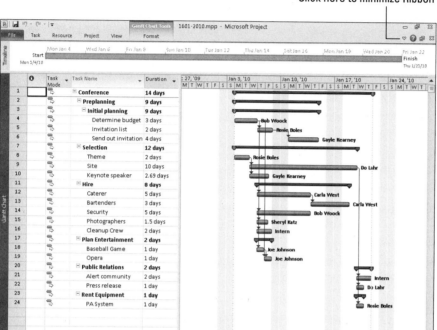

Follow these steps to add a predefined group from one Ribbon tab to another Ribbon tab:

1. Click the File tab and, from the Backstage view that appears, click Options.

2. In the Project Options dialog box, click Customize Ribbon.

3. Open the list box above the left column and select Main Tabs.

4. Click the plus sign beside the tab containing the group you want to add.

5. Click the group you want to add.

6. Click the plus beside the tab where you want to place the group you selected in Step 5.

7. Click the group you want to appear on the Ribbon to the left of the new group.

8. Click the Add button. Project adds the group you selected in Step 5 below the group you selected in Step 7 (see Figure 16.11).

9. Repeat Steps 4 to 8 as needed.

10. Click OK.

FIGURE 16.11

Adding the Task Views group to the Task tab.

Project adds the group you selected to the appropriate Ribbon tab; in Figure 16.12, the Task Views group appears to the right of the View group.

Also be aware that the group you added remains on its original tab; in this example, the Task Views group appears on both the Task tab and the View tab and performs the same function on both tabs.

Creating your own Ribbon group

You cannot add or remove buttons from predefined groups on a Ribbon tab, but you can create your own groups and place the buttons you want in the groups. Creating your own groups on the Ribbon can help you work more efficiently. For example, you can create one group on each Ribbon tab that contains the buttons on that tab that you use most often. If you place that group in the same position on each tab — say at the left edge of each tab — you won't need to search for the buttons you use most often; they will always be in the same position on each tab on the Ribbon.

When you add a group to a tab, you can assign a name to it that you find meaningful; then you can add whatever buttons you need to the group.

Regardless of the Ribbon tab on which you place your group, you can assign any name you want to the group; you even can use a group name that already exists on any Ribbon tab. You also are not limited to adding buttons to your group that appear on the Ribbon tab where you place your group; you can add buttons to your group that appear in some other group and even on some other tab.

FIGURE 16.12

Project's Task tab now contains the Task Views group found on the View tab.

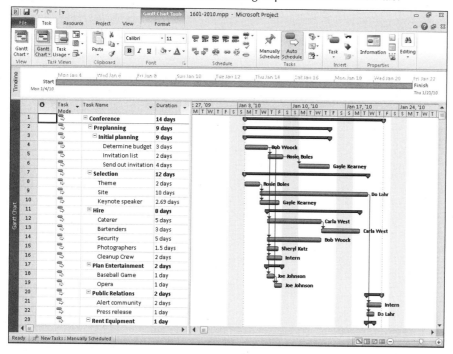

To create your own Ribbon group containing its own buttons, follow these steps:

1. Click the File tab and, from the Backstage view that appears, click Options to display the Project Options dialog box.

2. Click the Customize Ribbon tab.

3. In the right column, click the plus beside the tab to which you want to add a group.

4. Click the group you want to appear on the Ribbon to the left of the new group.

Tip

If you want your group to appear first on the tab, click the first group on the tab and, after you add your group, click the Up arrow on the right side of the right column to move your group up one position. ■

5. Click the New Group button below the right column. Project adds a new group to the tab below the group you selected in Step 4 and selects the new group (see Figure 16.13).

6. To assign a name to the new group, click the Rename button below the right column to display the Rename dialog box (see Figure 16.14).

FIGURE 16.13

The Project Options dialog box after adding a new group to the Task tab.

FIGURE 16.14

Use this dialog box to create a name for your new group.

7. Type a name for your group and click OK.

   Project assigns the name to your group and redisplays the Project Options dialog box.

8. To add buttons to your group, make sure that the group you created is selected in the right column.

9. In the left column, click a command. If the command you want does not appear in the list, click the list box arrow above the left column and select All Commands.

10. Click Add, and Project displays the command below the group you created.

11. Repeat Steps 9 and 10 for each button you want to add to your group (see Figure 16.15).

12. Click OK to save your changes.

    Your new group with its buttons appears on the Ribbon (see Figure 16.16).

If you change your mind about the location of your group, you can use the Up and Down arrows on the right side of the right column to move your group to another position on the same tab or to another tab altogether.

FIGURE 16.15

Adding buttons to a group.

503

FIGURE 16.16

The Task tab with a new custom group on it.

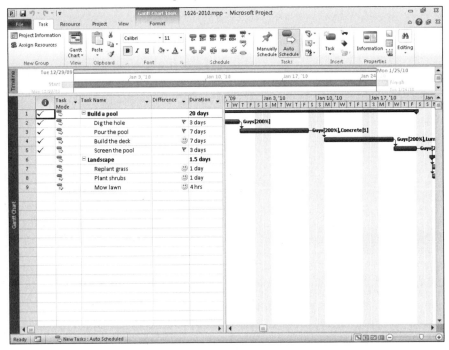

Those of you who prefer to use the keyboard instead of clicking buttons don't need to assign keyboard shortcuts; Project assigns them for you, based on the keys already assigned to commands that appear on the tab where you placed your group. Be aware that you can place the same button on two different tabs; if you do, Project assigns different keyboard shortcuts to that button on each tab.

Creating your own Ribbon tab

If creating your own Ribbon group isn't adequate for you, you can create your own tab on the Ribbon to help you achieve maximum efficiency. If you can create your own tab on the Ribbon, you can then add groups to that tab and store all the buttons you use most frequently from all the tabs on the default Ribbon. If you place your new tab to the left of the Task tab, then your tab will appear by default when you open Project, and you can leave the Ribbon positioned on your tab, saving you the time of locating the buttons you need on the various Ribbon tabs.

When you create a custom tab, Project automatically creates one group for you so you can quickly and easily add buttons to the new tab. You can assign names that mean something to you to both your tab and the group Project automatically creates. You also can add other groups to the tab; see "Creating your own Ribbon group" earlier in this chapter.

Tip

You are not limited to creating a single tab; you can create as many tabs as you want. ■

To create your own Ribbon tab, follow these steps:

1. Click the File tab and, from the Backstage view that appears, click Options to display the Project Options dialog box.

2. Click the Customize Ribbon tab.

3. In the right column, click the tab you want to appear to the left of the new tab.

Tip

If you want your tab to appear first on the Ribbon, click the Task tab; after you add your tab, click it and then click the Up arrow on the right side of the right column to move your tab up. ■

4. Click the New Tab button below the right column. Project creates a new tab below the tab you selected in Step 3, along with a new group on that tab (see Figure 16.17).

5. To rename the group Project added to your tab, click it and then click the Rename button below the right column. In the Rename dialog box that appears, type a name and click OK.

FIGURE 16.17

Creating a new Ribbon tab automatically adds a group to that tab.

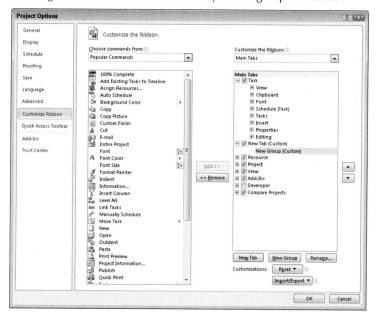

6. To rename the tab you created, click it and then click the Rename button below the right column. In the Rename dialog box that appears, type a name and click OK.

7. To add buttons to the group on your new tab, click the group.

8. In the left column, click a command. If the command you want does not appear in the list, click the list box arrow above the left column and select All Commands.

9. Click the Add button. The command appears below the group you created.

10. Repeat Steps 8 and 9 for each button you want to add to the group.

11. As appropriate, use the steps in the section, "Creating your own Ribbon group" to add more groups to your tab.

12. Click OK.

    The new tab appears on the Ribbon, along with the group(s) containing the buttons you added.

If you decide that you don't want to use the tab you created, you can hide it, which leaves the tab available should you decide you want to redisplay it. In the Project Options dialog box, on the Customize Ribbon tab, in the right column, remove the check that appears beside your tab.

If you decide you don't like the position of your tab, you can move it. In the Project Options dialog box, on the Customize Ribbon tab, in the right column, click your tab and then click the Move Up or Move Down buttons as appropriate; these buttons appear on the right edge of the right column.

Using Custom Fields

In Chapter 7, you read about outline codes, which are custom fields in Project. Custom fields enable you to create pick lists, which are useful for ensuring accurate data entry, creating formulas to perform calculations on custom data, and inserting icons to indicate graphically that a field contains custom data.

Tip
Consider customizing fields to help create standardization within your organization. If all projects in your organization use the same standards, you avoid problems when you merge or consolidate projects or move them into Project Server. ■

Customizing data entry

Suppose that your boss wants your best guess about whether you'll keep to the schedule on a task-by-task basis. You can set up a custom field and provide the information on any sheet associated with a task-oriented view of Project. Think of this process in two parts:

- Creating a custom field
- Using the custom field

Creating a custom field

For this example, we'll create a custom field that contains a *pick list*. A pick list is, well, a list containing choices from you which pick to set the value for the custom field. To create a custom field, follow these steps:

1. Click the Project tab.

2. In the Properties group, click Custom Field to display the Custom Fields dialog box (see Figure 16.18).

FIGURE 16.18

Select a custom field type.

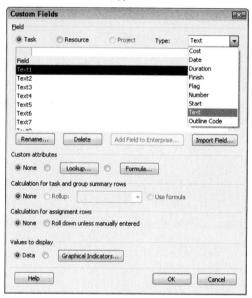

3. Select an option button — Task or Resource — that describes whether you want to create a custom field related to tasks or to resources.

4. Open the Type list box and choose the type of field that you want to customize.

   The type you choose determines the values that you can include in the pick list. Choose Text to include only alphanumeric characters in the pick list. If you choose Date, Start, or Finish, you must include date-formatted numbers in the pick list. If you choose Number or Cost, you can include only numbers in the pick list. If you choose Flag, you can include only Yes or No in the Value List dialog box. For this example, I chose Text because I want to set up a value list that contains Yes, No, and Maybe.

5. To provide a meaningful name for the code or custom field, click the Rename button and type the new name. Then click OK to redisplay the Custom Fields dialog box.

   You can use any name that Project isn't already using. (In this example, I named the field Best Guess.)

6. Click the Lookup button to display the Edit Lookup Table for Field Name dialog box (see Figure 16.19).

   Using this dialog box, you create the entries that appear in the custom field's pick list.

FIGURE 16.19

Use this dialog box to define the values you want Project to display in the pick list during data entry.

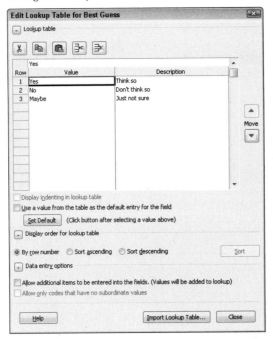

7. In the Value column, type a value that you want Project to display in the list.

   The values that Project lets you include in the value list depend on the field type that you chose in Step 4. If you chose Text, you can include only combinations of letters and numbers. If you chose Date, Start, or Finish, you must include date-formatted entries. If you chose Number or Cost, you can include only numbers in the value list. If you chose Flag, you can include only Yes or No in the value list.

Note

If you chose Flag, you need to substitute Yes or No for standard flag choices, such as True and False or On and Off. ■

8. (Optional) In the Description column, provide a description of the value.

9. Repeat Steps 7 and 8 for each list value that you want to define.

10. You can set a default value to appear as the entry for the field. Click the value in the list that you want selected by default and click the Set Default button.

    Project displays the selected value and its description in blue, bold text.

11. You can specify the order for the values in the list in the Display Order for Lookup Table section; click the plus sign (+), which changes to a minus sign (–) to display sort options.

12. In the Data Entry options section of the dialog box, you can opt to permit the user to enter values other than those in the list and add those values to the value list.

Note

Although you can allow users to enter information not stored in the value list, using that information can be troublesome. If users misspell entries or don't use entries consistently, you won't be able to filter or group effectively. ■

13. Click Close to save the value list and redisplay the Custom Fields dialog box.

14. Click OK to redisplay your project.

Using a custom field for data entry

Now that you've created a custom field that uses a list of acceptable values, let's walk through the process of using it for data entry.

To use the custom field, you need to display it as a column in a sheet view. Follow these steps:

1. Select a view that corresponds to the type of custom field you created.

   If you defined a task field, you can use any task sheet view; if you defined a resource field, use any resource sheet view.

2. To display the custom field in a column on a table view, slide the vertical view splitter bar to the right enough so you can see the Add New Column column on the table.

3. Click the Add New Column column heading and, when the list appears, type a few characters of the name you provided for your custom field.

   The more letters you type, the closer Project comes to displaying the custom field you selected.

4. When Project displays your custom field (see Figure 16.20), press Enter to select it and add it as the rightmost column in the table.

FIGURE 16.20

Adding a custom field to a sheet view.

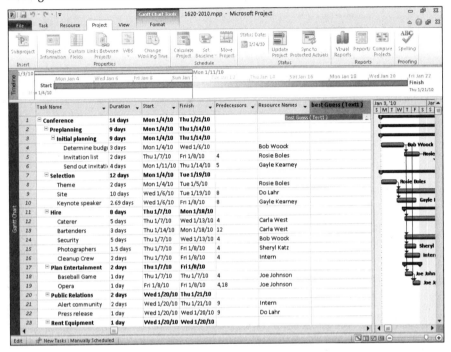

5. To move the column, click its heading; Project selects the column. Drag the column heading to the left; as you drag, a vertical bar marks the proposed location of the column. Release the mouse button when the column appears where you want it.

    I placed my custom field to the right of the Task Name column (see Figure 16.21).

When you click in the field, a list box arrow appears. When you open the list box, the pick list you established appears. Select a choice from the pick list, or simply type it in the custom field's column.

In my example, if you try to enter a value that doesn't exist in the list, Project displays an error message instructing you to use a value from the list.

Caution

You can't use custom fields to create value lists for regular Project fields. For example, suppose you've decided that you don't want to use all 1,000 of Project's priorities. In fact, you want your people to use only five possible priorities: 100, 200, 300, 400, and 500 (100 being the lowest priority and 500 being the highest priority). You can create a Number custom field (called Priority Lvl, for example) that allows the entry of only these five values in a sheet view. However, users can open the Task Information dialog box and assign any priority value in the Priority field — and Project permits the assignment. The custom field Priority Lvl is not substituting for the actual field Priority, and users can circumvent the custom value list. ■

FIGURE 16.21

As you fill in the field, select from the pick list.

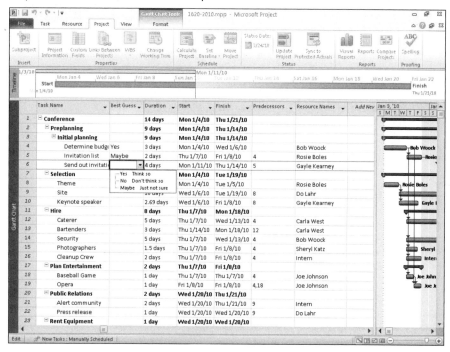

Using formulas in custom fields

Suppose that your manager tells you that part of your evaluation in project management depends on the accuracy of your cost estimates. Under these circumstances, you may want to monitor the tasks for which cost exceeds baseline cost. You can set up a custom field to help you easily identify those tasks. Follow these steps to do so:

1. Click the Project tab and, in the Properties group, click Custom Fields.

   Project displays the Custom Fields dialog box, shown previously in Figure 16.18.

2. Select either Task or Resource and then open the Type list box and choose the type of field that you want to customize.

   For this example, I choose Task and Cost because I want to compare task cost values.

Tip

The type of field you select from the Type list matters in a different way when you're creating a formula instead of a value list. If you select the wrong type when creating a value list, you can't set up the appropriate values for the list. However, if you select a type that doesn't match what you're trying to calculate in a formula, Project lets you create the formula but displays ERROR in the custom field column on the table. For example, suppose that you want to calculate a cost and you select Date from the Type list. Project still permits you to create the formula, but because the formula doesn't make sense, you see the message ERROR when you display the custom field column. ∎

   3. To provide a meaningful name for the field, click the Rename button and type the new name.

   You can't use any name that Project is already using; in the example, I named the field Difference. Then, click OK to redisplay the Custom Fields dialog box.

   4. Click the Formula button to display the Formula For dialog box.

   Figure 16.22 shows the formula I set up for this example.

FIGURE 16.22

This dialog box lets you create a formula; Project displays the results of the formula when you display the custom field.

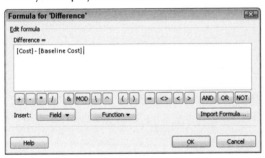

   5. Create a formula in the text box by selecting fields or functions. To select a field, click the Field button; Project displays a list of field categories. Select the appropriate field category, and Project displays a list of the available fields (see Figure 16.23). To select a function, follow the same process by clicking the Function button.

   6. To make a calculation, use the operators that appear above the Field and Function buttons.

Cross-Reference

In Appendix C, you find three tables. Table C-1 contains a list of all available Task fields, and Table C-2 contains the same information for Resource fields. Table C-3 lists the functions you can include in a formula as well as a description of each function's purpose. ∎

FIGURE 16.23

Select a field or a function to include in the formula.

Tip

If you've created this formula in another project, you can import the formula from the Global template (assuming you saved the formula in the Global template), or you can open the project that contains the formula before you create the formula in the new project. When you click the Import Formula button, Project displays a list of available templates or open Project files. Select the appropriate location, field type, and field name. Then click OK. ■

7. In the Formula For dialog box, click OK. Project warns you that it will discard any information that was previously stored in the custom field and replace the information with the calculated values based on the formula.

8. In the Custom Fields box, click OK to save the formula and redisplay the Custom Fields dialog box.

9. (Optional) Assign the formula to summary rows.

If you click OK at this point, Project calculates a value for the formula. You can see the value if you display the custom field in a column on a table, as I did in Figure 16.24. Based on the formula I created, positive values represent tasks where Actual Cost exceeded EV (BCWP) (budgeted cost of work performed) — and technically, my Difference column is nothing more than the Variance column of the Cost table.

When you display the column for a custom field containing a formula, you see the result of the formula.

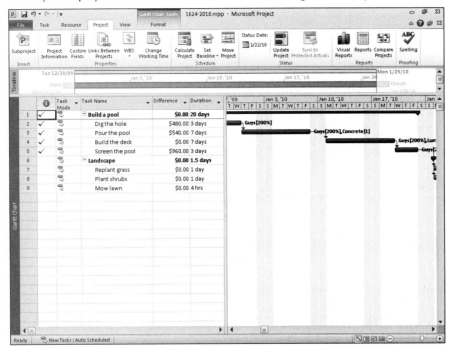

Suppose that you don't want to eyeball figures to find the problem tasks. You can insert icons to represent positive and negative values (and make the job of identifying the problem tasks much easier) by following these steps:

1. Click the Project tab and, in the Properties group, click Custom Fields.

2. In the Custom Fields dialog box, highlight the custom field that you created and click the Graphical Indicators button (refer to Figure 16.18).

   Project displays the Graphical Indicators dialog box (see Figure 16.25).

3. Choose the type of row to which you want to assign an indicator: Nonsummary, Summary, or Project summary.

4. In the Test For section, set up the test that Project should use. In each column, you can choose from lists. In the Value(s) column, you can compare the formula result to the value of another field or to a numeric value.

   In my example, if the result of the formula is greater than 0, I want to see a red flag, because the actual cost of the task exceeds the baseline cost. If, however, the actual cost is less than or equal to the baseline cost, things are fine, so I want to see a happy face (you can find other indicator choices in the Image list).

FIGURE 16.25

Set up the test that Project should perform on the formula's result and the indicator to display, based on the test results.

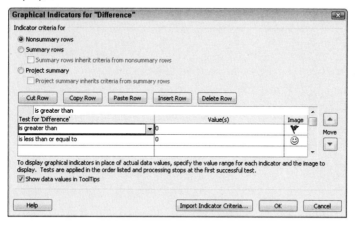

Tip

If you've set up graphical indicators in another project, you can import the criteria from either the Global template (assuming that you saved the formula in the Global template) or from another open project. When you click the Import Indicator Criteria button, Project displays a list of available templates or open Project files. Select the appropriate location, field type, and field name. Then click OK. ∎

5. To see the mathematical results of the formula in a ToolTip when you point the mouse at the indicator, select the Show Data Values in ToolTips check box.

6. Click OK to redisplay the Custom Fields dialog box.

7. Click OK again to redisplay your project.

If necessary, display the column for the custom field as described in the section, "Using a custom field for data entry." When Project displays the column, it will contain an indicator (see Figure 16.26). If you selected the Show Data Values in ToolTips check box, you can point the mouse at an indicator to see the results of the formula. (The ToolTip hides the icon on-screen; otherwise I'd show you the ToolTip.)

FIGURE 16.26

The custom field column contains an indicator.

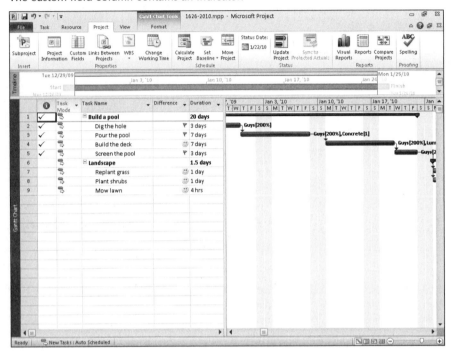

Summary

In this chapter, you found out how to do the following:

- Customize the status bar
- Set Project's options for saving files
- Use Project's Organizer to share tables, views, and other elements between projects.
- Control the way Project displays icons on the Windows taskbar for open projects
- Customize the features (Ribbon and QAT) that you use to get things done
- Work with custom fields to create data entry value lists and formulas

In the next chapter, you can read about creating macros and VBA scripts, which can streamline the repetitive tasks you perform to create and track a schedule.

Using Macros to Speed Your Work

Macros are small programs that carry out repetitive tasks you perform frequently. You may have used macros in a word-processing program. Macros work the same way in Project as they do in your word processor.

Don't let the word *program* in the preceding paragraph deter you from getting to know macros. Although you can work with the macro programming code, Project provides an easier way for you to write a macro, which I present in this chapter.

In addition to recording a macro, you can produce even more powerful automation by writing your own Visual Basic for Applications, or VBA, code. This chapter shows you how to write VBA code to filter all tasks on the project's critical path that should have finished by the current date, but have not. This example of VBA code is not intended to be a comprehensive VBA reference guide for Project. Instead, its purpose is to introduce you to many concepts of automating Project and to help you get your feet wet in the world of writing custom code.

Using Macros

Macros are most useful when you need to perform any repetitive task. In particular, you can use Project macros to do the following:

- Display frequently used tables
- Display frequently used views
- Switch to a custom view
- Generate standard reports

As you become comfortable using Project, you'll identify steps you take over and over again; these tasks are excellent candidates for macros.

Recording Macros

Project stores macros in the Visual Basic for Applications (VBA) programming language. And if you're adept at programming, you can write your macro directly in the VBA programming language. Figure 17.1 shows a sample, in Visual Basic, of the instructions stored in a macro.

Most people prefer to record a macro. When you record a macro, you have Project memorize the steps you want to take and then store those steps. That is, you do whatever it is you want Project to do. Project then converts those actions into Visual Basic statements and stores the statements in a macro. Later, when you want to take that action again, you run your macro, which I discuss in the next section.

Before you record a macro, you should run through the steps you want to take. You may even want to write down the steps. That way you are less likely to make (and record) mistakes.

FIGURE 17.1

A sample set of instructions stored in a macro.

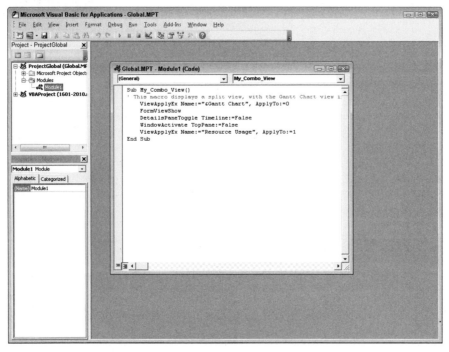

Suppose that you find yourself often displaying a split view with the Gantt Chart on top and the Resource Usage view below. Because you do this often, it would make a useful macro. First, walk through the process to create the view so that you know what steps you take:

1. Click the Gantt Chart view shortcut.

Tip

By selecting the view first, you force Project to start your macro from the Gantt Chart view, regardless of the view you were using before you ran your macro. ■

2. Click the View tab and, in the Split View group, select the Details check box to open the bottom pane that shows, by default, the Task Form view.

3. Click the left edge of the bottom pane to select the Task Form view.

4. On the View tab, in the Split View group, click the Details list box arrow.

5. From the menu of views that appears, click More Views to open the More Views dialog box.

6. Select the Resource Usage view.

7. Click Apply.

Now that you know what you intend to record, use the following steps to record the macro:

1. To help you see what's happening while it happens, right-click the status bar and make sure a check appears beside Macro Recording. If you don't see a check, click Macro Recording to display the Macro Recording button on the status bar. In Figure 17.2, I displayed the Macro Recording button — it appears to the right of the Ready button — and I opened the Customize Status Bar menu to show you that a check appears beside Macro Recording.

2. Click the Macro Recording button on the status bar to open the Record Macro dialog box (see Figure 17.3).

3. Enter a name for the macro in the Macro Name box.

Tip

The first character of the macro name must be a letter, but the other characters can be letters, numbers, or underscore characters. You can't include a space in a macro name or use any words reserved by Project. You can use an underscore character as a word separator in your macro's name, or create a one-word name but capitalize the first letter of each important word. ■

Note

You can optionally assign the macro to a keyboard shortcut, but that's only one way to ultimately run a macro. In the section "Using Shortcuts to Run Macros," later in this chapter, you can read about other methods to play back a macro, as well as how to assign a keyboard shortcut after you've recorded and stored your macro. ■

Customize the status bar to display the Macro Recording button.

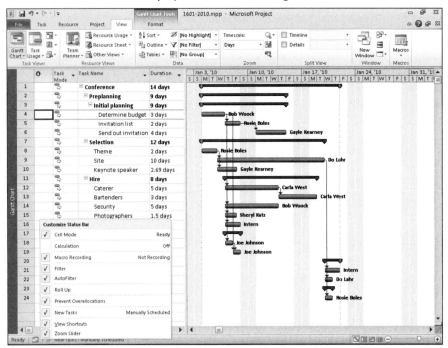

The Record Macro dialog box.

4. In the Record Macro dialog box, open the Store Macro In list box and click the location where you want to store the macro. You can store the macro in the Global File or in the current project. To make a macro available to all projects, select Global File.

Note

The Global File is also called the Global template file and it acts the same as the Normal template in Word or the Book1 template in Excel. Any customized features (such as macros, toolbars, or menus) that you store in the Global File are available to any project file. On the other hand, customized features that you store in an individual project file are available only to that file and you must use the Organizer, described in Chapter 16, to copy an element from one individual file to another. ∎

5. Type a description of the macro or the function that it performs in the Description box. This description appears whenever you run the macro from the Macros dialog box.

6. If you select cells while running a macro, use the options in the Row references and Column references sections to control the way that the macro selects rows and columns. For rows, the macro always selects rows — regardless of the position of the active cell — because it records relative references to rows. If you want a macro to select the same row every time, regardless of which cell is selected first, select Absolute (ID).

Note

For columns, the macro always selects the same column each time that you run the macro — regardless of which cell is selected first — because the macro records absolute references to columns. If you want a macro to select columns, regardless of the position of the active cell when you run the macro, select Relative in the Column references section. ∎

7. Click OK, and Project redisplays your project. You don't notice any differences except that the appearance of the Macro Recording button on the status bar has changed. Project is now recording each action you take.

8. Take all the actions you want to record.

9. Click the Macro Recording button again to stop recording your macro.

Running Macros

To use a macro you have recorded, simply run the macro. Some people refer to this action as "playing back" the macro because they associate recording and playing back with the process of recording a TV program on a DVR or a VCR and then playing back the recording.

If your macro makes substantial changes to your project, you should save the project before you run the macro. With unlimited Undo capabilities, you could undo its effects, but I doubt you'd find that fun. Just closing the project and reopening it would be much easier. To run a macro, follow these steps:

1. Open the project that contains the macro. If you stored the macro in the Global template file, you can open any project.

2. Click the View tab and, in the Macros group, click the Macros button to open the Macros dialog box (see Figure 17.4).

FIGURE 17.4

The Macros dialog box.

3. Select the macro you want to run from the Macro name list.

4. Click Run. Project performs the steps you recorded in the macro.

Tip

If your macro is long and you want to stop it while it's still running, press Ctrl+Break. If your macro is short, it will probably finish before you can stop it. ∎

Using Shortcuts to Run Macros

Although you can run macros by selecting them from the Macros dialog box, if you use a macro on a regular basis you may want to shorten the method for running the macro. You can create one of the following to do so:

- A Ribbon button that runs the macro
- A Quick Access Toolbar button that runs the macro
- A keyboard shortcut that runs the macro

Adding a macro to the Ribbon

You can add a button to run your macro to a custom group on any tab of the Ribbon. You can't add buttons to existing groups, although you can add buttons for macros to custom tabs you create. This section shows you how to add a button for a macro to the View tab.

Caution

If you add a button for your macro to the Ribbon tab and you reset that tab, the button you added will disappear. ■

Cross-Reference

See Chapter 16 for more information about customizing the Ribbon. ■

Follow these steps to add a command that runs your macro to a menu:

1. Right-click anywhere on the Ribbon and, from the menu that appears, click Customize the Ribbon. The Project Options dialog box appears, displaying the Customize Ribbon tab.

2. In the right column, click the plus beside the tab to which you want to add a group.

3. Click the group you want to appear on the Ribbon to the left of the new group.

Tip

If you want your group to appear first on the tab, click the first group on the tab and, after you add your group, click the Up arrow on the right side of the right column to move your group up one position. ■

4. Click the New Group button below the right column. Project adds a new group to the tab below the group you selected in Step 3 and selects the new group (see Figure 17.5).

5. To assign a name to the new group, click the Rename button below the right column to display the Rename dialog box.

6. Type a name for your group and click OK. Project assigns the name to your group and redisplays the Project Options dialog box.

7. To add a button for your macro to the group, make sure that the group you created is selected in the right column.

8. Open the list box above the left column and choose Macros (see Figure 17.6). Project changes the contents of the left column to display all available macros.

9. Click the macro you want to add to the Ribbon.

10. Click the Add button between the columns, and Project displays the command below the group you created.

11. Click OK to close the Project Options dialog box.

FIGURE 17.5

The Project Options dialog box after adding a new group to a tab.

FIGURE 17.6

Display all available macros.

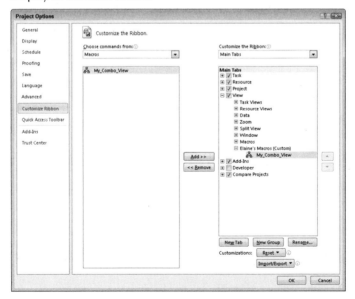

A new group appears on the selected Ribbon tab, and a button for your macro appears in it (see Figure 17.7).

In this example, I added my macro to a custom group on the View tab called Elaine's Macros.

Assigning a macro to a Quick Access Toolbar button

Suppose that you're a fan of Quick Access Toolbar (QAT) buttons and you create a macro that you use a lot. You find yourself wanting a QAT button you can click to make your macro run. Well, you can get your wish by adding a button to the QAT for your macro.

Caution

If you add a button to the QAT and you reset the QAT, the button you added disappears from the QAT. ∎

1. Click the customize Quick Access Toolbar arrow at the right edge of the QAT.
2. From the menu that appears, click More Commands. The Project Options dialog box appears, displaying the Quick Access Toolbar tab.
3. Open the list box above the left column and choose Macros (see Figure 17.8). Project changes the contents of the left column to display all available macros.
4. Click the macro you want to add to the QAT.
5. Click the Add button. Project displays the button in the list on the right, which contains commands already on the QAT.
6. To reorder the buttons on the QAT, click a command in the right-hand column.
7. Click the Move Up or the Move Down buttons, which appear to the right of the list on the right.
8. To change the name of the button, click the button in the right column and then click the Modify button below the right column to open the Modify button dialog box (see Figure 17.9).
9. Type the name, exactly as you want it to appear on the toolbar button, into the Name box; you can include spaces.
10. To change the button image for your macro that appears on the QAT, click a different image in the Modify Button dialog box.

FIGURE 17.8

Adding a button for a macro to the QAT.

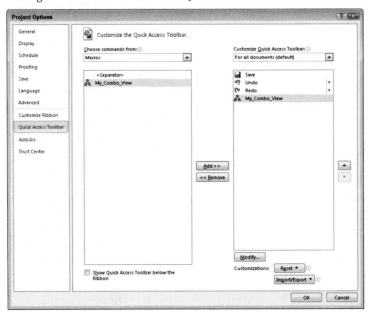

FIGURE 17.9

Use this dialog box to change a macro button's name.

Tip

If you prefer to use an image instead of text, click Default Style on the Modify Selection pop-up menu and then click Change Button Image to select a button image. ∎

11. Click OK. Project updates the macro button name and image, if you selected a different image (see Figure 17.10).

12. Click OK to save your changes and close the Project Options dialog box.

A new button for your macro appears on the QAT (see Figure 17.11). When you point the mouse at the button, the ScreenTip displays the name you assigned to the macro button.

FIGURE 17.10

I renamed the button Gantt/Resource Usage and picked a different button image.

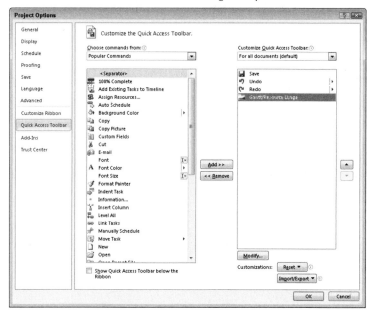

FIGURE 17.11

The new button after dropping it on the toolbar.

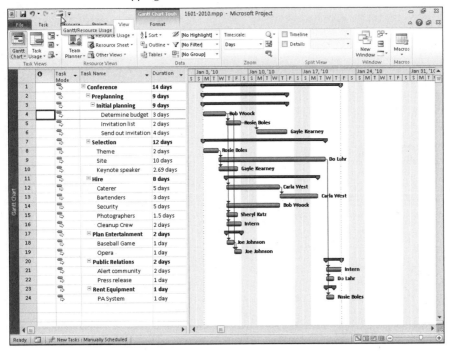

Assigning a keyboard shortcut to a macro

Suppose that after you experiment, you decide that you really want to run your macro from a keyboard shortcut. Furthermore, suppose that you didn't set a shortcut when you created the macro. Follow these steps to add a keyboard shortcut to the macro after you create it:

1. Open the project that contains the macro. If you stored the macro in the Global template file, you can open any project.

2. Click the View tab and, in the Macros group, click the top of the Macros button to open the Macros dialog box (see Figure 17.12).

Tip
You can also press Alt+F8 to display the Macros dialog box. ∎

3. Highlight the macro to which you want to add a keyboard shortcut.

4. Click Options to open the Macro Options dialog box that appears in Figure 17.13.

FIGURE 17.12

The Macros dialog box.

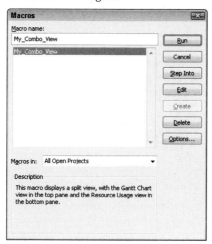

FIGURE 17.13

Set a keyboard shortcut for a macro from the Macro Options dialog box.

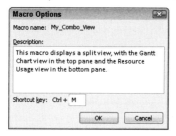

5. Place the insertion point in the Shortcut key box and type a letter.

6. Click OK. If the combination that you selected (Ctrl plus the letter that you typed) is not in use by Project, Project displays the Macros dialog box again. If Project is using the combination that you selected for another macro, Project asks you to try a different combination.

7. Close the Macros dialog box.

To run your macro, press the keyboard combination you assigned. If you decide that you don't want to run your macro by using this keyboard combination, you can change the combination by using the preceding steps, or you can remove the keyboard combination you assigned by reopening the Macro Options dialog box and deleting the letter from the Shortcut key box.

Creating VBA Code

As a project manager, you must be able to easily identify the tasks in your project that are falling behind schedule. In particular, if a late task is on the project's critical path, the late task is having a direct impact on your ability to complete the project on schedule.

You can use VBA to easily identify the tasks on your project's critical path that should have finished by the current date, but have not. After you have identified these tasks, you can filter the list of tasks for a particular resource — you can identify late critical-path tasks by person.

Recording a macro to create a filter for critical tasks

Recording a macro that captures the basic steps of the process is an excellent technique for producing the foundation for the VBA code you will ultimately need. After you've recorded the basic VBA code in a macro, you can customize the code to accomplish your exact requirements. In Figure 17.14, you see a project with all its tasks visible.

FIGURE 17.14

A project with all its tasks visible.

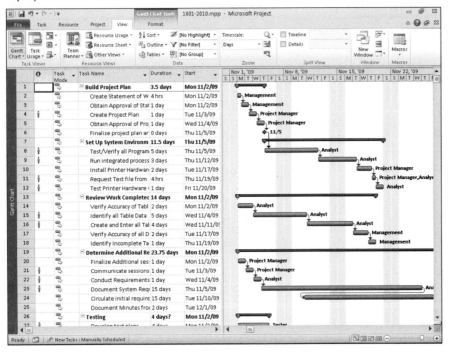

Use the following steps to create a filter that shows only the tasks in the project that should have finished by the current date and are on the critical path:

1. Start Project and open the `Example 1.mpp` file.

On the Web site
You can find `Example 1.mpp` **on the Project Bible Web site. ■**

2. If the Macro Recording button is visible on the status bar click it; otherwise, click the View tab and, in the Macros group, click the bottom of the Macros button and choose Record Macro. The Record Macro dialog box appears.

3. In the Macro name box, enter **FilterCriticalTasksByDateAndResource** (as shown in Figure 17.15) and click OK. The macro recorder will now capture all your actions.

FIGURE 17.15

The Record Macro dialog box.

4. On the View tab, in the Data group, open the Filter list and choose More Filters to open the More Filters window.

5. Click the New button to open the Filter Definition dialog box.

6. Complete the Filter Definition dialog box, shown in Figure 17.16, and click Save. Project redisplays the More Filters window.

Note
The text in the Value field `Today` **is automatically translated to the current date when you run the macro. ■**

7. Click the Apply button in the More Filters window.

8. If the Macro Recording button is visible on the status bar click it to stop recording the macro. Otherwise, on the View tab in the Macros group, click the bottom of the Macros button and choose Stop Recording. At this point, your recorded keystrokes have filtered the project to show only critical tasks that have not yet been completed.

FIGURE 17.16

In this figure, you're using the Filter Definition dialog box to set up the macro to filter for critical tasks for the Developer resource.

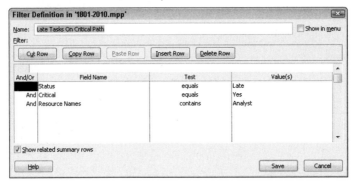

Compare Figure 17.17 with Figure 17.14. Notice that only late tasks on the critical path are now visible.

FIGURE 17.17

The project has been filtered to show only the critical tasks that are late.

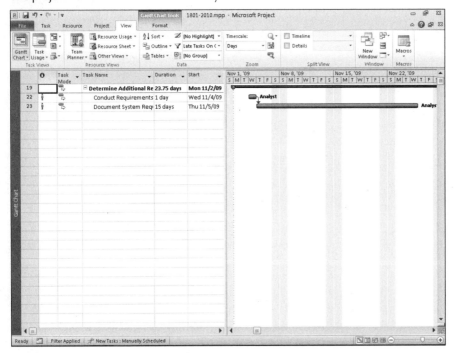

Editing the macro to show only specified resources

The macro you just recorded works fine for the Developer resource, but you would really like to be able to run this same code for any resource in your project. To add this flexibility to the code, you must add a few additional lines to the macro to prompt the user to enter the name of a resource to include in the filter. Use the following steps:

1. Click the View tab and, in the Macros group, click the top of the Macros to open the Macros dialog box.

2. Select the `FilterCriticalTasksByDateAndResource` macro and click the Edit button to open the Visual Basic Editor. See the sidebar "Key Components of the Visual Basic Editor" for a description of the window and its elements.

Note

The terminology may seem a bit confusing: You use the Visual Basic UserForm window to create dialog boxes or windows that will be a part of your user interface. The windows or dialog boxes you create in the UserForm window are known as UserForm objects and are usually called simply UserForms. In this chapter, whenever you see UserForm by itself, the term refers to a UserForm object. All references to the window will appear as UserForm window. ■

3. Close the Project Explorer window and the Properties window (if open) by clicking the X in the upper-right corner of each window. The Code window now occupies the full screen, as shown in Figure 17.18.

Note

The Code window contains the VBA code that was generated when you recorded your macro. The macro code is known as a sub-procedure. A sub-procedure is a set of instructions in your program that is executed as a unit. The code between the lines `Sub FilterByCurrentDateAndCritical()` **and** `End Sub` **are the instructions that create a filter programmatically. The lines with the green text (it really is green, even though you can't tell because the book is black and white) that begin with an apostrophe are comments used to document the code.** ■

4. In the Code window, modify the sub-procedure by adding the following lines and changes that appear in boldface:

```
Sub FilterCriticalTasksByDateAndResource()

Dim strResourceName As String
' Macro FilterCriticalTasksByDateAndResource
' Macro Recorded Sun 5/4/03 by Administrator.
    strResourceName = InputBox("Please enter the resource name:")
    FilterEdit Name:="Late Tasks On Critical Path",
    TaskFilter:=True, Create:=True, OverwriteExisting:=True,
    FieldName:="Finish", Test:="is less than", Value:="Today",
    ShowInMenu:=False, ShowSummaryTasks:=True
```

```
  FilterEdit Name:="Late Tasks On Critical Path",
  TaskFilter:=True, FieldName:="", NewFieldName:="Critical",
  Test:="equals", Value:="Yes", Operation:="And",
  ShowSummaryTasks:=True
  FilterEdit Name:="Late Tasks On Critical Path",
  TaskFilter:=True, FieldName:="", NewFieldName:="Resource
  Names", Test:="contains", Value:= strResourceName,
  Operation:="And", ShowSummaryTasks:=True
End Sub
```

On the Web site

This module is available on the Project Bible's Web site at www.wiley.com; search for the Project Bible. To add the module instead of creating it manually, download it from the Web site. Then, display the VBA Code window and choose File ⇨ Import File. Browse your hard drive for the file module1.bas. ∎

FIGURE 17.18

The Code window displays the VBA code generated by recording a macro.

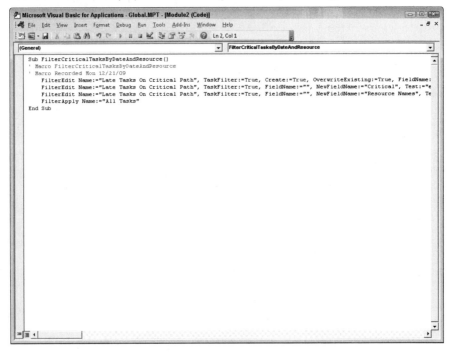

Key Components of the Visual Basic Editor

The Visual Basic Editor is the common programming environment used in all Microsoft Office applications, including Project 2010. Some of the key components of the Visual Basic Editor, shown in this figure, are as follows:

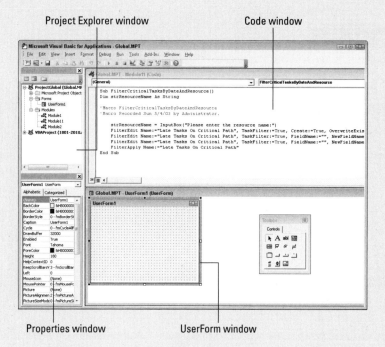

Project Explorer window   Code window

Properties window   UserForm window

- **Project Explorer window:** The Project Explorer window displays a hierarchical list of the projects and all the items contained in and referenced by each of the projects.

- **Properties window:** The Properties window lists design-time properties for selected objects and their current settings. An *object* is a piece of the application that can be manipulated; in Project, entities such as a task, a resource, or an assignment are objects. In fact, the entire application — Project itself — is considered an object. A *property* is a value that you can set to determine the object's appearance or behavior. For example, the Start date and Name are properties of a task object.

- **Toolbox:** The Toolbox displays the standard Visual Basic controls, such as list boxes, text boxes, and labels that can be added to a dialog box.

- **Code window:** Use the Code window to write, display, and edit Visual Basic code. The Code window occupies the same screen area as a UserForm.

- **UserForm window:** In the UserForm window, you create the windows or dialog boxes (called UserForm objects) in your project.

Testing the code

Now you can run the modified code to test the changes you made. Use the following steps to do so:

1. Click the Run Macro button in the toolbar at the top of the Visual Basic window shown in Figure 17.19. The Macros dialog box appears.

Click the Run Macro button to run the VBA sub-procedure.

Run Macro button

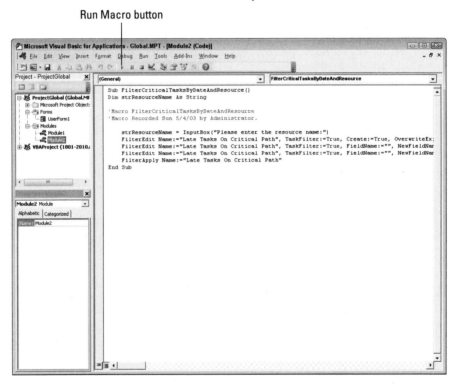

2. Select the FilterCriticalTasksByDateAndResource macro and click Run.
3. The screen switches to the Project window and the Microsoft Project dialog box opens (see Figure 17.20). At the prompt to enter the resource name, enter **Project Manager** and click OK.

FIGURE 17.20

Type a resource whose tasks you want to view.

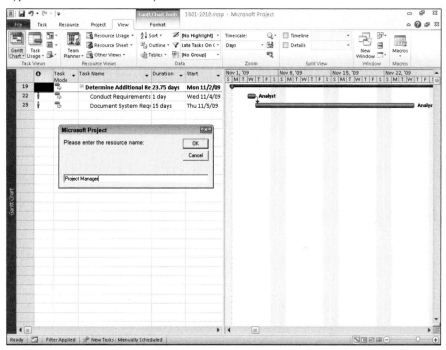

The Visual Basic for Applications window reappears; use the Windows taskbar to switch back to Project. You'll find that Project applies the filter so that you can view only the tasks in the project that are late, on the critical path, and assigned to the resource called Project Manager (see Figure 17.21).

Let's review the changes you made to the code so that you can understand the purpose of each change. The line that begins with Dim declares a variable that VBA uses to store the resource name that the user types into the dialog box. The variable that you created is known as a *string variable*, which is designed to store text.

The line strResourceName = InputBox("Please enter the resource name:") displays a dialog box known as an InputBox. The InputBox prompts the user to type in the resource name, and VBA stores the name that the user enters in the variable strResourceName.

On the last line that begins with FilterEdit, you substituted the text Analyst with the variable strResourceName. VBA uses the name that the user entered in the InputBox as the filter value for the Resource Names field.

After adding the filter, you can view tasks that are on the critical path for the specified resource.

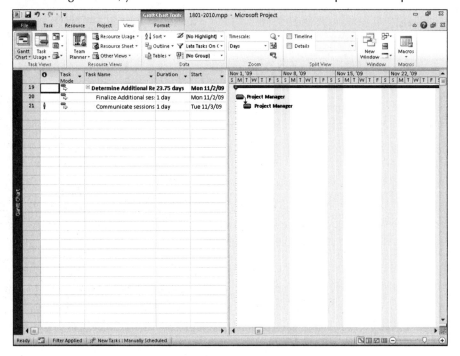

Tip

You can run your macro by assigning it to a QAT button or adding it to the Ribbon as described earlier in this chapter. ■

Summary

In this chapter, you found out how to use macros in Project. In particular, you now know how to do the following:

- Create macros
- Use macros
- Assign shortcuts to macros to make them easy to run
- Edit macro code in Visual Basic for Applications

Importing and Exporting Project Information

S ometimes you need to move information in and out of Project. In
many cases, you can simply copy and paste information. But, you will
find times where you need to make these moves by using Project's
import and export functions. You can import and export information using
various file formats. For example, you might find it convenient to start a
project in an Excel workbook, a SharePoint Project Tracking List, or
Outlook's Task List and later import that project into Project.

Using Copy and Paste

Importing is the process of bringing information into a Project file from
another program. *Exporting* is the process of sending information from
Project to another program. Copying and pasting information is a simple
way to import and export information.

The Copy and Paste functions in all Office 2010 programs have been vastly
improved to make it exceedingly easy for you to share information across
Office programs.

Copying Project data into other Office programs

Copying data from Project into another Office program is easy. Say, for
example, that you want to copy a list of tasks from Project to another Office
program or from another Office program to Project, copying and pasting
works exceedingly well. Figure 18.1 shows a project in the Gantt Chart view
in Project, and Figure 18.2 shows the project's task list — the information
from the Entry table in Figure 18.1 — in a Word table.

FIGURE 18.1

The Entry table of a project's Gantt Chart view in Project.

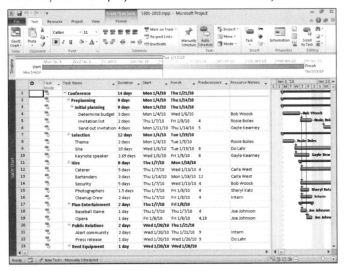

FIGURE 18.2

The Entry table information in a Word Table.

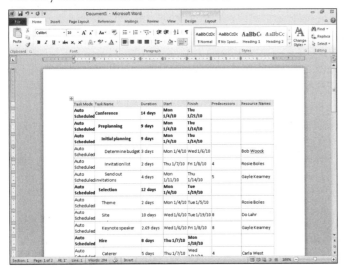

Here's how I got the information from Project to a Word table:

1. In Project, click the Select All button above Row 1 and to the left of the Indicators column at the upper-left corner of the table. Project selects all data in the table.

Tip
If you don't want to copy all the information, select the information you want to copy. ∎

2. Click the Task tab and, in the Clipboard group, click the Copy button.

3. Switch to Microsoft Word and position the insertion point at the location in the document where you want the Project table information to appear.

4. Click the Home tab and, in the Clipboard group, click the Paste button. The table information from Project appears in your Word document.

That's all there is to it. You can perform the same steps to paste the information into an Excel workbook, an Access database table, a PowerPoint slide, a Visio diagram, or in the Notes section of an Outlook task, appointment, contact, or e-mail message, as you can see from Figures 18.3, 18.4, and 18.5.

FIGURE 18.3

Project information pasted into an Excel workbook.

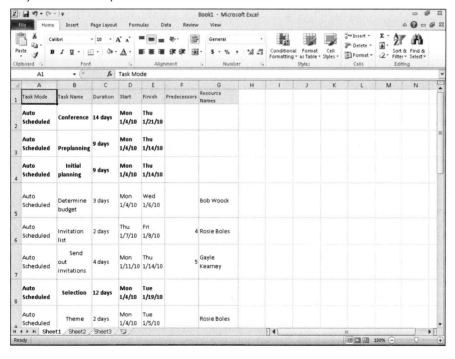

FIGURE 18.4

Project information pasted into an Access database.

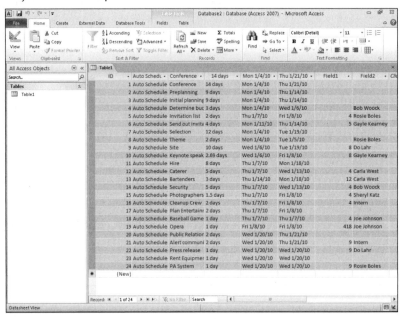

FIGURE 18.5

Project information pasted into an Outlook e-mail message.

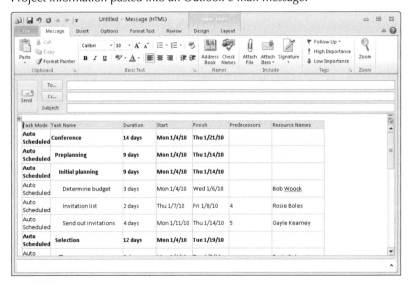

Although you can copy some of the graphic information in Project, such as a Resource Graph, to Office programs that are graphically oriented in nature, such as PowerPoint and Visio, the results aren't as good as those you get when you copy tables. Figure 18.6 shows a Resource Graph for one of the resources in a project; Figure 18.7 shows that graph sitting on a PowerPoint slide. Note that the distinction of each day's bars is pretty much lost in PowerPoint. If the slide were longer, we'd see a better graph.

Copying data from other Office programs into Project

So far, you've seen how to take information from Project to another program. But you can reverse the action and take information from another program and paste it into Project. Suppose you started jotting down task names in an Excel workbook and then realized you really needed them in a Project file. In this example, you would follow these steps:

1. Click the Select All button in the Excel workbook to select all of the information on the worksheet; the Select All button is located above Row 1 and to the left of Column A.

2. On Excel's Home tab, click Copy.

3. Switch to Project and select a table.

4. Click in the Task Name column and, on the Task tab in the Clipboard group, click the Paste button.

FIGURE 18.6

A Resource Graph in Project.

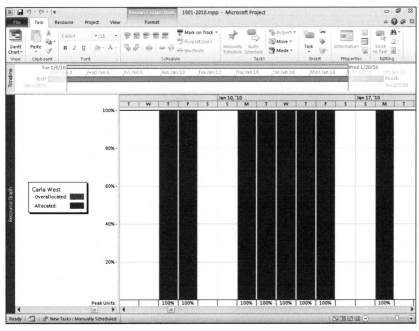

FIGURE 18.7

The same Resource Graph on a PowerPoint slide.

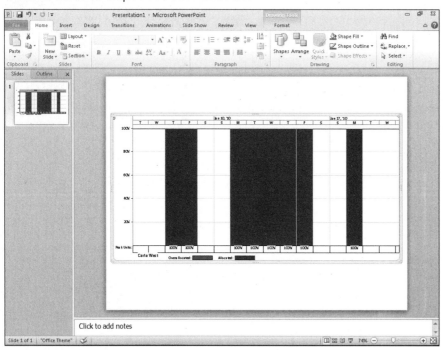

Be aware that your Excel workbook might have a blank cell in A1 if you included column headings in Row 1. When you paste the information, you'll get an error from Project. Continue the Paste operation anyway; in Project, you'll get a blank row that you can simply delete.

Note

If you supplied more information in the Excel file than just the Task Name, pick a table in Project that appropriately supports your Excel file information. If no table supports your existing information, consider importing the information as described later in this chapter. ∎

Exporting Information

If you need more control over the process of getting data out of Project and into another program, you can use Project's import and export features. A wizard walks you through the process, during which you use an import/export map. Think of an *import/export map* as a template that Project uses to correctly translate information from one program to another. An import/export map defines the information that you want to import or export and enables you to describe how to match the information in the Project file with the information in the other program's file. Whenever you import or export, you can use one of the predefined maps that comes with Project; you can edit a predefined map if necessary, or you can create a custom map.

You can export information to Microsoft Office products, such as Excel workbooks, Access databases, or Word documents. And you can export information to XML, text (.txt), or comma-separated value (.csv) files. You also can export project reporting data to an OLAP cube or an Access database, and in this section we'll start with this process.

Note

OLAP stands for Online Analytical Processing and it's a way to handle data to answer multi-dimensional queries. ■

Saving reporting information in an OLAP Cube or an Access database

Project automatically creates OLAP cubes and an Access database when it produces visual reports, but you don't have direct access to the data when you create a visual report. In addition, when you close your project, Project automatically deletes these OLAP cubes and Access databases. If you want access to the cube or the database Project creates so that you can prepare reports outside the context of visual reports, you can save the OLAP cube and the Access database.

To save an OLAP cube, start by clicking the Project tab. Then, in the Reports group, click Visual Reports. In the Visual Reports – Create Report dialog box that appears, click the Save Data button to see the Save Reporting Data window (shown in Figure 18.8).

FIGURE 18.8

You can create a reporting OLAP cube when you create any visual report in Project.

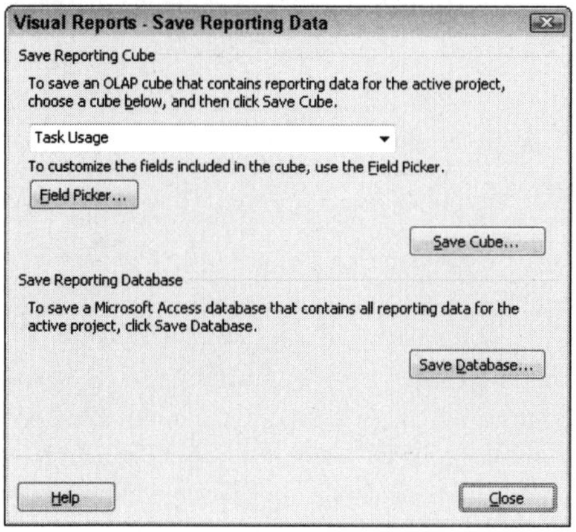

You can create and save any of the following cubes:

- Task Usage
- Resource Usage
- Assignment Usage
- Task Summary
- Resource Summary
- Assignment Summary

You also can customize the fields that will appear in the cube you select; click the Field Picker button in the Save Reporting Data window to display the Field Picker dialog box shown in Figure 18.9.

FIGURE 18.9

Use this dialog box to identify the fields you want to include in the selected OLAP cube.

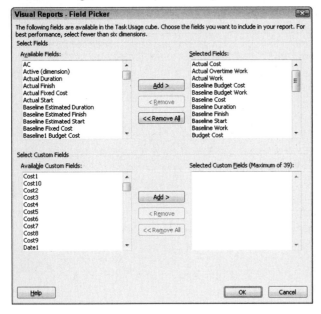

The fields that appear in the Field Picker dialog box depend on the type of cube you selected; only task-related fields appear in the Task Usage and Task Summary cubes when you choose to create either of these cubes; you won't see any resource fields. To add a field, select it in the left column and click the Add button. To remove a field, select it in the right column and click the Remove button. To add and remove custom fields, use the same techniques in the bottom of the dialog box. Click OK when you finish to redisplay the Save Report Data window.

To save the cube, click the Save Cube button; Project displays the Save As dialog box (see Figure 18.10), supplies a default filename, and automatically sets the file type to `.cub`. If you want, change the filename; then click Save to save the cube file.

Saving cube data.

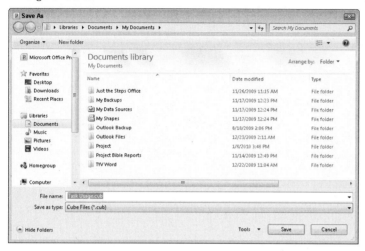

To save your Project file data in an Access database, click the Save Database button in the Save Reporting Data window shown previously in Figure 18.8. Project again displays the Save As dialog box, this time setting the file type to an Access database file (`.mdb`). You can change the default name suggested for the file; click Save to save the database.

Exporting Project data

You can export information to Excel workbooks. Or, if you have a program that can read either a text (`.txt`) file or a comma-separated value (`.csv`) file, you can export information from Project to that program, saving your Project data as either a comma-delimited or tab-delimited file.

Note

Although the steps for exporting each file type vary slightly, the process is generally the same. ■

If you intend to use your Project data in an older Office file format (such a `.xls` for Excel 2003) or you want to create a comma-delimited or tab-delimited file in either `.txt` or `.csv` format, you need to enable use of legacy formats in Project. Follow these steps:

1. Click the File tab and, from the Backstage view that appears, click Options to display the Project Options dialog box.

2. Click the Trust Center tab (see Figure 18.11).

The Trust Center tab of the Project Options dialog box.

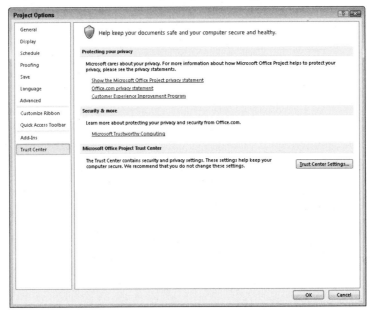

3. Click the Trust Center Settings button to open the Trust Center dialog box (see Figure 18.12).

4. Click the Legacy Formats tab.

5. Click either the Prompt When Loading Files With Legacy Or Non-default File Format option or the Allow Loading Files With Legacy Or Non-default File Formats option.

6. Click OK twice to save your settings.

To see how the predefined export maps work, let's walk through exporting a Project file to Excel. Each of the predefined export maps produces an Excel file that contains different elements of your Project file. If none of the predefined maps suits your purpose, you can export using a map you define yourself, and we'll look briefly at the process of creating a map after we walk through the exporting process using a predefined map.

FIGURE 18.12

Use the Legacy Formats tab of the Trust Center dialog box to control how Project treats older Office file formats and non-default file formats.

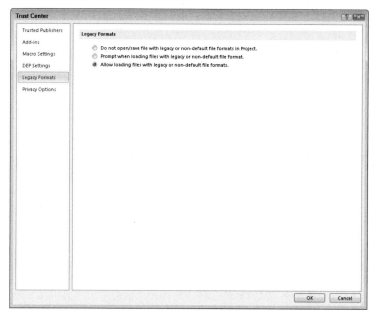

The Import/Export Wizard guides you through the export process; follow these steps:

1. Open the Project file that contains the information that you want to export.

2. Click the File tab and, in the Backstage view that appears, click Save As to open the Save As dialog box.

3. Enter a name in the File Name list box for the file that you want to export.

4. Open the Save As Type list box and select one of the Excel Workbook formats; for this example, I chose Excel Workbook (*.xlsx).

5. Click Save. Project starts the Export Wizard. Click Next.

6. Choose Selected Data and click Next.

Note

You can choose Project Excel Template to export the all data in the Project file to Excel. ∎

7. Choose Use Existing Map to display the Map Selection dialog box (see Figure 18.13).

8. Select a map and click Next. The Export Wizard displays the Map Options dialog box.

9. Select the type of data to export (see Figure 18.14). The boxes you select determine which wizard screens subsequently appear when you click Next as well as the type of data Project exports.

FIGURE 18.13

Use this dialog box to select the map you want to use to export your data.

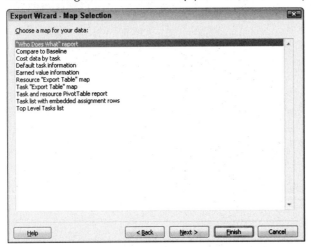

FIGURE 18.14

Select the type of data to export in the Map Options dialog box.

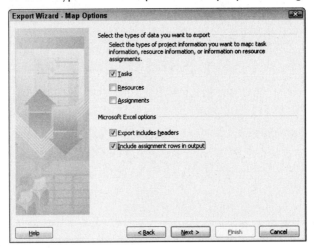

Note

The map you selected in Step 8 contains a predefined collection of data. The boxes you check in Step 9 identify the type of data to export within the predefined collection. ■

Tip

If you want your Excel workbook to contain assignments that are listed under tasks or resources, similar to the Task Usage or Resource Usage views, select the Include Assignment Rows in Output check box. ∎

10. When you click Next, you see one of the mapping dialog boxes. In this example, I selected Tasks in the Map Options dialog box. The Task Mapping dialog box appears (see Figure 18.15) and includes the following options:

FIGURE 18.15

As you add fields in the Task Mapping dialog box, a preview of the Excel worksheet you're creating appears at the bottom of the Task Mapping dialog box.

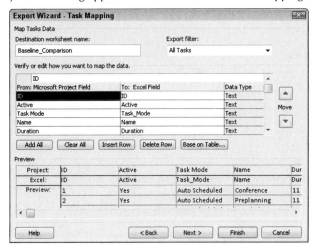

- **Destination Worksheet Name:** This box contains the name that Excel will assign to the sheet in the workbook. You can change this name.

- **Export Filter:** Use this list box to select the tasks that you want to export. By default, Project assumes that you want to export all tasks, but you can export, for example, only completed tasks, critical tasks, overbudget tasks, or tasks with a cost greater than an amount you specify. The list is quite long; experiment with it to see what you get.

- **From: Microsoft Project Field:** Under this column, click any blank cell to add fields to export one at a time. After you click, a list-box arrow appears; you can use it to view a list of fields available for exporting, and to select a field.

- **To: Excel Field:** Select a field to export and click the column next to the field you added. Project suggests a column heading for the field in the Excel worksheet; you can change this heading.

- **Data Type:** You can't change the data type for the field in the destination program, which appears in this column.

- **Add All:** To quickly add all the fields in the Project file, click the Add All button.

- **Clear All:** To remove all the fields you added, click the Clear All button.

- **Insert Row:** If you decide to add a field between two existing fields, click the row you want to appear below the new field. Then click the Insert Row button, and Project inserts a blank row above the selected row.

- **Delete Row:** To delete a field, click anywhere in the row that contains the field and click the Delete Row button.

- **Base on Table:** To add all the fields in a particular Project table, such as the Entry table or the Cost table, click the Base on Table button. Project displays the Select Base Table for Field Mapping dialog box, from which you can select a table. When you click OK, Project adds all fields contained in that table to the list of fields you want to export.

- **Move:** You can use the Move buttons on the right side of the dialog box to reorder fields. Click the field you want to move and then click either the Move Up arrow or the Move Down arrow.

Note

If you selected the Resources and the Assignments check boxes as well as the Tasks check box in the Map Options dialog box (shown previously in Figure 19.14), when you click Next, the Export Wizard displays additional boxes that are almost identical to the Task Mapping dialog box, but for each of these data types. ∎

11. After you finish defining your map, you see the final box of the Export Wizard (see Figure 18.16). If you elect to save your map by clicking the Save Map button, Project displays the Save Map dialog box, as shown in Figure 18.17. Provide a name for the new map in the Map Name text box and click Save.

FIGURE 18.16

In the final dialog box of the Export Wizard, choose whether to save the map you've defined.

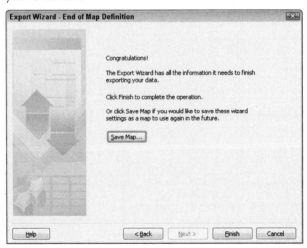

FIGURE 18.17

If you decide to save the map, provide a name for it in the Save Map dialog box, which displays a list of all existing maps.

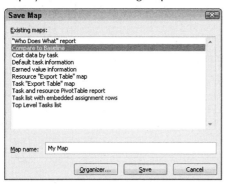

To see what Project exported, simply open the Excel file. In Figure 18.18, you see the result of exporting to Excel using the Compare to Baseline map. In this case, the workbook contains only one sheet, but, in many cases, a predefined map creates multiple worksheets in a single workbook.

FIGURE 18.18

An Excel workbook created using the Compare to Baseline map.

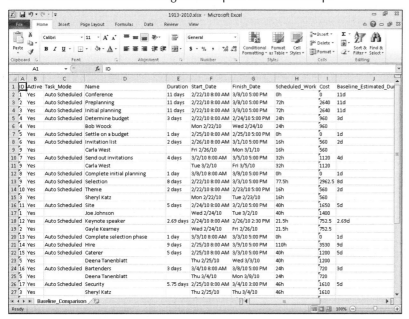

Now's let's examine the differences between exporting using a predefined map and exporting using a new map that you create. In this case, let's also assume that you want to create a comma-separated file.

This process uses the Export Wizard and closely resembles exporting information to Excel or Access. Complete the preceding steps with the following exceptions:

- In Step 4, select Text or CSV, whichever format works best in the program to which you're exporting, in the Save As Type box.
- In Step 7, choose to create a new map and click Next. Project displays the Map Options dialog box (see Figure 18.19). Select the options for the export map and click Next. You see at least one of the mapping dialog boxes. The one(s) you see depends on the information that you chose to export. Select the export filter you want to use and then add Project fields to export.

FIGURE 18.19

Select the options for the export map.

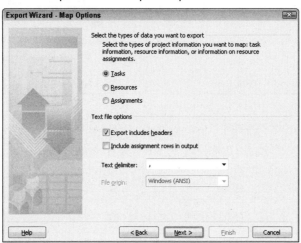

Importing Information

You can bring information into Project from another Project file or from Microsoft Excel, or Microsoft Access. You also can import information created in any program that can save text (.txt) files or comma-separated value (.csv) files. And, you can import XML files into Project. When you import any of these types of files, you use an import/export map to define the data that you want to import.

The process to import XML files is similar to importing other types of files. In the Open dialog box, select the XML file. Project launches the Import Wizard, where you choose one of three options: to append the data in the file to the active project, to merge the data in the file with the data in the active project, or to import the file as a new file.

Bringing Excel workbook or Access database information into Project

Want to start your project in Excel or Access? You can use the Import Wizard to bring your Excel or Access data into Project. The process for importing either file type is very similar. In the steps that follow, you walk through importing an Excel file.

Note

You can't import an Excel PivotTable into Project. ■

1. In Project, click the File tab and, from the Backstage view that appears, click Open to display the Open dialog box.

2. Open the list box beside the File Name box and select Excel Workbook.

3. Navigate to the folder that contains the Excel workbook you want to import, highlight the workbook, and click Open. Project starts the Import Wizard.

4. Click Next. In the Map dialog box, choose New Map.

Note

If you choose the Use existing map option, Project displays the list of maps from which you can choose. After you select a map, Project imports your data. ■

5. Click Next. In the Import Mode dialog box, select the As a New Project option button.

Note

If you select the Append the Data to the Active Project option button, Project imports the data and places it after any existing tasks in the Project file. If you select the Merge the Data into the Active Project option button, you'll complete Steps 6 and 7, but in the Task Mapping dialog box, you'll click the Set Merge Key button to identify the field that's found in both the Excel file and the Project file. ■

6. Click Next. In the Map Options dialog box, select the types of data you want to import (see Figure 18.20).

7. Click Next. In the Task Mapping dialog box, select a worksheet from the Source Worksheet Name list box, and Project attempts to resolve the column names in the worksheet with Project fields (see Figure 18.21). Verify that Project selected the correct fields. For fields that contain "(not mapped)" in the To: Microsoft Project field, enter the Project field name or select that name from the list that appears when you click in the To: Microsoft Project field.

FIGURE 18.20

Select the types of data you want to import.

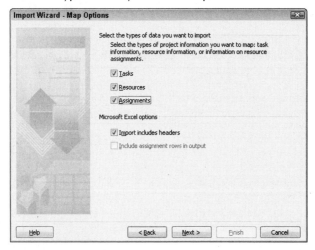

FIGURE 18.21

The Task Mapping dialog box shows the fields that Project expects to import from your workbook.

Cross-Reference

For a complete list of the purpose of each field in this dialog box, see the section "Exporting Project data," earlier in this chapter. ∎

8. Click Next. The final box of the Import Wizard appears, and here you can elect to save the map you just defined.

Note

If you selected the Resources and the Assignments check boxes as well as the Tasks check box in the Map Options dialog box (shown previously in Figure 18.20), then the Export Wizard displays additional dialog boxes for each of these data types when you click Next. The additional dialog boxes are almost identical to the Task Mapping dialog box. Perform Step 7 in each dialog box. ■

9. To save your map, click the Save Map button, and Project displays the Save Map dialog box. Provide a name for the new map in the Map Name text box.

10. Click Finish and Project imports the Excel file.

Bringing Outlook task lists into Project

Perhaps you started a task list in Outlook's Task List and now you realize that your list of tasks is really a project, and you need the scheduling and cost features in Project. You don't need to start over; you can import the Outlook Task List into Project by following these steps:

1. In a new project, click the Tasks tab and, in the Insert group, click the bottom of the Task tab.

Tip

You can import the tasks from Outlook into an open project that already contains tasks; in this case, Project appends the Outlook tasks to the task list. ■

2. From the menu that appears, choose Import Outlook Tasks. Project displays the Import Outlook Tasks dialog box (see Figure 18.22), which shows all the possible tasks you could import from Outlook.

3. Check the tasks you want to import and click OK. The tasks appear in Project.

FIGURE 18.22

In this dialog box, mark the tasks you want to import into Project.

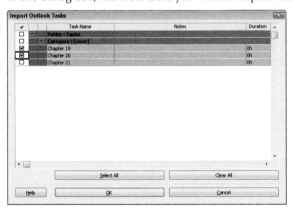

Note that the task names appear in Project; if you assigned any dates to the tasks, that information does not appear in Project.

Importing other files

If the information you want to import comes from a program that can produce either Microsoft Project Exchange files or text files, you can import that information. Microsoft Project Exchange (.mpx) files are of the ASCII, record-based file format.

You can use the MPX file format to import information from older versions of Project into Project 2010. Some other project management software packages also support the MPX file format; if you need to import information from another project management software package, you can save it as an MPX file and import it into Project. Importing an MPX file is similar to opening any project. The method currently recommended for interchanging Project data with other products is XML.

If you have a program that can create either a text file or a comma-separated value file, you can import information from that program into Project. You need to save the information that you want to import as either a text file or a CSV file in the native program. The Import Wizard walks you through the process. If the map that you need doesn't exist, you need to create it.

Follow the steps that appear in the earlier section, "Bringing Excel workbook or Access database information into Project," with only one change: In the Open dialog box, display Text (*.txt) or CSV (*.csv) files and select the file you want to import.

Troubleshooting

Importing and exporting can be tricky operations. Little things may go wrong, causing these operations to fail. This section suggests ways to solve some of the problems that you may encounter while importing or exporting.

On a general note, use some common procedures when you export or import data. For example:

- Create a table on which to base your export/import map.
- Include unique identifier fields in export/import maps whenever possible to ensure traceability.
- Include descriptive fields to make the export/import easy to read.
- Save any maps you create so you can compare the data easily.
- When updating existing project data, first import to a new project and use the Compare Project Versions utility to confirm correct mappings. Open one of the projects. Then, click the Project tab and, in the Reports group, click Compare Projects. Project displays the dialog box you see in Figure 18.23. Select the other project you want to compare, and then select the Task and Resource tables you want to compare.

FIGURE 18.23

Use this box to select two projects to compare.

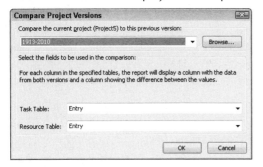

Cross-Reference

See Chapter 14 for details on comparing projects. ■

None of the preceding techniques is trouble-free, but getting in the habit of creating repeatable and verifiable maps will help you avoid many problems.

Project imports incorrect times in data from Microsoft Excel

In Excel, when you assign a date to a cell, Excel assigns a default time to the cell of 12:00 a.m. You may not see that time, but Excel has attached it to the cell. If the data you import from Excel to Project contains dates without specific times, Project automatically uses Excel's default time of 12:00 a.m. If you don't want to use Excel's default time in Project, enter times in Excel before you import.

Linked or embedded objects don't import or export

You're not imagining things. Project does not import or export linked or embedded objects when exchanging data with Microsoft Excel or Microsoft Access. You need to relink or re-embed the objects after you complete the import or export operation.

The export file contains more or less information than expected

The information you find in your exported file depends on the import/export map you select, the table you choose, and the filter you apply. If you export more or less information than you expect, check the map, table, and filter.

Export/Import Maps are created and edited using the Export Wizard; you won't find an "Edit Map" menu command or button. To troubleshoot an existing map, follow these steps:

1. Choose File ⇨ Save As and specify a filename and file type to start the Export Wizard.

2. On the Export Wizard – Map dialog box, select Use Existing Map and click Next.

3. On the Export Wizard – Map Selection dialog box, select the map that was used to generate the export file in question and click Next.

4. On the Export Wizard – Map Options dialog box, do not change any settings; simply click Next.

5. Review the fields selected and the Export Filters on the Task, Resource, or Assignment Mapping dialog boxes.

Project imports invalid information

Project checks data you import to ensure that the data types for each field are valid. If necessary, Project may modify the values of some fields to handle inconsistencies.

If Project warns that you are trying to import invalid data, check the import/export map you've selected to make sure you are importing the correct type of information into a Project field. Also, check the data in the import file and make sure that the field values are valid and within the acceptable range for the Project field into which you intend to import the data.

The values of imported information change

This situation is similar to the previous one, in which Project determines that the information you're trying to import is invalid. Project checks and, if necessary, changes the data you import to ensure that the data types and the values for each field are valid. Project may also change data to make sure that it falls within ranges that are valid for Project fields and doesn't create inconsistencies between fields that depend on each other. Project also overrides values you attempt to import into calculated fields by replacing the imported data with the calculated value.

The imported project is empty

As you know, importing depends on the import/export map that you select. If you choose the wrong map, no data may import. Also, make sure that you're looking at the correct view after importing. If you import task information, you may not see it if you're looking at a resource view.

Project displays imported information in the wrong fields

When imported information appears in the wrong Project field, you should check the import/export map. Make sure that you select the correct map and that the table you used contains the correct fields. Finally, check the mapping of the fields between the import file and your Project file.

Summary

In this chapter, you found out how to import and export information in Microsoft Project. In particular, you should now know how to do the following:

- Create and edit import/export maps
- Export information to Excel, Access, and Word
- Export information to graphics files, text files, HTML files, and other project management software files
- Import information from another project; from Excel, Access, or Word; or from text files
- Solve common problems that occur when you export or import information

In Chapter 19, you explore ways to coordinate multiple projects without using Project Server.

Part VII

Working in Groups

Coordinating Multiple Projects Outside Project Server

L arge projects are the most difficult to manage. Organization is a cornerstone to good project management — and in a large project, the sheer number of tasks makes the job more difficult than usual. In Microsoft Project, you can use the concept of consolidated projects to break projects into smaller, "bite-sized" pieces and then combine the smaller projects to view the bigger picture.

Consolidating Projects

When you're faced with a complex problem, finding the solution typically becomes easier if you can simplify the problem. Similarly, when you need to manage a complex project with many tasks, you may find it easier to organize the process if you deal with a limited number of tasks simultaneously.

Microsoft Project makes it easy for you to take this approach to planning large, complex projects. By using Project's consolidation features, you can create *subprojects*, which you can think of as the tasks that constitute individual portions of your large project. When you create a subproject, you save it as a separate project file. You can assign resources and set up each subproject with links and constraints — just as if it were the entire project and not just a subset of a larger project. When you need to view the bigger picture, you can consolidate the subprojects into one large project. When you consolidate, you're inserting one project into another — therefore subprojects are also called *inserted projects*.

Note

If you're a Project Professional user who also uses Project Server, you may be wondering whether consolidation applies to you. Although views in Project Server can "roll up" project information, you still need consolidation techniques if you want to see one critical path across all consolidated projects. Also, I describe resource pooling in this chapter. This concept applies more to Project Standard users than Project Professional users using Project Server. Project Professional users using Project Server can use the Enterprise Resource Pool in Project Server. ■

When you work in a consolidated project, you can focus on just the desired portion of the project. Subprojects appear as summary tasks in the consolidated project, and you can use Project's outlining tools to hide all the tasks associated with any subproject.

Cross-Reference

See Chapter 3 for more information on outlining. ■

From the consolidated project, you can view, print, and change information for any subproject — just as if you were working with a single project.

Preparing to use consolidation

Consolidation can help you achieve the following objectives:

- Tasks in projects that different people manage may be interdependent. Through consolidation, you can create the correct dependencies to accurately display the project's schedule and necessary resources while still allowing independent project management.

- A project may be so large that breaking it into smaller pieces can help you to organize it. Later on, when you want to view the big picture, you can use consolidation to combine the smaller pieces.

- You may be pooling the resources of several projects and find that you need to level the resources. Consolidating enables you to link the projects sharing the resources so that you can level the resources.

Note

If you're using Project Standard, you can't take advantage of the Enterprise Resource Pool that's available in Project Server — therefore the resource-pooling techniques I describe in this chapter apply to you. If you're using Project Professional and Project Server, however, you may want to use the Enterprise Resource Pool instead; to do so, see Chapter 21. ■

When should you decide to use consolidation? It doesn't really matter. You may realize right away that the project is too large to handle in a traditional way — or you may only discover later on, as you work on the project, that it's bigger than you originally thought. Suppose, for example, that the Marketing department of a software company decides — midway through the development cycle — to bundle various products under development. Doing so introduces dependencies where none originally existed — and provides an interesting opportunity for using consolidation.

If you decide to use consolidation before you start your project, simply create separate Microsoft Project files for various portions of the project. These files act as subprojects when you consolidate. Be sure to set up each subproject file so it's independently complete — and to create links within each subproject file as necessary. This chapter explains techniques for consolidating the subprojects and linking them.

If you start a project and then decide you want to use consolidation, you can create subprojects by following these steps:

1. Save your large project file.

2. Select all the tasks that you want to save in your first subproject file and click the Copy button on the Task tab in the Clipboard group.

3. Click the File tab and, from Backstage view, click New; if appropriate, select a template.

4. Click the Create button to start a new project.

5. Click the Project tab and, in the Properties group, click the Project Information button to display the Project Information dialog box (see Figure 19.1), where you can set basic project information, such as the project's start date and scheduling method.

FIGURE 19.1

Use the Project Information dialog box to set basic project information.

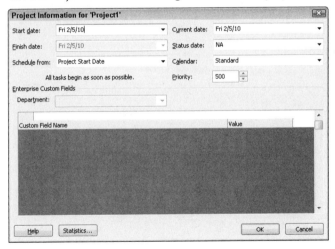

Tip

To make the Project Information dialog box appear automatically each time you start a new project, click the File tab — and then, from Backstage view, click Options to display the Project Options dialog box. Click Advanced on the left ; then, in the General section, put a check mark in the Prompt for Project Info for New Projects check box. ■

6. Click OK.

7. Click the Paste button; the tasks you copied in Step 2 appear in the new project.

8. Save the subproject and close it.

9. Repeat Steps 2 through 6 until you have saved several separate files that contain portions of your larger project.

Edit each subproject file that you create to make it an independently complete project. Then you can use the techniques that are explained in the following section to consolidate the subprojects and link them.

Inserting a project

To combine project files into one large project, you insert projects into a host project file, often referred to as the *consolidated project file*. Each project that you insert appears as a summary task in the consolidated project file, and, by default, Project calculates inserted projects the same way it calculates summary tasks. An icon in the Indicator field identifies an inserted project (see Figure 19.2).

FIGURE 19.2

A special icon in the Indicator field identifies inserted projects.

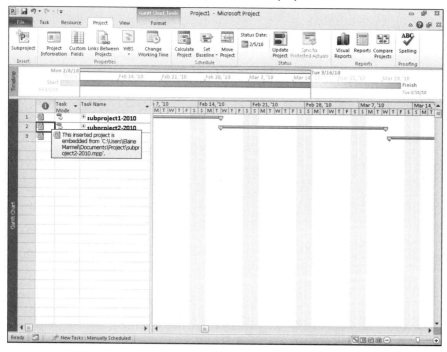

You can insert projects at any outline level. The level at which an inserted project appears depends on the outline level that appears where you intend to insert a project. Select the task in the target project that you want to appear *below* the newly inserted project. Insert the new project. Project places the inserted project above the task you selected to identify where it should go.

Typically, an inserted project appears at the same level as the selected task. If the task that is above the selected task in the outline is indented farther than the selected task, the inserted project appears at the same level as that indented task. If the task that's above the selected task is at the same level as the selected task (or outdented farther than it is), the inserted project appears in the outline at the same level as the selected task. Compare Figures 19.3, 19.4, and 19.5.

FIGURE 19.3

Here I expanded the Initial Planning Meeting task and then chose the Selection task when I inserted subproject2. This subproject appears at the same outline level as the Send Out Invitation task that's above it.

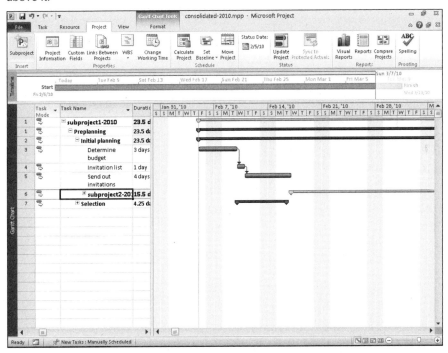

FIGURE 19.4

Here I collapsed the Initial Planning Meeting task and then chose the Selection task when I inserted sub-project2. This subproject appears at the same outline level as the Initial Planning Meeting task.

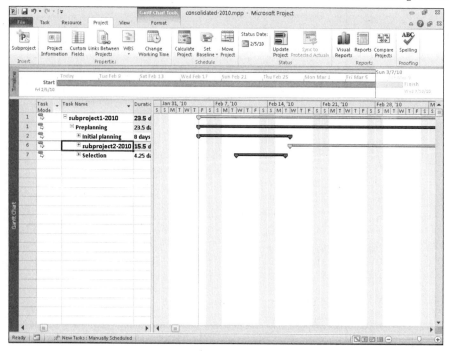

To produce a consolidated project in which the inserted projects line up at the highest outline level (as shown in Figure 19.6), make sure that you collapse the project you've inserted so you can't see its tasks when you insert the next subproject.

FIGURE 19.5

Here I selected the Determine Budget task and then inserted subproject2. This subproject appears at the same outline level as Determine Budget because the task above — Initial Planning Meeting — is outdented farther than Determine Budget (the selected task).

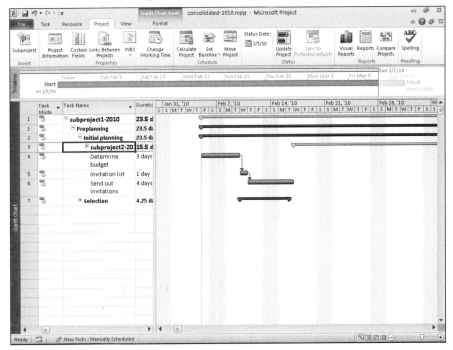

Tip
You can hide or show tasks after you insert a project by clicking the summary task's outline symbol — the plus or minus sign next to the task name. ∎

FIGURE 19.6

When subproject3 was inserted, subproject2 was selected and its subordinate tasks were visible, but the subordinate tasks of subproject1 were not visible.

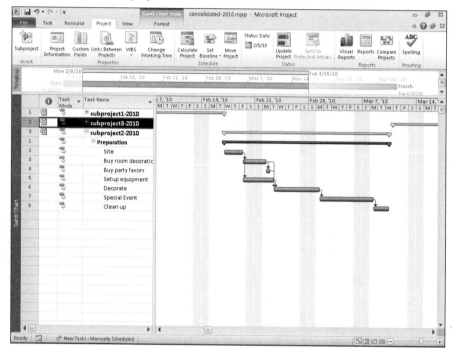

To insert a project, follow these steps:

1. Open the project in which you want to store the consolidated project.

2. Switch to the Gantt Chart view.

3. Click in the Task Name column on the row in which you want the inserted project to begin.

Note
When you insert a project, Project puts it immediately above the selected row. Therefore, if your consolidated project already contains tasks, click the task that you want to appear below the newly inserted subproject. ■

4. Click the Project tab and, in the Insert group, click the Subproject button to display the Insert Project dialog box (see Figure 19.7).

FIGURE 19.7

The Insert Project dialog box works the same as the Open dialog box.

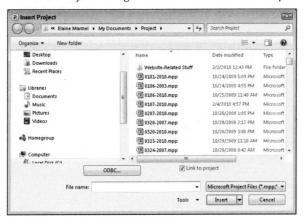

5. Navigate to the folder that contains the project you want to insert, and then select the file you want to insert.

Note

If you remove the check from the Link to Project check box, Project doesn't link the inserted project to its source project. If you choose Insert Read-Only from the Insert drop-down menu, Project doesn't change the source project when you change the inserted project. ■

6. Click Insert (or Insert Read-Only). Project inserts the selected file into the open project. The inserted file appears as a summary task, with its subordinate tasks hidden.

Using inserted projects and their source files

You can link an inserted project to its source file, as you saw in Figure 19.2. If you don't link an inserted project to its source file, any changes that you make to the inserted project while working in the consolidated project file don't affect the source file. Similarly, any changes that you make to the source file don't affect the consolidated project file that contains the subproject. Therefore, why wouldn't you want to link the files? You may want to create a consolidated file just so you can generate a report quickly.

In many circumstances, linking the files makes updating easier. Linking gives you the opportunity to ensure that any changes you make in one of the linked files — the consolidated project or the subproject — will affect the other file: When you save, Project prompts you to update the linked files. The link you create when you insert a project and link it to its source file works like any link between two files in the Windows environment. For example, if you rename the subproject file (or move it to a folder other than the one in which you originally saved it), you have to update the link to the consolidated project; otherwise the link doesn't work. If you move a file you've linked, you can update the link on the Advanced tab of the Inserted Project Information dialog box for the inserted project (see Figure 19.8). Double-click any inserted project's task name to display this dialog box; then click the Browse button beside the Link to Project check box to browse to the new location.

FIGURE 19.8

The Advanced tab of the Inserted Project Information dialog box.

Tip
You also can unlink subprojects from their source files by using the Advanced tab of the Inserted Project Information dialog box. To do so, deselect the Link to Project check box. ■

Or you can simply attempt to expand the inserted project in the consolidated project file. When you click the plus sign next to the subproject, Project automatically displays a dialog box that looks like the Open dialog box. Use this dialog box to navigate to the new location of the file and click OK after you finish, reestablishing the link between the files.

Consolidating all open projects: A shortcut

Follow these steps to consolidate several subprojects at the same time:

1. Open all the subprojects you want to consolidate.

2. Click the View tab and, in the Window group, click New Window to open the New Window dialog box (see Figure 19.9).

FIGURE 19.9

Use the New Window dialog box to quickly consolidate open projects.

3. Press and hold down Ctrl, and then click each project that you want to consolidate.

4. Click OK.

Project creates a new consolidated project that contains the projects you selected in the New Window dialog box; they appear expanded by default in the consolidated project. Project inserts the subprojects into the consolidated project in the same order in which they appear in the New Window dialog box.

Moving subprojects within a consolidated project

You can move subprojects around in the consolidated project by cutting a subproject row to delete it and then pasting the row where you want it to appear. When you select a summary row that represents a subproject and click the Cut button on the Standard toolbar, Project opens the Planning Wizard dialog box (see Figure 19.10).

FIGURE 19.10

The Planning Wizard dialog box appears when you try to delete an inserted project represented as a summary task.

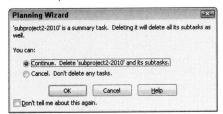

Select the Continue option button and click OK. The summary task that represents the subproject disappears, along with all its subordinate tasks. When you paste the subproject, Project places the subproject immediately above the selected row. Therefore, in the Task Name column, you must click the task that you want to appear below the subproject. Then click the Paste button on the Standard toolbar. Project reinserts the subproject at its new location.

Tip

If you intend to move many tasks, you may want to select the Don't Tell Me About This Again check box to avoid viewing the Planning Wizard dialog box. ■

Understanding Consolidated Projects and Dependencies

Typically, in a consolidated project, you have tasks — either in the consolidated project or in one subproject — that are dependent on other tasks in another subproject. You can create links between the projects in a consolidated file, and (if necessary) change the links you create.

Linking tasks across projects

You can create four different types of dependencies: finish-to-start, start-to-start, finish-to-finish, and start-to-finish. In addition, these types support lead and lag time. The process of linking tasks with dependencies across projects is much the same as the process of creating dependencies for tasks within the same project. Starting in the consolidated project file, follow these steps:

1. Click the Gantt Chart on the View bar.
2. Select the tasks you want to link, selecting the predecessor before the successor.

Tip

To select noncontiguous tasks, press and hold down Ctrl as you click each task name, in the order in which you want to link the tasks. ■

3. Click the Link Tasks button in the Schedule group on the Task tab of the Ribbon. Project creates a finish-to-start link between the two tasks.

Tip

You can create the link in the consolidated project file by dragging from the middle of the Gantt bar of the predecessor task to the Gantt bar of the successor task; watch the mouse pointer change to a small chain link. ■

You also can link tasks by typing in the Predecessors field, using the format project name\
ID#. The project name should include the path to the location of the file as well as the filename,
and the ID# should be the ID number of the task in that file. In Figure 19.11, the *Buy room decorations* task, Task 2 in a Project file called subproject2-2010.MPP, is linked as the successor to
the *Site* task, which is Task 8 in a Project file called subproject1.MPP. If you display the Entry
bar (just below the Ribbon), as I did in Figure 19.11, you can see the complete pathname of a
linked task in the Entry bar when you click in the Predecessors column for the task.

FIGURE 19.11

You can type in the Predecessors field to create a link between tasks across Project files, but exercise
care that you type everything correctly.

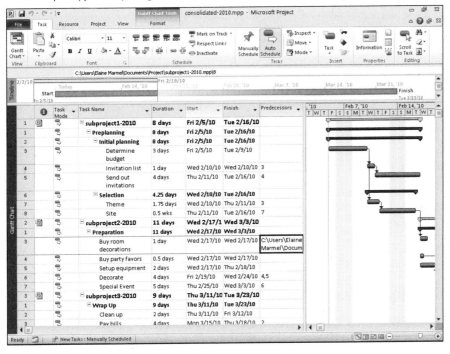

When you link tasks between projects, the task links look like standard links in the consolidated
project. However, when you open either of the subproject files, you see that Project has inserted an
external task (see Figure 19.12). The name of each externally linked task appears gray — as does
its Gantt Chart bar. If you point at the Gantt Chart bar, Project displays information about the task,
including the fact that it is external.

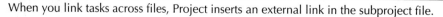

FIGURE 19.12

When you link tasks across files, Project inserts an external link in the subproject file.

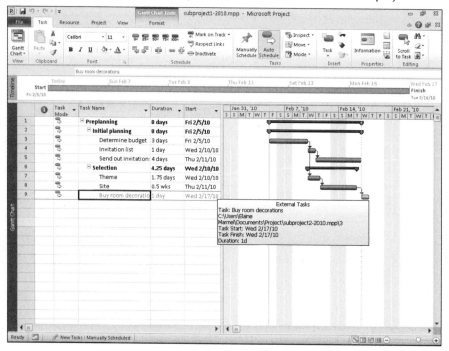

If you double-click the task name of the external task, Project opens the subproject that contains the task to which the external task is linked. In my example, double-clicking the *Buy Room Decorations* task in `subproject1.MPP` results in Project opening `subproject2.MPP`.

Changing links across projects

After you link tasks across projects, you may need to change information about the link. For example, you may want to change the type of dependency from the default finish-to-start link, or you may want to create lag time.

You can modify a link between tasks in different subprojects from the subproject or from the consolidated project. In the subproject, double-click the line that links an internal task to the external task (see Figure 19.13). In the consolidated project, double-click the line that links the two tasks (see Figure 19.14). In both cases, Project displays the Task Dependency dialog box.

In a subproject, double-click the link line between the internal task and the external task to display the
Task Dependency dialog box.

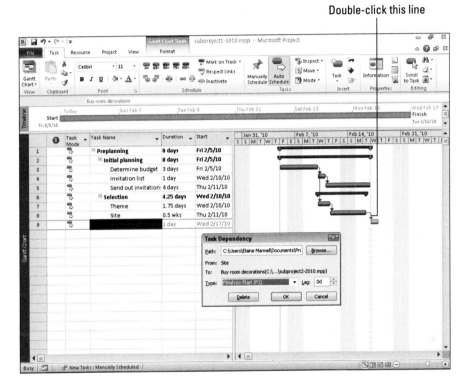

Consolidated projects: To save or not to save

You don't have to save consolidated project files unless you want them. You can create the consolidated project file by choosing either Window ⇨ New Window or Insert ⇨ Project — both methods are described earlier in this chapter. You can use the consolidated project to create links and even reports, and then close the consolidated project file without saving it. For example, suppose that you created the consolidated project by inserting projects and the inserted projects are not open. If you linked the inserted project to its source file, then Project asks whether you want to save the consolidated project when you start to close that project. Whether you choose to save the consolidated project doesn't change Project's behavior; Project next asks whether you want to save changes you made to the inserted projects (see Figure 19.15). If you've made changes in the consolidated project that you want to retain, be sure to save the inserted projects.

FIGURE 19.14

In a consolidated project, double-click the line that links the tasks to display the Task Dependency dialog box and change the dependency information about tasks that are linked across projects.

Double-click this line

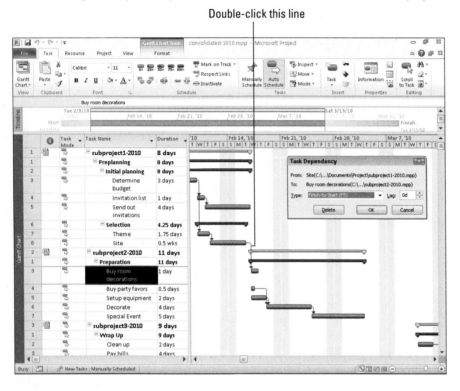

FIGURE 19.15

When you close a consolidated project that you created by inserting projects, Project asks whether you want to save changes — including links — that you made to each subproject.

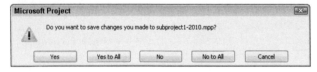

Project treats a subproject file the same as any other Project file; when you close a subproject, Project asks whether you want to save changes to the file.

If you save the changes to the subprojects — even if you don't save the consolidated project — external tasks, such as the one that you saw previously in Figure 19.12, appear in the subproject files when you open them.

Viewing Multiple Projects

Creating a consolidated project makes your work easier because you can display and hide selected portions of your project. The consolidated project that appears in Figure 19.16 contains three inserted projects. As you can tell from the outline symbols, you can't see all the tasks in this consolidated project in the figure; the tasks for subproject3 are hidden.

Suppose you want to focus on the middle portion of the project. As Figure 19.17 demonstrates, you can easily focus on the portion of the project that currently needs your attention: Just click the outline symbols to the left of each summary task to expand only the portion of the project that you want to view. Notice that task numbering within each subproject begins with Task ID 1.

FIGURE 19.16

This consolidated project contains three inserted projects.

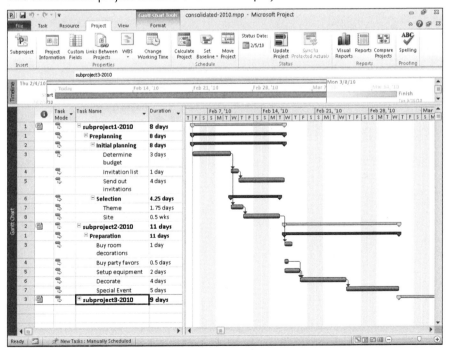

FIGURE 19.17

When you want to focus on a portion of a consolidated project, close inserted projects so just their summary tasks appear.

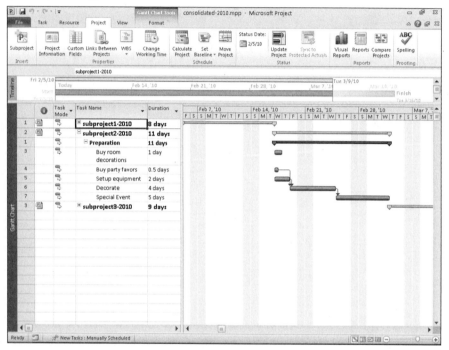

Viewing the Critical Path across Projects

When you consolidate projects, by default Project calculates inserted projects in the same way it calculates summary tasks — effectively showing you the overall critical path across all the projects by using the late finish date of the master project to make calculations. This behavior can make subprojects within the master project look as though they don't have critical paths of their own. For example, in Figure 19.18, Only Subtask 7, which is part of the subproject called Task2-2010, is on the critical path. No tasks in the subproject Task1-2010 appear to be on the critical path.

FIGURE 19.18

By default, Project treats inserted projects as summary tasks; you don't see critical paths for individual inserted projects.

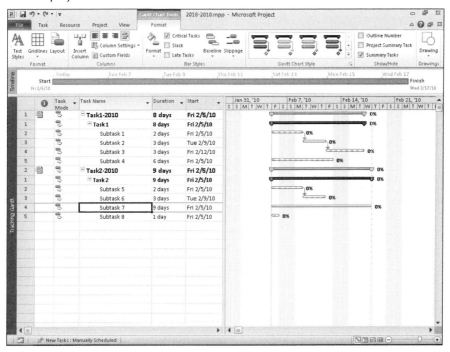

Suppose you want to see each subproject's critical path while viewing the consolidated project. To do so, you think, "I'll turn on multiple critical paths in the master project." That's the right idea, but because multiple critical paths apply only to tasks that are owned by the project, nothing changes. In this example, the tasks in Figure 19.18 (Task 1 and Task 2) are owned by subprojects, so turning on multiple critical paths in the consolidated project won't have any effect.

You can, however, tell Project to *stop* treating subprojects as summary tasks. If you do, Project uses the late-finish dates that the subprojects pass along to the consolidated project to determine the critical path. And you're likely to see each subproject's critical path in the consolidated project as the critical paths appear in each subproject (see Figure 19.19).

FIGURE 19.19

When Project doesn't treat inserted projects as summary tasks, you're likely to see multiple critical paths in a master project.

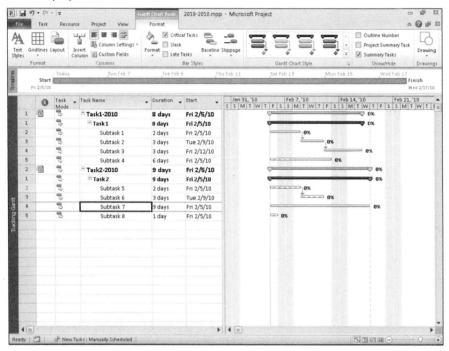

To change Project's behavior in the master project, click the File tab and, from Backstage view, click Options. In the Project Options dialog box, click Schedule on the left. Then, in the Calculation Options For This Project section, remove the check from the Inserted Projects Are Calculated Like Summary Tasks check box (see Figure 19.20).

FIGURE 19.20

The Inserted Projects Are Calculated Like Summary Tasks check box controls whether Project uses the sub-projects' late-finish dates or the master project's late-finish date for calculations.

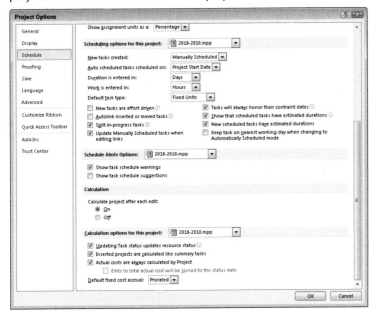

Sharing Resources Among Projects

Creating a resource pool can be useful if you don't use Project Server and you work with the same resources on multiple projects. A *resource pool* is a set of resources — both human and inanimate — made available to any project. You can use resources exclusively on one project, or you can share the resources among several projects.

If you work in an environment in which several project managers use the same set of resources on various projects, consider using a resource pool. Setting up a resource pool in Project can be a good way to schedule resources and resolve resource conflicts.

Cross-Reference

See Chapter 11 for more information on other techniques you can employ to resolve resource conflicts. See Chapter 21 for information about using the Enterprise Resource Pool feature of Project Server. ■

Creating a resource pool and sharing the resources

Setting up a resource pool in Project can facilitate resource management, especially if several projects share the same resources. To create a resource pool, you simply set up a project file that contains only resource information.

If you have already set up a project that contains all the resources presently available, you can use that project as a model. After you identify a project that can serve as the resource pool, you designate it as the *resource pool project* by using the following steps:

Note

No need to delete all the tasks in the project that serves as the model for the resource pool. Just make sure you have the resource information in the file. ■

1. Open the project that contains the resources and that will serve as the resource pool file.

2. Open the project that will use the resource pool (that is, the project on which you want to work).

3. Click the Resource tab and, in the Assignments group, click the Resource Pool button.

4. From the drop-down menu that appears, click Share Resources. Project displays the Share Resources dialog box (see Figure 19.21).

The Share Resources dialog box.

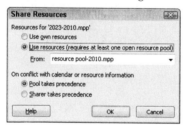

5. Click the Use Resources option button. Then in the From list box, select the resource pool project to indicate that you want to use the resources defined in that project.

Note

If you open only the project on which you want to work, the Use Own Resources option button is the only choice available; you can't share resources with the resource pool. The first time you want to enable resource sharing, you must open both the project you designated as the resource pool and the project on which you want to work. In addition, if you have any other projects open, they appear as candidates for the resource pool project when you open the From list box. That's because Project enables you to select from any open project when you identify the resource pool. ■

6. Select an option to tell Project how to handle calendar conflicts.

   If you select the Pool Takes Precedence option button, the resource calendars in the resource pool file take precedence when conflicts arise. If, however, you select the Sharer Takes Precedence option button, the resource calendars in the file you're updating take precedence over the resource calendars in the resource pool file when conflicts arise. Using the Pool Takes Precedence option helps ensure that Project calculates allocations across projects the way you would expect.

7. Click OK.

If you switch to the Resource Sheet view of the file that you want to update, Project displays all the resources in the resource pool file — along with any resources you may have set up in your project file.

You can now continue working in your project, or you can save your project and close it. You can also close the resource pool file.

Opening a project that uses a resource pool

At some point, you will save and close your file and then come back to work on it at a later time. You don't need to open the resource pool file at that time. Instead, when you open your file after you've set it up to share resources, the Open Resource Pool Information dialog box appears (see Figure 19.22).

FIGURE 19.22

The Open Resource Pool Information dialog box.

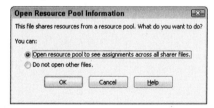

When you select the first option, Project opens the resource pool file in addition to your file. If you select the second option, Project opens only your file, and Project does not transfer to the resource pool any changes that you make to the resources in your file because the resource pool file isn't open.

Note

When you select the first option in the Open Resource Pool Information dialog box, Project opens the resource pool file automatically, as a read-only file. This action enables you to make changes to your project without tying up the resource pool file; therefore multiple users can use the resource pool simultaneously. ■

Updating information in the resource pool

If you make changes to resource information while you're working on your project, you must update the resource pool file so others who are using the resource pool have the most up-to-date information. To update the resource pool, follow these steps:

1. Make sure that the resource pool file is open, even if it's open in read-only mode.
2. Click the Resource tab and, in the Assignments group, click the Resource Pool button.
3. From the drop-down menu that appears, click Update Resource Pool (see Figure 19.23).

FIGURE 19.23

The Update Resource Pool command is available if you set up resource sharing and you make a change in your project while the resource pool file is open.

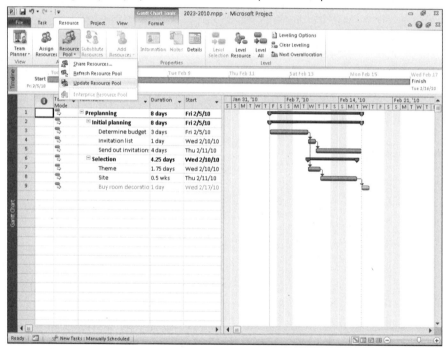

When you open only your project and make changes to the resources, the Update Resource Pool command is not available. Furthermore, if you open only your project, save and close your project, and then open the resource pool file, this command is still not available. To ensure that Project incorporates the changes in the resource pool that you make to resources in your project, be sure to open the resource pool file when you open your file.

Tip

To ensure consistency and avoid arguments in the workplace, consider making one group or person responsible for updating the resource pool. ■

If you forget to update the resource pool after you make a change in your project that affects the resource pool, Project displays a message, shown in Figure 19.24, when you save your project. Click OK to save changes you made in your project to the resource pool project.

FIGURE 19.24

If you forget to update the resource pool, Project alerts you when you save your project.

Note

Project stores the relative paths to projects that are linked to resource pools. If you move one or the other, Project can still open the files. ■

Quit sharing resources

Suppose you decide that you no longer want to use the resource-pool file. Follow these steps to disable the resource pool for a specific project:

1. Open that project. (Opening the resource pool isn't necessary, but it's okay to have it open.)
2. Click the Resource tab and, in the Assignments group, click the Resource Pool button.
3. From the drop-down menu that appears, click Share Resources.
4. Select the Use Own Resources option button in the Share Resources dialog box (refer to Figure 19.21).

However, suppose you decide you want to disable the resource pool in general for all files that are sharing the resources of one resource pool. Do you need to open each file and disable resource sharing? No. Follow these steps to disable the resource-pool file in general:

1. Open the resource pool file in read-write mode by using the Open dialog box — the same way you would open any file. Project displays the Open Resource Pool box (shown in Figure 19.25). Choose the middle option or the last option in this dialog box to open the file as a read-write file; then click OK.

FIGURE 19.25

Use this dialog box to determine whether you open the resource pool file as a read-only file or a read-write file.

2. Click the Resource tab and, in the Assignments group, click the Resource Pool button.

3. From the drop-down menu that appears, click Share Resources. Project displays the Share Resources dialog box (see Figure 19.26).

4. Select the project(s) you want to exclude from the resource pool. You can select multiple noncontiguous projects by pressing and holding Ctrl when you click the mouse, or you can select contiguous projects by pressing and holding Shift when you click the mouse.

FIGURE 19.26

The Share Resources dialog box.

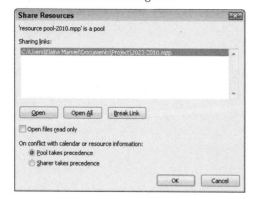

5. Click Break Link.

6. Click OK.

Collaborating Using SharePoint

In addition to the methods discussed so far in this chapter, you can use a SharePoint site to aid collaboration on projects.

As with other Office products, you can save a Project file to a list on a SharePoint site so others with access to the site can open, view, and download the project. Here's how it's done:

1. Open the file in Project and then click the File tab.

2. From Backstage view, click Save & Send (see Figure 19.27).

3. From the Save & Send list, click Save to SharePoint.

4. Click Save As and navigate to the location on your SharePoint site to which you want to save the project.

5. Provide a file name and click Save.

FIGURE 19.27

Use the Save to SharePoint command to upload a project to a SharePoint site.

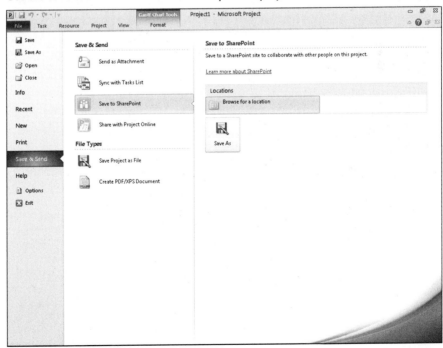

Even handier (and perhaps more interesting) is the capability to create tasks in either SharePoint or in Project — and then synchronize the tasks listed in the two products.

Setting up a list for project tasks

You can add a list to your SharePoint site that is specifically designed to support creating tasks. In Figure 19.28, I've already set up the Proposed Projects list, which can be used as a generic location where those with access to the SharePoint site can enter task information about projects they think should take place.

FIGURE 19.28

The general appearance of a SharePoint list that can be used to enter task information.

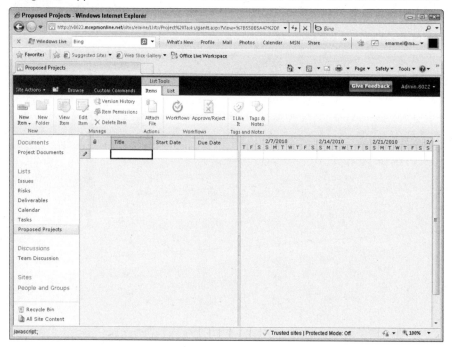

Follow these steps to set up a SharePoint list that supports entering task information:

1. On your SharePoint site, click the Lists link in the Quick Launch pane on the left side of the window.

2. At the top of the All Site Content window that appears, click the Create button.

3. From the Create window that appears (see Figure 19.29), click Tracking in the All Categories group in the left pane to view the SharePoint elements that support tracking efforts.

FIGURE 19.29

View the SharePoint elements that support tracking efforts.

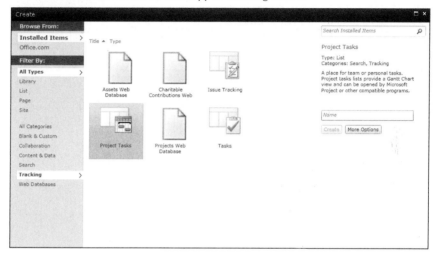

4. Click Project Tasks.

5. At the right side of the window, supply a name for the SharePoint list; I called mine "Conference Project."

Tip

If you want to provide a description for the list, you can click More Options and fill in the description. ∎

6. Click Create.

A new list appears in the Quick Launch pane; it has the same format as the list shown in Figure 19.28. To enter information into a Project Task list, click in the Title column and type a name for a task. If appropriate, enter Start Date, Due Date, % Complete, Task Status, Priority, Predecessors, and Assigned To information.

Note

Entering Start Date and Due Date information causes a Gantt bar to appear. ∎

If you prefer data entry in a form, click the Items tab on the Ribbon and, in the New group, click the bottom of the New Item button to choose between entering a task or a summary task. If you opt to enter a task, you see a window like the one shown in Figure 19.30.

FIGURE 19.30

You can add tasks using a form.

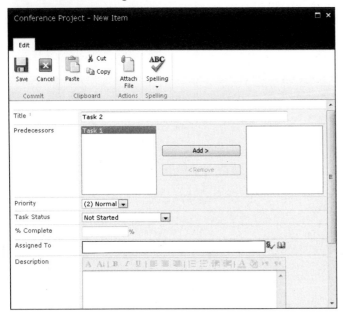

Synchronizing a SharePoint Project Task List with Project

The Project Task lists you can create in SharePoint provide a skeleton for a project, as you can see in Figure 19.31.

When you're ready to do some work in Project, you can synchronize the list information from SharePoint into a Project file. Follow these steps:

FIGURE 19.31

Set up a skeleton project task list in SharePoint.

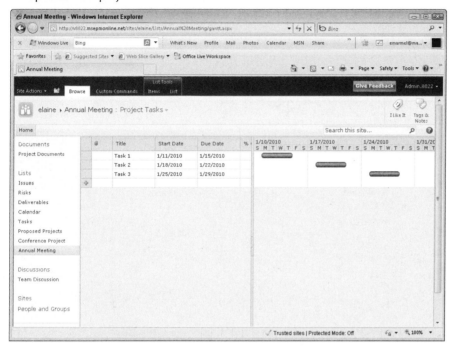

1. Open the Project file in which you want the tasks to appear.

2. Click the File tab and, in Backstage view, click Save & Send.

3. Click Sync with Tasks List (see Figure 19.32).

4. Click Validate URL.

5. If prompted, supply the credentials needed to connect to your SharePoint site. The available project task lists on your SharePoint site appear in the list box, immediately below the Validate URL button.

6. Select a list to synchronize with the open project.

7. Click Sync.

FIGURE 19.32

Use this page in Backstage view to connect to your SharePoint site and select a list with which to synchronize the open project.

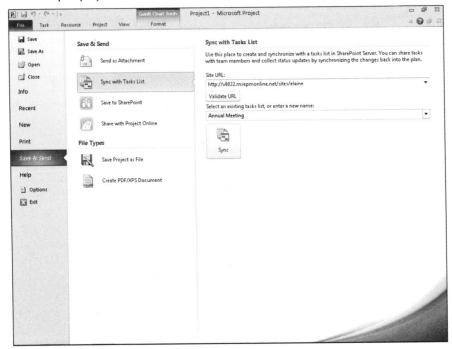

The tasks from the SharePoint list appear in Project (see Figure 19.33).

The synchronization goes in both directions; if you make changes in Project, you can synchronize those changes back to SharePoint.

If you start a project like the one shown in Figure 19.34 in Project, and then want team input, you can synchronize the project to SharePoint using the same technique.

FIGURE 19.33

The tasks from SharePoint appear in Project.

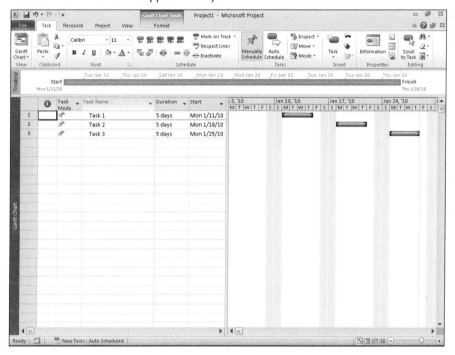

FIGURE 19.34

A project before synchronizing to a SharePoint project task list.

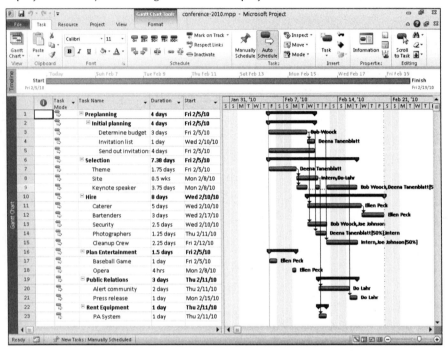

Be aware that

- The synchronization converts automatically scheduled tasks to manually scheduled tasks, and

- Only Summary tasks will appear in SharePoint.

After I synchronize, my project in Project looks like the one shown in Figure 19.35.

FIGURE 19.35

The project in Project after synchronizing.

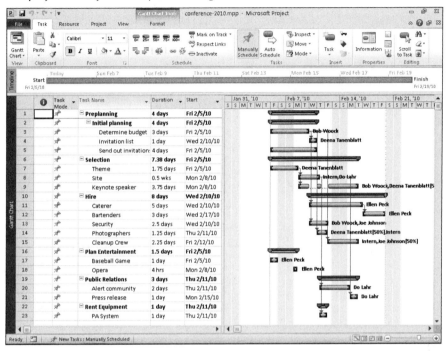

In addition, I see the summary tasks of my project in my SharePoint list (see Figure 19.36).

FIGURE 19.36

Project's summary tasks appear in the SharePoint list.

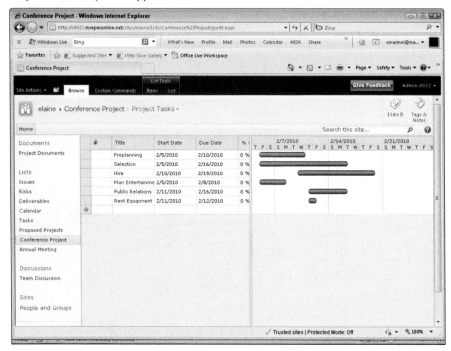

Summary

This chapter described how to consolidate projects and pool resources. You should now know how to do the following:

- Insert projects

- Understand and work with consolidated projects and dependencies

- Manage the view of a consolidated project

- Display multiple critical paths for consolidated projects

- Share resources

- Work with projects on a SharePoint site.

Chapter 20 introduces Project Server.

Preparing to Use Project Server

Y ou'll be tempted, but please don't skip this chapter. I know it sounds like double-talk when talking about project management software, but planning the implementation of Project Server (a project) is the single most important action that you can take to ensure a successful venture.

Implementing Project Server isn't only about hardware configurations and installing software. It's about planning for the needs of your organization so you can configure Project Server correctly. It's about assessing where your organization is today and where it plans to go. It's about identifying the players, their needs, and their roles in the process. It's about figuring out what needs to be done, who has the skills and availability to do it, when it needs to be done, and what else depends on it getting done.

In this chapter, you review the process to follow so your organization can accept the changes that using Project Server will bring — and make those changes as successfully and painlessly as possible.

Understanding Project Server and Project Web App

The concept behind Project Server is that *all the projects that your organization manages affect each other in some way*, if only because they share resources, and the need for collaboration on projects is greater than it has ever been.

As the number of projects and the size of your organization grow, so does the need to *manage the management* of projects. Project Server enables you to store all projects and all resource information for your organization in one central database on your company's local-area network (LAN) or intranet so that limited resources can be matched efficiently to projects. Only the project manager, the resource manager, and the administrator must actually install and use Project Professional. All other resources involved in the project use Project Web App (PWA), a browser-based product, to view the project data stored in the Project Server database. Using Project Server and Project Web App (and without using Project Professional), team members, managers, and executives can accomplish the following:

- Enter and view time sheet information
- View a project's Gantt Chart
- Receive, refuse, and delegate work assignments
- Update assignments with progress and completion information
- Attach supporting documentation, such as budget estimates or feasibility studies, to a project
- Receive notices about task status
- Perform analysis and produce organization-wide reports
- Carry out basic management of issues and risks
- Send status reports to the project manager

Cross-Reference

For more detail about the roles of managers, team members, and executives, see Chapters 22, 23, and 24, respectively. ■

Here's how the process works in general. The network administrator (or someone with similar skills and network privileges) installs Project Server on a Web server or in a server farm. The project manager creates a project in Project Professional. When the project manager is ready to store the project in Project Server, he or she publishes the project information. At this point, anyone with Internet Explorer 7.0 (or a later version) who has access to Project Server and proper viewing rights can view the project information as it appears in Project Professional by using Project Web App, the browser-based client side of Project Server.

Tip

Installing Project Server is not a simple process. I believe your interests will be best served if you hire a Microsoft Project Partner to assist you in the installation and configuration process. ■

Using a variety of tools, the project manager can assign resources to the project using a company-wide pool of available resources whose information is stored in the Project Server database. Using Project Web App, the project's team members can see the assignments they've received, update work assignments, send status reports to the project manager, and even set up to-do lists.

Note

The project manager uses both Project Professional and Project Web App, but other resources involved in the project typically use only Project Web App. ■

Project Server enables you to create consistent projects that use the same custom settings. Using the Enterprise Global template, each project you create contains all the same fields, maps, views, tables, reports, filters, forms, toolbars, groups, and calendars that are stored in the global template file included in Project Professional, along with additional enterprise-only fields. Project Server administrators can define whether fields are required and can create look-up tables and value lists for fields. Because the settings are stored in the Enterprise Global template, they can be used repeatedly without having to re-create information.

The Project Server Database

Each Project Server database actually consists of four databases:

- The Draft database
- The Published database
- The Archive database
- The Reporting database

The Draft database is a "holding tank" area where project managers using Project Professional can store projects that they don't yet want the general public to view. Only users of Project Professional can view draft projects.

The Published database is the location where projects are available to users of Project Web App (PWA). Using PWA, team members can update time sheets, update project information, and view reports, based on their PWA credentials.

The Archive database contains older and backed-up versions of published projects.

The Reporting database holds the data used in reports; in this database, Project Server generates reports and OLAP cubes. This database is optimized to generate reports, and Project Server updates the information in the Reporting database almost as soon as information changes.

Project Server 2010 is very dependent on elements in SharePoint Server 2010, such as the Project Detail Pages, Enterprise Project Types, workflow, and so forth. Although you can restore a server using Project's four primary databases, several features will be nonfunctioning until you restore the content database associated with a Project Server site and reconnect things. Microsoft promises to have lots of documentation on this subject.

Does your organization need Project Server? The following is a list of scenarios for which Project Server would work well:

- You manage many different projects using the same resources.

- Your organization has determined that the time of project managers *and* resources would be used more efficiently if resources could record their time directly in the project schedule instead of providing it to the project manager, who then updates the schedule.

- Your executives want better organization-wide reporting and analysis tools than you can currently provide.

- Your managers need to model what-if scenarios.

- Your users need access to project data anywhere in the world.

Project Server was originally designed as a LAN-based product. If your organization uses a LAN and wants one central database to store both projects and resources, Project Server should meet your needs.

Suppose your organization uses a wide-area network (WAN). You can use Project Server configured in a server farm. To improve performance, you may want to use additional software such as Terminal Services or Citrix, although using active cache may diminish this need. *Active cache* is a local cache that Project Professional uses to interact with Project Server. Active cache manages updates to project and Enterprise Global Resource Pool information. In addition, active cache uses message-based updates that transfer only the differences between files (rather than the whole files) to Project Server.

Planning the Implementation

Getting Project Server up and running is not a simple task; I strongly recommend that you work with a Microsoft Project Partner. Microsoft Project Partners are experienced in project management and in using and implementing project management systems using Microsoft Project Professional and Project Server. In this section, I provide a high-level overview of the process and issues you should consider. Because each organization's needs are different, installing and setting up Project Server is rarely an "out-of-the-box" experience. In no way should you consider the information in this chapter complete; a seasoned professional will make sure that you consider issues specific to your organization.

Tip
On this book's Web site, you'll find links to the sites of many Project Partners. ∎

If you think about the implementation of Project Server the same way you think about planning other information technology projects, you won't be surprised to find out that you need to take the same actions:

- Assess system and organizational requirements
- Design the system
- Develop an implementation strategy

You can upgrade from Project Server 2003 or 2007 to Project Server 2010. You also can run Project Server 2010 in Compatibility Mode to enable the server to accept connections from Project Professional 2007, but keep in mind that running in Compatibility Mode disables some of the new features available in Project Server 2010.

Software requirements

Most software requirements are for servers; project managers need Project Professional on their client machines; the client machines of other project team members should run Internet Explorer 7 or higher.

For basic use of Project Server, you need, at a minimum, 64-bit editions of Windows Server 2008 Standard, Enterprise, or Data Center, Release 2 or later.

To support Project Web App, you'll need Internet Explorer 7 or 8.

For your database engine, you need either SQL Server 2005 – SP3 CU4 or SQL Server 2008 RTM CU5, and you'll need to install the following components of SQL Server:

- Database Engine
- Analysis Services
- Reporting Services
- Management tools
- Connectivity components

Whether you use SQL Server 2005 or SQL Server 2008, you must install the SQL Server 2005 Native Client and the SQL Server 2005 Analysis Management Objects (AMO) on the server. You also need to install the SQL Server 2005 Native Client on the computer running Analysis Services.

Project Server depends on the SharePoint Server 2010, so the hardware you choose to use must support all SharePoint Server requirements in addition to Project Server requirements, and you must install SharePoint 2010 Server before you install Project Server 2010.

Hardware requirements

Again, most hardware requirements are for servers; Microsoft recommends that each client machine meet the requirements for running Windows 7. You can check the Microsoft Project home page for more information:

```
http://office.microsoft.com/project/
```

The recommendations for servers come from Microsoft and depend largely on the number of services you intend to install. Server machines should, at a minimum, be 3GHz, 64-bit, dual processors and contain at least 4GB of RAM, an 80GB hard disk, a DVD-ROM drive, a Super VGA (800 × 600) or higher-resolution monitor, and a Microsoft Mouse–compatible pointing device.

Typically, you install Project Server on the company's server or in a server farm. If you're planning to use the bare-minimum hardware, you should load only Project Server on that computer. Other components, such as SQL Server, should run on separate computers.

Cross-Reference
See the section "Considering software/hardware scenarios" later in this chapter for some information on load balancing and improving performance. ■

Assessing the network environment

The following factors directly impact amount of traffic that you can expect on your network:

- The total number of users
- The number of concurrent users updating the Project Server databases
- The number of projects that you store in the Project Server databases

Using older network architecture (10Base-T) in a heavily trafficked environment will undoubtedly result in complaints that the system is slow. You may want to plan to upgrade your network infrastructure.

Project Server is designed as a local-area network–based product that can provide one central location to store projects and resource information. To use Project Server across a wide-area network (WAN), you may need to use Terminal Services or Citrix software to improve performance. Note, however, that Project Professional 2010 connects to Project Server 2010 much more efficiently than earlier versions — diminishing (if you're lucky) the need to use Terminal Services or Citrix.

Considering software/hardware scenarios

The hardware/software configuration that works most effectively in your environment is influenced by multiple factors that affect the overall performance of Project Server, including, but not limited to, these:

- The total number of users
- The number of concurrent users
- The number of assignments per project
- The number of projects that you want to store in the Project Server databases
- The features of Project Server that you want to use

Note

To improve performance, Project Professional 2010 interacts with Project Server 2010 through a local active cache that manages replicating the Enterprise Global Resource Pool information and updating projects. When you make changes in Project Professional and upload them to Project Server 2010, the active cache delivers message-based differences between files rather than entire files. ∎

Because Project Server 2010 depends on SharePoint Server 2010, you have some choices about how you configure the hardware on which you will load the software, and your choices will affect the performance of Project Server. You can use a single server or a server farm.

In the server farm, you can place various components and services on several networked computers to balance the load. The server farm also improves how well (and how gracefully) your organization can handle present network needs or expand to meet growing needs. And when you use a server farm, you limit the impact created when a single component or service fails.

Microsoft makes various recommendations about server-farm configurations; the Microsoft Project Professional you hire to help you install and implement Project Server can help you determine which of these configurations is best for you. The guidelines Microsoft publishes address factors such as the number of tasks, resources, and assignments in your projects; the number of projects you have; and whether most of your projects are small, medium-size, or large in nature. The beauty of the server-farm concept lies in the ease with which you can expand any tier within the farm to improve performance.

Assessing organizational requirements

Determining your organization's direction and needs may be the most important phase of the implementation process, because the Project Server design ultimately depends on the information you gather about your organization.

Start by setting up a team to implement the system. You'll need people who are good at gathering information, making design decisions, and managing implementation. Be sure to include people who are experienced in using enterprise project management systems. You'll need a mix of business people and technical people to address the various facets of implementing Project Server. The business people should include senior project managers and staff with experience using Project. The technical people should include those who are experienced in your company's network architecture and hardware configuration. To customize or automate Project Server functions, you should include at least one technical person with skills in developing object models for Project. Everyone on the team should be familiar with your company's standards.

Tip

If you find yourself missing key team members, check this book's Web site, which provides links to the sites of many Project Partners — companies that are experienced in project management and in using and implementing project management systems, Microsoft Project Professional, and Project Server. ∎

The team should set milestone dates and task durations for each of the activities described in the next five sections.

Identify the people who will approve the Project Server design

As with any project, it's important to identify the decision-makers as soon as you start. If possible, include one or more of them on the team so they're part of the process — and so they feel ownership for the system that you ultimately design.

Identify staff members to interview

Identify people who fill the following roles. Note that in some environments, some or all of the following roles might be shared by one person:

- **Team members:** People to whom work is assigned.
- **Project managers:** People who prepare and manage project plans. Don't forget to include those who have used tools other than Project to manage projects.
- **Resource managers:** People who delegate work to team members and monitor project progress and resource utilization.
- **Portfolio managers:** People who compare proposals against business needs, financial constraints, and other deciding factors, and are familiar with company standards.
- **Executives:** People who view reports on projects and resources.
- **Administrators:** People who manage changes and access to the Project Server database. The people who start the administrator job may ultimately phase out of the job because the job changes over time. Initially, the administrator installs and sets up Project Professional, Project Server, and SQL Server and may use both Project Server and SQL Server tools to meet the needs of users. Eventually, the administrator role becomes a maintenance function, for which knowledge of Project Server administrative functions is the only prerequisite.

Create a requirements definition questionnaire

To effectively conduct an interview, the team should create a questionnaire to obtain information about how people work. To gather information for your questionnaire, use the reports that your company currently uses to record project performance. Evaluate each report to identify the resources and projects that are (or should be) included on the report; how tasks, projects, and resources are categorized; and who uses each report. To help you produce your questionnaire, you may want to download Microsoft's Enterprise Implementation Framework (EIF), a series of documents that describe implementing Project Server from the perspective of project managers, not that of IT professionals. In particular, the EIF Interview spreadsheet provides sample questions and codes them based on who should answer the question. The EIF's Requirements

Specification document assigns each question to a category that helps you identify how each question can help you with some aspect of the implementation. You can download the EIF (eif.exe) at the following Web site:

```
http://www.microsoft.com/downloads/details.aspx?FamilyId=6CC5B2D6-
    FBB6-4BE0-8046-21B57590F465&displaylang=en
```

The EIF was originally created for Project 2002. Although some portions of the EIF no longer apply, the concepts that it uses to help you determine your requirements are still valid.

Tip

Some of the Project Partners have developed their own questionnaires to help define requirements and design the system. For example, Project Server Support, Inc. has created the EWQ (Enterprise Web Questionnaire), which is role-based and customizable and includes reports. ∎

Conduct interviews

When you conduct interviews, be sure to include more than one person in each role. Because no two people are identical, any two people filling the same role will do things differently and potentially have different needs.

Calculate ROI

As part of your organization's consideration of using Project Server, you should calculate your return on investment (ROI). Implementing Project Server requires software and role-based training for resources; it may also require investments in hardware. Don't skip this important step; use whatever technique your organization has developed to calculate ROI to assess the costs and benefits of implementing Project Server.

Designing the system

You design your Project Server database using the information that you gathered while defining requirements. This information should help you identify which features in Project Server you want to implement.

Note

The System Design workbook in the EIF applies to Project 2002; you can use the workbook as a reference point to help you transfer your requirements information into Project Server database elements, but it will require updating, because Project 2010 contains features not available in Project 2002. ∎

As a part of the design process, the implementation team must also address issues that are not directly related to the construction of the Project Server database. For example, as mentioned earlier, Project Server requires certain software, and the hardware you use affects the performance of Project Server. You must evaluate the software and hardware you have, as well as your network architecture, and factor in the costs and timelines for upgrading as necessary.

Establishing and enforcing organizational standards

To effectively use an organization-wide project management tool, you should use consistent terminology across projects. All managers should apply the same processes and procedures to their projects. If your organization doesn't already have standardized language, processes, and procedures in place, you should develop them. If your organization has established standards, your existing standards may or may not work within the framework of Project Server.

Project Server contains several features that can help you establish and enforce standards in your organization's project management efforts. The Enterprise Global template — comparable to the Global template in Project Professional — contains a collection of all default settings used by projects across your organization. Someone with administrative privileges in your company should customize the Enterprise Global template so that it contains the calendars, views, custom fields, and look-up tables for outline codes that meet the needs of your organization. That way, as project managers create new projects, basing them on the Enterprise Global template enforces standard usage across all the organization's projects. The Enterprise Resource Pool helps you ensure that resource names, definitions, contact information, and calendars are consistent across all projects.

Custom fields

You can create and use custom fields to meet some specific need concerning the data that your organization uses in its projects. Project enables you to create custom fields to assign to either resources or tasks. Because Project Server stores custom fields in the Enterprise Global template, you can enforce standards across projects by setting up custom fields for all project managers to use on all projects.

Cross-Reference

In Chapter 21, you find out about creating custom fields. ■

Outline codes

You can use outline codes to produce work breakdown structures or organization breakdown structures to provide different ways of looking at tasks, resources, and projects. Project uses outline codes to help create these different structures. You can standardize outline codes, also stored in the Enterprise Global template, by using look-up tables for the values that are available for the outline codes. In this way, projects remain standardized because everyone uses the same set of outline codes.

Cross-Reference

In Chapter 7 you find out about outline codes. ■

Views

The administrator creates views in the Project Server database to control the information that various Project Web App users see. For each view, the administrator specifies the format of the view, the grouping of information visible in the view, any filters for the view, and the categories to which the view belongs.

Cross-Reference
In Chapter 21 you find out about creating views. ■

Note
Views that the project manager creates and uses in Project Professional are based on the Global template. The fields used to create views in Project Web App are stored in the Publish database and are unique to Project Web App. Creating a view in Project Professional does not duplicate the view in Project Web App. ■

Calendars
Project makes use of the following four types of calendars:

- **Base calendar:** Provides the source information for the other three types of calendars. Project provides the following types of base calendars (you can customize others):
  - Standard (Monday through Friday, 8 a.m. to 5 p.m., with an hour break)
  - 24-hour
  - Night-shift

Cross-Reference
Chapter 3 covers base calendars. ■

- **Project calendar:** The base calendar that is assigned to a specific project.
- **Resource calendar:** Assumes the working and nonworking times of the project calendar for a resource and can be customized to show the following resource data:
  - Nonstandard working times
  - Planned time off

Cross-Reference
Chapter 10 covers resource calendars. ■

- **Task calendar:** Assumes the working and nonworking times of the project calendar for a task and can be customized to show nonstandard working time.

  The task calendar is useful for situations such as shutting down a server for maintenance during nonbusiness hours.

Cross-Reference
Chapter 4 covers task calendars. ■

Enterprise resource pool
By using an enterprise resource pool, you can share resources among projects and identify conflicts between assignments in different projects. An enterprise resource pool is simply a central repository of all available resources. By storing information about all resources, their calendars, and their

assignments in one place, you can manage resource utilization and sharing more easily because resource information across your company is standardized; every project manager knows the skills and availability of every resource.

Cross-Reference

You find out more about the enterprise resource pool in Chapter 22. ■

Training

Chapters 22 through 24 describe the ways that various organizational members may use Project Server. Each role player requires training to fill his or her role successfully. Factor both the time and the cost of training into your project plan.

Developing a strategy for implementation and configuration

To successfully implement Project Server, you should plan the implementation as a phased process.

Consider first creating a prototype of the system, and from your requirements document, identify a few projects and project teams to participate in the prototype test. Make sure that you select users who represent all the various roles that were identified earlier so you can fully test the system. Also, select projects that don't depend on other projects that won't be a part of the prototype. Design and develop the prototype system, and demonstrate it to the implementation team. Make modifications to the prototype design based on input from the implementation team, and demonstrate the prototype to senior management. Again, make changes as needed.

Caution

Don't assume that project managers who have been using Project Professional for years can build plans that are suitable for the enterprise. For portfolio analysis and resource management to have meaning across the enterprise, plans and resource management must be consistent and standard across projects. ■

After you complete the prototype, you need to develop training materials — and, once again, select projects and project teams that represent each of the roles identified earlier — to participate in the pilot phase. Reset the Project Server database and load the pilot projects. At this stage, you should include at least one project that has external dependencies to another project to test that aspect of usage, and then make adjustments as needed. Train the pilot group and allow its members to use Project Server for at least four reporting cycles. Be sure to solicit feedback so you can address all the issues that arise.

Identify groups to which you can open the system, and plan the timing of each group's introduction to the system. As you introduce each group, you need to add that group's projects to the Project Server database and provide training to the group. Allow enough time for each group to get up and running before introducing the next group.

When you're satisfied that you've ironed out any kinks identified during the prototype and pilot phases, expand the user base of the system again — adding projects to the Project Server database from the groups you identified — and train each new group that begins to use the system. Allow each group to work through at least three reporting cycles before you add any more groups. Remember, as you add new groups, you must provide training to users if you expect a successful implementation.

Avoiding the Pitfalls

You need to consider one last subject: avoiding the known pitfalls associated with implementing Project Server.

When you define requirements, be sure that you ask how many projects each project manager expects to be managing at any one time — and determine the average size of the project. You may discover that some project managers define a project differently than others. This situation presents a problem only if you find that project managers tend to manage many projects — and that each project has only one or two tasks. In cases like these, defining these projects as separate entities in Project 2010 will make maintenance difficult. You may want to combine these smaller projects into one larger Project 2010 file.

Also ask both project managers and team members about the current reporting process. Ask whether the process works or whether people regularly bypass it. If people bypass the reporting process, try to determine why. The process may need to be changed to better suit the needs of those who are using it. If you expect to produce accurate reports and forecasts, the information that you provide to Project 2010 needs to be accurate and timely.

Determine whether your organization considers available resources when it accepts projects. If it does not, it will probably experience changes regularly in project scope, costs, and resources — in which case, Project 2010 won't provide accurate information about resource requirements and availability. Try to get senior management to agree to new methods that include the evaluation of resource needs when considering new projects.

Ask different role players how they deal with problems that arise on projects. If you get different answers from different people, then you don't have a company-wide mechanism in place that deals with resolving problems. In such cases, only some projects will be accurately reporting status, and any comparison or forecasting that you do will be inaccurate. To solve this problem, find a method of reporting status that you can standardize across the organization. Define the tools to use to look for problems, when to use these tools, the options available to solve problems, and who needs to be in the loop to resolve problems.

Note
Don't forget to establish a method to deal with problems while implementing Project Server — that is, make sure that the implementation project itself has a mechanism for addressing problems. ∎

Ask project managers about the methods they use to analyze performance. Determine whether they use earned value, and if so, identify the method of earned value. Project supports only the Percent Complete and Physical Percent Complete methods. If the organization is using some other method or uses methods inconsistently throughout the organization, you can't accurately analyze performance across the organization.

Phase the introduction of Project Server into your environment to avoid disrupting your regular business process — but don't let more than six months pass without introducing a new group to Project Server. The goal is to interrupt your business only minimally, without losing the momentum of the implementation.

Identify the criteria that the implementation team must meet to have the system accepted by management as well as by team members. Keep those criteria in mind through all phases of the process.

Summary

To implement Project Server successfully, you must think of the process as a project in its own right that must also be managed. By its nature, this project is an information-technology (IT) project that affects the majority of your organization.

In this chapter, you reviewed the following items:

- Understanding the basic functioning of Project Server and Project Web App
- Defining requirements
- Using requirements to identify the elements needed for the Project Server database
- Developing a strategy to implement the Project Server database
- Avoiding pitfalls while implementing Project Server

In Chapter 21, you explore the administrative tasks associated with customizing the Project Server database to support your organization.

Project Server and the Administrator

I n Chapter 20, you reviewed design issues and approaches to successfully implementing Project Server. This chapter presents a high-level overview of the kinds of activities a Project Server administrator might perform while setting up and customizing the Project Server environment to meet your organization's needs. This chapter is not intended to cover everything a Project Server administrator might do.

During this stage, you need the skills of the following types of people — and you might use only one person with both sets of skills or you might use multiple people:

- An information technology (IT) person with background in hardware, networking, and connectivity

- A project management (PM) person with extensive knowledge of your organization's needs while managing projects

After the design and implementation team has identified certain components that your organization will use, the IT person can work independently on some tasks while, at the same time, the PM person works independently on other tasks. To complete the setup, these individuals will probably work together. As you read the tasks in this chapter, you can decide who should perform each task.

This chapter is organized to present tasks in the order that they need to be done. Doing things in order when setting up and customizing the Project Server environment can make the implementation run smoother. And you'll find that some of the tasks overlap. For example, you add users to groups and groups to users. In these cases, it really doesn't matter which you do first, because you'll complete one task when you complete the other task.

Note

In the chapter, I used sample data provided by Microsoft and customized for a fictitious company called Contoso. This sample data appears in a virtual machine hosted for me by Project Hosts, a company that provides on demand Microsoft Enterprise Project Management (EPM), CRM, and SharePoint Server (MOSS). You can read about Project Hosts at www.projecthosts.com. ∎

After you have Project Server up and running, you will need to make occasional changes to the environment. For these types of changes, the Project Server administrator should be someone with project management background rather than someone whose experience is only in information technology. The role of administrator for the Project Server environment over time will fall to someone who is more intimately involved with your organization's approach to project management; at that point, it becomes a maintenance job.

Specifying Project Server Features for Your Organization

The Project Server environment contains many useful default values and settings, and you use Project Web App to check and change those settings. Launch Project Web App by starting Internet Explorer and entering the URL for your Project Server environment. The Project Web App home page for the Project Server administrator appears (see Figure 21.1). The Quick Launch pane runs down the left side of the screen.

Note

In earlier versions of Project Server, Project Web App was called Project Web Access. Because you can customize the appearance of Project Web App (and because Project Server 2010 was under construction at the time I wrote this chapter), the figures in this chapter might not match exactly what you see in your own installation of Project Server. For example, the screens still show Project Web Access. ∎

Project Web App Home page for the administrator contains an additional link in the Settings section of the Quick Launch pane: the Server Settings link. From the Server Settings page that appears when you click the Server Settings link, you can manage and customize the Project Server environment and Project Web App (see Figure 21.2).

FIGURE 21.1

The Project Web App home page of the Project Server administrator.

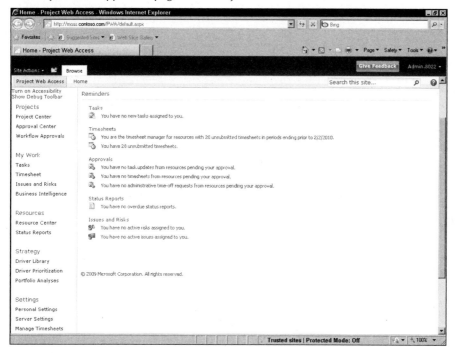

Note

Unless otherwise specified, all the tasks I describe in the following sections assume that you begin by logging on to Project Web App as administrator and then clicking the Server Settings link in the Settings section of the Quick Launch pane. ■

FIGURE 21.2

The Project Server Administrator manages most settings in the Project Server environment from the Server Settings page.

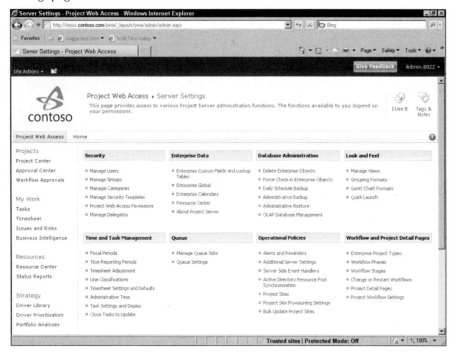

The top portion of the Additional Server Settings page appears in Figure 21.3; you display this page by clicking the Additional Server Settings link in the Operational Policies section of the Server Settings page. On the Additional Server Settings page, the administrator can determine whether your organization will do the following:

- Maintain compatibility with Project Professional 2007.
- Specify the versions of Project Professional that can connect to the server.
- Allow master projects in the Project Server environment.
- Allow projects to use the local base calendar instead of the Enterprise base calendar.
- Set a default currency and decide whether to enforce a uniform, single currency in the Project Server environment (you specify the currency in the Enterprise global template) or permit projects to be published in a variety of currencies.
- Establish resource capacity settings that specify the number of months behind and ahead that the report database maintains data for resources. You also set a schedule for maintaining forward-looking data. This setting helps you manage the size of the reporting database, which affects the speed of producing reports.

- Specify the basis for the resource plan work week; choose to calculate full-time equivalents for your resources, whether from resource base calendars or by setting a number of hours per week.

- Enable task synchronization with Exchange Server.

- Define the default task mode — automatic or manually scheduled tasks — and control whether manually scheduled tasks can be published on the server to team members and whether users can override the default task mode in Project Professional.

FIGURE 21.3

The features on this page control some basic enterprise features in the Project Server environment.

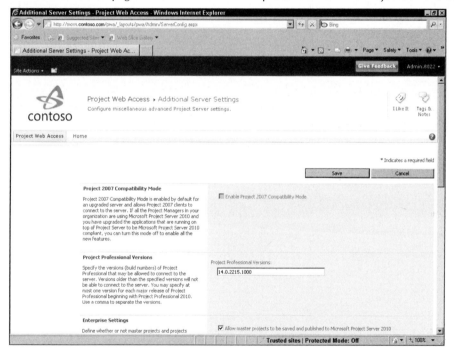

Managing Security Settings

To manage security settings, Project Server uses security templates, groups, and categories.

Managing security templates

The Project Server environment contains some default security templates, which are sets of permissions. You use security templates to assign a set of permissions to a user or a group of users.

You'll find security templates for each of the predefined groups in the Project Server environment. You can modify the default security templates or create your own; click the Server Settings link in the Quick Launch pane and then click Manage Security Templates in the Security section of the Server Settings page. On the Manage Templates page that appears, click the name of the template you want to modify or click New Template at the top of the page. As you can see in Figure 21.4, security templates contain a long list of information — including Category permissions and Global Permissions. You include or exclude permissions in a template by selecting the Allow or Deny check box for that permission.

Note
Typically, you don't "deny" a feature because denying can have far-reaching consquences; instead, you either select or deselect the Allow box. Denying a feature for one user in Group A can result in denying the feature for the same user in Group B, even if you set the permissions for that user to Allow in Group B. ■

Note
Read more about categories later in this chapter. ■

FIGURE 21.4

Use security templates to create sets of permissions.

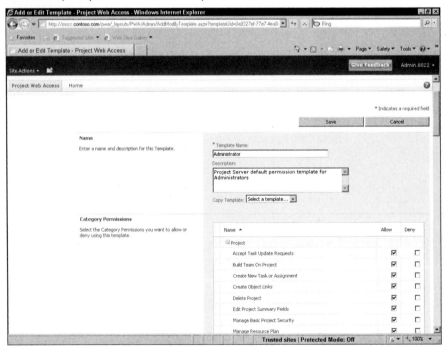

Managing groups

Groups are collections of users. Project Server enables you to group users in some fashion that is logical in your organization. Grouping users makes it easier to assign security permissions, and you can assign one user to more than one group. You find the following predefined groups in the database:

- Administrators
- Executives
- Portfolio Managers
- Project Managers
- Resource Managers
- Team Leads
- Team Members

Double-check the predefined groups and make sure that you have groups that accurately reflect the structure of your organization. Display the page that appears in Figure 21.5 by clicking the Server Settings link in the Quick Launch pane on the left side of the Project Web App window. Then click the Manage Groups link in the Security section of the Server Settings page.

FIGURE 21.5

The groups defined by default in a new Project Server environment.

When you create a new group or modify a group (by clicking the group name), you can add users to the group, assign categories and category permissions to the group, assign global permissions to the group. In Figure 21.6, you see a portion of the Global Permissions part of the Add Groups page. At the bottom of the Global Permission section, you can set permissions using an existing template, and all the available templates appear in a list box next to the Set Permissions with Template button.

FIGURE 21.6

You can assign users and categories to groups.

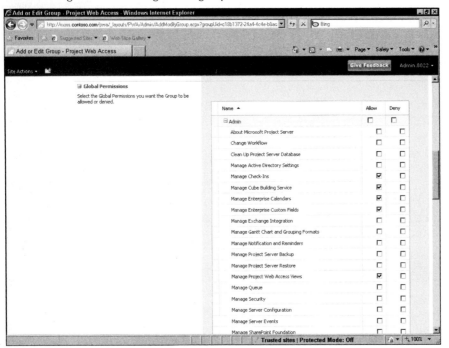

Note

I realize that you're double-checking the groups before adding users to the Project Server environment, so you can't add users to groups. Don't worry, though. When you add users, you get the opportunity to assign them to groups, so you don't need to assign users to groups when you create or modify groups. ∎

Working with categories

Categories are security tools you use to map users and groups to the projects, resources, views, and custom fields the users and groups can see in Project Web App. In other words, in a category, you identify the resources, projects, project views, Project Center views, Portfolio Analyzer views, Resource Center views, and Resource Assignments views to include in the category. The Project Server environment includes, by default, the following categories that are tied to the default groups that were identified in the section "Managing groups," earlier in this chapter:

Note
While it is possible to add a user directly to a category it is highly preferred to add users to groups and groups to categories to simplify security administration. ■

- **My Direct Reports:** Includes all projects and views that are worked on or managed by a user and resources that are managed directly by a user. This category includes the Resource Managers group.

- **My Organization:** Includes all projects, all views, and the following groups: administrators, executives, portfolio managers, project managers, proposal reviewers, and resource managers.

- **My Projects:** Includes all projects that are worked on or managed by a particular user, and the Project Managers, Resource Managers, and Team Leads groups.

- **My Resources:** Includes the projects worked on by resources who report to a specific user, as well as views for those projects. Resource Managers belong to this group.

- **My Tasks:** Includes all projects to which a user is assigned, a view of the assignments for those projects, and the Team Members group.

To create a new category or edit an existing category, Click the Server Settings link in the Quick Launch pane on the left side of the Project Web App window. Then, Click the Manage Categories link in the Security section of the Server Settings page. On the Manage Categories page that lists the categories I just described, click New Category to create your own category or click any category name to edit that category.

If you click an existing category, you see the Add or Edit Category page (the top of the page appears in Figure 21.7), where you select the users and groups that you want to include in this category and the projects that users in this category can view.

Use this page to define the groups you want to include in the category and the projects that users in this category can view.

As you select groups to include in a category, a permissions grid appears that identifies the actions a group can take with projects and resources included in that category. This grid changes as you select different groups, based on the permissions established for the group.

Scroll down and identify the resources whose information will be visible by users included in the category and specify the resource security permissions that Project Server should apply to the resources you select.

Note

I realize that you haven't added users yet, so specifying resources for a category may seem to pose a problem. However, when you add users in the next section, you see that you can assign a user to a category. So you get the opportunity to "double back" and connect the category with the user. ■

Scroll down further, and you can specify the views you want to include in the category; in this section, the views are broken down by Project, Project Center, Resource Assignments, Resource Center, My Work, Resource Plans, Team Tasks, Team Builder, Timesheet, Portfolio Analyses, and Portfolio Analysis Project Selection. In Figure 21.8, I've shown you only a portion of the views you can select to include in a category.

FIGURE 21.8

Specify the views you want to include in the category.

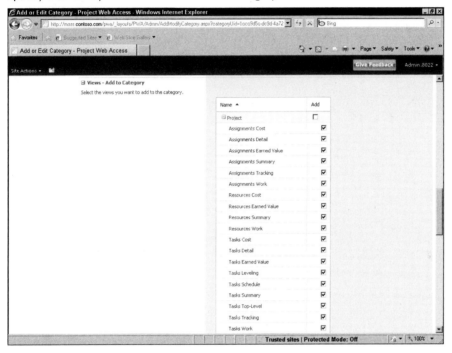

Managing Users

To enable people to use Project Web App, you need to add users. Click the Server Settings link in the Quick Launch pane on the left side of the Project Web App window. Then click the Manage Users link in the Security section of the Server Settings page to display the Manage Users page (see Figure 21.9).

FIGURE 21.9

Use this page to add or modify users.

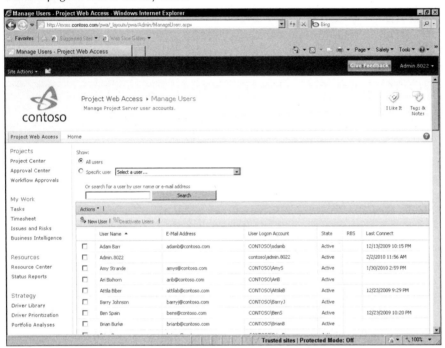

From this page, the Project Server administrator can add, modify, or deactivate user accounts. In addition, the administrator can merge two usernames into one account if a user appears twice in the Log On list under two different names.

Tip

You can print the list of users or export the list to Excel if you click the Actions button above the list of usernames. ■

To add a user, click New User at the top of the list of users. To edit a user, click the user's name. When you add or edit a user, you see a page on which you specify the user's name and other identification information, the type of authentication to use (Windows Authentication or Forms authentication), the user's assignment attributes, Exchange Server details, departments, resource custom fields, security groups, security categories, global permissions, group fields, team details, and system identification data. In Figure 21.10, you see the top of the Edit User page.

FIGURE 21.10

At the top of the page, supply basic user identification information.

Assignment attributes and resource custom fields will be specific to your organization, but typically they include information that indicates whether the resource can be leveled, as well as that resource's base calendar and the default booking type. Similarly, group fields, team details, and system identification data will be specific to your organization.

Security groups and categories include the information discussed previously in this chapter in the sections, "Managing groups" and "Working with categories." You can read about global permissions in the section "Managing security templates."

Tip

To manage security effectively, don't set permissions for individual users. Instead, set permissions in security templates; then assign the security templates to categories and groups. Then, assign users to groups; In this way, individual users inherit the permissions set for a category and group. ∎

Working with Views

A *view* contains a set of fields and filters that Project Web App uses when displaying project information. Through views, the administrator controls what you see in Project Web App because views enable users to examine project information in different ways.

The Project Server database contains many default views. The administrator uses the Manage Views page, shown in Figure 21.11, to create new views and modify or delete existing views. Display this page by clicking the Server Settings link in the Quick Launch pane on the left side of the Project Web App window. Then click the Manage Views link in the Look and Feel section of the Server Settings page.

Before you make changes here — either to create a view or to modify an existing view — I suggest that you continue customizing until you can load a project into the Project Server environment. With a project in the database, you can view that project using each default view that's available in the Project Server environment. You may find that Microsoft has already created the view you want — or a view that's close enough to the one you want that you can modify an existing view.

FIGURE 21.11

On this page, you can create a new view or modify or delete an existing view.

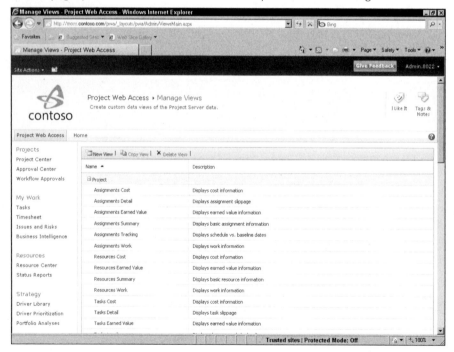

To add a view, click the New View link at the top of the Manage Views page. And, although you can directly edit an existing view by clicking its name, I suggest that you click Copy View at the top of the page to Duplicate the view and then edit the copy.

In Figure 21.12, you see the top of the Edit View page when editing a Project view. When you edit a view, you can't change the View Type at the top of the page, but this field is available when you create a new view. You can select the following view types: Project, Project Center, Resource Assignments, Resource Center, My Work, Resource Plan, Team Tasks, Team Builder, Timesheet, Portfolio Analyses, or Portfolio Analysis Project Selection.

The type of view you select determines the choices that appear as you scroll down the page to create the view. For example, for Project, Project Center, and Resource Assignments views, you can choose any of several Gantt Chart formats that are not available for other views. In Figure 21.13, you see the bottom of the Edit View page when modifying a Project view.

FIGURE 21.12

At the top of the page, specify the type of view, the view name, the tables and fields that you want to appear in the view, and some of the view format options.

FIGURE 21.13

At the bottom of the page, select other view format options, including outline levels, grouping and sorting options, filter options, and security categories.

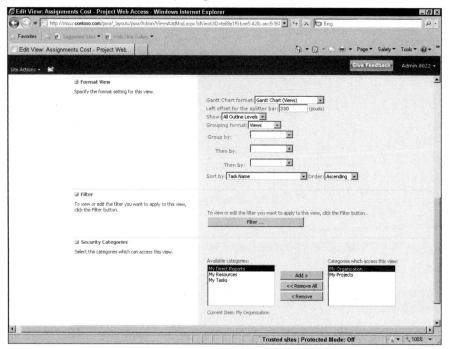

Working with the Enterprise Global Template

You can compare the Enterprise Global template to the Global template in Project Professional. Both serve the same purpose — to store a collection of all default settings that are used by projects across your organization. Each new project is based on the Enterprise Global template, enforcing standard usage across all the organization's projects.

Working with the Enterprise Global

Someone with administrative privileges in your company customizes the Enterprise Global template so it contains the custom fields and calendars that meet the needs of your organization. When you customize the Enterprise Global template, it opens in Project Professional (note the title bar in Figure 21.14 reads "Checked-out Enterprise Global"), where you can customize fields, groups, and filters, just to name a few elements.

Note

A complete list of the elements that you can customize in the Enterprise Global appears on the Configure Project Professional page in Project Web App, which appears when you click the Enterprise Global link in the Enterprise Data section of the Server Settings page. ■

You can customize the Enterprise Global using Project Professional.

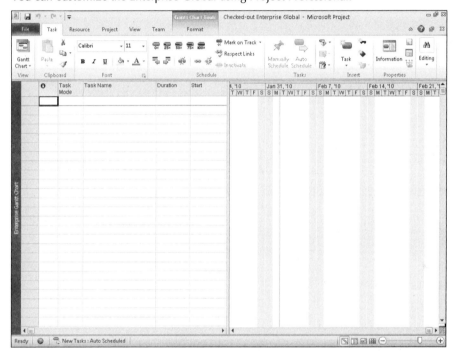

To open the Enterprise Global in Project Professional, click the Server Settings link in the Quick Launch pane on the left side of the Project Web App window. Then, click the Enterprise Global link in the Enterprise Data section of the Server Settings page; the Enterprise Global page appears. Click the Configure Project Professional button.

When you finish, Click the File tab and, in Back Stage view, click Close. You'll be prompted to Check in the Enterprise Global. Click Yes to save your settings and make the Enterprise Global available in Project Web App.

Defining Enterprise custom fields

You set up enterprise custom fields and outline codes in essentially the same way you set up custom fields, as I describe in Chapter 16, and custom outline codes, as I described in Chapter 7, but you use Project Web App.

Click the Server Settings link in the Quick Launch pane on the left side of the Project Web App window. Then, Click the Enterprise Custom Fields and Lookup Tables link in the Enterprise Data section of the Server Settings page. The Custom Fields and Lookup Tables page appears (see Figure 21.15), listing all custom fields that currently exist in the Enterprise Global. Further down the page, you also see a list of defined lookup tables. In the Enterprise Custom Fields table, you can identify the lookup table assigned to a given custom field in the Lookup Table column.

Tip

When you create a custom field and a lookup table, give them the same name so you can easily identify what goes with what. ■

FIGURE 21.15

The list of existing custom fields.

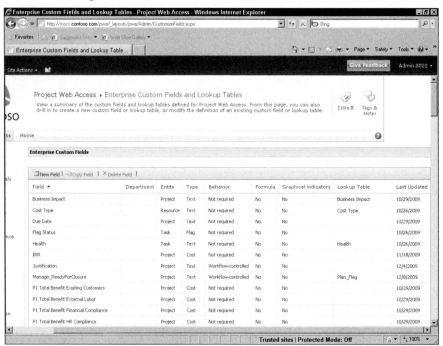

You can edit an existing field by clicking its name; if you want to create a new custom field based on the definition of an existing custom field, click anywhere on the row of the existing custom field and then click the Copy Field button above the list of fields. Or you can click the New Field button to create a new custom field.

For all custom fields, you supply a name. For the Entity, you can select Project, Resource, or Task, and, for the Type, you can select Cost, Date, Duration, Flag, Number or Text. In the Custom Attributes section, you can assign a look-up table or a formula to the custom field. You can opt to assign a custom field to a department. In the Values to Display section, you specify whether you want to see data or graphical indicators; in the Behavior section, you can specify whether the user must supply data for the field.

If you select Task or Resource as the Entity, you can specify calculation methods for both assignment rows and summary rows.

You can click the New Lookup Table button to define a look-up table; the process is the same as the one described in Chapter 16.

If you've already stored information about resources in the Enterprise Resource Pool, you might need to edit that information to assign a value to each resource for the new custom field. Follow the steps described in the section "Creating the Enterprise Resource Pool," later in this chapter, to assign values for the custom field to resources that are stored in the Enterprise Resource Pool.

If you have not yet stored resources in the Enterprise Resource Pool, edit the resources in Project Professional in the usual way. When you import the resources to the Enterprise Resource Pool, you have the option of including the custom fields.

Creating Enterprise calendars

Assign a calendar to the Enterprise Global template to enforce common workdays and work times across all projects. Resources in the Enterprise Resource Pool can use the calendar in the Enterprise Global template unless you override that calendar by assigning a resource-specific calendar.

You set up the calendar for the Enterprise Global template the same way that you set up a calendar for a project, but you start in Project Web App. Click the Server Settings link in the Quick Launch pane on the left side of the Project Web App window. Then, Click the Enterprise Calendars link in the Enterprise Data section of the Server Settings page to display the Enterprise Calendars page, which lists the calendars defined in the Enterprise Global.

You can edit an existing calendar by clicking anywhere on the line where its name appears and then clicking the Edit Calendar button above the list of calendars. If you want to create a new calendar based on an existing calendar, click anywhere on the row of the existing custom field and then click the Copy Calendar button. Or you can click the New Calendar button to create a new calendar. When you edit or create a calendar, Project Web App opens the Change Working Time dialog box in Project Professional (see Figure 21.16).

FIGURE 21.16

You work in Project Professional to create or edit an enterprise calendar.

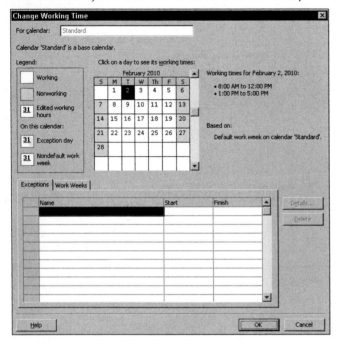

Cross-Reference

For details on making calendar changes, see Chapter 3. ■

Setting Up and Editing Enterprise Resources

The Enterprise Resource Pool is a single repository that project and resource managers can use when assigning resources to their projects. The Enterprise Resource Pool includes resource base calendars and any enterprise resource fields. Project managers borrow resources from the Enterprise Resource Pool to assign them to a project. The Project Server administrator can set the permissions for others to add, edit, and delete resources from the Enterprise Resource Pool. Project Server manages the check-out/check-in operations.

Creating the Enterprise Resource Pool

The easiest way to set up the Enterprise Resource Pool is to use a project that already contains the resources that you want to store in the Enterprise Resource Pool. Then a wizard walks you through setting up the Enterprise Resource Pool.

1. Open Project Professional and make sure that you connect to the Project Server environment; you'll see the Login dialog box, where you enter your username and password and click OK.

2. Open the project containing the local resources you want to load into the Enterprise Resource Pool.

3. Click the Resource tab and, in the Insert group, click the Add Resources button.

4. From the drop-down menu that appears, choose Import Resources to Enterprise. The Import Resources Wizard pane appears on the left side of the Project window (see Figure 21.17).

FIGURE 21.17

Use this wizard to copy local resource fields and resources to Project Server.

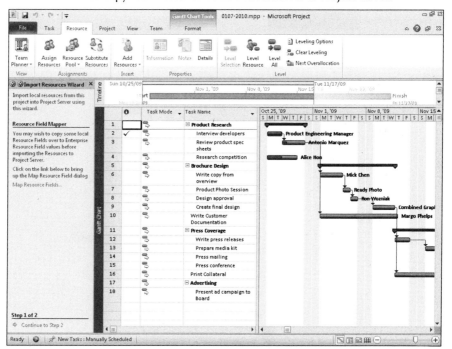

5. If you've created local custom fields for resources, click the Map Resource Fields link to match those local custom fields to custom fields in the Enterprise Global template before you import the resources. That way, Project Server can map the resource fields to the resources when you import the resources.

Note

Custom fields and values for local resources don't appear in the Enterprise Resource Pool unless you map them to enterprise resource fields. ∎

6. Click Continue to Step 2 at the bottom of the Import Resources Wizard pane. The Import Resources Wizard determines the number of local resources in your project and identifies any errors, such as missing information required in the Enterprise Global.

Note

If necessary, double-click a resource name to edit the resource's information and supply any needed information. ∎

7. Identify the resources you want to upload to the Enterprise Resource Pool by choosing Yes in the Import column (see Figure 21.18).

FIGURE 21.18

Identify the resources you want to store in the Enterprise Resource Pool.

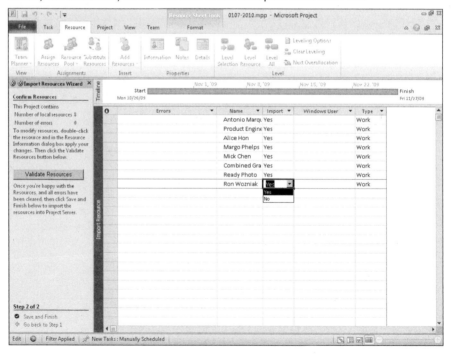

8. Click Save and Finish at the bottom of the Import Resources Wizard pane. Project copies the information for each of the chosen resources to the Enterprise Resource Pool in the Project Server environment.

Editing resources in the Enterprise Resource Pool

After you've stored the information for a resource in the Enterprise Resource Pool, what happens if you need to make a change to that resource? Suppose, for example, that you create a new custom field and you need to assign a value for the field to a resource in the Enterprise Resource Pool. You can edit the resource's information in Project Web App by checking it out, making the change, and then checking it back in. While resources are checked out, others can't make and save changes to the resources.

To make edits, follow these steps:

1. Click the Resource Center link in the Quick Launch pane and display the Resource Center (see Figure 21.19).

The Resource Center.

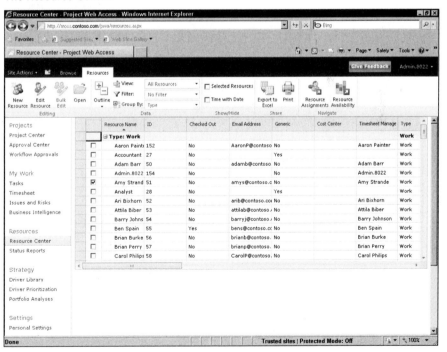

2. Place a check beside the name of the resource you want to edit.

3. In the Editing group on the Resources tab of the Ribbon, click the Edit Resource button to display the Edit Resource page for the selected resource.

4. Make your changes and click Save.

Tip
When you want to edit multiple resources, check each of them. ∎

Managing Timesheet and Task Settings

Project Server contains a variety of timesheet and task settings that you can manage through Project Web App.

Timesheet Periods

Use the Time Reporting Periods page to create reporting periods. When users want to record time spent on project tasks, they will select a time period. You can create 52 weekly time periods, 26 biweekly periods, and 12 monthly periods. You should create periods that match the way project managers want users to report time spent.

To display the Timesheet Periods page, click the Server Settings link in the Quick Launch pane on the left side of the Project Web App window. Then, Click the Time Reporting Periods link in the Time and Task Management section of the Server Settings page.

On the page, define the type of periods you want to create; you can create several periods simultaneously instead of creating periods one at a time. In the bottom portion of the page, you can insert a single period before or after an existing period, and you can delete any period that doesn't have any timesheets associated with it. Note that you can't leave gaps in dates when you set up time periods.

Line classifications

Use this page to set up classifications that match, for example, account codes or cost codes that your company uses in its general ledger. On timesheets, Project Server assigns each timesheet line to a classification so you can match lines that appear on timesheets with account codes or cost codes in your general ledger to help you track project costs.

To display the Edit or Create Line Classifications page, click the Server Settings link in the Quick Launch pane on the left side of the Project Web App window. Then, Click the Timesheet Classifications link in the Time and Task Management section of the Server Settings page.

Timesheet Settings and Defaults

Using the Settings and Defaults page, the administrator can set a variety of default settings related to timesheets. To display this page, click the Server Settings link in the Quick Launch pane on the left side of the Project Web App window. Then, click the Timesheet Settings and Defaults link in the Time and Task Management section of the Server Settings page.

Using this page, you can control whether users enter data against projects or against assignments, and you can set the default timesheet unit. You also can set the default reporting units, set reporting limits per timesheet if appropriate for your organization, set policies regarding reporting of future time or unverified timesheet lines, enable or disable timesheet auditing, and established fixed approval routing (which requires that the same person approve each timesheet).

Task Settings and Display

From the Task Settings and Display page, you can set a variety of options that control the way tasks function and display in Project Web App. To display this page, click the Server Settings link in the Quick Launch pane on the left side of the Project Web App window. Then, click the Task Settings and Display link in the Time and Task Management section of the Server Settings page.

On this page (the top of the page appears in Figure 21.20), you can set the default tracking method for projects that are published to the Project Server environment and permit project managers to select different tracking methods when creating their projects. Project offers four possible ways for users to record actual work in Project Server:

- **Percent of Work Complete:** This method is the fastest way for resources to record time, but it's also the least accurate because it's based on the resource's estimate of the total amount of work to be done, along with the amount that is actually completed. Resources enter the percentage amount.

- **Actual Work Done and Work Remaining:** This method is the middle-of-the-road method. It is both moderately accurate and moderately fast. Resources enter the hours, days, weeks, and so on of the amount of work done and the amount of work remaining to be completed.

- **Hours of Work Done per Time Period:** This method is the most accurate but also the most time-consuming. Resources enter the actual hours worked on each task for a specified time — typically, a day.

- **Free Form:** This method allows users to report by using any available method.

You also can specify whether project managers must use the method you set and whether project managers can change actual time worked. In addition, you can specify how often users should report their hours.

FIGURE 21.20

The administrator can select a default tracking method for published projects and allow managers to choose a different method.

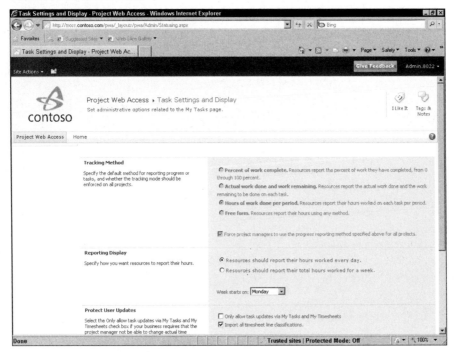

Note
On the Close Tasks to Update page, you can identify tasks to which users can no longer record time. ■

Setting Up Administrative Time

Administrative time is a fact of life, and you use the Administrative Time page (see Figure 21.21) to set up administrative time categories that users can use to record administrative time on timesheets.

To display this page, click the Server Settings link in the Quick Launch pane on the left side of the Project Web App window. Then, click the Administrative Time link in the Time and Task Management section of the Server Settings page.

These categories represent reasons that a resource may not be available for work — for example, vacation, sickness, jury duty, or bereavement. When you check the Always Display box, the administrative time category appears on each resource's timesheet with a work assignment of 0 hours. The resource can fill in time as needed.

FIGURE 21.21

From this page, you can create administrative time categories.

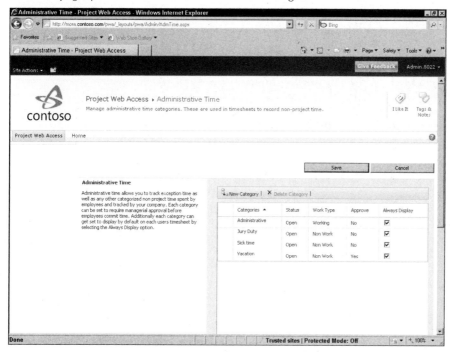

Customizing Project Web App

The administrator can customize Project Web App in the following ways:

- Control the appearance of the Quick Launch pane.
- Control the formatting of Gantt task bar styles and the timescale.
- Establish grouping formats for the timesheet and views in the Project Center and the Resource Center.

Control the appearance of the Quick Launch pane

From the Edit Quick Launch page, you can control what appears in the Quick Launch pane as well as how the Quick Launch pane items appear. To display this page, click the Server Settings link in the Quick Launch pane on the left side of the Project Web App window. Then, click the Quick Launch link in the Look and Feel section of the Server Settings page.

By default, all choices appear in each section of the Quick Launch pane, but you can choose to display only the main headings; then, if you click a main heading, the subordinate headings for that section appear. You also can choose to hide or display SharePoint menu items in the Quick Launch pane.

In addition, you can reorganize or hide default menu items in the Quick Launch pane and, if you click the New Link button, you can add a new menu item to the Quick Launch pane.

Selecting the Gantt taskbar styles and timescales

Using the Gantt Chart Formats page (see Figure 21.22), the administrator can control the appearance of taskbars on Gantt Charts for some or all Gantt Charts that team members and managers view in Project Web App. To display this page, click the Server Settings link in the Quick Launch pane on the left side of the Project Web App window. Then click the Gantt Chart Formats link in the Look and Feel section of the Server Settings page.

FIGURE 21.22

The administrator can modify the appearance of Gantt taskbars on timescales in Project Web App.

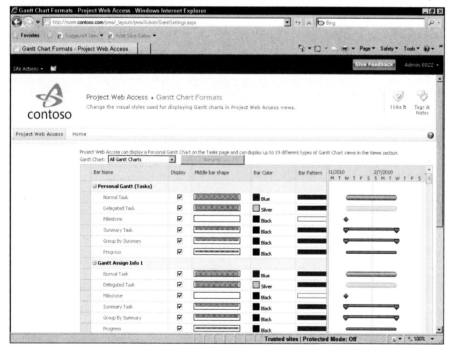

Selecting grouping formats

Using the Grouping Formats page (see Figure 21.23), the administrator can format the appearance of grouped information on the timesheet. The administrator can also define the appearance of up to ten groups for views in the Project Center and the Resource Center. To display this page, click the Server Settings link in the Quick Launch pane on the left side of the Project Web App window. Then click the Grouping Formats link in the Look and Feel section of the Server Settings page.

FIGURE 21.23

Establish grouping formats for the timesheet and for views that appear in the Project Center and the Resource Center.

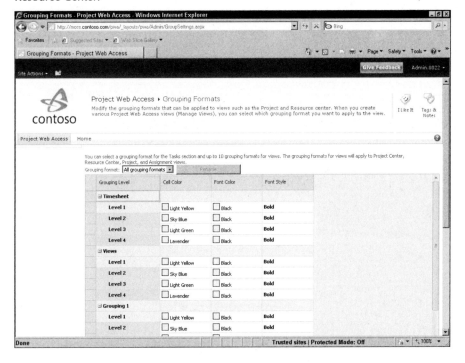

Setting Up Project Detail Pages

Project Server and Project Web App use Project Detail Pages (PDPs) to define the project data that can be viewed and captured in Project Web App. When a user drills down into a project from the Project Center, a set of links appears in a box in the upper-left corner of the page. The project name is the title of the box. In Figure 21.24, the project name is Apparel ERP Upgrade, and the project lists four links, each of which represents a PDP.

FIGURE 21.24

Available Project Detail Pages appear in a box in the upper-left corner of the page when you open a project from the Project Center.

The Project Server administrator can create or modify PDPs; click the Server Settings link in the Quick Launch pane on the left side of the Project Web App window. Then, click the Project Detail Pages link in the Workflow and Project Detail Pages section of the Server Settings page to display the page shown in Figure 21.25.

To edit any particular page, click its name. To add a new page, scroll to the bottom and click the Add Document link. When you create a PDP, you decide what information appears on the page.

FIGURE 21.25

The list of Project Detail Pages defined in the sample company.

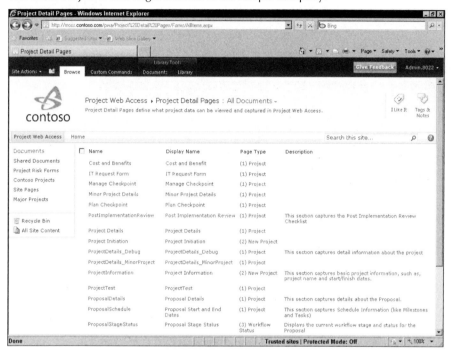

Establishing Enterprise Project Types

The Project Server administrator uses the Enterprise Project Types page (see Figure 21.26) to establish the types of projects available in the Project Server database; Users with appropriate credentials can create projects and associate them with an Enterprise Project Type. When you define an Enterprise Project Type, you define the types of projects users can create, you specify whether the project type is associated with a workflow, and You indicate whether the project type is associated with one or more departments.

FIGURE 21.26

The list of Enterprise Project Types defined in the sample company.

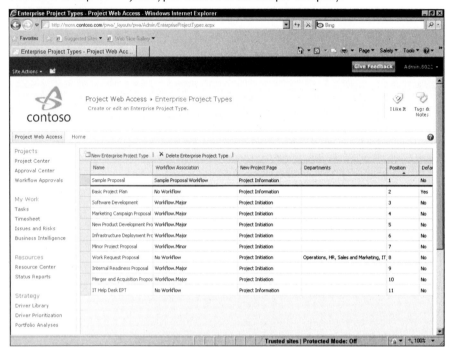

If you opt not to associate an Enterprise Project Type with a workflow, then you select the PDP that users see when they create a new project of this type. If you opt to associate the Enterprise Project Type with a workflow, then the PDP that appears when a user opens the project in the Project Center is driven by the workflow.

To create an Enterprise Project Type, click the Server Settings link in the Quick Launch pane on the left side of the Project Web App window. Then, click the Enterprise Project Types link in the Workflow and Project Detail Pages section of the Server Settings page. On the page that appears, click the New Enterprise Project Type button and fill in the form.

Workflow Phases and Stages

Using the Workflow Phases link in the Workflow and Project Detail Pages section of the Server Settings page, you can create the workflow phases your organization wants to use or modify existing workflow phases. For each phase, you supply a name and an optional description.

Using the Workflow Stages link in the Workflow and Project Detail Pages section of the Server Settings page, you can create workflow stages associated with a given phase; you can incorporate deliverables as workflow stages. When you create a workflow stage, you provide a name and optional description. You also can supply a description that users see when they submit workflow information.

You associate the workflow phase with a workflow stage and you select the Project Detail Page that appears as the introduction page when the project enters the workflow stage. You also can:

- Select and order the Project Detail Pages that are visible during the workflow stage
- Set workflow-specific descriptions for those Project Detail Pages,
- Specify whether a particular Project Detail Page requires user attention.

On occasion, the Project Server administrator may need to make modifications to workflow, changing or restarting the workflow for a particular Enterprise Project Type, or skip to a specified workflow stage for a particular Enterprise Project Type. To make such changes, use the change or Restart Workflows link in the Workflow and Project Detail Pages section of the Server Settings page.

Housekeeping Chores

As you would expect, some housekeeping tasks need to be done to keep the Project Server environment in good working order:

- On occasion, check in projects and resources
- Delete information from the Project Server databases
- Back up and restore the Project Server databases

Checking in enterprise projects and resources

Occasionally, as administrator, you may need to check in projects or resources. For example, after hours, you may be planning maintenance to the Project Server environment and someone may have left work without closing a project.

Instead of tracking down the machine of the person who checked out the project, you can use the Force Check-in Enterprise Objects page. To display this page, click the Server Settings link in the Quick Launch pane on the left side of the Project Web App window. Then click the Force Check-in Enterprise Objects link in the Database Administration section of the Server Settings page.

Note
When you force check-in, none of the edits made by the person who checked out the project will be saved. ∎

You can check in Enterprise projects, resources, custom fields, calendars, look-up tables for Enterprise custom fields, and resource plans. Use the list box at the top of the page to select the type of object you want to check in. Then check the object and click the Check-In link.

Managing information in the Project Server databases

The administrator can (and should) periodically delete old information from the Project Server environment, because response time from the database increases as the database grows in size. To help maintain speed for team members when they work in Project Web App, the administrator can delete old, unnecessary information by using the Delete Enterprise Objects page (see Figure 21.27). To display this page, click the Server Settings link in the Quick Launch pane on the left side of the Project Web App window. Then, click the Delete Enterprise Objects link in the Database Administration section of the Server Settings page.

Click the option buttons next to the type of items that you want to delete; then, select the objects you want to delete and click the Delete button.

Tip
If a project site exists for a project you are deleting, you probably want to delete both the project and the site. ∎

FIGURE 21.27

Use this page to reduce the size of the database and speed the processing in the database.

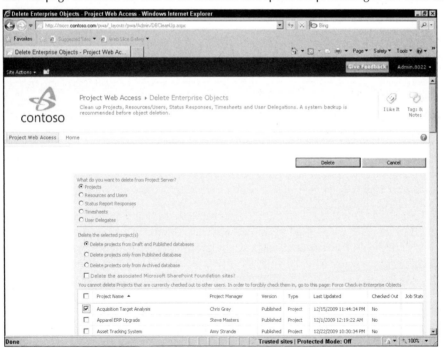

Backing up and restoring

Backing up and restoring the Project Server database is one of the most important actions you can take to protect your data. The backups you create in Project Web App are item-level back-ups designed to work with SQL Server database backups — not in place of SQL Server database backups.

From the Daily Backup Schedule page, you can set up a schedule for backing up items in the Project Server environment, and you can specify the number of versions of the backup that you want to keep. Project Server stores the backups in the Archive database, and the more versions you keep, the larger the Archive database becomes.

To display this page, click the Server Settings link in the Quick Launch pane on the left side of the Project Web App window. Then click the Daily Schedule Backup link in the Database Administration section of the Server Settings page.

The administrator can back up items in the Project Server databases outside the daily schedule using the Administrative Backup page. To display this page, click the Server Settings link in the Quick Launch pane on the left side of the Project Web App window. Then click the Administrative Backup link in the Database Administration section of the Server Settings page and select the items you want to back up.

When you need to restore a backup, use the Administrative Restore page. To display this page, click the Server Settings link in the Quick Launch pane on the left side of the Project Web App window. Then click the Administrative Restore link in the Database Administration section of the Server Settings page. From the Item list box, select the type of object you want to restore. You can selectively restore projects; to do so, click a project and then click the Restore button.

Managing the queue

Project Server uses a service to queue work requests until the server becomes available to act on the request. This functionality works very much the way a print queue works and improves the performance of Project Server.

You can control the behavior of the queue. Using the Queue Settings page (see Figure 21.28), you can establish or change settings for the Project queue or the Timesheet queue. You can set the maximum number of job processor threads, the polling interval, the subjob retry interval, the sub-job retry limit, the SQL retry interval, and the SQL retry limit for both types of queues.

To display this page, click the Server Settings link in the Quick Launch pane on the left side of the Project Web App window. Then click the Queue Settings link in the Queue section of the Server Settings page.

FIGURE 21.28

Establish or modify queue settings.

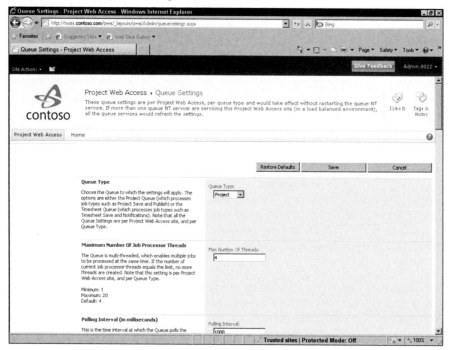

Using the Manage Queue page, you can view the current status of queued jobs and, if you want, retry or cancel jobs. To display this page, click the Server Settings link in the Quick Launch pane on the left side of the Project Web App window. Then click the Manage Queue link in the Queue section of the Server Settings page.

Managing the OLAP cube

You can use the OLAP Database Management page to create, configure, build and delete OLAP database cubes used for reporting. To display this page, click the Server Settings link in the Quick Launch pane on the left side of the Project Web App window. Then click the OLAP Database Management link in the Database Administration section of the Server Settings page.

Click the Configure button to display the Database Configuration page (see Figure 21.29). From this page, you can establish cube building settings, configure the cube's dimensions, built-in measures, and calculated measures. You can add custom fields as dimensions, measures, or calculated members.

FIGURE 21.29

The page you use to configure an OLAP database cube.

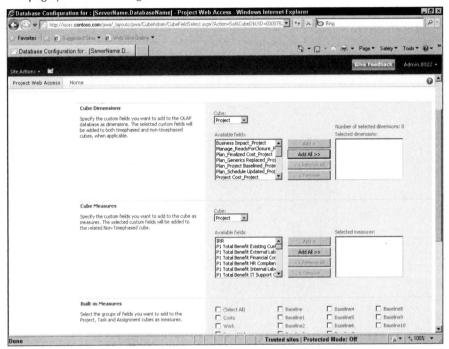

Tip

Use SQL Server Analysis Services to give users access to the OLAP cube. ∎

Managing operations

The Project Server administrator also can control a variety of operational policies.

For example, using the Alerts and Reminders page the administrator can set up the SMTP mail server used in the E-Mail Notifications and Reminder feature of Project Server, and customize the default e-mail message that is sent. To display this page, click the Server Settings link in the Quick Launch pane on the left side of the Project Web App window. Then click the Alerts and Reminders link in the Operational Policies section of the Server Settings page.

Using the Active Directory Enterprise Resource Pool Synchronization page (see Figure 21.30), you can select an Active Directory Group with which to synchronize the Enterprise Resource Pool, check the status of the synchronization, schedule synchronization, and choose to reactivate inactive users. To display this page, click the Server Settings link in the Quick Launch pane on the left side of the Project Web App window. Then click the Active Directory Resource Pool Synchronization link in the Operational Policies section of the Server Settings page.

The Operational Policies section of the Server Settings page contains three links related to the SharePoint-based Project sites that you can use in Project Server:

- The Project Sites page
- The Project Site Provisioning Settings page
- The Bulk Update Project Sites page

Using the Project Sites page, the Project Server administrator can create a SharePoint site, change the address of a site, delete a site, and synchronize access to sites. To display this page, click the Server Settings link in the Quick Launch pane on the left side of the Project Web App window. Then click the Project Sites link in the Operational Policies section of the Server Settings page.

FIGURE 21.30

Use this page to establish synchronization settings for the Enterprise Resource Pool and an Active Directory Group.

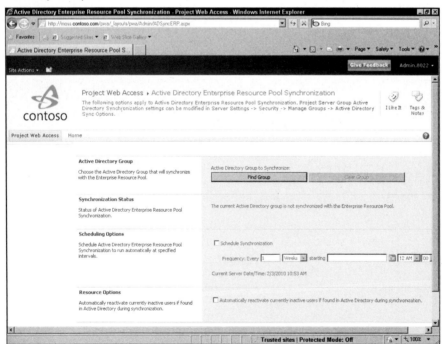

On the Project Site Provisioning Settings page, the Project Server administrator can perform several essential tasks:

- Select the default Web application and site URL under which SharePoint project sites are provisioned
- Establish default site properties
- Select a provisioning mode when projects are published
- Identify the way Project Server grants access to project sites.

To display the Project Site Provisioning Settings page, click the Server Settings link in the Quick Launch pane on the left side of the Project Web App window. Then click the Project Site Provisioning Settings link in the Operational Policies section of the Server Settings page.

On the Bulk Update Project Sites page, the Project Server administrator can

- Update URL paths to one or more project sites
- Repair broken content-type links
- Decide whether Project Server synchronizes permissions to project sites while updating site paths.

Summary

Customizing the Project Server environment to meet your organization's needs is a task that initially requires the joint efforts of a person with project management background and a person with information technology background. Some of the customization tasks are performed in Project Professional and the rest are performed in Project Web App. When the database is set up, the Project Server administrator's role becomes mostly occasional maintenance.

In this chapter, you reviewed tasks a Project Server administrator can use to customize the Project Server environment to meet the needs of your organization.

In Chapter 22, you see how the Project Manager works with Project Professional and Project Web App.

Project Server and the Project Manager

Project Server offers a wide variety of tools to help project managers shepherd their projects to completion more effectively. In this chapter, you learn how to connect to Project Server, create a Web-based project, use the Enterprise Resource Pool to assign resources to your project, track project progress, and update workflows while managing projects.

Note

In the chapter, I used sample data provided by Microsoft for a fictitious company called Contoso. This sample data appears in a virtual machine hosted for me by Project Hosts, a company that provides on-demand Microsoft Enterprise Project Management (EPM), CRM, and SharePoint Server (MOSS). You can read about Project Hosts at www.projecthosts.com. ■

To use a desktop client version of Project and Project Server, you must be using Project Professional; if you are using Project Standard, you can't use Project Server and Project Web App.

Note

In earlier versions of Project Server, Project Web App was called Project Web Access. Because you can customize the appearance of Project Web App (and because Project Server 2010 was under construction at the time I wrote this chapter), the figures in this chapter might not match exactly what you see in your own installation of Project Server. For example, the screens still show Project Web Access. ■

The information in this chapter is only an overview of the kinds of things a project manager can do using Project Professional and Project Web App.

Using Project Web App to Manage Projects

The *project manager* (PM) is the person who builds and maintains the project schedule and makes task assignments — in effect, the project's "boss." The PM can use either Project Professional or Project Web App to create the schedule and make assignments to team members to track their activities. In this section, we take a look at a few of the things you can do using Project Web App.

Cross-Reference

To log in to Project Web App, you use the same method as team members use; see Chapter 23 for details. ■

Updating a schedule in Project Web App

You can make changes to a project schedule using Project Web App. When you log in to Project Web App, your Home page appears; it will look similar to the one shown in Figure 22.1

FIGURE 22.1

The Home page of Project Web App.

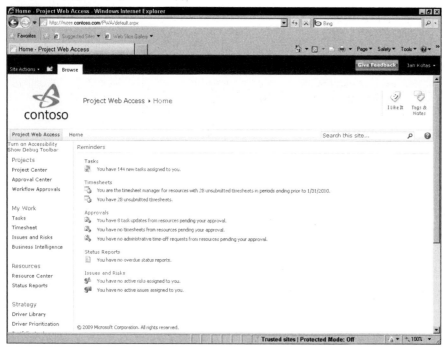

To adjust a project schedule, start by clicking the Project Center link in the Quick Launch on the left side of your Project Web App Home page. Assuming that your company takes advantage of the Workflow feature of SharePoint Server in much the same way as the sample company, Contoso, does, the Projects by Phase view of the Project Center lists each of your projects by workflow phase (see Figure 22.2). You can use the Views list box in the Data group on the Projects tab of the Ribbon to switch to any other available views of your list of projects and their tasks.

To work with a particular project, click the link in the Project Name column. Project Web App displays a project detail page, and the page you see depends on your Project Server settings. In Contoso, you see the Project Detail Pages – Schedule page, which lists the tasks in the project; the tasks are collapsed to a summary task level. You can click the Outline button in the Data group on the Schedule Tools Task tab of the Ribbon to expand the outline and view the tasks under each summary task, or you can click the plus sign beside a summary task name to expand that summary task, as I did to the *Scope* and *Documentation* summary tasks in Figure 22.3.

FIGURE 22.2

The Summary view of the Project Center.

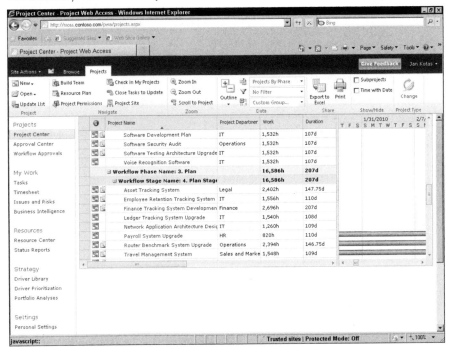

FIGURE 22.3

A Project Detail Pages – Schedule page.

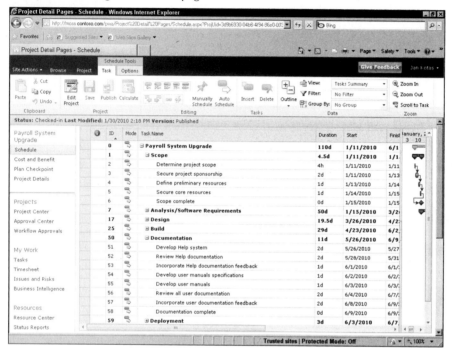

To modify anything about a particular project plan, first you have to check the project out. Click the Edit Project button in the Project group on the Schedule Tools Task tab of the Ribbon, and Project Web App displays the project's status below the Ribbon (see Figure 22.4).

You change a task in Project Web App the same way you change a task in Project Professional. For example, you can change a task's duration by simply typing in a new duration.

To add a task, click the name of the task below the place where you want to insert a new task. Then, on the Schedule Tools Task tab of the Ribbon, in the Tasks group, click the Insert button. A new row appears; type a task name and assign a duration. To link the task to another task, select the tasks and click the Link Tasks button in the Editing group of the Schedule Tools Task tab on the Ribbon.

FIGURE 22.4

Once you check out a project, the project's status appears just below the Ribbon.

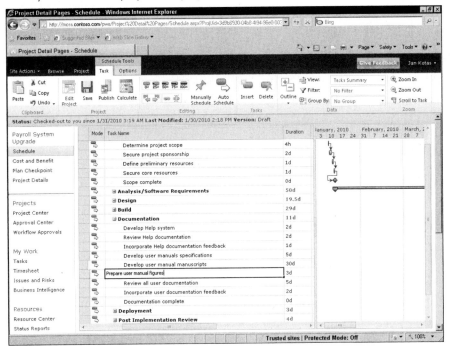

Saving changes

To save the changes you make to a project schedule, click Save in the Project group on the Schedule Tools Task tab. To publish the changes to the Project Server database, click Publish in the Project group on the Schedule Tools Task tab.

When you finish working with a project schedule, you should check it in so others can work with it. Click the Project tab on the Ribbon and, in the Project group, click Close. Project Server prompts you to check in the project (see Figure 22.5). Click Yes, and the Project Center reappears.

FIGURE 22.5

FIGURE 22.5

Check in a project after you finish working with it.

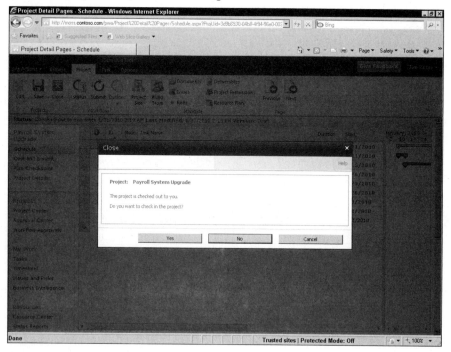

Assigning resources using Project Web App

In addition to modifying a schedule, you can assign resources to a project by following these steps:

1. Log in to Project Web App.

Tip
The Home page that appears in Project Web App is customizable; see Chapter 23 for details. ∎

2. Display the Project Center page by clicking Project Center in the Quick Launch pane on the left side of the page.

3. Click the name of the project for which you want to build a team. Project Web App displays the appropriate Project Details page for the project.

4. Click the Project tab on the Ribbon.

5. In the Navigate group, click the Build Team button. Project Web App displays a list of resources on the left side of the Build Team page (see Figure 22.6). You see only the resources you have permission to view within your RBS code. On the right side of this page, you see the resources already at work on your project.

Note

You read more about RBS codes later in this chapter in the section, "Replacing generic resources with real resources." ■

Tip

You can use a filter to find resources with specified skills. Click the Filter button in the Data group on the Team tab of the Ribbon and select or create a filter. ■

FIGURE 22.6

Build a team for a project using Project Web App.

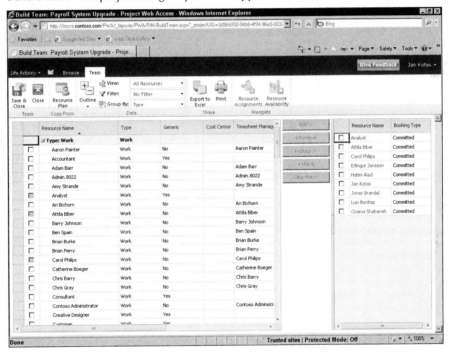

6. In the list on the left, select the resources you want to add to the project.

7. Click the Add button.

8. To assign the resource, click the Save & Close button on the Build Team page. But before you assign the resource, read on.

You can replace generic resources easily. Check the box beside the generic resource on the right and then click the Match button. Project Web App displays, on the left, real resources with the same skills as the selected generic resource (see Figure 22.7). To replace the generic resource, check the box on the left side of the window beside the real resource you want to assign to your project, and then click the Replace button.

Note
You read more about generic resources later in this chapter in the section, "Replacing generic resources with real resources." ∎

Before you add a particular resource to your project, you can check whether he or she is available by viewing an availability graph: Place a check beside the resource in the list on the left, and then click the Resource Availability button in the Navigate group on the Team tab of the Ribbon (refer to Figure 23.7). Project opens a separate page to display the Resource Availability graph (see Figure 22.8).

FIGURE 22.7

Finding a match for a generic resource.

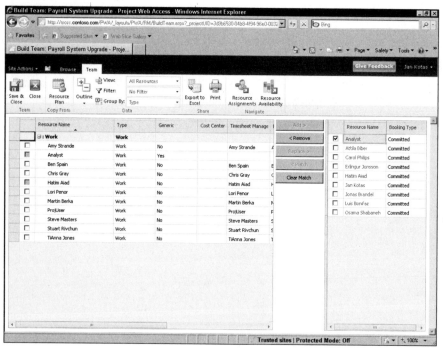

FIGURE 22.8

The View Resource Availability graph you see when you click the Availability button.

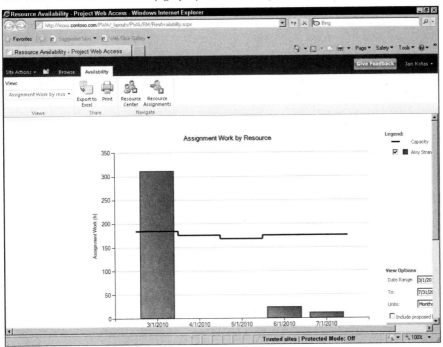

You also can view the resource's assignments from the Build Team page: Place a check beside the resource's name in the list on the left, and then click the Resource Assignments button in the Navigate group. Or, on the Resource Availability page, click the Resource Assignments button in the Navigate group. Either way, Project Web App displays assignments for the selected resource on a separate page that shows assignments for all selected resources (see Figure 22.9).

You can click the X in the upper-right corner to return to the Build Team page. From there, you can click Save & Close to save the changes you made to the project's resource team. When you finish working with the project, don't forget to click the Projects tab and check in the project; see the preceding section for details.

FIGURE 22.9

View assignments for a selected resource.

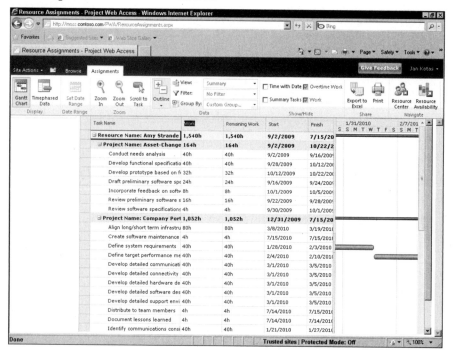

Opening a published project in Project Professional

You might find, while working with a project in Project Web App, that you really need some Project Professional tools. For example, you might want to use the Team Planner as you build your resource team. You can open the project in Project Professional (as described in the next section) or you can use Project Web App to open the project in Project Professional by following the steps given here:

Note

The method you choose for opening the project is strictly a matter of personal preference; neither method is better than the other. ■

1. Click the Project Center link in the Quick Launch pane.

2. Click in the Project Name box to select the project you want to open.

   Be sure you don't click the link representing the project's name; instead, click a white space *near* the name to select the box.

3. On the Projects tab, in the Project group, click the Open button (see Figure 22.10).

4. Click In Project Professional for Editing.

   Project Web App opens Project Professional and displays the project you selected (see Figure 22.11).

Using Project Web App to open a project in Project Professional.

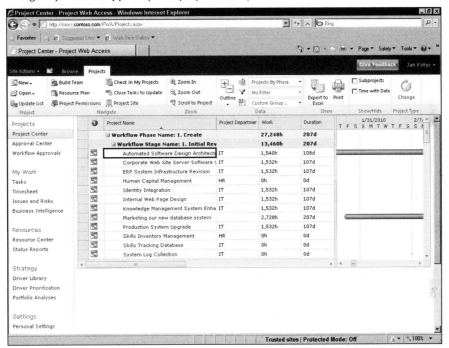

Work with the project as needed; when you finish, save and publish the changes (as described in the sections, "Storing a draft project in the Project Server database" and "Publishing project information"). Then check the project in, as described in the section, "Closing a project stored in the Project Server database."

After you check the project in and close Project Professional, you return to your Project Web App session.

FIGURE 22.11

The project selected in Project Web App opens in Project Professional.

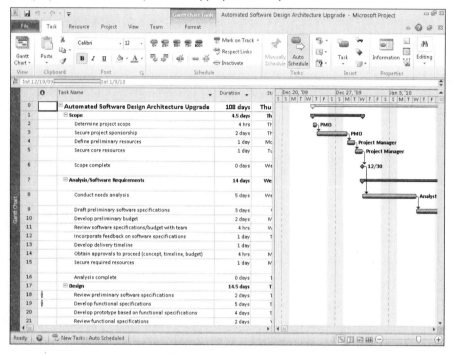

Working with Web-Based Projects in Project Professional

Although you can use Project Web App to perform some project management tasks, other activities — such as creating a new Web-based project and resolving resource overallocations — are best suited to Project Professional. This section provides a look at how you use Project Professional with Web-based projects.

Connecting to Project Server

If you plan to use Project with Project Server (as opposed to using Project in a standalone environment), you need a Project Server account — which enables you to log in to Project Server while working in Project Professional.

Creating a Project Server login account

You can easily create your own Project Server account from within Project after you know the URL for your Project Server environment; your Project Server administrator will most likely give you this URL. Unless your organization uses multiple instances of Project Server, creating your Project Server account is, essentially, a one-time activity; when you have a Project Server account, you use it every time you want to log in to the Project Server database.

To create a Project Server Account, follow these steps:

1. Start Project Professional.

2. Click the File tab and click Info.

3. Click the Manage Accounts button and, from the drop-down list that appears, click Configure Accounts. You see the Project Server Accounts dialog box (see Figure 22.12).

FIGURE 22.12

Use this dialog box to add a Project Server login account and to specify connection state detection options.

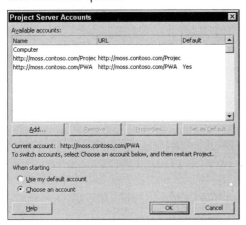

4. Click the Add button. You see the Account Properties dialog box (see Figure 22.13).

5. In the Account Name box, enter a name for the account. You must use a name that no other user is already using — for example, your own name.

6. In the Project Server URL box, enter the URL for the location of your Project Server database.

7. (Optional) If you intend to create more than one account and you want the current account to be your default login account, select the Set As Default Account check box.

FIGURE 22.13

Use this dialog box to create a new Project Server account.

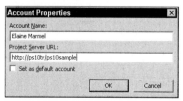

Note

Why create another account? Well, if your company uses more than one instance of Project Server, you need more than one account to access the correct database. ■

8. Click OK. You see the Project Server Accounts dialog box again.

9. At the bottom of the box, choose whether you want to log in automatically using your default account or select an account manually.

   If you choose the Use My Default Account option button, Project attempts to detect the Project Server database when you open Project in the future. If you choose the Choose An Account option button, Project prompts you to select a login profile each time you open Project in the future, giving you the opportunity to choose the account that you want to use to log in to Project Server.

Logging in to Project Server from Project Professional

If you opted (in the preceding section) to choose a Project Server account when you start Project Professional, then you have the option of working with a project while connected to Project Server or working with the project in a standalone environment.

For example, suppose you use Project from a notebook computer while traveling. If you opt to choose a Project Server account when you open Project (as described in the preceding section), you can click the Work Offline button in the Login dialog box (see Figure 22.14) and open Project Professional without connecting to Project Server. If you chose to detect the connection state automatically, you won't connect to Project Server when you start Project if your computer isn't connected to the network.

Tip

If you are connected to the Project Server environment and you see a message that indicates that you're not allowed to log in because the environment is unavailable, double-check with the Project Server administrator and make sure you've been set up in Project Server as a user who belongs to a group with login privileges (Project Managers or higher). ■

FIGURE 22.14

You see this dialog box if you choose to select a Project Server account when opening Project Professional.

Understanding the structure of the Project Server Database

The Project Server database I keep referring to is actually a collection of databases. As a project manager, you interact with several of these databases — and most of the interaction is invisible to you. You'll work better, however, if you understand the interactions that deal with draft projects versus published projects.

Whenever you create a project in Project Professional, you can — and should — save a copy of it to your local hard drive (as described in Chapter 3). At some point, you'll want to place the project in the Project Server database — but you might not be finished working with your project, and not yet ready for the world at large to have access to it. At this point, you save a draft project in the Project Server database. You can continue to work with the draft project stored in the Project Server database and modify it, and the project won't be visible to other users.

When you're ready to let the world see your project, you publish it. At this point, two versions of your project reside in the Project Server database — the draft version and the published version. You can continue to work with your project in Project Professional; typically, you'll work with the draft version and ultimately republish it to update the version that everyone else sees.

When you work with draft or published projects in Project Professional, you take advantage of the local cache introduced in Project 2007; the local cache speeds up the interaction of Project Professional and the Project Server database.

Enabling task reassignment for team members

You can control whether team members can reassign tasks in your project in Project Web App. In Project Professional, follow these steps:

1. Open the project.

2. Click the File tab and, from Backstage view, click Options to display the Project Options dialog box.

3. Click Advanced on the left (see Figure 22.15).

FIGURE 22.15

Set task reassignment permission in the Project Options dialog box.

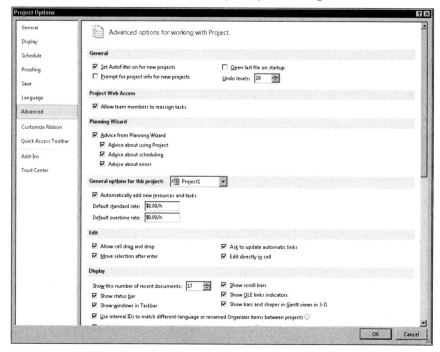

4. To permit task reassignment in Project Web App, select the Allow Team Members to Reassign Tasks check box. You find the check box under the Project Web Access heading.

5. Click OK to save your settings.

Storing a draft project in the Project Server database

You can store draft projects in the Project Server database before you're ready for the world of Project Web App users to view those projects. You must first create this draft version before Project Professional will let you publish your project. When the "published" state is assigned to a project, the world of Project Web App users can view it. To store a project in the database, open Project Professional and log in to Project Server (refer to the section "Logging in to Project Server from Project Professional," earlier in this chapter). Then open the project you want to store in the Project Server database, and click the File tab. From Backstage view, click Save As. The Save to Project Server dialog box appears (see Figure 22.16); any custom fields stored in the Enterprise Global template appear at the bottom of the box.

FIGURE 22.16

When the Enterprise Global template contains custom fields, the Save to Project Server dialog box displays them.

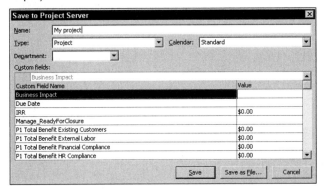

Publishing project information

When you're ready for the world to see your project, you publish it. Save it first, using the technique described in the preceding section. Then, to publish it, click the File tab and, from Backstage view, click Publish. You see the Publish Project dialog box shown in Figure 22.17.

When you click Publish, Project saves the project to the Project Server database and anyone with proper credentials can view your project. In addition, a SharePoint site is created by default for your project.

FIGURE 22.17

When you click Publish in this dialog box, your project appears in the Project Server database and everyone with privileges can view it.

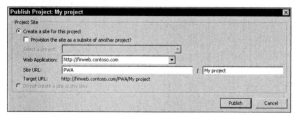

Opening a project

Even if you're connected to the Project Server database, in Project Professional you have the option of opening the original project schedule stored on your hard drive, or you can open either the draft version or the published version stored in the Project Server database. Click the File tab and, in Backstage view, click Open to display the Open dialog box (see Figure 22.18).

FIGURE 22.18

Using this dialog box, you can open an original .mpp file or open the draft or published project stored in the Project Server database.

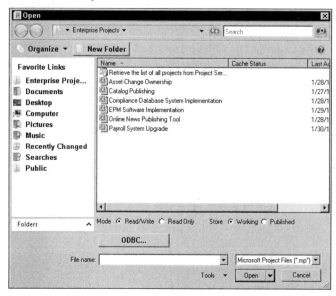

To open the original Project .mpp file, use the links on the left side of the dialog box to navigate to the location where you stored the .mpp file on your hard drive, click that file, and then click Open.

Opening a project stored in the Project Server database takes a bit more thought because you have to decide whether you want to open the draft version or the published version of the project. But before I discuss those choices, I have to address the fact that the first time you display the Open dialog box, no projects appear at all.

Understanding the Open dialog box

The first time you display the Open dialog box, no projects appear in it; instead, you see only one item — the Retrieve the List Of All Projects from Project Server item. Don't panic. This condition exists only because you haven't opened a project stored in the Project Server database yet. The situation I'm about to describe reminds me of the age-old question: "Which came first, the chicken or the egg?" (and makes my head hurt, I might add).

When you are connected to the Project Server database and you open a project in Project Professional, Project Professional stores a copy of the project in the local cache; the local cache serves the purpose of improving performance when exchanging information between Project Professional and the Project Server database.

The Open dialog box lists projects stored in the local cache. So you won't see any projects listed in the Open dialog box until you've opened a project; the *next* time you display the Open dialog box, the project you opened will appear in the list, along with the Retrieve the List of All Projects from Project Server item. If you see only one item — the Retrieve the List of All Projects from Project Server item — in the Open dialog box, then you simply haven't opened any projects yet, so none are stored in your local cache.

You can easily view all the available draft or published projects by double-clicking the Retrieve the List of All Projects from Project Server item.

Opening a draft project or a published project

The Mode options and the Store options at the bottom of the dialog box help determine both the projects you can open and the way in which you can work with those projects. These options work together.

The Store options determine whether you select a draft version of a project or a published version of a project. *Working* represents the projects stored in the draft database, whereas *Published* represents the projects stored in the published database. So, to view and open projects in the draft database, you click the Working option, and to view and open published projects, you click the Published option. By default, Project displays draft projects in the Open dialog box; you can view published projects by switching the Store option. And yes, if you don't see any difference between the two lists, all draft projects have been published.

The Mode options determine whether you can save changes to a project you open — but the Mode options work with the Store options. When you select Working as the Store option, you'll notice that you can choose either Read/Write or Read Only as the Mode option. But when you select Published as the Store option, your choices for the Mode option are narrowed to the Read Only option. By implication, you can make changes only to a project stored in the draft database, which is the default database from which to open projects.

If you open a draft project, you can save the changes you make to it in the Project Server database by saving and then publishing the project (as described earlier in this chapter).

If you open a published project, you cannot save changes to it directly, but you can save them in a roundabout fashion. . You might want to use a published version to create a draft version with which to work. Open the published version, which will be a read-only copy, and then follow the steps provided earlier in this chapter to save a draft version; when you supply the filename, use the same name as that of the published version. You'll see a prompt that indicates that you'll be over-writing an existing project. If you choose to proceed, your draft copy will be the same as the pub-lished copy.

Tip
You can use the same technique to create a local .mpp version of a project, whether draft or published. Open a project from the Project Server database, click the File tab and, from Backstage view, choose Save As. In the Save to Project Server dialog box, click the Save as File button. ■

Closing a project stored in the Project Server database

When you close a Web-based project, Project prompts you to check in the project (see Figure 22.19). When you opened the project, you checked it out, and while a project is checked out, nobody else can open it in Project Professional and work on it. So, when you close the project, Project Professional prompts you to check the project in, and you should check it in.

FIGURE 22.19

Checking in a project opened in Project Professional.

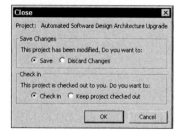

If the project remains checked out, you can check it in from Project Web App. In the Quick Launch pane of Project Web App, click the Project Center link. Then, in the Navigate group of the Projects tab, click the Check in My Projects button. Project displays the Force Check-in Enterprise Objects page, where you place a check beside the project you want to check in and then click the Check In button.

Cross-Reference

See Chapter 21 for more information on using the Force Check-in Enterprise Objects page. ■

Assigning Resources to Projects

If your organization uses Project Server, managers have some additional powerful tools at their disposal to assign resources and manage resource use. Your organization will probably use the Enterprise Resource Pool that's available in Project Server — a comprehensive list of your organization's resources, both human and inanimate. The Project Server administrator initially builds the Enterprise Resource Pool and imports existing projects to Project Server. If you have appropriate permissions, you can add resources to the Enterprise Resource Pool.

Cross-Reference

Typically the Project Server administrator sets up the Enterprise Resource Pool. See Chapter 21 for details. ■

You can assign resources to Web-based projects the same way you would assign them to standalone projects (as detailed in Chapter 5). Or you can use the Team Builder feature and the Enterprise Resource Pool to select resources for a project. You also can assign generic resources to your project and then use the Team Builder feature to help you replace the generic resources with real resources.

Cross-Reference

See Chapter 5 for information on creating generic resources. ■

In addition, if you manage more than one project at a time, you can take advantage of the Resource Substitution Wizard to identify the best possible use of limited resources.

Adding enterprise resources to your project

You can use the Build Team dialog box to view the resources in the Enterprise Resource Pool and assign them to your project. Click the Resource tab and, in the Insert group, click the Add Resources button. From the drop-down list that appears, click Build Team from Enterprise. Project displays the Build Team dialog box (see Figure 22.20).

Use this dialog box to select resources to assign to your project.

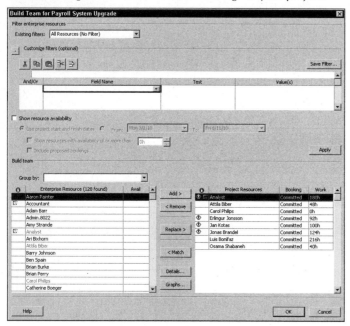

By default, you see all resources, but you can limit the resources that you see by applying filters. Use the Existing filters drop-down list and click the plus sign (+) that appears next to Customize filters to choose fields by which to filter. In the figure, I've already clicked the plus sign, so it appears as a minus sign (–) and you can see the additional space for specifying filters. You also can filter by available hours to work for a given time period.

Tip

You can filter by RBS (Resource Breakdown Structure) code, and you can set as many filters as you want. By using the And choice, you reduce the number of possible resources that Project displays. ∎

After you select resources and click OK, the resources appear on the Resource Sheet of your project and you can assign tasks to them. When you republish your project, the Enterprise Resource Pool is updated to reflect the assignments.

Replacing generic resources with real resources

If your organization uses generic resources, you can use the Team Builder to match a generic resource in your project to a real resource that has the same skill set that you defined for the generic resource. Project Server matches generic resources to real resources by using an enterprise resource custom outline code with a value list for the field, where each value represents, for example, a set of skills. After you assign the appropriate value to each resource by using the custom field, you can use the code to match skills that are required by generic resources with skills that are possessed by real people when project managers run the Team Builder.

Note

You'll find one enterprise resource custom outline code that the staff at Microsoft prenamed — the RBS code. Conceptually, you can compare this code for resources to a WBS code for tasks. Your organization may want to use the RBS code to establish a skill set, or your organization may want to use the RBS code for a different purpose, such as assigning a resource's geographic location. Regardless of the enterprise custom outline code that you choose, the concept I'm about to describe is the same. ∎

Cross-Reference

The Project Server administrator typically creates the enterprise custom fields and outline codes in Project Server. Anyone who has security rights to update the Enterprise Resource Pool can assign the appropriate RBS code to each resource. To find out how to set up and assign enterprise custom fields and outline codes, see Chapter 22. ∎

To use the Team Builder to replace generic resources with real resources, filter the Enterprise Resource Pool so that it displays only those that match the generic resource. Follow these steps to filter the Enterprise Resource Pool:

1. In Project, open the published version of the project containing generic resources that you want to replace.

2. Click the Resource tab and, in the Insert group, click the Add Resources button.

3. From the drop-down list that appears, click Build Team from Enterprise. Project displays the Build Team dialog box.

4. In the list on the right side of the dialog box, click the generic resource for which you want to search for a replacement.

5. Click the Match button. Project displays, in the left side of the dialog box, those resources that match the selected generic resource (see Figure 22.21).

FIGURE 22.21

Replace a generic resource in your project with a real resource from the filtered Enterprise Resource Pool list.

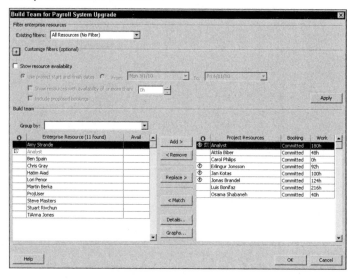

6. To assign a real resource in place of a generic resource, click the name of the resource that you want to use in your project; it appears in the list on the left.

7. Click the Replace button. Project replaces the resource in the Team Resource list with the Enterprise resource you selected. When you click OK, Project also updates the project by replacing the generic resource with the real one you selected.

Notifying resources of assignments

The project manager assigns work to resources. To notify the resources of the work assignments, the project manager publishes the assignments. At a minimum, the team members receive notifications of new or updated assignments on the Home page in Project Web App. If your organization chooses, team members may also receive e-mail notifications.

Using the Resource Substitution Wizard

Suppose that you manage multiple projects with the same set of resources and you want to try to smooth work assignments and reduce overallocations across one or more projects. You can use the Resource Substitution Wizard to help you find resources to fill your needs.

The Resource Substitution Wizard can use different criteria to substitute resources. For example, the wizard can simply consider the resources in the projects that you select and reallocate them to better use their time. Or, the wizard can use the RBS (Resource Breakdown Structure) code that is assigned to resources to match skills required by resources that are already assigned to tasks and then substitute other resources with the same RBS code.

Note

The Project Server administrator typically creates the RBS custom field code; the person who creates the resource — often the Project Server administrator — assigns the custom field to the resource. To find out how to set up and assign custom fields, see Chapter 21. ■

Follow these steps to run the Resource Substitution Wizard:

1. Open the project(s) for which you want to substitute resources.

2. Click the Resource tab and, in the Assignments group, click the Substitute Resources button. The first screen of the Resource Substitution Wizard appears.

3. Click Next. Check the project(s) that you want the wizard to consider while substituting resources (see Figure 22.22).

FIGURE 22.22

Each project that you have open is listed.

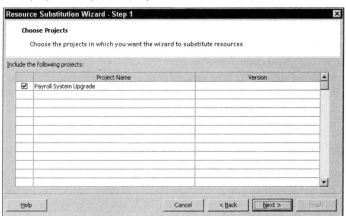

4. Click Next. Identify resources for the wizard to consider when rescheduling projects (see Figure 22.23).

FIGURE 22.23

Use this screen to identify the resources that the wizard should consider when making substitutions.

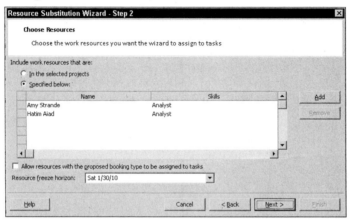

5. Click Next. Choose related projects to consider when rescheduling.

6. Click Next. Specify options for the wizard to use when rescheduling (see Figure 22.24). You can set the priority or choose to use resources from the pool or from the project.

FIGURE 22.24

Specify options for rescheduling.

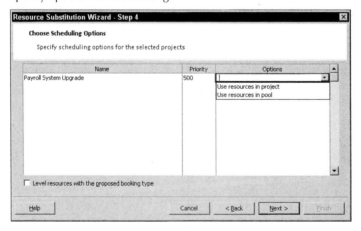

Tip

By selecting the check box at the bottom of the figure, you can also level the resources set up with a booking type of "proposed." ∎

7. Click Next. You see a summary of the options you've selected (see Figure 22.25).

After you set up your options, the wizard displays a summary.

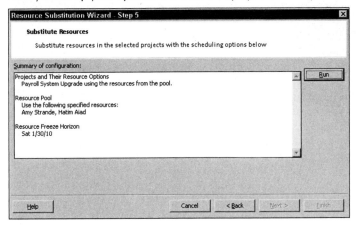

8. Click the Run button to run the wizard with the options you've selected.

   The Run button changes to the Stop button while the wizard runs.

9. When the Run button reappears, click Next.

   The wizard displays a grid of assignments that it has changed (see Figure 22.26) and gives you two possible options:

   - Review the results.
   - Back up and change the wizard's options to try again.

   After you make your decision(s), click Next.

10. You see the Update Options screen of the wizard, where you can choose to have Project update the projects considered by the wizard based on the results of the wizard. You also can choose to save the results of the wizard to a file. When you click Next, a final page appears.

FIGURE 22.26

The wizard's suggested changes.

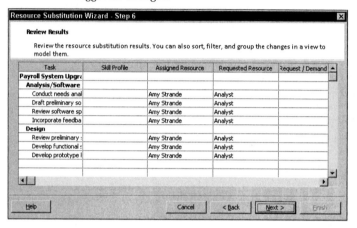

11. If you aren't satisfied with the results you get from the wizard, simply close the affected projects without saving them.

The Resource Substitution Wizard can also help you select resources for more than one project at a time, so you can quickly develop staffing models. As Step 3 demonstrated, you can select the open projects that you want the Resource Substitution Wizard to consider. To do so, simply open each project before you start the wizard. After the wizard has finished, don't forget to level the projects to see how the wizard's resource assignments change project finish dates and resource use. If you aren't satisfied with the results you get from the wizard, simply close the affected projects without saving them.

Tracking Progress

After you've set up a project and uploaded it to Project Server, you have to track the progress of your project. To effectively track progress in an enterprise environment, you should do the following:

- Set up a status report form for team members to complete.
- Receive updates from team members as they update the project in Project Web App.
- As appropriate, adjust actual work.

Setting up status reports

As a manager, you can create the layout for the status report that you want to view from your team members using Project Web App. When you create a status report layout, you specify how often you want status reports, when reporting should begin, which resources should report, and the section you want included in the report.

To create a standard layout for a status report, click the Status Reports link under Resources in the Quick Launch pane to display the Status Reports page (see Figure 22.27). The Status Reports page lists existing status report request layouts and status reports responses you need to submit.

FIGURE 22.27

The Status Reports page lists all information concerning status reports.

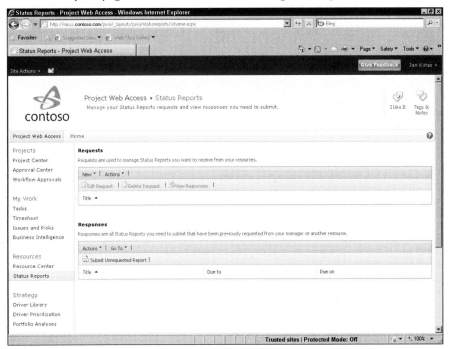

To create a layout for a status-report request, follow these steps:

1. Click the New button in the Requests section and then click New Request. The Status Report Request page appears.

2. On the top of the page, you assign a name to the status report, establish a frequency and a start date, and identify the resources you want to submit reports (see Figure 22.28).

3. At the bottom of the page (see Figure 22.29), establish the sections that should appear in the report. You can add a section by clicking the Insert Section button. Project Web App adds blank lines in which you enter the section names.

4. Click Send when you finish; Project Web App creates the status report and sends a skeleton of the status report to the selected team members, requesting a status report. The team members can then use the skeleton to fill in the information you want to see.

FIGURE 22.28

Identify the team members who should submit the status report.

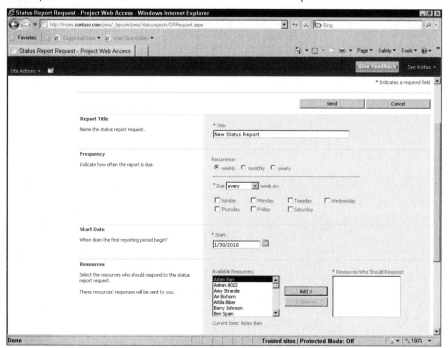

FIGURE 22.29

Identify the information that should appear in the report.

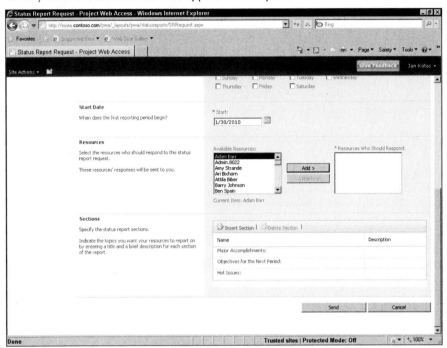

Receiving updates from team members

If you manage resources and approve their time, then your Project Web App home page indicates, in the Approvals section, how many task updates from resources are pending your approval (see Figure 22.30).

To review and accept or reject task updates, click the link in the Approvals section. Or, when you open Project Professional, You'll see a message indicating that task updates are waiting. You can then let Project open the appropriate project and display the updates, which you can then accept or reject.

FIGURE 22.30

In the Approvals section, Project Web App indicates the number of task updates that await your approval.

Reviewing and updating the project workflow

Many organizations use workflows to govern a project's progress through its lifecycle. The workflows help ensure that all the company's goals are met as a project progresses.

Note

Workflows are an option of Project Server, not a requirement. ■

Using SharePoint features, your organization can incorporate workflows into the lifecycles of its projects to check progress on a project along the way. And you, as a project manager, might be charged with providing workflow information. The information you submit is reviewed by appropriate people in your organization; if it's approved, your project moves along the workflow path.

The imaginary Contoso organization uses four workflow phases: Create, Select, Plan, and Manage. Some of the workflow phases are broken down into more than one workflow stage.

Note

Enterprise reporting in Project Server uses aggregated workflow phases rather than the workflow stages. ∎

To view workflow information for a project, start in the Project Center. Click your project's link in the Project Name column to display workflow status information (see Figure 22.31).

FIGURE 22.31

Workflow status information for a project.

This project is in the Manage phase of its workflow; the interactive grid at the bottom of the figure shows deliverables that must be completed during this stage. To view details on any of these deliverables, you can click any of these three items:

- The deliverable's name in the grid.
- The Next button in the Page group on the Project tab of the Ribbon.
- The deliverable's corresponding link in the upper-left corner of the page, just below the project name and the Project group on the Ribbon.

Part VII: Working in Groups

It's important to understand that the deliverables displayed change, depending on the phase and stage of the project to reflect the rules governing the workflow stage of the project.

If you scroll down (as I've done in Figure 22.32), you can see detailed information about the workflow in a grid that's not interactive but does list all the stages — and all deliverables associated with each stage.

FIGURE 22.32

Detailed information about the workflow.

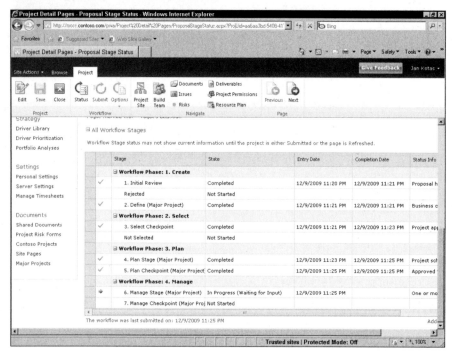

Check marks appear in the Workflow Stage grid to identify completed phases. The arrow in the left column beside Stage 6 identifies the project's current position in the workflow.

As a project manager, you might be expected to provide workflow-status information. You do so by clicking the link associated with the appropriate deliverable; then you click the Edit button in the Project group (on the Project tab of the Ribbon) to check the project out and complete any information requested.

When you finish entering information, you submit it for approval. Someone higher up the food chain reviews the information you provide and decides whether the project can move to the next workflow stage.

Handling project issues and risks

You can create and track issues and risks that are associated with a project in general or with specific tasks in a project. Issues and risk notifications can be initiated by anyone with proper permissions; the idea is to promote collaboration on the project team.

Think of *issues* as unexpected things that occur on projects. They may be problems or they may be opportunities. When they arise, you can create an issue notification, let others on the team review the issue, assign the issue to someone to address, and monitor the progress of the issue.

Risks are possible events or conditions that could have a negative impact on a project. Risks have not yet occurred but *could occur*. Essentially, a risk is an issue before it happens.

You set up an issue or a risk for tracking by using your project's SharePoint site. From the Project Center, click the project's name to drill down into the project. Then, on the Ribbon, click the Project tab and, in the Navigate group, click Project Site. The project's SharePoint site appears (see Figure 22.33).

FIGURE 22.33

A project's SharePoint site.

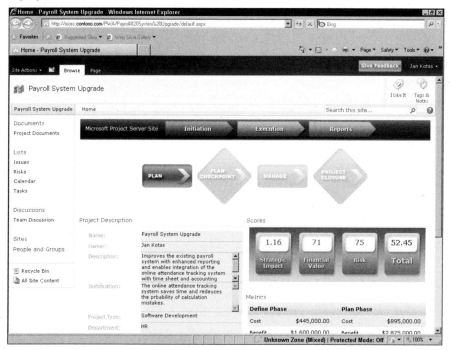

Using the Quick Launch pane on the left, you can click the Issues link to view existing issues or the Risks link to view existing risks. To create a notification of a new issue or risk, click the appropriate link — and, on the page that appears, click the Add New Item link. A window appears, in which you supply the information associated with your issue or risk. In Figure 22.34, you see a typical Issues window.

FIGURE 22.34

Defining an issue for a project.

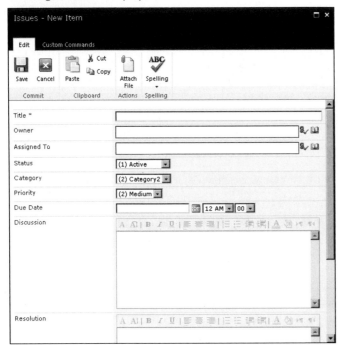

Assign a title, status, and priority to the issue; assign the issue to someone; identify the issue owner; set a due date; describe the issue; and (if possible) provide a resolution for it. You also can attach files to the issue notification, or link it to tasks within the project. Click Save when you finish filling in the screen.

Note
You edit an issue by clicking its link. You can filter issues by clicking the View button at the top-right edge of the Issues list. ■

If someone assigns an issue to you, you see a notification on your Home page when you log into Project Web App. You can click the Issues and Risks link in the Quick Launch pane to view the issues and risks assigned to you.

Tip
SharePoint sites for project open in a separate browser instance. To return to Project Web App, close the SharePoint browser instance. ■

Summary

In this chapter, you read about how to address your primary concerns as a project or resource manager who deals with Web-based projects. You found out how to do the following:

- Log in to Project Server
- Create a Web-based project
- Manage resource assignments for Web-based projects
- Track the progress of Web-based projects
- Manage issues and risks associated with projects

For information about the behind-the-scenes tasks that helped create your Project Server environment, read Chapter 21. For more information on the day-to-day tasks that your team members can perform, see Chapter 23. To see how an executive can take advantage of Project Web App, see Chapter 24.

Project Server and the Day-to-Day User

A t this point in the book, you've probably realized that the world of project management has moved beyond the traditional pencil-and-ruler war room and into the world of technology. Nowhere is this shift more evident than in the many ways project managers can take advantage of the Internet to communicate with others, present information, and gather data.

If your organization uses Project Server, then you, as a team member, should read this chapter to find out how you can make use of Project Web App — the browser-based interface that connects to the Project Server database — to view the tasks you need to accomplish, update the schedule with work completed, and even enter new tasks that may arise.

Note

In earlier versions of Project Server, Project Web App was called Project Web Access. Because you can customize the appearance of Project Web App — and because Project Server 2010 was under construction at the time I wrote this chapter — the figures in this chapter might not match exactly what you see in your own installation of Project Server. For example, the screens still show Project Web Access. In addition, your company might customize Project Web App to display information differently. ∎

In this chapter, you read about how the average team member can connect to Project Server, update timesheets and task status, and report to the project manager. You also can submit proposed projects.

Note

In the chapter, I used sample data provided by Microsoft customized for a fictitious company called Contoso. This sample data appears in a virtual machine hosted for me by Project Hosts, a company that provides on-demand Microsoft Enterprise Project Management (EPM), CRM, and SharePoint Server (MOSS). You can read about Project Hosts at www.projecthosts.com. ■

Logging on to Project Web App

To log on to Project Server by using Project Web App, a resource needs to know the URL for the Web database. The project manager should notify the resource of the URL. To log on to Project Server, open Internet Explorer and, in the Address box, enter the URL of the Web database, press Enter, and your Project Web App Home page appears.

Tip

Save the URL in your Favorites list — or, if you use Project Web App more than any other Web page, set it up as your Home page so Project Web App appears whenever you open Internet Explorer. To set Project Web App as your Home page, enter the address into the Address box and press Enter. Then choose Tools ⇨ Internet Options. On the General tab, click the Use Current button in the Home Page section and click OK. ■

Reviewing the Home Page

The Project Web App Home page serves the same function as most home pages on the Web (see Figure 23.1). It introduces you to Project Web App; in the Reminders section, you'll see summary information such as the number of new tasks you have, the number of unsubmitted timesheets you have, the number of overdue status reports you have, and the number of issues and risks assigned to you.

You can use the Quick Launch pane that appears on the left side of the screen to navigate to other areas of Project Web App.

If you click a link in the Quick Launch pane and want to redisplay your Home page, you can click the Project Web App button or the Home button if they are visible; otherwise, if you see the Ribbon, you can click the small folder, which navigates up one level, and select either Project Web App or Home.

A typical Project Web App Home page, from which you can navigate to other areas of Project Web App.

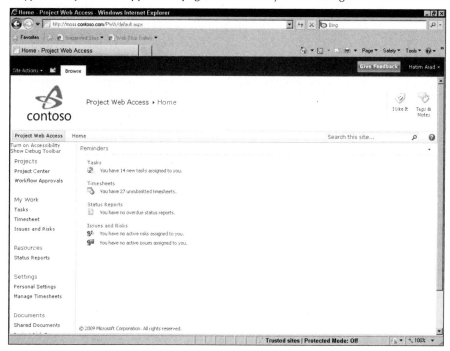

Customizing the Home Page

You can customize the appearance of your Project Web App Home page either temporarily or permanently using the Web Part menu that appears on the Home page beside each part. Each Web Part menu is a small, downward-pointing caret at the right edge of a section on the Home page; in Figure 23.2, the mouse pointer is pointing at a Web Part menu.

You can close a section of the Home page temporarily: Click the Web Part menu and choose Minimize. To redisplay the information, click the Web Part menu and choose Restore.

FIGURE 23.2

You can minimize sections on the Home page to hide the information temporarily.

If you want to remove a section from the Home page on a more permanent basis, click the Web Part menu and choose Close. Project Web App removes the section from your Home page entirely.

You can add sections to the Home page. For example, if you close the Project Workspaces and then change your mind, you can add it back. The following steps explain how:

1. Click any Web Part menu and choose Edit My Web Part. Project Web App displays the Home page in Edit mode (see Figure 23.3).

Tip

You also can click your name in the upper-right corner of the Project Web App screen and choose Personalize this Page to add, remove, or reorganize the information on your Home page. ∎

FIGURE 23.3

The Home page in Edit mode.

2. Click an Add a Web Part button on your Home page and Project Web App displays the Ribbon above your Home page and below the Project Web App browser tab (see Figure 23.4). The Ribbon includes two tabs related to editing your Home page: The Page Tools Insert tab and the Web Part Tools Options tab. The information you see also appears on the Web Part Tools Options tab.

3. Below the Ribbon on the left, in the Categories list, click a category related to the element you want to display on the Home page. The items in the Web Parts section change to match the category you selected.

FIGURE 23.4

You can add a Web part to the Home page.

4. Click a Web part and then click the Add button at the right side of the Ribbon. Project Web App redisplays the Home page, still in Edit mode; the Home page now includes the element(s) you added.

5. Click OK at the bottom of the Reminders pane that appears down the right side of the window to display your new Home page.

If you want to reorganize Home page elements, you can drag the title of a section to a new location, using the same screen shown in Figure 23.4.

Tip

You can use the techniques described here to modify the appearance of most pages in Project Web App. ∎

Viewing and Recording Information

The Project Center displays individual projects — typically, those on which you've assigned work (see Figure 23.5). Different views of the Project Center are available; Figure 23.5 shows the Projects by Phase view. To switch views of the Project Center, use the Views list box in the Data group on the Projects tab.

On each line of the Projects by Phase view, you see a Gantt taskbar that shows you the duration of the project and the progress that's been made on the project so far. To find a particular project, click the icon in the Information column on the left and then, in the Zoom group on the Projects tab of the Ribbon, click Scroll to Project.

Note
You must have appropriate permissions from the Project Server administrator to display the Project Center, and the Project Server administrator determines which views are available to you in the Project Center. ■

FIGURE 23.5

In the Project Center, you see entries representing projects stored in the Project Server database.

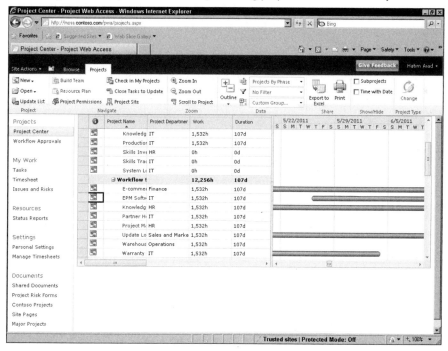

You can organize the projects by using the Filter, Group, and Sort options in the Data group on the Projects tab of the Ribbon. You can open a particular project in Project Web App by clicking the link that appears when you point the mouse at the project's name in the Project Name column.

Note
If you have proper permissions, you can view and edit resources and resource assignments from the Resource Center; typically, project managers and resource managers have permission to view the Resource Center, but team members don't have permission. ■

Working with your tasks

Work assignments go from Project Professional to team members via Project Web App. If your organization chooses, the Project Server administrator can set up e-mail notifications so Project Server generates e-mail notices and reminders of events, such as past-due tasks. These e-mail notices and reminders appear in your regular e-mail client's inbox.

As you saw, however, when you log on to Project Web App, the Home page also indicates whether you have new task assignments. You can view your task assignments by clicking the link in the Tasks section that identifies new tasks assigned to your or by clicking Tasks in the My Work section of the Quick Launch pane (see Figure 23.6).

As life would have it, you may not work on only one project at a time. The My Tasks page lists the project and, indented, each task assigned to you on the project. Beside each project, you'll see either a plus or a minus sign; you can click the symbol to toggle between the plus and minus sign. When you see a plus sign, your tasks on the project are hidden; click the symbol to change it to a minus sign and view your tasks on the project.

Tip
Using the Layout button in the Display group on the Tasks tab of the Ribbon, you can view your tasks using the Gantt Chart view, the Timephased Data view (shown in Figure 23.6) or the Sheet view. ■

New tasks have a small "new" icon beside their names in the Task Name column; in Figure 23.6, the first task is new.

Tip
You can filter the view to display only new tasks; on the Ribbon, in the Data group, open the Filter list box and select Newly Assigned Tasks. ■

Entering time on tasks

If you click a task name, Project Web App displays the Assignment Details page (see Figure 23.7). From this page, you can see the details of the task, including the planned work, and, if you scroll down the screen, any task history, attachments, contacts, related assignments, and notes.

FIGURE 23.6

The Tasks page lists your task assignments, both new and existing.

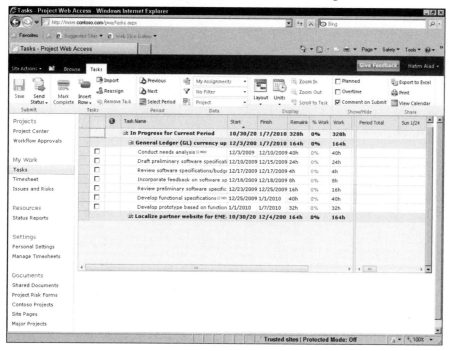

Tip

Use the Attachments section to attach a document, issue, or risk notification to a task. ■

You also can report time spent on the assignment from the Task Center. If you are viewing the details of a task, click the back button to redisplay the list of your tasks.

Using the left side of the grid, you can record Actual Work or, using the right side of the grid, you can record work on the day it occurred. After you type a value, click the Save button on the Ribbon.

Note

Any work you record from the Tasks page also appears on the Timesheet page, as you'll see later in this chapter. ■

FIGURE 23.7

Displaying the details of an assignment in Project Web App.

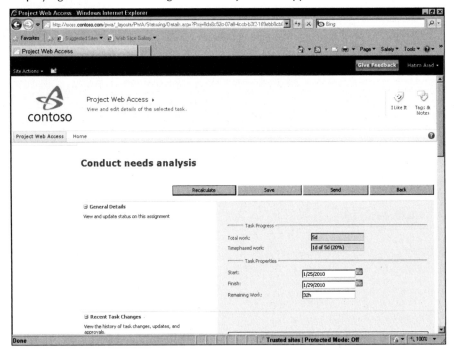

Submitting task updates

Saving a task update doesn't send it to the project manager. You can check the Process Status column to identify updates you have not yet submitted; use the scroll bar below the left side of the Tasks page to scroll to see the Process Status column. In Figure 23.8, one task has recorded work that has not yet been submitted to a manager.

You can submit status information for all or selected tasks. For each task you want to select, click the check box in the leftmost column. To submit updates, click the Send Status button in the Submit group on the Tasks tab of the Ribbon and choose whether to send all or only selected updates.

FIGURE 23.8

Review the Process Status column to identify updates you haven't submitted.

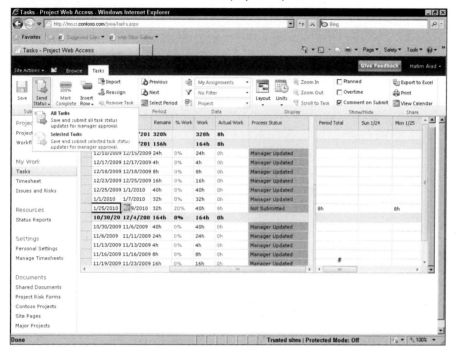

Adding tasks

As a team member, you may realize that what you're doing requires more work than the manager anticipated — and may even call for tasks that the manager didn't assign to you. If your Project Web App privileges permit, you can add a task from the Tasks page. In the Tasks group on the Tasks tab, click the Insert Row button and choose Create a New Task (see Figure 23.9). Project Web App displays the Add Task page (see Figure 23.10).

FIGURE 23.9

Use the Insert Row button on the Ribbon to add a task to a project.

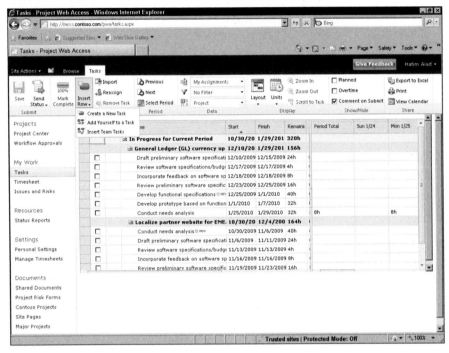

From the Add Task page, follow these steps to add a new task:

1. Select the project to which you need to add the task from the Project drop-down list

2. Select the task's level in the outline using the Summary Task drop-down list.

3. Supply a task name and estimated start and/or end dates and Total Work information.

4. Optionally, provide a comment about the task.

Tip

To assign the task to yourself, use the Tasks page; select the task and then click the Insert Row button From the drop-down list that appears, click Add Yourself to a Task. ■

5. Click the Send button, and Project Web App adds the task to your Tasks page and sends information to the project manager about the additional work.

FIGURE 23.10

Fill out information about a new task from this page.

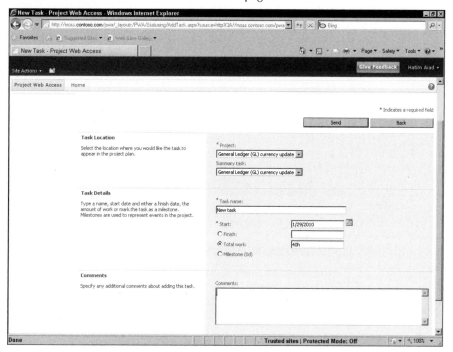

Reassigning a task

You're overloaded with work and you can't possibly complete everything you've been assigned. But — luckily for you — management just approved your request to hire an intern to help you. Now you need to reassign some of your tasks — and keep your project manager informed of the change in assignments.

Note

You can reassign tasks only if you have the correct permissions. ∎

To reassign tasks, follow these steps:

1. Click the Tasks link in the Quick Launch pane.

2. In the Tasks group on the Tasks tab of the Ribbon, click the Reassign button.

   The Task Reassignment page appears (see Figure 23.11).

3. On the line of the task you want to reassign, select a resource in the Reassign To column.

4. Provide a start date for the new task and, if you want, scroll down to provide any comments about the assignment.

5. Click the Submit button.

Project Web App redisplays the Tasks page; the task you reassigned still appears in your task list, but at the bottom of the list with a list drawn through it (see Figure 23.12).

To notify your manager of the reassignment, select the task by clicking the check box to the left of the Information column beside the task name and clicking the Send Status button; from the drop-down list, click Selected Tasks; after the project manager approves the reassignment, the reassigned task appears on the Microsoft Project Web App Tasks page of the affected recipient. The reassigned task remains on the Tasks page of the person who reassigned it; that person can remove the task using the Remove Task button in the Tasks group on the Tasks tab.

FIGURE 23.11

Select a resource for the appropriate task.

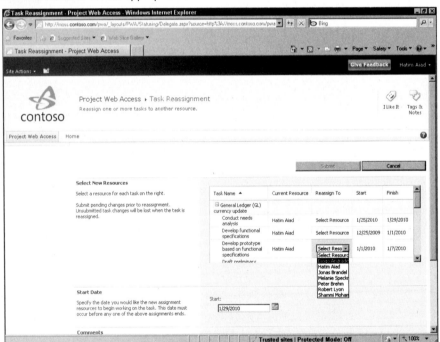

FIGURE 23.12

Reassigned tasks appear with a line drawn through them.

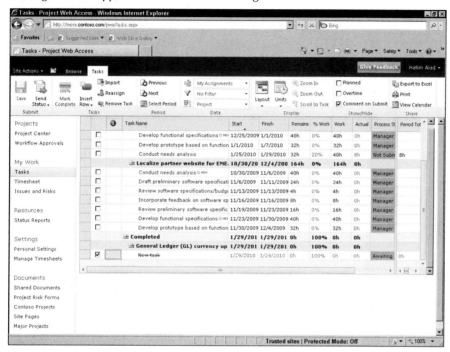

Working with your timesheet

Some organizations and some users prefer to record the time worked on tasks using a timesheet. In these cases, the Project Server Administrator sets up Project Web App so that timesheets for appropriate periods appear when you click Timesheet in the Quick Launch pane to display the Timesheet page, which lists each task to which you are assigned.

Your Project Server administrator can set up the Tasks view to show timephased fields, and the Timesheet view shows timephased fields automatically on the right side of the view. Depending on your organization's defaults, you can view planned work for the task as well as record actual work. The left sides of the two views differ.

In the Timesheet view, the left side of the view displays columns for the project name, task name, comments, billing category, and process status for any entries. You can view the timesheet in the Timesheet view by using the View drop-down list in the Data group on the Timesheet tab of the Ribbon (see Figure 23.13). From the Timesheet view, you enter work using timephased fields only.

FIGURE 23.13

The Timesheet view of your timesheet.

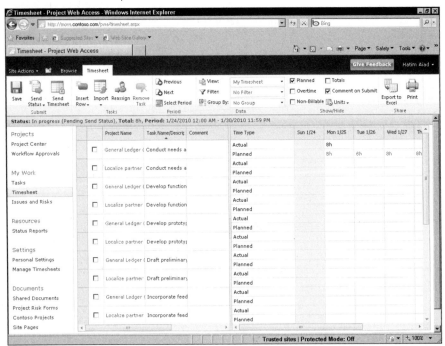

The Task view contains the same columns on the left side as the Timesheet view, as well as additional columns for Start Date, Finish Date, Remaining Work, % Work Complete, Work, Actual Work, and Duration; using these additional columns, you can record information at a task level instead of using timephased fields. On the right side of the view, you can use the timephased fields to enter work. In Figure 23.14, I've scrolled the left side of the view so that you can see some of the additional columns available; remember that the name of each task to which you are assigned appears at the left edge of the left side of the view and in the figure, task names aren't visible.

The period for which you are entering work appears just below the Ribbon; you can select a timesheet period in which to enter work if you click the Select Period button in the Period group of the Timesheet tab of the Ribbon. Project Web App displays the Select Period dialog box (see Figure 23.15). Click the calendar and navigate to the period for which you want to record time.

The Task view of your timesheet.

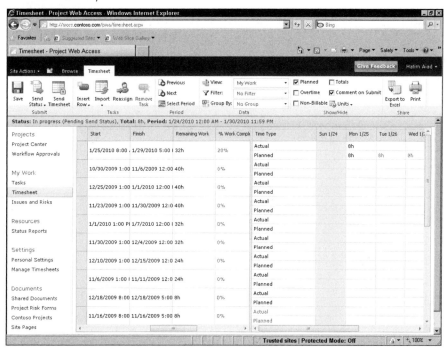

Select a period for which to record work.

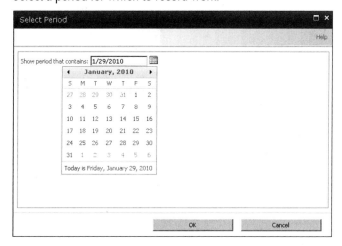

Tip

If your organization set up administrative time for you, it appears at the bottom of the timesheet. ■

Entering time

Using the Task view, the numbers that you can enter on the left side of the view depend on the settings that your project manager or your organization has selected. You might be able to fill in the percentage of work completed, the actual work done and the work remaining, or the hours of work done per day.

Using the timephased fields on the right side of the My Work view and the My Timesheet view, you can enter work manually. In addition, depending on your permissions, you might also be able to replace actual with planned work.

To record time manually, click in the box that represents the intersection of the date for which you want to record work and the task on which you want to record work. Then type the number of hours you want to record on the Actual row.

Tip

Using the check boxes in the Show/Hide section, you can control the values that appear as rows on the timephased side of the view. ■

If your permissions allow you to import time, you can replace actual work values with planned work values for an entire row. Place a check in the leftmost column of the task and then click the Import button in the Tasks group of the Timesheet tab. From the drop-down list that appears, click Replace Actual with Planned. Project Web App notifies you that you're about to replace regular work you've already reported with planned values from the assignment's scheduled tasks.

Tip

To view overdue tasks, open the Filter list in the Data group and select overdue tasks. ■

Saving timesheet entries

You don't typically finish recording all information on a timesheet at one time. You can click the Save button on the Timesheet page to save your entries but keep the timesheet available for further updating; you'll want to take this approach as long as your working dates fall in the period covered by the timesheet.

When the timesheet period no longer covers your working period, click the Send Timesheet button to save your work and submit your timesheet for approval. If you need to send a status on selected tasks, check the boxes in the leftmost column beside those tasks and then click the Send Status button; from the drop-down list, click Selected Tasks.

Tip

You can print your timesheet at any time; view it and click the Print icon in the Share group at the right edge of the Timesheet tab of the Ribbon. ∎

Reporting administrative time

Suppose that you've just been selected for jury duty — and, of course, you're scheduled to work on a project at the same time. It happens — something comes up, and you are not available to work during the time you had been scheduled to work. From the Timesheet page, you can report actual administrative time, using the pre-established administrative time tasks that appear at the bottom of your timesheet, and you fill in these tasks in the same way you report work you performed on a task.

Submitting a Project Proposal

Suppose that you've got an idea for a project that you think would be beneficial to your company and you'd like to propose the project. Your Project Server administrator can set up Project Server and your permissions to enable you to submit project proposals.

The proposal you submit will be built on templates designed by your organization so that you provide all the information your management needs to evaluate your proposal and determine whether it will, indeed, be beneficial to your company.

Your proposal will move through a workflow — again, established by your company — of the various stages of the approval process established by your company, and Project Server will keep track of your proposal and where it stands in the approval process.

To propose a project, follow these steps:

1. Navigate to your Project Web App Home page and click the Project Center link in the Quick Launch pane.

2. On the Ribbon, click the New button in the Project group on the Projects tab.

3. From the drop-down menu that appears, select the type of project you want to propose (see Figure 23.16).

   The choices that appear will be those your company makes available in your version of Project Server.

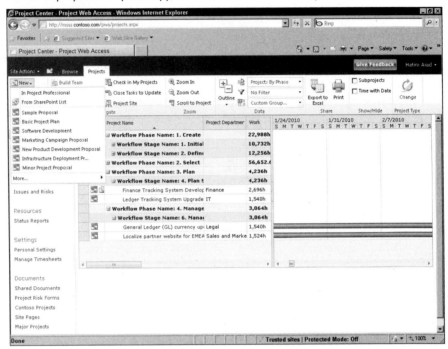

FIGURE 23.16

Available proposal templates appear on the New button's drop-down list.

After you make a selection, a proposal request form appears; typically, the form focuses on collecting the information needed for the type of project you are proposing (see Figure 23.17).

4. Supply a name for the proposed project and a proposed start date, along with other information requested on the form.

By default, your name appears as the proposed project's owner.

FIGURE 23.17

Complete a proposal form.

5. When you finish filling in the proposal form, click the Save button on the Ribbon.

   Project creates the proposal and displays the Workflow Status page for the proposed project; you can see the top of a sample page in Figure 23.18 and the bottom, which details the process, in Figure 23.19. The statuses that appear on this page depend on the workflow statuses your company sets up in Project Server.

6. When you finish reviewing the details of your project, click Close; Project Web App prompts you to check in the proposed project; click Yes.

FIGURE 23.18

The top of a typical Workflow Status page.

As your proposal proceeds through the approval process, you can review the details of where it stands at any time by returning to the Project Center and drilling down into your proposal. As your proposal moves through the approval process, it will appear in different workflow stages in the Project Center.

FIGURE 23.19

The bottom of a typical Workflow Status page.

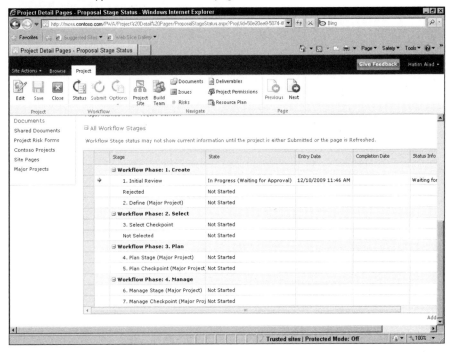

Working with Documents

Project Server is built on SharePoint Server; using SharePoint features, project managers with appropriate privileges or the Project Server administrator can create a workspace for a project. In this workspace, anyone with proper privileges can store project-related material, such as supporting documents or pictures. This feature comes in handy, for example, when you have a budget justification or a feasibility study or some other supporting document that you want to be able to "grab" whenever the need arises.

Note

SharePoint Server is a feature-rich product that supports a wide variety of team-oriented functions to facilitate document sharing and team communication. You can post documents in the Shared Documents folder, available from the Project Web App Home page; Shared Documents is a public, company-wide space that anyone in the organization can access. ∎

To post documents related to a specific project, the project must have a workspace. By default, in the project's workspace you'll find the `Project Documents` folder; only those with access to the project workspace also have access to the documents in this folder.

To attach and view the documents for a particular project, click the Project Center link in the Quick Launch pane; in the Project Center, click in the Information column beside your project. Then, on the Projects tab of the Ribbon, in the Navigate group, click Project Site. If a site exists for the project, Project Web App displays a page similar to the one shown in Figure 23.20.

FIGURE 23.20

From this page, you have access to SharePoint features associated with your project.

In the Quick Launch pane that runs down the left side of the screen, click the Project Documents link to view the list of documents shared by the team (see Figure 23.21).

The contents of the Project Documents library.

You can add a document to the Project Documents folder by following these steps:

1. Click the Add New Document link.

2. In the Upload Document dialog box shown in Figure 23.22, click the Browse button and use the Choose File to Upload dialog box that appears to navigate to the document you want to upload.

3. Click OK, and SharePoint uploads the document.

Tip

To upload multiple documents click the Upload Multiple Files link and use the Windows Explorer–like view to select multiple documents. ■

FIGURE 23.22

Use this dialog box to navigate to and select a document to upload.

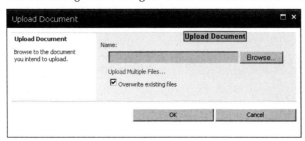

A window like the one shown in Figure 23.23 appears, enabling you to update the properties of the document you uploaded by supplying a title, owner, and status. You also can link project tasks, risks, or issues to the document you upload.

4. Click Save after you finish adding information via this window.

FIGURE 23.23

Use this dialog box to supply properties for the document you upload.

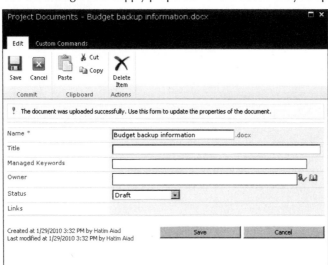

5. To view a document, click its name.

The program that created the document opens it in Project Web App and you see the contents of the document (see Figure 23.24).

FIGURE 23.24

An Excel document open in Project Web App.

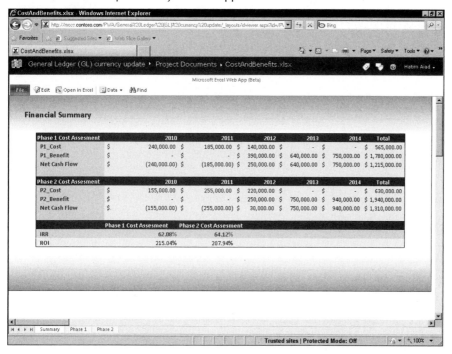

Tip

To return to Project Web App, use the navigation bar above the Ribbon; in Figure 23.24, I clicked General Ledger (GL) Currency Update, which is the project name, to redisplay the SharePoint site for the project. Then I clicked the Navigate Up folder (refer to Figure 23.21) and selected Project Web App from the drop-down list that appeared. ∎

Reporting Status

Project Web App provides you with status reports you can send to your project manager.

Tip

Don't forget: If you have appropriate permissions, you can create an issue or a risk notification if you've run into something unexpected that you want to report; other team members, as well as your project manager, can see and comment on the issue or risk notification. ∎

You've already seen how Project Web App enables you to send work assignment updates from the Tasks page or the Timesheet page. But you can also send both solicited and unsolicited status reports to your project manager. Click the Status Reports link in the Quick Launch pane to display the Status Reports page (see Figure 23.25).

The Status Reports page.

If your project manager has requested a status report, you'll see a link to the requested report on the Status Reports page. If you don't see a status report link, you can still submit a status report; click the Submit Unrequested Report button to display a status report form that you can complete and submit (see Figure 23.26).

Fill in the report, supplying a title and selecting resources to receive a copy of your report. You can define the starting and ending timeframe for the report, and then add sections at the bottom of the report in which you can type report information. When you're ready to submit the report, click the Send button.

FIGURE 23.26

You can create your own status report.

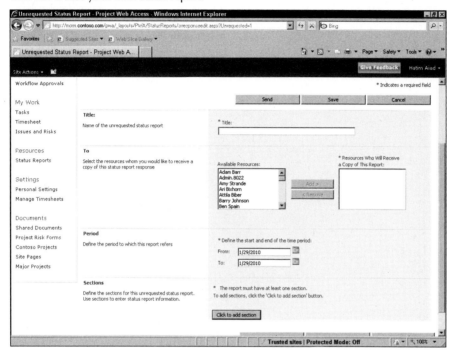

Summary

In this chapter, you read about how the day-to-day user typically interacts with Project Server using Project Web App. The user can view and update tasks, fill in timesheets, provide status reports, and create documents. If the user has appropriate permissions, he or she can submit proposals for new projects and follow the proposals through the approval process.

In Chapter 24, you see how executives use Project Web App.

Project Server and the Executive

Executives can use Project Web App to review the portfolio of work that is happening across the organization. Using analysis tools, you can review projects at varying stages in the project lifecycle. You can also define the elements that drive your business from your perspective — and then evaluate the projects in progress, as well as proposed projects, to find the collection of projects that best helps your organization meet its goals. This chapter presents a high-level overview of the Project Web App areas that might interest an executive.

IN THIS CHAPTER

Logging in to Project Web App

Using workflows to manage projects

Analyzing possible project portfolios

Note

In earlier versions of Project Server, Project Web App was called Project Web Access. Because you can customize the appearance of Project Web App — and because Project Server 2010 was under construction at the time I wrote this chapter — the figures in this chapter might not match exactly what you see in your own installation of Project Server. For example, the screens still show Project Web Access. ■

Logging into Project Web App

You open Project Web App the same way other users open it: Use Internet Explorer and navigate to the IP address supplied by your Project Server administrator. Project Web App displays your Home page. If your organization uses Windows authentication, you see your Home page immediately (see Figure 24.1). You navigate in Project Web App using the Quick Launch pane on the left side of the screen; you can control and customize the information that appears in the pane to the right of the Quick Launch pane by using the techniques described in Chapter 23.

The Project Web App Home page.

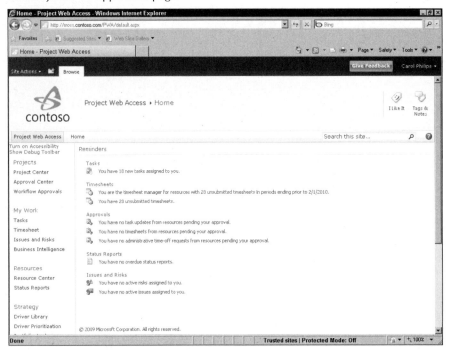

Note

In this chapter, I used sample data provided by Microsoft and customized for a fictitious company called Contoso. This sample data appears in a virtual machine hosted for me by Project Hosts, a company that provides on-demand Microsoft Enterprise Project Management (EPM), CRM, and Microsoft Office SharePoint Server (MOSS). You can read about Project Hosts at www.projecthosts.com. ∎

Using Workflows to Manage Projects

When you click the Project Center link in the Quick Launch pane, you see the Project Center (see Figure 24.2). The Project Center provides a high-level picture of all the projects that you have security permissions to view. Your organization can create custom views for the Project Center, each providing you with different kinds of information; use the View list box on the Projects tab in the Data group of the Ribbon to see the views that are available to you.

FIGURE 24.2

The Project Center.

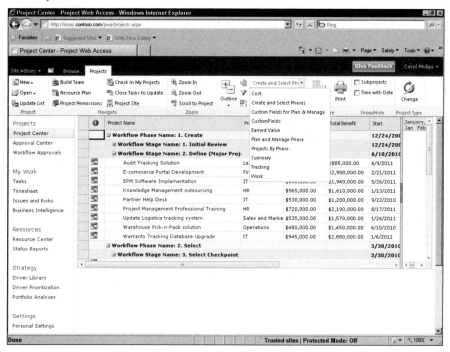

As part of managing projects, your organization might opt to use the SharePoint features available with Project Server to set up workflows to manage and govern projects and potential projects through their lifecycles, helping to ensure that all the company's goals are met as a project progresses.

Note

Workflows are an option in Project Server, not a requirement. ∎

One phase in a workflow might be an evaluation phase, where you focus on determining whether a project would be feasible (as well as profitable) for your organization. For any project under consideration, many companies build a business case that contains the information needed to evaluate the project.

If your organization uses the workflow feature, then clicking any name in the Project Name column brings up the Workflow Status information for the project (see Figure 24.3).

FIGURE 24.3

Typical Workflow Status for a project.

Using Project Server, you can capture a wide variety of information as part of a business case. For example, Contoso, the sample company, includes a Project Details description, a Strategic Impact statement, a cost/benefit analysis, and a risk evaluation in its business case.

Tip

The Cost and Benefit form appears as an Excel template within Project Server 2010, and the Risk Evaluation form uses an InfoPath Forms Services survey to generate a risk score and a risk weight that are saved as custom fields in Project Server. ■

You can view details about any of these deliverables by clicking any of these:

- The deliverable name in the interactive grid shown in Figure 24.3.
- The Next button in the Page group on the Project tab of the Ribbon.
- The deliverable's corresponding link in the upper-left corner of the page, just below the project name and the Project group on the Ribbon.

Note

The deliverables that appear on-screen change, depending on the particular phase and stage of the project, to reflect the rules that govern the workflow stage of the project. ■

If you scroll down (as I've done in Figure 24.4), you can see detailed information about the workflow in a grid that is not interactive but lists all stages and all deliverables associated with each stage. Click the plus sign (+) beside All Workflow Stages to display the grid.

Check marks appear in the Workflow Stage grid to identify completed phases. The arrow in the left column (beside 3 Select Checkpoint) identifies the project's current position in the workflow.

Project Server uses the information Contoso collects in its Strategic Impact statement, cost/benefit analysis, and risk evaluation to prioritize projects when you start building possible project portfolios for your company.

Tip

You can click the Resource Plan button in the Navigate group on the Project tab of the Ribbon to build a high-level resource plan for a project during its evaluation stage that incorporates probable resource cost and availability information while assessing the project's feasibility. ■

FIGURE 24.4

Detailed information about the workflow.

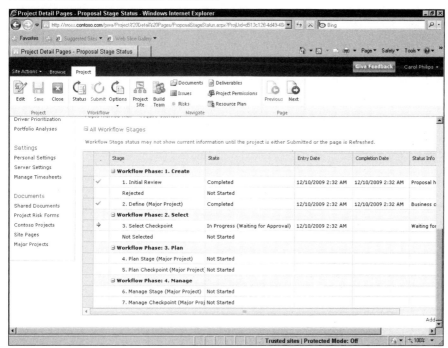

When you finish reviewing information for a project, click the Close button in the Project group on the Project tab of the Ribbon to redisplay the Project Center.

Analyzing Possible Project Portfolios

Project Server includes analysis tools that you can use to help you identify the optimal portfolio of projects for your company, considering various constraints on both cost and resources.

Reviewing the Driver Library

If you click the Driver Library link in the Quick Launch pane, you can view the existing factors that drive your business (see Figure 24.5). Not all factors apply to all projects; in the Driver Library, you identify all possible factors that might drive your company's activities so that you can use them when you evaluate potential projects.

FIGURE 24.5

A typical business driver library.

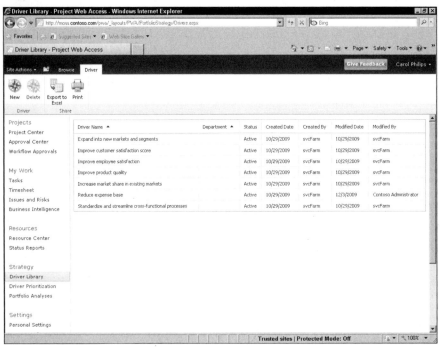

If you click the New button in the Driver group on the Driver tab of the Ribbon, you can create a new business driver for your organization (see Figure 24.6). When you create a new driver, you supply the following information for it:

- Driver name & description.

- Departments, which can be used to associate a particular driver with certain departments within your company.

    Skip the Department field if your organization uses a single set of business drivers for the entire organization.

- Project Impact Statements, which are ratings (None, Low, Moderate, Strong, and Extreme) applied to a project to assess how strongly a particular project affects the business driver.

FIGURE 24.6

Information stored in a business driver.

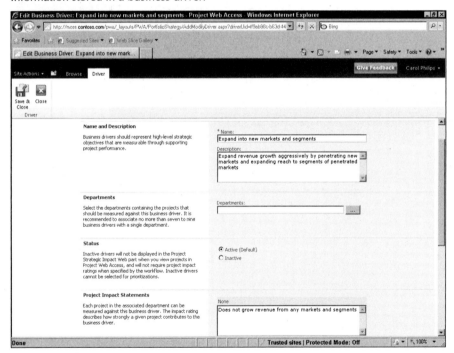

Prioritizing business drivers

As you would anticipate, not all drivers affect all projects equally. Project Server enables you to set up a variety of prioritizations; click the Driver Prioritization link in the Quick Launch pane to display the list of existing prioritizations (see Figure 24.7).

To view a particular prioritization, click its name; to create a new prioritization, click the New button in the Prioritizations group on the Prioritizations tab of the Ribbon.

When you create a new prioritization, you supply a name and description, department, and prioritization type (calculated or manual); then you select the drivers to include in the prioritization. Remember that not all prioritizations apply to all projects or to all people doing the prioritizing.

After selecting the drivers, you see a grid like the one shown in Figure 24.8. Click anywhere in the Select a Rating box to assign a priority to the driver on the left when compared to the driver on the right. You repeat this process for each driver you include in the prioritization.

FIGURE 24.7

The list of available prioritizations.

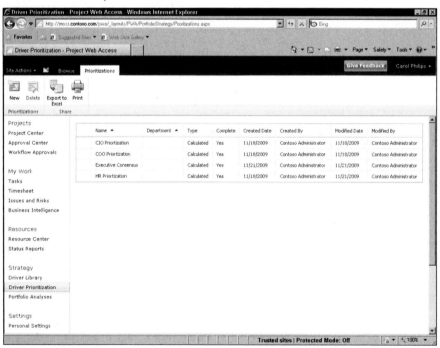

FIGURE 24.8

You use a grid like this one to identify how business drivers relate to each other.

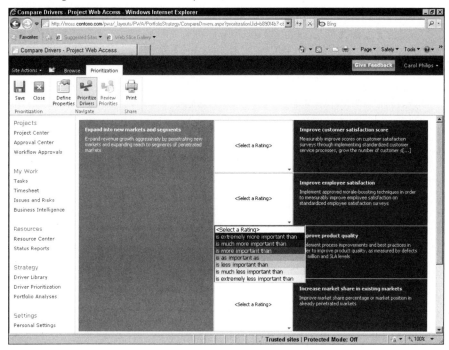

When you finish, you click the Prioritize Drivers button and Project Server assigns a percentage priority to each driver you included in the prioritization.

Tip

Project Server also evaluates the logic of the priorities you select and lets you know if you were inconsistent in your assessments. ∎

A typical prioritization looks like the one shown in Figure 24.9.

FIGURE 24.9

A typical prioritization.

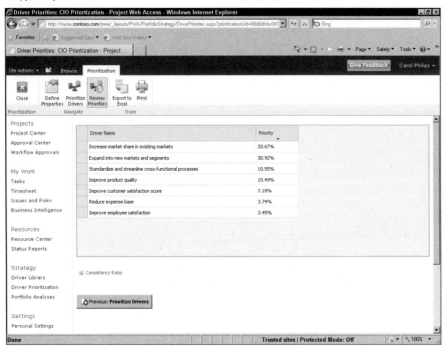

Creating a portfolio

Using Project Server analysis tools, you can create portfolio scenarios to help you identify the optimal mix of projects for your organization to undertake. Project Server considers the priorities you establish for prospective projects, the costs of each project, and the resource constraints that might be imposed by each project. You also can change the parameters of a portfolio, modifying the cost constraints and the resource constraints.

Tip
You might consider creating a "pie in the sky" portfolio that includes all possible projects with no cost or resource constraints and then making modifications to cost constraints, resource constraints, or both. ■

To create a potential portfolio, click the Portfolio Analyses link in the Quick Launch pane to display existing analyses (see Figure 24.10).

FIGURE 24.10

The list of possible portfolios modeled so far.

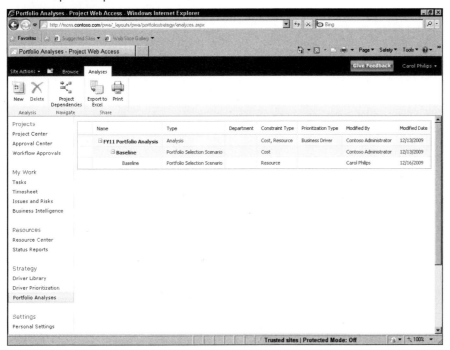

Tip

If you click the name of any existing analysis (one that has "Analysis" in the Type column), you can see the parameters used to create that portfolio. ■

Then, click the New button in the Analysis group on the Analyses tab of the Ribbon. Provide a name and description for the analysis and, if appropriate, select a department if you want to limit the portfolio to that particular department. You can prioritize by business driver — the recommended approach — or by custom field. You can select up to 800 projects to analyze, but Microsoft recommends that you limit any one analysis to no more than 200 projects.

You also must select a primary budget constraint; the default is internal rate of return (IRR), but the available list from which you can choose is lengthy.

If your organization has a defined organizational capacity and you've assigned resources — whether through a resource plan or project assignments — you can opt to have the analysis consider timephased resource requirements against organizational capacity.

Viewing the results of the analysis

After you've set the parameters of the portfolio, Project Server creates the portfolio and you can begin analyzing. The Navigate group on the Analysis tab of the Ribbon walks you through this process:

- Click the **Define Properties** button to display the page where you set up the parameters of the portfolio.

- Click the **Prioritize Projects** button to see the Impact matrix (see Figure 24.11), which shows how the projects in the portfolio, listed on the rows of the matrix, support the business drivers listed on the columns of the matrix.

- Click the **Review Priorities** button to display the priority by cost that Project Server calculated for each project (see Figure 24.12). Each project is competing for the dollars you have to spend, and this matrix prioritizes projects according to their costs.

Analyzing and adjusting the cost

Click the Analyze Cost button in the Navigate group on the Analysis tab of the Ribbon to display the Cost Constraint view, which you can use to review the total cost of your portfolio (see Figure 24.13).

FIGURE 24.11

A sample Impact matrix.

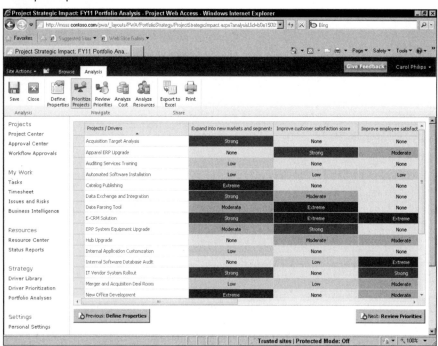

FIGURE 24.12

Projects prioritized by cost.

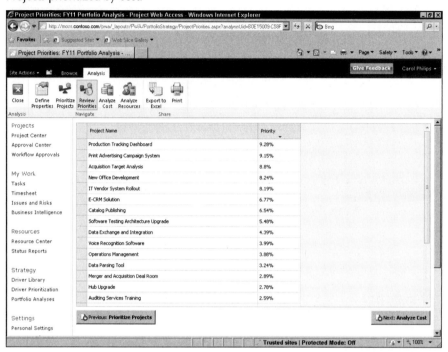

In the Projects section, you see the cost of each project included in the portfolio along with the total cost of the projects. You can use the Force In/Out column to force Project Server to include or exclude a particular project in the analysis.

The Metrics section on the left side of the page shows you how much the projects in the portfolio will cost — and how much value you can expect to gain from doing them. In this example, it will cost Contoso approximately $20,000,000.00 to achieve 100% of the strategic value of the 23 projects in the portfolio. You toggle the Metrics section on or off using the Hide Metrics button in the Projects group of the Analysis tab on the Ribbon.

You also can toggle the chart that appears in the Metrics section between the Strategic Alignment chart shown in Figure 24.13 and the Efficient Frontier chart, which compares the importance of each driver to its total cost.

Using the Metrics portion of the page, you can make changes to the portfolio. You can modify the constraints of the portfolio by changing the constraints being used, the total cost, or the projects included in the portfolio. Assuming you used IRR as the constraint for the portfolio, you can add or use other constraints by click the Modify link beside Cost Limits.

FIGURE 24.13

Reviewing the cost of the portfolio.

You can change the Total Cost value by typing in the box; the idea here is, "What would I get if I spent X instead of the value shown?" For example, you might want to try reducing the cost to see which projects remain in the portfolio.

If you make changes, click the Recalculate button in the Portfolio Selection group of the Analysis tab on the Ribbon. You can save the recalculated portfolio by clicking the Save As button in the Portfolio Selection group of the Analysis tab on the Ribbon.

Tip

You also can compare various analyses by clicking the Compare button in the Portfolio Selection group of the Analysis tab on the Ribbon. ■

Evaluating resource constraints

In addition to modeling various financial scenarios, you also can see the resource constraints a proposed portfolio will impose:

- For any given skill set, you can identify the resources you need and those you have in abundance.

- You can change project start dates to adjust your use of your resources.

- You can consider the cost of hiring more resources.

To begin evaluating resource constraints, click the Analyze Resources button in the Navigate group on the Analysis tab of the Ribbon. The Resource Constraint Analysis view appears (see Figure 24.14).

This view lists, in priority order, the projects in the Cost Constraint Analysis. In priority order, Project Server determines resource demand and resource availability and then identifies the projects you can complete based on the resources you have. These projects appear in the Selected group of the view.

To analyze why some of the projects have not been selected, you can use the Requirements Details view; this view, shown in Figure 24.15, helps you compare the resources you need with available resources. In the Projects group on the Analysis tab of the Ribbon, click the Requirements Details button.

FIGURE 24.14

The Resource Constraint Analysis view.

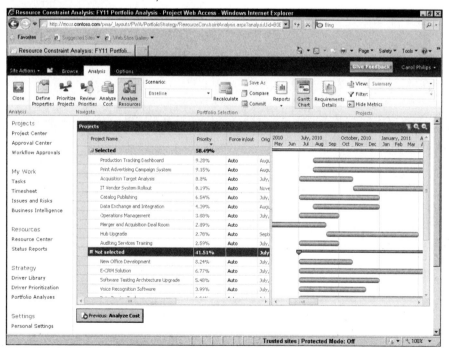

FIGURE 24.15

The Requirements Details view.

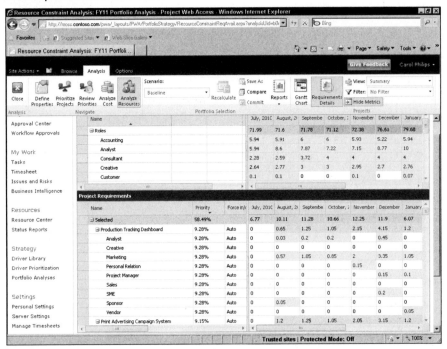

In the top pane of this view, you see available resources by role; in the bottom pane, you see the resource roles you need to fill, arranged by project.

At the right edge of the Resource Availability portion of the view, you can check the Highlight Deficit box to identify resource shortages. You might find that you could alleviate some of the deficits if you were able to change the start dates of some projects.

You can change a project start date using the Project Requirements portion of the grid on the bottom of the view. On the left side of the grid, scroll to the right or drag the vertical divider bar (as I did) to see the Original Start and New Start columns and make a change (see Figure 24.16). Then, click the Recalculate button in the Portfolio Select group of the Analysis tab on the ribbon.

FIGURE 24.16

You can change start dates for proposed projects to smooth resource availability.

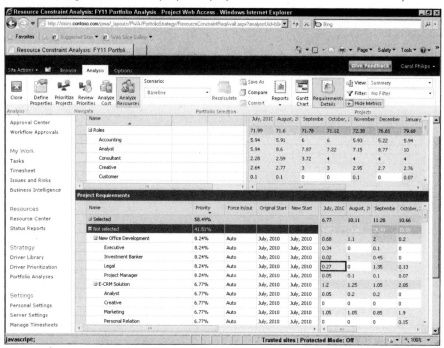

You also can see the impact of hiring additional resources: In the Projects group on the Analysis tab of the Ribbon, click the Hide Metrics button to display the Metrics section of the view on the left. In the Hire Resources row, type the number of resources you would like to hire — and then click the Recalculate button in the Portfolio Selection group of the Analysis tab on the Ribbon. If Project Server adds projects to the Selected group, you can use the Hired Resources Report to identify the resources you need to hire and the potential cost of using them. In the Portfolio Selection group of the Analysis tab on the Ribbon, click the Reports button; from the drop-down list that appears, click Hired Resources Report. The report appears on the right side of the Resource Constraint Analysis view (see Figure 24.17).

FIGURE 24.17

The Hired Resources report shows the resource roles you need and their cost.

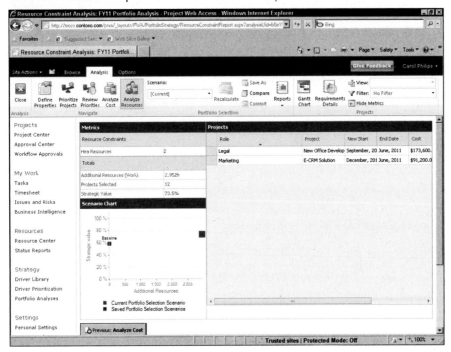

Tip

You can save resource scenarios by clicking the Save As button in the Portfolio Selection group of the Analysis tab on the Ribbon. ■

Summary

In this chapter, you've seen how executives can use Project Web App to manage projects and model various portfolios of projects to identify the one that will offer the greatest return for the investment made in them. When modeling, you can make changes to the proposed cost of a portfolio, the projects included in the portfolio, and you can analyze resource utilization and evaluate the cost of adding resources to include a project in your portfolio.

Part VIII

Appendices

What's on the Web Site

T he *Project 2010 Bible* Web page offers links to the sites of Microsoft Project partners who offer software that enhances Microsoft Project and assistance in using Microsoft Project. At several of the Web sites, you'll find Web-based demo products. All author-created material from this book is available at the book's companion Web site, which is located at www.wiley.com/go/project2010bible. You'll also find a list of links to some Project partners who are knowledgeable and might be of assistance to you.

This appendix lists and describes what you can expect to find at the Web site. Each listing includes contact information so that you can buy the software directly from the vendor.

Software Products

The links on the book's Web site take you to the latest version of these third-party products or services, which may or may not have been upgraded to be compatible with Project 2010 at the time you visit.

Planview Open Suite for Microsoft Project

Vendor: Planview

Description: Planview OpenSuite ensures seamless data transfer between Planview Enterprise and Microsoft Project through fully-supported, two-way integration. Users can import, or check-in, Microsoft Project schedules and resource assignments directly into Planview Enterprise. Once this data has been modified, users can then check the data out for use in Microsoft Project.

Company Web site: `http://www.businessengine.com/`

Live demo: `http://www.planview.com/products/opensuite/microsoft-project.aspx`

Graneda

Vendor: American Netronic, Inc.

Description: Take data from your Microsoft Project plan and chart it using this popular charting program. You can modify a variety of formatting of nodes, dates, and even the logic of the data representation.

Company Web site: `http://www.netronic.com/`

Downloadable trial version: `http://www.netronic.com/products-for-users/planning-software/graneda-dynamic-download.html`

Hans Tff TimeReg 98

Vendor: Hans Tff Management Systems A/S

Description: If you deal with simple, smaller projects, this software can help you see an overview of your project details and information about your resources' workflow in one project — or across several projects.

Company Web site: `http://www.torsleff.dk/`

Live demo: `http://www.torsleff.dk/Løsninger/IPWTimeReg/tabid/66/Default.aspx`, click on the IPW Timereg logo to start the demo

Innate Multi-Project

Vendor: Innate, Inc.

Description: Innate describes Multi-Project as an alternative to Project Server. They offer Web-based spreadsheets of your Project data with an Excel-like interface.

Company Web site: `http://www.innateus.com/`

Downloadable documentation: `http://www.innate.co.uk/documentation/useful-documents.html`

Innate Timesheets

Vendor: Innate, Inc.

Description: Record how employees are spending time on projects and track expenses with this easy-to-use software. Compare actual hours spent on projects to your estimates.

Company Web site: http://www.innateus.com/

Downloadable documentation: http://www.innate.co.uk/documentation/useful-documents.html

Innate Resource Management Software

Vendor: Innate, Inc.

Description: Avoid resource bottlenecks by using this software to reallocate resources to the highest-priority tasks. Improve your management of time, resources, and costs on your projects.

Company Web site: http://www.innateus.com/

Downloadable documentation: http://www.innate.co.uk/documentation/useful-documents.html

Milestones

Vendor: Kidasa Software

Description: The Milestones family of software includes Milestones Professional, Milestones Simplicity, and Milestones Project Companion. All focus on enhanced reporting and charting of your Project data.

Company Web site: http://www.kidasa.com/

Downloadable trial software: http://www.kidasa.com/download/index.html

PERT Chart EXPERT

Vendor: Critical Tools

Description: If PERT charts make your day, try out this software, which enables you to produce a variety of PERT charts based on your Project information. You can use this program as a standalone product or as an add-on to Project.

Company Web site: http://www.criticaltools.com/

Downloadable trial software: http://www.criticaltools.com/download.htm

WBS Chart for Project

Vendor: Critical Tools

Description: WBS Chart Pro is to WBS what PERT Chart EXPERT is to PERT charts. This software helps you draw tree-like charts based on your project's WBS structure, useful for top-down planning.

Company Web site: http://www.criticaltools.com/

Downloadable trial software: http://www.criticaltools.com/download.htm

Project Kickstart Pro

Vendor: Experience in Software

Description: Project Kickstart Pro helps you to brainstorm your initial Project plan. It's touted as easy to use and a good, inexpensive way to handle initial project planning.

Company Web site: http://www.projectkickstart.com/

Dowloadable trial software: http://www.projectkickstart.com/downloads/download_free_trial.cfm?s=navft

ProjectCommander

Vendor: Project Assistants, Inc.

Description: Provides a step-by-step approach to planning and managing your project adding a set of functions to Microsoft Project. ProjectCommander lets you get your project plan going more quickly and streamlines certain activities.

Company Web site: http://www.projectassistants.com/

Enterprise Advantage Toolset

Vendor: Artemis/Artemis Views

Description: Artemis gives you an overview of your enterprise project governance, planning, and scheduling that is useful for decision-making. Artemis Views is a project management suite for planning, time reporting, and managing earned value.

Company Web site: http://www.aisc.com/

Project Connect Online

Vendor: Project Hosts

Description: A Web-hosted solution for online collaboration on projects.

Company Web site: `http://www.projecthosts.com`

Downloadable trial: `http://www.projecthosts.com/pol.asp?source=ewpus`

EPM Live

Vendor: EPM Live

Description: Publish schedules and collaborate online. Suite of tools helps with tasks such as reporting and managing multiple projects.

Company Web site: `http://epmlive.com`

Videos and documentation (requires that you sign up): `http://kb.epmlive.com/Logon.aspx?SessionId=ggkw433kdyv04qm2hm2amsqe`

Organizations, Web Sites, and Blogs

Further useful information about Project is available online from these sources.

Microsoft Project Users Group (MPUG)

`www.mpug.com`

A great resource for connecting with other Project users and getting advice and tips about project management.

Brian Smith's Microsoft Office Project Support Blog

`http://blogs.msdn.com/brismith/`

An especially useful site for users of Project Server with special guest bloggers offering a variety of Project expertise.

Christophe Fiessinger's Blog

`http://blogs.msdn.com/chrisfie/`

Fiessinger provides useful support for the Microsoft Project community, including developers writing applications for Project.

Microsoft Project Team Blog

`http://blogs.msdn.com/project/`

Get your advice direct from Microsoft's Project team.

The Project Management Institute

`http://www.pmi.org`

A professional organization offering accreditations in project management and PM standards.

ProjectManagement.com

`http://www.projectmanagement.com`

A good all-around Web site for all things related to project management.

Project Sample Files

The Web site also contains three sample files that give you a head start on typical projects. Copy these sample files to your hard drive, open them, save them with your own project name, and then add, delete, and change settings for the various tasks included here.

You need to create your own resources and assign them to tasks and add timing and dependency relationships between tasks. The three sample files are as follows:

- **Publication sample file** (`Publish.mpp`): This sample file is useful for any kind of publishing project, from a simple brochure to a product documentation manual. Phases for writing and editing content, design, layout, printing, and distribution give you the basis for your own publishing project.

- **Meeting sample file** (`Meeting.mpp`): Everybody plans meetings. Whether it's a regular weekly staff meeting or your company's annual meeting, this sample file provides the tasks you need for planning meetings; you can arrange for location, transportation and lodging, invitations, catering, equipment, and speakers.

- **Facility sample file** (`Facility.mpp`): You can use this sample file to set up a new facility or to move to a new space. Tasks include planning space, coordinating movers, managing utilities, and setting up computer networks.

Tip
Project 2010 comes with some predefined templates on which you can base projects. These templates, like my sample files, provide a starting place for projects that you enter into Project. ∎

Project Management Worksheet

This appendix provides worksheets that help you plan every phase of a project. Feel free to make copies of these pages and fill them in as you work through your project to be sure you've covered all the bases.

On the Web Site

You can find a copy of this appendix on the Project 2010 Bible companion Web site in .PDF (Adobe Acrobat) format to help you print and use these forms. ■

Phase I: Research

In this phase, you gather information about the scope and goals of your project; you determine parameters, such as dates, resources, and money available for your project; and finally, you specify deliverables.

1. Ask the following people or groups of people to define the goal of this project. Note any discrepancies in their goal statements — and resolve them before you begin planning your project:

   - Your manager.

   - Your staff.

   - The manager of finance.

   - The person who manages the product or service that pertains to your project. For example, if you are setting up a new manufacturing unit, contact the production-line supervisor. If you are organizing the move to a new facility, contact the office or facilities manager.

Write their responses here:

_____

_____

_____

_____

2. In the space provided, sketch the organizational chart of those who will implement your project. Indicate who reports to whom (a) within your general organization and then (b) specifically for this project (these two hierarchies may differ slightly). Who will expect to receive reports, communications, and deliverables?

3. To help you begin to build a project team, list the resources you may have available for your project in the following table, noting each resource's department, expertise, and availability.

Project Resources Table

Resource	Department	Expertise	Availability

4. Research the timing for this project and answer the following questions:

- How long have similar projects taken in your organization or your experience?

_____

- Are any of the dates related to your project unchangeable, such as a yearly inspection by an outside organization or the end of your fiscal year? List them here. Also make note of holidays and vacation times.

_____

_____

_____

_____

- Rank the priority of the three major areas that typically affect a project: time, quality, and cost. In a crunch, the criterion that you rank highest here will take precedence.

___Time

___Quality

___Cost

Phase II: Planning

In this phase, you take some of the information that you gathered in Phase I and begin to see how those details will come together to form a project plan that can be the basis of your project schedule.

1. Write a goal statement. This one-sentence description states the desired result of all the efforts in your project. A sample goal statement may be as follows: "Our goal is to successfully launch a new software product into the marketplace."

_____

_____

_____

2. Write a scope statement. This statement should broadly outline the parameters of your project. A sample scope statement may be as follows: "We will finalize the software according to our internal quality standards and launch it in three major markets by the end of this fiscal year, at a cost not exceeding $1.2 million."

_____

_____

_____

_____

_____

3. List the major phases of your project:

_____

_____

_____

_____

_____

4. List any milestones in your project. Milestones are tasks that mark a significant moment or accomplishment in your project.

_____

_____

_____

_____

_____

_____

_____

_____

5. Create a contact list for your project, including each resource's name, title, and department; each resource's manager, contact information, hourly rate or fee; and any other information that you consider useful. You can create this list in a word-processing program, such as Microsoft Office Word, or begin to enter this resource information into Microsoft Office Project. Use the following entry as a model:

Resource Name: John Smith
Title/Department: Engineer/manufacturing department
Manager: Sally Jones, manufacturing manager
Phone: (444) 555-1111
E-mail: jsmith@org.com
Rate: $35 per hour
Comments: Not available in December due to professional association commitments; assistant is Bob James, ext. 5567.

_____

_____

_____

_____

_____

_____
_____
_____
_____
_____
_____
_____
_____
_____
_____
_____
_____
_____
_____
_____
_____
_____
_____
_____
_____
_____
_____
_____

6. Outline the standards that you will use for entering information into Microsoft Office Project, including the following:

- How will you name resources (by name or title)?

  _____

- Who will track progress and how often?

  _____

- What are your organization's standard work hours and fiscal year? This information enables you to create an accurate calendar in Project.

  _____

- What regular reports will you generate and to whom will they go?

  _____

- How will you track and account for overtime?

  _____
  _____

Phase III: Creating Your Project Schedule

In this phase, you enter information to begin building your project. Use this checklist to be sure that you are creating a comprehensive and accurate schedule.

Checklist for creating a project schedule

_____ Enter general project information, such as the project name, start date, and finish date.

_____ Make any calendar settings for your project based on your organization's workday, week, or year.

_____ Enter the names of major phases of your project.

_____ Enter the first level of individual tasks in each phase, including task name and timing. If this level of tasks will have subtasks, don't bother to enter timing because the task timing will be derived from subtasks.

_____ Enter any subtasks and include timing information.

_____ Enter any regularly recurring tasks, such as monthly project meetings.

_____ Add resource information to individual tasks, including costs and availability.

_____ Establish dependencies between tasks.

_____ Study and resolve resource conflicts by using the resource leveling and contouring tools in Project.

_____ Determine whether Project is giving you an acceptable finish date. If it isn't, consider using the following actions:

- Add resources to reduce duration. (However, this action is likely to add costs.)
- Request additional time to complete the project.
- Use resource downtime more efficiently.
- Adjust dependencies.
- Start the project earlier.

_____ If possible, add some slack time to tasks to allow for delays.

_____ Set up any workgroup resources with whom you will be using Project's TeamAssign, TeamStatus, and TeamUpdate features.

_____ When the project schedule is acceptable, set the baseline and save the file.

Phase IV: Tracking Your Project

Tracking your project involves entering actual time expended on tasks. Use this checklist to help in tracking projects. Don't forget to set a baseline before beginning to track activity on your project.

Tracking procedures checklist

____ Enter actual start and finish dates for tasks that have been completed.

____ Enter resource effort expended on tasks.

____ Enter actual fees or charges incurred on tasks.

____ Set remaining durations and percent complete for individual tasks.

____ Use various tracking views in Project, information about earned value and resource usage, and filters (such as critical paths) to analyze the status of your project. Pay careful attention to how much time and money remains by comparing your original estimates and actual activity on the project.

____ Make any adjustments necessary to keep your project on track, such as adding or reassigning resources, extending your final deadline, or reassessing the remaining budget available for the rest of the project based on cost overruns.

____ Send out TeamStatus and TeamUpdate messages to keep your team informed of project progress.

Phase V: Preparing for the Next Project

After you've completed a project, don't forget to analyze the project's activities so you can improve your estimation and tracking ability for your next project. Use this worksheet to analyze your completed project.

1. List your baseline start and finish dates and actual start and finish dates for your entire project:

   - Baseline start:_____

   - Baseline finish:_____

   - Actual start:_____

   - Actual finish:_____

2. Write a statement about the major factor that affected your timing and a conclusion about whether you could have anticipated or avoided that factor. Be honest about your own failings. It's the best way to become better at what you do.

   _____

   _____

   _____

3. Enter your baseline total costs and actual total costs for the project:
   - Baseline costs:_____
   - Actual costs:_____

4. Write a statement about the major factor or factors influencing your final costs, including what you can do to avoid cost overruns on a future project (or, if you're lucky, what you can do to have similar cost savings on future projects). What did you do or not do to keep costs in line?

   _____

   _____

   _____

5. Analyze how resources performed on your project. Are there people or vendors you would *not* recommend for use on future projects? Are there people or vendors you feel did exceptionally well? Make a record of them so that you and others in your company can plan resources for future projects appropriately.

   - Vendor issues on current project:

     _____

     _____

     _____

   - Recommended resources for future projects:

     _____

     _____

     _____

6. List three things you can do more efficiently as a project manager on your next project to improve performance and efficiency:

   _____

   _____

   _____

7. List three things your manager or organization could provide you to make your next project more successful:

   _____

   _____

   _____

8. List three ways you can improve your tracking procedures on future projects:

   _____

   _____

   _____

9. Write statements of what worked and what didn't work in your management of resources in these areas:

- Communication:

  _____

  _____

  _____

- Accuracy of time estimates for resources to complete tasks:

  _____

  _____

  _____

- Resource management:

  _____

  _____

  _____

Available Fields and Functions for Custom Field Formulas

This appendix contains three tables that help you identify the fields and functions you can use when creating formulas to include in custom fields. Table C.1 contains a list of all the Task fields you can include in a formula. The fields are listed according to the respective submenus on which they appear when you click the Fields button in the Formula dialog box. Table C.2 contains the same information for Resource fields. In each of these tables, the first column contains a field category. The second column contains either fields within the category or those that occupy a subcategory. If the second column contains a subcategory, then the fields appear in the third column. Table C.3 lists the functions you can include in a formula, as well as a description of each function's purpose.

IN THIS APPENDIX

Task fields

Resource fields

Functions available

TABLE C.1

Task Fields Available for Custom Field Formulas

Category	Subcategory or Field	Field
Cost	Actual Cost	
	Actual Overtime Cost	
	ACWP	
	Baseline Cost	Baseline Cost, Baseline1 Cost – Baseline10 Cost, Baseline Budget Cost, Baseline 1 Budget Cost – Baseline10 Budget Cost
	BCWP	
	BCWS	
	Budget Cost	
	Cost	
	Cost Variance	
	CPI	
	Custom Cost	Cost1 – Cost10
	CV	
	CV%	
	EAC	
	Enterprise Custom Cost	Enterprise Cost1 – Enterprise Cost10
	Enterprise Project Custom Cost	Enterprise Project Cost1 – Enterprise Project Cost10
	Fixed Cost	
	Overtime Cost	
	Remaining Cost	
	Remaining Overtime Cost	
	SPI	
	SV	
	SV%	
	TCPI	
	VAC	
Date	Actual Finish	
	Actual Start	
	Baseline Finish	Baseline Estimated Finish, Baseline1 Estimated Finish – Baseline10 Estimated Finish, Baseline Finish, Baseline1 Finish – Baseline10 Finish

Category	Subcategory or Field	Field
	Baseline Start	Baseline Estimated Start, Baseline1 Estimated Start – Baseline10 Estimated Start, Baseline Start, Baseline1 Start – Baseline10 Start
	Constraint Date	
	Created	
	Custom Date	Date1 – Date10
	Custom Finish	Finish1 – Finish10
	Custom Start	Start1 – Start10
	Deadline	
	Deliverable Finish	
	Deliverable Start	
	Early Finish	
	Early Start	
	Finish	
	Finish Variance	
	Late Finish	
	Late Start	
	Preleveled Finish	
	Preleveled Start	
	Resume	
	Scheduled Finish	
	Scheduled Start	
	Start	
	Start Variance	
	Stop	
Duration	Actual Duration	
	Baseline Duration	Baseline Estimated Duration, Baseline1 Estimated Duration – Baseline10 Estimated Duration, Baseline Duration, Baseline1 Duration – Baseline10 Duration
	Custom Duration	Duration1 – Duration10
	Duration	
	Duration Variance	
	Finish Slack	
	Free Slack	

continued

TABLE C.1 (continued)

Category	Subcategory or Field	Field
	Leveling Delay	
	Remaining Duration	
	Scheduled Duration	
	Start Slack	
	Total Slack	
Flag	Active	
	Confirmed	
	Critical	
	Custom Flag	Flag1 – Flag20
	Effort Driven	
	Estimated	
	External Task	
	Group By Summary	
	Hide Bar	
	Ignore Resource Calendar	
	Level Assignments	
	Leveling Can Split	
	Linked Fields	
	Marked	
	Milestone	
	Overallocated	
	Recurring	
	Response Pending	
	Rollup	
	Subproject Read Only	
	Summary	
	Task Mode	
	TeamStatus Pending	
	Update Needed	
ID/Code	Custom Outline Code	Outline Code1 – Outline Code10
	ID	
	Outline Number	
	Predecessors	
	Successors	
	Unique ID	

Appendix C: Available Fields and Functions for Custom Field Formulas

Category	Subcategory or Field	Field
	Unique ID Predecessors	
	Unique ID Successors	
	WBS	
	WBS Predecessors	
	WBS Successors	
	GUID	
	Deliverable GUID	
Number	% Complete	
	Constraint Type	
	Custom Number	Number1 – Number20
	Deliverable Type	
	Fixed Cost Accrual	
	Objects	
	Outline Level	
	Physical % Complete	
	Priority	
	Resource Type	
	Status	
	Type	
Project	Date	Creation Date
		Current Date
		Default Finish Time
		Default Start Time
		Last Update
		Project Finish
		Project Start
		Status Date
	Number	Minutes Per Day
		Minutes Per Week
		Resource Count
		Task Count
	Text	Author
		Project Calendar
		Subject
		Title

continued

TABLE C.1	(continued)	
Category	**Subcategory or Field**	**Field**
Text	Contact	
	Custom Text	Text1 – Text30
	Deliverable Name	
	Enterprise Custom Text	Enterprise Text1 – Enterprise Text40
	Enterprise Project Custom Text	Enterprise Project Text1 – Enterprise Project Text40
	Hyperlink	
	Hyperlink Address	
	Hyperlink Href	
	Hyperlink SubAddress	
	Name	
	Notes	Task name, Resource name
	Project	
	Resource Group	
	Resource Initials	
	Resource Names	
	Resource Phonetics	
	Subproject File	
	Task Calendar	
	Deliverable Name	
Work	% Work Complete	
	Actual Overtime Work	
	Actual Work	
	Baseline Work	Baseline Work, Baseline1 Work – Baseline10 Work, Baseline Budget Work, Baseline1 Budget Work – Baseline10 Budget Work
	Budget Work	
	Overtime Work	
	Regular Work	
	Remaining Overtime Work	
	Remaining Work	
	Work	
	Work Variance	

TABLE C.2

Resource Fields Available for Custom Field Formulas

Category	Subcategory or Field	Field
Cost	Actual Cost	
	Actual Overtime Cost	
	ACWP	
	Baseline Cost	Baseline Cost, Baseline1 Cost – Baseline10 Cost, Baseline Budget Cost, Baseline1 Budget Cost - Baseline10 Budget Cost
	BCWP	
	BCWS	
	Budget Cost	
	Cost	
	Cost Per Use	
	Cost Rate Table	
	Cost Variance	
	Custom Cost	Cost1 – Cost10
	CV	
	Overtime Cost	
	Overtime Rate	
	Remaining Cost	
	Remaining Overtime Cost	
	Standard Rate	
	SV	
	VAC	
Date/Duration	Available From	
	Available To	
	Baseline Finish	Baseline Finish, Baseline1 Finish – Baseline10 Finish
	Baseline Start	Baseline Start, Baseline1 Start – Baseline10 Start
	Custom Date	Date1 – Date10
	Custom Duration	Duration1 – Duration10
	Custom Finish	Finish1 – Finish10
	Custom Start	Start1 – Start10
	Finish	

continued

TABLE C.2 *(continued)*

Category	Subcategory or Field	Field
	Start	
Flag	Can Level	
	Confirmed	
	Custom Flag	Flag1 – Flag20
	Linked Fields	
	Overallocated	
	Response Pending	
	TeamStatus Pending	
	Update Needed	
ID/Code	Custom Outline Code	Outline Code1 – Outline Code10
	ID	
	Unique ID	
Number	Accrue At	
	Custom Number	Number1 – Number20
	Max Units	
	Objects	
	Peak	
	Type	
Project	Date	Creation Date
		Current Date
		Default Finish Time
		Default Start Time
		Last Update
		Project Finish
		Project Start
		Status Date
	Number	Minutes Per Day
		Minutes Per Week
		Resource Count
		Task Count
	Text	Author
		Project Calendar
		Subject
		Title

Appendix C: Available Fields and Functions for Custom Field Formulas

Category	Subcategory or Field	Field
Text	Base Calendar	
	Code	
	Custom Text	Text1 – Text30
	E-mail Address	
	Group	
	Group By Summary	
	Hyperlink	
	Hyperlink Address	
	Hyperlink Href	
	Hyperlink SubAddress	
	Initials	
	Material Label	
	Name	
	Notes	
	Phonetics	
	Project	
	Windows User Account	
Work	% Work Complete	
	Actual Overtime Work	
	Actual Work	
	Baseline Work	Baseline Work, Baseline1 Work – Baseline10 Work, Baseline Budget Work, Baseline1 Budget Work – Baseline10 Budget Work
	Budget Work	
	Overtime Work	
	Regular Work	
	Remaining Overtime Work	
	Remaining Work	
	Work	
	Work Variance	

TABLE C.3

Functions Available for Custom Field Formulas

Function Category	Function	Description
Conversion	Asc(string)	Returns an Integer representing the character code corresponding to the first letter in a string.
	CBool(expression)	Coerces an expression to a Boolean.
	CByte(expression)	Coerces an expression to a Byte (0–255).
	CCur(expression)	Coerces an expression to a Currency value.
	CDate(expression)	Coerces an expression to a Date.
	CDbl(expression)	Coerces an expression to a Double.
	CDec(expression)	Coerces an expression to a Decimal.
	Chr(charcode)	Returns a string containing the character associated with the specified character code.
	CInt(expression)	Coerces an expression to an Integer.
	CLng(expression)	Coerces an expression to a Long.
	CSng(expression)	Coerces an expression to a Single.
	CStr(expression)	Coerces an expression to a String.
	CVar(expression)	Coerces an expression to a Variant.
	DateSerial(year, month, day)	Returns a Variant (Date) for a specified year, month, and day.
	DateValue(date)	Returns a Variant (Date).
	Day(date)	Returns a Variant (Integer) specifying a whole number between 1 and 31, inclusive, representing the day of the month.
	Hex(number)	Returns a String representing the hexadecimal value of a number.
	Hour(time)	Returns a Variant (Integer) specifying a whole number between 0 and 23, inclusive, representing the hour of the day.
	Minute(time)	Returns a Variant (Integer) specifying a whole number between 0 and 59, inclusive, representing the minute of the hour.

Function Category	Function	Description
	Month(date)	Returns a Variant (Integer) specifying a whole number between 1 and 12, inclusive, representing the month of the year.
	Oct(number)	Returns a Variant (String) representing the octal value of a number.
	ProjDateConv(expression, dateformat)	Converts a numeric value to a date in an optionally specified format.
	ProjDurConv(expression, durationunits)	Converts a numeric value to a duration value in the specified units.
	Second(time)	Returns a Variant (Integer) specifying a whole number between 0 and 59, inclusive, representing the second of the minute.
	Str(number)	Returns a Variant (String) representation of a number.
	StrConv(string, conversion, LCID)	Returns a Variant (String) converted as specified.
	TimeSerial(hour, minute, second)	Returns a Variant (Date) containing the time for a specific hour, minute, and second.
	TimeValue(time)	Returns a Variant (Date) containing the time.
	Val(string)	Returns the numbers contained in a string as a numeric value of appropriate type.
	Weekday(date, firstdayofweek)	Returns a Variant (integer) containing a whole number representing the day of the week.
	Year(date)	Returns a Variant (Integer) containing a whole number representing the year.
Date/Time	Cdate(expression)	Coerces an expression to a Date.
	Date()	Returns a Variant (Date) containing the current system date.
	DateAdd(interval, number, date)	Returns a Variant (Date) containing a date to which a specified time interval has been added.
	DateDiff(interval, date1, date2, firstdayofweek, firstweekofyear)	Returns a Variant (Long) specifying the number of time intervals between two specified dates.

continued

TABLE C.3 *(continued)*

Function Category	Function	Description
	DatePart(interval, date, firstday-ofweek, firstweekofyear)	Returns a Variant (Integer) containing the specified part of a given date.
	DateSerial(year, month, day)	Returns a Variant (Date) for a specified year, month, and day.
	DateValue(date)	Returns a Variant (Date).
	Day(date)	Returns a Variant (Integer) specifying a whole number between 1 and 31, inclusive, representing the day of the month.
	Hour(time)	Returns a Variant (Integer) specifying a whole number between 0 and 23, inclusive, representing the hour of the day.
	IsDate(expression)	Returns a Boolean value indicating whether an expression can be converted to a date.
	Minute(time)	Returns a Variant (Integer) specifying a whole number between 0 and 59, inclusive, representing the minute of the hour.
	Month(date)	Returns a Variant (Integer) specifying a whole number between 1 and 12, inclusive, representing the month of the year.
	Now()	Returns a Variant (Date) specifying the current date and time according your computer system's date and time.
	ProjDateAdd(date, duration, calendar)	Adds a duration to a date to return a new date.
	ProjDateDiff(date1, date2, calendar)	Returns the duration between two dates in minutes.
	ProjDateSub(date, duration, calendar)	Returns the date that precedes another date by a specified duration.
	ProjDurValue(duration)	Returns the number of minutes in a duration.
	Second(time)	Returns a Variant (Integer) specifying a whole number between 0 and 59, inclusive, representing the second of the minute.
	Time()	Returns a Variant (Date) indicating the current system time.

Function Category	Function	Description
	Timer()	Returns a Single representing the number of seconds elapsed since midnight.
	TimeSerial(hour, minute, second)	Returns a Variant (Date) containing the time for a specific hour, minute, and second.
	TimeValue(time)	Returns a Variant (Date) containing the time.
	Weekday(date, firstdayofweek)	Returns a Variant (Integer) containing a whole number representing the day of the week.
	Year(date)	Returns a Variant (Integer) containing a whole number representing the year.
General	Choose(index, expression1, expression2,…)	Selects and returns a value from a list of arguments.
	IIf(expression, truepart, falsepart)	Returns one of two parts, depending on the evaluation of an expression.
	IsNumeric(expression)	Returns a Boolean value indicating whether an expression can be evaluated as a number.
	IsNull(expression)	Returns a Boolean value that indicates whether an expression contains no valid data.
	Switch(expression1, value1, expression2, value2,…)	Evaluates a list of expressions and returns a Variant value or an expression associated with the first expression in the list that is True.
Math	Abs(number)	Returns a value of the same type that is passed to it specifying the absolute value of a number.
	Atn(number)	Returns a Double specifying the arctangent of a number.
	Cos(number)	Returns a Double specifying the cosine of an angle.
	Exp(number)	Returns a Double specifying e (the base of natural logarithms) raised to a power.
	Fix(number)	Returns the integer portion of a number. If the number is negative, Fix returns the first negative integer greater than or equal to number.

continued

TABLE C.3 *(continued)*

Function Category	Function	Description
	Int(number)	Returns the integer portion of a number. If the number is negative, Int returns the first negative integer less than or equal to the number.
	Log(number)	Returns a Double specifying the natural logarithm of a number.
	Rnd(number)	Returns a Single containing a random number.
	Sgn(number)	Returns a Variant (Integer) indicating the sign of a number.
	Sin(number)	Returns a Double specifying the sine of an angle.
	Sqr(number)	Returns a Double specifying the square root of a number.
	Tan(number)	Returns a Double specifying the tangent of an angle.
Microsoft Office Project	ProjDateAdd(date, duration, calendar)	Adds a duration to a date to return a new date.
	ProjDateConv(expression, Dateformat)	Converts a numeric value to a date in an optionally specified format.
	ProjDateDiff(date1, date2, calendar)	Returns the duration between two dates in minutes.
	ProjDateSub(date, duration, calendar)	Returns the date that precedes another date by a specified duration.
	ProjDateValue(expression)	Converts a numeric value to a date.
	ProjDurConv(expression, durationunits)	Converts a numeric value to a duration value in the specified units.
	ProjDurValue(duration)	Returns the number of minutes in a duration.
Text	Asc(string)	Returns an Integer representing the character code corresponding to the first letter in a string.
	Chr(charcode)	Returns a String containing the character associated with the specified character code.
	Format(expression, format first-dayofweek, firstweekofyear)	Returns a Variant (String) containing an expression formatted according to instructions contained in a format expression.

Appendix C: Available Fields and Functions for Custom Field Formulas

Function Category	Function	Description
	InStr(start, string1, string2, compare)	Returns a Variant (Long) specifying the position of the first occurrence of one string within another.
	LCase(string)	Returns a String that has been converted to lowercase.
	Left(string, length)	Returns a Variant (String) containing a specified number of characters from the left side of a string.
	Len(string)	Returns a Long containing the number of characters in a string or the number of bytes required to store a variable.
	LTrim(string)	Returns a Variant (String) containing a copy of a specified string without leading spaces.
	Mid(string, start, length)	Returns a Variant (String) containing a specified number of characters from a string.
	Right(string, length)	Returns a Variant (String) containing a specified number of characters from the right side of a string.
	RTrim(string)	Returns a Variant (String) containing a copy of a specified string without trailing spaces.
	Space(number)	Returns a Variant (String) consisting of the specified number of spaces.
	StrComp(string1, string2, compare)	Returns a Variant (Integer) indicating the result of a string comparison.
	StrConv(string, conversion, LCID)	Returns a Variant (String) converted as specified.
	String(number, character)	Returns a Variant (String) containing a repeating character string of the length specified.
	Trim(string)	Returns a Variant (String) containing a copy of a specified string without leading and trailing spaces.
	UCase(string)	Returns a Variant (String) containing the specified string, converted to uppercase.

Project Management Resources

Project management is a detailed methodology and intricate system of requirements that has evolved over many years for various industries and disciplines. Project management as a topic encompasses concepts of leadership and team building, charting and analysis of data, cost and schedule control, and more.

Many useful resources for project management information, tools, and support can help you work with Microsoft Project. This appendix contains five resource categories: Associations, Publications, Education, Online, and Software Products. It provides phone numbers and, when available, address and fax information. As you can see from this list, project management is an extremely international discipline. Remember to dial country codes before dialing any phone number outside the United States.

Associations

The following associations provide support and information for both general and industry-specific issues in project management.

- **Association for the Advancement of Cost Engineering:** Counts among its membership those interested in cost engineering and cost estimating.

  209 Prairie Ave., #100
  Morgantown, WV 26505
  Phone: (800) 858-COST
  http://www.aacei.org/

- **Association of Proposal Management Professionals:** Can assist you in developing proposals for your projects, whether you bid for government or industry contracts. APMP has local chapters, as well as a newsletter and task force on Electronic Procurement.

  APMP
  P.O. Box 668
  Dana Point, California 92629-0668
  http://www.apmp.org/

- **Association for Project Management:** Based in England, the Association for Project Management has chapters in both the United Kingdom and Hong Kong. This association has a certification program for project management professionals.

  Ibis House, Regent Park
  Summerleys Road
  Princes Risborough
  Buckinghamshire
  HP27 9LE
  Tel: 0845 458 1944
  Fax: 0845 458 8807
  International tel: +44 (0)1844 271 640
  International fax: +44 (0)1844 274 509
  info@apm.org.uk
  http://www.apm.org.uk/

- **American Society for Quality:** Focuses on quality issues in project management. This organization offers certification in a variety of specializations related to quality.

  P.O. Box 3005
  Milwaukee, WI 53201-3005
  or
  600 North Plankinton Avenue
  Milwaukee, WI 53203
  U.S. Phone: (800) 248-1946 (United States and Canada only)
  International Phone: 1+414-272-8575
  http://www.asq.org/

- **Construction Management Association of America:** As its mission statement, this organization "promotes professionalism and excellence in the management of the construction process."

  7918 Jones Branch Drive, Suite 540
  McLean, VA 22102
  Phone: (703) 356-2622
  Fax: (703) 356-6388
  info@cmaanet.org
  http://cmaanet.org/

- **Educational Society for Resource Management:** Formerly the American Production & Inventory Control Society (and still referred to as APICS), the Educational Society for Resource Management specializes in support and information for those wanting to improve or maximize their skills in resource management.

  8430 West Bryn Mawr Avenue
  Suite 1000
  Chicago, IL 60631
  Phone: (800) 444-2742 or (773) 867-1777
  Fax: (773) 639-3000
  service@apics.org
  http://www.apics.org/

- **International Project Management Association (IPMA):** A multinational nonprofit confederation of project management associations based primarily in European countries. It offers international conferences on project management.

  International Project Management Association
  PO Box 1167, 3860 BD Nijkerk, The Netherlands
  Tel: +31 33 247 3430
  Fax: +31 33 246 0470
  info@ipma.ch
  http://www.ipma.ch/

- **Project Management Institute:** The premier United States project management association. It has chapters across the country, educational programs, a long list of publications, and online discussion forums. In addition, PMI has a monthly magazine called *PM Network* and a quarterly called *Project Management Journal*. Its publication, *A Guide to the Project Management Body of Knowledge* (PMBOK Guide), is a bible in the project management world.

  Project Management Institute Headquarters
  14 Campus Boulevard
  Newtown Square, PA 19073-3299
  Phone: (610) 356-4600
  Fax: +610-356-4647
  customercare@pmi.org
  http://www.pmi.org

PMI Special Interest Groups

PMI offers a variety of special interest groups, or SIGs, that focus on different aspects of project management. SIG members are required to pay a small fee to support the group, and all members must also belong to PMI.

These SIGs are either currently available or under consideration:

- Aerospace & Defense
- Automation Systems
- Design-Procurement-Construction
- Diversity
- eBusiness
- Education & Training
- Financial Services
- Government
- Healthcare Project Management
- Information Systems
- Information Technology & Telecommunications
- Manufacturing
- Marketing & Sales
- Metrics
- New Product Development
- Oil, Gas & Petrochemical
- Pharmaceutical
- Program Management Office
- Quality in Project Management
- Risk Management
- Service & Outsourcing
- Students of PM
- Troubled Projects
- Women in Project Management

Publications

A great many books, newsletters, and journals are devoted to project management and its many facets. Some of the publications in this list are from small presses or associations. You can use the ISBN number — a publishing industry code — to order many of the books from your local bookstore.

Books

The following books provide guidance on project management — both general principles and industry-specific advice. You can search for these books, read descriptions of them, and find their locations by using the ISBN database available at `http://isbndb.com/`.

- *The AMA Handbook of Project Management,* **2nd Edition**
  Author: Paul C. Dinsmore, Jeannette Cabanis-Brewin
  Publisher: Amacom Books, A Division of AMA
  ISBN: 978-0814472712

- *Cost Estimator's Reference Manual*
  Authors: Rodney D. Stewart, James D. Johannes, Richard M. Wyskida, eds. Publisher: John Wiley-Interscience
  ISBN: 978-0471305101

- *Effective Project Management Through Applied Cost and Schedule Control*
  Authors: James A. Bent and Kenneth K. Humphreys
  Publisher: CRC
  ISBN: 978-0824797157

- *5-Phase Project Management*
  Authors: Joseph W. Weiss and Robert K. Wysocki
  Publisher: Project Management Institute
  ISBN: 978-0201563160

- *Fundamentals of Project Management,* **3rd Edition**
  Author: James P. Lewis
  Publisher: Amacom Books, A Division of AMA
  ISBN: 978-0814408797

- *Managing High-Technology Programs and Projects,* **3rd Edition**
  Author: Russell D. Archibald
  Publisher: John Wiley & Sons, Inc.
  ISBN: 978-0471265573

- *Project Management: Strategic Design and Implementation,* **3rd Edition**
  Author: David I. Cleland
  Publisher: McGraw-Hill Professional Book Group
  ISBN: 978-0070120204

- *Project Management for the 21st Century,* **3rd Edition**
  Authors: Bennet P. Lientz and Kathryn P. Rea
  Publisher: Academic Press
  ISBN: 978-0124499836

- *Project Management Memory Jogger: A Pocket Guide for Project Teams*
  Author: Paula Martin
  Publisher: Project Management Institute
  ISBN: 978-1576810019

Journals and magazines

Many of the associations listed in the first section of this appendix publish magazines or journals. Some of those are listed here, along with a Web site for additional information. Note that many of these publications are available only to members of the sponsoring organizations.

- *APICS Magazine*
  Association for Operations Management
  `http://www.apics.org/resources/magazine/default.htm`

- *International Journal of Project Management*
  Elsevier Science
  `http://www.elsevier.com/wps/find/journaldescription.cws_home/30435/description#description`

- *Journal of Quality Technology*
  Quality Management Journal
  Software Quality Professional
  Quality Engineering
  Technometrics
  Journal for Quality and Participation
  Quality Progress
  Six Sigma Forum Magazine
  American Society of Quality Control
  `http://www.asq.org/pub/index.html#journals`

- *Project Management Journal*
  PM Network
  PMI Today
  Project Management Institute
  `http://www.pmi.org/Resources/Pages/Our-Publications.aspx`

Online

You could spend days online and never run through all the Web sites devoted to — and associated with — project management. The following list, however, offers a few good places to begin surfing. Please note that Web sites and addresses change frequently; those listed here were current as this book went to press.

- **American Production and Inventory Control Society:** `www.apics.org`

- **Architecture, Engineering, Construction Business Center:** `www.aecinfo.com`

- **Center for Coaching and Mentoring:** `http://coachingandmentoring.com/`

- **Earned Value Management:** Sponsored by the Office of the Under Secretary of Defense (Acquisition & Technology) Systems Acquisition/Performance Management. `www.acq.osd.mil/pm`

- **FedWorld:** www.fedworld.gov/
- **Heuristic Management Systems:** http://www.hmssoftware.ca
- **The Project Management Forum:** www.pmforum.org/
- **Project Management Institute:** www.pmi.org

Software Products

This section lists some other project management tools worthy of investigation:

- **Innate Multi-Project:** Innate Multi-Project extends Microsoft Project to a complete system of program management — giving a view across projects, offering resource capacity planning, and supporting your business processes whether top-down or bottom-up.

  Innate, Inc. Saracens House
  25 St. Margarets Green
  Ipswich, Suffolk IP4 2BN
  England
  E-mail: mikew@innate.co.uk
  www.innate.co.uk
  Phone: +44 (0) 8456 123 145

  Innate Inc.
  5807 Nelson Road
  Oconomowoc, WI, 53066
  +1 888 371 3350

- **Knowledge Relay Solution:** Knowledge Relay Solution, a modular product, helps accelerate the business decision-making cycle by reducing the time between collecting data and acting upon it. The Knowledge Relay Solution delivers pertinent information on a timely basis, putting it into the hands of those who make operational decisions in a format meaningful to them using information from a variety of sources, including Microsoft Project.

  Knowledge Relay, Inc.
  5836 Corporate Avenue
  Suite 130
  Cypress, CA 90630
  Phone: (800) 447-2633

- **Artemis:** Offers a two-way interface between Microsoft Project and the Artemis Views product for enterprise-level project and resource management.

  Artemis Management Systems
  Newport Beach, United States
  Telephone: 800.477.6648
  Fax: 949.660.7020
  www.aisc.com

- **Hans Tørsleff IPW TimeReg:** A time registration system that updates Microsoft Project with Actual Work entered by individual resources, sparing the project manager the manual update of the project plan and making more time available for real management of the project.

  Hans Tørsleff Management Systems A/S
  Gl. Kongevej 161
  1850 Frederiksberg C
  Denmark
  Phone: +45 70 20 08 16
  Fax: +45 70 22 08 07
  E-mail: mail@htms.dk
  http://www.htms.dk/

  EPK Suite & EPK-MPPlus: EPK Suite offers an integrated approach to planning for your projects and managing your portfolio. You can take an inventory of resources, prioritize projects, control business processes, and more. EPK-MPPPlus enhances an organization's utilization of Microsoft Project.

  EPK Group LLC
  6671 W. Indiantown Rd.
  Suite 56, PMB 153
  Jupiter, FL 33458
  (561) 310-7279
  (561) 658-0979 Fax
  Web: http://epkgroup.com/

- **Smart EPM:** Offers an end-to-end EPM solution, built using the Microsoft Office System stack. Smart EPM offers specific functionality and benefits for demand management, portfolio management, project management, operational management, collaboration, and business intelligence.

  LMR Solutions Inc.
  5860 Owens Ave, 130
  Carlsbad, CA 92008
  Phone: (760) 603-9990
  Fax: (858) 225-0685
  http://www.lmrsolutions.com/
  info@lmrsolutions.com

Glossary

ACWP (actual cost of work performed) Cost of actual work performed to date on the project, plus any fixed costs.

ALAP (as late as possible) A constraint placed on a task's timing to make it occur as late as possible in the project schedule, based on its dependency relationships.

ASAP (as soon as possible) A constraint placed on a task's timing to make it occur as early in the project as possible, based on its dependency relationships.

BAC (budget at completion) The total of planned costs to complete a task (also referred to as *baseline costs*).

BCWP (budgeted cost of work performed) Also called *earned value;* this term refers to the value of work completed. A task with $1,000 of associated costs, when 75 percent complete, has a baseline value of $750.

BCWS (budgeted cost of work scheduled) The planned completion percentage multiplied by the planned cost. This calculated value reflects the amount of the task that is completed and the planned cost of the task.

CV (earned value cost variance) This variance indicates the difference between the planned costs (baseline costs) and the costs after taking into account actual costs to date and estimated costs going forward (scheduled costs). The difference between these two values produces either a positive (overbudget) or negative (underbudget) cost variance.

EAC (estimate at completion) The total scheduled cost for a resource on a task. This calculation provides the costs incurred to date plus costs estimated for remaining work on the task.

WBS (work breakdown structure) Automatically assigned numbers for each task in a project outline designed to specify an order to complete the project. Government project reports often include WBS codes.

actual A cost or percentage of work completed and tracked as having already occurred or been incurred.

actual cost of work performed See *ACWP.*

as late as possible See *ALAP.*

as soon as possible See *ASAP.*

Automatically scheduled task For tasks using this mode, Project automatically calculates the task's Start and Finish dates using its duration or, conversely, Project calculates the task's duration based on its Start and Finish dates. Any changes you makes that result in a change to the dates of an automatically scheduled task also affect successor tasks and the project schedule. Also see *Manually scheduled task.*

base calendar Also called the Project calendar, the default calendar on which all new tasks are based, unless a task or resource-specific calendar is applied.

baseline The snapshot of a project plan against which actual work is tracked.

baseline cost The total of all planned costs on tasks in a project before any actual costs have been incurred.

budget at completion See *BAC.*

budgeted cost of work performed See *BCWP.*

budgeted cost of work scheduled See *BCWS.*

Glossary

calendar The various settings for hours in a work-day, days in a work week, holidays, and nonworking days on which a project schedule is based.

circular dependency A dependency among tasks such that each depends on the other(s), creating an endless loop that can't be resolved.

collapse To close a project outline to hide subtasks from view.

combination view A Project view with the task details showing at the bottom of the screen.

constraint A rule that forces a task to fit certain parameters. For example, a task can be constrained to start as late as possible in a project.

cost A cost can be applied to a task in a project. The cost of the task may be fixed, or you can apply a cost to a task by assigning resources, which can be equipment, materials, or people with associated hourly rates or fees.

critical path The series of tasks that must occur on time in order for the overall project to meet its deadline.

critical task A task on the critical path.

crosstab A report format that compares two inter-secting sets of data; for example, you can generate a crosstab report showing costs of critical tasks that are running late.

cumulative cost The planned total cost for a resource to date on a particular task. This calcula-tion provides the costs already incurred on the task, plus the costs planned for the remaining, as yet uncompleted, portion of the task.

cumulative work The planned total work of a resource on a particular task. This calculation pro-vides the work already performed on the task plus the work planned for the remaining, as yet uncom-pleted, portion of the task.

current date line The vertical line in a Gantt Chart indicating today's date and time.

demote To move a task to a lower level in the project outline hierarchy.

dependency A timing relationship between two tasks in a project. A dependency can cause a task to happen after another task, to happen before another task, or to begin at some point during the life of the other task.

detail task See *subtask*.

duration The amount of time it takes to complete a task.

duration variance A field displaying the variation between the planned (baseline) duration of a task and the current estimated task duration, based on activity to date and remaining activity to be performed.

earned value Also called *budgeted cost of work performed*. Earned value refers to the value of work completed. For example, a task with $1,000 of associated costs, when 75 percent complete, will have a baseline value of $750.

earned value cost variance See *CV*.

effort-driven An effort-driven task has an assigned amount of effort to complete it. When you add resources to these tasks, the effort is distributed among those resources.

elapsed duration An estimate of how long it will take to complete a task, based on a 24-hour day and 7-day week.

estimate at completion (EAC) The total scheduled cost for a resource on a task. This calculation provides the costs incurred to date, plus costs estimated for remaining work on the task.

expand Opening a project outline to reveal sub-tasks as well as summary tasks.

expected duration This calculation estimates the actual duration of a task based on performance to date.

external task When tasks are linked between projects, Project displays tasks from the external project in the current project. The external task represents the linked tasks without having to leave the current project.

finish date The date on which a project will be completed.

finish-to-finish relationship A dependency relationship in which the finish of one task depends on the finish of another task.

finish-to-start relationship A dependency relationship in which the start of one task depends on the finish of another task.

fixed cost A cost that does not increase or decrease based on the time a resource spends on a task. A consultant's fee or permit fee are examples of fixed costs.

fixed date A task that must occur on a certain date. Fixed-date tasks do not move earlier or later in the schedule because of dependency relationships.

fixed duration The length of time required for a task remains constant, no matter how many resources are assigned to it. Travel time is a good example of a fixed-duration task.

float See *slack*.

Gantt Chart A standard project management tracking device that displays task information alongside a chart that shows task timing in a bar chart format.

gap See *lag*.

ID number The number assigned to a task based on its sequence in the schedule.

Inactive task a task that is no longer part of the project, perhaps because of a change to the project's scope; inactive tasks can remain part of the schedule so that you don't lose their information, but they don't affect the project schedule or resource availability.

lag The result of dependency relationships among tasks. Lag is a certain amount of downtime between the end of one task and the start of another.

leveling See *resource leveling*.

linking Establishing a connection between two tasks in separate schedules so that changes to tasks in the first schedule are reflected in the second. Linking is also a term applied to establishing dependencies among tasks in a project.

Manually scheduled task For tasks using this mode, Project does not calculate any Start date, Finish date, or Duration information. The project manager can completely control the task's schedule. Any changes to the dates of a manually scheduled task do not affect successor tasks or the project schedule.

milestone A task, typically of zero duration, that marks a moment of time in a schedule.

network diagram A standard project management tracking form that indicates workflow among the tasks in a project.

node Boxes containing information about individual project tasks in the Network Diagram view.

nonworking time Time when a resource on a project is not available to work. On the project calendar, time specified as time resources won't be working.

outline The structure of summary and subordinate tasks in a project.

Glossary

overallocation Occurs when a resource is assigned to spend more time than its work calendar permits on a single task or combination of tasks occurring at the same point in time.

overtime Any work scheduled above and beyond a resource's standard work hours; overtime work can have a different rate assigned to it than a resource's regular rate.

percent complete The amount of work already accomplished on a task, expressed as a percentage.

predecessor In a dependency relationship, the task that is designated to occur before, or precede, another.

priorities Project uses the priorities that you assign to tasks when it performs resource leveling to resolve project conflicts; a higher-priority task is less likely than a lower-priority task to incur delay during the leveling process. You also can assign priorities to projects.

progress lines Gantt Chart bars that overlap the baseline taskbar and indicate tracked actual progress on the task.

project A series of steps to reach a specific goal. A project seeks to meet the triple constraints of time, quality, and cost.

project management The discipline that studies various methods, procedures, and concepts used to control the progress and outcome of projects.

promote To move a task to a higher level in a project's outline hierarchy.

recurring task A task that is repeated during the life of a project. Typical recurring tasks are regular meetings of project teams or regular reviews of project output.

resource A cost associated with a task. A resource can be a person, piece of equipment, materials, or a fee.

resource contouring Changing the time when a resource begins work on a task. You can use contouring to vary the amount of work that a resource does on a task over the life of that task.

resource-driven A task whose timing is determined by the number of resources assigned to it.

resource leveling A process used by Project to modify resource assignments to resolve resource conflicts.

resource pool A centrally located, shared collection of resources. Many organizations share the resources in their resource pool among all their projects.

roll up The calculation by which all subtask values are "rolled up" or summarized in a summary task. The summary task displays the duration of all subtasks it summarizes.

slack Also called *float*. The time you have available to delay a task before that task becomes critical. You have used up slack on a task when any delay on that task will cause a delay in the overall project deadline.

split tasks When progress on a task is interrupted or delayed because the task has been placed on hold, you can split the task into two tasks. When you split tasks, the downtime between the two is not allocated to the total time taken to complete the task.

start date The date on which a project, task, or assignment begins.

start-to-finish relationship A dependency relationship in which one task can't finish until another task starts.

start-to-start relationship A dependency relationship in which the start of one task depends on the start of another task.

subproject An inserted copy of a second project that becomes a phase of the project in which it is inserted.

subtask Also called a *subordinate task*. A task providing detail for a specific step in the project. This detail is rolled up into a higher-level summary task.

successor In a dependency relationship, a successor task is scheduled to begin after another task in the project.

summary task A task in a project outline that has subordinate tasks beneath it. A summary task rolls up the details of its subtasks and has no timing of its own.

task An individual step to be performed to reach a project's goal; a project is composed of tasks.

template A format in which a Project file can be saved; the template saves elements such as calendar settings, formatting, and tasks. New project files can be based on a template.

timescale The area of a Gantt Chart or time-phased view that indicates the units of time being displayed.

tracking The act of recording actual progress in terms of both work completed and costs accrued on tasks in a project.

variable rate A shift in a resource's cost that can be set to occur at specific times during a project. For example, if a resource is expected to receive a raise or if equipment lease rates are expected to increase, you can assign variable rates for those resources.

work breakdown structure See *WBS*.

workload The amount of work that any resource is performing at any given point in time, taking into account all tasks to which the resource is assigned.

Index

SYMBOLS AND NUMERICS

Index

Index

Index

Index

Index

Index

Index

Index

Index

Index

Index

Index

Index

Index

Index

Index

Index

Index

The books you read to succeed.

Get the most out of the latest software and leading-edge technologies with a Wiley Bible—your one-stop reference.

978-0-470-55419-7

978-0-470-56813-2

978-0-470-50909-8

978-0-470-55481-4